Lords of Darkness

Lords of Darkness

A History of the 45th Avn Bn (Sp Ops) and OKARNG Aviation

COL Billy R. Wood, U.S. Army (Retired)

iUniverse, Inc.
Bloomington

Lords of Darkness
A History of the 45th Avn Bn (Sp Ops) and OKARNG Aviation

iUniverse books may be ordered through booksellers or by contacting:

iUniverse
1663 Liberty Drive
Bloomington, IN 47403
www.iuniverse.com
1-800-Authors (1-800-288-4677)

ISBN: 978-1-4620-2724-8 (sc)
ISBN: 978-1-4620-2723-1 (hc)
ISBN: 978-1-4620-2722-4 (ebk)

Library of Congress Control Number: 2011909962

Printed in the United States of America

iUniverse rev. date: 08/10/2011

CONTENTS

Preface xi
Introduction xvii

Caribbean Coup d'état 1986 1
Chapter 1   Territorial Militia to Thunderbirds.......................8
Chapter 2   The Patriarchs of OKARNG Aviation and Birth of
             Army National Guard Aviation 34
Chapter 3   The Godfather of ARNG Aviation..........................90
Chapter 4   Transitioning to the Current Era....................122
Chapter 5   Name That Unit 148
Chapter 6   Lexington Army Aviation Support Facility..............231
Chapter 7   Tulsa Flight Activity 1978 – 1984 and Tulsa
             Army Aviation Support Facility 1989—present........255
Chapter 8   Army Aviation Advisors 279
Chapter 9   OKARNG Aviation Medicine.............................312
Chapter 10   "No, We Are Not Invincible" 341
Chapter 11   Jackpot at Caesar's Palace 369
Chapter 12   Golden Palace on Cincinnati 382
Chapter 13   Counter-Terrorism or Special Operations? 407
Chapter 14   Troop Command (Aviation).............................422
Chapter 15   The Stories You May Not Have Heard 433
Chapter 16   1st Battalion, 245th Aviation
             (Special Operations)(Airborne) 461
Chapter 17   Lest We Forget 516
Chapter 18   Don't Forget to Turn Out the Lights 553
Appendix A   Military Abbreviations and Acronyms................584
Appendix B   OKARNG State Aviation Officers 599
Appendix C   The Adjutants General of the
             Oklahoma National Guard 601
About the Author...605

To the Patriarchs and the men and women whom they served.

Acknowledgement

I could never list the all of the names that have made a contribution to make this book possible, however, some were indispensable. Thanks to my daughter, Angela L. Wood for her editing talents. A special thanks to Joseph Seymour and LaTasha Gatling at the U.S. Army Center for Military History, 45th Inf Div Museum, Oklahoma Military Department Hqs & Staff, COL Gail Lusty, Oklahoma Guard Public Affairs Office, Ms. Cheryl Thomas and the former members of the unit we called the "Lords of Darkness."

Preface

In the autumn of my life, I've discovered that with age comes the realization that sometimes I really don't know what I don't know. One of the reasons for writing this book was the realization that I didn't know the events and specific facts of how a particular secret counter-terrorism aviation unit, the 45th Aviation Battalion (Lt Hel Cbt), of the Oklahoma Army National Guard (OKARNG) came into being. Also, I didn't know why key military figures and political leaders selected the Oklahoma Army National Guard (OKARNG) as the 45th Aviation Battalion's home. My primary purpose is to give you the story, along with the facts, of this unit's beginning, its evolution and eventual deactivation. It would be wrong to do this without also presenting the history of the OKARNG Aviation.

Years ago, I found it confusing when I would ask someone about any aviation unit in the OKARNG. The majority of every Oklahoma aviation unit designation and redesignation included the numerals four and five, as I suppose they should. Here are several examples: 45th Avn Bn (Lt Cbt Hel), or Co B 45th Avn Bn (there was more than one), 145th Avn Co, 445th Avn Co, 245th Air Ambulance, 145th ATC, 45th Avn (Sp Ops) (Abn) or the 1/245th Avn.

This causes an enormous amount of puzzlement for a normal soldier and even a military historian. As a pretty good genealogist and historian, I thought that I understood lineage, but I was quite surprised with the explanation from a true military historian, and unit lineage expert, Joseph Seymour. Mr. Seymour works at the U.S. Army Center for Military History, in Fort McNair, Washington, D.C. He told me, "ARNG history follows the personnel and geography, not the unit designation; because in the Guard, designations come and go, but the personnel remain the same, and it is through personnel and localities that we trace the history, not the designations."

My attempt to keep track of OKARNG aviation units, as we move into this twenty-first century, is exacerbated when aviation force structure personnel add unfamiliar designations within the plethora of new OKARNG aviation units and their lengthy unit names of today. I hope, through this book, to help you reduce some of the perplexity associated with numerical unit designations of the *earliest OKARNG aviation units*. The research for this book has taken seven years; the work has been enjoyable and productive.

Aviation isn't just a bunch of flyers and maintainers. Aviators, crew chiefs and mechanics, although intelligent, are all leaders. There are those in our midst who are placed in charge—we call them "leaders." You cannot go through a single day without noticing the efforts and the results of leadership—good or bad. But what makes a good or great leader? Is it popularity? Do you have to "get your ticket punched" by attending and graduating from the Dale Carnegie "School of Charm?" Is it the individuals who always come in "number one," or that finish the course at the top of the list? If you graduate in the middle of your class, does that mean you'll be a mediocre leader?

Or is it the ability to lead? Do you need "courage of steel" to be a great commander? What happens if mortar shells or tracers land next to you, causing your ears to ring or bleed and you can't run fast enough for the nearest shelter because you are scared? Should that prevent you from being a combat leader? Or is it always being honest and never telling a lie? Does your ability to get results guarantee you will be a respected leader? Does being humorous or having the ability to tell a great joke improve your chances?

Is it the books you have read or how you talk that causes other men to be willing to follow you? The fact that you once got a horrible Officer Efficiency Rating (OER) or that you got fired or relieved, does that mean you can't become or never were a good military leader?

General Douglas MacArthur's mother lived at the Thayer Hotel along the Hudson River while her son attended West Point; she was just a stone's throw from her son's dormitory on the West Point campus for four years. Was he a "momma's boy"? Perhaps, but he also became a tremendous leader and the most highly decorated soldier of WWI. MacArthur was known to have lied, perhaps frequently, to promote his own cause. General Dwight D. Eisenhower probably never lied. President Harry Truman fired MacArthur. Yet we still admire and recount his military victories and his leadership abilities. Later didn't Eisenhower have difficulty making a decision, such as "Do I want Nixon again as my vice presidential running mate?" Things change.

Each year a young Army National Guard (ARNG) officer is chosen from hundreds of nominations nationwide and awarded the coveted General Douglas MacArthur Leadership Award for excellence. It is my honor to have worked with and to have known several of these awardees from Oklahoma. One is still today a great leader and soaring above the rest! In the near future, I expect him to invite Carolyn and me to his pinning when he makes Brigadier General!

MacArthur's, Eisenhower's and other military icon's leadership skills are still recognized and promoted. Why? Because leadership is the key required element resulting in progress.

Whenever we have seen major progress in OKARNG organizations and units, it is because the leaders have made courageous decisions! And because the soldiers who get things done, the NCOs, were up to the task! A leadership position doesn't automatically give a person courage. But courage can cause them to be given a position of leadership. Courage isn't the absence of fear anymore than peace is the absence of war! Courage is doing something in spite of your fears! Billy Graham says, "Courage is contagious." Courage displayed by a leader inspires others to follow. A leader who has no followers is like the Tin Man without a heart, he can wish, but can't get anything done.

The Roman Historian, Tacitus said, "The desire for safety stands against every great and noble enterprise." However, courage opens doors, it is often seen by others, sometimes emulated, greater results are achieved, and missions are accomplished that ordinary men would not have fathomed! Courage can give ordinary men the ability to accomplish extraordinary things.

Our OKARNG patriarchs were courageous; they must have had broad shoulders, thick skin, tenacity, devotion, and the ability to dream! But were they like the statue of young David carved in marble by Michael Angelo – perfect in every way, without blemish, fearless and combat ready? No.

The leaders you will read about in this book are much like you and me. First, I suspect that they put their trousers on one leg at a time. You wouldn't find their face on the cover of *GQ* or *People* magazine. A few began as privates in the enlisted ranks and later earned the rank of colonel, and several became brigadier generals. Although all were members of the exclusive club we call "aviation" and were Army National Guard (ARNG) officers, men and women. Many of them also served on active duty at one time or another. Often they served on active duty before the Guard,

xiii

but sometimes they were activated and deployed during their service with the ARNG. Not only did they actively serve, but they participated with distinction in WWII, Korea, Vietnam, Central America, Bosnia, Kosovo, Somalia, Haiti, Kuwait, Afghanistan or Iraq. Many of them served in two or more wars and were awarded Air Medals, Purple Hearts, Bronze or Silver Stars. Some were awarded the Distinguished Flying Cross.

Scores of them weren't 'spring chickens' when they " . . . saw the elephant." Some of them made as many or more mistakes than you and I put together. They drank too much on occasion or with regularity; some were overweight, too tall, or too short. That's not where I am heading in this book and I don't intend to go there. These were men – regular men, but each had a little something "extra." They inherited at birth an extra dose of tenacity and they were visionary!

They dreamed that Oklahoma's ARNG Aviation Program would one day far exceed that from whence it began; that it would grow and that it would become relevant. That something extra, which several of them had, was the ability to translate their dreams into words, schemes and plans that others could see and transformed them into reality, where the skids touched the ground. Those arrogant and courageous aviators caused those elaborate dreams to come true. Leadership is key to your success!

In addition to some of our patriarchs, there were some challenging aviation leaders who believed that you and I ought to be able to fly precision night formation, lights out, during modest nocturnal illumination. They said, "With these new 'first and second generation' night vision goggles (NVGs) we can traverse over long, difficult routes into unfamiliar and foreign places." We had faith in our flight leaders; we believed we could avoid enemy detection and deliver a special operations client on target, and arrive at the agreed destination within plus or minus thirty seconds.

Well, if you believe that, you've either got to be a blithering idiot and I want to check your security clearance or . . . . you have been a part of Special Operations Aviation or one of our customers. Perhaps you heard about or worked with the OKARNG's Special Operations Aviation unit known as *the Lords of Darkness the 45th Avn (SO)(A)*.

The subsequent pages of this book are merely an account of one man's research, his conclusions, and his opinions. Those opinions were derived from 28½ years of military service, 13 years in OKARNG aviation and a total of 22½ years active duty. Research for this book includes many hours of tape recorded interviews, days of arduous research regarding OKARNG aviation history in general, and specifically our one and only covert Special Operations Aviation unit in Oklahoma. The aviation history of the OKARNG and the history of the 45th Aviation Battalion's clandestine beginning, organization, training, evolution and its deactivation, as I have determined it, will be presented as you turn these pages.

There are some regrets associated with a military career of 28½ years. One is spending too much time away from home; eventually contributing to a divorce. Two, there were times that I may have shouted my position or opinion on a certain subject, and in doing so, may have damaged a working relationship or a friendship. In my naivety, I may have created more discord than existed beforehand. In retrospect, what I considered a mountain at the time was only a mole hill. I and others, fought hard and long for the best training opportunities, tables of distribution and allowances (TDAs), modified tables of organization and equipment (MTOEs), the best and newest equipment, more modern aircraft and significant wartime missions. I don't regret that one iota. However, the way in which we went about it could have been more civilized. Some of us remember a few bitter disagreements, confabs and petty jealousies between aviation and the other guys at the OKARNG headquarters. A precious amount of time was wasted because of those jealousies and I regret that. I also regret that I was often much to blame for those disagreements.

As I researched page after page of the 45th Avn Bn and Trp Cmd (Avn), Department of the Army (DA), National Guard Bureau (NGB) and Oklahoma Military Department (OMD) files, concept plans, modernization plans, year-round-training plans, ODT and exercise files, I recall the endless hours we spent swimming upstream.

The sun came up each morning, so that we could see again the eyes of the miserable "S.O.B.s" we were going to try and whip that day. Pulling on olive drab (OD) or camouflage fatigues and spit-shined boots, so we could fight again and achieve the victories we sought that week – TDAs, newer NVGs, modified Blackhawks, Chinooks, Aviation Qualification Course (AQC) quotas, flight engineer quotas, etc. By late evening, sometimes the darkness of morning, our bodies crashed! We never had trouble sleeping. On occasion at the 45th Avn Bn's Sperry Armory, I unfolded my Army cot and slept next to my desk. The routine was "get-up, battle all day, eat, sleep, get-up, battle all day, eat, sleep . . ." – you get the idea. For certain, I was not the only one – no, many other OKARNG soldiers, staffers, and commanders, were dedicated to their own units and causes.

Robert Strauss said, "Success is a little like wrestling a gorilla. You don't quit when you're tired – you quit when the gorilla is tired!" If you want your team to succeed, you have to keep pushing beyond what you think you can do. It's not the first step, but the last step in a relay race, the last shot in the basketball game – that's where the race and the game is won!

Let's revisit the stories and rediscover the mission of these soldiers, their nocturnal missions, their boldness and stealth – all of which qualified them to be special warriors.

"Understanding our past, shapes and sustains memory, which is essential to our perception of who we are. Without it we have no sense of community as individuals," stated by curator Gila Hurvitz in an exhibit in Tulsa entitled "Abraham to Jesus." He who would know the future, must study the past. For all of you aviators and citizen soldiers who desire to foretell the events forthcoming, I would advise you to become students of history, and (in this case) military history – Oklahoma military aviation history to be more precise. By knowing where the OKARNG has been, you will impress your fellow soldiers as well as your mentor.

The following pages incorporate some of the secrets, scars, sacrifices, soaring successes, a few tall tales and sketches of the senior leadership of the OKARNG's Special Operations Aviation unit—the *"Lords of Darkness."*

Remember, the leadership in you effects everyone with whom you work and serve.

Introduction

During the first year of combat in Iraq, we lost 486 service men and women. As of February 2011, we have lost 4,439 U.S. service men and women in Iraq. We have also lost 1,464 men and women in Afghanistan since 2001. Thirty-two thousand U.S. forces were wounded in Iraq and 9,971 wounded in Afghanistan since each war began.

More than any other persons on earth, soldiers want peace, but not without honor. To serve in the military is an honor, and sacrifices are necessary. As the motto of the 1st Bn, 245th Special Operations Aviation stated, [. . . it is] "Not For Ourselves Alone."

During October 2005, 80,000 of the Guard and Reserve forces were deployed in 40 nations. The largest portion was in Iraq, where Guard units accounted for eight of 15 Army combat brigades. Since then so many, many Army National Guard and Army Reserve (USAR) units have been deployed to Afghanistan, Kuwait, Iraq, Egypt, Africa, Bosnia and Kosovo. What was unexpected, however, was that later they would be re-deployed again back to combat areas. Some Guard or Reserve units and individuals have been deployed to combat zones three different times within a three—to four-year period. Still the opinion of the senior leadership in the Active Army, and that of former Secretary of Defense Rumsfeld, stated that, "We don't need to increase the endstrength of the active services. We have sufficient manpower to meet our political and military goals."

When I was first on active duty in 1963, as an enlisted field artillery soldier, I called a friend of mine in the Army Reserve a "weekend warrior." Many young, American males in the mid-1960s were attempting to get military deferments; those who couldn't get a deferment tried to get into the National Guard. The rest were either drafted into the Army or enlisted so that they might get to choose the area in which they would serve in the military. Our nation was engaged in a conflict in Southeast Asia and so many young men were concerned with avoiding Vietnam all together!

As the years flew by, our nation engaged in hostilities that my fellow soldiers called "war," but politicos called "conflicts" – Vietnam, Grenada, Panama, the Persian Gulf. My personal thoughts about the Army National Guard changed dramatically! The idea of a National Guard unit and its men and women being "part timers" or "weekend warriors" evaporated, and those insulting terms were no longer part of my vocabulary.

Being an Army aviator, I knew that you could not maintain aviation skills and proficiency (as an aviator or crewmember) by attending drill once a month. Nearly all Army National Guard or Army Reserve aviation men and women drill a minimum of four to six days a month, and these same aviators will rack up more than 90 days of active duty each year.

As aviators and crewmembers, during my time in the OKARNG, we were authorized four additional flight training periods (AFTPs) each month. Four AFTPs per month was the norm. There were periods of time in Special Operations Aviation that we were authorized six to eight AFTPs per month, allowing us to get much more hands-on training and provide more Special Operations Forces (SOF) aviation support to the active duty Special Operations (SO) community. How can we call National Guard or Reserve aviation personnel "part timers" or "weekend warriors"? Although they aren't full-timers, they didn't deserve the slurred label of weekend warriors. The terms are no longer meaningful, yet they remain derogatory and uncouth.

Prior to Operation Desert Storm, it was the exception that an Army Guard or Reserve unit was activated. Eisenhower called up the Arkansas ARNG in Little Rock in 1957. In the late 1970s and most of the 1980s, deployment of reserve component (RC) units was not necessary and rarely done. The men and women in the National Guard or Reserves never really expected to be deployed; that's one reason so many units were full and/or "overstrength." Most OKARNG guardsmen were ready to volunteer for deployment and many did; however, few were ever called. The endstrength of the Army National Guard and the Army Reserves was right where the Secretary of the Army wanted it – balanced between what congressional and state interests wanted and what the Department of Defense's (DOD) active component (AC) would tolerate! But as the world turns, new situations around the globe become violent and/or threatening. We are no longer looking at the old Cold War OpPlan (operational plan) of fighting two simultaneous wars on two different fronts.

During the 1970s and 1980s, the Department of Defense seemed to have no intention of using Guard or Reserves units for military operations, as this might give rise to showing "relevance" of reserve component units. We were there in the event of another major war and the Army and the Defense Department felt they had all the bases covered for simultaneous conflicts on two fronts. We were there so the active Army could demonstrate their largess, and dump the older equipment they no longer wanted, equipment they eagerly wanted to replace with new technology. The machinations and hardness of their conceit was inexorable. It was as though the reserve component might out shine the active component, heaven forbid! Therefore, due to the Army's egoism they would not ask us, the ARNG, to participate for fear that we would, and that we might do it quite well!

"Behold the turtle; he makes progress only when he sticks out his neck," said James Conant.

Many things have changed since the mid-1980s, when the Army chose not to use Oklahoma's premier, Army National Guard, Special Operations Aviation unit, in the Persian Gulf. Were senior leaders in the Army afraid someone would complain; even though an entire unit had volunteered for this combat mission in the Persian Gulf? Many members of the 45th Avn Bn (SP OPS) (ABN) had signed individual statements, volunteering for Active Duty and deployment in Operation Prime Chance in the Persian Gulf. Our unit, the 45th Avn Bn (SP OPS) (ABN), had at least as much (if not more) night vision goggle (NVG) flight experience than its sister SOA unit, Task Force 160, an active component Special Operations Aviation unit. These two SOA units, one active, one reserve component, were once called "mirror images" of each other. Yet they were held far apart by the Department of the Army (DA). The secrecy that encompassed both units and the exclusivity of P5 funding for SOF units may have worked against the 45th Avn Bn (SP OPS) (ABN), within the OKARNG and on a national level.

> Note: Military P5 funding was appropriated and designated for Special Operations units and could not be dispersed for anything other than Special Operations, unlike other funding that could be shifted from one area sometimes to another area. P5 funding could be utilized for ARNG mandays, travel, equipment, and it was almost unlimited for the 45th Avn Bn (SP OPS) (ABN) during the mid to late 1980s

Some people have difficulty admitting that they indeed are prejudiced and/or biased. Allow me the opportunity to state that I am prejudiced – against other military officers who look down their noses at me or my fellow National Guardsmen because they feel that being "Regular Army" or "active duty" is reason to believe they are better than everyone else and smarter. I am also quite biased that Army aviators normally have spent more time in military schools, education and training. Thus they have a unique, often more experienced and valid opinion on military subjects. Some combat branch officers may hesitate to engage an aviator because they are prejudiced against them. Well, even when not asked to participate, don't be surprised when an Army aviator tells you they have something to share. Not all Army aviators are good looking, well educated and soft spoken, just most of them.

Three things used to concern and scare me. First, when a second lieutenant said, "Sir, I've been thinking!" Second, when a young captain said, "Sir, in my opinion, we should . . . ." And third, the most frightening of all was when a young warrant officer aviator while flying a group of passengers would say, "Hey ya'll, watch this!"

Since retiring from the Army in July 1998, I have enjoyed my days, but I still miss the dedicated and hard charging soldiers with whom I worked. Although my retirement is fulfilling, there are days when I miss the thrill of battle, the clawing up hill, the pursuit of excellence, the seeking of victory and occasionally achieving both. However, in my maturity and in retrospect, I can see the faults I had (have) more clearly. I see that so many times, the other guy was indeed right in his deluded position, or in his ludicrous disapproval of my request(s). The volume of paper on which I wrote thousands, upon thousands of words, pages of ideas, point papers, information papers, proposals, concepts, recommendations, requests for equipment, and requests for redesignations, the hours spent arguing our position; in the end, it's the same kind of exercise one gets from shadow boxing, isn't it? A lot of activity, a bit of sweat, and often very little progress!

As a friend and former boss once said to me, "Progress necessitates change, but change does not necessarily mean progress!" The same applies to activity; activity alone doesn't mean progress. We need to share that with those close to us—our young NCOs and officers – tomorrow's leaders.

Did we stumble? Yes, sometimes, but we got right back up.

Did we fail? Yes, but not always.

Did we quit? Never! Wasn't it Churchill who told his fellow Brits, "Never, never, never, never give up"? And they didn't.

Did we achieve success? Yes, because we never gave up . . .

More importantly, did we learn? Yes (and I'm still learning). I've learned that success isn't final, and that failure isn't always fatal.

I believe that we should also learn to respect those with whom we disagree. Just because we disagree doesn't have to mean that we don't like each other. My hope is that even though you may disagree with what we did at the time, as you read the following pages, you will be able to see the reasons why we tried so hard. In the mid-1980s and early 1990s, I saw a humbling number of OKARNG aviation soldiers wanting in the fight, and not the interstate wars between Tulsa and the Oklahoma Military Department, but the real ones. Our young (and not so young) men were volunteering for the war in the Persian Gulf – they deserved the opportunity to fly their Little Birds and fight, because they had trained, met the special operations standards, they had volunteered, and they were ready. Most often what we did was right, but even when we were wrong, the loyalty of those behind us was unswerving – it's called camaraderie and esprit de corps. The 45th Avn Bn (SO) (A) and OKARNG Aviation had both!

The leadership and aviators of Task Force 160 had a great deal of respect for the soldiers and aviators of the 45th Avn Bn (SP OPS) (ABN). This was apparent when at one time our NVG flight instructors were asked to conduct NVG flight training for aviators of the Task Force (TF). TF 160, U.S. Special Operations Command (USSOCOM), and all of the Special Forces Groups (SFG) whom we regularly supported recognized the 45th's relevance, our skill and our professionalism. When the active component's operational tempo (OPTEMPO) was extremely high, we were often asked and performed maintenance on TF 160's MH-60 and MH-47 aircraft, because they were stretched too thin and P5 funding was available. They would gladly have had us in the Persian Gulf Theater, flying the very same mission! And the members of the 45th Avn Bn respected our brethren in Task Force 160.

Our active duty forces and reserve component forces are to complement each other, not compete with each other.

Today, we hear almost daily, of yet another National Guard unit being re-deployed to Iraq or Afghanistan. These guard units are not just in a combat service support (CSS) role, they are combat units, with a major war fighting role! The military pendulum has now swung far to the left and slammed into the ridiculous. The Defense Department and Congress, hide their heads in the sand like an ostrich rather than increase the Total Army's endstrength, or instead of re-instituting a much needed military draft. They have chosen to over-utilize the majority of its war-trained reserve component units and individuals!

From about 2008-2009, the U.S. Army forced about 50,000 soldiers to continue serving in Iraq or Afghanistan after their voluntary stints ended under a policy called "stop-loss." The policy applied to soldiers in units due to deploy for the Iraq and Afghanistan wars. The Army said 'stop-loss' was vital to maintain units that were cohesive and ready to fight. Some experts said it ('stop-loss') showed that the Army was stretched too thin and that it could further complicate efforts to attract new recruits. Under the policy, soldiers who normally would leave when their commitments expire must remain in the Army, starting 90 days before their unit was scheduled to depart, through the end of their deployment and up to another 90 days after returning to their home base.

That "handful," without a doubt, includes the Army National Guard and Army Reserve – they, their families, and their employers are making a tremendous sacrifice!

As I'm writing this, my thought is that our U.S. Army is spread thinly around the globe with 138,000 U.S. troops in Iraq alone. Forty percent (40%) of that number is Army Guard and U.S. Army Reserve soldiers and units. We have 37,000 troops strategically positioned in South Korea, other forces in Bosnia, Europe, Afghanistan, varied Southwest Asia and Mid-east locations, as well as the Horn of Africa. These countries and locations I've mentioned are the majority, but there are others that you and I aren't supposed to know about.

Does today's leadership of the Army still elect to ignore the relevance of its reserve component units? At the moment there is a tremendous need for the rebirth of another SOA group, such as the OKARNG's 1st Bn, 245th Avn Bn (SP OPS) (ABN). Why is that?

Christmas Day 1991 is noted as the "fall of the Soviet Union," which ended 45 years of Cold War between the United States and the Soviet Union. Prior to 25 December 1991, the U.S. Department of Defense maintained a Cold War military establishment and created the two-war doctrine, which states that the U.S. military must be prepared to fight two simultaneous Gulf War-like campaigns on opposite sides of the world. Today the U.S. military spends 85% of what it did during the Cold War.

Shouldn't that be beneficial? Our military operational plans (OpPlan) have changed. Shouldn't we now feel better prepared and protected against current threats; for example, North Korea's nuclear capabilities and its lunatic leader, Kim Jong Il and Iran's President, Mahmoud Ahmadinejad and his lies about building nuclear power plants?

We now have new OpPlans. In the opinion of military strategists, there are only two regions outside Europe where broadly perceived threats, interests, and alliances converge to make large-scale intervention seem plausible: Korea and the Arabian Peninsula. We might add Pakistan and India to the list as an area of interest. Certain countries we have long considered our allies hate all U.S. citizens around the world and want to kill American "infidels." We no longer even make "over flights" of North Korea for fear of losing an Air Force pilot. Special Operations Aviation units would be utilized to recover a U.S. pilot from enemy territory, except that we don't have sufficient Army Special Operations Aviation units with which to meet all of the services' military requirements. This is in spite of the fact that the Air Force's own special operations' community feels that it can handle all known and unforeseen requirements for all of the DOD!

Buried deep in a 2006 Report of The Secretary of the Army on page 88, is the following note:

> In addition, we are rebalancing the mix between Active and Reserve Component force structure and adjusting the quantities of certain military specialties. We expect through this process to realign more than 100,000 positions across the Active and Reserve components. In response to Secretary of Defense guidance, we already have addressed approximately 10,000 slots. The Army National Guard is on track to divest about 19,500 spaces of less frequently used force structure, which will help to resource critical, high-demand units, such as military police, civil affairs and special operations forces. We project that our rebalancing efforts will convert another 80,000 slots of lower-priority force structure, 26,000 of which should be completed in FY 2005.

My belief is that the Secretary of the Army wanted to "steal" 19,500 spaces from the Army National Guard to be utilized for active component military police, civil affairs and special operations forces!!!

Why was the 1st Bn, 245th Avn Bn (SP OPS) (ABN) deactivated if the Army today wants more special operations forces? Or am I just being overly prejudiced and just confused?

Our Army National Guard and Army Reserve aviation and ground units incorporate a vast amount of experience, and much of it is combat experience—something that should be noted! In the decade of the mid-1980s to mid-1990s, OKARNG's 1st Bn, 245th Avn (SP OPS) (ABN) aircrews had as much NVG flight time as their active duty comrades, and had a much higher total flight time average than most aviators on active duty! Why was this valuable experience ignored? Why was this not considered advantageous by the Army Staff?

Is there an unspoken competition between Active Component and Reserve Components within the Total Army? In the Pentagon, not out in the field, leaders used to use the term "seamless Army." I suppose the term was meant to present an image of the active Army, Army National Guard and the Army Reserve, all being one big, happy family; because we all wore Army green and all knew the words to the Army Song, (. . . *as the caissons go rolling along!*) we would always agree with the active Army's position or statements. This was not the case at all! The Guard and the Reserves want to be considered equal players in the game, both having played real hard ball before; but more often than not, we sat on the bench with little or no prayer of ever getting to start or even fill in during the game!

We are teetering on the verge of catastrophe, with our military services being spread too thin and worldwide threats and international terrorism on the rise. I believe that the Army has dumbed down, and has lowered enlistment standards to meet unrealistic recruiting goals for an "all volunteer" Army. We, as Americans, should be ashamed and demand that the Department of the Army immediately raise the requirements for all volunteers wanting to enlist in our U.S. Army. It could be (soon I pray) that political doves and hawks choose to re-establish conscription by military draft. Having personally felt this way for the last 25 years or so, I would contend that a non-discriminatory draft, with absolutely no exceptions, no exclusions, where everyone is eligible to be called to 24 months governmental and military service would benefit this nation and its young adults! A program of such wisdom would save our country billions of dollars per year! Yet, I digress; the issue of a military draft for the United States of America is the subject of another book.

The importance and relevance of the Oklahoma Army National Guard's former highly skilled, counter-terrorism aviation unit, the 45th Avn Bn (SO)(A) (later redesignated 1st Bn, 245th Avn Bn (SO)(A) was almost totally ignored – WHY? Was this earlier, one-of-a-kind Army Guard unit deactivated in 1994 because of political reasons? Who, if anyone, might have gained from this decision? Would the 1st Bn, 245th Avn Bn (SO) (A) be considered relevant and utilized in Iraq if it existed today? I say a resounding, "Hell yes!"

This book isn't about an assault helicopter battalion, and it isn't about a traditional Army National Guard unit. It is about the men and a few women of the OKARNG and the decisions to organize, to train, and the evolution of a one-of-a-kind, covert, black, Special Operations Aviation unit within the reserve component, specifically the Oklahoma Army National Guard. The 45th Avn Bn (SO)(A) and the 1st Bn, 245th Avn Bn (SO)(A) was an outstanding aviation unit, which flew extremely small, light, highly maneuverable, almost silent helicopters in the dark of night, over short or long distances, avoided radar and enemy detection, and had unbelievable mission parameters that would still be difficult to meet today, "to deliver unique passengers and/or cargo to a designated target within plus or minus 50 feet and within plus or minus thirty seconds!"

The aviators, men and women of this organization were rightfully called . . .

Original art work by Rebecca Bond

Caribbean Coup d'état 1986

The green glow of the digital LED clock indicated 2300 hours Zulu. In the dim lit red-glow of the cargo area of a C-130 Hercules, somewhere over the Caribbean, our troops did what seasoned troops always did when given the opportunity—they slept while they could. During the first hour of flight, the 45th Aviation Battalion (SP OPS) (ABN) soldiers and aviators were reviewing night vision goggle (NVG) flight 'route sheets'; there was excitement in the air, as well as concern about this 'secret mission.' As the three C-130s droned over a darkened sea, these Lords of Darkness silently visualized the mission, going over again in their minds, each leg and check point of this mission—a "Little Bird extraction."

The Special Forces mission commander made the rounds, carefully stepping over sleeping soldiers, talking with each of the MH-6 pilots. He received assurance from the 45th Avn Bn Air Mission Commander (AMC), MAJ Richard Murphy, that our MH-6 "Little Birds" would be on target, plus or minus thirty seconds.

The Hercules had left the old USAF Strategic Air Command (SAC) base, known today as Hunter Army Airfield near Savannah, Georgia at sunset and was proceeding south toward Puerto Rico, 1,380 miles down range at about 300 knots and 20,000 feet. This airplane was one of three Air Force C-130s supporting the 7th Special Forces Group (SFG) in a very complex operation that would last only one night, and cover a lot of ground – if all went as planned.

This classified mission (a situation of concern) was brought about by Cuban insurgents and circumstances involving a senior U.S. government official who was taken hostage just three days earlier. United States Special Operations Command (USSOCOM) at Fort Bragg had been tasked by the White House, through the Department of Defense and had given the mission to 7th SFG to " . . . go in and rescue our man and bring him home, alive and pronto!" An "A Team" of the 7th SFG, supported by the 45th Aviation Battalion (Special Operations) of the Oklahoma Army National Guard and the Air Force was tasked for this operation. The 45th Avn Bn, with its compliment of AH-6's and MH-6's, for the past two days had been carrying Special Forces (SF) soldiers on clandestine operations all over Georgia and Florida as they made practice night raids against simulated radar sites and practiced hostage snatches. Our U.S. government official and his staff had been imprisoned on the small Puerto Rican island of Vieques (see map below). The area was very remote and the jungle canopy thick. Isabel Segunda Port on the northern shore of Vieques holds the distinction of being the last fort built by the Spaniards in the New World.

Puerto Rico politicos claimed not to know the captors, or their demands, but they had gained knowledge of where they were keeping the hostages. It was suggested that rebels sympathetic with Castro's Communist ideology were attempting to take control of remote parts of the Caribbean from the U.S. friendly Puerto Rican government. It was believed that the majority of the local people would lend their assistance to the U.S. supported forces if they thought we were winning. The CIA believed that if this senior U.S. official could be rescued then flown back to a secure area to make a radio broadcast; subsequently the Puerto Rican people would rise up against the insurgents.

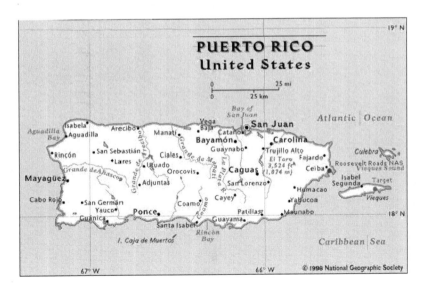

The Special Operations Aviation mission that evening would involve three C-130 aircraft and two MH-6 helicopters. The MH-6 "Flight Lead" was CW2 Tommy "TK" Klutts, one of the high time NVG aviators/instructor pilots within the 45th Avn Bn. One C-130 Hercules carried 45th Avn Bn aviators, ground support personnel and two MH-6's, plus an Air Force pathfinder detachment. Our "Little Bird" Air Mission Commander (AMC), MAJ Murphy, had portable "SATCOM" (satellite communications) radios onboard the C-130 and was able to have secure commo with our headquarters back at Hunter AAF, as well as the Special Forces FOB.

The other two cargo planes carried a company of Army Rangers. The plan was for the first C-130 carrying our 'Little Birds' and Special Forces Pathfinders, to fly at altitude along the commercial airway near Vieques, thus simulating an international airliner. The other two C-130's would trail the first C-130 dropping down below radar coverage about 50 miles out of Vieques. As the first C-130 passed by the island, the Special Forces Pathfinders with their steerable chutes would make a HAHO (High Altitude High Opening) jump onto the airfield at Vieques. When they landed, they were to remove any obstructions on the runway such as trucks, barriers, guards, etc. and prepare NVG compatible lighting for the landing of the Air Force C-130s. At about the same time another SF 'A' Team which had been covertly inserted the night before by parachute—was to attack the area where the hostages were being held. This was about seven nautical miles from the airfield. This would cause a diversion allowing the SF Pathfinders to do their work almost unnoticed.

When the strip was clear, two low-level C-130's would land and offload the Rangers on the strip to secure the airfield. Rangers would then reinforce the SF and attack the 'jungle prison' from the opposite side. When word was received that the airfield was secure, the first C-130, which had began descending as soon as the SF Pathfinders jumped, would land and offload the two MH-6 'Little Birds.' If things went as planned, the SF would complete the snatch and bring our U.S. official and two members of his staff to the MH-6 helicopters. Then they would be flown northwest across the strait to the mainland and make a broadcast to the people from a radio station that the SF had captured. The C-130's would then pick up the Rangers, SF and any remaining captives and fly them to Roosevelt Roads Naval Station[1], an airfield on the eastern coast of Puerto Rico, 15 nm northwest of the target on Vieques. All this was to be covertly accomplished during morning darkness using AN/PVS-5B Night Vision Goggles (NVGs); after refueling the airplanes and helicopters at 'Rosy' we would all return to Hunter Army Airfield (AAF), landing before daylight.

Our C-130 landed hot, didn't turn, nor leave the runway, but stopped hard on the white center line, feeling like the nose of the aircraft would lurch down and grind on the dark asphalt. The C-130 tail ramp was lowered almost before we stopped. The "Little Bird" tie-downs were released from the 'D-rings' in the floor of the Hercules; ground handling wheels raised into place and the MH-6s were quickly off-loaded. As the MH-6s rolled down the rear C-130 ramp, each of the MH-6's four rotor blades were unfolded, positioned, pinned and rechecked. The whine of two small Allison 250-C20 turbines began and within two minutes the two 45th Avn Bn (Lt Hel Cbt) MH-6s were airborne. The Lords of Darkness Air Mission Commander (AMC) received a short, cryptic signal to begin the inbound approach to pick up "passengers."

The AMC then 'challenged' the originator on the ground. No further radio communications were made; "chem-lites" marked the aircraft as the pax were assisted walked to and boarded on the MH-6s. The aircrews then signaled the SF commander with the chem-lites to confirm that passengers were loaded onto the "planks" and departure had begun. The "Little Birds" swiftly and silently lifted into the thick Caribbean night air at tree top level over the pitch black jungle. The flight then continued 15 nm across water to the eastern end of the main island and within minutes approached "Rosy" for landing . . .

This very extraordinary and realistic 'training mission' was an EDRE[2] ARTEP[3] for the 7th Special Forces Group, and included elements of the 75th Ranger Regiment, the 45th Avn Bn (Lt Hel Cbt) and several USAF C-130 and C-141 aircraft and aircrews. The exercise segment we performed, rescuing the hostages, was called by the Special Forces a 'Snatch.' That event was successful; no one was hurt and everyone returned to the airfield in Puerto Rico with smiles on their sweaty, exhausted, but happy faces! They had been up, excitedly awake and 'running' for about 20 hours now and were expecting some well-earned rest.

Upon our arrival back in "PR" things went downhill rather quickly. All of our 45th Avn Bn personnel were prepared for a "quick-turn-around" and an Air Force lift back to Hunter Army Airfield, former Strategic Air

Command base, at Savannah, GA. Thereafter, the senior commander would announce "ENDEX" (End of exercise) and all personnel would return to their respective home bases. This was not to happen as planned, nor as scheduled.

While the 'Snatch' was taking place on Vieques, the USAF C-130s flew over to Roosevelt Roads Naval Air Station and positioned themselves for an engine running refuel, all except the C-130 to carry our "Little Birds" and 45th Avn Bn personnel. He taxied up to a tie down spot and began shutting down all four engines. There was an Air Force Major on board who was liaison to the 7th SF. LTC Leroy A. Wall, 45th Avn Bn Commander, asked the Air Force LNO, "Hey, Major, what's was going on?" Wall then talked to the Air Force Captain, AMC of our C-130 and he stated rather sarcastically that, " . . . this airplane is staying over [in Puerto Rico] because by the time we would get back to Hunter [AAF, GA] we would be into "crew rest." Crew rest is an aviation term which limits aircrews to "no more than X hrs of flight time in X hrs of a duty day. Each service, Army, USAF, USN and USMC having their own limitations for "crew rest." It was a nauseating, excuse, often employed by USAF crew so they could "RON" (remain over night) at their favorite 'hang out.' Nothing that LTC Wall or the USAF liaison said or could do would change the C-130 pilot's mind. As you know rank doesn't mean anything in the Air Force, except in this case to the Air Force C-130 pilot it meant that LTC Wall received more military pay at the beginning of the month than he did. It was obvious that they had already made plans to party in Puerto Rico.

LTC Wall made a wise decision to pack all 45th Avn Bn personnel onto the other two C-130 airplanes that were returning that night to Savannah and left a handful of guys there to see that our helicopters got back to Hunter AAF the next day.

As all military planners know, especially Army planners, you seldom get 100 percent cooperation and support from the Air Force. There is never any "dedicated air support" with the Air Force! This was another one of those 70 percent missions. Just like so many, many previous joint military operations and JA/ATTs[4]—if things can go wrong, they will.

Lessons Learned: "The first lesson learned was—you must always anticipate what Clausewitz referred to as 'friction'—those unknown forces that impede and force changes in the midst of battle. Another lesson learned was that there is going to be built-in resistance when you have different services involved on the same mission with differing values and attitudes towards mission accomplishment. This comes to light when you recall past efforts to do away with Marine aviation. The Marines have learned the hard way that when the chips are down, you can count on your own people (not the Navy, not the Air Force, nor anyone else)."

Most of these Oklahoma Special Ops Aviation soldiers, the "Lords of Darkness," had other jobs, high school teachers, funeral director, plant managers; many of them had civilian flying jobs: American Airlines, off-shore helicopter pilots, Oklahoma City or Tulsa Police Department Pilots. Their military job was "Army Special Operations Aviator." This meant they specialized in flying at night, utilizing extraordinary, cutting edge Night Vision Goggles (NVG), special GPS navigational equipment and deadly accurate armament. The NVGs allowed them to become highly proficient night flyers in the absence of normal available light, like the great horned owl, also a nocturnal and superior owner of the night.

These unique aviation personnel performed an average of 110—130 days Active Duty per year. The average age for 45th Avn Bn aviators was 28 years old, 15 years of education, about 3,500 flight hours of which approximately 350 were NVG and already had accumulated 10-14 years of military service. Many were veterans of one or two combat tours in Vietnam and elsewhere as Army aviators. All were highly trained, skillful, fearless Army soldiers who flew specialized helicopters at night and didn't quit! Most had flown missions in many different foreign countries, in support of U.S. and foreign governments.

The Lords of Darkness were a one-of-a-kind Army National Guard, Special Operations Aviation unit within the Oklahoma Army National Guard and many had already "seen the elephant[5]." The adage which states, "The sum of the whole is greater than any one individual" is true; the combined talent and capabilities of this unit was far greater and beyond the efforts of any one aviator or soldier. "You can count on me . . . ," didn't need to be stated, it was understood.

This story is based on a mission flown as part of a real Special Operations exercise called "Casino Gambit '86." The original 'recollection' was provided by COL (ret) Leroy A. Wall, who was Commander of the unit at that time and part of the original crew and mission. The author has edited the original version.

---

1.   Roosevelt Roads Naval Air Station is now an inoperative, former United States military air base in the town of Ceiba, Puerto Rico. It was officially closed in 2004.

2   Emergency Deployment Readiness Exercise (EDRE)

3   Army Readiness Training and Evaluation Program (ARTEP)

4   JA/ATT: Joint Airborne/ Air Transportability Training - a method by which Army units could request USAF airlift (C-130, C-141, C-5As) airlift for training missions.

5   "I seen the elephant" was a Civil War phrase for a soldier's first glimpse of combat.

Chapter 1

Territorial Militia to Thunderbirds

"Wars always begin with cheers. The tears begin later!"

Joe Curreri

Oklahoma Army National Guard Aviation traces its origin to the United States Congress of 1890, which authorized one regiment of organized militia for the Oklahoma Territory. It included only six counties and covered a mere 5,000 square miles of prairie lands. Later in the congressional session of 1895, provisions were stipulated, allowing for the organization and development of the Volunteer Militia with an authorized strength of approximately 500 members, which we today call the Oklahoma Army National Guard (OKARNG).

The Oklahoma Territorial Militia was loosely organized in 1890, and was officially reorganized as the Oklahoma Territorial National Guard on 8 March 1895. The first National Guard consisted of infantry companies, cavalry troops and artillery batteries. There was neither pay nor benefits for its members; officers were required to furnish their own uniforms and horses. This militia served an important purpose in maintaining peace and assisting in emergencies within the territory. It also stood ready to serve the nation if war was to come . . . and it did.

A single gunshot on 22 April 1889 signaled the opening of a vast area of the plains land to white settlers. In less than a day, the Oklahoma Land Run, which had started at dawn, by nightfall, had created a tent city of 10,000, soon to be called Oklahoma City. The Oklahoma Territorial capitol was established in Guthrie.

And only a few brief years after the Oklahoma Land Run, Wilbur and Orville Wright flew successfully for the first time. It was on 17 December 1903, that between them they made four successful flights in a power-driven aircraft at Kitty Hawk, NC. Aviation in America had begun, yet it would be nearly a half century before it became part of the Guard in Oklahoma.

The Territorial Militia grew in the years prior to 1907, when Statehood was granted. Federal allotments to support the troops doubled and the Territorial legislature voted to expand support by increasing money and manpower.

Years passed, Indian Territory (I.T.) and Oklahoma Territory were combined, and in 1907, the new state of Oklahoma had its first elected Governor, Charles Nathaniel Haskell (1907-1911). Born in Putnam County, Ohio in 1860, Haskell moved to Muskogee, I.T. in 1901 where he practiced law and promoted railroads. Oklahoma was a much larger body of land by this time, covering an area of 69,919 square miles and was ranked 18th by area. With statehood came the end of the Territorial Militia and the beginning of the Oklahoma National Guard. Progress meant change, and in 1911 the Territorial Capital was moved to Oklahoma City. In later years, the OKARNG endstrength would eventually grow to about 8,500.

While on active duty in Washington, D.C., on occasion I enjoyed running at Fort Myers, VA, not far from the Pentagon. Jogging on post there, I was able to combine two of my favorite things – seeing some historical military architecture and experiencing that euphoric sense of peace, while running. My route took me through an old, red brick, military community with giant red oak trees lining the streets and gentle, rolling hills. Adjacent to Fort Myers are acre upon acre of grassy slopes, pierced with thousands of small white crosses, honoring American soldiers. Arlington National Cemetery is without a doubt the most impressive final resting place honoring our fallen heroes and veterans that I have ever visited. In the summer of 1995, at Arlington National Cemetery I attended the solemn military funeral of fellow OKARNG aviator, Chief Warrant Officer Four Dennis Laffick, killed on duty in Oklahoma while flying for the Drug Enforcement Agency (DEA) and the Oklahoma Bureau of Narcotics (OBN).

Each year in October, at the base of a hill on which Arlington's carillon tower stands, a very distinctive and unique race begins – the United States

Marine Corps (USMC) Marathon. Over the years and further proving my madness, I ran and completed the USMC Marathon four times, nearly setting a record – slowest time ever recorded.

Parking was always a problem at the Marine Corps marathon and Fort Myers was one of the best places to find a spot. Once this was accomplished, a fairly long walk was necessary to reach the official starting line. One crisp October morning prior to the marathon I parked east of the Fort Myers Post Exchange next to a stone wall that separated Myers from Arlington National Cemetery. As I got out of my car I noticed a brass plaque on a stone pillar of the wall. It described a fatal Army aviation accident with which I was not familiar: "IN MEMORY OF FIRST LIEUTENANT THOMAS E. SELFRIDGE . . . first military casualty of powered flight on a U.S. military installation." On 17 September 1908, First Lieutenant Selfridge was granted permission from President William Taft to fly with Orville Wright during a military demonstration flight at Fort Myers, VA. Selfridge was assigned to the 1ˢᵗ Field Artillery Regiment and detailed to the Signal Corps for aviation duties. The Wright Brothers plane crashed, killing Selfridge and putting Orville Wright in the hospital for several months. Thomas Selfridge is buried at Arlington National Cemetery.

The United States contracted for its first military aircraft when the Signal Corps announced it would receive bids in December 1907. Records show that the Army took delivery of its first complete airplane, a Wright Type B Flyer on 2 August 1909 and produced its own aviator, Lieutenant Frederick Erastus Humphreys. LT Humphreys, Engineer Corps, was the first Army officer to make a solo flight in a heavier-than-air craft. This three-minute solo occurred on 26 October 1909. COL Humphreys was from Summit, NJ and born on 16 September 1883. He was a member of the New York Army National Guard.

While the early growth of this fledgling state called Oklahoma and its new National Guard was somewhat slow, U.S. military aviation was dramatically slower in its beginning. Congress voted the first appropriation for military aviation in 1911, when Oklahoma City became the capital of the state. Soon thereafter, Army aviation leaders rejected a proposal to separate their service from the Signal Corps, thus delaying progress some 70 years before the Army finally established Aviation as a separate combat arms branch.

The First Aeronautical Division of the U.S. Army was established in August of 1907. By 1914 it had grown to six airplanes. This provisional Air

Squadron was formed to support the Punitive Expedition under General John J. Pershing on the Mexican border in 1916. This was a dismal failure because of poor equipment and bad maintenance.

The importance of military aviation was established with its role in Europe during World War I (WWI). Dirigible balloons were used for artillery spotting and airplanes for reconnaissance over enemy lines. Both made a decisive contribution; they had proven effective at bombing. Every army sought control of the air, and great battles between the knights of the air became the pages of romance. A doctrine for aerial warfare was beginning to emerge. For example, Army commanders began to distinguish between strategic air operations, deep in an enemy's territory, directed at his vital war-making industries and civilian morale, and tactical operations against his ground forces.

At the time of America's declaration of war against Germany on 6 April 1917, the Army's Aviation Section was marginal at best. The Army's 1,152 aviation officers and men had very little, if any, knowledge of the air war in Europe. The Army's aviation section had 55 airplanes and 5 balloons, none of which could have survived long in combat. The United State's aircraft manufacturers had up to that time produced 1,000 planes. Yet, when France asked the U.S. to provide an air force of 4,500 airplanes and 50,000 men, there was no hesitation. With more enthusiasm than wisdom, U.S. Secretary of War Newton D. Baker asked for and received $640 million from Congress for Army Aviation. The result was a fiasco. By the spring of 1918, it was clear that the Signal Corps, who was responsible for aviation at the time, had failed to produce any organized aviation force.

The War Department then set up an Air Service consisting at first of two agencies reporting directly to the Secretary of War: One was headed by a civilian whose function was to deal with the manufacturers, and one was under a military officer who was to train and organize units. This new activity, begun in April and May of 1918, was consolidated in August, when President Woodrow Wilson appointed John D. Ryan, Second Assistant Secretary of War, as Aviation Czar to straighten out the mess and consolidate the whole thing under the aegis of the Air Service. The U.S. Army signed a contract with the Wright Brothers for the first Army airplane on 10 February 1918.

"Aeroplane No. 1, Heavier-than-Air Division, U.S. Aerial Fleet" was officially accepted by the U.S. Army on 2 August 1909. Eight hundred pounds of bamboo, wire and cloth, and a 30 hp engine connected to propellers by bicycle chains had cost the government $30,000. Included in the contract was the requirement for the Wright Brothers to train and certify two military officers as pilots. These were to be Lieutenants Lahm and Foulois; the latter, however, was dispatched to attend the International Congress of Aeronautics in Europe, and Lieutenant Frederick E. Humphreys was detailed to take his place.

Vacant land near College Park, Maryland, was leased and cleared where a temporary hanger was erected. Wilbur Wright undertook training the two officers in early October.

Shortly after 8 a.m. on 26 October 1909, a mechanic held a gasoline-soaked rag over the engine intake while another cranked the engine into life. Wilbur Wright hurriedly ran to a nearby shed for window sash weights to replace his weight in the passenger seat. When a catapult weight dropped, aeroplane and pilot were launched for a three-minute flight. After a little more than three hours of actual flying time, Lieutenant Humphreys became the first military student pilot to be told he was ready to "take her up on your own."

Two more flights were made by Lieutenant Humphreys that day, the next eight and one half minutes, and the last one lasting twenty-four minutes. Lieutenant Lahm also soloed for three flights, and Wilbur Wright pronounced both certified pilots. Over the next few days the two pilots flew practice flights together and separately, until 5 November, when they crashed the plane. American military aviation came to an ignominious but temporary end.

Winter weather was setting in, Lahm's detail from the Cavalry was about to expire, and there were no funds left for repair of the aircraft. Humphreys returned to the Corps of Engineers, and the broken plane was shipped to Fort Sam Houston, Texas, where Foulois attempted to put in back together in his spare time while teaching himself to fly by correspondence course.

Foulois would later become a Major General and Chief of the Air Corps, Lahm and Humphreys, Brigadier Generals in the Air Corps and New York National Guard respectively. By 1911, Aeroplane No. 1 was no longer serviceable and was donated to the Smithsonian Institution.

General Humphreys suffered a fatal heart attack on 20 January 20 1941, at the age of 57.

In the end, the only American achievement in the field of aircraft production was the Liberty engine. At the time of the Armistice on 11 November 1918, almost all of the 740 U. S. aircraft at the front in France were European-made. Still, the Air Service of General Pershing's American Expeditionary Forces, organized by Major General Mason M. Patrick and Brigadier General William (Billy) Mitchell, had distinguished itself in action against the Germans.

U.S. air power played an important role in WWI, resulting during the 1920s and 1930s in a movement within the military to create an independent air force. Great Britain had done so early in 1918, combining its Army and Navy air arms into the Royal Air Force (RAF) under the Air Ministry. Since the Army's leaders saw the airplane primarily as a weapon for supporting the infantry, they gave the Air Service branch a status comparable to that of the field artillery or the engineers, responsible for procuring equipment and training units. Local ground forces commanders, none of them aviators, directed the aviation units assigned to them. A series of boards and commissions studied and restudied the question of air organization, with no result other than the name change to the U.S. Army Air Corps in mid-1926.

As has been said prior to this writing, "Adjutant Generals come and they go, but the Guard made little progress . . ." This was true in Oklahoma in the earliest part of the 20th century, but that too was about to change with the growth of our nation, the addition of states in the west, the fluctuation of economics and world-wide dramatic changes soon to occur. The National Defense Act of 1920 created the authority to form the 45th Infantry Division (Inf Div) from four states: Oklahoma, Colorado, Arizona and New Mexico. Organization of the division was started by 1923, and in 1924, Oklahoma guardsmen bivouacked together for the first time at Fort Sill, Oklahoma. The fourth, fifth and sixth decades of Oklahoma's 1900s saw the anthesis of the National Guard and the maturation of aviation within its boundaries.

The story of the 45th Division's Thunderbird shoulder sleeve insignia (SSI), or patch, is unique. For the first 15 years of the division's life, the soldiers of the 45th wore a yellow, broken cross (some called it a swastika) on a square background of brilliant red. This ancient American Indian symbol of *good luck* recognized the heritage of the first Americans; the red square symbolized the early Spanish

Div's first
patch

13

culture of the four Southwest states[1] from which the division's soldiers had been drawn. But by the mid-1930s, the broken cross had become so identified with Adolph Hitler's German National Socialist Party (Nazi) swastika[2] and fascism that the 45th could no longer use it, and they quickly discarded their original patch.

For many months, division soldiers had no SSI patch while a board of officers considered a variety of new proposed designs. The division held a contest, and many ideas for a new patch were submitted. In 1939, the 45th Inf Div adopted the Native American's Thunderbird as its new insignia.

45th Inf Div's second patch

Native American mythology recalls that the Thunderbird was a huge, eagle-like bird capable of producing thunder, lightning and rain as it wildly flapped its wings. This American Indian symbol means "sacred bearer of happiness unlimited." In keeping with tradition, the original red-and-yellow colors of the old insignia were retained in the new Thunderbird patch. The division's motto is – *Semper Anticus* ("Always Forward").

Ninety miles southwest of Oklahoma City is Lawton, OK – home of the U.S. Army's Field Artillery Center and Henry Post Army Airfield (AAF), which was the first home of Army Aviation. This western outpost was established by Major General Philip H. Sheridan in January 1869 to protect settlers in Texas and Kansas from hostile Indians. Later, after we had broken every single treaty made between the United States and all of the North American Indian nations, we would recruit descendants of these fierce warriors to fight with us against our national enemies and we called these citizen soldiers and ourselves Thunderbirds!

General Sheridan conducted a major winter campaign in 1869, which included such notables as "Wild Bill" Hickok, "Buffalo Bill" Cody, Jack Stilwell and Ben Clark. A distinguished unit of Buffalo Soldiers, a part of Sheridan's tactical troop, constructed most of the stone buildings that surround the original post quadrangle and housed some of the 7th Cavalry, the 19th Kansas Volunteers and the 10th Cavalry.

The early plains garrison was first called Camp Wichita and known to the local Native Americans as the Soldier House at Medicine Bluffs. MG Sheridan later named the outpost in honor of a classmate from West Point, Brigadier General Joshua W. Sill, who had been killed in the Civil War.

Henry Post Army Airfield was indeed once the home of all Army Aviation Training before the Army moved it to Camp Rucker, AL. Since Army Aviation training began at Henry Post AAF before there was a separate Air Force, this airfield was also the first home of Air Force aviation.

Henry Post AAF is a very historic airfield. The first aircraft in the Army Air Corps were assigned there and before that military balloons (dirigibles) were flown and hangared there. Dirigibles were used in WWI for adjustment of field artillery and as aerial observation platforms. They might as well have had large, red, circular targets painted on them, because the enemy soon learned to destroy them as they were launched and tethered! As a matter of fact, there is a balloon hanger at Fort Sill that still supports the airfield's rotating beacon and is listed as a Historic Landmark, as is the old Harrison Aviation Clinic adjacent to the airfield.

During 1923 and the following years, several committees and boards reviewed the issue of a separate Air Service and other major military issues, and at least two conflicting recommendations were made. In accordance with the views of then President Woodrow Wilson, the Morrow Board recommendation rejected the idea of a Department of Defense and a separate Department of Air. It did recommend, however, that the Air Service be renamed the *Army Air Corps* to allow it more prestige, that it be given special representation on the General Staff, and that an Assistant Secretary of War for Air Affairs be appointed.

Congress accepted the Morrow Board proposal, and the Air Corps Act was enacted on 2 July 1926. The legislation changed the name of the Air Service to the Army Air Corps, "thereby strengthening the conception of military aviation as an offensive, striking arm rather than an auxiliary service." The act created an additional Assistant Secretary of War to help foster military aeronautics, and it established an air section in each division of the General Staff for a period of three years. Other provisions required that all flying units be commanded by rated aviation personnel and that flight pay be continued. Two additional brigadier generals would serve as assistant chiefs of the Army Air Corps. The position of the air arm within the Department of War remained essentially the same as before. The flying units were under the operational control of the various ground forces corps commands and not the Army Air Corps, which remained responsible for procurement of aircraft, maintenance of bases, supply and training. Once more the hopes of Air Force officers had to be deferred.

A promising aspect of the Air Corps Act was the authorization for a five-year expansion program. However, lack of funding delayed the beginning of this five-year expansion program until 1 July 1927. The goal adopted was 1,800 airplanes with 1,650 officers and 15,000 enlisted men, to be reached in regular increments over a five-year period. But even this modest increase never came about as planned because adequate funds were never appropriated in the budget.

Nevertheless, just as in the RAF, the formulation of strategic bombing theories gave new impetus to the argument for an independent air force. Strategic or long-range bombardment was intended to destroy an enemy nation's industry and war-making potential, and an independent service would have a free hand to do so. Amid intense controversy, BG Billy Mitchell came to espouse these views and, in 1925, went to the point of martyrdom before a court-martial to publicize his position. But despite perceived obstruction from the War Department, the Army Air Corps made great strides during the 1930s. A doctrine emerged that stressed precision bombing of industrial targets by heavily armed long-range aircraft. The next major step toward creation of a separate air force was taken in March 1935 with the creation of a centralized operational air force, commanded by an aviator and answering to the Army's Chief of Staff.

Imagine all the machinations going on within the military during these early days: very strong feelings for a totally separate air service; those desiring an internal air branch and other bizarre theories. About 1941 another name change occurs from Army Air Corps to Army Air Forces.

Over the years and with zero state-appropriated funds, the Works Progress Administration (WPA) built 52 armories across the plains, upon the prairies and near the pine-covered mountains of Oklahoma. These military armories are 100 percent Oklahoma-made buildings. Thirty-three armories were constructed of stone cut and blasted from Oklahoma quarries. Eighteen were built of brick molded from bright red, Oklahoma clay. All of the steel used in these structures was manufactured in Oklahoma City plants and Oklahoma citizens were employed in their construction. However, to my knowledge, the WPA did not build any hangars for the OKARNG.

An armory program had long been needed in Oklahoma. Guard units had forever been inadequately housed. Some of them occupied abandoned barns and/or garages. Thousands of dollars worth of equipment was stolen from many insecure Guard quarters. Providing quarters for Guard units was just one of the armory's functions.

A large drill hall was the principal enclosure of each of these huge buildings. At one end of the hall was a spacious stage. Each hall seats approximately 2,000 persons; therefore, they could accommodate conventions and other assemblies, which otherwise could not be held in these communities. The armories were open to all civic gatherings.

The WPA activities were confined to the erection of the buildings. The interior furnishings and fixtures were contributed by interested individuals and groups in the communities in which these armories were located. In most cases, citizens of the towns and cities showed their appreciation by raising funds from which the interiors were decorated and offices and recreation rooms were generously furnished.

The first dirt turned or ground breaking for an Oklahoma Armory was on 8 October 1935 at Wewoka, OK. The governor, state administrator and other state, federal and military officials were in attendance. The brick structure at Wewoka was dedicated on 18 February 1937 and housed a Medical Detachment and Battery A, 160th Field Artillery. The armory is still in use as a warehouse.

In 2008, in a time when closings and consolidations of many armories is a common subject, there remain 130 OKARNG military units, including maintenance shops, located in 63 different Oklahoma cities/towns, at least 63 armories.

Prior to World War II (WWII), aviation in the Oklahoma Guard was non-existent. Organic Army Aviation first entered combat during WWII in November 1942 on the coast of North Africa.

Because aerial support was vital for artillery fire adjustment and the Air Corps fire support aircraft were not always available, field artillery officers became interested in using light aircraft organic to the artillery units. The Army experimented with using small, organic aircraft for artillery fire adjustment and other functions. The Army's L-4 Grasshoppers, as these light, spotter planes came to be called, proved to be much more effective than the larger Air Corps planes used for the same purposes. The

Grasshoppers and a few larger L-5 Sentinels were used to adjust artillery fire, gather intelligence, support naval bombardment; direct bombing missions and perform other functions.

In 1942, following the name change from Army Air Corps to Army Air Forces, a final series of experiments with organic Army Grasshopper (spotter) aircraft were conducted. The Secretary of War ordered the establishment of organic air observation for field artillery – hence the birth of modern Army Aviation on 6 June 1942. Three Army L-4 Grasshoppers launched on 9 November 1942 from the USS Ranger for the sole purpose of artillery adjustment in Northern Africa. Fratricide was the fate of these spotters and none returned.

The Army also became interested in an aircraft that might not need a runway and could take-off and land vertically. Army funding for helicopter research began in the 1920s, but the first U.S. military helicopter flight did not take place until 20 April 1942. On this date Igor Sikorsky demonstrated his prototype helicopter.

The helicopter was in its infancy during WWII and Korea; they were used to perform artillery adjustment and aerial medical evacuation (medevac). Most training of both pilots and mechanics was conducted by the Department of Air Training within the Field Artillery School at Fort Sill, Oklahoma, although the Army Air Forces conducted some primary training of organic Army Aviation personnel.

Because of the shortage of helicopters and the reluctance of the U.S. Army Air Force to purchase them for the ground forces, the Army did not acquire its first helicopter, an experimental model of the two-place OH-13 Sioux, until 1947. Following initial testing of this aircraft, the Army requested authorization to purchase 150 more and recommended the development and acquisition of cargo helicopters. The Army was able to acquire a total of 74 OH-13 observation helicopters during the following three years and it didn't acquire its first cargo/utility helicopters until 1952. Helicopters were in short supply during the years of the

Bell OH-13 'Sioux' helicopter ca 1950

Korean conflict. Therefore, largely because of the lives saved by heroic medevac pilots flying the OH-13, the helicopter became a viable presence on the modern battlefield.

It was just as helicopters were coming into the Army in much greater numbers that the Army National Guard (ARNG) Aviation Program came into being in 1948. Nearly ten years later, the ARNG inventory was made up of about 1,100 Army aviators, a little more than 600 fixed-wing airplanes and just 100 observation helicopters. Not the largest military fleet in the world, but a beginning!

Both during and following the Korean War, several Army leaders called for the use of helicopters in new tactical missions. General James Gavin published a challenging and stimulating article in April 1954, "Cavalry, and I Don't Mean Horses." The article called for the use of helicopters in air cavalry operations to provide the needed mobility that Army cavalry forces had lacked in Korea. Much of the conceptual basis for doctrinal development of the helicopter during the 1950s came from General Gavin's vision of a Sky Cavalry unit. Keep in mind that while this new air mobile concept was growing during 1954, Army planners were testing new Infantry and Armored Division force structure, which would include aviation companies in each division headquarters battalion.

In the scorching Oklahoma heat during June 1950, a newsman on WKY television in Oklahoma City reported that, "Communist North Korea has attacked and invaded South Korea and the United Nations had declared a police action." This police action was to members of the 45th Infantry Division the Korean War, as opposed to the Korean Conflict. After the initial invasion by Task Force Smith, President Truman called four National Guard Divisions to active duty for a two-year period, including the 45th of Oklahoma. The 45th was one of two National Guard divisions to see combat in the Korean War. The other was the 40th Division from California. As the 45th Infantry Division was mobilized at Camp Polk, 70

Cessna O-1A 'Bird Dog' ca 1951

percent of the soldiers were veterans of World War II, most of who had served with the 45th.

The Korean War provided new challenges and opportunities for Army Aviation. Organic Army Aviation had acquired its first helicopters, thirteen OH-13 Sioux, in 1947, before the U.S. Air Force became independent of the Army. In Korea, the Army employed the O-1 Bird Dog and other improved fixed-wing planes, but also helicopters. The Army used its OH-13s and OH-23 Ravens primarily for artillery adjustment, medical evacuation and transport of lightweight and valuable cargo. Because of the rugged terrain of the Korean peninsula, the value of helicopters came to be recognized by all the services; the demand for both helicopters and trained aviators exceeded the supply.

Sikorsky UH-19 'Chickasaw' ca 1951

The Army began organizing five helicopter transport companies and training warrant officer aviators in 1951. There was an ongoing rivalry between the Army and the new Air Force concerning responsibility and resources for the aerial support of ground forces. Because of this rivalry, and also because of the shortage of helicopters, only two Army transport companies were supplied with H-19 Chickasaw helicopters in time to participate in the Korean

OH-23B—CPT C.L. Strance Tulsa 1960

War. Transport helicopters nevertheless proved their value by moving cargo and personnel during the final months of the war and then by participating in prisoner exchanges and other functions after the cessation of hostilities.

Credit is given to the Transportation Corps for introducing the cargo helicopter program during the Korean War. This brought about two significant facets within aviation. The first was to bring Army Aviation into a high-cost arena with a larger and new type of helicopter. i Secondly, the cargo helicopter program brought about the start of the Warrant Officer Aviator Program. Warrants were to become recognized as the true professional pilots in Army Aviation.

Prior to the mid-1950s, the Army Air Forces/U.S. Air Force had provided primary training for Army Aviation aviators and mechanics. During the Korean War, the Department of Air Training at Fort Sill expanded, and in 1953, it became the U.S. Army Aviation School. As a result of the expansion of both aviation and artillery training, Fort Sill became overcrowded, and the Army decided to move the Army Aviation School to a different post. When no satisfactory permanent Army post was found, a temporary post, Camp Rucker, AL was chosen. The Army Aviation School moved from Fort Sill, Oklahoma, to Camp Rucker, Alabama, in 1954. Camp Rucker became Fort Rucker, and the U.S. Army Aviation Center (USAAVNC) was established there the following year.

In 1956, the Department of Defense (DOD) gave the Army control over all of its own training. Gary Air Force Base (AFB) and Wolters AFB in TX, where the Air Force had been conducting this training, were also transferred to the Army. Lacking adequate facilities at Fort Rucker, Army Aviation continued primary fixed-wing training at Camp Gary until 1959, advanced or tactical fixed-wing training at Fort Sill and primary rotary-wing training at Fort Wolters until 1973.

Amidst the turmoil of the fighting in Korea, the Oklahoma Military

LT Karl M. Frank Gary AFB
San Marcos, TX

Department was established in 1951 at Oklahoma City. It continues to serve there as the administrative agency for all matters concerning the Oklahoma National Guard and other military organizations.

In April 1954, Gov. Johnston Murray welcomed 45th Infantry Division soldiers home from Korea, as they returned to their homes in Bartlesville, Wewoka, Ada, Guthrie and other small Oklahoma towns. The historic and famed 45th Division was disbanded that year and the 45th Infantry Division (NGUS), which was organized in the OKARNG, received the official division colors from the original unit. NGUS was dropped from its designation. It appears that not until after our fighting Thunderbirds of the 45th Infantry Division fame in WWII and the Korean War returned to Oklahoma did we first see Army aircraft in the OKARNG. There is the possibility of a lone L-4 Grasshopper at Norman, prior to Korea, but I can't prove or disprove such.

In 1956, the Army Aviation Center began assembling and testing armament systems on Army helicopters and developing air cavalry tactics. These tests were conducted while the Air Force still theoretically had exclusive responsibility for aerial fire support and led to the development of armament systems for Army helicopters. Later, OKARNG Aviation (Avn) would see the UH-1M gunship along with other UH-1 Hueys arriving in Oklahoma in the 1970s.

The first U.S. Army Armed Helicopter Company was activated in Okinawa in 1962. It was deployed to Thailand and then to Vietnam, where it flew escort for lift helicopters. The Department of Defense did not abolish mission restrictions on the Army's rotary-wing aircraft, and thereby authorized the Army to arm its helicopters until 1966. At the same time, January 1962, helicopters were first used to transport Vietnamese troops.

The Howze Board, headed by Lieutenant General (LTG) Hamilton H. Howze, was established in 1962 to develop and test the concept of airmobility. This was also referred to as the Tactical Mobility Requirements Board. After test exercises, war games and concentrated study and analysis, the Howze Board recommended that the Army commit itself to organic airmobility—later known as Air Assault. Many active duty and National Guard soldiers would later attend OKARNG's Air Assault School at Camp Gruber, OK in the 1990s. OKARNG aviation provided continuous helicopter support to the Air Assault School during its several years of existence.

The Howze Board completed its work in August 1962. It concluded, "Adoption by the Army of the airmobile concept is necessary and desirable." The board recommended the creation of five air assault divisions in a 16-division Army force structure. Each of these air mobile divisions was to include an air cavalry squadron that replaced 2,339 of its ground vehicles with 459 aircraft.

The Howze Board recommended the extensive use of helicopters to transport infantry troops, artillery and supplies, as well as to provide local aerial fire support. These recommendations were tested by the 1st Air Assault Division (Test) from 1963 to 1965. In 1963, the 11th Air Assault Division tested the concept at Fort Benning, Georgia and other places. In 1965, the first airmobile division, the 1st Cavalry Division (Airmobile), was organized and sent to Vietnam where it demonstrated the validity of the airmobile concept in actual combat. Although the concept of air mobility was developed with a mid-intensity European conflict in mind, it proved to be valid for the low-intensity conflict in Southeast Asia.

Both Army Aviation and the helicopter came of age during the conflict in Southeast Asia. From the arrival in Vietnam of the first Army helicopter units in December 1961 until the completion of the disengagement and Vietnamization processes in 1973, it was America's helicopter war.

In late 1965 the ARNG created provisional divisions of full-strength ready units, which could be activated upon short notice in the event of another war. This evolved due to an ever increasing manpower need of the war in Vietnam. These units were called Select Reserve Forces (SRF). They drilled twice a month and were told, "Be ready to mobilize on short notice." Troop units of the OKARNG's 45th Div comprised about one brigade of SRF. The SRF units were still part of the 45th Inf Div and were given accelerated training support. OKARNG Aviation provided aircraft support and aviation training for the Oklahoma SRF units. No OKARNG units were mobilized and the program was later discontinued. One company size unit, Trp "D", 145th Calvary became an Air Cavalry Troop and was stationed at Marlow, OK. About half of Oklahoma Army National Guard aviators served in this unit from 1965 to 1968.

The National Guard Bureau, in 1968, conducted a reorganization of the entire Army National Guard and several divisions were eliminated, including Oklahoma's 45th Infantry Division. Final reorganization was on 1 February 1968, and the 45th Infantry Division became a separate infantry brigade (SIB), with numerous combat support and combat service support organizations. The new designation was the 45th Inf Bde (Sep), sometimes referred to as the 45th SIB, and it comprised one half of the total ARNG troop strength authorized to Oklahoma in 1968. In the Army's effort to further convolute things in this 21st century, the 45th SIB was reorganized and redesignated the 45th Brigade Combat Team (BCT).

There is no 45th Infantry Division today. Its former history is magnificent; you and I should ensure that its history is not forgotten.

In the post-Korea days of OKARNG aviation, there was not yet a separate aviation unit within the state boundaries. Initially each of Oklahoma's major commands, the 45th Infantry, 45th Field Artillery and Engineers, had a slice of the aviation support pie. As previously mentioned, these were called aviation sections. There was a young Army Guard lieutenant or captain at each headquarters who was assigned the additional duty of aviation liaison (Avn LNO). He was responsible for requesting aviation support and the individual who would be blamed when the general wanted to go inspect a subordinate unit and the damn airplane didn't show up, or when it was late, and in the dismal case—should it crash with the general on board. The Avn LNO always got the blame, but never any credit!

One weekend each month OKARNG units drilled at Oklahoma City, Tulsa and about 50 small Oklahoma armories. Aviators would be assigned an aircraft and a mission by Gus Guild—"Hey C.L., why don't you go up to Edmond and see if you can gin up some flying business with the infantry this weekend?" Or "Dan (Batey), you ought to take the OH-13 down to Lawton and see if you can fly one of their second lieutenant forward observers out to the range and adjust a few rounds of 105mm!"

So what would these young adventuresome aviators do with the airplanes or helicopters in between drill weekends? There weren't any additional flight training periods (AFTPs) in the National Guard yet. Many guardsmen had told their wives they didn't get paid for belonging to the Guard, they just did it because there were patriotic individuals. These wives smiled and poured another cup of coffee for their strong, dedicated husbands.

In fact in the very beginning, National Guardsmen didn't get paid; it was a volunteer militia. That changed over time, however. Today traditional guardsmen are paid quite well and can receive reenlistment bonuses, recruiting bonuses and other major benefits, including the G.I.

Bill. They can even sign up for a program called College First in which the ARNG pays for their education before they go to a unit.

Aviators and flight crew members today are authorized to receive flight pay when they are assigned to a flying slot in a unit. Unit's personnel authorizations are note in the Table of Distribution and Allowances (TDA) or the Modified Table of Organization and Equipment (MTOE) line-position, one day's flight pay for each day of active duty or each Unit Training Assembly (UTA) performed. Also included are two Additional Flight Training Periods (AFTPs) per month, which equate to two days military pay, and then there's the pot of gold at the end of 20 years military service – a retirement check each month! Thank you Jesus!

Circa 1960, the OKARNG had received perhaps one OH-13 Sioux and several OH-23 Raven helicopters. Both of these types of whirly birds were used proudly in the Korean War and greatly reduced the number of casualties killed in action (KIA) or seriously wounded in action (WIA) as a result of quick, prompt airborne medical evacuation from the battlefield to a mobile army surgical hospital (MASH). Medical personnel would later say that Army helicopters, which carried the wounded from the battlefield to a MASH, prevented so many individuals from going into shock, thus saving their lives and reducing the results of serious wounds by getting them into triage more quickly. Although it would be years before Medical Evacuation Aviation units came into existence and became common in the Army, these aircraft and the brave, heroic aviators who flew them under fire, in the mountains and at night, eventually became members of the Oklahoma Army National Guard. Many of the aviators from Korea came home and joined the OKARNG, continuing to fly as they had on active duty.

In the late 1950s, early 1960s, many of my high school contemporaries considered themselves beer wizards. They could name 50 or more different brands, where they were brewed, etc. One beer of great interest to those of us living out on the plains of Oklahoma was Coors. Its slogan was "brewed with pure Rocky Mountain spring water." In 1959, Adolph Coors introduced the first all-aluminum beer can and introduced recycling. They offered one penny for each aluminum can returned to their brewery. I wanted to drive up to Colorado each weekend and get my six cents refund!

At this time, most kids east of the Mississippi had never known Coors beer. It just wasn't available. Many college entrepreneurs made small fortunes bootlegging Coors back to colleges and universities in the east, as the brewery didn't distribute east of the muddy Mississippi. Coors transitioned from a regional to international brewer in the 1970s when the company began expanding to new markets. Until then, Coors produced one beer, Original Coors, for distribution in just 11 Western states. In1981 Coors distribution crossed the Mississippi River, and not until 1991 were Coors products available in all 50 states.

Why all this talk about beer? Well, this isn't about Coors beer. It's about geography—on which side of the Mississippi River you happen to be. Oklahoma I believe is still on the west side of the Mississippi, but this has been open to debate at times. You see, our first Army helicopters in the ARNG were the OH-13 Sioux and the OH-23 Raven. In the late 1950s, OKARNG had one OH-13 and several OH-23, plus a plethora of fixed-wing aircraft. The OH-13 was manufactured by Bell Helicopters back east in the state of New York. And the OH-23 was manufactured by Hiller on the left coast in Palo Alto, California. In the Army's infinite wisdom, OH-13s were initially fielded to states and military units east of the Mississippi and OH-23s only west of the mighty Mississippi. Therefore, if you had OH-23s parked on your ramp, you must be west of the Mississippi. The Army's helicopter wizard at the Pentagon was convinced there were no highways, railroads or airplane freight deliveries across the Mississippi.

Several years later he was promoted up and out. His replacement was a little brighter and someone showed him a couple of photos of bridges going across this Mississippi River with a Consolidated Freight eighteen-wheeler crossing the bridge. Sooo, just maybe, we can ship aircraft parts both directions across this formidable barrier. Another breakthrough for modern man and today's Army!

Most aviators, Army, Air Force, Navy or Marine, who flew in WWII, or Korea and/or later in Vietnam, never lost the love of flying or the desire to continue flying. I can name quite a few former aviators[3], who retired militarily from OKARNG Aviation at age 60, yet remain very active as civilian aviators, some well into their 70s! Military aviation isn't a hobby, it is a way of life and some would still fly just for groceries!!!

Within the OKARNG a major reorganization came about in January 1969, when the former WWII 45th Division was restructured into three major commands: an infantry brigade, an artillery group, and a support command, with a state area command headquarters (STARC) providing general administrative and logistical support. All OKARNG members continued to wear the Thunderbird SSI and carried on the Thunderbird traditions. The division did not receive a call for service in the Vietnam War. Although four National Guard Divisions had been called to serve in WWII by President Truman, not one ARNG Division was activated for the war in Vietnam.

There were other aircraft in the years that followed; later more helicopters came into the OKARNG than airplanes. There were some large rotor-wing aircraft added to the inventory: H-19s Chickasaws, with R-1300 Wright 700 hp radial engines; they red-lined or VNE (velocity not to exceed) at 112 mph and had a max range of 330 miles. Then there were the CH-34 Choctaws, a medium utility transport helicopter with a Wright R-1820-84 radial engine, and could carry 12 to 16 troops. With these two additions came a great carrying capacity, but also an increase in our maintenance program. Additional personnel were needed to keep them flying. Aviation personnel didn't want to leave them outside and didn't want to perform maintenance on them outside, and soon that too changed.

A hangar was leased at the Naval Flight Training Base on Max Westheimer Field in Norman, OK. This was a blessing for all involved.

Even the passengers would have been happy to know that when SGT Davis removed the engine out of the chopper, hardly any dirt got into the transmission since we moved it into the hangar! The addition of this hangar improved the ability of Aviation to provide safer and timelier maintenance on aircraft. It also allowed OKARNG

Max Westheimer Naval Air Station, Norman, OK ca 1944

Avn to better support the major military units of the OKARNG. A few more years passed, new aviators came from the active Army and other services. Some guardsmen within the OKARNG were able to get quotas to attend the Initial Entry Rotary-Wing (R/W) Flight School. This was very significant progress. At the same time a number of OKARNG aviation personnel had accepted full-time employment in Baja Oklahoma (Texas) as civilian rotary-wing flight instructors for Southern Airways, a military flight contractor with the Army at Fort Wolters, Texas, near Mineral Wells.

Some of the very earliest military helicopters at the Army's primary rotary-wing flight school still had wooden blades. Many of the early OKARNG aviators who worked for Southern Airways were flight instructors in the OH-23B, or C model. Hiller can attest to this fact.

Located in the counties of Palo Pinto and Parker, Fort Wolters'[4] history dates back to the days of old Camp Wolters, created in 1925 as a National Guard training area under the guidance of General Jacob F. Wolters.

On 13 October 1940, the U.S. Army activated Camp Wolters as an Infantry Replacement Center, with the support of Mineral Wells' community leaders. Additional lands were bought or donated to the Army by local residents to expand the camp to more than 7,500 acres. In less than four months, more than 100 buildings were constructed. The original buildings of old Camp Wolters were converted into a prisoner of war (POW) camp for German prisoners from North Africa. The prison camp was closed on 15 August 1946, as the last prisoners were returned to their homeland.

At its peak, Camp Wolters was home to more than 30,000 soldiers per training cycle. Among notable war heroes that passed through the camp were Lieutenants Jack Knight and Audie Murphy, both of whom were awarded the Congressional Medal of Honor.

After World War II, Fort Wolters was deactivated as an Army Training Facility and reactivated in 1951 as Wolters Air Force Base. In 1956, it was designated Camp Wolters Army Base, and was used for helicopter flight training with more than 1,000 helicopters stationed at three different heliports. The base expanded to cover 722,000 acres of land for flight training purposes. In 1963 it was designated Fort Wolters. The fort also became the site of a Nike missile installation until it reverted once again to the National Guard after the Vietnam War. Fort Wolters was closed for military service on 1 February 1973.

The UH-1 Iroquois or Huey was sent to Vietnam in significant numbers in 1964; before the end of the conflict, more than 5,000 of these versatile aircraft were introduced into Southeast Asia. They were used for medical evacuation, command and control and air assault; to transport personnel and materiel; and as gunships. The AH-1 Cobra arrived in country in 1967 to partially replace the Huey gunships. Other important helicopters in Vietnam included the CH-21 Shawnee, CH-34 Choctaw, CH-47 Chinook, the OH-6 Cayuse (Little Bird), the OH-58 Kiowa, and the CH—54 Tarhe. In the mid to late 1960s Bell Helicopter's UH-1 Huey, the most recognized aircraft of the Vietnam War, began to replace some of Oklahoma's older, outmoded, reciprocating engine helicopters. We were moving on up.

Although the concept of airmobility had been developed with a mid-intensity European conflict in mind, Army Aviation and the helicopter had proven themselves during the low-intensity conflict in Southeast Asia. Afterwards, the Army turned its major attention back to the threat of a mid or high-intensity conflict in Europe, and doubts reemerged about the value of helicopters in that sort of arena.

The creation, implementation and consolidation of the Army Aviation Branch dominated the 1980s. Prominent aviators as well as other Army leaders had debated the establishment of Aviation as a separate branch since the time of the Korean War.

The opposition to a separate Aviation branch had resulted in part from Army attitudes regarding the Army Air Corps and the U.S. Air Force. In Army circles, both of these aviation organizations were believed to have been unreliable in performing their mission of supporting the ground forces—even after having been given resources to do so. Since Army Aviation had demonstrated its commitment to the support of the ground battle in Vietnam, however, opposition to a separate Aviation branch began to wane.

Some military leaders believed that the helicopter could not survive and perform an essential role in a heavy combat environment. In order to gain general acceptance and ensure further success, Army Aviation continued to develop new doctrine, tactics, aircraft, equipment and organizational structure. New or radically modified aircraft adopted during the 1980s consisted of the AH-64 Apache, the CH-47D Chinook, the UH-60 Black Hawk, and the OH—58D version of the Kiowa.

Also, Army Aviation had grown in size and technological sophistication. This growth caused complex problems in training, procurement, doctrine development, proponent responsibility and personnel management. Many non-aviators as well as aviators became convinced that these problems could be solved more effectively by the creation of an aviation branch.

Both Department of the Army (DA) and U.S. Army Training and
Doctrine Command (TRADOC) conducted extensive studies of the
separate branch question during the 1980s. Army Aviation having begun
in 1942, it was 41 years later, in 1983, that there was a near consensus
among Army leaders, and the Secretary of the Army signed an order
creating the Army Aviation Branch. It was the Commanding General
of the U.S. Army Aviation Center and School, Major General Bobby J.
Maddox[5], who announced the new Aviation Branch, with an effective
date of 12 April 1983.

Aviation Officer Basic and Advanced Courses were begun at Fort
Rucker in 1984, and a gradual consolidation of aviation-related activities
followed. In 1986, the U.S. Army ATC Activity became part of the branch;
the following year, an NCO academy was established at Fort Rucker. In
1988, the Army Aviation Logistics School, which had been dependent
on the Transportation Center at Fort Eustis, was incorporated into the
Aviation Branch.

In today's Army (2010) an Army soldier should be able to complete
flight school within 12 calendar months. However, it may take up to 24
months to graduate as an Army Rotary Wing Aviator. This is due to an
extreme backlog in the training pipeline. During this bottle neck, aviation
flight school candidates might now expect to attend Officer's Basic Course
(OBC), Survival, Escape, Resistance and Evasion (SERE), Resistance
Training Lab (RTL), and other aviation-related courses before beginning
their actual academic and flight line instruction.

In 1988, the Army Aviation Modernization Plan was given final
approval and implemented. The modernization plan called for a gradual
reduction in the number of Army aircraft as older models, such as the
UH-1 Huey and the OH-58 were replaced by modern ones. Aircraft
adopted or planned during the late 1980s and 1990s included the OH-58D
Kiowa Warrior, the RAH-66 Comanche, and a new training helicopter.
The RAH-66 contract has since been cancelled, having been deemed too
expensive and obsolete before production began. By 1990, the Army's
aviation assets exceeded 8,800 aircraft along with 24,000 aviators and
23,000 enlisted aircrew. The Army's new utility helicopter, the UH-72
Lakota by Eurocopter was fielded in 2008/2009.

Army Aviation's role of providing the indispensable vertical dimension
to the modern battlefield has come to be universally recognized. Army
aviation units were involved in all major contingency operations during

the 1980s and 1990s. In Operation Urgent Fury, the American invasion of Grenada in October 1983, both the Marine Corps and the Army used helicopters. For the Army, Urgent Fury was the first combat test of the new UH-60 Black Hawks, which were used for assault, medevac and transport during the operation. Three Army aviation battalions took part in Operation Urgent Fury.

Another new Army helicopter, the OH-58D Kiowa Warrior, was employed in the Persian Gulf in 1987, for Operation Prime Chance. The Army armed 15 of these aircraft with Hellfire missiles and stationed them on U.S. Navy ships in the Persian Gulf to protect shipping during the war between Iran and Iraq. Task Force 160 was the covert side of U.S. involvement in the Gulf, because of its armed AH-6 Little Birds. OKARNG's 45th Avn (Lt Hel Cbt) was highly trained and available, but not mobilized, much to the disappointment of many, including the Pentagon.

About 160 Army helicopters took part in Operation Just Cause, (the American invasion of Panama) beginning in December 1989. AH-64 Apaches self-deployed from the United States and engaged in combat for the first time. Other Army aircraft performing attack, assault, transportation and observation roles in Operation Just Cause included Cobras, Black Hawks, Chinooks, Kiowas, Hueys and MH and AH-6s. The invasion of Panama employed the largest number of Special Operations aircraft (65 helicopters, including Little Birds and 20 fixed-wing planes) ever employed by United States forces. There was general agreement that Special Operations' aviation support was the best that had ever been provided. Operation Just Cause enabled Army aviators to demonstrate in combat that, through the use of the night vision devices with which they had

GARY A.F. B.
SAN MARCOS, TEX.

trained, they could own the night, and they did.

The morning of 17 January 1991, an Army aviator fired the first shot of Operation Desert Storm from an Army helicopter. Within a few minutes, two teams of Apaches destroyed two Iraqi radar stations, paving way for the air war over Iraq to be conducted with relative impunity.

Army aviation didn't drift across the Red River into Oklahoma, nor did it blow in from Amarillo because two strands of a three-strand barbed wire fence were down. It was brought onto the plains and prairies of our great state by Army aviation pioneers and patriarchs – true leaders, men of vision and integrity, great examples for others to emulate. Our OKARNG aviation patriarchs are men such as Lieutenant Colonel August Lee "Gus" Guild, Brigadier General Chester A. "Chet" Howard, Colonel Charlie R. Jones, Brigadier General Dana D. Batey and Colonel Leroy A. Wall.

Oklahoma Army Aviation training and support began in the mid-20th century with reciprocating, antiquated, but war tried and tested aircraft, flown by cocky, sometimes arrogant, but always confident Army aviators. These men brought us from the Da Vincian days of just dreaming about flying, through the throws of creating and supporting Counter-terrorism and Special Operation Aviation units. They led us from the stark, simplistic valleys of near non-existent aviation force structure (days of the Avn Sec), into, through and out of the fog-covered mountains and darkest nights of Special Operations. These patriarchs orchestrated small trios and quartets of mismatched, antiquated airframes into magnificent, multi-missioned fleets of modern, turbine-powered, nocturnal, workhorses and then complemented these with sleek, superb, twin-turbine powered fixed-wing airplanes capable of transporting a commander's immediate staff half-way across these United States.

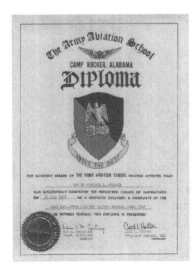

Strance—RW Camp Rucker diploma Jul 1955

Our Oklahoma Army Guard Aviation patriarchs brought us from only dreaming of aviation to a hay day peak of over 600 personnel and 65 aircraft, with real worldwide aviation missions in the 1990s.

Our earliest Oklahoma Army National Guard aviators were trained while on active duty, either in the Army Air Corp or later the Air Force. Before Camp Rucker even became Fort Rucker, many Army aviators trained at Gary Air Force Base, San Marcos, Texas. On this and the previous page are two truly wonderful examples of deco artwork for a 1955 Army Primary Flight Training

Graduation from Gary AFB, TX and a July 1955 Army Aviation School graduation diploma from Camp Rucker, AL. Both were provided courtesy of C.L. Strance, Collinsville, OK, former member of the OKARNG Aviation Program and a Lords of Darkness (45th Avn (SO)(A)) aviator.

1. Arizona, Colorado, New Mexico and Oklahoma.

2   The swastika was officially adopted by the National Socialist Party in 1935.

3   George Senne and C.L. Strance, both in their 70s; Clay Clarkson and Leroy A. Wall are also men who continued to fly after their military careers. Batey, Senne, Clarkson, Wall have well over 10,000 flight hours. LTC Jay "Tommy" Evans had over 10,000 flight hours, as did Douglas Gandy and Samuel T. Hinch. Some are very close to 10,000 hours, like Bobby Lane and Tommy Klutts. A few OKARNG aviators quit logging flight time after they reached 25,000 hours, like CW4 Joe Patterson, formerly a WWII B-24 pilot and later a member of Det 1, HHC, 45th (Sep) Inf Bde Avn Section.

4   State of Texas historical marker near the entrance to the Mineral Wells Industrial Park, Mineral Wells, TX. The newly refurbished entrance gate to Fort Wolters was dedicated in March 2011.

5   Major General Maddox is the brother of former OKARNG aviator, CW4 Orbie J. Maddox of McKinney, TX.

Chapter 2

The Patriarchs of OKARNG Aviation and Birth of Army

National Guard Aviation

"The world is divided into people who do things and people who get the credit. Try, if you can, to belong to the first group. There's far less competition . . ."

Dwight Marrow

Any organization, especially a military unit, will never rise higher than the leader's own abilities, visions or dreams!

"Everything rises and falls on leadership[1]."

Have we forgotten that "Leaders determine the level of an organization"?[2] This maxim is 100% true. This isn't to say that the leader does all the work or that he/she should get all the credit – far from it! Take a moment and recall any unit in which you have served and consider its commander. With the exception of one headed by a complete ignoramus, remember the standards that were set for the unit, and those reached by that unit. Weren't the results achieved often beyond your imagination?

Much of what your unit accomplished can be attributed to the motivation of unit personnel, the vision and imagination of your leader(s). The adage, If you can dream it—you can achieve it, is not far off the mark. An organization's level of accomplishment is attributable to those in leadership positions. Success or failure can often depend on the combined efforts of a commander, senior NCO and the staff. However, the whole ballgame rises and falls on the credibility, efforts and dreams of the leader!

We've heard that the whole is only as strong as the weakest link. While that saying is true in most circumstances, a track relay team or a highly motivated military unit will often disprove the point. However, teamwork can overcome many weaknesses. Positive motivation, leading from the front, giving credit to the team, not the individuals (or to the leader), and enabling each component to function as part of the whole, creates an atmosphere in which great things can be accomplished. Sometimes we can judge our success by how much we had to give up achieving it. Great leaders often have to give up the glory and the credit, besides their blood, sweat and tears!

The aspirations and the efforts of our early leaders, the true patriarchs of Army Aviation in the Oklahoma Army National Guard, were such that our evolution was more than just noteworthy. By recounting their stories we can support two important tenants of leadership: The cream rises to the top, and "The strength of any organization is a direct result of the strength of its leaders."[3]

As you read on, you decide, was there a special connection and/or camaraderie that Oklahoma Aviation shared with the Pennsylvania ARNG Aviation (PAARNG) program and personnel? Was it imaginary; did it really exist? Was the state of Pennsylvania considered a stepping stone, or the next rung up the ladder of success? How was it that some of our finest OKARNG aviators worked in PAARNG Aviation, even rising to the rank of General Officer, to the benefit of or credit of OKARNG and Aviation? When Pennsylvania was in dire need of aviation leadership and expertise . . .

Was it Texas that came to the rescue? No!

Was it California? No!

If you were about to answer, "Oklahoma," you are correct!

Prior to Korea, there were very few aviation resources in Oklahoma and the National Guard. Light observation or spotter aircraft was all that was available. The Army had given the Guard a few L-15 Scouts manufactured by Boeing, several going to Oklahoma. The fact that the Army's first flight school was located at Ft Sill, OK didn't hurt anything either. There would be no separate OKARNG aviation units in existence for several years following the war in Korea and the return of the 45th Infantry Division.

We know of only a few Army aviators in the OKARNG prior to Korea. These men were: Chief Warrant Officer Perry H. Papa Tango Townsend, Chief Warrant Officer Bill Tingle, Chief Warrant Officer Jack Ray, and Captain August Lee "Gus" Guild. These men,[4] Oklahoma Army Aviators, were in the OKARNG before Korea, were activated with the 45th Infantry

Division (Inf Div), deployed to and flew in Korea, and returned. After the war they continued to fly in the Oklahoma Guard Aviation program.

During the time that the 45th Inf Div was in Korea (1950–1953) there were several L-19s assigned, primarily used for artillery adjustment. These were in Avn Sections, such as the Div Arty (Avn Sec), Inf Div Hqs (Avn Sec) and the 45th Inf Div Regiments (179th, 180th and 279th).

It was a thing of true beauty, that aluminum-skinned 1950 Cessna, L-19A Bird Dog. The Department of Defense had received a bargain contract price of $30,000 each for this Cessna aircraft, which later become a collector's item. This is coincidentally the same price as the Army contracted and paid for its very first Wright Brothers aircraft in 1908. The standard Table of Organization and Equipment (TOE) for every Army Field Artillery Battalion (active duty) included an aviation section of two Bird

LTC August L. "Gus" Guild—First Okla. Avn Officer in Charge

Dogs. These fixed-wing observation aircraft were the commander's extra eyes and legs, used not only for artillery adjustment, but liaison as well. At this time, the Army had a grand total of 56 helicopters (utility and observation). No cargo helicopters existed in the Army yet.

Major August Lee "Gus" Guild was Oklahoma Army National Guard Aviation's first true patriarch. Gus was Scot-Irish, gruff and tough, had a ruddy complexion, and was built close to the ground. He wore his hat kind of cocky. He was stout, but more slender than stocky; he had dark hair with a receding hair line. Born to Reid and Pearl Guild, in Hugo, OK, on 11 May 1916, Gus had three siblings: two older sisters, Elizabeth and Mildred, and later his little brother Hershel, who joined the clan in 1919. He attended and graduated high school in Norman, OK in 1935.

Gus Guild and his wife, Dora were living in Norman, OK, near where Gus was to pursue his military aviation career. In 1940, Gus enlisted in the Army Field Artillery as a private. At that time he was 128 lbs and 5' 7" according to his military entrance physical.

Private (PVT) Guild rose up through the ranks. He had that don't give up attitude. Before the term State Aviation Officer (SAO) was even thought of, Gus was the man in charge of airplanes, helicopters and aviators in the Oklahoma Guard immediately after the Korean War.

Gus graduated from Field Artillery OCS in 1942 and received a commission as a second lieutenant on Christmas Eve 1942. Not long after, he became an Aviation Cadet and completed cadet pilot training in 1943. He served 29 months during WWII in the Pacific Theater in 1943-45. He was discharged from the Active Army in 1947.

Having joined the OKARNG after WWII, Gus was promoted on 22 August 1950 to the rank of Major and was the Div Avn Officer of the 45th Inf Div at Fort Polk, LA. He served as the Div Avn Officer in Korea for the 45th in 1951-52. He was once again released from Active Duty on 9 August 1952 at Fort Sill, OK.

MAJ Guild was again reassigned as the OKARNG Div Avn Officer, 45th Inf Div, Oklahoma City, OK, from 15 September 1952 to March1959.

Following the end of the Korean War, the 45th Inf Div was released from active duty on 30 April 1954. Prior to that, in 1951, the Oklahoma Military Department (OMD) came into existence and in the following years, Major General Roy W. Kenny, the Adjutant General of Oklahoma (OKTAG), authorized three full-time aviation manning positions. MAJ Guild was hired as the first of three full-time OKARNG aviation employees. The other two were aircraft maintenance positions, filled by Sergeant Lloyd R. Ormiston and Sergeant Marvin Davis. MAJ Guild's military assignment was as the 45th Inf Div Aviation Officer. At this time there were three aircraft in the OKARNG: two L-19 Bird Dogs and one OH-23 B Raven.

MAJ Guild's full-time position with the OKARNG was as Aircraft Maintenance Officer, with Ormiston and Davis doing the actual work on the aircraft. In those days, the Aviation Maintenance Officer was under the State Maintenance Office (SMO) in Norman. MAJ Guild supervised the scheduling, utilization, and maintenance of OKARNG's aircraft and its small host of vintage aviators. Gus was a perfectionist and aviation maintenance was his forte. The aircraft were hangared at the old Air National Guard hangar at Will Rogers Airport, on the southwest quadrant of Oklahoma City, long before it became an international airdrome.

On a windy, hot, Oklahoma morning, ca 1956-57, MAJ Guild cranked up the only OH-23 B helicopter OKARNG had at the time.

He flew a short cross-country VFR route southwest from Will Rogers down to the South Canadian River to a Boy Scout Camp called Camp Kickapoo. The BSA Camp had made a request for a Guard helicopter to come down and do a static display, and Gus took the mission. He landed at the camp, shut down the Raven, and was inundated with Tender Foots, first and second class Boy Scouts and ten thousand questions, all of which he attempted to answer. After having lunch with the Scouts in their mess hall, Gus went back to the chopper, and instructed an adult BSA leader to keep everyone back at least 100 feet. Damn good thing. As soon as he lifted off the ground to a hover, he intended to turn 90 degrees left and take off into the wind. He turned 90 degrees left and the tail rotor blades struck a telephone pole that had been there no less 5-7 years and was quite set on staying there. There was a lot of noise for about 20 seconds as the pole splintered and helicopter parts spewed all around and floated to the ground. As you might guess, the helicopter was destroyed. Gus wasn't seriously hurt and thankfully no Boy Scouts were hurt either.

Slowly at first, a few more aircraft were authorized and assigned to Oklahoma. Mostly, they were the Army's leftovers from Korea, seven or eight L-19 Bird Dogs (later designated O-1s) and about three L-20 DeHaviland Beavers (later designated as U-6As). Of course the Bird Dogs were light, single engine, two-passenger observation airplanes; the Beavers were larger, four-passenger utility airplanes with a maximum speed of 141 kts (163 mph) according to the book, although some say, "I never saw a U-6A do more than 110 kts in cruise and 130 kts in a screaming dive!" The Beaver was said to have a maximum range of 455 miles, which from Oklahoma City, allowed full flight coverage of the state.

Gus was the caretaker for Oklahoma Guard Aviation in the mid-to-late 1950s. Although his expertise was aviation maintenance, he recruited many new soldiers into the aviation program, which made a significant difference at the time, and a dramatic impact down the road. He was constantly marketing OKARNG Aviation.

Clarence L. "C.L." Strance got into the OKARNG as an aviator in February 1957 in Norman. He remembers this little tidbit about Gus: "I got along with Gus really well; some of the guys didn't like him. He was always saying to me, "I'm gonna burn your ass!" because he knew I was always taking people for helicopter rides. [He was] kind of a thin built guy; he had flown in Korea. He had this nervous twitch in his throat and some called him Gulping Gus."

MAJ Guild was promoted to the rank of Lieutenant Colonel on 1 February 1956. He attended the Avn Maint Officer course at Fort Eustis, VA, in 1956-57.

The 45th Avn Co came into being 1 May 1959. Lieutenant Colonel Guild was assigned as Commander and given the title Div Avn Officer from 16 May 1959 to March1963. In 1959 OKARNG conducted annual training at Fort Hood, TX. Gus also attended a 4th Army Instructor Pilot course in 1959.

On occasion, the air boss, LTC Gus Guild, would get a phone call notifying him that a new aircraft was being issued to OKARNG and was to be picked up at Fort Sill, OK or at Camp Rucker, AL, or some other location. Gus would then call two aviators at home and asked if they were interested in a ferry mission. They eagerly accepted and he would assign them as the crew for that mission. They packed their small suitcases for a brief Temporary Duty (TDY) excursion and on the day of departure, Gus assigned them an aircraft from the hangar at Will Rogers Airport and they began flight planning. They completed their map recon, grabbed their TDY orders and a letter of authorization to pick up the new aircraft, and off they went. Sometimes they even filed a flight plan. A few days later the new aircraft was ferried back to Oklahoma, much to the delight of several awaiting aviators and the two full-time aviation mechanics.

Everyone was energized and anxious to see what new-fangled radios or other improvements these aircraft might have. These were often battle weary airframes and there was nothing new about them at all. Yet they were assets that Oklahoma didn't have the day before and now they did! They learned to be thankful for what they had! The fleet was growing, not exactly by leaps and bounds, but the hangar now had several aircraft parked inside, which greatly reduced the echo.

Gus had the guts and character to be the leader – he knew maintenance, inside and out, and he knew he had to keep this ball rolling. He convinced MG Kenny to allow him to move the Army Aviation aircraft out of the Air Guard hangar at Will Rogers, down to Max Westheimer airfield in Norman, which was a very wise move. It was a large, wooden Navy hangar divided it into four groups. Navy Operations had one quarter of the hangar; University of Oklahoma Aviation had one quarter; Aero Commander (a private corporation) had one quarter; and OKARNG Aviation had the other quarter. Our offices were on the second floor, against the outside walls, with a common balcony connecting them. We had a twenty-five year lease for $1 consideration. This hangar was the same wooden-two-story style as the one that Trp Cmd (Avn) shared with the USAR from 1986 until 1993 at Westheimer (located on Westheimer Drive).

"The OKARNG would later build a new fixed-wing hangar at Westheimer in the 1962-63 timeframe," stated Dana D. Batey.[5] This became the current C-12 and Reconnaissance Air Interdiction Detachment (RAID) hangar on the north end of the airfield in the late 1980s and 1990s.

In 1961, Gus was about to get a little raise in salary, albeit somewhat complicated in how it happened. A new full-time position was authorized in aviation – an Operations and Training Officer position at each facility. The new position paid more than the Maintenance Officer position that Gus was in and had held since Moses was a baby! Guild and others had noticed another very sharp young man, another up and comer, in the Field Artillery Brigade at Enid: a young captain by the name of Charles R. Jones. He was asked to accept the new position, which he did and was hired as the new, full-time Operations and Training Officer at Max Westheimer Airfield. The position was a state employee slot and paid a salary of $7,700 per year. "It was an easy decision," stated Charlie, who had been teaching in Enid for $4,500 per year.

"It's interesting what happened," he said. "They created the Operations and Training Officer slot at each aviation facility/activity in a state. When they advertised this position it was first a state position, meaning state payroll, but that soon changed. They called me and wanted to know if I would be willing to come on board as the maintenance officer and let August Guild take the new Ops & Tng Officer position because it paid more. And would I be willing to switch with him? In other words, I'd do the Ops & Tng business and he'd continue to do the Maint Officer work. That was fine with me. I accepted the position and left right away for the Aircraft Maintenance Officer Course (AMOC) at Fort Eustis, VA."

"Also of interest at this time, each full-time aviator in the OKARNG was an instructor pilot on State orders. It was not at all unusual for anyone of our patriarchs to be on orders as instructor pilot for four, five or more different aircraft, rotary-wing and/or fixed-wing at any one time! "Charlie, you're going to be the IP on this aircraft and they'd cut the orders at OMD and that was it." Jones added, "When they came out with the idea of standardization at a later point, I was rotary-wing and fixed-wing rated, and was working full-time as an IP. They wanted us to attend a one—to three-week course at Fort Wolters, TX for standardization. We were fortunate that several instructors at Wolters ('Southern Airways'[6]) were also members of the OKARNG aviation program. One of the things that we had to do in those days was to give an annual check ride. We got standardized by the people at Fort Rucker and we learned from them. It was the beginning of a very exciting time."

"When I came into the OKARNG we had L-19s and OH-23B models and OH-13 Bells. The [active] Army decided that they wanted to get rid of the H-19s. A guardsman out in Fresno or Stockton, CA had gone through some kind of transition course on the H-19. And they cut temporary dut orders on Batey and me to fly out to California and do a transition with the California guardsman for a week or two, and then we were designated the IPs in the H-19s. We came back to Oklahoma and transitioned everyone that needed it. We got much more proficient as time went on, but in those days things were a bit looser. Of course when I left for Washington D.C. in 1970, I was an IP in 7 different types of aircraft. You had to be on your toes to make sure you were doing everything right," recalls Jones.

According to Colonel Leroy A. Wall, "the ARNG Aviation accident rate in the [early] 1960s timeframe was 58 mishaps per 100,000 hrs."

Judge Ron Howland (former OKARNG aviator and retired colonel) recalls that, "Gus Guild was an outstanding contact aviator and I remember having a check ride with him where he made me over control the [U-6] Beaver so that we were going down the runway on one [main] landing gear! I was petrified."

Without a doubt Gus was a good guy, but a stern and dedicated soldier. He was also an outstanding fixed-wing aviator. Gus could do anything with the O-1 Bird Dog or the U-6 Beaver. But according to one very trustworthy source, he learned to fly helicopters because he was the maintenance officer and therefore had to be able to test fly them. It seems that many Army aviators, including Gus, all of whom had received fixed-wing training first and later were told they had to also transition into rotary-winged aircraft, never had that basic love affair with helicopters. For this reason Gus is not remembered as being very proficient regarding rotor-wing aircraft. It seemed he always had trouble following the written pre-flight guide for a helicopter. Several old timers stated, "Over the years, he had started the engines of so many OH-23's with the blades still tied down to the tail boom that the mechanics began following him to the aircraft." This new practice saved the OKARNG State Maintenance Office a small fortune and prevented LTC Guild from being burned at the stake.

LTC Guild was assigned as the Aircraft Maint Officer for HHD OKARNG from April1963 to May 1965. From June1965 to June1966 he was Avn Ops Officer for HHD OKARNG.

Colonel Charles R. Jones stated that, "Gus was what we called a long time lieutenant colonel, which means old school, not very open to new ideas; he was set in his ways. He selected good people and insisted upon good work. He was a perfectionist, maintenance was his forte. We'd prepare all kinds of things, new ideas and go in to brief him and before we were half way through, he'd say, "Nope, we're not going to do that." He had a good heart, even though he was rough and hardnosed, he was still sympathetic to a lot of individual problems."

Even while he worked tirelessly as an instructor pilot and the maintenance officer, Gus continued to recruit for Guard Aviation, always looking for experienced, enthusiastic and good personnel, even if they out ranked him or were smarter. Gus was referred to as the Aviation facility commander there in Norman.

LTC August L. Gus Guild was a loyal, patriotic veteran and a true patriarch of OKARNG Aviation. Gus was awarded the Senior Army Aviator badge on 18 February 1952. He was the OKARNG State Aviation Officer from 10 June 1965 to 16 January 1968. Guild's long-time wife, Dora, became an invalid in 1980. Gus cared for her the next 18 years. She passed away in the summer of 1998. LTC Guild passed away in Oklahoma City on 1 January 1999, a very short six months after his wife, Dora.

Captain Charles R. Jones had been a school teacher, then an elementary school principal at Enid, OK. Jones met and married a gorgeous young lady, DeJuana Hale, from Marksville, LA. They both were attending Bethany College, in Bethany, OK when they were married in 1951. In 1952 Jones was drafted into the regular Army and became a radar operator (SCR-584) for an anti-aircraft artillery (AAA)

DeJuana & COL Charles R. Jones

unit in Okinawa. "They couldn't keep our SCR-584 radars operating long enough for us to do any good, so I asked to be transferred to the Chaplain's office. I later worked for the Chief of Chaplains [there in Okinawa] as a clerk and directed the choir. Then they put out an announcement that they wanted people to work at the Armed Forces Radio Service. I tried out for that and worked the remainder of my two year tour as an announcer for Armed Forces Network (AFN). We were a strong signal for all the planes coming back from Korea; they could navigate by our signal. We came home to Oklahoma the summer of 1954," recalls Jones.

Jones resumed his academic goals and graduated from Bethany College with a Bachelor of Arts in Music in 1955. Later he earned a master's from Oklahoma State University in Public School Administration ca 1960.

When asked how he got into the OKARNG, Jones said, "There were two or three teachers on the staff at Enid High School who were in the OKARNG, in fact Div Arty was located at Enid and the one star of the 45th Inf Div Artillery, Brigadier General Otwa T. Autry, was the junior high principal. When I was practice teaching I got to meet him. These two friends mentioned that with my education and prior military service, I could get a direct commission in the OKARNG. So I said, "OK." I applied and BG Autry,[7] 45th Div Arty Commander, approved it and gave me a direct commission in the Field Artillery (FA) in 1956."

"A year or so later, BG Autry called me in and asked, 'Jones what are you going to do? Are you going to be a communications officer or just what?'"

Jones said, "Sir, looking at your manning chart, I see you are short three or four aviators. I sure would like to go to flight school."

Autry said, "Oh hell, you don't want to do that, you'll be a lieutenant the rest of your life."

"Well, I've always wanted to fly."

And then BG Autry said, "Well, OK, go for it!"

"I got a leave of absence from the School Board at Enid and went to fixed-wing flight school at San Marcos, TX. The first six months, were called primary and were at Gary AFB, San Marcos, and then the advanced phase was at Fort Rucker. I graduated in 1958, Class # 57-17," stated Jones. He attended rotary-wing flight school in 1959 at Ft Wolters, TX and Ft Rucker, AL.

Jones was born 29 June 1930 in Nacogdoches, TX, but the Jones' home burned to the ground when he was just two months old. The family then moved to his mother's hometown of Lufkin, TX where he attended Lufkin High School, along with an older brother. Charlie graduated from high school at the age of 16. A guardian angel said to him, "Stand up tall Charlie; you've got a lot to accomplish!"Jones reflected, "Maybe a year or two later (ca 1962-63) they (the National Guard Bureau [NGB]) decided that all these [full-time] aviation positions ought to be Civil Service. And then they decided that they wanted to have a facility commander and instructor pilots. It was fortuitous for me because they hired Chet Howard to be the facility commander in Norman in 1965 and hired me and August

MAJ Charles R Jones, Norman, OK ca 1968

Guild as instructor pilots. I say that it was fortuitous because Chet would become OKSAO in 1968 and he was key in setting up all these facilities in a certain way that they would function so well. He came in and reorganized the maintenance program at the facility so that the aircraft that we flew on AFTPs and weekends was driven by the maintenance department, rather than by operations. He set up the AFTP program in Oklahoma with Guild and me, so that we were available for the weekends.

I remember clearly he took me to coffee there at Westheimer Field and said, "I need to talk to you a little while Charlie." He told me what he proposed, that I would have my pilots come for a weekend and Gus Guild would come in and help me. And then Gus Guild would have his weekend and I'd help him. Then [in addition] we would have our weekend drill training. Of course I was bollixed because that was three weekends [a month] and I said, "Chet I can't do that, those are all my weekends." He never withdrew and said, "Well, Charlie what are you going to do for a living?" The reason I say all this is that Chet was a mastermind at setting all these things up. When I left for Washington, D.C. in 1970, I left with all that in my mind and helped set it up all across the country because it was such a good program!"

"Chet had a real sense of humor," remembers Jones. "Best example I can think of right now, when he took command of the 45th Avn Bn, he inherited a Bn CSM, and he came to Norman, OK. I guess it was cold weather; I won't say [when] but let's say it was February. Chet had just put out some bulbs and the guy laughed and said, "I guess it'll be six months before you see any flowers." Chet said, "No, no, in three weeks they'll be up and blooming." The guy said, "Oh, I don't believe that." Now I don't know if they had a bet or what. Everyday Chet would dig the bulbs up [that were in the ground] and go down to the flower shop and buy some a little bigger and taller. In those three weeks, the guy checked every day and the flowers indeed got bigger every day, sure enough they got taller and taller. At the end [of the three weeks] Chet had planted bulbs that were already blooming. That's how far Chet would go to carry out one of his stories!"

"While he (Chet) was the facility commander, myself and Guild were IPs, Second Lieutenant Dana Batey was hired as the full-time Aviation Maintenance Officer. That was the team. Dana was a fabulous aviation maintenance officer and I'm sure made an outstanding commander as he progressed through his various assignments. He was very people-oriented, attention to detail, etc." stated a very humble Jones.

2LT Batey had become a rotary-wing aviator in 1959-60. He earned his fixed-wing rating at Fort Rucker, AL on 21 March 1961, with a military occupational specialty (MOS) in 1990. Batey, an infantry officer at this time, was a member of the 45th Avn Co in Norman, OK. His fixed-wing class was OFWAC 60-9.

Captain Batey, as the full-time aviation maintenance officer in Norman, had participated in an aerial photography mission, a traffic engineering study for Tinker AFB in September 1966. Seeing his first branch, the Air Force and Tinker AFB from the air, must have generated a lot of ideas and dreams. These were dreams and plans that eventually would be put into effect.

During the mid-to-late 1960s, "We tried to get in the Vietnam war, but LBJ didn't want to activate the National Guard," reflected Jones. The Army forced the National Guard to turn in a lot of the L-19s or O-1As, as they were called then. Ross Aviation out of Fort Sill, OK had a contract to ferry new airplanes and helicopters from various nearby factories to different Army installations. We ferried them from Oklahoma to Wichita,

KS to be refurbished, and then crews from the OKARNG would fly them out to Stockton, CA and other locations.

"Five of us made some extra money as ferry pilots flying for Ross. There was Dale Martin, Dana Batey, Pete Phillips, Jerry Bourassa, and Charlie Jones. We flew Cessna Bird Dogs out of the Cessna plant at Wichita, KS; U-21s out of Beech; O-3 pusher/puller out of the Cessna plant. We flew Cobras out of Fort Worth and Hueys and Chinooks out of Corpus Christi, TX, and I put in somewhere around 2,500 to 3,000 hrs doing that. We would do these ferry flights on weekends and holidays," remembered Dana Batey.

Although some ARNG units were activated for Vietnam, no ARNG divisions or ARNG aviation units were.

It was while Vietnam was just beginning that the Army started transferring CH-34s to the ARNG. Oklahoma got its slice of the pie! Then before you could say CH-34 Choctaw, OKARNG began receiving UH-1 Hueys and returning aviators from Vietnam. Each year, National Guard Association United States (NGAUS) has an annual ARNG Conference, which Jones attended annually, without fail. "One year about 1969, the conference was in Washington, D.C., I flew up with our crew and was seated at the table with Major John J. Stanko Jr. He and I started talking Aviation Safety and by the time that conference was over," Stanko says, "I want you to come back to Washington, D.C. and make a tour all of the states. Come up a month early and write your own Aviation Safety Briefing program and then tour all the 4th Army, 5th Army, Area Conferences and put on a Safety Briefing for each of the states." I did this on a 90-day temporary tour and then went back to Oklahoma," remembers COL Jones.

Stanko recalled those days, "Okay, so when I'm about to leave the Pentagon in 1970, I call up Chet Howard, 'Hey Chet, old buddy, you remember that guy that you promised me 90-day temporary tour? I need him.'"

Stanko said to Chet Howard, "Okay, send your guy [meaning Batey] out here. Well, what I didn't know was that Batey's daughter had had a serious automobile accident and he was taking care of her and his family. He couldn't possibly go TDY right now. But I didn't know that. Chet

COL John J. Stanko

Howard didn't want to disappoint me so he sent Charlie Jones in place of Batey. So in comes Charlie Jones for his 90-day tour. I think this was in 1968 in July or August."

Stanko continued, "We had 90 days to use our quotas, two classes in 10 days and then two classes every four weeks—every two weeks."

"Here's what had happened. I was trying to break loose and petition for quotas from Fort Rucker. I wanted 500 quotas for the Guard. And when we started phasing down from Vietnam, no one remembered that. And I said 'hell.' Nobody remembered that and I pulled out the paperwork and showed the DCSPER people and their concurrence and comments and so forth. I went to General Greenlief and Greenlief said, "John, you get all the quotas you can get!"' Major General Francis S. Greenlief, a decorated WWII infantry veteran from Nebraska, was ordered to duty in the National Guard Bureau in 1960 as Executive Officer, Army Division, NGB. As a brigadier general, he was designated Assistant Chief, Army, NGB in November 1962. The following year, Major General Greenlief

was named Deputy Chief, NGB. As a brigadier he became an Army Aviator. He was appointed as Director, Army National Guard in 1970 and became Chief, National Guard Bureau in 1971.

Stanko continued, "After about two weeks of harassing and haranguing both DCSPER and DCSOPS, they [at last] agreed to give the Reserve Components 326 quotas and that was all; half for the Guard and half for the Reserve. There was no equality with the Guard and Reserve. So anyway, I said, "Fine, okay." But the catch was the first class started within 10 days. And you had two classes every two weeks, so many [candidates] in Warrant Officer Qualification and so

MG Francis S. Greenlief

many in Officer Qualification. But they never would send the paperwork down. So I went to Colonel Santangelo at DCSOPS and said, 'Sir, I want to send a message to the states to tell them to get ready.'"

"The same day I said to Greenlief, 'What about the money Sir?'"

"He said, 'Don't worry about the money, you just get all the quotas you can get John.'"

"So I did. We got less than half the quotas that we needed for the Guard. I had about 75 applications on file, aviation people out in the states that were ready to go to flight school. I go to Tommy Hill, DAC Chief of Schools Branch and he said, 'John, don't accept any quotas inside of 40 days, 45 days notice.'"

"And I said, 'Why?'"

"He said, 'Well, because the states can't respond that fast.' He explained, 'It takes us over five weeks to get a flight physical over to the surgeon and get it back. To get it over to the Surgeon General's office and get it back and get an approval.'"

"I said, 'Oh shit, I'll take care of that.'"

"The states won't respond," Hill said. To Tommy Hill, flight school was just another course."

Stanko decided to go to COL Santangelo and said, Colonel, you ought to let Aviation [Branch] run this school's quota thing for flight school.'"

"John, it's a schools thing. Let them handle it."

"He and I walked back to Tommy Hill's office. Five weeks to get an approval on a flight physical and we've got about 75 applications on file . . . we don't have enough quotas, time, or anything!"

"Santangelo said, 'The states won't respond, they can't respond that quickly.'"

"I'm looking at Santangelo and he says, 'What about the approval for flight physicals?'"

Stanko said, "I'll take care of that." Stanko's intention was that he would be responsible for resolving the ludicrous amount of time it had been taking to get one measly flight physical approved.

So, Santangelo said to Tommy Hill, "Tommy, I think the Major here's got the right idea. I'm going to let Aviation run this on the flight school quotas."

Santangelo added, "Give him Joseph McGuire here to help."

Tommy Hill had a small complement of worker bees, a deputy named Eve Delphin, a character worth two and a half pages of narrative just by herself, and one program analyst named Joseph McGuire. Mr. McGuire was a GS-9 and handled combat branch schools, including aviation.

Stanko admitted, "I had not thought that out, the technical, administrative details involved between NGB and the State POTOs with regards to authorizing Guard personnel to go active for schools. McGuire was a blessing."

Mr. McGuire came to work for MAJ Stanko at Aviation. "You know that I reduced that flight physical approval time, right? [Dramatic pause] . . . Stanko announces: "Got it down from five weeks to two hours!!!"

Stanko elaborated, "Here's the thing—I get things done, right? It took three or four hours to find the person that approved those physicals. That's all it is, someone that just checks the box and makes sure everything's there. It was a Major George Brindell, a ring-knocker from West Point who had taken a sabbatical, and was now the flight surgeon at the Surgeon General's Office over in the Forrestal Building [on Independence Ave. SW] in Washington, D.C. He was the one who approves these flight physicals. I got a hold of him, talked to him, told him what my situation was."

"Major Brindell said, 'You bring 'em over and I'll just approve 'em right away.'"

"I took two bags full over the first time. You know these little airline handbags, satchels. I went over to his office [about 3½ miles from the Pentagon] and just sat there. Watched him pull out his rubber stamp Approved, and went to the next one, went through it, Approved, went through the next one."

"Hey, there's something missing here," Brindell said with surprise.

"Okay, I'll get that taken care of, I'll get the missing piece," Stanko assured him.

"Lieutenant Colonel Don Andrews (active duty), my new aviation branch chief, wrecked his Volkswagen, broke his hip and was in the hospital. So I'm running the Aviation Branch all by myself. And there's five Army area conferences coming up. And at the aviation breakout session I had prevailed on USAABAR to give a safety presentation for us. But just on the aircraft that we had, not on the Cobras (AH-1) and the new stuff that the Guard didn't have. They put on a safety program, and sent somebody to make presentations at our Army area conferences."

"I'm trying to manage all of the aviation quotas for flight school by myself and then out of the blue USAABAR calls and says 'John, we're going to have to re-nig on our commitment to come out. We're having trouble in Europe and we can't furnish anybody for you.'"

Stanko queried USAABAR, "If I send a guy (Charlie Jones) down there, can you give him platform experience and teach him to make the presentation and give him the equipment and everything he needs?"

So Charlie Jones reports in at the Pentagon, [in July 1970] "He shows up at my office one day. And I had met Charlie once or twice before. [I say to myself,] 'Hey, here's this water walker from Oklahoma.' So then I say, 'Hey Charlie, look here. You go downstairs to the Army Library and for the next week or so research Army Aviation Safety. Find everything you can with a background on safety. Here's what you're going to do, you're going to each of the five Army Area Conferences and at the Aviation breakout you're going to brief Aviation Safety.'"

"Charlie does his research and a couple of weeks later he comes back and says, 'Now what?'"

"So I send him down to Rucker, and I say to him, 'They'll give you everything you need down there for making your presentations at the Army Area Conferences.' He does that and then he goes to the Army Area Conferences. Charlie finishes the area conferences and is about ready to go home and comes in and we talk and I don't have too much time for him, to spend with him."

"Meanwhile, I go to visit Art DeLone, who was the Aviation Officer up at Office of the Chief Army Reserves."

He says, "Hey John, you want all of my quotas for the first two classes?" (He was talking about flight school quotas.)

And I said, "Yeah, I'll take em."

DeLone says, "I can't even get out the word to the units in this short amount of time. You know I've got to go through Forces Command and all different sorts of levels just to get down to the units."

And Stanko said, "Yeah, I just go direct to the state, that's all I have to do."

"I was taking one course over at the University of Maryland on campus and I would drive over from the Pentagon, over to the University of Maryland after work. And I'd make telephone calls from the phone booths along the highway to different State Aviation Officers and tell 'em, 'I need so many guys to fill quotas.'"

"Every week or so Art DeLone would call up and say, 'Hey John, you want half my quotas for the first class—for the next class?'"

"And I'd say, 'Yeah, I'll take 'em.'"

"Mid-week he'd say, 'You want three quarters of 'em?'"

"Yep, yep."

"So on Friday before the class would start on Monday, he'd offer me up all of the quotas for that class and I'd take 'em, all of 'em!"

Then Stanko called James R. Sulpizi from Delaware and said, "Hey Jim, I need help, I need you to come down here on a 90-day tour."

Sulpizi said, "John, I'm a bachelor, I have a condo here at Ocean City for July, August, and September. You want me to give those 90 days up? Just to come down to the Pentagon, you think I'm crazy?"

"Two days later Jim would show up. And without Jim I just couldn't have done it. See Fort Rucker hadn't had a National Guard guy down there in five years. They didn't know what to do with National Guard guys. You know, the regular Army would send a guy to school 10-12 days ahead of the class start date, and our NG guys would show up at Rucker on a Saturday or a Sunday to start school on Monday and no patches, no uniforms."

"Jimmy, you go down to Rucker, get you a rental car and you meet these kids that are showing up for Warrant Officer Candidate School and for Officer Flight School and you meet them and you husband them." James R. Sulpizi was not an ordinary aviator!

"Eventually we got it where the U.S. Property and Fiscal Office would authorize a couple of travel days so that the kids would have a little bit of leeway when they showed up at Rucker."

"Well, anyway, when it was all said and done, the Guard put . . . . out of 326 quotas, the Guard put 324 men in to flight school. That has always been my perspective on the difference between the Guard and the Reserve."

"So Charlie Jones goes home and I thank him for his service. I never did follow up and ask the State Aviation Officers from the different Army areas how he did."

"Now it's time for me to leave and no one wants to come in to this job at the Bureau. So I talk to Charlie Jones and said, 'Hey Charlie, you ought to think seriously about coming out here to the Pentagon and taking this job. You ought to consider taking the Aviation Staff Officer job and taking my place.'"

Stanko recalled, "I know that Chet Howard is going to be mad at me but, What the hell. At first Charlie was a little bit reluctant, but quickly he decided 'Yeah, okay.'"

"Then I said, 'Hear this one thing, Charlie, if you come here as a major, then you're going to have to wait four years before you get promoted.' He was due to be promoted to lieutenant colonel in about five months. I said, 'Look, I'll stay here six more months and hold that chair down. You get promoted to lieutenant colonel, then you'll come in here but you'll be the junior lieutenant colonel. So Don Andrews has another year to go here on his tour so when he leaves and the Army sends another active major in here, you'll be the ranking man as lieutenant colonel and you'll be the new [Avn] branch chief. And the active Army guy will be the worker bee. And after that it'll rotate between the Guard and the active Army as far as the branch chief goes.'"

Stanko says, "I spent six more months in that goddamn BOQ at Bolling AFB, running the show, which I loved, waiting for Charlie to get promoted and come in. Oh, one more thing, before we had that influx of quotas, MG Greenlief convened a thing called The Graham Committee. The Graham Committee came in to create the [Army] Aviation Support Facilities (AASFs) and the maintenance shops and to get rid of the old stand alone maintenance shop concept, kind of like the Air Guard. I learned a lot from the Air Guard. I used a lot of their stuff."

Charlie Jones remembers that, "MG Francis S. Greenlief, DARNG, was in flight school at the time or had just graduated. They [Greenlief and Stanko] were pleased with what I did and what I had to offer. John asked me to come back and accept a four-year NGB Tour to take his place. Stanko's four-year tour at the Pentagon was just about up [and would end in May 1970]. They called the state [OKARNG] and got everything set up and we moved up here in July of 1970. I was 40 years of age and have been here ever since. I had talked it over with Chet Howard and he was quite supportive and went so far as to say, 'Whatever money you need Charlie, just let me know and I'll help you make this move.'"

Charlie continued, "In 1970, at the age of 40, my first assignment at the Pentagon was as an Aviation staff officer in the Aviation Branch of NGB-ARO or Operations. The first thing I had to do was to learn how to operate at that level in the Pentagon. That wasn't an easy task; we had a lot of telephone calls. Up to a certain point I always had to say, 'Let me check on that . . . ' I finally got to the place I could answer a question. Then you had to learn the ins and outs of working with the NGB staff and I will say this, that it was a very pleasant transition as a new guy coming in. They took me in and were like a big family, wonderful people. I was in the Pentagon for nearly three years."

On 22 November 1970, in a small Pentagon ceremony, Major Charles R. Jones was promoted to the rank of LTC/0-5.

"MG Francis S. Greenlief had just finished flight school; LTC Don Andrews (active duty) NGB Aviation Branch Chief, and MAJ (P) John Stanko were kind of bored with flying with him so much. Since Greenlief was required to always fly with an IP, they asked would I go out and fly him. I had just gotten out of the U-6 back in Oklahoma and now was getting into the U-6 with Greenlief, flying out of Andrews AFB. He and I hit it off and soon he solicited an Air Guard Cessna 310 (U-3A) and sent me through the U-8 transition so I could be a U-8 [multi-engine] instructor pilot. Then I flew quite a bit more with him in the 310. We spent a lot of time, a lot of cross country, talking about aviation and safety. He was very interested in safety and always on me to do more. But then when LTC Don Andrews finished his tour, Greenlief said, 'Charlie, I want you to take Aviation.' That's how I got to be Chief of the NGB Aviation Branch ca 1970-71."

When asked about when and how the new NGB Aviation Branch became an NGB Division, MAJ Jones replied that "Until this time, ARNG Aviation consisted of a numbered of qualified Army Aviators, scattered about the several states in a variety of ground units. Thankfully, there were a few leaders at NGB who could envision ARNG as a professional military element that could one day be a vital asset for the U.S. Army, the NGB and the United States. That's why this period is so important."

MAJ Jones continued, "Major General LaVern E. Weber had been the OKTAG and then was selected to be the Director of ARNG (DARNG). When he moved up to the Pentagon, he decided that aviation had become paramount, with all of the combat veteran aviators coming back from Vietnam and joining the National Guard. So many new aircraft also coming to the NG, UH-1s, CH-54s, and CH-47s; it was a very exciting time."

"MG Weber said, 'Charlie, a Branch won't do it, let's create an Aviation Division. Charlie, [you] put together a wiring diagram of what you think ought to be in an Aviation Division.'"

"John Stanko was heading up the brand new Aviation Logistics and Maintenance portion of it up at Edgewood, MD, and I thought that [Avn Log] ought to be part of the Division, so I wrote a plan with a Commander,

Deputy Commander, Ops & Tng, Logistics, Admin and Flight Surgeon set up the [NGB] Aviation Division. General Weber bought it and the only thing he scratched off was the nurse. He then said, 'I'll buy that . . . form it up and I want you to run it.'"

"I had a [temporary] flight surgeon on staff, [on a] 90-day tour [at the Pentagon], Bob Stockton from Texas, [he] made himself available [and was a part of the new NGB-AVN Division]," remembered Jones.

I asked MAJ Jones, "How did you become the first Chief, NGB Aviation Division?"

"The decision to make [NGB] Aviation a separate division had much to do with the tremendous influx of Vietnam aviators and aircraft coming home. John Stanko and his maintenance people had one end of the building at Edgewood [OAC] and I was sitting almost by myself on the other end. Then I hired all the people who would fill the various positions," recalled Charlie Jones.

Mrs. DeJuana Jones, COL Charles R. Jones, New Chief NGB Avn Div and MG LaVern E. Weber—Pentagon

MAJ Jones continued, "We couldn't put the new NGB Aviation Division in the Pentagon because of limited space and personnel requirements so we set it up at Edgewood Arsenal, MD (Aberdeen Proving Grounds) and we moved up there."

"A lot of things were happening all at once. Weber made me the Chief of the Division first and then promoted me to Colonel," reflected COL Charlie Jones.

Based on the stories of Colonel John J. Stanko and COL Charles R. Jones and the DA 2-1, Officer Record of Assignments, of Charles R. Jones, the records show a change of assignment to [NGB] Director, Army Aviation Division as of 17 November 1973.[8] Charles R. Jones, the very first Director, NGB Avn Division, was promoted to the rank of COL/0-6 on 4 February 1974, by MG LaVern E. Weber.

Originally, when the infant NGB Avn organization was part of the Army's Logistics Division (ARL), it was in the Pentagon. The Army and NGB created a totally separate organization [NGB Avn Logistics Branch 1972], not an Aviation Logistics Division; it was separate from the NGB Logistics Division. It was decided to move the new organization, set it up at Aberdeen Proving Grounds, MD, near Edgewood. The old Nike-Hercules site, building #4430, was an old wooden, WWII, two-story building. After the initial move to the Nike-Hercules site, other NGB organizations joined and it became an OAC. There were approximately 200 personnel at the OAC, which included the Avn Div, Environmental Div, Engineer Branch, Schools, Training, Manpower and administrative personnel. 'Jones and company' set up the NGB Avn Division at the OAC ca 17 November 1973. Later Stanko's bio says he became Chief of NGB Avn Division in 1976 and retired in 1993. The fact Ms. Debi Horne said Jones hired her in 1974 adds credibility to the November 1973 date.

Charlie Jones explained, "These WWII offices of NGB-AVN and a few other NGB sections at Edgewood were called the Operating Activities Center (OAC). The decision to make Aviation a separate division had much to do with the tremendous influx of Vietnam vets (aviators) and aircraft coming home. John Stanko and his maintenance/logistics people had one end of the building at Edgewood, and I was sitting almost by myself on the other end. Then I hired all the people who would fill the various positions. I also hired Ms. Deborah (Debi) Horne as the executive secretary [ca 1974]."

Jones continued, "A lot of things were happening all at once. He made me the Chief of the Division first and then he set about to get me promoted to colonel. We needed to become part of the Maryland Army National Guard in order to get the manpower spaces that he needed for the NBG Avn Division." Charlie Jones had become the first Chief of the National Guard Bureau Aviation Division, from Enid, OK, and he led ARNG Aviation from 1972 until 1976.

Following his years as Chief, NGB-AVN at Edgewood, COL Charles R. Jones attended the U.S. Army War College and graduated in 1978, then worked at the NGB Policy Division for one year. During that time he wrote the entire Mobilization Plan for all of the ARNG. In 1979, Lieutenant General Weber asked Charlie to go to the Army Concept Analysis Agency, the Army's Think Tank. He did this, and worked on intriguing concepts for the defense of Alaska and the Panama Canal. The results of which were surprising – they can't be defended! After the Think Tank, Charlie accepted a position as the District of Columbia State Aviation Officer at Davison AAF. He was instrumental in obtaining D.C.'s first Aviation Battalion.

The 1970s were a transition period in the Army National Guard, not just regarding aircraft, not just with personnel, but with our organization and future! "We moved out of a laid back, devil-may-care attitude, from the days of the Old Flying Club to that of new challenges and new requirements. aviation safety was now being emphasized from the top down, not just talked about," said Charlie R. Jones.

"And not be taken lightly are the contributions to accident prevention that Generals Greenlief and Weber made to the program. No one in the program today has likely heard of these accomplishments. But today they walk in the footsteps of these who help guide the program where it is today. COL Chester A. "Chet" Howard, with his ability to organize, laid the groundwork for the [modern combined] AASF and I took it with me when going to the Bureau. MG Greenlief was determined that the accident rate would be reduced or eliminated, and MG Weber took up that banner. My job [the first Chief NGB Aviation Division] was to carry out what ideas they had, initiate the orders/regulations and make suggestions for change. It worked," COL Jones added.

In the late 1970s, Charlie became the SAO for the DCARNG and served in that position at Davison Army Airfield for nine to ten years. He retired in August 1987 from the military with 33 years total military service. He and his wife, DeJuana, live in Virginia, near Mt. Vernon, in the same house they bought in 1970. COL Charles R. Jones is an outstanding soldier, musician, Master Army Aviator with 6,000+ flight hours, and he is an honorable veteran. Let us not forget his service and contributions – another true patriarch of OKARNG Aviation!

While COL Jones was there at Davison AAF, another gentleman was commanding the airfield and a group of VIP helicopters and the U.S. Army Priority Air Transport (USAPAT) – Colonel Jerry A. Simmons. COL Simmons was the Davison AAF Commander from January 1976 to January 1978. He was responsible for the air movement of the President's administration and the Executive and Legislative branch personnel to an underground, secure location, not far from D.C., near Camp David. Included in COL Simmons' responsibilities were the five or six Army VIP fixed-wing aircraft located at Andrews AFB. These were [and are today] used to provide airlift to the very senior Army leadership, who are required to fly military airlift, rather than commercial air.

I meet Jerry A. Simmons, at my 174th Assault Helicopter Company (AHC) Association's annual reunion at Fort Walton, Florida. The 174th was the second unit I served with in Vietnam in 1967. Major Simmons was a platoon leader in the 174th AHC from November 1965 to March 1966 in Vietnam. While visiting with COL Simmons in 2007 at Fort Walton Beach, I discovered that he lived at Fort Washington, MD, which is just across the Potomac River to the east of Mt. Vernon – not but a few miles from Fort Belvoir, and hardly a mile from where Charlie R. Jones lives today! They both remember each other and prove what a small, small world we live in.

In September 1955, another full-time manning position was authorized.

Airman Dana D. Batey
ca 1951

SGT Dana D. Batey, who had served the previous four years in the U.S. Air Force and accumulated 3,000+ hours as a B-24 and C-124 mechanic/flight engineer, dressed in his Air Force Class A blue uniform went to the 45th Inf Div Hqs to meet with MAJ Gus Guild. The 45th's headquarters was in the rock building on 36th St., which is now the 45th Inf Div Museum. After a short visit and after Gus had reviewed his military files and saw his CAA airframe and powerplant (A&P) license, he was hired as the fourth aviation maintenance technician in Norman, OK.

Young Dana Batey had grown up on the family farm east of Oklahoma City, later moving to Midwest City's (MWC) east side. He and most of his ten siblings attended elementary school at Midwest City. Arthur A.B. Batey, Dana's father, worked at Tinker AFB during WWII and later for the Engineering Department of Midwest City. They lived on a 180-acre farm that was under water most of the time.

Dan Batey attended Jarman Junior High School, just a mile or so north of S.E. 29th Street, near the landmark red and white checker board

(USAF color pattern) water tower in MWC. During the school year, Dan drove his robin egg blue, 1932 Ford Roadster, with yellow spoke wheels, to and from the Midwest City Bombers High School. Often the Roadster's rumble seat was carrying another couple behind Dan and his current girlfriend. Having grown up on a farm, he participated in Future Farmers of America (FFA) and sports at MWC high school; he graduated in May 1951.

Batey had seven sisters and two brothers. One brother was a Marine and the other was in the Army. In June of 1951, right out of high school, Dan Batey enlisted in the USAF and was sent to Lackland AFB, San Antonio, TX for USAF basic training. He had applied to attend advanced training at Spartan School of Aeronautics in Tulsa, OK, but due to the needs of the service, the USAF sent him to Oakland, CA to Cal Tech for further aviation schooling. After some fun in the sun at Cal Tech, he traveled east to Chanute AFB, IL, another USAF aviation training base, where he received maintenance training on the B-24. While at CAL Tech, Airman Batey received the practical/hands-on training for his A&P license. He later took the written test for his A&P rating in Oklahoma and passed. Dan held a Civil Aeronautics Administration (CAA) A&P rating at the time he was hired by Gus Guild.

The Federal Aviation Administration (FAA) didn't exist when Dan Batey was hired at Norman in 1955; however, its predecessor, the Civil Aeronautics Administration (CAA) was the government controlling agency for aviation. The Federal Aviation Act of 1958 anticipated the introduction of jet airliners; then a series of midair collisions expedited this enactment. The new legislation transferred CAA's functions to the new Federal Aviation Agency (FAA), which had broader authority to investigate aviation hazards. The Act took safety rulemaking from the Civil Aeronautics Board (CAB) and entrusted it to the new FAA. It also gave the FAA sole responsibility for developing and maintaining a common civil-military system of air navigation and air traffic control – a responsibility that the CAA had previously shared with others.

Although there weren't any company sized (or larger) separate aviation units within the OKARNG during this time period, traditional aviation sections (Avn Sec) existed at the 45th Infantry Division Headquarters and its major commands. The 45th Inf Div Arty, known as the Div Arty had an Avn Sec at Enid, OK. Small Avn Sections were assigned to each of the three 45ᵗʰ Inf Div Regiments, one at the Engineer Battalion and another at the 700ᵗʰ Support Company.

Prior to the 1960s, if you were (or wanted to be) an Army aviator in the OKARNG, and wanted to get an aviation slot in a unit, you had to go talk the battalion and/or regimental commanders and convince them that they needed you! You'd get in your car and drive around to these different places that had aviation slots and find one that was vacant and willing to take you. It was up to you to convince them, "I'll make you a good troop if you'll let me go to flight school." And that's the way it was back then. You had to promote yourself, go out and find those aviation slots and interview for them..

In the 1958-63 era, there were three to four OH-23B Ravens, three OH-23Cs, about seven or eight L-19 Bird Dogs, one L-17 Navion and two or three L-20 Beavers, all located at Max Westheimer Airfield, Norman, OK. The older OH-23B model Hiller had a slanted bubble,

1LT Dana D. Batey

unlike the newer, rounded bubbles on the later models. Both the B and C model Hillers had wooden blades that absorbed water and became unbalanced when it rained or sat with the blades tied to the tail boom for an extended period. This maintenance anomaly was an area of constant concern for SGTs Batey, Davis and Ormiston. Of course there were rules, and naturally, Army regulations, but not very many concerning usage of Army aircraft in those days. The few regulations that did exist were sometimes overlooked. Thus the question, "What did they do with the aircraft between drills?" The answer lay somewhere between the honor system and let's use a little common sense, sort of in that gray area in the middle. In between drill weekends, aviators often flew their aircraft home and kept them at their local airports until next month's drill. This was a common practice across the country in the Guard. In the late 1940s, 50s, and 60s you could land on a grassy field and park near the Phillips 66 sign or next to the Mobil station at the end of Main Street. Then, with a couple of borrowed five-gallon cans of 20-cent gasoline and a little help from Joe Bob, the station attendant, you could refuel your Bird Dog or OH-13 with the same gas you put in your Oldsmobile Sky

Rocket. With your fuel quantity gauge indicating at least half full, you could now safely fly on to the headquarters for your next mission. Or you could fly back home until next drill!

Within the next several years, Dana D. Batey, having been promoted to MSG, went to Infantry Officer Candidate School at Ft Benning, GA, in April 1958. After graduating from Fort Benning's NG OCS-1 on 5 May 1959, Batey went concurrently to flight school at Fort Rucker and became an Army rotary-wing aviator. Lieutenant Batey appeared to be quiet, but on the inside wheels were turning—a thousand and one ideas about how to move the OKARNG Aviation Program forward. He was always thinking beyond today, next week, and even next year! Weekly he gave his subordinates more things to do than they could possibly accomplish. He was a true visionary and became an aviation icon both in the State of Oklahoma and at NGB.

On 1 May 1959, the 45th Avn Co. was organized at Norman, OK. Its home was an old WWII wooden hangar on Westheimer Airfield. Another WWII building, a two-story wooden barracks, was used for an office and meeting place. Captain Butcher was the first commander. Butcher did not get promoted to major, and resigned from the Guard.

The lack of higher grades within OKARNG aviation was a very limiting situation. With only one true MAJ/0-4 aviation slot in the OKARNG, many aviator captains stayed onboard in the Guard as captains, and had no place to go if they wanted to be promoted to major, except the SAO position, and it was already taken! A very few would get out of aviation and move to an administrative MAJ/0-4 position to be promoted.

There seems to have been a lot of personnel turnover, and with a severe lack of higher aviation headquarters to provide greater supervision and oversight, there were many aviation accidents. Older aircraft? Yes, but that's no excuse. Part of the reason appears to have been the lack of an Aviation Safety Program, and a failure of what leadership there was to address safety issues, such as: proper pre-flight and post-flight inspections, weather forecasts, personnel limitations, crew rest, risk assessment, and inadvertent Instrument Meteorological Conditions (IMC). IMC is a relatively new term meaning Instrument Flight Rules (IFR), but in the case of the OH-23s and OH-13s, they weren't capable of instrument flight. We could have picked another acronym instead of IMC, like CSS (Can't See S___), but IMC is what we got, so we'll just go with it. With very little guidance and emphasis until now, aviation accidents weren't just isolated occurrences.

Sad, but true, with the older aircraft from the Army and no aviation safety program or aviation safety officer, the nation's Army National Guard Aviation Safety statistics were atrocious. There were many accidents and many fatalities. Promoting OKARNG aviation was a full-time job, and the need to have an Aviation Safety Program was recognized. Before there was a Safety Program or Safety Branch at the National Guard Bureau, the handwriting was on the wall. Someone was keeping track of accidents, and it was not a good rate they had recorded. The national NGB aviation accident rate was about 25-30 accidents per 100,000 flying hours. This was atrocious.

CPT Charles R. Jones became the first OKARNG Aviation Safety Officer in Norman, OK. In 1965 Charlie attended the Aircraft Accident Investigation Course at the University of Southern California (USC), which was a three-week course at that time. Charlie shared with me, "It served me well; I dealt with accident prevention from then on in some form or another. It was an additional duty when I went to NGB at the Pentagon in 1970. They wanted me to continue to work that area, as well as being on the Aviation Staff [at NGB]." CPT Jones was a keen student of aviation according to some of the former aviators.

However, Charlie was not your typical good ole boy. Some said he was a bit dry, perhaps. Some considered him too serious, and said he was somewhat self-centered, perhaps. Was it because of his desire to be militarily correct and his teaching background, that some mistook him as arrogant? Perhaps. I think he was morally upright, his talk matching his walk, and he has a delightful sense of humor. This 5'10", 200 lb, former driver's education, health and safety teacher and elementary principal from Enid, OK, must have been a savvy salesman, as well as an excellent aviator to have been hired by Gus. Charlie's military assignment was with the 45th's Div Arty Avn Sec. Several years down the road, Charlie commanded the 245th Air Ambulance (Clearing Co) at Norman. Later, many of his OKARNG contemporaries were totally surprised when they heard news of gigantic proportions – CNGB, MG Francis S. Greenlief, was about to announce a new COL/0-6 position dealing with NGB Aviation; something about someone being selected as the new Chief of Aviation! But that story will have to wait until later.

But I must regress slightly and tell of another new face, MAJ Chester A. Chet Howard. MAJ Howard would soon prove his significance in Oklahoma and ARNG Aviation. Having been in the OKARNG for about nine years, he was the very first commander of the 45th Aviation Battalion, which was organized on 1 April 1963. MSG L.T. Lantz was his senior NCO at summer camp at North Fort Hood, TX in 1963. Howard became

COL Chester A. Howard

a federal technician in 1965 and was hired as the commander of the Oklahoma Army Aviation Support Facility at Max Westheimer Airfield Norman, OK. He was born in Hollister, MO on 25 July 1917 to O.L. and Chloe Howard. Chet and his older brother Frank grew up in Dustin, OK in Okfuskee County, where he graduated high school in 1935. Chet's wife, Chlokeeta (Miller) was from Ada, OK, and they married in Tulsa, OK on 5 October 1962. He had three daughters from his first marriage to Corene (Connie) Hines: Chloe Ann, Martha J. and Mary Lynn.

This wasn't Chet Howard's first rodeo. His military career began with the Aviation Cadet Program of the U.S. Army Air Corps on 13 October 1942. He completed flight training, and received his pilot's rating and commission as second lieutenant on 12 March 1944. Soon thereafter he completed the B-24 Liberator transition program and was designated a B-24 aircraft commander. Then in June 1944, he was assigned to combat air crew duty and reported to the Italian Combat Station, 15th Air Force in September 1944. During WWII Chet flew combat bombing missions over Germany. He served overseas for 21 months during WWII and once again in Europe from 1952-53.

While on his 15th mission on 16 November 1944, his aircraft was shot down on a bombing run over the Munich railroad marshalling yards. As the aircraft commander, First Lieutenant Howard was the last to parachute out of his Liberator just 700' above the ground, landing hard in a tree. The tree saved his life, but he sustained a neck injury on landing. He cut his shroud lines and dropped into five feet of snow below. Chet spent the next six months in Deutschland as a military prisoner of war. The Germans tried to outrun the Allied Army, marching their weak, hungry POWs from camp to camp. 1LT Howard and fellow POWs were liberated by Lieutenant General Patton's Third U.S. Army on 18 May 1945.

Chet returned to the States and was honorably discharged from the Army Air Corps on Christmas Eve 1945. Although home from the war, which had ended, Chet's memory was forever etched with his experiences as a POW. These experiences caused his devotion, dedication, loyalty, and patriotism for this great country to be even greater, which he demonstrated for the rest of his life!

In 1946 Chet Howard constructed the Tri-City Airpark in Okemah, OK and established an FAA and VA-approved flight school where he gave flying lessons. Howard joined the Air Force Reserve in 1948 and was called to active duty in January 1949 prior to the Korean conflict. He was assigned to the 6th Bomber Wing, Walker Air Force Base, in Roswell, NM. In addition to his flight duty in B-29, B-36, and B-50 aircraft, he was assigned to supervise and coordinate the transition of classified facilities under a new Air Force regulation, effecting not only Walker AFB, NM, but also RAF bases in Mildenhall and Lakenheath, England. Captain Howard was released from active duty 13 July 1954.

It is indeed a small world and Okemah, OK is just a small part of the larger whole. Yet many of its residents have served in the OKARNG. One soldier who grew up in Okemah is CW5 Tommy T.K. Klutts. Tommy joined the OKARNG at the age of 14 at the WPA Armory in his home town of Okemah. At that time, back in the old days, "We drilled every Monday night. And we did that four times a month. That's how we got our drill," recalled Klutts.

Part of the old stone armory structure had been an American prisoner of war camp for German POWs during WWII. Tommy recalls, "I remember Chet Howard from Okemah when I was just a kid. He came to our house and was either a postman or the milkman. He was a true man's man and a gentleman."

Chet entered into the Oklahoma Army National Guard on 29 July 1955 in Norman, OK as a fixed-wing aviator. While serving in the OKARNG as an M-Day aviator, he was soon hired to be an Army Instrument Flight Instructor at Fort Sill, Oklahoma. Ultimately, he became the chief flight instructor responsible for standardization and acceptance of instrument flight instructors for Fourth, Fifth, and Sixth U.S. Armies. In 1959 he was employed as a test pilot for Page Aircraft Maintenance, at Fort Sill. Then in 1960, Chet became the Director of the School of Flight, Spartan School of Aeronautics in Tulsa, OK. He attended the rotary wing Q Course at Camp Wolters, TX in 1960. In 1962 he established and served as general manager and chief pilot for Charter Flight, Inc., also in Tulsa, OK. Then in 1964, Chet, still an M-Day soldier, was a co-founder and owner of Aircraft Repair & Service Co. at Tulsa, OK, until he became a federal technician in 1965 in Norman, OK.

He was the Bn Cdr of the 45th Avn Bn from 31 March 1964 to 31 January 1968.

About 1965-66, a young CPT Robert M. Morgan (later to become the Adjutant General of Oklahoma in November 1978) commanded Company A, 2/279th Infantry. This was a split-company, two platoons in Okemah and two platoons and the headquarters section in Wewoka. Klutts said that, "My commander in the Okemah split off was a First Lieutenant Kenneth Clark." He, Klutts, wanted to become an officer. Morgan recommended that Klutts apply for Officer Candidate School (OCS). He did, was accepted, and graduated from OKARNG's OCS. The new butter bar Second Lieutenant Tommy T.K. Klutts called the State Aviation Officer, Lieutenant Colonel Chester A. Howard, and requested his assistance in getting into the Army's Officer Rotary Wing Aviation Course (flight school). During the Vietnam war, quotas for the Army's rotary-wing flight training program were maxed out. In fact, for several years there were zero flight school quotas available to all of the ARNG; then the quota restriction eased up somewhat and the ARNG and USAR got about 200 quotas total per year. Due to sufficient quotas for the ARNG, 2LT Klutts had to wait a couple of years, but Howard kept his word—T.K. went to flight school, graduated in July 1970, and returned to Oklahoma.

Although Gus Guild had been there in the OKARNG from the beginning of ARNG aviation in 1948, the OKTAG, MG LaVern Weber, hired MAJ Howard in 1968 as the first OKARNG State Aviation Officer and to be the Flight Support Activities Cdr, over Gus Guild. Howard was the first official State Aviation Officer for Oklahoma and served from 1 February 1968 until 11 February 1972. In Norman, a new, strong team was forming – with all the right players: Charlie Jones and Gus Guild were rehired (Civil Service) in the new instructor pilot slots and the up and comer Dana Batey was hired as the new maintenance officer.

"Chet was a mastermind at organization and setting all these things up," said Charlie Jones. "When I left and went out to Washington to work in the Pentagon with NGB, I left with all that in my mind and helped set it up all over the country because it was such a good program!"

Some referred to Chet as an odd duck by certain standards. His family heritage was Scottish, and he had a full head of blond hair, which was turning white. He was probably six foot tall, somewhat stocky, with a ruddy complexion and quite good natured. "Chet Howard could talk to a telephone pole and get a conversation going," recalled Brigadier General Dana D. Batey. Everyone that knew Howard recognized his skill as an aviator, his talents in operations, planning, and that he was good at recruiting. He continued to bring many more aviators and soldiers into the OKARNG Aviation program.

The OKARNG Aviation program was definitely moving forward. Each day progress was being made in the areas of recruitment, operations, training, safety, and improved maintenance. Oklahoma was not only at the very center of the map at NGB's Pentagon headquarters, OKARNG's Aviation leadership was at or near the center of the radar with the aviation staff at NGB.

Some years later, CPT Batey followed Gus as the OKARNG aviation maintenance officer. I believe that Batey had ideas early on that one day he'd somehow take that L-17 Navion up to Oklahoma City and put it on a display pole at the 45ᵗʰ Inf Div Museum. Chet Howard had some major, visionary ideas for ARNG aviation too.

As a CPT, Batey earned the designation of Senior Army Aviator while serving in Tulsa with the 145ᵗʰ Avn Co on 21 February 1968.

During the Territorial Militia days, none of the (National Guard) volunteers were paid. After the war in Korea, our Army National Guard aviators didn't get paid for flying. It was also during this time in Oklahoma that Army aviation was called by many a *flying club*. These cocky, blond-haired, blue-eyed, weirdoes in their orange Army flight suits would go down to Norman on their own time and fly – just for the pure joy of it and the personal satisfaction! Why risk your life, without remuneration, without any insurance – WHY? Because they loved it. Most of these guys would've flown just for sex, maybe for groceries, but you didn't even have to pay these bums! These wacky aviators did it because it was exciting and brought them closer to . . . something?!?! As Captain Ishmael of the sea knows, there's always a degree of risk involved, and the alluring adventure of the unknown draws sailors to seek the mysteries of the sea; the same magnetism draws aviators to soar into the air. Perhaps it's a love affair with flying?

During the *flying club* days (into the early 1980s) there was little, if any, tactical aviation training done at all. There was some night flying; however, very, very little, as this was *truly dangerous!* What a contrast to today's Army Aviation who . . . owns the night! Aviation mission requests back then did exist, but few were for a real military-type mission. Most were submitted from one of the major commands because *CPT Ima Jerk* had never been in a helicopter before and wanted to experience soaring with the eagles for himself!

Later, it was Chet Howard, as State Aviation Officer of the OKARNG (OKSAO), who lobbied NGB around 1968 and helped obtain paid additional flight training periods (AFTPs) for Oklahoma's aviators! Within a short time period, additional progress was seen at the Norman support facility with the addition of blue box *Link Trainers*, along with staff (instrument trainers) and full-time flight instructors.

As the OKSAO, Chet Howard was at the controls when NGB Aviation centralized States' aviation assets (aircraft, maintenance, avionics, and training) into the Army Aviation Support Facilities (AASF) ca 1970-71. Prior to that, the OKARNG Avn Operations in Norman was technically called an aviation activity. This change gave OKARNG some admin force structure and added some full-time manning and funding. About this time, Sergeant George Droescher was the flight operations specialist at Westheimer Airfield. These changes, which occurred during Howard's tenure as SAO, were quite noticeable as well as beneficial. These were positive steps and the beginning of a metamorphosis that changed OKARNG Aviation from a *flying club* into a professional military aviation program!

Chet Howard was also an instructor pilot and a tremendous and challenging fixed-wing instrument flight examiner (IFE), most likely from several years experience as an instrument instructor at Fort Sill, OK in the late 1950s. He was often known to give his students a back course ILS at Will Rogers Airport in the Beaver on aviator's annual instrument check ride. This instrument approach required the aviator to correct his inbound course opposite the needle. This was demanding, stressful, and very tricky; it was also a true confidence builder, assuming you passed.

When I say confidence, I mean it gave you confidence after landing and parking, to walk straight back to the flight ops area; whereas, if you flunked, you might just go to your car, head lowered, not speaking to anyone and hoping they didn't see you.

About May 1966, Chet was once again requested by name to do a 90-day TDY temporary tour at NGB in the Pentagon. During the previous four or five years, MAJ John J. Stanko Jr. at NGB had heard about, worked with, and visited several times with Howard, and was quite impressed with this Scotsman from Oklahoma. During Chet's temporary tour Stanko introduced him around at the Pentagon and to the TAG in Pennsylvania.

Stanko recalled the TDY of Chet Howard, "He came in for a 90-day temporary tour. I'd go in to work at the Pentagon every day, from my BOQ at Bolling AFB, and I had this big old '59 Oldsmobile. I had bought it new for Pinky. So I got to use that car going back and forth to Washington."

"So Chet, me and several other people would meet at the Bolling AFB O Club for breakfast. Then I'd take him over to the Pentagon to work. Of course, Chet and I got to know each other real well."

"So Chet put the Aviation [AASF] site survey thing together and we had eight three-man teams. For example, three aviation officers from the northeast would go and do site surveys in the southwest. Chet put together the checklist and it was exhaustive. Airfield surveying, checking orders, and safety; a tremendous piece of work. This had never been done before."

"Now what happened was the state's aviation offices knew what was happening. As we were preparing the orders, they were out there doing their homework."

Stanko continued, "So as the teams went around they would send their reports back in to me and I would sort them into the five Army areas. I had these five areas and I wasn't finding that many deficiencies. Because as the teams were going out there, people had been making preparations for this survey and they were checking things and also calling back and calling their buddies in other states. It was a great effort. This was just a wonderful idea. It continues to this day."

"We have the AASF surveys that the states do for each other. We just made that a regulatory thing."

COL John J. Stanko Jr. added, "Chet was a fun guy. He had a real sense of humor. Chet Howard added, 'You know John, I got a young guy out in Oklahoma. If you ever need a guy for a 90-day tour or something, just let me know. I'd like for him[9] to come out here and work for you for 90 days. Just let me know. And [he can] get some real experience out here at the headquarters. But you can't keep him John; he's our future out here in Oklahoma. He is the future of Oklahoma Army National Guard Aviation, John.' He said, 'You'll enjoy him, but please John, would you do that for me.'"

From May 1972 until September 1972 Chet served as Army National Guard Staff Officer at the U.S. Continental Army Command, known as CONARC, serving as Army Aviation Coordinator between the Army and the Army Aviation Reserve components.

After Chet's return to Oklahoma, word on the flight line at Westheimer Field was – "Chet Howard is transferring to the Pennsylvania ARNG."

LTC Chet Howard didn't see much ahead for himself in Norman. To him it appeared that he had gone as far up the ladder of success that he could in Oklahoma; there were no full COL/O-6 slots in aviation in the OKARNG. Chet wasn't near ready to be put out to pasture; he wasn't even thinking about quitting! He visited with Major General Matthews, OKTAG, and was assured that he would support his move to the Pennsylvania Army National Guard (PAARNG). Chet had done his homework and made a lateral transfer to Pennsylvania.

Any aviation major in the ARNG is always looking for a LTC/O-5 slot and would like to be promoted. Wouldn't you? At least one person instantly saw an LTC/O-5 vacancy about to open. MAJ Charlie Jones had to be thinking about maneuvering for position, looking for upward mobility and hoping that he might be selected to take Chet Howard's place as OKSAO. Why shouldn't he be selected?

A few days before Chet left for Pennsylvania, MG David C. Matthews selected Major Pete Phillips as the State Aviation Officer for OKARNG; Lieutenant Colonel Phillips was SAO from February 1972 to January 1976. Pete was eventually

COL Pete Phillips

promoted to colonel and later reverted to Chief Warrant Officer. He was one of the most congenial soldier aviators that OKARNG ever had; he always had a smile and continued to fly rotary-wing and fixed-wing aircraft until he retired from the Guard at age 60. He was killed in a civil aviation accident on 25 June 1992, near Konawa, OK.

The SAO of Pennsylvania in 1970 was Colonel William Gardner Bill Prowell. Bill was a native of the keystone state and was born on 18 July 1918. At the age of 22, Prowell joined the PAARNG cavalry as a corporal in Harrisburg, PA, in February 1941. As of 1970, COL Prowell had been Pennsylvania's only SAO up to that point . . . He had a lot in common with Gus Guild, in that both men had been around in Guard Aviation since the true beginnings of ARNG aviation in 1948, and they both headed their own state's aviation programs, before the Bureau had authorized State Aviation Officers.

Unfortunately, COL Prowell was diagnosed with prostate cancer by his civilian physician. He didn't want to let this fact be known by the flight surgeon just yet, as it would mean losing his flight status and being grounded and forced to retire from his full-time job as SAO.

In May 1970, John J. Stanko Jr. was promoted to lieutenant colonel; his wife Pinky pinned the silver oak leafs on his khaki uniform in a small ceremony held in the Pentagon's outer E ring office of the DARNG, MG Greenlief. On 1 October 1970, he became the New Cumberland AASF Cdr, and within the following months he was called to the State Headquarters by Major General Richard Snyder, the PATAG. In light of the serious and deteriorating physical condition of COL Prowell, MG Snyder asked LTC Stanko to become the de facto State Aviation Officer and gave him the necessary authority to conduct aviation business on behalf of him and COL Prowell. However, Prowell and Snyder required this issue somehow be kept quiet.

How do you do that? Stanko never let Prowell's health condition become a problem and agreed "to do the job without getting the pay, the title (or recognition)." John J. Stanko Jr. was not concerned about getting any credit, and he gave his friend, Prowell, 150% support. He too was interested in promoting the Pennsylvania Army National Guard Aviation Program. Stanko continued to perform his assigned duties as AASF Cdr at New Cumberland and functioned in the office of SAAO until the fall of 1972. It became evident that Prowell's situation was not improving and that he would have to retire. Prowell was hospitalized in December of 1972, and was in and out of the hospital for the next few years. He passed from this life in January 1975 in Mechanicsburg, PA at the age of 56 years 5 months. He had served the PAARNG as SAO from 1 December 1948 until 31 December 1972.

During this chaotic time, LTC John J. Stanko Jr. demonstrated great leadership and was making plans for PAARNG Aviation that were visionary. One of those plans took a pair of balls the size of Dallas to brief the PATAG. So Stanko said, "Sir, I think we should close Lancaster, Harrisburg, and Allentown Aviation Support Facilities and build one [large AASF] at Fort Indiantown Gap."

MG Richard Dick Snyder's face turned just as white as snow.

Within a short period of several weeks, Stanko briefed and convinced Snyder that he would be able to sell this very costly, but ingenious idea to MG Francis Greenlief, the DARNG.

Long story short, Greenlief bought into Stanko's idea and ordered Snyder to get the engineers and architects going. But in the meantime . . .

The State of Pennsylvania had a tough situation! They were in a bit of a bind and asked the [NG] Bureau, "Who do you have that we can get to come out here and straighten this [aviation] program up?"

"We," said Charlie Jones, who was at NGB during this critical time, "recommended Chet Howard for the position of PA SAO!"

After Matthews became TAG for Oklahoma, Stanko remembers, "Chet did a short tour at the Continental Army Command down at San Antonio. No, Fort Monroe, Virginia. And he worked with a guy named Bobby [G.] Hanna, an active Army guy, who was the Aviation Officer at CONARC."

"When I left Pennsylvania, Major General Harry Mier was set; he wouldn't hear of Snellbecker becoming the next SAO. I had brought along Snellbecker to be the aviation officer."

"So," Charlie Jones said, 'Hey John, General Weber said we got to do something for Chet Howard. We can't get him another extension for his tour down there at CONARC, and he needs a couple more years before he retires.'"

"So I said, 'Hey, I have an idea. Why don't I take him? Why don't I fly MG Weber up to visit with MG Mier; he'll [Mier] do handsprings to have the Chief [CNGB] come up and visit. Then let the two visit and let

General Weber tell Mier that he'd like for him to take Chet Howard as the new State Aviation Officer for Pennsylvania.'"

"I go down to the Pentagon and get General Weber and somebody else, fly them up to Fort Indiantown Gap, and fly back down to Fort Monroe. So that's the way Chet got the job as State Aviation Officer in Pennsylvania," says John J. Stanko Jr.

"Chet came into Pennsylvania and one of his greatest contributions was building the big AASF facility at Indiantown Gap. See, when I left it was approved and so were the engineering drawings. But Chet was the guy that pushed it on through, that lived through it," complements Stanko.

"Howard initially had trouble from above and below, among those hard-headed Pennsylvanians who had been doing it their way for a long time. He had to convince a state-level staff what they now had to do for PA aviation. He also had to convince the people in the field, at the facilities, how they were to conduct themselves. He had to sell them. But he did a good job. Yes, we had a good relationship; we, DeJuana and I, went up to FITG there fishing several times and would visit Chet and Chlokeeta from time to time," said Charlie Jones.

"I first met Chet Howard before he became SAO in PA. I was a second lieutenant AASF Commander in Washington, PA. On LTC Howard's way to Harrisburg, Chet stopped by and introduced himself, stated he was from Oklahoma, and asked 'What do you do here?' He didn't mention that he would shortly become the State Aviation Officer of my home state, Pennsylvania," recalls Brigadier General Cecil Hengeveld, PAARNG.

After this meeting with Hengeveld, Chet replaced LTC John J. Stanko Jr. as the AASF Cdr at New Cumberland, PA [in August 1972] for a short period while he learned about the PAARNG and Prowell was closing up shop. New Cumberland AASF was at the Capital City Airport just south of Harrisburg on the western shore of the Susquehanna River. The Adjutant General of Pennsylvania, MG Richard Snyder, called Howard and told him to report to Fort Indian Town Gap (FITG), PA; he was then officially appointed as the State Aviation Officer in Pennsylvania on 1 January 1973 and served until 15 March 1976. COL Howard restructured the PAARNG Aviation Program, built new facilities, and started many new programs.

Howard came along when turbine engine helicopters were being fielded and older reciprocating aircraft were being phased out. As PA

COL Billy R. Wood, U.S. Army (retired)

SAAO he caused outdated, obsolete aircraft to be turned in and more than one hundred modern, up–to-date turbine engine aircraft eventually were on hand in PA. After Stanko had sold the idea of closing three PA AASFs and consolidating them into one large AASF (on behalf of Prowell), not just to the TAG of PA, but also to the DARNG, Chet was the man who as SAAO carried out the project and completed it! He was the primary force to bring about construction of the largest Army Aviation Support Facility in the United States – Fort Indian Town Gap, PA.

CW4 Darrell Larhs worked directly for Chet Howard in Pennsylvania and remembers Chet and Chlokeeta. Chief Warrant Officer Larhs worked in the SAO office with COL Howard from 1972 until 1976 and had the highest regard for this citizen soldier. Mr. Larhs currently works as a contractor at FITG AASF.

Many new programs were instituted in Pennsylvania by Howard, such as *Nap-of-the-Earth*, *Instrument Pilot*, and *Night Training* programs. He was responsible for Pennsylvania becoming the first state to authorize the new and coveted UH-1 Synthetic Flight Training System, which provided ongoing instrument training for more than one thousand (1,000) rotary-wing aviators in the northeastern United States.

Colonel Bobby G Hanna followed Chet as PA SAO on 1 April 1976 and held that position through 19 September 1980.

Howard's sights were set on becoming the chief of NGB Aviation and perhaps of making brigadier general sometime in the near future.

Many of Chet Howard's contemporaries thought of him as a fun guy and a practical joker. John Stanko tells a story about Chet while he was PASAO, living just outside of Fort Indian Town Gap, about seven miles to the southeast at Jonestown, PA. It happened that Chet's neighbor had just bought a new Oldsmobile 88 and insisted on showing it off to Chet. Later that week, in the cool, quiet of a summer night, Chet retrieved a five-gallon can of gasoline from his own garage, then slipped across the street and added gas to the tank of the new Oldsmobile 88.

Several days later he repeated his nighttime adventure. The next day after work, he inquired of his neighbor, "How's that new salmon and white colored Oldsmobile doing?"

His friend smiled, shook his head somewhat sheepishly and replied, "Chet, you're not going to believe this, but my mileage is out of sight!"

Chuckling, and with a smile, Chet asked, "What the hell do you mean buddy?"

"Well, I've driven this 88 back and forth to work every day since I bought it and haven't had to add one drop of gas. I'm getting over 50 miles per gallon so far."

Chet smiled and just scratched his head. Later that night, he went to his garage, not to get more gas, but this time to get a short length of hose and an empty five-gallon gas can. He slipped across the silent street, up the driveway of his friend, and began to siphon several gallons of gas from the Olds. He did this again each of the next three nights.

On the fourth day, his neighbor was waiting for Chet as Howard pulled into his own driveway in Annville from work. "What's up bud?" asked Chet.

"I can't figure this out. My new Olds was doing just great!"

"What do you mean Fred?" Chet was having trouble not bursting a gut, but maintained his casual demeanor.

"I don't know Chet, she was doing 50 mpg or better, then all of a sudden it just reversed. Seems like I'm having to fill up the tank every other day," reported our friend Fred.

Chet, being the sharp individual he was and an Army aviator to boot said, "You know Fred, if I were you I'd take this little beauty back to the dealer and have them look into this. You might ruin the motor if you keep driving it."

Well, of course Fred did take it back to the Oldsmobile dealer, and as you might expect, the service department couldn't find anything wrong with the 88's fuel system, carburetion or fuel tank. Fred was furious and just knew there was a major problem! He demanded to speak with the owner. He did and after explaining how great the car was and receiving no explanation regarding what was causing his low gas mileage now, Fred justifiably required that the dealership refund his money and he gave them back their lousy salmon and pink Oldsmobile 88.

While Chet was in Pennsylvania, he was contacted by another Okie, Major Tommy Klutts, a young, robust, up and comer who had decided to try his wings in the beautiful and mountainous back country of Fort Indiantown Gap (FITG). Tommie went out to Pennsylvania, applied for an instructor pilot position and was hired by Chet Howard to work at the new FITG AASF. Shortly after Chet retired, Tommy came back to

Oklahoma and went back to work full-time for OKARNG aviation at Tulsa.

Chet had learned a lot in Oklahoma, but he also learned a lot from his friends at NGB. Those TDY conferences with the high-muckity-mucks (NGB guys) were more beneficial than they appeared. Rubbing elbows with the right guy(s) and finding a mentor might truly pay large dividends in the future! Aviation folks in the know knew that many future National Guard generals, including a few aviators as well, came from the Pennsylvania Army National Guard. For an aviator, this meant a prerequisite tour as PAARNG State Aviation Officer, and years later would include an alternative tour as commander of the Eastern Army Aviation Training Site (EAATs) at Fort Indiantown Gap, PA.

COL Chester A. "Chet" Howard received a Pennsylvania ARNG promotion to brigadier general before he retired and left Fort Indian Town Gap. He was awarded the Master Army Aviator designation on 29 January 1967, and during his flying career he flew more than 18,500 hours. He was an affable, positive leader and officer. He always got the job done. He retired militarily as the SAO of Pennsylvania on 19 March1976 at FITG, PA. He and his wife Chlokeeta first moved to Rogers, AR where they lived for 17 years, and later they bought a getaway trailer at Branson, MO, where his older brother Frank lived.

Chlokeeta and Chet began to visit the Rio Grande Valley in 1985 and called themselves *winter Texans*. In 1993, as they watched the birds fly south, the Howard's also chose to move south to Mission, TX, near McAllen. It was there in about 1995 that Chet was diagnosed with glaucoma, which resulted in his being declared legally blind. He attended two schools for the blind and took a computer class at the Veteran's Administration Hospital in Waco, TX. Chlokeeta said, "These VA schools and classes helped Chet very much. They are available to any veteran who is losing or has lost their sight."

Circa 1991, Brigadier General Chester A. Chet Howard wrote a letter of sincere appreciation for a poem called "Wave On," written by the Reverend T.J. Finley, of Branson, MO in 1989. The patriotic piece was about the *Stars and Stripes*, representing the courage and bravery of American fighting men and those who died for our freedom.

Chet closed his letter of gratitude with these humble words . . . ."As an aged and blind Veteran, I will never again see the American flag, but those colors, properly arranged, are embedded in my memory. And when the National Anthem is played, I will never again turn my head to shield the moisture in my eyes from view, but will stand erect in the military position, facing forward, allowing the tears to flow freely down my face. And when that little chill starts creeping up my spine, that ever present arthritic pain will be unnoticed," signed simply – Chester A. Howard.

Chet volunteered and worked at the Casa Amparo (*House of Shelter*) orphanage across the border from McAllen, TX, in Reynosa, Mexico. Ten Catholic sisters cared for the young orphans, who called him Abuelo (Grandfather). His work was not only of benefit to the young ladies at

MG David C. Matthews

Casa Amparo, but to himself as well. In the autumn of his life, he was admitted into the hospital to receive an angioplasty and stint implant. While in the recovery room, he had a heart attack and died at McAllen Medical Center on Wednesday, 10 December 2003, at the age of 86. COL Chester A. Howard, a Master Army Aviator, had been awarded the Legion of Merit, Purple Heart Medal, Distinguished Flying Cross, Air Medal, Prisoner of War Medal, Army Commendation Medal, and Good Conduct Medal, among others.

Chester A. Howard is an honored Army Veteran and true patriarch of OKARNG Aviation.

MG David C. Matthews[10] was born in Tupelo, OK, in 1914, just southeast of Ada. He earned a BS in 1938 and an LLB in 1942 from Oklahoma University. Then in 1942 he entered the Navy's V-5, Aviation Preparatory Program at Annapolis and Princeton. He served as an ensign in the Navy in the European and Pacific theaters, until his release from the active duty in January 1946 as a Navy lieutenant. He joined the OKARNG in October 1946 as a captain in the infantry. Matthews was appointed as the Adjutant General of Oklahoma in 1971, and in late 1975 as his term as TAG was about to end, he instructed his executive secretary to call CPT (P) Dana Batey at Norman. She told him that the TAG wanted to see him.

"When?" Batey asked.

"Right away CPT Batey!" Matthew's secretary replied.

Batey wasn't sure what this office call was about. He perceived something big was about to happen, and he went to the latrine area, showered and put on a clean uniform, then scrabbled up to the Oklahoma Military Department in Oklahoma City.

Matthews tells Batey, "Dana I want you to replace Pete Phillips as State Aviation Officer." CPT (P) Batey was shocked, but remained humble and asked what the TAG's game plan was to be. MG Matthews said, "I or my successor will run the state and the major issues, you will draft the plans for the future of aviation in Oklahoma, I'll approve them, and you'll run with the ball. Any questions?"

Batey was almost speechless and said, "No sir. Thank you, sir." He officially became OKSAO on 13 January 1976. At that time the SAO's office was at Westheimer Airfield, in building 7-K, a long, rectangular Army barracks, adjacent to the State Maintenance Office (SMO) at Norman.

Ten years earlier, CPT Batey had been a hard charger, an up and comer. He had the attention and notice of his superiors; one in particular became a life-long friend and was instrumental in many, many major aviation events, and manpower plus ups for OKARNG Aviation – LaVern E. Weber. In a State of Oklahoma Military Department letter, dated 15 June 1966, Weber wrote to a young CPT Dana D. Batey: "Seeing the [Oklahoma] State Headquarters' L-20 [Beaver] at Fort Chaffee [annual training] was indeed a pleasant surprise. The new paint job and interior renovations are fabulous. I particularly like the color, the seats and the carpeting. I certainly appreciate your efforts and hard work in the improvements of the plane. Your actions as Shop Supervisor have raised the maintenance conditions of our aircraft to an unprecedented high level. For this we are most grateful to you. Signed, Sincerely, L.E. Weber, Major General, OKARNG, the Adjutant General."

Under the aegis of Dana D. Batey, things just kept improving! He too was an enthusiastic recruiter and brought many aviators and soldiers into aviation at Norman. These, along with those brought on board by Guild and Howard, created the beginning of a professional military aviation organization. Batey had started out as the Commander of the 445th (Avn) Maintenance Detachment. Then he moved up to 45th Inf Bde Aviation Officer at Edmond, OK. When Chet Howard left Oklahoma, Batey was tabbed as the Facility Cdr at Norman.

As SAO, Batey took the ball and ran with it; those intangible ideas came forth and became lists of improvements and then became task lists for his loyal subordinates to accomplish. Although not perfect, Batey was always thinking ahead of ya! He could think up more than you could do! I don't think he owned a watch, nor did he ever watch the clock. He kept working and expected you to do the same. The job was over only when he got the new force structure, or aircraft and/or full-time manning that he had requested!

Batey recalls, "I think I was the first facility commander at Lexington and the SAO at the same time, depending on who the AG was, but most of them liked to have the SAO in the building at the Oklahoma Military Department (OMD) in OKC. After Colonel Pete Phillips, former SAO, reverted to chief warrant officer, then the title of Facility Cdr and the SAO were [normally] one in the same. Later, when we added a second facility (Tulsa) then we had two AASF Cdrs and an SAO. At Lexington they wanted to pull the Norman hangar out from under us. Said we didn't need both Lex and Norman; John [Stanko] kind of supported that. Well, my friend the airport manager said, 'There's a little rule book – FAA – that says if you're a tenant on an airport you have to have aviation assets to function and participate in airfield business.' I told him to tell the chain of command and he did. He called Colonel Rex Wilson, Director, POTO, at the time and the TAG said 'Batey come up here, we need to put something in that hangar in Norman.' So I suggest we put the UH-1 *static display* trailer in the hangar. Not too long after that, the head shed wanted me to put some aviation [aircraft] in there, so that's when we got back into the fixed-wing business."

Batey continued, "Eventually, we began supporting the Drug Enforcement Agency (DEA) and the Oklahoma Bureau of Narcotics (OBN) drug programs. Our first twin fixed-wing was an old Tulsa Air National Guard's (ANG) *Blue Canoe* Cessna U-3A. Pete Phillips and I went up and transitioned in it for about a week. The Chief of the Oklahoma Bureau of Narcotics office was at Will Rogers [Int'l Airport]. Stu [Stewart] Earnest was his name, a government agent. Visiting with him we got to see his [airplane] 'shopping list' and found several 'excess' drug aircraft, which we could support and maintain through NGB. Following that we got the U-8s (L-23s) [Beech Queenaire]. We went through two or three series of those [U-8s]. Once we got operating with the narcotics division then we got the C-310s."

MAJ Dana D. Batey, Transportation Corp, became a Master Army Aviator on 21 March 1976. The letter of designation from NGB is signed by COL Charlie R. Jones, Chief, ARNG Aviation Division.

As those who had the pleasure of working with COL Dana D. Batey know, he wasn't a quitter. Batey had the additional duty of Commander, Troop Command (Aviation) from 1 November 1983 to 30 October1987. When he would ask Stanko, or others at NGB Aviation for something, they would often say, "Dana . . . . watch my lips! Not NO, *but HELL NO!*" His brain wasn't wired to understand the word "no." To him, no just meant not yet! So we'd stay a bit longer, he'd change the subject and come back to the real issue 30 minutes later. After several no's, the person being asked would finally say, "Batey, if I agree to what you are requesting, would you please go home?" I know for a fact this worked, even though Batey would never admit it. He just felt that his logic was reason enough to get things approved, regardless.

We had an appointment with COL John J. Stanko Jr., Chief, NGB-AVN at Edgewood, MD one clear, wintry morning in 1984. After several minutes of pleasantries and coffee there at the Operating Activities Center (OAC), Batey told Stanko why we were there. He spoke very slowly, "J-o-h-n, we've got this Cessna 310, an N model, really nice, from DEA (Drug Enforcement Agency) for one dollar." Then he laughed gently, as was his manner. "All we need to get it up to the TAG's standards are a new King-NAV [avionic/navigation] package and a Colemill[11] conversion (for each engine)." I recall that the Colemill conversion cost was about $60K at Cornelia Fort Airpark, northeast of downtown Nashville, TN, and I believe the new King radio Nav-Package was about $30K. With total seriousness, Stanko stared at Batey, smiled and said, "Dana, you know I can't do that, don't you?" That was early morning. We didn't leave Edgewood until late that evening. When we returned to Oklahoma, Batey had me fly the C-310 N to Nashville for the installation of the King radios and for the Colemill conversions, which had been finally authorized by Stanko after the sun had set!

Within six weeks of having brought the C-310 home from Nashville, with upgraded engines and three bladed props just purring, and the new King radios also working great, Batey asked Stanko for money to paint the aircraft. I thought I could see the telephone melting in Batey's hand as I overheard the other end of the conversation. True to form, however, within the next few days we had NGB approval to get the C-130 repainted olive drab and white, with black numerals and letters. The paint job was fantastic. Batey had several of his AASF guys go over to Downtown Airpark, in the heart Oklahoma City, and help do the prep work, which lowered the cost. Downtown Airpark also did a complete new interior and the paint job at a cost of $18,000. Floyd Ormiston and Jay Pierce did a fantastic job of sheet metal work building the new wing lockers. The OKARNG C-310N was a beautiful, single pilot, IFR aircraft.

Batey was never emotionally down, never in a bad mood; he always had a smile on his face. If he was down, at least he never let it show. His contemporaries recall that he was a gentleman. He always aimed for the stars! Although he might appear to be quiet, he was deep in thought, thinking, planning how he could get more aviation force structure for OKARNG. He spoke slowly, but he was a fast thinker! He loved his troops and he took care of them!

COL Batey was also the person that solicited, lobbied, and on occasion could out last the naysayers at NGB. These were the same people who gave OKARNG the aviation reorganizations, aviation battalions, companies, platoons, detachments, and aircraft he had dreamed of having! He saw his dream come to fruition of three ARNG aviation facilities (Norman, Lexington, and Tulsa) being built in Oklahoma. He was a *signatory* for the organization and activation of the first and only Counter-Terrorism Aviation Battalion, ever, in the ARNG. This stealth helicopter unit later became the 45th Avn Bn (Lt Hel Cbt) and afterwards was redesignated 1st Bn 245th Avn (SO)(A) at Tulsa, OK. He was also very instrumental for nearly a dozen OKARNG Army aviators being promoted to full colonel before their retirement.

"I greatly admire him and his talents. He's a real people person. Just does a laudable job picking people and helping them get done what he wants them to get done!" said Charlie R. Jones.

"Dana D. Batey's a person you just can't dislike. You like Dana the minute you meet him, and the way he talked—"Jooohhnn" [long, slow and soft]. There was just an affinity there, the way he loved the Aviation program. You could tell that Batey was really something. Dana is such a wonderful person and I just love him dearly, he's just one of my favorite people," stated John J. Stanko Jr. at his home in Danville, PA.

Ms. Deborah Horne, first secretary of the NGB Aviation Division at the OAC in Edgewood, MD (hired by COL Charlie R. Jones in 1972) made the unsolicited statement regarding COL Dana D. Batey, "When

COL Batey would come out to NGB, and he was always a gentleman, always very professional, polite, soft spoken and courteous. He was a good friend of COL John J. Stanko Jr."

BG Dana D. Batey is a wonderfully obsessed man, whose military career of 39 years rotated around and was focused on how he could make the OKARNG Aviation Program better. He was eternally working on ideas, plans, and schemes, whereby he might get OKARNG Aviation additional force structure; his dearest dream was an Aviation Brigade Headquarters for Oklahoma. He almost succeeded in getting an Aviation Brigade Headquarters, during our involvement in the Special Operations arena. BG Batey was loyal, dedicated, and always working for the advancement of aviation in Oklahoma and the OKARNG.

BG Batey was the third OKSAO from 13 January 1976 to 27 October 1988. He was appointed Assistant Adjutant General for the OKARNG on 28 October 1988. He has accrued approximately 16,000 total flight time in this lifetime. After his retirement from Federal Civil Service and the OKARNG, BG Batey became the Director of the Oklahoma Aeronautics & Space Commission, and served in that position from March 1991 to September 1998.

BG Batey remains very civic-minded and nurtures his love of the military and his former comrades through the 45th Inf Div Museum in OKC and his former service as OKC Chapter Commander of Military Order of World Wars (MOWW) 1999-2000 and as Vice Commander, Fort Worth Regional Headquarters of MOWW. He also served on the Board Directors for the Oklahoma Military Hall of Fame. He was inducted into the Midwest City High School Wall of Fame in 1997, and the Oklahoma Aviation Hall of Fame in June 2004. On 13 August 2004, Batey was awarded the George Washington Honor Medal, from the Freedom's Foundation at Valley Forge, PA.

BG Dana D. Batey
October 1988

BG Batey earned a bachelor's degree in Aviation from Southeastern Oklahoma State College in Durant, OK in 1968. He earned a master's degree in Aerospace Management from the University of Southern California at Los Angeles in 1978. He is also a graduate of the Army's Command and

General Staff College, Fort Leavenworth, KS. He was inducted into the Fort Benning Infantry Officer Candidate School (OCS) Hall of Fame on 31 March 2006.

BG Dana D. Batey's military awards and decorations are numerous, but include the following: Legion of Merit, Meritorious Service Medal (2nd award), Army Commendation Medal, Air Force Good Conduct Medal, Armed Forces Reserve Medal w/Gold Hourglass Device, General Staff Badge, Master Army Aviator badge, Royal Thai Army Master Army Aviator badge, Oklahoma Distinguished Service Medal with two oak leaf clusters, Oklahoma Meritorious Service Medal, and numerous other awards and citations for meritorious service, distinguished and exceptional service to include the National Patrick Henry Silver Award (MOWW).

Winston Churchill said, "We make a living by what we get, we make a life by what we give." One of the Oklahoma's Army Aviation patriarchs, BG Dana D. Batey, gave us so very, very much. It may be hard for you to ever know how long or hard was the row that he plowed to get us there!

BG Dana D. Batey is a true patriarch of OKARNG Aviation.

Although I've had many bosses during my military career, I've only had a few mentors. In times past I considered myself a good pilot. In my wallet were civilian FAA ratings for airline transport pilot (airplane single engine land), commercial privileges (airplane multi-engine land; rotorcraft-helicopter; instrument airplane/ helicopter), type rating SK-58, single/ multi-engine land/instrument, commercial flight instructor instrument. When I returned from the Army's UH-1 Instructor Pilot course I felt like I was "ten feet tall and you can't touch me". Well, with age, I've been blessed with some maturity, some senility, wisdom and a sprinkle of humility. I've actually forgotten how good I was, but now I realize and remember quite a few that were far more skilled and better aviators than I ever dreamt of being. If I had it to do over again, there are a couple of men that I would endeavor to emulate – Leroy A. Wall is at the top of my list.

COL Leroy A. Wall
ca 1988

You might disagree with my selection of the four patriarchs of OKARNG Aviation. And that is your right and privilege. I will respect your opinion, although we disagree and I'm still right. Leroy came up from the ranks in the OKARNG, and he grew up in Guard Aviation. He got his Master Army Aviator Wings, 12,000 plus flight hours and rank of colonel the old fashioned way – he earned them!

Besides being my superior, my boss, and my mentor, Leroy has always been my friend since I joined the OKARNG. When I joined the Guard at Lexington, OK, Leroy was a senior Chief Warrant Officer (CW4) wearing a two-piece olive drab, Nomex flight suit, waiting on federal recognition for a direct commission and promotion to major in the Transportation branch. I knew at that time he was very intelligent, honest, and was a hard charger.

When Batey stepped up to the Deputy AG position for OKARNG, Leroy was appropriately selected for the position of OKARNG State Army Aviation Officer. He became the fourth SAO for Oklahoma on 1 December 1988.

Ever since I met Leroy at Lexington, OK, he has been one of two great story tellers I've known; the other being Brigadier General Paul D. Pete Costilow. You will find these pages brightened with a few of Leroy's stories and wit. Leroy could always tell it better than I could, so below I have incorporated a presentation he gave at the 1995 OKARNG Annual Safety Stand-down.

COL Leroy A. Wall was the State Army Aviation Officer at the time and addressed the aviation safety conference with these thoughts and words in January 1995:

Since I began my career in Army Aviation in 1964, I have seen and been a part of many changes that have occurred throughout these 30 years. This seniority, more aptly described as old age, at least gives me some perspective as to the progress we have made and perhaps the challenges that we face in these times of uncertainty and more rapidly changing scenarios.

In 1964, my vision was 20/20 uncorrected and focused on getting into and finishing flight school. In the Guard at that time we had the Hiller OH-23 B and C models, Cessna L-19s, Bird Dogs and DeHaviland L-20 Beavers. Our only base was at Norman where the Fixed-Wing [C-12] Flight Detachment is today. As I recall, there were one or two majors, three or four captains, some lieutenants and a few enlisted men in Aviation.

Seven or eight people were full-time; most were Korean War veterans and a few were WWII veterans.

They were all old—late 30s or 40s. We had only recently begun drilling on the weekends rather than Monday[12] nights. There was some talk that we might even get some extra drills for aviator proficiency—additional flight training periods (AFTPs) they were called. This meant that we could maintain our own currency instead of coming in once a month and flying the first trip around the pattern with an IP.

At that time we had two very distinct groups of pilots. One group was pure fixed-wing and they were sure that the helicopter was simply a passing fad. The other group flew helicopters—something that real gentlemen would never do. Most of these slightly crazy helicopter pilots were Southern Airways IPs at Fort Wolters, Texas, and needless to say they could really fly the helicopters.

In April 1964, I reported to Fort Wolters and began flying the almost new 1956, 1957 more powerful OH-23D models. Later at Fort Rucker, we marveled at the slick new UH-1As and Bs that we would later fly after we mastered the Sikorsky UH-19 Chickasaw. In January 1965, I graduated from flight school and returned to Oklahoma. A few of my classmates had orders to Vietnam, at that time, a small police action in a foreign country that was beginning to have ominous overtones.

In the drawdown after the Vietnam War, the Guard entered the turbine era. New and used UH-1 B, C and Ds came in. Fort Wolters was on the closure list. I had been working there as an instructor pilot for five years. I went to work for the Oklahoma Guard in 1971. The O-1As and the U-6s began to phase out and we became largely an all helicopter outfit. Those pilots who never accepted the helicopter slowly faded away.

In 1975, having outgrown Norman, we moved to a new facility at Lexington. Some pilots did not move and got on with the Army Reserve unit still in Norman. We got some new units; the biggest was the 445th Aviation Company (Assault Helicopter). It had 23 UH-1s and about 400 people [authorized]. The infantry brigade, engineers, and artillery had aviation sections and flew OH-58s. Gradually these small organizations were absorbed into a provisional battalion, and we began a real Aviation training, standardization, and safety program.

During the late 1970s and early 80s there was rapid growth in OKARNG Aviation. In a visionary move by COL Batey, all aviation assets were consolidated into an aviation headquarters. We signed up a real flight surgeon (Colonel John Dille) and hired a physician's assistant (Chief Warrant Officer Three Floyd Todd). They collectively put together, piece by piece, a professional Aviation Medicine Program in the Oklahoma Guard.

In April 1983, Army Aviation became a branch. Aviation officers no longer had to split their careers two ways. The terrible price and sacrifices of the Vietnam aviators and the job that they did demonstrated to everyone that the helicopter was just as essential to the modem battlefield as the tank or artillery piece.

Meanwhile, aviation training in the Guard had become serious business. All pilots became 100% instrument qualified. NOE (Nap-of-the-earth) was next and then Night Hawk. Some said, " . . . flying was not fun anymore." In fact, it was downright risky.

Other dramatic changes included the conversion of a small attack helicopter company at Tulsa in 1982 to a small Special Operations helicopter battalion; flying OH-6s at night using the PVS-5 night vision goggles. We began pioneering NVG flight in the Oklahoma Guard. Two UH-60s came in for the maintenance company. The battalion grew in size and in capability. Two deployments a month were common. The first ODT was Honduras. It occurred one year before it was announced that Oklahoma's 160th Artillery would be the first National Guard unit to train in that country. The 45th Aviation Battalion won the AAAA NG Aviation Unit of the Year in 1987.

Colonel Leroy Wall's presentation to OKARNG Annual Safety Stand-down in 1995

Although COL Wall mentioned the 45th Avn Bn winning the Outstanding Aviation Unit of the Year Award in 1987, the following wasn't part of his presentation. Below are several paragraphs extracted from the Spring 1987 issue of *On Guard*, written by CPT Pat Scully, the Assistant Public Affairs Officer for the OKARNG at that time.

"The 45th Avn Bn Special Ops unit was honored as the Outstanding Aviation Unit of the Year by the Army Aviation Association of America during ceremonies held in Fort Worth recently. The award is given to outstanding aviation units . . . that have demonstrated the highest degree of professionalism and accomplishment."

"The 45th Aviation Battalion, headquartered in Sperry [OK], was given the award for their performance of mission citing the unique organization of the unit. 'The 45th Aviation Battalion is one of the most innovative aviation units in the Army National Guard,' said Lieutenant General Charles D. Franklin, commander of the First U.S. Army and presenter of the prestigious award."

"Accepting the award was Battalion Commander Lieutenant Colonel Leroy Wall and Sergeant Major Charles B. Connell. 'We are proud to accept this honor on the behalf of the men of the 45th Aviation Battalion,' Wall said. 'The men have worked long, hard hours enduring many hardships and I'm proud they are being recognized for their efforts.'"

"'This is a highly specialized unit,' Lieutenant General Franklin said. 'It is 100 percent air deployable, participating in continuous exercise programs in support of special operation forces units.'"

More ODTs followed. The 45th SOA became 1/245th SOA. The assault helicopter company at Lexington [Co B 149th Avn Co] became part of the battalion and a major reorganization resulted in conversion from OH-6s to UH-60s. In 1989, the Barr Barlow Aviation Complex at Tulsa was completed. The 1/245th became the best (but least known) aviation unit in the National Guard. Deployments to support the Special Forces and JRTC were commonplace. Deployments outside the U.S. were frequent.

We mission-trained and maintenance-trained our crews in UH-60s. We began training hard to receive the Special Operations Chinooks.

In 1989, disaster struck. It was rumored that the Soviet Union was on the verge of collapse. The collapse of the Berlin Wall proved the rumor to be fact. Suddenly, our favorite arch enemy had retired from the field, leaving our entire military industrial complex at the mercy of Congress and the taxpayers. Just as quickly, the U.S. military began to downsize, only interrupted for a short period by Operation Desert Shield and then Operation Desert Storm. Unlike the past, when the active components downsized and the Reserve Components increased, AC and RC alike were downsizing (i.e. 1 September 1994 we lost the *1/245th* Avn Bn).

It is of some consolation that we were the best, and we reached training levels that were unheard of in the National Guard.

At this time, there were numerous *problems* facing aviation in the OKARNG:

1. Headquarters of aviation Tulsa units are in Kansas.
2. Headquarters of Lexington units are in Texas, Wyoming, Washington, D.C.
3. One-year gap between deactivation of 1/245th and activation of other units.
4. Large variety of aircraft and missions.
5. Loss of 198 aviation personnel spaces—112 people excess.
6. Pending loss of Det 3 and Co A 1/132nd with 15 aircraft and 72 personnel in FY96.
7. Loss of aviation support to the state with 34 aircraft and 345 Aviation personnel.
8. Coordination problems with so many headquarters out of state.
9. Dual tasking the physician's assistant, decrementing the aviation medicine program.

And there were also numerous *challenges* facing aviation:

1. Maintaining a positive attitude, especially among the key aviation personnel.
2. Maintaining a safe and effective aviation force.
3. Learning new missions and new aircraft.
4. Providing support service, but avoiding the old taxi service game.
5. Continuing to educate the National Guard in aviation use, training, and doctrine.

The most important function of a senior leader is institution building. Establishing the organizational vision – *what the organization is all about* and communicating that vision to the organization. Nowhere is this more important than in the military, which must be uniquely institutional rather than occupational.

The following are some of COL Wall's military aviation aphorisms and philosophies:

1. "Aviation is a technically skilled area. It requires people who are highly trained, self—disciplined and motivated."
2. "Aviation leaders must be competent, honest, and more energetic toward the success of the organization and welfare of the people."

3. "OKARNG Aviation must be used efficiently and legally to support the OKARNG program."
4. "Each Aviation soldier must feel that they have a stake in the safety and success of Aviation."
5. "Everyone must know that any illegal or irresponsible act may reflect unfavorably on Aviation and damage the organization."
6. "Aviation must willingly meet any challenge given it by the higher headquarters."
7. "Aviation must ensure that there is documented credibility. There must be no pencil whipping of aircraft operational rates, readiness rates, minimums, APFT, etc."
8. "Aviation people have a reputation of working harder, being smarter, going the extra mile and spending the extra time in order to increase the success of the mission or the organization."

In 1978 COL Wall was awarded the Army Aviator of the Year Award by the Army Aviation Association of America (AAAA) for the 5th Army Area. In 1988 he graduated the Army's Air Assault School. He earned a master's degree from Oklahoma State University in 1991. COL Leroy A. Wall was the OKARNG SAO from 1 December 1988 until 1 March 2000. Among the many honors and military awards he received, he holds the Meritorious Service Medal, the Oklahoma Star of Valor, and the Legion of Merit. He has been an enlisted soldier, a warrant officer (WO-1 through CW4), and a commissioned officer. He is a Master Army Aviator with 12,000 + accident-free flight hours. COL Leroy A. Wall retired from civil service and the Army National Guard as the OKARNG State Aviation Officer in March 2000 with 43 years of military service. Most importantly, he is a true American patriot and for us, he is an Oklahoma Army National Guard Aviation patriarch who won't be forgotten!

By the way, Leroy didn't really *retire*. He went from a military uniform in March 2000, to a dark blue flight suit with a black soldier holster for his pistol. He continues to work and fly today for the Oklahoma Bureau of Narcotics.

Let us remember our OKARNG patriarchs and their desires, dreams, and goals for OKARNG's Aviation program. Remember that immense achievement, like great love, involves great risks! What they achieved they did it the old fashion way, they worked smart and earned it!

Regarding the patriarchs of OKARNG Aviation, Colonel Jerry D. Bourassa, former dual-rated OKARNG aviator, instructor pilot, unit commander and Lexington, OK AASF Commander said, "Those four guys were really the people that got this thing started. Professionalism is contagious! OKARNG Aviation grew from a non-paid, on your own time operation in the late fifties . . . through the addition of paid AFTPs and structured leadership and reorganization into a professional trained flying organization. It improved with support from the State, NGB resources and local leadership. They made amazing improvements in the OKARNG Aviation Program."

The reputation of OKARNG Aviation (sometimes referred to by NGB-AVS staffers as the Oklahoma Mafia) improved over the years and was envied by many. Through these changes, growth has occurred and " . . . resulted in going from one LTC/O-5 [aviation slot] in the state and two MAJ/O-4 [aviation slots] while everyone else were captains and warrant officers, to four [OKARNG Aviation] people being promoted to brigadier generals[13] and at least a dozen [promoted to] colonel. To me that shows leadership way back there, even though it may have not been recognized at the time," said COL Jerry D. Bourassa.

The old Headquarters, State Area Command (HQs OKSTARC), OKARNG shoulder sleeve insignia (SSI) and distinctive unit insignia (DUI) (or crest) with the above design was redesignated in October 2003 to "OKARNG Element, Joint Force Headquarters" SSI and DUI insignia.

1. Reprinted by permission. John C. Maxwell, "Leadership Promises For Everyday (A Daily Devotional)," (Nashville, TN: Thomas Nelson Inc.), 15. All rights reserved.

2. Ibid

3. Ibid

4. The author was able to verify only four OKARNG aviators who went to Korea with the 45th INF DIV. It is very possible there were more.

5. Personal interview Brigadier General Dana D. Batey, 22 December 2006.

6. Telephone interview CW5 Clarence R. "Clay" Clarkson recalls there were about 20 or so OKARNG aviators who were also rotary-wing flight instructors at Fort Wolters, TX, working for "Southern Airways" in the mid-late 1960s. Those included: Leroy A. Wall, Emmett Doyle McElwain, Don Key, Sid Morse, Don Harvey, Tom Nissen, Don Heath, Gwen Shepherd, Donald Wolgamott, Keith Owens, Regan Popplewell, Lance Fletcher, Mitch Johnston, Emery Lamunyon, John Dollins, Preston Perry, George Forrester, Don Hayes, and Richard Spurlock.

7. Brigadier General O.T. Autry commanded the 45th Inf Div's 189th FA during WWII and also during Korea, and he was promoted to Brigadier after Korea. He was inducted into the Oklahoma Military Hall of Fame in November 2006.

8. Date of assignment/date of rank for Charles R. Jones to COL/0-6 provided by Ms. Henrietta L. Massenburg, D.C. Guard, Archives Mgr telephone conversation 7 January 2008 and DA 2-1.

9. Chet Howard was referring to Dana D. Batey.

10. General Matthews was TAG of Oklahoma from 2 October 1971 to 12 January 1975. He enlisted in the OKARNG as a private in HHB, 158th Field Artillery, 45th Inf Div, OKARNG. While attending Oklahoma University, he took two years of Army ROTC and completed the U.S. Navy V-5 Aviation Preparation Program. In addition to his active Navy service during WWII, he served with the 45th Inf Div in Korea from December 1951 until 12 July 1952.

11. Colemill Conversions in Tennessee did engine upgrades on light twins. The new, overhauled and improved engines, with three-bladed props provided greater power and dependability.

12. Early on Oklahoma Army National Guard drill used to be every Monday night for four hours (one Unit Training Assembly [UTA]); thus four Monday evening drills equaled four UTAs or one drill weekend, as is done today. Monday evening drill ended ca early 1970s.

13. Bourassa is referring to Brigadier General Chester A. "Chet" Howard, Brigadier General Dana D. Batey, Brigadier General Paul D. "Pete" Costilow and Brigadier General Terry R. Council.

Chapter 3

The Godfather of ARNG Aviation

"Everything rises and falls on leadership."
John C. Maxwell

Without imagination, creativity, vision, or reliability, how can there be dynamic, stellar leadership? But when all of these leadership characteristics are present, along with the confidence and determination of the whole team, you will notice that the highest expectations and highest standards are achievable; some who have seen this style of leadership have called the actions and results a *legacy*.

Did you ever have a boss say, "Listen up, here's the Big Picture"? One of my favorite military bosses, a true gentleman and a fabulous mentor, would remind me on occasion, "You can never satisfy all of NGB's 54 entities (one for each state, territory[1] and the District of Columbia), regardless of how hard you try."

As Henry David Thoreau prophetically stated, *"The question is not what you look at . . . but what you see." One of the most interesting things about life isn't about the destination, but about the journey – what you see and experience enroute. It's like the difference of taking a vacation in a car—or experiencing a road trip on a motorcycle. The car gets you there and back, but on the motorcycle you become intimately familiar with the smells, feel the changes in temperature or moisture, and you can hear – quite differently than in a car. On a motorcycle, the rain or sleet stings just a little when it touches your face as you lean into and out of each curve on a winding road, but you've made a commitment and are experiencing an adventure. Bugs rarely get between my teeth, but they hurt like hell when they hit my forehead just below my helmet visor and just above my glasses. Riding the bike is the closest thing to flying while still remaining in contact with the ground.*

How did these men, these patriarchs, these chiefs or godfathers – reach their destinations? How did they achieve such pinnacles, such high-level positions; having sometimes literally performed the impossible? Others might say it was luck. What did they see; what was their vision?

On a scale of 1 to 10, (1 being at the top of the scale) each Guard State will adamantly proclaim they are Number One, or that they should be the *top priority*, and declare that they should receive everything on their military *want list*. Everyone in Lexington, Edmond, Tulsa, Oklahoma City, and all of the towns across Oklahoma, today are striving to obtain the best force structure, the best training opportunities, and the newest equipment and best rewards for Oklahoma ARNG units and their soldiers. They work hard to obtain more and greater educational and retirement benefits for all of our citizen soldiers, especially those who have already served our country in the Global War on Terrorism or who will be in the near future. And so did their predecessors 30, 40, and 50 years ago. (Note: The new Obama Administration has cast away the term Global War on Terrorism, and has changed it to a new and unrelated idea—Overseas Contingency Operation.

Is it working today? Allow me to address those still in the military for just a moment. Are you working for every soldier in your unit and for the future of the ARNG or just a paycheck?

It's sorta like my wife says about church – "Are we going to be doing just *church work* or are we going to do the *work of the church?*" A person can spend an entire day at his desk and may appear to be busy, but that doesn't mean that busy work is productive. Far from it.

Oklahoma is one among 50 states. How is it that Oklahoma carried so much clout within the ARNG in earlier days? How is it that Oklahoma's aviation leaders made such an impact on ARNG Aviation at the national level? How is it that Oklahoma provided some of the most successful and dynamic general officers at the highest levels within the Army and Army National Guard? You are possibly aware of them all; or perhaps not. You may not be able to name any of them or how they climbed the ladder to such heights.

Before the ink on this page dried, another Oklahoma General Officer moved up to accept a new challenge at the national level.

LTG Harry M. Wyatt III

Major General Harry M. Bud Wyatt III served notably as the Adjutant General of Oklahoma from 13 January 2003 to 3 February 2009. President George W. Bush nominated Wyatt for promotion to lieutenant general in early 2009, and he was then confirmed by the Senate and pinned. Lieutenant General Wyatt was then reassigned to NGB, Washington, D.C. as the Director of the Air National Guard 3 February 2009. Major General Wyatt served as commander of the 138th Fighter Wing in Tulsa and as the Oklahoma Guard's Chief of Staff for the Joint Headquarters before becoming Adjutant General.

"This is a great honor for General Wyatt and a great honor for Oklahoma," said Gov. Brad Henry. "I've always said we had the best adjutant general in the country and the latest announcement is confirmation of that."

MG Myles L. Deering

Gov. Henry then appointed a young combat infantryman from Ada, OK, Major General Myles L. Deering, as the new Adjutant General of Oklahoma. Major General Deering was commissioned in 1976 through the Texas Army Guard OCS program. He later transferred to the OKARNG and rose through the ranks, serving as commander of the 700th Support Battalion, and in nearly all of the key OMD staff positions. He was promoted to brigadier general (line) on 10 February 2005. He deployed to New Orleans in the aftermath of hurricane Katrina and Rita in September 2005 as Commander of the Oklahoma National Guard's Joint Task Force. Once in New Orleans he assumed command of Task Force Orleans, providing disaster relief operations to the people of New Orleans. In October 2007, Brigadier General Deering mobilized his 45th Inf Bde and deployed to Iraq where he served as commander of the Joint Area Support Group-Central in Baghdad, Iraq. He returned from Iraq in November 2008 and was assigned as Director of Manpower and Personnel at the National Guard Bureau headquarters in Washington, D.C. He was promoted to major general (line) 13 November 2008, and Gov. Henry selected and appointed the young general officer as the Adjutant General of Oklahoma.

This chapter is about transition, imagination, creativity, vision, and leadership. It leads us from the good ole days into a new realm of military aviation. It is also about ARNG Aviation at the NGB level: the who, what, when, and how it all happened. Follow along as the maturation occurs from primary aviation and we transition into the advanced portion of ARNG Aviation development.

Were there growing pains/problems? Damn right there were! Were their successes just chance or happen-stance? Or was it just plain luck, being in the right place at the right time? Was it destiny, part of the plan, part of the big picture? If you are a soldier still, I offer you the opportunity to make your own conclusion(s).

In the previous chapter on Patriarchs we introduced, August Lee "Gus" Guild, who was considered the first (unofficial) State Aviation Officer (1965-68) of Oklahoma, before the term SAO came into being, before the TDA position existed. We also discussed one of OKARNG's finest aviation gentlemen, who became the first official SAO, Chester A. Howard (1968-72). You learned about a school teacher, Charlie R. Jones, who became a full-time aviator at Norman and went to the front of the class at the national level. Then we came to know the man who thus far had the longest tenure as SAO in OKARNG history, Brigadier General Dana D. Batey. Batey was OKSAO from 1976 until 1988. I doubt anyone now or in the future will exceed his time in office as SAO (12 years 9 months 14 days.)[2]. Brigadier General Batey's reputation is legendary, as he is and was so well-liked and appreciated by his subordinates, contemporaries, and superiors within Oklahoma and at NGB.

Brigadier General Batey brought the OKARNG Aviation Program from the piston days of reciprocating-engine helicopters and airplanes into the modern days of turbine aviation. As SAO he brought to the OKARNG Aviation program a plethora of new types/models of aircraft. He opened the very first AASF, with collective operations, training and maintenance shops, all combined in one facility! He was at the helm when Oklahoma received the UH-1 helicopter, OKARNG's first turbine aircraft in the 1970s. What a major step and challenge in aviation maintenance and aircrew training. As the state aviation officer, as an aviator, as an aviation headquarters commander, he had pride, imagination, creativity, and vision. He was thinking outside the box, before the box was even invented. But he wasn't flying solo . . .

The big war, World War II, aroused many a young American to serve in the armed forces and work in the military industrial complex. They came from farms, colleges, large, impersonal cities, and far away little towns. Most were young men, but not all. Most volunteered because they loved this country of ours and they hated what Hitler, Mussolini and Imperial Japan were doing overseas. These young Americans chose to fight in Europe then, rather than waiting for the war over here, on our shores, later. As you know, the Fighting 45th Infantry Division of Oklahoma Army National Guard fame fought most honorably in WWII and received tremendous accolades. Many OKARNG soldiers were highly decorated, including with the Congressional Medal of Honor, and they were recognized as tremendous leaders.

LaVern E. Weber was born on 3 September 1923, in Lone Wolf, OK. After graduating from high school, he attended Oklahoma University and the Louisiana Polytechnic Institute. Weber enlisted in the U.S. Marine Corps Reserve on 9 November 1942 to enter the Navy V-12 Program[3], and was commissioned a second lieutenant, USMC, upon graduation from Officer Candidate School on 21 November 1945. His active duty continued until 9 May 1946. He served in the Marine Corps Reserve until 21 July 1948.

Weber graduated from East Central State College in Oklahoma with a Bachelor of Science Degree in Education in 1948. In addition to being a soldier, he became a schoolteacher, a coach, and a farmer/rancher in southwestern Oklahoma. After volunteering and serving as a lieutenant in the Marine Corps during WWII, he returned to Oklahoma and joined the Army National Guard as a second lieutenant in 1948.

On 29 July 1948 Weber was appointed a second lieutenant, infantry, Oklahoma Army National Guard, and was assigned as company commander, Headquarters Company, 180th Infantry Regiment, 45th Infantry Division. He served in that capacity through mobilization of the division on 1 September 1950, to include the training of the division at Camp Polk, LA and Hokkaido, Japan, preparatory to combat service in Korea. During this period, GEN Weber also attended the Infantry Officer's Associate Advanced Course.

While on active combat duty in Korea, GEN Weber served as the operations and training officer, S-3, of the 2nd Battalion, 180th Infantry Regiment, and was promoted to the rank of major on 1 May 1952. Upon release from active duty on 12 June 1952, he reverted to National Guard status in the Oklahoma National Guard.

On 15 September 1952, when the 45th Infantry Division was reorganized, he was assigned as S-3, 179th Infantry Regiment.

General Weber graduated from the U.S. Army Command and General Staff College on 18 December 1955 and was assigned as assistant G-2, 45th Infantry Division. On 15 December 1958, he assumed the duties of Division Intelligence Officer.

He was promoted to lieutenant colonel on 15 May 1959 and on 1 April 1961 was assigned as G-1, 45th Infantry Division, serving in this position until 17 November 1964, when he became chief of staff with his promotion to colonel on 18 November 1964.

On Main Street in Norman, OK, is the office of the *Transcript*, a suburban, university town newspaper. In the late 1950s and early 1960s, a man named Joe E. Burke worked for the *Transcript*. He was a staunch Republican, very patriotic, and he believed in the military, so much so that he enlisted in the OKARNG. Joe was outspoken, audacious, and was quick to give his opinion – and did so frequently.

In 1962, another Republican, also a marine and farmer from Billings, OK, ran for governor of Oklahoma. Henry L. Bellmon served in WWII from 1942-46, and he won the Silver Star for action in Saipan and the Legion of Merit for action in Iwo Jima. Bellmon asked Burke to become his publicity and public relations chairman for his gubernatorial election. Burke accepted. Bellmon won the race and became the first Republican governor of Oklahoma. He was inaugurated in January 1963.

For a couple of years the status quo remained unchanged in the OKARNG. However, since Burke had done a marvelous job on his campaign and was a member of the Oklahoma Guard, Bellmon offered him a direct commission to second lieutenant and later asked him if he wanted to become the new adjutant general, replacing Major General Roy W. Kenny. Burke replied, "Hell no, I don't want to be the AG, I just want to select the next one." Bellmon agreed.

Burke was about 15-20 years junior to LaVern E. Weber, a tall, stout, rancher and infantry commander in the 45th Inf. It is said that Burke was given his wish, and he selected the next adjutant general – LaVern E. Weber. Weber became the Adjutant General of Oklahoma on 8 March 1965.

Several years later, David Hall, a Democrat, was elected governor of Oklahoma and took office in January 1971. Colonel David C. Matthews, from Perry, OK, a strong Democratic supporter and commander of the 179th Infantry, wanted very much to become the OKTAG and had some strong, stealthy, political connections. It happened that David Hall chose him to be the next OKTAG. What some staunch supporters of Weber saw at this point was that Major General Weber was about to be without a military job. His military leadership potential went well beyond TAG of Oklahoma. Behind the scenes others had been working and soliciting support for Weber at the national level.

However, in the meantime, the new adjutant general, Matthews, had an agenda. One of the first things Matthews did was to fire two people – "Two of many . . . ," it has been said. He fired Colonel Burke as commander of the 279th Infantry. And he fired Chet Howard, then OKSAO, who just happened to be attending the resident Command & General Staff College (CGSC) course at Fort Leavenworth, KS, during this transition.

Did firing these officers end their careers or their dreams?

No, sir, it did not.

"Don't take it personally, it's just politics!"

In the mid-1960s, the General Officer staff positions at the National Guard Bureau were fewer and different than they exist today. There was a Chief, NGB (CNGB), by the name of Major General Winston P. Wimpy Wilson (1963-71), and his deputy was Major General Francis S. Greenlief. There was not a Director NGB (DARNG), but the position was called the Assistant Chief NGB for Army, and that was Brigadier

General Charles Southward. There was also an Assistant Chief NGB for Air Force, Brigadier General John Pesch.

Sometime in the early 1970s another general officer staff reorganization took place at NGB. The Deputy Chief, NGB position was traded for two major general positions: a new position and title were created—Director, NGB (DARNG) and Director, ANG (DANG). Brigadier General Pesch was promoted to major general as the DANG and Major General Greenlief was reassigned as the first Army Director (DARNG).

After Weber was replaced by Matthews as the OKTAG, and in view of Weber's stellar record, performance, and legacy, Gov. Hall, the new OKTAG, Major General Matthews, and others sought to promote Weber as the next DARNG with the other governors and CNGB staff. In the early 1970s, the new position of Director, ARNG was selected by a majority vote of the 50 states' governors. The distinguished name of LaVern E. Weber, the former Adjutant General from Oklahoma, had been suggested and Major General Weber's leadership potential was recognized at the national level. He was selected and called to serve as the Director, Army National Guard, by a majority vote. He served as DARNG at the Pentagon from 1971-74. "I don't know that Joe E. Burke had any influence getting Weber selected as DARNG, but he did get him selected as the OKTAG under Bellmon," stated BG Batey.

This famous Oklahoma general, LaVern E. Weber, then rose to serve as the Chief of Army National Guard 1974-82. He was promoted to lieutenant general in 1979, after his first four-year term as CNGB,

 upon the recommendation of President Jimmy Carter, becoming the first Chief, National Guard Bureau to be promoted to lieutenant general.

Lieutenant General Weber almost served longer than any other individual as CNGB. He and Major General Wilson (1963-71) were the two generals to serve as CNGB for eight years each. Wilson was a combat pilot and the first member of the Air National Guard to become CNGB. Major General Wilson died 31 December 1996, age 86, at Baptist East Memorial

LTG LaVern E. Weber

Hospital in Memphis, TN, after suffering a stroke. Major General Greenlief followed Wilson as CNGB.

Following his tenure as Chief, NGB, Weber served at Army Forces Command (FORSCOM) Headquarters at Fort McPherson, GA., as Deputy Commanding General for mobilization and as Executive Officer of the Reserve Forces Policy Board.

Weber retired on 30 June 1984 after 42 years of military service. General Weber was appointed as the full-time Executive Director of the National Guard Association of the United States (NGAUS) effective 1 July 1984, a position he held for nine years.

While serving as CNGB, he founded the LaVern E. Weber National Guard Professional Education Center (PEC) at Camp Robinson, Little Rock, AR, a facility dedicated to building proficiency at all levels of staff and command in the Guard.

His military decorations include the Distinguished Service Medals from the U.S. Army and Air Force, the Legion of Merit, and the Combat Infantry Badge.

Lieutenant General LaVern Erick Weber died 30 December 1999, after an accident at his ranch near Perry, OK, at the age of 76. His family said heavy fence panels fell on him as he was preparing to work at the ranch. He was laid to rest in Oklahoma City's Union Soldiers Cemetery on 5 January 2000.

Retired Lieutenant General Herbert R. Temple, former CNGB, told those attending LaVern E. Weber's memorial in D.C. that, "No two people were more philosophically opposed on issues than LTG Weber and I. Yet, we met often, enjoyed each other's company, and were close friends."

"Perhaps that's a lesson for us all," Temple said. "We don't always have to agree. But there are issues that are important on the human side of life, which he understood and brought to me. I've lost a friend. I'm deeply hurt."

LTG Weber, not long before his death, was presented the Raymond S. McLain Medal of the Association of

LTG Raymond S. McLain

the United States Army (AUSA). LTG La Vern E. Weber was a man of imagination, creativity, tremendous vision, and undaunted courage. He was a leader of men, decisive, honest, and fair. He was indeed a citizen soldier.

Are you aware that LTG Weber was not the first Oklahoman to rise to three-star rank? Raymond Stallings McLain, who was born 4 April 1890, in Washington County, KY, was the first Oklahoman to rise to the three-star rank. He began his military service with the Oklahoma National Guard in 1912, later serving on the Mexican border, and in Europe during World War I. While pursuing a career in business in 1938, McLain attended the Special Command and General Staff Class for Guard and Reserve officers.

During WWII, he commanded the 45th Infantry Division Artillery in Sicily, where he earned the first of two Distinguished Service Crosses. At Normandy in 1944, McLain took command of the troubled 90th Infantry Division, transformed it into a first-class fighting formation, and led it across France. He then assumed command of the XIX Corps, becoming the only Army National Guardsman to command an Army Corps in combat.

For his distinguished service, McLain was appointed as a regular Army brigadier general, the first guardsman so honored. Later, he became the first comptroller of the Army. McLain later rose to the rank of lieutenant general.

At the time of his death in 1954 he was serving on President Dwight Eisenhower's National Security Training Commission. He died on 14 December 1954 at Walter Reed Army General Hospital, Washington, D.C at the age of 64.

In the words of George C. Marshall, "Lieutenant General Raymond S. McLain gave great distinction to the term *citizen soldier*. His service to his state and nation spanned more than forty years."

Were any of these men, the recognized leaders, movers and shakers of the Oklahoma Guard, Army Guard, and aviation leaders, doing these things alone, or in a vacuum? Batey as the SAO wasn't flying solo, any more than Weber as TAG was leading the Oklahoma National Guard by himself. They surrounded themselves with intelligent, successful, imaginative, tireless, and creative staff, soldiers, and aviators. Not *yes men*, but courageous soldiers who weren't afraid to tell their boss, "No Sir, that won't work, but here's how we can make it work!"

And, it isn't just about working hard, or blood, sweat and tears. Occasionally, a leader will admit that a portion, large or minute, of his/ her success, had to do with luck, fate, and/or just being at the right place at the right time!

Joe E. Burke was an individual from Oklahoma who, for most of his life, had lots of good luck. He learned that the further up the ladder of success you go, greater is the risk and distance that you might fall. Some have learned from experience, like Burke, of Norman, OK.

So, let's continue with Joe E. Burke's story. Three very impeccable aviation sources knew Burke and have related much more than I can share here. With respect for them, I have honored their wishes not to repeat or write certain things relating to Burke. Yet the stories they chose to tell me are quite interesting.

One good turn deserves another, doesn't it? Burke, a full colonel in Oklahoma, stated that he'd like to have a position at NGB and also wanted to become a one-star general. How did Burke get to the Pentagon?

Colonel John J. Stanko, Jr. offered that, "General Weber arranged for Burke to be called up to NGB as the new Division Chief of NGB-ARO (Operations). Burke followed Colonel Bob Cowan as Chief of ARO. COL Cowan was from Nebraska, as was GEN Greenlief. Greenlief moved Cowan up to NGB Chief of Staff. Cowan's demeanor was excellent for his job as chief of staff. He was Father Confessor, one who smoothed out conflicts, and was gentle when bad news had to be announced.

Following his duties as chief of staff, Cowan was appointed to head up the brand new Operating Activity Center (OAC) at Edgewood, MD, which was located at Aberdeen Proving Grounds, MD.

"In 1972 we opened the doors in Edgewood for what was then called the Aviation Logistics Office. The Aviation Logistics Office was created with the [enormous] influx of Hueys [from Vietnam], because it was no longer going to be manageable by people in ARL [Logistics]. So we set up 13 people to start managing the logistics for this huge influx of Hueys. Stanko was selected by [Major General] Francis Greenlief [CNGB] to be the Chief of that Aviation Logistics office. That's not the Aviation and Safety Division," said Ray Engstrand.[4] [Colonel Charlie Jones became Chief of the Aviation Division on 17 November 1973].

Mr. Engstrand later added, "Then Charlie Jones was appointed. Because by that time, GEN Weber, who was from Oklahoma, was the Director [of the ARNG]. Charlie Jones was his Aviation Officer and so — GEN Weber had a lot of respect for Charlie Jones. So that [aviation division] was created and then sometime later we added a Safety branch."

The new OAC incorporated the NGB's Combined Logistics Review Team (CLRT), Aviation Logistics Division, Military Education (Schools) Branch, Aviation Division, Safety Branch, Environmental Resources Branch, and Centralized Scheduling Section. The Centralized Scheduling Section later became the key focal point of the Army's Operational Support Airlift Agency (OSAA) at Fort Belvoir, VA, placing all 107 of the Army, ARNG, and Reserve fixed-wing passenger/cargo airplanes under one command at Fort Belvoir, VA beginning in 1995. Cowan was to coordinate with the active Army for buildings, for monies paid for space, and for making sure all functioned properly. He was perfect for the job; his low-key personality made things work. I'll discuss more about the OAC later.

But COL Cowan did not like Burke. According to my sources, almost everyone else liked Joe.

"Joe E. Burke had been a very successful businessman and Guardsman in Oklahoma. He may have made lots of money as a movie producer, among other investments, and may also have owned a very successful huge automobile distributorship," suggested Colonel John J. Stanko Jr.

Joe E. Burke was a very, very likeable individual and had expressed to Weber a strong desire to become a general officer. Weber wanted him appointed to brigadier general at the Bureau, but that didn't happen. John J. Stanko recalled, "When the Assistant Chief, NGB position was elevated to Director [DARNG], a one-star Deputy Director ARNG was created, and when the position came open, Joe E. Burke expected to be nominated and selected. All of us on the NGB staff were aware of the special relationship between the two Oklahomans [Burke and Weber] and no one thought ill of it. So you can imagine our surprise, MG Weber's shock, and Joe's rage when the Secretary of Defense office announced the appointment and promotion of Colonel Herb Temple to be the new Deputy Director, ARNG."

Stanko continued, "So he [Weber] sends Burke to the Virgin Islands and makes a *ghost headquarters*. He assigned the Army Guard band to the VI, the MPs, an administrative element, and all sorts of units."

BG Batey added, "It takes about 800-900 troops in a unit/headquarters for a one-star brigadier slot to be authorized." Orders were cut for Joe E. Burke to become a brigadier general (VI) and he was assigned as the TAG of the Virgin Islands[5] in July 1976.

Juan Luis was Governor of the Virgin Islands in 1980, the last year Burke was TAG. He and Burke became friends and Gov. Luis was present as Brigadier General Burke hosted his final military ball. Two significant accomplishments were noted at the Third Annual Military Ball of the Virgin Islands National Guard. The first accomplishment was the activation of the first ANG unit in the VI, the 285th Combat Communications Flight. The second was achieving the CNGB's recruiting goal of the 900 personnel in the VI Army National Guard on 25 January 1980.

Brigadier Burke stepped down as TAG of the Virgin Islands National Guard in July 1980.

Stanko recalled a story about the Virgin Islands, " . . . rumors kept surfacing regarding misuse of aircraft because BG Joe E. Burke, TAG, USVI ARNG, was visiting all sorts of places throughout Central America."

Several sources have stated that Burke, "Flew too near the edge, did some shady things . . ." It was stated that the USPF&O of the Virgin Islands filed formal charges against Burke for misuse of federal funds. This purportedly had to do with Burke (or a family member) using a military plane for personal use. One of Joe's military pilots may have been from the OKARNG.

GEN Weber remained a strong supporter of his Oklahoma friend, Burke. Stanko recalls, "I think the name of the first aviator assigned to fly the old Blue Canoe (old Air National Guard 'hand-me-down' U-3A [civilian C-310]) for VI, was CWO David Lusker from New York. He had worked in the Operations Branch at NGB-AVN and was a happy go lucky sort of a young Army aviator and ideal choice for that job. In the Virgin Islands, auto traffic drives on the left side of the road as they do in England. Lusker had the only automobile on the island that was of British origin. He also went native in dress, open toe sandals, shorts, etc."

The rumors began to circulate and indicated that Burke was somehow linked to a developing organization that was to grow feed in Central America for the LeDoug Chicken Production firm on the east coast in Maryland. "He may have been within the law at the time because the Virgin Islands position [or job description] for the AG was not as clearly defined as in the several contiguous states, in regard to restrictions on outside business involvement," added Stanko. However, someone was quiet unhappy with him and/or his activities.

Soon, when Burke [supposedly] showed up on the FBI Wanted List, GEN Weber turned Joe's picture to the wall.

There was also mention of an alleged banana republic incident involving Burke and a big land deal and development in Central America, involving another Oklahoma Guardsmen. At least one former high ranking officer from Oklahoma was involved in the Burke scheme to get rich. The deal went bad and some of the investors claimed it was a fraud. Joe never officially made his star! He was promoted to brigadier general by the Virgin Islands, but never received federal recognition as a general of the line.

COL John J. Stanko, Chief, NGB-AVN, was in a very difficult situation: "My recommendation [to the DARNG] for aviation support for the Virgin Islands ARNG was to create an element in the Puerto Rico [ARNG Avn] Unit and station it in St. Croix and [over a period of time] slowly grow an aviation culture. These Caribbean islanders were not a technological society, and recruiting anyone with any [aviation] experience was a long shot."

Following Burke's tour as TAG in the Virgin Islands (July 1976 – July 1980), Brigadier General Clifton B. Wingate became the new TAG. Wingate was followed by Brigadier General Carl E. Briscoe, and then came Major General Ernest R. Morgan (August 1983 – October 1987).

Brigadier General Morgan left the job of Assistant AG at the District of Columbia Army Guard to work at St. Croix. A fine man, with a lovely wife, they moved to the Islands and he served as the new adjutant general. Morgan was appointed TAG VI in August 1983 and served as such until October 1987. His first military aide de camp was Captain Caroline Adams, later the SAO of the VIARNG. According to Colonel Marion Petersen, USPFO VI, "Major General Morgan was the best qualified and most excellent leader we ever had to this date [12 July 2008]."

In December 1989, Captain Adams became the first and only female State Army aviation officer in the Army National Guard (in the United States and its territories), a position that she held until 2000. She was the first female National Guard pilot in the U.S. Virgin Islands. As a Master Army Aviator, with 4,000 plus flight hours, she was the first and only female in the armed forces to pilot the C-23B Sherpa aircraft, a 23-passenger airplane with a 7,000-pound capacity.

As of 2008, Colonel Caroline Adams was the J5/7 – Strategic and Joint Training Officer for the VI. National Guard and has set her sights on becoming the Adjutant General of the Virgin Islands National Guard, and one day opening her own flight school. I believe she will accomplish her goals.

John J. Stanko liked Morgan; however, the weight and power of the several previous adjutant generals in the VI overruled a colonel at the Aviation Division. The VI got their own aviation force structure (even though quite small), plus full-time personnel and several aircraft. "I was overruled and the evolution of an aviation program in the Virgin Islands was one of the most formidable and challenging assignments that was handed to me. Like everything else, I got it done, but it was not easy," mourned John J. Stanko Jr.

Over the years, the Virgin Islands have had a plethora of problems, not unlike some other ARNG states. I can attest to several incidents of alleged misuse of military aircraft in the VI during my watch as commander of OSAA. Major General William Navas, then the DARNG, directed me to travel to the Virgin Islands and discuss the proper and authorized use of military aircraft by the TAG of the VI. I did as instructed and visited with Major General Jean A. Romney and promised him, I did not threaten him, that the Virgin Islands C-23 aircraft would be withdrawn from the VIARNG if this misuse occurred again under my watch.

Why so much talk about adjutants general of the National Guard? Well, they comprise one of the most elite and powerful groups of military officers/officials in the world. Together, the size of the force they command is larger than the conventional military of every country in NATO except Turkey. And they rule their state militaries with unrivaled autonomy[6].

Together, these two-star generals command (as of 2008) an Army and Air Guard force of about 466,000 troops. Few military commanders anywhere are compensated so well.

The active duty military takes great care in training its future generals. They must rise through the officer ranks from lieutenant to colonel, take rigorous courses at military colleges, and command units as large as 5,000 troops. Not so in the National Guard. The Guard is the only place in the U.S. military where the top general isn't required to have had senior commands or to have led large numbers of troops. State Guard commanders can even skip two or three ranks to get this prized job.

And yet the National Guard's commanding generals usually make more money than the governors who are their commanders-in-chief. In the case of Connecticut, a former National Guard TAG earned more than twice as much as his boss, the governor.

"Becoming an adjutant general is like being coronated," says Major General Paul Monroe, former TAG who commanded the 20,000-member California National Guard, the nation's largest.

Several years back, General Hugh Shelton, then chairman of the Joint Chiefs of Staff, commanded 1.4 million regular troops, and was paid about $132,100 per year. Major General William Cugno, while serving as Adjutant General of Connecticut, earned about $166,300 while commanding a force of 5,000.

Adjutants general aren't chosen the same way as active duty or reserve military officers, who must rise through the ranks and compete nationally for promotions. In all but two of the 50 states, governors appoint their National Guard commanders. In South Carolina and Vermont, adjutants general are elected by the people and the legislature, respectively.

Sometimes, the selections backfire. Sometimes stuff just happens . . . .

In the past decade, adjutants general from at least nine states, including Oklahoma, have committed offenses that include strong-arming subordinates for campaign contributions, embezzlement, using military aircraft for personal use and vacations, improperly retaliating against officers reporting misconduct, and lying to federal investigators.

We may all be created equal – yet we aren't all paid equally. But nobody said life was going to be fair – did they???

Thus ends the story about Joe E. Burke. He died about 2002.

We need to regress in time back to 1942 and resume the story about John J. Stanko Jr . . . .

During 1942, there wasn't a town or city in America whose young men weren't talking about going off to war and fighting in WWII. A few of these young patriots were also quite eager to become flyers and rain down tons of bombs on the Third Reich's industrialized metroplexes. One such man had this dream and also a very unusual beginning . . .

Stanko's father was an iron worker; he built sky-scrapers and was called Jack. He lived in Scranton, PA, was a hard worker, a hard drinker, and loved to play poker. On payday, almost every Friday evening, the iron workers played their five-card poker game. This particular Friday, Jack, who also smoked like a chimney, won the last hand with a ten-high straight. The loser of that hand, a Mohawk Indian ironworker, didn't have enough cash to cover his bet, and Jack damn sure wasn't going to let him leave without his money. So Jack reluctantly agreed to follow this disheveled man home.

Once there, at the brown stone apartment, the man admitted he didn't have any cash in the house either. Jack was going to kill him, but the Mohawk fearfully said, "Wait, I'll give you my woman! She's a good woman! We ain't married, never have been."

After another swig from the half-empty bottle of booze, Jack staggered towards his home in eastern Pennsylvania. The Indian woman followed along behind him with all of her life's belongings in a cloth bag. Jack took her to his mother's place in Scranton. His mother insisted the Indian be baptized the next day, and told Jack, "You'll have to marry her right away! You won't be living in sin in my house." They were married and later moved to Ohio.

Almost nine months to the day, on 22 March 1922, there in Cleveland she gave birth to a healthy baby boy, who was initially called Junior, after his father, Jack. Eight months later, the Indian woman became sick. Her beautiful brown skin burned to the touch with fever, her frail body twisted with pain and was drenched in perspiration. She called out to a Great Spirit in the sky, "Come, come softly for me." Her dark, round eyes closed, she drifted into a far away sleep, a peaceful, thin smile the only adornment she wore. Within the hour, she silently passed, her spirit as free as the mighty eagle that soars above. Her son doesn't even know her name.

Jack then took his infant son, whom he had named, John J. Stanko Jr., only eight months old, to live with his mother back in Scranton, PA. J.J. would see his father occasionally.

J.J. was a mere eight years old, when on a Wednesday afternoon, 3:00 p.m., 23 July 1930, in Archbald, a small northeastern Pennsylvania town, near Scranton, Jack Stanko was electrocuted (while working) at the age of 33 years. To allow time for his oldest brother to travel from Detroit, the funeral was scheduled for the following Monday, 28 July. This was an unusually long wake because of the weekend.

John J. Stanko Jr. recalled "I can still see the continuous crowd of men on the front porch of the house on Jefferson Avenue each of the four nights that my father was [laid out] on display in the corner of the parlor.

No one paid much attention to me because there were no other children, and so I could listen to the stories being passed back and forth by these men, friends, comrades, and associates of my father, who had come to be part of this, his last event."

First communion, as part of the Catholic tradition, for young John J. Stanko Jr. would normally have been a very significant and emotional rite of passage, but it occurred the day prior to the funeral on Sunday, 27 July. This particular Sunday should have been an occasion for joy and celebration, but instead what occurred was a sobering thought for this eight year old boy, "My father is dead. Now John J. Stanko Jr. is an orphan."

J.J.'s grandmother, Pauline Stanko, was quite strict raising him; she never hesitated to discipline him when she felt he needed such. She insisted that he do well in school and wanted him to read a lot. She required him to join Boy Scouts several years later. Yet she loved this child and gave him not what he wanted, but everything he needed.

As the enormity of this war grew, so did its intensity. John J. Stanko Jr., at 20 years old, enlisted in the Army Air Corps in 1942.

On 11 and 12 January 2007, COL John J. Stanko told the author about his adventure of going to Aviation Cadet Program testing, the induction process, and Atlantic City, NJ.

I responded to Uncle Sam's invitation to become an Aviation Cadet in Newark, NJ, on October 16, 1942. It was quite a process and took several days. There was a two-day written examination, which was test of general knowledge, history, math problems, current events etc. If you were an "A" student in high school, and did a lot of reading, it was not too difficult. However, I noticed empty seats on the second day, [indicative of] men who did not want to continue on. Out of 55 applicants, only 5 of us passed the written exam that day.

The physical examination [for Aviation Cadet Training] was an experience. It was the first time I had ever had a complete physical examination and I was amazed at all the places and things on the human body that interested the medical people. Beyond the normal items still on a current Class One [aviation flight physical], were eye/hand coordination tests, solving puzzles, and finally the hour long visit with the psychiatrist.

One of the most interesting facts that began to surprise me was, what a small percentage of American males could become pilots. Well, I still had a long way to go, but I was through the first gate, and now a member of the Army Reserve, waiting for orders. A telegram from DA sometime in January informed me that I was expected to be at the Union Station, Newark, NJ at 0800 hours on 28 January to report for active duty.

The troop train had started sometime early in Bangor Maine, and had been picking up fellow reservists all the way down the East Coast, including one named Paul Sparber, at Penn Station, New York City, who through a series of unreal coincidences would wind up as my bombardier [in Europe].

On board the train were about 400 prospective [aviation program] candidates, the self-proclaimed experts were forecasting, "Basic training at Miami Florida." Looking forward to the long train ride down the coast and wintering on the sunny east coast beaches that the Army had taken over for military training.

There were not too many stops after Newark, perhaps only the Princeton/Summerville area, which netted a boisterous group of Rutgers students who were putting the rest of their education on hold to become Army pilots also. Just about the time the new additions, from the last stop, were settling in their seats and the earlier passengers, from way up East, were fast asleep, dreaming of happy times on those Florida Beaches, the train pulled into the station at Atlantic City. It then became involved in a series of railroad maneuvers, switching back and forth from track to track. This did not concern anyone because troop trains were always shunted aside to let mainline passenger trains fly on by.

However, when the several cars of our train came to a stop on a spur at the freight terminal, with all the noise and hissing steam, the engine was disconnected and went off without us. This created some curiosity. But no one was prepared for the announcement that was about to be delivered by a uniformed person of authority. "Quiet," he shouted repeatedly, until he had everyone's attention. Remember, we are still in civilian clothes, not quite one-day veterans yet.

There followed a brief, but succinct, series of shouted instructions, information, and a list of "'You WILL do this . . ." and "You WILL NOTs." Our first military briefing was followed by disembarking at our new duty station – Atlantic City, NJ. That was followed by a train side short-arm inspection and then a short trip to our new [military] home, the Knickerbocker Hotel, on the boardwalk in Atlantic City.

Basic Infantry Training took place at Atlantic City, NJ—there was no Army Post per se. The Army had taken over all of the hotels along the boardwalk to house the 50,000 troops there for training. The largest hotel, Hadon Hall, became a huge mess hall and supply center. Brigatine Beach, seven miles down the coast was the rifle range.

It was January, AND it was cold AND damp AND indeed misery was everywhere – very typical for an Army training location. As has been said many times, "misery loves company!" They were young and healthy, and many were on their way to be aviation cadets, so they sang as they marched – until the spinal meningitis hit.

Let me clarify one detail, not all 50,000 troops at Atlantic City were destined to become aviation cadets – this city had become a basic training facility. And in the words of PVT E-nothing John J. Stanko Jr., " . . . while we all thought we were something special, in reality, we were nothing more than a very large group of the lowest things in the military, not even [true] privates yet!"

While in New Jersey, John met Olga Katherine Petsko, from Newark.

Immediately, John started calling the love of his life Pinky. John and Pinky were married on 15 November 1942. They were blessed with two wonderful daughters, Sharon John Stanko and Katherine P. Stanko. The Stanko's have two grandchildren and three great-grandchildren. One granddaughter, Lynne, who also became an Army aviator in 1985.

John continued:

From Army Basic [Infantry] Training at Atlantic City, several hundreds of us were troop-trained to Seymour Johnson Field, in the Carolinas. I never unpacked my duffle bag, because I went from the train, to the military hospital with an ear infection.

Eight days in the hospital and my return to duty status was simultaneous with inclusion on the list being assigned to an Army Air Corps Cadet Aviation Training Detachment at Syracuse University, NY. Of all the cadet training detachments in the USA, Syracuse was the largest with 2,000 students. The program was designed to condense the first two years of an engineering curriculum into a nine month accelerated course by eliminating the nice to have electives and social amenities.

There were many interesting things happening in the Air Corps Cadet Training Program – resulting in 400 student Cadets being identified to further accelerate the already ambitious schedule, requiring the nine month program to be completed in a mere four months. I had the misfortune to make that cut.

Soon John was sent to Kelly AFB, San Antonio, TX to be processed at the Classification Center.

The urgency was an identified shortfall of 400 student pilots (cadets) in the Central Training Command. The fix? Transfer 400 from the Eastern Command to the Central Training Command.

First days at Kelly Field in early May were a wonderful experience, especially if you loved the sun. What an experience: shorts and sneakers, and throwing a football around from morning to dark. We processed through the classification system and [then moved] across the street to "Preflight!"

HELLO!!! This was a real wakeup call!

By August, the weather was beginning to change and I was on the troop list for Corsicana, Texas – Primary Flight Training in PT-19s (Fairchild 200hp/124mph VNE). During Primary we had civilian instructor pilots and military check pilots [examiners]. I was a hot shot in Primary: first Cadet to solo, ground school grades were excellent, etc.

Next I was off to Enid, OK for Basic Flight Training in BT-13 or BT-15, [called the Consolidated Vultee, unofficially called Vultee Vibrators] and everything turned 180 degrees south.

We transferred in early December [1943]; the weather was miserable and I caught a bad cold, which I never could completely shake. That led into a case of conjunctivitis. My flying suffered. The weather didn't cooperate, resulting in a lot of no fly days. Construction on one of the runways interfered with training schedules. This led to a poor decision by our cadre to risk using that runway for a low utilization training procedure, simply landing a few aircraft at the completion of dual instrument training flights.

Murphy's Law [kicked in] and as a result, I was involved in a fatality to a construction worker, and although I was not at all liable, as a witness, I had to be present at all the legal hearings, including the inquest.

I was dragging anchor now, but I was working hard to catch up with the class and almost there. On the last night for scheduled night training, six of us were dispatched to a satellite field to complete the requirements for night training. I needed about three hours and eight touch-and-go landings. That was the most of any one in the group. Everyone else completed their requirements that night, although we all had to return to the base about mid-evening when I succeeded in putting the satellite field out of commission on my second landing.

So, when you ask what I did at Enid AFB, OK—I survived!

Next? Further south in Oklahoma to Altus, to begin twin-engine Advanced Flight Training (Curtis AT-9s & UC-78s Bamboo Bomber).

Pinky and I enjoyed a 30-day leave upon graduation and now I had orders to Liberal, KS for B-24 Liberator transition. Liberal, KS was the finest aviation training I ever experienced. [The curriculum]—it was almost an engineering degree. Perhaps because I just loved that airplane; I enjoyed not only flying the aircraft, but the five military operating manuals that detailed all the systems, electronics, fuel systems, flight controls, troubleshooting, etc.

In April 1944, Cadet John J. Stanko Jr. was commissioned a second lieutenant and rated as a pilot in the U.S. Army Air Corp. He was assigned overseas to the 15th Air Force, 461st Bomber Group, 765th Squadron as a pilot and aircraft commander. He also flew B-29s before the end of the war in Japan. He returned from overseas and was released from active duty in November 1945.

After WWII, in 1945, he enrolled at Lehigh University in Bethlehem, PA, majoring in industrial engineering. After graduating from Lehigh, Mr. Stanko did graduate studies in personnel management at Penn State University. He also holds a BS degree in business management from the University of Maryland.

As a civilian, John J. Stanko Jr. joined the Air Force Reserves in 1945. He remained a member of the USAF Reserves until 1952, when he transferred to the Pennsylvania Army National Guard and accepted a commission as a first lieutenant and a rating as an Army aviator in the 104th Armored Cavalry Regiment.

In 1952 he and Pinky returned to Danville, PA to establish his own business. During the next 10 years (from 1952-61), he succeeded in business, and had an exciting career as an Army Guard officer and aviator. In his business endeavor, he became the major stockholder and CEO of the third largest sheet metal construction company in eastern Pennsylvania and the owner of a steel specialty manufacturing company.

Starting in about 1956, Mr. Stanko began building a large, ranch-style home for Pinky and the girls at 905 Red Lane in Danville, PA. He did nearly all of the work himself. Next to the house is the landmark red, turned-metal roofed barn, which he also built. Pinky and daughter Sharon, a registered nurse (RN), live there still.

In 1961, he retired from active participation in the sheet metal business in Danville, serving only in a consulting capacity until 1963.

Although Pennsylvania Army Guardsman First Lieutenant Stanko must have enjoyed getting back in the cockpit of a military airplane, his initial checkout in the L-19 Cessna was quite interesting, as was his ARNG instructor pilot (IP).

Stanko explained, "I was an M-day aviator in the Pennsylvania Army Guard (PAARNG); Major General Richard Snyder was the AG at the time. Pennypacker was the IP that checked me out in the L-19, after it taking 9 months to get my flight status from the Guard Bureau. There were 32 endorsements back and forth, back and forth. In those days, it took two days to take a flight physical. I went to Olmenstead AFB, took two days off work and six months later had to do it again. An aviation flight physical then was only good for six months! Nine months later I get my wings in the mail and now I'm an Army aviator."

Before my 2/20th Aerial Rocket Artillery, 1ˢᵗ CAV Div friend, Cecil Hengeveld, went to work full-time for PAARNG, he was a part-time IP at Allentown (Flight Activity), PA. On this particular day, Cecil was taking an annual check ride in an OH-23 and John J. Stanko Jr., the New Cumberland AASF Commander, was the instructor pilot.

"After completing the oral phase of the check ride, we began the flight portion of the check ride. Stanko never once touched the flight controls. It was several years later that I was told the reason why he hadn't! He had bursitis so bad he could hardly move!" stated Hengeveld, a retired brigadier general from Pennsylvania.

From COL Stanko's PAARNG guard days in 1952 until the late 1960s at the Pentagon, there were hundreds of Stanko stories to be told. I believe there is a book there that should be written – but it will have to be a very large book. So now we must fast forward from his days as a first lieutenant ARNG Bird Dog aviator in the Pennsylvania guard to a newly pinned lieutenant colonel as he left the Pentagon in 1970.

After aiding an ailing friend, the Pennsylvania State Aviation Officer, and recommending Colonel Chet Howard from Oklahoma to become the next Pennsylvania SAO, Stanko returned to the national level. Stanko was instrumental in assisting Colonel Charlie R. Jones in the establishment of this new NGB aviation division at the Edgewood, MD Operating Activity Center (OAC).

In July 1972, and Stanko was selected to organize the ARNG Aviation Logistics branch, prior to the new NGB aviation division becoming operational at Edgewood Arsenal (Aberdeen Proving Grounds), MD. Brigadier General Alberto Jimenez explained, "COL Charlie Jones was very good friends with COL Bob Cowan, now deceased, who was the first director of the OAC at Edgewood. This had some influence with Charlie getting the job of Chief Avn Div in November 1973. The OAC had a total of +/- 200 personnel, and in addition to the aviation division, also included the NGB Environmental Div, Engineer Branch, Schools Branch, Training, Manpower, and Administrative personnel[7]."

Ms. Deborah L. Debi Horne was a young, GS-2, clerk typist with the Procurement Directorate at Edgewood Arsenal, before she applied for the position with NGB-AVN. "There were more than 270 applicants for the [Avn Div secretarial] job and I got it," said Ms. Horne. "I was thrilled and grew up in the Avn Div."

Ms. Horne explained:

> In the beginning we had a Standardization and Training Branch. Larry Payne was the Chief. Wally Mueller was hired a month after I was, and we shared an office. Safety was already there under Captain Charles Strickland. LTC Stanko was Chief of Avn Logistics then. The key players initially were: Charlie Jones, Stanko, Al Marshall, and Ray Engstrand Logistics, and Major Charles Strickland in Safety."
>
> Charlie Jones had a small office nearest the parking lot to Procurement Directorate and I believe Stanko had the large office on the other end of the building, even though he was only Chief of Logistics at that time. There was much contention between the two of them. Stanko had a secretary; her name was Lydia Snyder. This was in the days of typewriters; Jones would hold our work up to the light to see if we had any erasures on them. If so, we had to retype. He trained us to perfection.
>
> I think anyone who ever come in contact with John J. Stanko Jr. would say that aviation and the Army National Guard was in his blood. He hated to hang up his uniform when he became a civilian and [he] always wore it whenever he had a chance to attend a military function, though. He kept his physical fitness routines to himself, but made sure everyone knew that he ran in place just outside the door of his apartment, or ran the steps, however many times, every day.
>
> Bill Badger was also my supervisor for a time. He was a pleasure to work with, but not a mover and shaker of the

same caliber as the others. Art Ries was a go-getter. He could be very excitable about things.

Eric Braman was also a rising star and Stanko adored him. I believe JJS was grooming him for much bigger and better things. LTC Mike McCourt was Chief of Safety and he was also very good. JJS liked him a lot. Mike could get things done.

Craig Bond was also one of the JJS' protégés. Stanko liked to bring young aviators in and train them. Bond was from the Maryland ARNG. Others that worked in NGB-AVN at the OAC before the move down south to the new Arlington Hall Readiness Center in 1993 included: Alberto J. Jimenez (later Brigadier General), Bill Francisco, Anna Marie Thomas, Richard Taylor, Ron Eaton, Jeanne Ulrich, Ron Briones, Jack Sink, Benny Cobb, Albert Bud DeLucien, Harry Gilman, Captain Michael P. Bishop, and a Captain Art Sosa. Jeanne Ulrich added the following OAC personnel that she remembers: Frank Thompson, Ray Engstrand, John Johnson, LTC Ken Boley, Larry Burbank, LTC Rod Hora, and Agnes J. Eisenhart. The list went on, as players come and go.

Ms. Horn was a longtime administrative assistant to Lieutenant Colonel Stanko before she later became an NGB Aviation Action Officer and subsequently went to work for the Corps of Engineers. She was (as of 2008) the Editor in Chief for the *APG News* (Aberdeen Proving Grounds, MD).

Alberto Jimenez continued to rise in the aviation division, from the Chief of Logistics, to later become the fifth Director of the NGB Aviation and Safety Directorate at Arlington Hall. Brigadier Jimenez, a Maryland Guardsman, as of 2008, was a Special Assistant to the Director, ARNG at the NGB's Readiness Center, Arlington Hall.

Ms. Jeanne Ulrich began working at the OAC at Edgewood early on for Al Marshall, who had become the Branch Chief of the Aviation Logistics Office. "He always came to work in a suit and he always made time each day for his daily exercise run, regardless of the weather," said Ms. Ulrich. Later Ms. Ulrich worked personally for COL Stanko.

Ms. Ulrich stated:

The aviation folks from the states who would visit us were surprised to find the NGB Aviation Division in a secluded area right outside of the Edgewood Post entrance. They expected a large, fancy building in town.

Over the years, I watched the NGB Avn Div evolve. During the early times secretaries answered all telephone calls, and then later, when individual action officers (AOs) got their own individual phone lines and answered their own calls. I watched the introduction of the personal computer into Army offices. Pretty interesting when most of the men didn't know the first thing about typing!

As time marched on, females were allowed to move up into Action Officers positions as interns. We were already familiar with the NGB Aviation Program, the aviation facilities and knew the AVCRAD Commanders and the State Army Aviation Officers of each of the states.

TDY travel was important in the Division. Mr. Stanko always said, "Get on an airplane and get out there and meet face to face with the people. More will get accomplished and people will do more for you if they know who you are."

A TDY story I remember about Alberto Jimenez and Bob Recker, our aviation maintenance and supply team, who traveled together regularly. Both Alberto and Bob were civilian technicians, who wore a coat and tie daily. They stopped by a Sears department store at the end of their TDY day. A woman walked up to Mr. Recker and asked him about some socks. He looked like a Sears sales manager with his suit on, so he answered her questions, then took out a pen and marked the price of the socks down. We laughed over and over when he told that story.

Mr. Stanko looked forward to the AAAA Conventions and other aviation gatherings. He worked with the Multi-Media Group at Fort Rucker who did a great job in setting up the ARNG aviation display booth. Mr. Stanko encouraged many ARNG Aviation personnel to attend the annual AAAA conventions and get out there to meet with other vendors/contractors and see their products first hand. He was a great speaker who always dressed his part. He had dark suits when he needed to have the *executive in charge* look, western suits when he went TDY out west, and casual suits when he was just being the Chief, Aviation Division. He was always proud of his people and gave them the authority to run their program.

He also had the gift of talk. If you were asked to come up to his office, you could expect to be there for awhile. Little did I know how much influence he would have and how much knowledge and experience we would learn from him. He would have stacks of papers in his office, but he would call when I was his secretary and tell me to "Look in the third pile halfway down," to find what he was looking for. And I would.

Most of the guys in the Aviation Division, especially the Logistics Office were also in the Mobilization AVCRAD Control Element (MACE) of the MDARNG, where they did their weekend warrior drills. Later on it would become the Aviation Depot Maintenance Roundout Unit (ADMRU) unit. The first commander of this unit was Alvin Marshall, followed by Ray Engstrand, and later on down the road Ron Eaton and Alberto Jimenez.[8] That makes four commanders who came out of the NGB Aviation Division—not bad!

One of Mr. Stanko's favorite restaurants was Georgetown North in Bel Air, MD. He would make a reservation and would make sure he had the table by the window. He took many visitors to this restaurant.

Ms. Jeanne Ulrich began her AO intern position as the Aircraft Readiness and Distribution Action Officer, taking over Richard Taylor's position as he was promoted up in the division. She now works at the Aviation Depot Maintenance Roundout Unit (ADMRU) in Maryland, as the AMCOM/NGB liaison officer.

In my opinion, it should be a requirement for aviation soldiers to learn as much as possible about the personalities, characteristics, leadership qualities, and especially the attitude of our patriarchs and godfathers.

Two of my all-time early American heroes are Captains Meriwether Lewis and William Clark and the story of their *Corps of Discovery*. Stephen

Ambrose, author of *Undaunted Courage*, the best book I've ever read about Lewis and Clark's expedition west, over the years wrote many non-fiction books on the military leaders of our nation. Ambrose noted that, "Each of them is quite different!"

You should never just have one person as a mentor. You should recognize the best qualities in each of your leaders whom you wish to emulate and learn best how you can achieve those leadership traits or qualities.

It's great to read books about Eisenhower, Patton, MacArthur, Bradley or Schwarzkopf, but don't just focus on one man. Don't get into a rut; read as much as you can about other famous leaders. Read books about today's heroes and leaders – Lieutenant General Dell Dailey, General Bryan "Doug" Brown, General Tommy R. Franks or General David H. Petraeus. We can also learn from their mistakes.

Great leaders will admit their shortcomings and failures. Life is too short to learn all of the pitfalls firsthand – learn from others' mistakes. GEN Stanley McChrystal was a great combat leader and made one bad, political decision—he talked to a news reporter. This led to the end of his military career. Life is hard enough, plow around the stumps.

Over the last 40 years, I've had the pleasure to become acquainted with and make friends with many active duty and ARNG aviators. I have learned that many members of the OKARNG formerly served as aviators in combat, either in the Army Air Corps in WWII, during Korea and/or in Vietnam. Besides John J. Stanko and Chester A. Howard, there was: Joe Patterson, a longtime member of Det 1, 45th Inf Bde Aviation who flew B-24s, and John Mitch Johnson, a WWII Navy Ace. Gus Guild, "Pappy" Devine, Perry Townsend, and Jack Ray all flew in Korea and later in the OKARNG. The list of Vietnam-era aviators in the OKARNG would be several pages long. The list of current combat tested aviation personnel in the OKARNG is even longer. However, to all of them, I say, "Welcome home. Thank you for your service."

Many men have gone before and blazed the trail for us to follow. These men did things that had never been done before. They asked, "Why not?" instead of sitting on their thumbs and accepting an answer that would mean no progress today! Life is not about waiting for the storms to pass. It's about learning to dance in the rain! Most of Oklahoma's former adjutants general have come and gone. One third of the OKARNG State

Aviation Officer's have passed. Yet we are fortunate to have most of our aviation patriarchs still with us.

A dear friend of mine, COL John J. Stanko, passed away at age 88 on 8 October 2010. We've been very blessed that our Army National Guard Godfather continued until this year to attend AAAA annual conventions, traveled to many different aviation meetings and conferences, and worked as a consultant into his 88th year.

COL John J. Stanko

Retired MAJ GEN Gus Hargett, the president of NGAUS, attended the memorial service and said, "The loss of John Stanko is a great loss to the entire Guard family. Not only was he the father of Guard aviation, but he was a friend and valued advisor to many of us. He will be missed."

COL Stanko was not shy, nor an introvert. He was confident and perhaps arrogant, but for certain he was knowledgeable and wanted to see Army National Guard Aviation grow. This was the longest and most common theme of his life, other than his family. He was always a mentor to young aviators and State Aviation Officers.

As a former Oklahoma Army National Guard aviator, I challenge you not to forget our own OKARNG patriarchs, and especially our true OKARNG Godfather – COL John J. Stanko Jr. He laid the tracks that allowed the aviation train to roll into the station in each state and territory. Oklahoma was always one of his favorite states, he told me at his home with a very special twinkle in his eyes.

COL Stanko was the single person most responsible for the development of the Army National Guard Aviation Program. A part of aviation since WWII when he was in the Army Air Corps, he became an Army aviator in his home state of Pennsylvania as a member of the National Guard.

For more than ten years he headed the first aviation logistics element of the National Guard. Then COL Stanko directed the Aviation Division, where he was responsible for safety, operations, and support of the ARNG's massive aviation program, which included more than 2,500 Army National Guard aircraft located in the 50 states and the separate territories of the U.S.

The following is a timeline of COL Stanko's service:

- **1942** At 20 years of age, enlisted in the Army Air Corps
- **April 1944** commissioned a second lieutenant and rated as a pilot in the U.S. Army Air Corp
- **November 1945** Released from active duty.
- **1945—1952** Member of the USAF Reserves.
- **1952** Transferred to PAARNG (Pennsylvania Army National Guard).
- **1952—1972** Various aviation assignments in the PAARNG and at the Pentagon and NGB's OAC at Edgewood, MD and Aviation Division at Arlington Hall.
- **1976-93** He served as the Director of Safety, as well as Director of the Aviation Division. These were later consolidated into NGB Aviation and Safety Division (NGB-AVS). COL Stanko was responsible for the ARNG's total safety program, continuously concerned with the safety of 400,000 Guardsmen, 100,000 with driving privileges and the safety programs at the myriad of armories, training sites, and maintenance installations throughout the 50 states.
- **1977** He retired as a colonel with 33 years of commissioned service, but continued in his position as a Department of the Army Civilian (DAC). He is the first and only civilian to be awarded flight status in the Army National Guard.
- **1980** COL Stanko was awarded the Meritorious Service Award by the National Guard Association of the United States for his outstanding contributions in the field of aviation. In 1980 he also received the AAAA Joseph P. Cribbins, Department of the Army Civilian of the Year Award (while at the OAC at Aberdeen Proving Grounds).
- **1982** Promoted to the rank of brigadier general in the Pennsylvania Army National Guard.
- **1983** Inducted into the Army [Aviation] Hall of Fame, Fort Rucker, AL. (He is the only individual elected to the Army Aviation Hall of Fame for contributions to Army Aviation as a Guardsman.)
- **1990** Awarded the National Guard Association's Distinguished Service Medal for sustained excellence throughout the decade.

- **1993** His last flight as an Army Aviator was 23 July 1993 at Fort Indiantown Gap, PA. At the time of his final retirement (on 3 August 1993) as Director of Aviation and Safety (NGB-AVS) in Arlington Hall, VA, he was directly responsible to the Chief of the National Guard Bureau for the administration and supervision of operations, proficiency training, and logistical support of the Army National Guard's aviation program. The 2,800 helicopters, 150 fixed-wing aircraft and 6,800 aviators in the Army National Guard made it the largest aviation program under one major command in the United States.
- Fifty-one years of continuous military flight status; fifty-one consecutive flight physicals!

We salute you and thank you, sir! You will indeed be missed . . .

---

[1] Although there are six US Territories, only three have ARNGs and adjutant generals: Guam, Puerto Rico, and the Virgin Islands.

[2] Batey's successor, COL Leroy A. Wall, came very close to doing so, with 11 years 3 months. 24 days in office as SAO.

[3] The Navy V-12 Program allowed students to complete bachelor's degrees at civilian universities and earn commissions in the Navy and Marine Corps during WWII.

[4] Personal interview COL Raymond Engstrand, 10 January 2007, at the ARNG Readiness Center. Mr. Engstrand was a functional analyst with NGB-AVS (Aviation and Safety Division) at Arlington, VA as of 2008.

[5] Brigadier General (VI) Joe E. Burke was the TAG Virgin Islands from July 1976 – July 1980, according to the VI ARNG History.

[6] Moniz, "Most Adjutants Make More than Governors," *USA TODAY*, (December 2001)

[7] The OAC was established at Edgewood because of the shortage of space at the Pentagon. NGB Headquarters was incorporated at the Pentagon before this time.

[8] Brigadier General Jimenez was the Special Assistant to the DARNG and also the Deputy Adjutant General for Maryland. Jimenez retired from the military in June 2010.

Chapter 4

Transitioning to the Current Era

Or Once we called them Good Ole Boys,

but they are Citizen Soldiers

*"Education is when you read the fine print. Experience is
what you get if you don't."*

Pete Seeger

There were few times in the history of OKARNG Aviation that things changed quickly; occasionally they did when one commander or senior NCO replaced another. An old warrior once told me, "Progress necessitates change, but change doesn't necessarily mean progress." For aviation in the OKARNG, progress, (learning new tactics, new technology and training methods) was not readily accepted and was not achieved overnight.

The evolution from small aviation sections into aviation companies, and then battalions, was a long and tedious development. The late 1950s and all through the 1960s into the 70s, many small changes, and a few monumental advancements, took place.

"When I joined [the OKARNG] off the street on 8 January 1966, the [Aviation] commander was Colonel Chester Howard. We were located on [Max] Westheimer Field, Norman, in a two-story barracks on Einstein street. Across the street was a one-story building that had monkeys that the University was observing. The aircraft [in the guard then] were H-19s,

122

OH-23s, OH-13s, a Bird Dog, and one other fixed wing," stated Chief Warrant Officer Five Daniel Danny Washa[1], formerly of the 45th (Sep) Inf Bde Avn Section.

"The first several summer camps, later called Annual Training, were at Fort Chaffee. First Lieutenant Emmett McElwain was a section leader, and I was his driver before I went to flight school. To name a few of the pilots: Captain Ron Howland, Major Pete Phillips, Major Bourassa, Chief Warrant Officers Leroy Wall, Clay Clarkson, Donald Day, and Joe Patterson," remembered CW5 Washa.

"When I returned from flight school in November, 1970, my [Bde Avn] section leader was Captain Dana Batey. By then we had turned in the H-19s for a couple of CH-34s. The 45th [Bde Avn Sec] started receiving the UH-1 around 1971, and the OH-58 in 1972," according to Washa.

Long-range planning was the desired method of scheduling unit training, but it was not the norm. Everyone knew you weren't going to be able to plan things much more than one or two drill weekends ahead. The obstacle to long-range planning was that aviation was considered in a support role, which meant 'do your thing, but only after you've provided aviation support to the rest of the Guard.' It took years before the paradigm was broken. It was a process of mutual understanding; some of the new, younger leadership in the Inf Bde aided in this process.

The most subtle (yet important) change was the snail-paced, but complete transformation in Oklahoma Guard Aviation's daily conduct of business. This metamorphic change began at the end of those days, often referred to as the *Flying Club Days*. The transition was (and is being) completed in the current era. Let's consider the mid-1980s as the beginning of what I refer to as the Current Era.

CPT Alfred F. Dreves & MSG Cleo F. Templin
ca 1980

Long-range planning may have been the desired result, but it wasn't the way training was handled. The old way of doing business was – Don't rock the boat, just show up for drill. Planning for drill seemed to occur on the Friday night before drill started on Saturday. "We damn sure don't want to go to the field and sleep in tents," was the common feedback unit trainers would hear.

Yes, there were monthly planning meetings held by the commander, first sergeant, full-time training NCO and/or AST (Admin, Supply Technician – a full-time military civil service employee). They would prepare a training schedule and it would include a few mandatory classes during drill (drug testing or the piss test) and the major, common tasks for all soldiers, such as annual weapons qualification. Nuclear, Biological and Chemical (NBC) training was one of my least favorite things. Then there was of course the most fraudulent event of every year, the annual physical fitness test (APFT) or annual walk as was done in the old days. I'm surprised that many OKARNG personnel in each unit (not just aviation) didn't go to jail for falsifying APFT scores. Those good ole boys took care of each other.

Not often were aviation commanders able to plan a complete year of individual and/or unit training in advance, prior to 1985. Was it their fault? NO! Was it their responsibility? YES! However, it was impossible for an aviation commander to plan a drill based on having 100% of your aviation personnel and aircraft for a full drill weekend (four back-to-back UTAs (unit training assemblies). Aviation units, such as Det 1, 45th Inf Bde Avn Sec and Co B, 149th Avn, were seen by the rest of the OKARNG as an aerial taxi cab service. "You call—we haul." No matter how unrelated to infantry training their mission requests were our aviation unit training was always secondary to their mission requests. This began to change slowly, but particularly around the late 1980s. After the Special Operations Aviation program was well under way, aviation unit training was scheduled on a long-range basis, although it too provided mission support to the Inf Bde and other support units.

A dedicated and professional aviation commander or platoon leader would require the crew of a single-aircraft mission to accomplish certain individual aviator and/or crew training requirements during most missions. Not all of the missions flown were what we used to call ash and trash (frivolous or not beneficial to aviator/crew training), but too many were.

124

You don't have to tell aviators today, "If it weren't for the boys on the ground, there wouldn't be a mission for aviation." This statement is true. However, aviation is a separate branch, a full member of the Combat Arms team. Aviation unit training isn't optional, it is mandatory, just as it is with any other unit. With imagination and cooperation, required unit training for an aviation unit can be accomplished in coordination with those units it is assigned to support within an ARNG state. An aviation unit's individual and unit training must be accomplished and cannot be sacrificed.

The priority for any ARNG aviation unit should always be, train today just like you will be expected to fight tomorrow, next week or next year. It's not *if* we are required to fight, it is *when*!

In years of the *Flying Club Days*, down at the corner of Comanche and

CW5 Charles H. Evans

Jones Streets, next to the old Cleveland County Courthouse in downtown Norman, OK, stood an Oklahoma Army National Guard reddish, stone armory. This two-story structure was built by the WPA in 1934 across from the train depot in the heart of Norman. For a good four decades it served the ARNG and the city of Norman quite well.

The two-story building, sort of a U-shaped structure, had an indoor firing range in the basement. It also had a large drill floor, which was used by the local population for roller skating on the weekend. The north side of this strong building was the two-story section, with lockers and offices upstairs. "And at one time it even had a hand-operated elevator or dumb waiter as they called it, which was large enough to put a four-drawer desk on it and crank it up to the second floor," offered Chief Warrant Officer Four Charlie Evans. Charlie was assigned there from December 1972 until 15 September 1975 with OKARNG aviation units.

Charles H. Evans joined the Army on 11 September 1958 and spent three years on active duty in the infantry with a heavy weapons section.

"In September 1961 I got out of Army, was assigned to 90ᵗʰ Control Group for the Reserve Component and started college at Ada. In February 1962 I received a notice that the local draft board was looking for me. So within the month, (26 February 1962) I joined the ARNG at Ada, stayed until October 1965. I graduated from East Central College at Ada and obtained a job teaching school. In those days (ca 1965-70) there was a waiting list in all the units and you couldn't just transfer to another guard unit because nobody had any openings. I got out in 1965 and in 1967 got back in the medical company at Ada and stayed until 1968, when they moved me to Oklahoma City and I got associated with Army aviation. We became the 245ᵗʰ Medical Company (Air Ambulance Clearing), part of the 120ᵗʰ Med Bn. I was a medical aid man in the aviation section there at the 2222 SW 44ᵗʰ St. OKC armory. It was reorganized in 1968, the first major reorganization in the OKARNG since WWII and Korea," Charlie added.

Charlie continued, "The National Guard was 'just gone' while the 45ᵗʰ Inf Div was in Korea. They were trying to reorganize aviation and they made detachments. Det 3 & 4 was at Norman. The aircraft and maintenance were assigned and stationed at Max Westheimer Field, Norman. Div Arty had an Avn Sec up at Enid, 120ᵗʰ Engineers had an Avn Sec down at Okmulgee and Det 1 (45ᵗʰ Inf Bde Avn Sec) at Edmond. They were all separate and didn't get combined all into one until, the FA and Eng [Avn Sec] went away and we absorbed those people into the aviation at Lexington. Det 1, 45ᵗʰ Inf Bde Avn Sec always stayed as a separate entity in aviation, but it was under aviation command & control for admin and training, except for AT. It was kinda a foggy period for OKARNG aviation from 1968—1972. The 445ᵗʰ Avn Co was one of 6 AHC in the ARNG (NY, MO, OH, OK, ??, ??) and was authorized 232 personnel. I was a full-time Technician, Sergeant First Class, M-day Plt SGT, Maint NCO (crew chief 67N40) from January 1973 to October 1978 and was then appointed a WO1 while in the 445ᵗʰ as the Unit Pers WO."

CW4 Charles H. Evans retired from the OKARNG on 31 March 1999 with 39 years, one month and 12 days total military service (24 yrs 11 months active duty). Mr. Evans has provided a wealth of information on OKARNG aviation, units and personnel.

"For many years, the large drill floor [at the old downtown Norman armory] was also used for roller skating on the weekends," said Judge Ron

Howland (retired colonel and OKARNG aviator), who skated there while he attended Norman High School. Other guardsmen from the Norman area also remember the skating on Friday and Saturday nights, which other ARNG armories in Oklahoma towns also allowed.

"The 45th Avn Company was organized in 1959, but in 1960-61, I remember that the 45th Avn Co drilled at the old stone armory in Norman. Captain David Vaughn was the commander then, Master Sergeant Lantz was the senior NCO and Sergeant First Class R. L. Eades was the full-timer at the armory," recalled Major C.L. Strance.

There is a granite memorial at the corner of Comanche and Jones that Professor Robert Goins helped design, which commemorates the old armory. It gives a modest history of the armory; on the reverse is an engraving of an old photograph of the armory. Goins related, "When I was a young boy, I used to roller skate there [at the armory] on the weekends. During my college days at Oklahoma University (OU), there were two primary units I remember that drilled there: Co D, 179th Inf and Co C, 120th Engineers. There was a medical unit that may have been there later. As a young man attending OU (ca 1948-50), I was in Co D 179th Inf when it was activated for the Korean War. At that time I was an architectural student at OU and was also in advanced ROTC. In fact, I was at Fort Belvoir, VA attending [ROTC] summer camp when the Korean War broke out. The 45th Inf Div was activated then, and I was given a choice by the Army of either going with the 45th or finishing my last year in advanced ROTC. I chose the latter and was discharged from the 45th as they were mobilized to go to Fort Polk, LA. Therefore I was commissioned into the Corps of Engineers after my fourth year of a five-year architectural degree program. I spent the next two years in the Army, most of that in Korea. I believe that the old armory was razed in 1979 when the Cleveland County court house was about to be expanded."

Bob Goins is Professor Emeritus for the College of Architecture at Oklahoma University, and his real love is the Department of Regional & City Planning. He is a planning consultant for many Oklahoma towns, one of which is Ada, my home town. Goins added, "On 1 March 2007, we [City of Norman] dedicated the fourth plaza, called The War Years in Norman as part of the Legacy Trail. This plaza commemorates the years 1941 to 1954. We designed and incorporated a one-fourth scale Stinson biplane as part of the display. The date of dedication relates back to 1 March 1946 when the Navy decommissioned the North Naval Base at

Max Westheimer Field and also the South Naval Base on the southern edge of Norman, near old highway 77.

From the memories of Colonel Ron Howland, "I was the Commander, a Major at the time, of the 45th Avn Co following Major Pete Phillips ca 1971-1972. Master Sergeant Faye C. Shepard was the senior NCO. We were meeting at that stone armory and it was not in very good condition when I commanded the unit. I would periodically conduct weekend inspections of the facility because the arms room was not very secure. This Company [45th Avn Bn] was inactivated and they tore down the old stone Armory across from Norman train depot. While it was used by the Guard, they were the sole user."

There is a stone monument on the northwest corner of the new Cleveland County Courthouse in downtown Norman, OK honoring the old stone Armory. The armory was built for Co D 179th Inf and Co C 120th Eng in 1934 and torn down in 1979.

Beginning in the mid-1970s, new OKARNG aviation facilities began

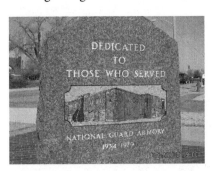

Old downtown Norman, OK Armory Monument

to be completed, thanks to the far reaching and visionary ideas of men such as Dana D. Batey and Leroy A. Wall. Brigadier General Batey envisioned a combined Aviation Support Facility (incorporating both aircraft maintenance and operations and training facilities), a new, modern, multiple-unit armory and an Organizational Maintenance Shop (OMS) on one tract of land. He accomplished this goal just east of Lexington, OK and dedicated these facilities in 1975. The OKARNG heliport is called Muldrow AHP in honor of Major General Hal L. Muldrow. Major General Hal L. Muldrow Jr., a Choctaw Native American, commanded the Division Artillery, 45th Infantry Division in Korea from December 10, 1951, to May 22, 1952.

During the *Flying Club Days,* the term aviator was almost a derogatory term or at least was often used as such by the infantry troops. Many said that becoming an aviator was a dead-end career. Aviators were not were known for their military bearing – few had military-like haircuts, few spit-shined their flight boots, or polished their brass. Rarely did you see an aviator wearing starched fatigues and just as few ever saluted. Many wore their MacArthur-style or Ray Ban sunglasses day and night. Aviators didn't like headgear, which was obvious. Yes, there were later, safety reasons and restrictions on the flight line – "No headgear, No saluting." But the fact remained that we were rarely accused of standing tall and ready for inspection, Sir! We were our own worst enemy!

In those days, the most difficult question posed at a monthly drill weekend in an aviation unit was, "Where are we going to fly today for lunch?" Sure we got some training benefit from flying cross country (to eat fish or steak near Muskogee, or barbeque near Sallisaw, OK). I recall several weekend IFR, formation flights, cross-country into Fort Smith Approach Control's airspace to an IFR intersection, then requesting a VFR vector to Wild Horse Barbeque, five miles south of Sallisaw. The owner wouldn't let us pay for our lunch. "The extra business your helicopters parked out front brings us is worth it to me!" Yes, there was some benefit from the hour or so of IFR formation flight, but our motives lacked military dedication.

It had taken a long, long time for our ARNG flight training to reach the point that instrument training was something that was seen as beneficial to Army aviators. Many of us had seldom filed IFR flight plans when flying Army helicopters in Vietnam and other remote areas of the world, before coming to the OKARNG. This VFR attitude was a paradigm that had to be broken. And it was about to happen.

During this time period (1960-84), there appeared to be a distinct lack of motivation to conduct tactical field training for aviation units in the OKARNG, other than perhaps a couple of nights in a general purpose (GP) medium tent at summer camp. This lack of motivation was internal, not external. Most company and field grade aviators didn't know how to write an operation order (Op Ord) or how to conduct a Field Estimate, or how to prepare a Logistical Estimate. They didn't know what FM 101-5 (Army Field Manual—Staff Organization and Operations) was about, nor did they even have a copy. Most didn't care. They knew what an S-1, S-2, S-3 or S-4 was, but 99% had never served as an aviation administrative, intelligence, operations or logistics staff officer for an aviation unit. Combined Arms and Services Staff School[3] (CAS[3]) had not yet become available to our OKARNG Aviation commissioned officers.

Not many aviation commissioned officers even bothered completing their branch advanced courses before aviation became a Combat Arms Branch within the Army on 12 April 1983. This was because if your branch was Field Artillery or Armor, it was extremely difficult to get a resident course quota and the Oklahoma Military Department was reluctant to send Joe Smo, Army Aviator to such a course because of the cost. Doing the Advance Course by correspondence was often unbelievably difficult and time consuming. I know because I completed the Field Artillery Advance course, as an OKARNG aviator, by correspondence, as well as the required Command and General Staff College (CGSC) course () by correspondence. The other reason was that aviators are lazy, not stupid; they just have their own priorities and time schedules.

Those commissioned officers who didn't want to do any additional work or educational courses had a bad philosophy – "Oh well, I'll just revert to warrant officer." That attitude was a terrible disservice and insult to the Aviation Warrant Officer branch. This gave warrant officers a bad image.

The fixed-wing hangar at Norman was more like a title or designation of a special unit. You would hear someone say, "I'm going down to the fixed-wing hangar" and people understood exactly which hangar you meant. OKARNG aviation personnel were quite familiar with the term. Oklahoma did not always have a dedicated maintenance and storage facility for its fixed-wing aircraft. In the late 1950s and 1960s, all of the olive drab O-1s or L-19 Bird Dogs and U-6 Beavers were parked outside on the ramp at Max Westheimer Field at Norman.

The OKARNG built a new fixed-wing hangar at Westheimer in the 1962—1963 timeframe, according to BG Batey in a December 2006 interview. This became what is today the OKARNG C-12 and Reconnaissance and Interdiction Detachment (RAID) hangar on the north end of the airfield. It has had a least one office addition/remodel since 1980.

Major Batey became the Norman Flight Activities commander in the early 1970s, before there was an AASF at Lexington. He became the OKSAO during 1976.

The first hangar at Max Westheimer dedicated to OKARNG fixed-wing aircraft was a small T-hangar leased by the USPF&O from the airport manager at Westheimer ca 1971. The first VIP twin-engine

OKARNG aircraft was an original U-3A Blue Canoe ca 1957 from the OKANG, and it was parked in that T-hangar.

During this time, out in California a young former Air Force F-4 mechanic was working as civil service technician and missile mechanic, for the California Guard and was about to be released. James Andrew Hall (Jim) came to Oklahoma in 1974 and was hired as a full-time RW mechanic for the OKARNG at Norman. Soon he was assigned to help Sergeant First Class Jay C. Pierce, the designated fixed-wing maintenance repairman there at Westheimer Field. Pierce would leave the Guard ca 1979, but not before a second fixed-wing passenger airplane arrived.

On 16 May 1978 the OKARNG received a very nice U-8F Seminole (Beechcraft QueenAire) at Westheimer. CWO Pete Phillips, former

colonel and OKSAO and CW4 Leroy A. Wall, future OKSAO, were photographed at the stairway entrance to this aircraft after they had received and ferried the airplane back to Norman, OK. Within the next four to eight months it received a new 45th Inf Bde blue interior. The color of the U-8F's interior

CW2 Pete Phillips & CW4 Leroy A. Wall
May 1978

was not of great importance, but it showed that Batey knew how to get Oklahoma to pay for the things he wanted to accomplish!

After Pierce retired from the OKARNG, Jim Hall took over as the full-time tech in charge of fixed-wing maintenance in 1979[2]. Over the years, depending on the amount of fixed-wing maintenance needed, for example: replacing props on both engines and doing some repairs to the belly of the C-310 after a 'main gear collapsed' on landing, Sergeant First Class Hall had some help from the Lex AASF. Some of these men that from time to time came to Norman to temporarily assist were: Staff Sergeant Rodney Smoothers, Staff Sergeant Robert Jensen, Sergeant Phil Sorrom, and Sergeant Eric Wilson.

Around 1989, OKARNG was instructed to turn in the several fixed-wing aircraft it had on hand, acquired from the Drug Enforcement Agency (DEA). Two C-310s were transferred, one to SD ARNG and the other to AZ ARNG. The U-8F was transferred to the Oklahoma Bureau of Narcotics (OBN) and is still flown on state government/OBN business by several former OKARNG aviators.

The turn-in of these aircraft was not without some emotions. Oklahoma never let an aviation asset go without having a replacement coming down the pike. In this case, OKARNG was awaiting pick up of a new turbo-prop C-12 King Air (T-tail). The C-12 element at Norman was later designated Det 46 of Operational Support Airlift Agency (OSAA) the Army's consolidated passenger/cargo/VIP fixed-wing unit. OSAA supports all military services' airlift needs, nearly worldwide, through centralized scheduling from its headquarters near the Pentagon at Fort Belvoir, VA. This C-12 aircraft made your mouth water; it was fast, high tech and had very long legs (range approximately 1,280 miles).

About 1993, OKARNG also received two C-23 Sherpa fixed-wing aircraft and a detachment from a tactical Army fixed-wing company MTOE. This Sherpa unit was designated as Det 3, HHC, 1st Bn 132nd Cmd Avn. These aircraft and a small contingent of AGR and contract maintenance personnel were also stationed at Max Westheimer field, Norman, OK.

Both the C-12 Det 46 and the C-23 unit, Det 1 Co A 249th Avn (today) fly almost daily OSAA missions. The C-12 was authorized to fly 50 hrs per month and the C-23s 70 hrs per month each. Both Detachments have been deployed and served in Operation IRAQI FREEDOM.

SFC James A. Hall

SFC Hall worked at Max Westheimer Field for the OKARNG aviation and fixed-wing program for 33 years. He was not out front in the public's eye, but worked a hellish schedule. If the airplane came back in late at night and another aircrew was scheduled to fly the next morning, it was Jim who got the aircraft refueled at midnight, did his required maintenance checks and filled out the log books before 0600 hrs the next morning. He worked weekends, holidays, and thousands of hours of overtime keeping one or more fixed-wing aircraft ready and available for flight. SFC Hall retired from the OKARNG on 26 June 2007 with 41+ years of military service. Thank you Jim for your loyal and dedicated service.

What happened to some of those older olive drab, reciprocating engine airplanes? Did we let them all go? Obviously, not on Dana D. Batey's watch! I can recall watching as at least two former OKARNG aircraft and one current OKANG aircraft were sling-loaded to the 45th Inf Div Museum's Thunderbird Park. The most interesting mission was to watch the final flight of the U-18 Navion by CW4 George Senne into Westheimer Field. Then I watched as it was rigged for a sling-load pick up by a UH-60 Blackhawk from Tulsa. CW4 Tommy Klutts, PIC of the UH-60, cautiously lifted the (now un-aerodynamic) sling-load to a high-hover, and then expertly picked up speed until the drag chute tied to the rear end of the Navion's fuselage inflated and gave some stability to the load. He and his fellow crewmen delivered it to OKC for a permanent pole-mounting at the museum.

For those of you who have not taken the time and opportunity to visit Oklahoma City's 45th Infantry Division Museum located at 2145 NE 36th Street, you must do so. It is well worth your time. Museum curator, Mike Gonzales, and his loyal crew of former 45th Inf Div veterans and former OKARNG guardsmen are extremely helpful and certainly know their subject!

When visiting the 45th Inf Div Museum, the first thing you will notice near the parking lot is the old stone building, which houses the thousands of treasured military items from WWII and Korea and the excellent exhibits Mr. Gonzales has created over the years. However, you can't help but notice the outside exhibits too!

That beautiful Oklahoma native stone building, which now houses the 45th Inf Div Museum, was once the headquarters for the 45th Inf Bde. Dana D. Batey had just gotten out of the USAF and in September 1955 met Lieutenant Colonel Guild there in the old stone building to be interviewed for a full-time aviation mechanic position at Norman. After a very short interview, Guild probably said to Batey, "Young man, welcome aboard!"

The numerous Army and Air Guard aircraft on static display is fun and amazing. The Thunderbird Park and its outdoor exhibits are situated on 15 beautiful acres surrounding the museum complex. In the park are more than 60 different types of equipment, including wheeled vehicles, full track vehicles, tanks, aircraft, including a U-6 Beaver, L-17/U-18 Navion, and an OH-6 Cayuse, plus several large artillery pieces.

In the late 1980s and 1990s, the attitude within OKARNG Aviation toward advanced military education changed. By this time most commissioned officers and warrant officers attended their Advanced Branch course and completed CGSC, as well as other optional military educational courses. Several senior Oklahoma Army Guard aviators decided to attend the U.S. Army War College or Senior Service College. This was beneficial to these highly competent individuals, as three of them, to date, have been promoted to the rank of brigadier general and have received federal recognition. I expect several more aviators to achieve the same results in the near future. The Aviation branch is a challenging career field and isn't for the run of the mill individual.

Aviation leaders will remind their Infantry or Field Artillery contemporaries that aviation schooling places a new aviator behind other young Army officers because of the length of initial training. This is especially true in the case of platoon leaders and company commanders. Many enlisted aviation maintenance and avionics courses take up to a year to complete and become MOS qualified. To become an Army aviator today, it may take up to 24 months. Getting those silver wings isn't easy. Just ask a recently appointed Aviation Warrant Officer Jonathan Council from Tulsa, OK, now stationed in Iraq with B Co 1/285th OKARNG.

Jonathon spent six weeks at the U.S. Army Aviation Center in the Warrant Officer Candidate program and then was appointed as an Aviation Warrant Officer. Then he attended a very demanding and trying course called Level C Survival Escape and Evasion (SERE) course, which takes approximately three weeks to complete, including the Resistance Training Lab (RTL) phase of SERE. This phase exposes aviation individuals to the most severe and hostile circumstances of captivity, interrogation, and mental and physical torture.

Former Night Stalker CW3 Michael Durant (of the 160th SOAR) was shot down by a rebel-fired RPG while in his MH-60 on 3 October 1993. Although he was injured and his fellow crewmembers were killed, he was held prisoner for 11 days in Mogadishu, Somalia. In his book, *In Company of Heroes,* Durant acknowledges the lessons he learned from

Colonel Nick Rowe's example and the SERE training he (Durant) had received while in the 160th SOAR.

Level-C SERE is designed for personnel whose "jobs, specialties or assignments entail a significant or high risk of capture and exploitation." AR 350-30 states: "As a minimum, the following categories of personnel shall receive formal Level-C training at least once in their careers: combat aircrews, special operations forces (e.g., Army Special Forces and Rangers, Marine Corps force reconnaissance units, Air Force special tactics teams, and psychological operations units) and military attaché." SERE, roughly three weeks in length, is now a requirement for graduation from the U.S. Army Special Forces Qualification Course and for Special Operations Forces aviators. The course is conducted at Camp Mackall, North Carolina.

After completion of the SERE and RTL training, WO1 Council attended dunker training. Dunker is military helicopter egress training in a water environment, simulating a crashed helicopter that is submersing and how to get out of the cockpit. This course was first conducted at Naval installations for Naval and Marine (brown shoe) aviators. Jackson NAS, FL, was a TDY location where the 45th Avn (SO)(A) took its dunker training. The Army now conducts its own training at Fort Rucker. This training is conducted over a three-day period and is a pass or fail course.

Today Army aviation students, warrant officers and commissioned officers have learned to be flexible. They may encounter a bubble between phases in flight school. These bubbles mean a delay in training, sometimes due to aircraft availability and/or instructor pilot availability. This creates further TDY time away from the student's unit and the continuation of his military career.

After dunker training, then Warrant Officer One (WO1) Council began 23 weeks of flight and academic training the U.S. Army's Bell TH-67 turbine helicopter trainer. This is an advanced, modern version of the older OH-58 Kiowa. After completing this phase of flight training, young Council entered Advanced Flight Training phase – in his case, UH-60 Sikorsky Black Hawks. Since December 2009 young WO1 Council has flown approximately 700 UH-60 flight hours in his B Co 1/285th OKARNG unit. Things have indeed changed in the Oklahoma Army National Guard.

Accuracy first, speed second. But always, the Aviation branch remains "Above the Best!"

As mentioned before, OKARNG Aviation had a humble and somewhat slow, low-key beginning. With a measured, but steady increase in the number and new types of aircraft added to the OKARNG inventory, military tactical training occurred, but it was individual training, not collective training at the company and battalion level. Remember that aviation companies weren't a reality in the OKARNG until the late 1950s.

Individual flight training in the OKARNG took place at Norman and although gradually, some emphasis was placed on rotary-wing instrument training in the late 1960s. There were no paid additional flight training periods (AFTPs) yet.

Although Army Aviation safety officers weren't part of early OKARNG aviation, it was recognized that you could die quickly if you flew inadvertently into instrument meteorological conditions (IMC) in a helicopter. This fear of IMC, and the very high accident rate for all of NGB aviation in the late 1960s, brought some needed progress to the Norman aviation support facility with the addition of the Blue Box *Link Trainers*. Not long after came staff (instrument trainers) and full-time flight instructors. To quote one former OKSAO, "When I went to work full-time at Norman, the flight ramp outside our wooden hangar looked like a WWII aviation museum."

"During the days after Korea, the old Blue Box Link trainer was installed on site at Max Westheimer Field at Norman," said Colonel Jerry Bourassa, " . . . and later we had them at Lexington for a while."

Simulation technology was developed by Edwin Albert Link in the late 1920s. Link had been an musical organ builder; his knowledge of pumps, bellows and valves gave him the idea for a motion simulator. Link produced more than 10,000 Blue Boxes during the 1930-50 period for all of the world's major powers, including the Japanese Imperial Navy. The ANT-18 (Army Navy Trainer 18) was the second model and provided motion through all three axes. This Link Blue Box wasn't phased out by the Army until the mid 1970s.

Individual instrument training for rotary-wing Army aviators was a real challenge in the 1960s. Graduating from flight school in 1965, my classmates and I were issued a tactical instrument ticket before leaving for Vietnam. This Tac ticket authorized us to fly IMC, and to legally file an IFR flight plan while assigned outside the continental United States (OCONUS). Oh, it also meant I could get my ass killed if I ever tried to fly IMC without a whole lot more training and practical experience! In 1966, we flew IMC in Vietnam during the monsoon season, not because we wanted to, but because it was the only option to get us back to base camp (An Khe). We flew several ground controlled approach (GCA) approaches into the Golf Course (1ˢᵗ CAV Div airfield at An Khe, named because of the all of the holes caused by mortar attacks) and on several night missions, we had to do tactical automatic direction finder (ADF) approaches to get back into our landing zones at night. You couldn't pay me enough money to ever do that again!

In the meantime, back in Oklahoma, Troop D, 1ˢᵗ Squadron of the 145ᵗʰ Cavalry was officially organized and federally recognized on 1 November 1965. This aviation squadron included a Flight Operations Section, an Aero Scout Platoon, and a Service Platoon. It was part of the 145ᵗʰ Armored Cavalry at Marlow, OK. During these days crushing the communists in Vietnam and giving that country democracy was the Army's highest priority. Someone at the Pentagon decided (or they were told) that Army National Guard units would not be activated for service in Vietnam.

Yet another someone decided to have a Plan B just in case. Plan B was to have a number of units, infantry, armor, and aviation units, trained up and ready to go at a moment's notice. These were called Special Reactions Forces or SRF units. Trp D at Marlow, OK was an SRF unit for about two years, 1965 and 1966.

They had a high priority for logistics, mandays and training, but no new aircraft. They were still flying OH-23s, OH-13s, and H-19s. It's hard to imagine them rehearsing for an aerial combat assault with OH-23s and OH-13s. Nearly 100% of the Army's Hueys (UH-1s) were already in Vietnam. Trp D drilled twice a month at Marlow and did 36 AFTPs per year against a standard 24 AFTPs per year.

During those SRF days down at Marlow, OK, many OKARNG guys would carpool together and try to save a buck or two. Here's an interesting and true story. Names have been provided by a former OKSAO:

"When we stayed at the Derrick Motel (as in oil derrick) in Duncan over drill weekend, we'd share a room to save money. Usually there'd be at least three, sometimes four guys to a room. Captain Keith Owens, who drove an older VW, he'd just gotten off active duty and was pretty sharp and straight laced. He once told me, 'Clem, it will be best for everyone if we just go ahead and use proper military courtesy and terms during drill weekend. You should address me as Captain Owens and I'll address you as CW2 Keyes or Mr. Keyes.' Warrant officers, especially Aviation warrants, were never known for their military appearance, military bearing or military courtesy. We always called each other and most of the Captains by their first names, rather than 'sir.' But I agreed to his request."

"That first night at the Derrick Motel, there were three of us in the room. It had two double beds. I was lucky and got a double bed all to myself. CPT Owens and another aviator, who just happened to be a warrant officer aviator (CW2 Don Keyes – a real jokester), got the other double bed. Everyone had turned in for the night and the lights were out."

"However, before anyone had gone to sleep, the warrant officer sharing the other double bed with our straight-laced captain said, "CPT Owens, Sir, since we're now sleeping together, would it be alright with you if I called you by your first name?"

Laughing is good for the soul, just as long as you don't get court-martialed.

Within the ARNG there wasn't going to be any instrument flight training conducted in the OH-23s or OH-13s. But within a few years that, too was about to change.

An Army study in July 1968 determined the technological feasibility of a Synthetic Flight Training System (SFTS) for transition, instrument and proficiency flight training of Army rotary-wing aviators. A training concept was developed to serve as a basis for an SFTS design that would provide effective training at minimal total cost. The concept utilized a device called the "2B24" Synthetic Flight Training System (SFTS), which had the cockpit of the UH-1 Army Iroquois. It was approved and began operations in the mid-to-late 1970s. At the time, OKARNG was part of the 5th Army area and Fort Sill was chosen to receive one of the new SFTS buildings, personnel, etc. OKARNG Aviation first conducted all of its SFTS training at Fort Sill, utilizing AFTPs.

In the early 1990s, the Army bought and began utilizing UH-60, CH-47 SFTS, and later the Army had Special Ops aircraft SFTS as well. Today, a UH-1B 2B24 SFTS would cost +/—$7.5 mil per cockpit. OKARNG SOA aviators later traveled longer distances TDY to get UH-60 and CH-47 SFTS training at Fort Riley, Kansas and Fort Campbell, Kentucky and other locations.

OKARNG aviation began to see its first UH-1 Hueys arriving from Vietnam in 1970-71. However, the Huey wasn't the first IFR helicopter in the OKARNG. The CH-34 Choctaw and the H-19 were also IFR aircraft and were assigned to the OKARNG before it had Hueys. At Fort Wolters we had a link trainer in flight school in mid-1965 that was based on the CH-34 Choctaw cockpit. I later flew IFR in CH-34s in Germany, after Vietnam. The real challenge for the Army was to:

Train enough rotary-wing flight instructors and get them instrument qualified.

Qualify them as Army rotary-wing instrument flight instructors/examiners so they could train the remaining aviators. (This was going to take the ARNG a very, very long time if they only did instrument flight training on drill weekends.)

Around 1969-70, the Army decided that all aviators should have a standard instrument rating, but it was several years later before NGB required the States to have rotary-wing aviators instrument qualified. Dana D. Batey, as the new SAO in 1976, assigned this monumental task to the one person who could not only handle it," but would give it to you "on time and within budget. This person was a true hard charger who had worked for Douglas Aircraft in Tulsa before he joined the Oklahoma Guard and later went to flight school. This aviator was CW3 Leroy A. Wall. He was intelligent, rock solid and had a military bearing that was exceeded by very few and a sense of humor on the other end of the spectrum. He was (and is today) an aviator extraordinaire.

Leroy's dad, Troy Wall, worked at Tinker AFB, while Leroy attended Southeast High School, in Oklahoma City and graduated in 1958. He joined the Oklahoma Guard in 1957 and was initially an "11 Bravo" infantryman assigned to HQs, 45th Div. Leroy married Tommie Eades in 1962 and then went to rotary-wing flight school at Fort Wolters and Fort Rucker as a warrant officer. He graduated as an Army aviator in 1964. Wall attended the fixed-wing transition in 1969. Between rotary-wing initial flight training and the fixed-wing course, WO Wall went to work for Southern Airways at Fort Wolters/Mineral Wells, TX, training Army helicopter pilots, most of which were headed for Vietnam. Leroy was one of about 20 OKARNG aviators who worked during the week at Wolters and drilled with the NG at Norman. Charlie Jones used to call the guys in the OKARNG who worked at Southern Airways gypsies because they lived, worked, and drilled in different places.

Leroy A. Wall went to work full-time for the OKARNG at Norman in 1971. Not only a straight shooter, he came onboard dual rated (R/W and F/W rated), multiengine, and instrument rated in fixed-wing, plus he was an instructor pilot. He obtained his R/W instrument rating soon after he came onboard full-time. Not long thereafter he went to the Army Aviation Safety Course and was one of the first OH-58 instructor pilots (IPs) in the OKARNG. That first year he logged 600 hours of IP time and had checked out all the OH-58 pilots.

Well, what was this high-level task that Batey wanted CWO Wall to do?

Pure and simple, Batey wanted Wall, "To provide instrument training to every OKARNG aviator, evaluate, and qualify them as instrument-rated Army aviators.

Being one of the few rotary-wing instrument-rated instructor pilots in the OKARNG, and already having been seen by LTC Batey as a true up and comer, CW3 Wall was given the job of putting the OKARNG R/W Instrument Qualification program together. Batey then sent Wall to the Instrument Flight Examiner Course. The IFE course is known worldwide as eight weeks of pure, unadulterated hell. You were made to feel like you didn't know squat about flying, instructing, and for certain – "You don't know squat about rotary-wing instrument flying."

When Wall returned from the IFE course, he trained some of the other pilots, assisted them in getting their instrument ratings and placed them on mandays to train other R/W pilots.

Colonel Leroy A. Wall stated, "I remember Butch Coale, Claude Guy, and a couple of others who did a great job as instructors. We conducted instrument classes five nights a week and flew about three hours each night per student in UH-1s. We did it at night to accommodate Guardsmen with civilian jobs. Not only did I instruct, but also gave the instrument check rides. The OKARNG R/W Instrument Qualification program lasted about a year. We achieved our goal – 100% of the OKARNG aviators became instrument qualified—the few who couldn't cut it got out." Oklahoma was likely the first ARNG State to achieve 100% instrument qualification for all aviators; both Batey and Wall agree that we were.

In the year after completing this major training project, CW3 Wall was recommended for the AAAA Aviator of the Year (1978). This was AAAA's Reserve Component 5th Army Area Aviator of the Year Award. Wall recalls, "I don't know who put me in for the award, probably COL Batey. I remember that I didn't have time to go to the awards ceremony at Corpus Christi, but I flew the Cessna 310 down there one afternoon. Lieutenant Colonel Ron Howland and Sergeant First Class Bill Rogers went with me. When the ceremony was over that night, about 2200 hrs, we flew back to Norman. We didn't know what 'crew endurance' was in those days."

Lieutenant Colonel Marvin Roberts, former active duty U.S. Marine Corps AH-1 Cobra gun pilot and later S-1, 45th Avn Bn (Sp Ops)(Abn), talked about the early gun platoon in his unit history, "Throughout 1979 Co D () 149th Avn Bn continued both its recruiting effort and a training program to bring the new recruits and appointees up to speed. In June 1979, the company went over the 100% strength mark for the first time since it had been reorganized as a company. In July, the company conducted its annual training (AT) at Fort Rucker AL and each member of the unit attended a formal Military Occupational Specialty (MOS) producing school or received Operational Job Training (OJT) alongside an active duty soldier of the same MOS. Our aviators trained with active duty IPs and became qualified on the weapons systems mounted on OKARNG UH-1M aircraft[3]."

Co D (-) 149th was organized on 1 October 1978 and stationed at Tulsa; D (-) was one half of an attack helicopter battalion headquartered in Arizona. The armament subsystems on the UH-1Ms included the M158 – 7 tube 2.75 in. rocket launcher, the M5 – 40mm grenade launcher and the M21 – 7.62mm mini-gun. It takes a special type of helicopter pilot, with an attitude, to become a gun driver. Here are a few memories about a couple of gun missions:

CW5 Samuel T. Hinch recalled this incident, "At summer camp at Fort Chaffee, AR, CW2 Richard Cooper and I left a permanent hole in one of the concrete helicopter pads. We had lost hydraulics and the mini gun flexed to full down while Cooper had the trigger depressed. We coughed concrete dust for a week after we returned from the range. We were lucky and the best thing was no one was injured!"

On another gunship training exercise, Sam related, "One time at Fort Sill, CW2 Larry "Bear" Smith and I answered a call for help and medevaced a kid that had been snake bit out on the gunnery range. We landed a fully loaded UH-1C [armed gunship] model Huey at the Medical Evacuation (Medevac) helipad at Reynolds Army hospital, Fort Sill, OK. What's the statute of limitations on that?"

During these days of evolution, it was Chet Howard, as State Aviation Officer of the OKARNG (OKSAO), who lobbied NGB ca 1968 and helped obtain paid AFTPs for Oklahoma's aviators. Paid AFTPs were a brand new prize in the Cracker Jack box. Few people knew the best way to administer or utilize them. Then you could only do one AFTP per day.

Major Charlie Jones became the first Aviation Safety Officer at Norman. According to Leroy A. Wall, "Jones and I were working at cross purposes. If we got off work at noon on an AFTP weekend, we would drive up and do a Friday evening AFTP. Charlie didn't like to work Friday nights, but occasionally it was his turn. When that happened, he had everything planned out. We had to be there at exactly 1800 hrs, get his safety briefing, then preflight, fly, etc. I guess he was right. However, he was ahead of his time and certainly ahead of ours. Most of the Guard pilots were mavericks to say the least and working for Charlie, with his disdainful attitude, made the situation worse."

Leroy continued, "The pilots, including me, wanted to come in somewhere between 1800—1930 hrs, get a tail number, fly, and be at the local watering hole by 2100 hrs. Consequently, the pilots became even worse because they wanted to aggravate Charlie. They came in late, left early, padded flight time, etc. I remember once, Charlie had us in for the safety briefing. Again Charlie tried to do a good job, but he just pissed everybody off. He wanted to talk about emergency egress. He began by asking if anyone knew what 'egress' meant. Being a young smart aleck, I said, 'Yes sir, a large white bird.' He said, 'No that's not it.' Did I mention that Charlie had no sense of humor? The other guys said, 'Wall is right, it's a big white bird.' Then one guy said, 'They can be blue also.' Another guy said, 'No you're thinking about a Blue Heron.' Charlie not catching on, said, 'No, *egress* not egrets.' Then one guy said, 'Oh more than one Egret.' Then Charlie began to get red in the face and said, 'I'm talking about exiting from an enclosed place – egress.' One of the guys said, 'Oh, like a bird cage. Egrets are too big for bird cages.' At this point, Charlie gave up and issued tail numbers. We flew and then laughed ourselves silly at Ole

Blues. Charlie later went to NGB where he excelled as a safety officer and got more respect."

Progress necessitates change, and sometimes it is the slow changes that bring the best results and the most change.

Prior to 1983-84, it appeared to me that OKARNG Aviation was tactically still in its infancy. Training was making some notable changes. We were getting to where we broke the code on getting aviation unit training out of the short-term column and made great headway in planning long-term.

Co B, 149ᵗʰ Avn saw major changes in the way it trained beginning in 1984. Operations orders were staffed, written, briefed, and executed. Night unit training was conducted, time on target insertions and exfils were planned, rehearsed, and executed. After Action Reports for just completed missions became the norm. You could see and sense an attitude change. It was no longer a *Flying Club*, and aviators had begun to take pride in their appearance and how they were perceived by others. Pride had become something you wanted to see in your fellow aviators and in yourself too!

For certain, one of Oklahoma's newest aviation units, the 45ᵗʰ Aviation Battalion, (Special Operations) (Airborne), which was organized and federally recognized on 1 May 1982, was establishing training programs that were extraordinary. Their MH/AH-6 aircraft qualification training program was far reaching (coast to coast) and the night vision goggle (NVG) training programs were demanding as well as astonishing. But I'll elaborate more on these subjects in later chapters.

Later, COL Leroy A. Wall was passed the baton by Dana Batey and became the fifth Oklahoma Army National Guard State Aviation Officer on 1 December 1988. COL Wall, having been the third Commander of the 45ᵗʰ Avn Bn (Lt Hel Cbt), continued a legacy of excellence. Leroy, the company commanders, staff, and dedicated Special Operations Aviation personnel who preceded him in the 45ᵗʰ Avn Bn, worked from an old WPA stone armory in Sperry, OK, and shared hangar/ramp space with the Oklahoma Air National Guard at the Tulsa International Airport. When the 45ᵗʰ Avn Bn was first organized in 1982, it shared an armory in downtown Tulsa with the 279ᵗʰ Infantry.

Leroy completed the Tulsa aviation facilities/armory/OMS task began by Batey, then oversaw the dedication and opening of the new $6 million dollar Tulsa Army Aviation Support Facility and separate but equally impressive new $2.2 million dollar Armory for the recently designated 1st Bn, 245th Avn (SOA)(Abn) on 26 August 1989. The new OMS #18 at the Tulsa AASF was dedicated on 2 May 1988.

Progress or change is sometimes quite spectacular. Unit personnel who moved the 1/245th Avn (SOA) unit headquarters, companies and staff offices from the old stone armory in downtown Sperry, OK to the modern, expansive, masonry armory, with tiled floors, air conditioning, large classrooms, a physical fitness room, etc., to its new location on the northwest corner of Tulsa International Airport in 1989 were not only in shock, but amazed at the change they were experiencing first hand! Imagine the same cultural shock experienced by the guys at Norman when they moved in 1975 to the new facilities at the Lexington, OK, AASF.

As the transition from the *Flying Club Days* continued into the Special Ops Aviation era in OKARNG Aviation history, the new aviator and crew were required to specialize in night flying. They would use cutting edge night vision goggles, special GPS navigational equipment, and deadly accurate armament. The NVGs allowed them to become proficient flyers in the absence of normal available light, like the great horned owl, a nocturnal and predator of the night. Their charge was to own the night and become the best warriors of the night!

These unique individuals performed an average of 110—130 days active duty per year. The common age for 45th Avn Bn aviators was 28 years old, with 15 years of education, 3,500 flight hours (of which about 350 were NVG hours), and 10-14 years of military service. Many were veterans of one or two combat tours in Vietnam. All were highly trained, skillful, fearless Army soldiers who flew specialized helicopters at night and didn't quit! Most had flown missions in many different foreign countries in support of U.S. and foreign governments.

The Lords of Darkness were a one-of-a-kind Army National Guard, Special Operations Aviation unit within the Oklahoma Army National Guard, and in the whispered voice of the warrior, had already " . . . seen the elephant."

Although these few examples are not the complete story of our transition, they represent the type of progress that did occur, and some of the changes – all of which brought about a new, more tactically sound and professional attitude in OKARNG Aviation. In the early days, when you came to the AASF and signed in, you were issued an aircraft, given a key, matched up with a co-pilot (or instructor pilot), and were assigned a support mission or a training scenario. You planned your mission, checked the current and forecasted weather, and then filed a flight plan. From Flight Ops, you took your helmet bag, gloves, flight jacket, and maps to the flight line, did a pre-flight of your aircraft, and away you went for the next hour and a half or so. You might perform one AFTP in the morning and one in the afternoon or evening.

With the coming of Oklahoma of Special Operations Aviation – to say that things changed significantly was indeed the understatement of the day. An average NVG-qualified aviator, coming in to Tulsa from several hundred miles away for an AFTP, might spend 3-4 hours planning a single-ship, NVG, low-level route, and then log one to one and a half hours of flight time. Planning a multi-ship, NVG, formation mission required a lot more time. Getting an AFTP now had a very new meaning – you got it the old fashioned way, you earned it!

Most of these Oklahoma aviation soldiers and Lords of Darkness had other jobs. Today we proudly refer to them as *citizen soldiers*. Sure some were (and are still are) full-time federal technicians. Beginning in the 1980s, some became full-time AGRs (Army Guard-Reserve on Title 32) operations officers, instructor pilots or unit admin/training NCOs. However, the large majority, the M-day side of the house, then and today, include high school teachers, funeral directors, plant managers, U.S. Postal Service employees, county extension managers, insurance agents/adjusters, sheet metal workers, HVAC contractors, full-time college students, FAA employees, doctors, nurses, lawyers, and Indian Chiefs.

Not surprisingly, many of these citizen soldiers had civilian flying jobs: American Airlines, off-shore helicopter pilots, Oklahoma City or Tulsa Police Department pilots, EMS or Medevac pilots. A few had no fear and were weekday Ag pilots (flying crop dusters), the bravest of them all. And then there were a few real entrepreneurs of the day, who we called *Guard Bums*. It wasn't a derogatory term; it simply meant rather than working a real job, they would take their chances and fly AFTPs until they ran out, and then would volunteer for whatever mandays and active duty for training missions were available. They did well; at least I did on several occasions.

These citizen soldiers remain the backbone of the Army National Guard. Not only do they receive accolades from the civilian side in their chosen fields, but for their volunteer efforts in support of their communities and their families. They leave jobs or their home in work clothes or civilian attire, and after driving several hours, they pass through the security gates, and a transformation takes place – from citizen to soldier. Their military job was/is Army aviator or Army Special Operations Aviator, crew chief, flight engineer, electrician, avionics specialist or helicopter repairman. All of them are equally important.

When they left the town in which they work or live, it might just be for the afternoon, perhaps for a weekend drill or for a two-week summer camp (annual training). Yet within the past six to eight years that too has changed dramatically. The citizen soldier may have been called to active duty; he and his fellow unit members might be mobilized into service along side active duty units. It is no longer the exception, being called to active duty to serve for 12-15 months in Kuwait, Iraq, Afghanistan or wherever the need of the Army is at that time. It is not uncommon that today's *citizen soldier* has already served two or three overseas deployments in the period of five, perhaps six years. Don't ever call him or her a weekend warrior – he is a *citizen soldier*, if you please.

The old adage which states, "The whole is greater than the sum of its parts," might be stated another way – one plus one equals three. The combined talent and capabilities of this unit was far greater and beyond the efforts of any one aviator or soldier. "You can count on me," didn't need to be stated, it was understood.

By the mid-1980s, we had graduated from the old days of "Kick the tires, light the fires, let's go . . ." A new attitude existed, incorporating the qualities of PRIDE and PROFESSIONALISM. It was like the old field artillery adage: "Mission always, but safety first, then accuracy and then speed." Practice and train as you intend to fight!

What a change from the 1960s, when men join the ARNG or USAR today, they do so knowing that going into combat with your guard unit isn't just a probability, it is almost a guarantee that he/she will serve in a combat environment in the near term. Yet they chooses to join, they aren't forced to, nor were they drafted. They volunteered.

Your Oklahoma Army National Guardsman today deserves to be called a *citizen soldier*. That is who he is . . .

1. Emails received from CW5 Daniel "Danny" Washa. Danny retired from the OKARNG on 1 June 05 with 39 years and 5 month's military service. All of that was OKARNG except for three years with the Army Reserves at Norman. He continues to fly the UH-60, UH-1H/N, CH-47D as a flight test pilot for Corpus Christi Army Depot. In 2003, Danny went with the Chinook company (G Co., 149 AVN) in 2003 to Kuwait. He currently has over 8,500 flight hours.

2   Telephone interview Sergeant First Class James A. "Jim" Hall, 5 January 2008.

3   UH-1Ms were simply UH-1Cs with the T53-L-13B engine upgrade and had several armament systems added.

Chapter 5

Name That Unit . . .

"The legacy of heroes is the memory of a great name and the inheritance of a great example."
Benjamin Disraeli

Part I – Chronology

Have you ever been to a cemetery and read some of the epitaphs on the markers? Did you notice on most of the grave markers there were two dates, usually the date of birth and the date of death of the person buried beneath the stone? But notice closely, there is usually a dash between the two dates. Have you wondered about the meaning of that dash?

If that dash could talk, it would tell the story of that person's existence, his or her life story, no matter how long or short. The dash represents what happened after the birth, through the years, up to the death or end of that person's existence in this earthly world. How did Oklahoma Guard Aviation evolve from three or four aircraft from the late 1940s and early 1950s, into numerous, modern, relevant, combat aviation units in this new 21st century?

What occurred with those early Bird Dog and Hiller/Bell aviation sections and how did they develop into such skilled, tactical and proficient aviation companies and battalions? Many years and much blood, sweat and tears were involved. Tenacity, hard work, and vision were at the core of our Oklahoma aviation leader's dreams and plans. They were visionary, long before that term was first seen on an Officer Efficiency Report (OER) or NCOER.

In this chapter, my goal is to describe to you some of the major events that influenced the growth and advancement of the aviation units within the Oklahoma Army National Guard and give, as accurately as possibly, the names of those aviation units from the end of the Korean War (the birth of aviation in Oklahoma) up to the deactivation of the 1st Bn, 245th Avn (SO)(A) on 1 September 1994.

The evolution of Guard Aviation in Oklahoma didn't occur within a matter of six days and on the seventh they rested. It took 70 years for OKARNG to get its first real TOE aviation company, but they did! And that unit grew; another replaced it, then another. Eventually, an Aviation Command and Control Headquarters came into being and we learned and benefited from that experience, maturing with each step.

Oklahoma Army National Guard Aviation force structure had a dawdling beginning. There wasn't a big bang or any fanfare. It steadily developed through its long infancy, competing for resources, striving for relevance. Korea is the most logical point from which to begin to tell the story of Oklahoma ARNG Aviation force structure and its growth. Why start with Korea? There was no aviation force structure in Oklahoma before Korea, only dreams! Also, Korea was such a significant event in OKARNG history. We cannot and will not forget the 45th Infantry Division's contributions and participation in WWII, which caused it to be the most decorated combat division in U.S. Army history. However, concerning the starting point for OKARNG Aviation, Korea is the logical point in time.

It is hard to imagine, but the number of OKARNG guardsmen having been mobilized and served in Afghanistan (Operation Enduring Freedom) and/or Iraq (Operation Iraqi Freedom) may have already exceeded the total number of Oklahoma Thunder Bird soldiers (roughly 12,000) who were first mobilized to serve with the 45th Inf Div in the Korean War (1951-52). "Since 9-11 we have mobilized and deployed approximately 18,695[1] Oklahoma National Guardsman[2]," stated COL Walter E. Fountain[3], Master Army Aviator and full-time J-3, Deputy Chief of Staff for Plans and Operations at Oklahoma's Joint Forces Headquarters.

As of April 2006, more than 39,000 U.S. Guardsmen were serving in Operation IRAQI FREEDOM (139,733 to date); 14,000 in Operation ENDURING FREEDOM (Afghanistan) (37,700 to date) and 652 in Operation NOBLE EAGLE (homeland security). Since 9-1-1, more than

248,000 soldiers have been mobilized under USC Title 10 authority (federal orders) and 337,000 under Title 10 or Title 32 (federal and state orders).[4]

The war in Korea, almost as painful as Vietnam, took the lives of 50,000+ U.S. servicemen; other U.S. casualties included 92,000+ WIA, 8,100+ MIA and 7,200+ POWs. The cause had its roots in the political history of Korea under Japanese rule from 1910 to 1945. The Japanese were very aggressive task masters during this period of domination. They cut many trees for Japanese ship building, the taller ones being used for masts. The remaining trees were burned on the peninsula so the Koreans could build nothing, which eliminated their ability to keep warm in the bitter cold of winter.

In 1945, after WWII had ended, U.S. and Soviet troops went into Korea ostensibly to liberate the Korean people from the Japanese and accept surrender from the Japanese in 1945. What occurred was a three-year occupation characterized by uncertainty and confusion.

This co-occupation force, U.S. and Soviet, was of little help to the embittered Korean people, much like today's de facto civil war in Iraq, except with less bloodshed. The U.S. Army placed military occupational forces, led by LTG John R. Hodge, into the south, while the Soviets put theirs into North Korea, presumably waiting on the UN to decide the independence issue of the peninsula. The U.S. and Soviets agreed to temporarily divide the Korean peninsula along the 38th parallel, occurring on 15 August 1945. This may have prevented a civil war in Korea at the time. However, a few months later, in October 1945, the Korean Communist Party was resuscitated.

U.S. strategists began to question the long-term defensibility of South Korea, a difficult question, which remains today. The division of the country at the 38th was very much a disadvantage to South Korea, as all the industry, especially the fertilizer plants and electrical generating plants were in the north. Most of the industry and mining in Korea had been owned and operated by Japan. When the U.S./Soviet occupation occurred, some 700,000 Japanese were allowed to leave Korea; therefore, nearly all the mines, factories, and industrial plants were without leadership, managers, technicians, and operating capital.

On 15 August 1948, the Republic of Korea was proclaimed and Syngman Rhee became the first president. During the next month, September 1948, the South Korean Army came into being. Over the years it became one of the most, if not the most, disciplined and fierce fighting group with which this author has ever been associated.[5]

By 29 June 1949, U.S. occupation forces had been withdrawn, except a few military advisors, and Korea had been placed outside of the U.S. perimeter of defense. It remains a political hot potato and most difficult location to defend still today. Since the 1990s, the South Koreans no longer want U.S. military personnel in their country, but they don't want to lose the strong, protective arm of their big brother and his financial underpinning of their economy.

On 25 June 1950, the North Korean Army crossed over the 38th parallel, invading South Korea, and hoping to reunite the peninsula. President Truman believed that the North Koreans were puppets of the communist Soviet Union. Later in October 1950, the Chinese Army shocked the world by sending a massive army across the Yalu River into North Korea, as UN forces immediately fell back. The war had begun in earnest.

Oklahoma's 45th Infantry Division was mobilized and activated for the Korean War on 1 September 1950. The 45th Inf Div's units included: HHC Co., 45th Recon Co., 45th QM Co, 45th Signal Co., 45th MP Co., 700th Ord/Maint., 45th Replacement Co., 45th Div Band, 179th Inf Regmt, 180th Inf Regmt, 279th Inf Regmt, and the Division's Field Artillery. The 45th's Div Arty included: HHB, 158th FA Bn, 160th FA Bn, 171st FA Bn, 189th FA Bn and the 145th AAA AW Bn. Notice there were no aviation units, no aviation force structure within the division.

The Army National Guard mobilized 140,000 soldiers during the Korean War. However, "The 45th Inf Div OKARNG was mobilized at Fort Sill, OK in 1950 and the 45th's approximate authorized strength was 15,000. Of course they were well under that strength [perhaps 10,000-12,000]. And then the Division was rounded out with soldiers from the General Replacement Depot. They spent a year in training at Fort Polk, LA and Hokkaido, Japan[6]. And . . . . they fielded about 15,000 soldiers, [when] they entered into the conflict itself and moved onto the peninsula of Korea through Inchon in December 1951," explained Mike Gonzales

"At the end of a year [ca December 1952] the Oklahoma Army National Guard component of the 45th Division had served its allotted time. So all, well most of the Oklahomans, went home. And the [45th Inf] Division's strength was replaced with soldiers from the General Replacement Depot and from other units in the theater. The [45th Inf] Division's colors stayed in Korea until the cessation of hostilities. But the Oklahoma National

Guard [personnel] came back to Oklahoma. So there was a period of time there when you had technically two 45th Inf Divisions – the 45th Inf Div deployed in Korea and the 45th Inf Div of the Oklahoma Army National Guard. The Division colors stayed in Korea," said Mike Gonzales.

A few of Oklahoma's 45th Inf Div soldiers stayed overseas for the duration of the war. Most were deployed for 12 months and then returned home. Sergeant Major Bill Stearns couldn't leave Korea at the end of his 12 months due to an extreme shortage of Army sergeants major. Stearns later became CW2 Stearns and worked as COL Dana D. Batey's State Aviation Coordinator in Oklahoma in the late mid-1980s to early 1990s. He retired from the Guard, and in 2006 was inducted into Oklahoma's Military Hall of Fame.

On 27 July 1953, the United States, North Korea, and China signed an armistice, which ended the war but failed to bring about a permanent peace. Technically, North Korea is still at war with the United States. Believe me, North Korea's Kim Jong Il awakens today with thoughts of how to proceed in his war against the United States of America. Should you have the opportunity to visit the Pacific Rim of Southeast Asia, stop by the DMZ in Korea, as I did in April 1998, and visit the Joint Security Area at Pan Mun Jong; without a doubt what you will see will convince you that the North Koreans want to kill you right now.

The Fighting Thunderbirds of the 45th Inf Div were released from active duty 30 April 1954. On 1 February 1968, the 45th Inf Div was federally reorganized and redesignated as Hqs 45th Inf Bde, later redesignated a Separate Bde. Recently the 45th Inf Bde (Sep) became the 45th Brigade Combat Team (BCT). In 2007, BG Myles L. Deering deployed with his 45th BCT to Iraq and returned in late 2008. On 17 December 2008, he was promoted to major general, at the Blue Room in the Oklahoma State Capitol by Gov Brad Henry and MG Harry M. Wyatt III.

A concise study of early OKARNG and Army Aviation history uncovers an interesting fact. There were no designated, separate aviation units within the Army, or in the ARNG, before the Korean War.

Yes, we had a few fixed-wing aircraft in the Oklahoma Guard before Korea, but no helicopters. Officially, Army National Guard Aviation began in 1948, but basically devoid of any aviation force structure. The ARNG received quite a few L-19s from the Army before 1950. From 1951 until 1954, with the exception of the two H-19 transport companies in Korea, there weren't any other aviation companies, or any assault helicopter companies fielded in the Army or ARNG. There was, however, Army aircraft assigned to the various states and to aviation sections. There wasn't a standard size, set number of aircraft, or number of aviators for an aviation section (Avn Sec). At the division level, the G-3 decided who got what aircraft, how many aviators, and what their mission would be.

In our own 45ᵗʰ Inf Div, as I mentioned earlier, there were Aviation sections in the division headquarters, each of the Infantry regiments and the Field Artillery (Div Arty). These were small sections and primarily used for reconnaissance and artillery adjustment. Also mentioned in the previous chapter, some of our first OKARNG aviators were CPT Gus Guild, CWO Perry H. Papa Tango Townsend, CWO Bill Tingler and CWO Jack Ray, who went to Korea with the 45ᵗʰ Inf Div. They returned from Korea and stayed in the Oklahoma Guard and helped the aviation program grow.

The development of atomic warfare in WWII, led to an evolution of newly designed Army divisions and separate brigades. After the war in Korea, former General of the Army, President Dwight D. Eisenhower, USMA Class 1915, adopted a military philosophy and posture that emphasized nuclear capability through air power rather than ground combat. Several major considerations were under review: limited resources, world commitment to contain communism, and a desire to reduce defense spending. With a decline in the number of ground combat troops following the end of WWII and Korea, the Army fielded fewer divisions. Yet with the threat of nuclear war, Army leadership wanted to rebuild new units that could fight and survive on a nuclear battlefield, as well as a conventional one. The divisions developed by the Army for these two combat environments were smaller than in the past, and they were authorized equipment and weapons not yet in the inventory.

In April 1954, Army Chief of Staff, General Ridgeway, under continuing pressure from the Department of Defense (DoD) to create smaller units, shifted the emphasis of the divisional studies taking place at that time. Under the newly designed ATFA-1 (Atomic Field Army) the Infantry and Armored divisions were very similar. Within each division's headquarters battalion were new, never before seen units – aviation companies and reconnaissance companies. The strength of the new division stood at 13,500 officers and enlisted men, a cut of nearly 4,000 from the divisions of 1953.[7]

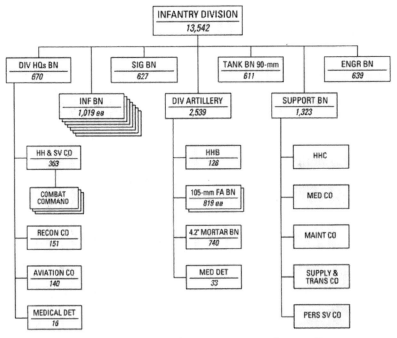

Atomic Field Army Infantry Division October 1954[8]

Within both newly designed divisions, Infantry and Armor, the designers of the ATFA-1 introduced some significant changes. Now all aircraft (and aviators) were gathered from the former aviation sections into an aviation company in the headquarters battalion.

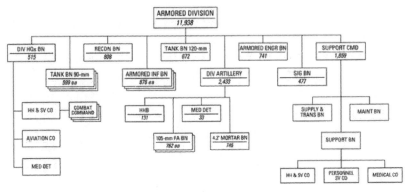

Atomic Field Army Armored Division October 1954[9]

The reality of actual OKARNG Aviation force structure in 1955-56 was that none existed. CW4 Nate Franke, longtime Oklahoma Guardsman recalls, " . . . during this time period, OKARNG Aviation had three sections: Div Arty Avn Sec, Inf Div Avn Sec and 700th Spt Co. Avn Sec. The Div Arty Avn Sec had two OH-23 Hillers and two pilots – warrant officers Don Nave and Bill Imboden."

In 1956, the U.S. Continental Army Command (CONARC), which replaced Army Field Forces, distributed some revised tables of organization (TOEs) for Atomic Field Army Divisions for review and comment. The Atomic Field Army Studies, some of which (Armored Division Tests) were being conducted at Fort Hood, TX. No dramatic changes were recommended in the Armored Division; however, it was recommended that an Aviation company be added for greater flexibility in the use of aircraft.

One of our fellow OKARNG aviators, at that time (1954-55) Second Lieutenant C.L. Strance, was at Fort Hood flying O-1A Bird Dogs. C.L. graduated in 1953 from Oklahoma University at Norman, accepted a

CPT C.L. Strance ca 1965

commission in the Army direct from ROTC and attended Officer Basic Course (OBC) in the Engineer Branch at Fort Belvoir, VA. He then went to fixed-wing flight school at Gary AFB, San Marcos, TX, and tactics at Fort Sill, OK. He was now part of the Army's Armored Division Tests involving the new aviation company in the division. C.L. was involved in many of the various and lengthy tests involving aviation and its relationship in a support role of the Armored Division. C.L. left Fort Hood in 1955 for a three-year accompanied tour in Germany. While there, he was involved in a unique aviation mission involving an overturned U.S. atomic canon. That's a story for later . . .

In 1957, Army literature soon included reports on such ideas as convertiplanes[10], which combined the advantages of rotary-wing and fixed-wing aircraft; one-man flying platforms; and the adoption of pentomic divisions, which fielded nuclear weapons. And during 1958, the

Army bolstered the aviation company with an aircraft field maintenance element, an avionics repair team, and approach control teams. This would lead to the Air Traffic Control (ATC) platoon, and later the ATC Company.

Armored division tests in 1960 led to a number of minor adjustments. These included moving the reconnaissance and surveillance platoon in the reconnaissance squadron to the Aviation company, providing a transportation aircraft maintenance detachment to support the aviation company, and reorganizing the reconnaissance squadron as in the Infantry division.

Oklahoma Army National Guard Aviation began ca 1949-50 with a few aircraft, i.e., the L-14 Army Cruiser (Piper) and the L-15 Scout (Boeing)[11], an OH-23 Hiller or two, and several of the small Aviation sections. As described earlier, it wasn't until in 1954 and after that the Army designed, developed, tested, and implemented the aviation company in the revised and smaller Infantry and Armored divisions.

In the 1957 timeframe, OKARNG Aviation could boast of having Aviation sections at the Infantry Brigade Headquarters, Division Artillery, the Infantry Regiments, Engineer Battalion, and 700th Maintenance Battalion. OKARNG aircraft inventory on hand included three OH-23B model Hillers, several L-19/O-1A Bird Dogs, and a few other light observation fixed-wing aircraft.

Note: All of the following, actual unit names, designations, dates of organizational authority, and federal recognition were obtained by the author from the U.S. Army Center for Military History, located at Fort McNair, Washington, D.C. The primary document that formed and officially stood up a new unit or reorganized or redesignated one, was the organizational authority order number. This does not apply to TDAs formed or reorganized within the Oklahoma State headquarters.

Photo courtesy of COL Karl M. Frank family

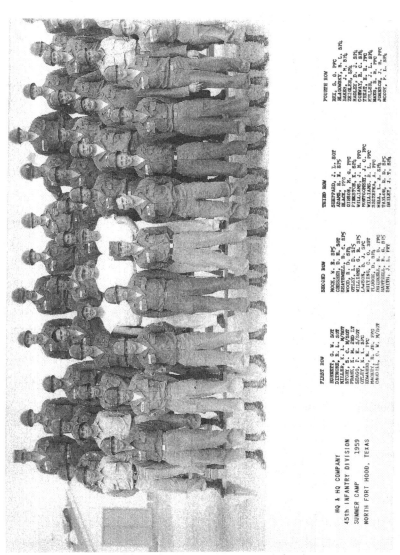

Photo courtesy of COL Karl M. Frank family

Photo courtesy of MAJ (ret) Clarence "C.L." Strance

159

Photo courtesy of MAJ (ret) Clarence "C.L." Strance

1959

The very first organizational-size aviation unit in the OKARNG was

designated the 45th Aviation Company. It was activated and federally recognized on 1 May 1959 at Norman, OK, per organizational authority (OA) 100-59 dated 10 July 1959. Annual training was at Fort Hood, TX, in 1959.

"Everybody, especially the U.S. Air Force, had all kinds of patches. Myself [C.L. Strance] and several others conducted a small contest to determine the best design for a 45th Avn Co unit patch. So we did and had a patch made up. It was simple and had '45th Avn Co' embroidered on it, and we put 'em on our flight suits. We showed up for drill and stood in morning formation outside the old barracks there at Westheimer Field. CPT Butcher (our company commander) stood in front and waited for LTC Gus Guild to come out and speak to us. Guild said, 'Well, I want to commend you guys for the patch. It looks nice! But these patches are not authorized, so take them off.' We got to wear them for that one formation," stated C.L. Strance.

45th Avn Co
(unofficial patch)

According to a former unit member[12], CPT Butcher was the first commander (Cdr) of the 45th Avn Co in 1959. For whatever reason, poor performance or lack of higher grade slots, he didn't get promoted to major, and he got out of the OKARNG. CPT David Vaughn followed Butcher as the next commander ca 1960-62. Vaughn was from Oklahoma City (OKC) and he also didn't get promoted to major; soon he too got out of the OKARNG. Then in the 1962-63 timeframe, a lawyer from Norman, Captain Coy McKinsey was the third commander until the unit was reorganized. Perhaps his luck and timing were better than his two predecessors.

LTC Guild was assigned to the 45th Avn Co from 16 May 1959 to March 1963; his duty position/title was Div Avn Off.

Over the next several years[13] [ca 1958-1963], OKARNG Aviation received several more Hillers for a total of seven helicopters. The inventory was increasing and included a variety of 18 aircraft:

- Four OH-23 Hillers
- Three OH-13 Bells
- One L-17 Navion
- Three L-20 Beavers[14] (later designated as U-6As)
- Seven or eight L-19 Bird Dogs (later designated O-1As)

Our early aviation patriarchs were building the fleet, adding much needed force structure and increasing the aviation support provided to the state's other Guard units. OKARNG Aviation was ever enhancing its own visibility both within Oklahoma and at the national level.

Note: The older OH-23B model had a slanted bubble, unlike the newer rounded bubbles on the "C" and later models. Both had wooden blades that absorbed water and became unbalanced when it rained or if they sat with the blades tied to the tail boom for an extended period.

Thus, in 1959, OKARNG Aviation likely was structured as shown below:

45th Avn Co, Norman, OK
45th Inf Div Hqs [Avn Sec], Edmond, OK
45th Inf Div Arty [Avn Sec], Enid, OK
Avn Sec 1, Bde 45 Inf Div – 179th Inf Regmt
Avn Sec 2, Bde 45 Inf Div – 180th Inf Regmt
Avn Sec 3, Bde 45 Inf Div – 279th Inf Regmt

1960-1961

Annual training was at Fort Hood, TX in 1960 and at Fort Chaffee, AR in 1961.

There were no known or major changes in OKARNG Aviation force structure. Following are the types of aircraft at Norman ca 1960:

- H-19
- L-20 Beaver
- L-19 Bird Dog
- OH-23 Hiller

1962

Annual training was at Fort Polk, LA in 1962.
In 1962[15] Div Arty Avn Sec had the following aircraft:

- OH-23B Hiller
- OH-13 Bell
- L-19 Bird Dog

There were no known or major changes in OKARNG Aviation force structure.

1963

CPT Chester A. Howard is listed on OMD orders as a fixed-wing aviator in HHB, (Unk) How Bn, 30th Arty, Bartlesville, OK. He is promoted to major on 8 May 1963 and became the Bn Cdr, HHC, 45th Avn Bn on 1 May 1963. He served as such until 31 January 1968.

Annual training was at Fort Chaffee, AR in 1963.

The second Aviation unit in the OKARNG was Co B, 45th Aviation Battalion, with federal recognition granted on 1 April 1963 at Oklahoma City, OK, per OA 89-64 dated 19 March 1964. This appears to be quite convoluted; in essence, Co B 45th Avn Bn received federal recognition on 1 April 1963, but the organizational authority (OA) order for the federal recognition wasn't issued until 19 March 1964. Co B 45th Avn Bn was reorganized and formed from the former 45th Avn Co.

A few of the members of Co B, 45th Avn Bn included: MSG E-7 Robert F. Jones Jr., CPT Jerry D. Bourassa, CPT Charlie R. Jones, CW2 Perry H. Townsend Jr., 2LT Emmett D. McElwain, 1LT Richard E. Bailey, 1LT Marlin W. Shears, and CPT Karl M. Frank.

Thus, in 1963, OKARNG Aviation likely was structured as shown below:

HHC, 45th Avn Bn, Norman, OK
Co B, 45th Avn Bn, Norman, OK
45th Inf Div Hqs [Avn Sec], Edmond, OK
45th Inf Div Arty [Avn Sec], Enid, OK
Avn Sec 1, Bde 45 Inf Div – 179th Inf Regmt
Avn Sec 2, Bde 45 Inf Div – 180th Inf Regmt
Avn Sec 3, Bde 45 Inf Div – 279th Inf Regmt

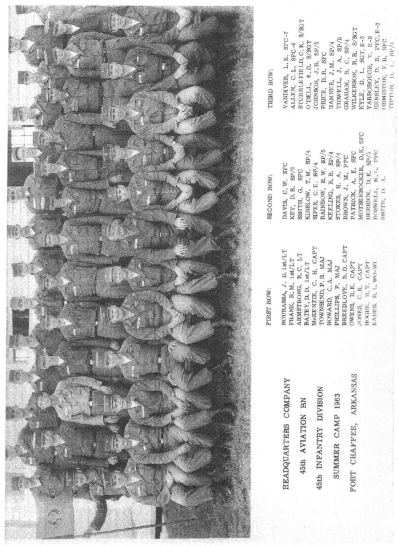

HEADQUARTERS COMPANY

45th AVIATION BN

45th INFANTRY DIVISION

SUMMER CAMP 1963

FORT CHAFFEE, ARKANSAS

FIRST ROW:

BOURASSA, J. D. 1st/LT
FRANK, K. M. 1st/LT
ARMSTRONG, R. C. LT
BATEY, D. D. 1st/LT
McKENZIE, C. H. CAPT
TOWNSEND, P. H. MAJ
HOWARD, C. A. MAJ
PHILLIPS, P. MAJ
BREEDLOVE, B. D. CAPT
OWENS, R. K. CAPT
JONES, C. R. CAPT
HOGUE, R. T. CAPT
KADER, R. L. WO-WI

SECOND ROW:

DAVIS, C. W. SFC
KEY, D. R. SP/5
SMITH, G. SFC
KINSLOW, T. M. SP/4
SIPES, C. E. SP/4
RAINBOW, R. W. SP/5
KEELING, R. B. SP/4
STOKES, H. A. SP/4
BROWN, J. M. PFC
PATRICK, A. E. SFC
MOTSENBOCKER, D. K. SFC
DERRICK, D. E. SP/5
BOSWELL, M. L. PFC
SMITH, D. A.

THIRD ROW:

VANDIVER, L. E. SFC-7
ALLEN, C. L. SFC-6
STUBBLEFIELD, C. K. S/SGT
O'DELL, E. D. S/SGT
JOHNSON, J. B. SP/5
PRICE, D. R. SFC
HAMNER, J. M. SFC
TIDWELL, J. A. SP/5
GRAHAM, B. C. SP/4
WILKERSON, R. R. S/SGT
KYLE, D. L. SGT, E-5
YARBOROUGH, T. E-2
HENSLEY, D. B. PFC, E-3
ORMISTON, F. R. SFC
TIPTON, D. L. SP/4

Photo courtesy of MAJ (ret) Clarence "C.L." Strance

164

Photo courtesy of MAJ (ret) Clarence "C.L." Strance

1964

Annual Training was at Fort Chaffee, AR in 1964.

On 31 March 1964, a Headquarters (Hqs) Detachment (Det) 45th Aviation Battalion was added at Tulsa, OK, per OA 66-64 dated 17 March 1964. This organization was formed from the former Co B, 45th Avn Bn at the same as the 45th Inf Div was undergoing major revisions. OA 89-64 (dated 19 March 1964) extended federal recognition to the old Co B 45th Avn Bn, the new HHD 45th Avn Bn is formed and the issuance of federal recognition to Co B 45th Avn Bn, likely a paperwork correction.

LTC Howard was the first 45th Avn Bn Cdr. Major Pete Phillips[16] was the Executive Officer (XO), CPT C.L. Strance was the S-1, CPT/MAJ Ron Howland was the S-2, CPT/MAJ Robert C. Armstrong was the S-3, and CPT ____ Jackson was the S-4. CPT Robert C. Bob Armstrong was the UA (unit administrator) for the HHD 45th Avn Bn at Tulsa.

A few of the known members of the 45th Avn Bn included: LTC Howard, MAJ Pete Phillips, CPT Dana D. Batey (Maint Off), CPT Ronald L. Howland and CPT Robert C. Armstrong.

SP4 Donald E. Derrick was discharged from the OKARNG at the end of April 1964. However, 2LT Donald E. Derrick was assigned to Co B 45th Avn Bn at Norman as of 1 May 1964, having just graduated from OCS.

In 1964, OKARNG Aviation likely was structured as shown below:

HHD, 45th Avn Bn, Tulsa, OK
Co B, 45th Avn Bn, Norman, OK
45th Inf Div Hqs [Avn Sec], Edmond, OK
45th Inf Div Arty [Avn Sec], Enid, OK
Avn Sec 1, Bde 45 Inf Div – 179th Inf Bn
Avn Sec 2, Bde 45 Inf Div – 180th Inf Bn
Avn Sec 3, Bde 45 Inf Div – 279th Inf Bn

1965

Annual Training was at Fort Chaffee, AR in 1965.

We can see that in 1965, there were more than just a handful of Aviation sections, at least five, plus the Hqs Det, 45th Avn Bn and Co B 45th Avn Bn. Another organizational change took place on 1 November 1965; a new unit was formed – Troop (Trp) D, 1st Squadron (Sqd), 145th Cavalry (CAV) at Norman per OA 89-65 (dated 6 January 1965). This again was a reorganization and redesignation from the former Co B 45th Avn Bn. This unit was an SFR (Special Reactions Forces) element of the 145th Armored Cavalry unit at Marlow, OK. Trp D drilled twice a month at Marlow in OH-13s and H-19s and did 36 AFTPs per year against a standard 24 AFTPs per year. The new Armored Cavalry Aviation unit is shown with the other known OKARNG Aviation units below.

"Trp D was . . . . a split unit; Norman had the maintenance part and we at Marlow had the fighting (guns) part, the Aero Rifle platoon. SFC Bill Ferrell was the AST at Norman, a redheaded guy. I was the 1SG at Marlow. I started off in Marlow in 1953," said Lloyd Todd.[17]

"Don Harvey was the last commander [of Trp D]. Karl Frank had it for a while. Then we had one that lasted for ten minutes! His last name was Hawk. He was one of the IPs at Fort Wolters. Carl Bankman, who was the [ARNG State] auditor, scheduled us for a change of command. I think this was when [CPT] Don Harvey was leaving. They had Hawk scheduled to take command and he had to be there at 10 o'clock that morning to sign the property book as the new commander. And he never showed up. We got to calling and found out the guy (Hawk) had committed suicide that morning. That's when they hollered at Karl Frank to be the commander. It was kinda a quickie deal. Karl was a super commander and so was Don Harvey. We were blessed with some good pilots back then . . . . Don Day, Popplewell, Leroy Wall. The majority of those guys were IPs down at Fort Wolters," added Lloyd Todd.

Major Karl M. Frank was commander[18] of Trp D from 1966-68. Karl retired from the OKARNG in 1983 as a full colonel. Karl had enlisted in the Navy in 1949/50 for two years, and then joined the OKARNG in 1954. In about 1963, COL Frank attended rotary-wing flight school at Camp Wolters and Camp Rucker.

At this same time, some of the known members of Co E, 700th Maint Bn (Avn Maint) included: CPT Jay T. Evans, CPT Thomas R. Nissen[19], CPT Ralph L. Mayfield, 2LT Gwynne L. Sheppard,, 2LT Jimmy A. Watt, CW3 Benny E. Hurd, WO1 Don R. Heath, and WO1 Samuel G. Yates.

In 1965, Captain Robert C. Armstrong was assigned to Co E 700 Maint Bn.

"1965, Co D 700th Spt was Aviation Maintenance, still part of 45th [Inf] Div. At that time, I think we only had the 45th Avn Bn. That's where we got a whole bunch of maintenance people when they reorganized in 1968 – Leo Keenan, Joe D'Amico, come over to 45th Avn Bn. . . . It was Army Aviation is what it was. And they were working around Guard Bureau programs and everything to keep aviation in Oklahoma. . . . You know that's what Batey spent his whole life doing, keeping aviation in Oklahoma," emphatically stated by Charlie Evans.[20]

Following are the OKARNG Aviation units and sections that were substantiated in 1965 by OAs and individual general, special and permanent orders. Note the unusual names given to the 45th Inf Div Bde Avn Sections:

HHD, 45th Avn Bn, Tulsa, OK

Co B, 45th Avn Bn, Norman, OK – (deactivated by the reorg of Trp D)

45th Inf Div Hqs [Avn Sec], Edmond, OK

45th Inf Div Arty [Avn Sec], Enid, OK

Avn Sec 1, Bde 45 Inf Div – 179th Inf Bn

Avn Sec 2, Bde 45 Inf Div – 180th Inf Bn

Avn Sec 3, Bde 45 Inf Div – 279th Inf Bn

Trp D, 1st Sqd, 145th CAV

Flight Opns Section

Aero Scout Platoon

Service Platoon

Co E 700 Maint Bn, Ardmore, OK (there was no official name attached, such as Avn Sec or Avn Maint)

1966

Annual training was at Fort Chaffee, AR in 1966.

During the mid-1960s, what could be described as a turf war took place between the U.S. Army and U.S. Air Force. The Air Force argued that they were the military branch tasked with providing air resources, and that they should rightfully be operating the CV-2 (Army Caribou). In 1966, that debate was concluded with the transfer of all the Army Caribou units in Vietnam to the Air Force. Army Caribous were CV-2As and CV-2Bs; USAF changed the designation to C-7A and rapidly took over all in-country operations. Initially, there were six C-7A squadrons; two at Vung Tau, two at Cam Rahn Bay, and two at Phu Cat. By the end of the war, combat losses had reduced the squadron count to five; four at Cam Rahn and one at Phu Cat. The USAF never did provide unit-level cargo support or aerial delivery as promised.

There were no known or major changes in OKARNG Aviation force structure in 1966.

<u>1967</u>

There were no known or major changes in OKARNG Aviation force structure.

<u>1968</u>

Another totally new aviation unit was formed on 1 February 1968—the 245[21] Medical Company (Air Ambulance) at Norman, OK, per OA 88-67 (dated 31 December 1967). This new aviation company was formed from elements of the HHC 120[22] Engineers. These were new, additional slots added to OKARNG Aviation's force structure, taken from the HHC, 120th Engineers. It was located at Oklahoma City and Norman, OK. The authorized strength was 27 officers, 0 warrant officers and 121 enlisted men.

"This was the first major reorg in the OKARNG since WWII (and Korea). The National Guard was just gone while the 45th Inf Div was in Korea. They were trying to reorganize aviation and they put detachments . . . Det 3 and 4 at Norman. The aircraft and maintenance were at Norman. It was kinda of a foggy period there from '68-'72," remembered CW4 Charlie Evans.[23]

This Air Ambulance unit "was formed at the 2222 SW 44th Street Armory [in OKC] as part of the 120th Med Bn. I was assigned as a SP6 medic and was considered a crewmember. SP4 Jack Nation was assigned there also and had duties as a crew chief. We kinda worked our way up from there," said Charlie Evans.[24]

Simultaneously, another aviation reorganization and name change occurred. The second new unit in 1968 was the 145th Aviation Company[25], also activated on 1 February 1968, at Norman per OA 88-67 (dated 31 December 1967). This was a reorganization and redesignation formed from elements of the former Trp D, 1st Sqd, 145th CAV unit. CPT Dana D. Batey was a Plt Cdr in HHD 45th Avn Bn on 1 February 1968. The 45th Avn Bn was deactivated at this same time, 1 February 1968. The authorized strength was 14 officers, 24 warrant officers, and 97 enlisted men.

LTC J.R. Dome was an Army aviation advisor for the 145th Avn Co. and very respected by the OKARNG Aviation personnel. He was the Army Aviation Advisor assigned to OKARNG Aviation from 1967/68 to 1971.

MAJ Clarence L. C.L. Strance was the first commander of the 245th Medical Co (Air Amb) unit (February – May 1968), which was part of the 120th Medical Battalion in Oklahoma City. CPT Karl M. Frank was assigned as station commander[26] of the Norman element. The 1SG was Tommy J. Hawkins; CPT Jack E. Avant was the Flt Ops Officer, and SFC George Droescher was the Flt Ops Chief. CPT Jerry D. Bourassa was the Maint Plt Ldr; CPT James L. Smith was the First Helicopter Plt Ldr; CPT Donald L. Nave was the Second Helicopter Plt Ldr; CPT Karl M. Frank was the Third Helicopter Plt Ldr; and CPT Donald L. Taylor was the Fourth Helicopter Plt Ldr.

On 28 May 1968, MAJ Charlie R. Jones took command from MAJ Strance (May 1968—June 1970). MAJ Jerry Bourassa, from Wanette, OK, was the third original commander of the new 245th Med Co (Air Amb) at Norman, September 1970 – June 1973. Part of the unit was at the SW 44th St. Armory in OKC, and the remainder was at the Norman Armory. Jones was commander when SSG Charlie Evans left the unit in August 1968.

The 245th Med Co (Air Amb) had several H-19 helicopters and established a common load of mobile hospital items: cots, blankets, and medical supplies during 1968.

OMD orders, dated 16 January 1968, note that the first commander of the 145th Aviation Company was MAJ Pete Phillips, and although it is not listed on this order, CPT Ronald L. Howland was appointed Executive Officer on 11 March 1968. The Flight Operations Officer was CPT Frank Cory, General Support Platoon Cdr was CPT Jay T. (Tommy) Evans, Aero Scout Plat Cdr was CPT Dana D. Batey, and the Service Platoon Cdr was CPT Ralph Mayfield.

MAJ Pete Phillips was the XO of the 45th Avn Bn.[27] On 16 January 1968, MAJ Pete Phillips was released as XO, HQ 45th Avn Bn and assigned as Co Cdr 145th Avn Co. Pete was the first commander of the 145th Avn Co at Norman, OK. The Senior NCO for the 145th Avn Co was 1SG Ivel Cypert, appointed 1SG on 16 September, replacing 1SG Kenneth A. Inman. SSG Rudie Leippe was appointed Maintenance Supervisor also on 16 September, replacing SSG Arthur W. Rames.

Before its deactivation on 1 February 1968, some of the members of Trp D, 1st Sqd, 145th CAV included: CPT Don L. Hayes, 2LT Tommie Jones, CPT Patrick M. Goerig, 1LT Gwynne L. Sheppard, CW2 John M. Johnston, CW2 Reagan E. Popplewell, CW2 Frank L. Berry, CW2

Clarence R. Clarkson Jr., CW2 Billy W. Good, CW2 Leroy A. Wall, CW2 Donald R. Key, and WO1 John R. Dollins.

CPT Dana D. Batey, an Armor officer, was awarded the designation of Senior Army Aviator on 19 April 1968, signed by COL Francis A. Santangelo, NGB, Chief, Army Org. and Tng. Div. Batey was a member of 145th Avn Co, Tulsa, OK, according to the letter order.

Note: There was no aviation unit or section assigned or stationed a Tulsa, OK from February 1968, when 45th Avn Bn was deactivated, until January 1978, when Det 1, 445th Avn Co comes to "T town."

Therefore, here is a recap of what OKARNG Aviation should have looked like in 1968:

HHD, 45th Avn Bn[28] (45th Avn Bn ceases to exist on 1 February 1968)

HHC, 45th Inf Div Hqs [Avn Sec], Edmond, OK

HHB, 45th Inf Div Arty [Avn Sec], Enid, OK

Avn Sec 1 Bde 45 Inf Div [Avn Sec]—officially part of 120th Med

Avn Sec 2 Bde 45 Inf Div [Avn Sec]—officially part of 120th Med

Co E, 700th Maint Bn [Avn Sec], Ardmore, OK

Co E, 120th Engr Bn [Avn Sec] (aviators were assigned to Engineer slots as excess)

Trp D, 1st Sqd, 145th CAV (deactivated in December with the formation of 145th Avn Co)

Helicopter Platoon
Flight Opns Section
Aero Scout Platoon[29]
Service Platoon
Aero Weapons Section
245th Med Co (Air Amb)

145th Avn Company (formed from elements of the former Trp D, 1st Sqd, 145th CAV)

1969

1969 began the second year of both the 145th Avn Co. and the 245th Med Co. The 245th Med Co (Air Amb) is a subordinate organizational unit of OKARNG's 120th Medical Battalion.

In September, the 245th bivouacked at Goldsby Airport, south of Norman. In October they decided it was so much fun, they did another on the Lexington Game Reserve and also did a night march. These guys had become serious, thinking, hoping they might get a chance for Vietnam.

A change of command in the 145th Avn Co took place this year; MAJ Pete Phillips was reassigned to the 45th Inf Brigade Staff and CPT Jay T. Tommy Evans was promoted to major and appointed as company commander. Twenty-five aviators of the 145th maintained a high level of flight proficiency during 1969, while six officers, one warrant officer, and one enlisted man were accepted into U.S. Army Aviation flight school, after flight school had been closed to the National Guard for several years due to the Vietnam war.

In December 1969, five OH-13s and two CH-34 helicopters arrived at the 145th Avn Co., Norman, OK, location. However, the OKARNG had to turn in all of its O1-A Bird Dogs to the active Army, again for Vietnam.

MAJ Jones was the 245th Med Co (Air Amb) Cdr. The 1SG was Tommy J. Hawkins; CPT James L. Smith was the Flt Ops Officer, and SFC George Droescher was the Flt Ops Chief. CPT Jerry D. Bourassa was the Maint Plt Ldr and his Plt SGT was William "Bill" Rogers; CPT Donald L. Nave was the First Helicopter Plt Ldr; CPT Larry G. Schlotfelt was the Second Helicopter Plt Ldr; CPT Donald L. Taylor was the Third Helicopter Plt Ldr and 2LT Ronald K. Varner was the Third Plt Training Officer; and CPT Karl M. Frank was the Fourth Helicopter Plt Ldr and station commander. The Airfield Service Platoon was led by SGT Hugh E. McGovern Jr. CPT Jack E. Avant reverted to WO in 1969. And CPT Curtis R. Cline temporarily stood in as Acting Co Cdr for Charlie Jones while he did a 90-day tour of ADT at the Pentagon.

2LT Donald E. Derrick is listed as an Evac Pilot in (3rd and 4th Plts) 245th Med Co (Air Amb).

In 1969, OKARNG Aviation was structured as shown below:
HHC, 45th Inf Div Hqs [Avn Sec[30]], Edmond, OK
HHB, 45th Inf Div Arty [Avn Sec], Enid, OK
245th Med Co (Air Amb), OKC
HHC, 120th Med [Avn Sec], OKC
Co E, 700th Maint Bn [Avn Sec], Ardmore, OK
Co E, 120th Engr Bn [Avn Sec], Okmulgee, OK
245th Med Co (Air Amb), Norman, OK
145th Avn Company, Norman, OK

<u>1970</u>

The 145th Avn Company's air fleet increased with the addition of three CH-34 Choctaw helicopters and five OH-13 Sioux helicopters. "As the year ended, word had been received that sometime during 1971 the 145th Avn Co could expect the addition of at least three UH-1s [Iroquois]."[31] Unit strength grew to 129 in 1970. In September 1970, CPT Preston Perry became Plt Ldr for the Gen Spt Plt, and in December, CPT Clarence C. Buxton III, from Ada, OK, was appointed Maint Plt Ldr. CPT Tony E. Boyle was an Aero Scout Plt Ldr.

Later in 1970, CPT Dana Batey moved from the 145th Avn Co and was reassigned as the Section Leader of the 45th Inf Bde Avn Sec. The section was located at Norman and had +/- 6 OH-23s and +/- 3 OH-13s, according to CWO Frank Lillard Berry of Konawa, OK, who was an aviator in that section at this time.

On 26 May 1970, CPT Dale E. Martin replaced CPT Jerry D. Bourassa as 245th Med Co Maint Plt Ldr. CPT Donald E. Derrick is listed as the First Flt Plt Ldr. Then on 15 September, Bourassa replaced Charlie Jones as commander of the 245th Med Co, and CPT Bourassa was promoted to major on 19 October 1970. CPT Donald L. Taylor reverted to WO in December 1970.

"I went full-time for the Guard in 1970 . . . that was the year the Guard got Huey's and we still had aircraft like the OH-23 and OH-13 and some UH-19s and CH-34s. [Then] the unit moved to Tulsa in 1978 and became the [Co D (-) 149th Avn [Bn] with Huey gunships," stated Don McCarty.[32]

There were no known or major changes in OKARNG Aviation force structure in 1970.

<u>1971</u>

In the *Sunday Oklahoman*, dated 18 July 1971, an article appeared with the headline "State National Guard to Add Unit of Assault Helicopters," by Pete Feldman, staff writer. Governor David Hall is quoted, "The brand new unit, the 445th Aviation Co., is being formed. This will be an assault helicopter unit, with the Huey Cobra of Vietnam battle action as the backbone. The unit will have six of the Cobra attack helicopters backed up by another 31 Huey (UH-1) choppers under optimum conditions . . . The company, when fully formed, will have a component of 234 enlisted men, 14 officers and 55 warrant officers. Of the 69 officers and warrant officers, 68 will be helicopter pilots."

MAJ Karl M. Frank

The article goes on to add, "The 445th is commanded by Capt. Karl M. Frank of Moore, and based at the guard's Norman aviation center. The 145th Aviation Co. is also based there. Actual 445th headquarters will be in Midwest City. The 445th was the former 245th Air Ambulance Co."

Feldman noted that the Cobras cost $500,000 each and would "come through in fiscal year 1973." The 31 airlift evacuation choppers [UH-1s] cost $250,000 each.

The 445th Aviation Company was officially federally recognized at Norman, OK, per OA 98-71 (dated 14 May 1971). This reorganization and redesignation was created from the former 145th Avn Co and the 245th Med Co (Air Amb) units. This new aviation organization became the premier aviation unit in the OKARNG and the largest unit up until this time. Over the first several years of its existence, it received many, many accolades.

445th Aviation Company (Assault Helicopter) Norman, OK

	Auth/Assg
Company Headquarters	24/24
Operations Platoon	13/13
First Airlift Platoon	31/28
Second Airlift Platoon	31/30
Armed Helicopter Platoon	26/24
Service Platoon Hqs	17/14
Aircraft Sys Repair Sec	23/22
Aircraft Maint Sec	19/19
Aircraft Armament Sec	12/9
Avionics Repair Sec	15/9
Airfield Svc Sec	13/7

Flight Surgeon Detachment 5/5
Total auth/assg   229/204

The commanders of the 445th Avn Co were MAJ Jerry Bourassa[33] (ca 1968-1972), then MAJ Karl M. Frank while the unit was at Norman (ca 1973), and then when it moved to Lexington, OK, 15 September 1975. CPT Donald E. Derrick was a Plt Cdr in the first or second Air Lift (Armed Hel and Svc Plts) 445th Avn Co (Aslt Hel) at Norman. CPT Dale E. Martin was appointed as the Operations Officer for the 445th Avn Co at Norman on 15 May 1971. The 445th Avn Co moved from Norman to Lexington in September 1975, and Dale remained the Opns Officer until 20 February 1976. CPT Donald L. Nave was also a member of the 445th Avn Co in 1971.

Prior to the 445th Avn Co reorganization, a few known members of the 145th Avn Co. in 1971 included[34]: MAJ Ronald L. Howland, CPT Frank A. Cory, 1LT Morris W. Hale, 1LT Tommy Klutts Jr., 1LT Richard W. Wilson, CW4 Benny E. Hurd, CW2 Warren L. Applegate, CW2 Frank L. Berry, CW4 Joe Patterson (former B-24 pilot in WWII), CW2 Bobby J. Swink, CW2 Leroy A. Wall, WO1 Wayne R. Teague, WO1 Danny Washa, CPT Dana D. Batey (Flt Opns Off)[35], CW2 Douglas L. Gandy, and CW2 William N. Jackson Jr.

During August 1971, the 45th Field Arty Gp Avn Sec included: CW2 Bobby D. Breedlove, CW2 Bill J. Hensley II, CW2 Douglas W. Jones, CW2 Stephen Sneed, and WO1 Robert S. McGee.

That same August 1971, CPT Robert C. Armstrong was listed as being in Co D, 700th Spt Bn Avn Sec., and MAJ Tommy Evans was in the OMD Cmd Avn Sec.

According to CW5 Clarence R. Clarkson, "There were Artillery and Engineer Avn sections about the same time the Bde Avn Section began. CPT Bill Snyder was the Arty Avn Sec Cdr, Bobby Breedlove was in that section and so was CWO Roy Brown. Charlie Coats and "Sonny" Bishop were in the Eng Avn Section at Okmulgee. These two sections had five or six OH-58s then."

Therefore, in 1971, OKARNG Aviation was structured as follows:
HHC, 45th Inf Div Hqs [Avn Sec], Edmond, OK
HHB, 45th Inf Div Arty [Avn Sec], Enid, OK
HHC, 120th Med [Avn Sec], OKC
Co E, 700th Maint Bn [Avn Sec], Ardmore, OK

Co E, 120th Engr Bn [Avn Sec], Okmulgee, OK
245th Med Co (Air Amb), OKC (deactivated in May 1971)
145th Avn Company (deactivated in May 1971)
445th Avn Co (Asslt Hel), Norman, OK (OH-23s) (activated 15 May 1971)
Note: In October 1971, Aviation was moved out from under Hqs, 120th Medical Battalion control to the 245th Transportation Battalion at Ardmore, OK.

1972

"During the drawdown of [forces] in Vietnam, in1970-71 we [NGB] began to issue UH-1s to the states. We still have a few UH-1s flying [in the ARNG today]" stated BG Alberto Jose Jimenez, former Chief, NGB Aviation and Safety Division, former Special Assistant to the Director, ARNG, and former Assistant AG Maryland, during an interview on 10 January 2007.

Annual training for OKARNG Aviation was at Ft. Carson, CO in August 1972.

During March 1972, Smallbore rifle matches were held at the 23rd Street Armory, Oklahoma City. SFC Charlie H. Evans was listed among the participants from the 245th Med Co.

In 1972, OKARNG Aviation was structured as follows:
HHC (-) 45 Inf Bde (Sep) [Bde Avn Sec], Edmond, OK
HHB, 45th Inf Div Arty [Avn Sec] Enid, OK
HHC, 120th Med [Avn Sec], OKC
Co E, 120th Engr Bn [Avn Sec] Okmulgee, OK
Co E, 700th Maint Bn [Avn Sec], Ardmore, OK
445th Avn Co (Asslt Hel), Norman, OK
Note: According to OMD SO #265, 20 October 1972 ,there were 14 aviators assigned to HHC (-) 45 Inf Bde (Sep) [Bde Avn Sec].

1973

About April 1973, aviator qualification check rides and written examinations were conducted for the 445th Avn Co (Assault Hel). "Preparation was under way for Instrument Flight Training Classes to be conducted at the Army Aviation Support Facility Norman, OK, for six separate classes of thirty days duration scheduled to qualify all assigned aviators on instruments by December 1973."[36]

During June, MAJ Jerry D. Bourassa resigned as 445th Aviation company commander and transferred to HHD, OKARNG. CPT Karl M. Frank was assigned as the new commander, and CPT Donald E. Derrick was appointed as the Executive Officer.

In 1973, under the command of MAJ Karl M. Frank, with 1SG Kenneth Inman as the Senior NCO, the 445th Aviation Company (Assault Helicopter) won the prestigious and coveted 5th Army AAAA Outstanding Aviation Unit of the Year Award.[37]

CPT Donald E. Derrick was the Company Executive Officer from 25 June 1973 – 26 July 1976.

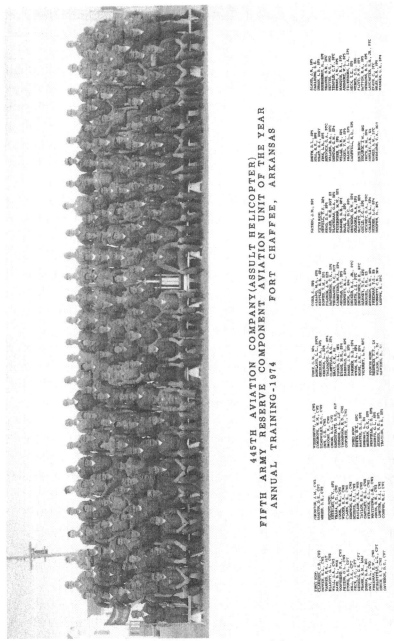

Photo courtesy of COL Karl M. Frank family

During the 1969-84 period, the Army Aviation Association presented an Outstanding Reserve Component Aviation Unit Award that recognized annual outstanding unit accomplishments within the Army National Guard and U.S. Army Reserve. The Army National Guard's aviation units won the award in 14 of the 16 years in which it was presented by the AAAA. In late 1985, the Association established separate Aviation Unit Awards for both the Army National Guard and the U.S. Army Reserve, with each trophy being sponsored by Honeywell.

There were no known or major changes in OKARNG Aviation force structure in 1973.

1974

The 445th Aviation Company (Asslt Hel) stationed at Norman, OK, replaced its OH-23s, H-19 Chickasaws and CH-34 Choctaws with UH-1 Hueys during the 1971-74 time period. There were numerous Vietnam vets in the OKARNG in 1974, and the 445th had a gun platoon along with a slick (lift) platoon. Some of the early Vietnam returnees were CPT Tony Boyles, from Tahlequah, OK, CPT John Burle, CPT Ray Brown, CPT Paul D. Pete Costilow , Yukon, OK and CPT Buck Buxton, from Ada, OK.

According to OMD SO #201(dated 20 August 1974) there were 13 aviators assigned to HHC (-) 45 Inf Bde (Sep) [Bde Avn Sec], at Norman, OK, and there were approximately 35 aviators on flight status assigned to OKARNG per OMD SO #131 (dated 1 June 1974).

There were no known or major changes in the OKARNG Aviation force structure in 1974.

1975

Captain Emmett D. McElwain was Aviation section commander of the

HHC (-) 45th Inf Bde (Sep) [Bde Avn Sec], assigned to Edmond, OK, with aircraft stationed at Lexington, OK, per OMD SO #190 (dated 8 August 1975). This section had about 13 aviators.

"Congratulations to each member of the 445th Aviation Company (Assault Helicopter), you are a definite asset to our Nations' Defense and a great credit to the Oklahoma Army National Guard." Those were the words of COL W.C. Milligan, Assistant Chief of Staff-Operations for Oklahoma as the unit [445th Avn Co] was presented with the National

Guard Bureau's Superior Unit Award for 1974 during the March [1975] drill assembly.

With the awards over, successful completion of the COMET inspection, and range firing near completion, the unit went back to the classroom for instruction and MOS-OJT training. Armed UH-1s fired rockets and mini-guns at Fort Chaffee during March 1975 in conjunction with aerial gunnery qualification.

The 445th Avn Co (Asslt Hel) was relocated from Max Westheimer Field at Norman, OK, to the new Army Aviation Support Facility located six miles east of Lexington, OK on 15 September 1975, per OA 422-75 (dated 26 August 1975). Since the new armory wasn't completed, a corner of the new AASF hangar floor served as temporary quarters for the 445th Avn Co. A request to reschedule the Annual General Inspection (AGI) in January 1976 was approved so that the 445th could begin nap of the earth training on the new Hal Muldrow Heliport land and the Lexington Wildlife Management Area.

LTC J. Robert Dille
flight surgeon

On 17 December 1975, LTC John R. Dille was appointed as the flight surgeon replacing LTC David J. Geigerman, who accepted a three-year Title 10 tour as the first flight surgeon for the newly formed NGB Aviation Division, under COL Charlie R. Jones.

There were very few other personnel changes for the 445th Avn Co this year.

In 1975, OKARNG Aviation was structured as shown below:

HHC (-) 45 Inf Bde (Sep) [Bde Avn Sec], Edmond, OK
HHB, 45th Inf Div Arty [Avn Sec] Enid, OK
HHC, 120th Med [Avn Sec] OKC
Co E, 120th Engr Bn [Avn Sec] Okmulgee, OK
Co E, 700th Maint Bn [Avn Sec] Ardmore, OK
445th Avn Co (Asslt Hel), Lexington, OK

There were no other known or major changes in OKARNG Aviation force structure in 1975.

1976

Lexington held its annual 89er Day Celebration, and the enthusiastic members of the 445th were there recruiting new members. This was the first public showing of Dana D. Batey's UH-1 Huey static display mounting on a two-axle trailer.

During the 11 July drill, MAJ Frank read orders to the members of the 445th Avn Co and said, "In an effort to increase the authorized strength of the 245th Transportation Battalion, the 445th Avn Co (Aslt Hel) will be assigned to the 245th Trans Bn effective 1 August 1976." Summer camp 1976, combined with elements of the Texas ARNG and the 445th Avn Co, was said to have been the best ever and achieved one of its highest levels of effectiveness in its history.

MAJ Donald E. Derrick became the company commander of the 445th Avn Co (Aslt Hel) on 26 July 1976 and served until 31 December 1977, when the unit was redesignated (see 1978).

In August 1976, an Instrument Qualification Course was conducted at home station (Lexington) during annual training, which qualified seven aviators.

The 445th Avn Co conducted ceremonies for the new Armory at Lexington on 24 October 1976, which included an open house and dedication ceremony. The unit was proud of its new armory. The day was cold and dreary, however, approximately 1,200 people, fellow OKARNG guardsmen, family and visiting dignitaries.

Changes during 1976 in the 445th Avn Co include the following: On 13 January, SP5 John T. Ashmore replaced SFC George Droescher as Flt Ops Chief; On 10 January, SFC Nathan D. Franke replaced 1SG Kenneth A. Inman as 1SG; On 25 January, SP6 Leo Keenan replaced SFC Dale Beets as Maint Sup. CPT Donald E. Derrick was appointed Commanding Officer on 26 June, replacing MAJ Karl M. Frank, who transferred to 45th Spt Cen (RAO). CPT Dale E. Martin became the new XO and CPT Tony E. Boyle was the new Flt Ops Officer. On 9 July, SFC Charles H. Evans was appointed as WO1 and assigned as Unit Pers Tech filling a new MTOE position. SP5 James E. Carpenter was assigned as Pers SGT, also filling a new MTOE position.

CW3 Leroy A. Wall was listed as the rotary-wing instrument examiner for the 445th. CW2 Bobby J. Swink resigned as Acft Maint Sec Ldr on 10 July and CW2 Ernest E. Eadelman was his replacement. CPT James C. Peck became the Plt Ldr for the Armed Hel Plt. CPT Gary A. Elliott became the First Sec Cdr of the Armed Hel Plt, and CW2 Robert E. Clark was appointed a captain and assigned as Second Sec Cdr of the Armed Hel Plt.

SP5 Rodney Smothers, SP5 Donald L. Combs, SP6 Leo Keenan, SP6 James W. Perry, and SP6 Harvey L. Roseberry were all in the Aircraft Maint Sec. SSG Jerry W. Kirby joined SSG Willis G. Bettes in the Aircraft Armament Sec. SSG Jimmy R. Nunley, SP5 Glen W. Red Rowland, SP4 Henry H. Lancaster, SP4 Roger D. Farley, and PV2 William E. Lee made up the Airfield Service Section.

There were no known or major changes in OKARNG Aviation force structure in 1976.

1977

The 445th Avn Co began 1977 with the recognition of a need to train for armed conflict in a mid-intensity environment, which prompted the Constant Change unit [445th] to request assistance from aviation personnel with real experience from the 101st Airborne Division (Air Assault). Three SMEs were sent from Fort Campbell, KY, to Lexington, OK, for 15 and 16 January drill. Further tactical training followed.

SGT Frank Wellner joined Airfield Services Section and CW2 Rex L. Bowen II was assigned as an Acft Repair Tech, replacing CW2 Eadelman on 1 April.

There were no known or major changes in OKARNG Aviation force structure in 1977.

1978

1978 was a red letter year for OKARNG Aviation. Several new aviation units were added or reorganized and another first – a real, organizational aviation unit in Tulsa. On 1 October 1978, Det 1, Command & Control Hqs was constituted and organized[38] at Lexington, OK. Det 1, C & C was, in

LTC Ronald L. Howland

182

COL Batey's terms (SAO at this time), a quasi aviation headquarters, but none the less it was more than had been on the ground before! It included a total of 21 personnel assigned and 14 personnel attached. Attached personnel are listed in the elements below Cmd & Staff:

> Cmd & Staff
> Flight Surgeon Detachment
> Aviation Fire/Crash Rescue
> Avionics Dir Spt Maint

As the Det 1, C & C Hqs existed for about 3 years, the list of commanders is not long either. The first Cdr was LTC Ronald L. Howland of OKC (ca 1978-1979), followed by LTC Donald Derrick (ca 1979–1980) and LTC Emmett D. McElwain, from Byars, OK (ca October 1980-82).

MAJ Donald E. Derrick was commander when the 445th Avn Co is reorganized on 1 January 1978, per OA 182-77 dated 25 October 1977 and remains at Lexington. The last company commander of the 445th Avn Co (Aslt Hel) at Lexington was MAJ Ray Brown in 1978.

And on 30 September 1978, Co B, 149th Aviation was formed at Lexington per OA 234-78 (dated 26 September 1978), from the old 445th Avn Co. The new Co B, 149th Avn was part of the Texas ARNG's 149th Avn Bn.

We can identify most of the Co B 149th Avn Co commanders: the first being MAJ James C. Jim Peck, from OKC (1 October 1978 – 16 June 1980), 1SG Jack Nation, MAJ Larry Graham, from Cache, OK (17 June 1980 – December 1982), 1SG Jack Nation, and MAJ Alfred F. Dreves Jr., from Lawton, OK, (ca 1983 – 85), 1SG Jack Nation. MAJ Michael D. Whitlow (ca 1985 – October 1987), and 1SG James W. Perry followed Al Dreves, and then MAJ Jackie L. Self from 1 November 1987 to 31 August 1991.

Also in January of 1978, Det 1, 445th Avn Co[39] received federal recognition. This detachment was located at the 15th Street armory in Tulsa, OK, with the 445 Aviation Company headquarters located in Lexington. Det 1 was a small gun unit with 50 personnel, three UHIM gunships and two OH58 aircraft. Det 1 was located at the 15th Street armory in Tulsa, OK, and preceded Co D (-) (Attack Helicopter) 149th Avn Bn.

"CPT Dale Martin and LTC Tommy Evans were both techs at the AASF in Lex and went to Tulsa as techs [for Det 1 445]. Don McCarty, Wheeler Parker, Ernie Moore and Greg Stilwell were all enlisted at that time and also went as Techs . . . . I think there were a couple of others, but that was a long time ago and I have slept some since then . . . and I think all four of them were appointed as WOs in the Guard. Tommy Evans was [assigned M-day] in the HQ OKARNG [but worked at the Tulsa Flight Activity]. I think since he was a lieutenant colonel, and at that time major was the highest [authorized] rank that 445th had," stated CW4 Charlie H. Evans.[40]

CWO Garry O. Bentley was one of the M-day members of Det 1, 445th Avn Co.

"They [Det 1, 445] weren't fully established and were flying [Hueys] from Lexington to Tulsa for drill and AFTPs . . . SFC McCarty, SSG Greg Stilwell, SSG Wheeler Parker, Dan Crocker, MAJ Tommy Evans, State Safety Officer, senior IP. I think they were all [Tulsa] full-timers at that time. They all transferred from Lexington to Tulsa. SSG Gene Paine was the UA (Unit Administrator). MAJ [Dale E.] Martin was the facility Cdr and the Det [1, 445] Cdr. That [unit] lasted until October '78 and then it became Co D (-) 149th Avn Bn. What happened was me and SGT Don Russell got hired [on] 26 September '78 as the first two full-time techs at Tulsa," explained Norm Crowe.[41]

"Well, the other half of Co [D (-) 149th] was in Arizona. A smaller detachment was there [in AZ, who had the XO] like one platoon . . . in Phoenix, AZ. We started forming up, enlisting a lot of people, getting new people in '78 & '79 we kinda built up. We started our [2.75mm] rocket program, shooting and everything. Our first AT was at Ft Rucker, AL the next year, like July '79," said Crowe.

Bobby Lane[42] stated, "[Initially] we drilled in Lexington, I drove back and forth the day of AFTPs and drilled at Lexington—in '79 I think we moved to Tulsa. We were [an] AAFA (Army Aviation Flight Activity) . . . we didn't have a full [AASF] facility. We used to fly—do Friday night AFTPs—kept one Huey up here. We'd [load up a Huey w/pilots] fly Friday night AFTPs . . . to Lexington, [and] we'd pick up helicopters and bring them up here, do our drill and we'd fly 'em back down there [to Lex] on Sunday drill and ride back in that one Huey, 'cause we didn't have the facilities to prepare or do [maintenance], we just had a

Flight Activities [status]. Didn't have very many people . . . . Then when we started getting the full AASF, they started keeping aircraft up here."

CPT Dale E. Martin commanded this unit from 1 January 1978 until it was reorganized and replaced in October 1978.

Then on 1 October 1978, another new unit, Company D (-) 149th Aviation Battalion was formed and redesignated from the former Det 1, 445th Avn Co. MAJ Dale E. Martin commanded Co D (-) from the beginning until 15 June 1980, at which time MAJ Vern R. Ashbrook took command. MAJ Martin (tech) was the Tulsa Flight Activity full-time commander. The unit had an authorized strength of 127 personnel, seven UH-1Ms, and six OH-58s; it remained located in Tulsa and the 15th Street Armory. OKARNG instructor pilots (IPs) and aviators became qualified on the weapons systems mounted on the OKARNG UH-1M aircraft[43]. These armament subsystems included the M158 – 7 tube 2.75 in. rocket launcher, the M5 – 40mm grenade launcher, and the M21 – 7.62mm 'mini-gun'. "Co D (-) was part of the Arizona ARNG Attack Battalion," according to COL John J. Stanko Jr.

On 24 October 1978, certain members of Co D (-) 149th Avn Bn, gun platoon flew a four-day AFTP trip from Oklahoma to Ft Bliss, El Paso, TX, to Yuma, then Phoenix, AZ, and back to LEX AASF. Purpose – "the long way . . . out to gun range. [The 149th Avn Bn] Arizona folks had an old car [out there] with a really old inter-spring mattress tied to the top to welcome the us Okies to Arizona!," remembered C.L. Strance[44]

Thus, in 1978, OKARNG Aviation was structured as shown below:

Det 1, Cmd & Control Hqs, Lexington, OK
Det 2, HHC (-) 45 Inf Bde (Sep) [Bde Avn Sec][45], Edmond, OK
HHB, 45th Inf Div Arty [Avn Sec] Enid, OK
HHC 145th Avn Bn (PROV), Lexington
445th Avn Co (Asslt Hel), Norman, OK (deactivated on 1 October 1978)
Det 1, 445th Avn Co Tulsa, OK (deactivated on 1 October 1978)
Co B, 149th Avn Bn[46], Lexington, OK–activated/replaced 445 Avn Co.
Co D (-) 149th Avn Co[47], Tulsa, OK
OKSTARC Fixed-wing section, Norman, OK

1979

There was one known and major addition to OKARNG Aviation force structure in 1979. The new TO&E unit was a significant addition to aviation in Oklahoma. The 145th Air Traffic Control (ATC) Platoon was constituted on 1 April 1979, at Lexington, OK per OA 61-79 (dated 15 March 1979) and federally recognized per OA 86-79 (dated 21 May 1979).

Former 145th ATC commanders include: CW2 Mike Patterson, who was the first commander in 1979 and MSG Levi Orphan was senior NCO, then came CW2 William "Bill" Rogers,[48] then MAJ James Crawford, who commanded from 15 December 1982 – 15 August 1984 with MSG David Keating. CPT Mayo Elliott was next (ca 1984-85), again MSG David Keating was senior NCO, then CPT Vicki Glass and MSG David Keating, followed by CPT Ramon Claudio Rivera with SSG Darryl Anderson as Senior NCO, and later 1LT Michael Thomason. This commander and senior NCO list is incomplete.

The 145th ATC became an ATS company (Co E 245th ATS). Then (ca 2006) it changed to Co F 211th Avn (ATS)[49]. "I can tell you that the Air Traffic Service Co is the most deployed aviation unit we have in Oklahoma. They've deployed three times. Recently, [they] deployed with us, the Bn Hqs, when we went to Tekrit, Iraq (August 2004 – December 2005) for OF3, and they've been to Bosnia a few times. This was Co E 245th ATS (Bosnia – June 1998 to February 1999 [air traffic controllers] and also Bosnia – November 2002 to October 2003)."

On 1 December 1979, MAJ Donald E. Derrick, who had been the XO, was moved up to the Bn Cdr position of 145th Avn Bn (PROV). He was promoted to LTC in September 1980 and stayed as Bn Cdr until 31 August 1981.

According to OKPA-O, DF (10 December 1979), subject ASED & TFOS Dates[50], there were about 47 aviators on flight status assigned to OKARNG.

The 45th Inf Bde Avn Sec Unit Alert Notification Roster, dated 1 October 1980, listed approximately 46 aviation personnel (off/wo/em) in this section.

Therefore in 1979, OKARNG Aviation was structured as shown below:

HHC 145th Avn Bn (PROV)
Det 2 HHC 45th Inf Bde (Sep) [Bde Avn Sec], Lexington, OK
Co B, 149th Avn, Lexington, OK
Co D (-) 149th Avn Co, Tulsa, OK
145th ATC Platoon, Lexington, OK

OKSTARC Fixed-wing section, Norman, OK

1980

Det 1 (later Det 2) 45th Inf Bde, which was most often referred to as the Brigade Avn Section, was perhaps the longest standing aviation unit in the OKARNG. Although this section had many different names/designations, it was referred to as the 45th Inf Bde Avn Sec. Here are most of its former commanders: 1LT/CPT Dana D. Batey had the honors (ca 1970-71). CPT Ronald Howland was commander from 1972-74 and was the Bde Avn Officer for a period of time. CPT Emmett D. McElwain was commander from 1974-75, and CPT Don Shroyer in 1978. MAJ Pete Costilow was commander and Bde Avn Officer from January 1979 to November 1980, followed by 1LT Richard Sackett, then CPT Roger Ferguson with 1SG Jerry McLaughlin as Senior NCO. 1LT Walter E. Fountain was Cdr April 1986 to August 1987, and 1SG Don Morris was his Senior NCO. Then CPT John M. Griffis commanded in 1989. This list is incomplete.

Ref Co D (-) 149th Avn Bn at Tulsa, "I took over in September/October of '80 as unit 1SG, and I got promoted [to 1SG] 1 October 1981. Dale Martin was there [Co D (-)] until about '80, then Vern Ashbrook picked up as unit commander. Dale went to state [OMD] of course. [CW2] Chance Whiteman[51] was our XO until he got killed. It happened right around the [OMD] Military Ball that year," recalled Crowe.

There were no known or major changes in OKARNG Aviation force structure.

1981

Once again, the designation HHC 145 Avn Bn (Provisional)[52] formerly Det 1 Command and Control, pops up at the aviation headquarters on OMD orders effective 11 March 1981. And the 45th Inf Bde Avn Sec became known as Det 2, HHC, 45th Inf Bde.

On 1 September 1981, LTC Derrick[53] was appointed (M-day) Dep ACofS Avn at OMD. He served as such until 1 January 1982, when he retired.

In 1981, OKARNG Aviation was structured as shown below:

HHC 145 Avn Bn (PROV) (formerly Det 1, Command & Control HQs), Lex, OK

Cmd & Staff
Flight Surgeon Detachment
Aviation Fire/Crash Rescue
Avionics Dir Spt Maint
(Total of 35 pers[54] assigned, none attached, to Det 1, C&C HQs)
Co B 149th Avn Bn, Lexington, OK
Co D (-) 149th Avn Co, Tulsa, OK (UH-1M guns)
Det 2, HHC, 45th Inf Bde (Sep) [Avn Sec], Lexington, OK
145th ATC Platoon, Lexington, OK
OKSTARC Fixed-wing section, Norman, OK

1982

Eureka! The dreamed about aviation force structure arrived. On 1 May 1982, the 45th Aviation Battalion (LT HEL CBT) was constituted and federally recognized at Sperry, OK, with 203 personnel authorized per OA 81-82 (dated 2 September 1982). Co D (-) 149th Avn Bn was the nucleus for this new black avn organization. This unit was requested by the Army DCSOPS and designated for a unique new role called Counter Terrorism. The statement heard repeatedly, "It will be a mirror image of Task Force 160, was made by an individual in DCSOPS at the Pentagon" to COL John J. Stanko, former Chief, NGB Aviation Division.[55]

The 45th Aviation Battalion, later (Special Operations)(Airborne) unit became the largest, single aviation unit within the OKARNG before and since 1982. It grew to an authorized personnel strength of 463 (in 1991) and had 30 aircraft assigned in the early 1990s. The 45th began with 25 OH-6 Little Birds (17 MH-6 lift and eight AH-6 attack), which were A models modified to MH and AH-6s. Later, modified UH-1s were attached from Co B 149th Avn. In October 1986, Co B 149th will be redesignated as Co B 45th Avn Bn. In time, UH-1s and MH-60s replaced the MH and AH-6s, and CH-47s replaced the UH-1s in Co B at Lexington.

Each year the Oklahoma Military Department (OMD) presented an annual report to the governor on the OKARNG for the fiscal year. The SAO office submitted a two-page section on Oklahoma Aviation to the governor's report. It was called the Army Aviation Division.

Following are some excerpts from the FY 1982 report to the governor from pages 122 and 123:

The State Army Aviation Office (SAAO) is responsible to the AG for all aviation operations . . . by the eight aviation elements and two AASFs. The [SAAO] is located in the OMD complex and consists of the SAO and Mgmt Asst.

The [145th] Prov Avn Bn Hqs is located at Lexington and consists of six federal technicians. Also at LEX is the AASF #1 . . . [which] employs 48 fed techs and six State employees. AASF #1 supports HHD OKARNG; HHC 145 Avn Bn; Co B (Aslt Hel)[149th Avn Bn]; 145 ATC Plt; and Det 2 45th Inf Bde." There were 26 UH-1H and 8 OH-58s, plus one 'float' aircraft at LEX.

AASF #2 (temporarily located with the ANG) Tulsa, is authorized 44 fed techs, 2 CFTM pers. and supports HSC, Co A and Co B 45th Avn Bn [(Lt Hel Cbt)] in Sperry, OK. Aircraft available for training at this location are programmed [to be] for six OH-6 [should have said AH-6s] and fifteen OH-6 [should have said MH-6s], two OH-6 Electronic Warfare Helicopters, and one float UH-1 for admin support, for a total of twenty-four aircraft.

One U-8F Cmd & Staff airplane is hangared at Norman awaiting completion of runway at the LEX AASF. One hundred percent of authorized aircraft assets are on hand for a state total of sixty aircraft.

The 45th Avn Bn's [training] emphasis . . . is tactical night training.

The report goes on to add:

There are " . . . seventy-eight aviators at LEX, fifty-six aviators at Sperry for a total of one hundred thirty four aviators. There are thirty-six enlisted crewmembers at LEX and eighteen enlisted crewmembers at Tulsa. The OKARNG Aviation program is in its 11th accident-free year and has accumulated 70,000 plus accident-free flying hours." Thus ends the reading from the FY 1982 Annual Report to the Governor, Amen.

Therefore, in 1982, OKARNG Aviation was structured as shown below:

HHC 145 Avn Bn (Provisional) HQs (Lexington, OK
45th Avn Bn (LT HEL CBT), Sperry, OK
HQ & Svc Co, 45th Avn Bn, Sperry, OK
Co A, 45th Avn Bn, Sperry, OK
Co B, 45th Avn Bn, Sperry, OK
Det 2, HHC, 45th Inf Bde (Sep) [Avn Sec], Lexington, OK[56]
Co B 149th Avn Bn, Lexington, OK
145th ATC Platoon, Lexington, OK
OKSTARC Fixed-wing section, Norman, OK

1983

There isn't today, there won't be tomorrow, and in 1983, there weren't enough Aviation Battalion Headquarters (or higher) force structure to go around. This was (and is) an ongoing command and control problem for NGB and ARNG state aviation units. It has become an accepted fact of life for all states with ARNG Aviation force structure. Every State Army Aviation Officer (SAAO) would like to have an aviation headquarters within their state to oversee and supervise the smaller, individual elements/ units.

Each and every one of the 54 ARNG entities has some aviation elements and/or units. But each entity (state/territory) cannot possibly have a battalion or regimental aviation headquarters. The total Army force structure isn't designed to provide wanted aviation headquarters.

Our visionary leader, COL Dana D. Batey, the OKSAO then, and dreamer that he was and still is, came up with a near perfect solution. In OKARNG it was called Troop Command (Aviation) [Trp Cmd (Avn)], and it filled the aviation force structure gap of not having a TOE (Table of Organization and Equipment) or MTOE (Modified Table of Organization and Equipment) Avn Hqs. Trp Cmd (Avn) was a TDA (Table of Distribution and Allowances), basically, a non-go-to-war state ARNG Aviation headquarters unit. It incorporated the normal headquarters positions—Cdr, CSM, and Staff (S-1, S-2, S-3, S-4), Avn Safety Officer, but also an Admin/Personnel section, Flight Surgeon section, Airfield Operations section (including refueling and crash rescue). COL John J. Stanko, Chief, NGB Aviation Division, liked this organization's template and capabilities. Other states with major aviation assets, but lacking TOE/ MTOE Avn Bn, and Avn Regimental Hqs, emulated the OKARNG Trp Cmd (Avn) TDA organization.

Trp Cmd (Avn), came into being 1 March 1983 at Lexington, OK, as a reorganization and redesignation from the former HHC, 145th Avn Bn (Prov) (formerly Det 1, Cmd & Control Hqs).

The Trp Cmd (Avn) commanders were: LTC Ronald L. Howland ca 1983, LTC Don Derrick ca 1984, LTC Emmett D. McElwain ca 1984, COL Dana D. Batey (all actual dates of command unknown), LTC James C. Peck 28 February 1986 to 1 September 1987, followed by ????, and then LTC Paul D. Costilow (February 1989 to August 1991), then LTC Leroy A. Wall (1 September 1987 to 30 September 1991) and LTC Billy R. Wood (1 August 1991 to 25 April 1993).

Here are some excerpts from the FY 1983 Annual Report to the Governor for the OKARNG Aviation program from pages 121 and 122:

> Troop Command (Aviation) is located at LEX and consists of eight fed techs and four AGR personnel. AASF #1 supports Hqs State Area Command (STARC), Trp Cmd (Avn), Co B 149th Avn Bn, 145 ATC Plt and Det 2, 45th Inf Bde. There are still 35 aircraft assigned to LEX. No change in numbers of full-time personnel at LEX and TUL. There are 24 aircraft assigned to TUL. Fifty acres and $3.5 million have been programmed for construction of a new facility in Tulsa.
>
> A[n Aviation Recruiting] trailer has been constructed with a permanently mounted [UH-1] helicopter to be used for static displays.
>
> . . . Night Vision Goggle (NVG) training has been introduced into our [45th Avn Bn] aviation program.
>
> There was no change in the total number of aviators or crewmembers (124/54).
>
> The OKARNG Aviation program is in its 12th accident-free year and has accumulated 70,000 plus accident-free flying hours. Thus ends the reading of certain excerpts from the FY 1983 Annual Report to the Governor.

Therefore, in 1983, OKARNG Aviation was structured as shown below:

Trp Cmd (Avn) , Lexington, OK

Cmd Staff & Admin sections

Airfield Operations section
Flight Surgeon Detachment
Aviation Fire/Crash Rescue
45th Avn Bn (LT HEL CBT), Sperry, OK
HQ & Svc Co, 45th Avn Bn, Sperry, OK
Co A, 45th Avn Bn, Sperry, OK
Co B, 45th Avn Bn, Sperry, OK
Co B, 149th Avn Bn, Lexington, OK
Det 2, HHC, 45th Inf Bde (Sep) [Avn Sec], Lexington,
OK
145th ATC Platoon, Lexington, OK
OKSTARC Fixed-wing section, Norman, OK

1984

Following are some excerpts from the FY 1984 Annual Report to the
Governor for the OKARNG Aviation program from pages 121 and 122:

AASF #2 [still] (temporarily located with the ANG,
Tulsa) is auth 40 fed techs and two CFTM pers (has 27 fed
techs and one CFTM per assigned). This facility supports
HSC 45th Avn Bn, Co's A, B and C 45th Avn Bn in Sperry,
OK. Aircraft available for training at this location (TUL) is
five AH-6 helicopters, twenty MH-6 helicopters and two
UH-60s (not yet assigned), for a total of 27 aircraft.

One U-8F and one U-3K, Cmd and Staff airplanes are
hangared at Norman . . . Rehabilitation of hangar space at
Norman is currently underway. Total number of aircraft
within the state is 64 and 62 assigned; . . . . 76 aviators at
LEX and 64 aviators at Sperry for a total of 140 [and] 36
enlisted crewmembers at LEX and 5 at Tulsa.

The OKARNG Aviation program is in its 14th major
accident-free year and has accumulated 85,000 plus
accident-free flying hours. Thus ends the reading of certain
excerpts from the FY 84 Annual Report to the Governor.

Trp Cmd (Avn) performed its annual training from 2-16 June 1984 at
Fort Chaffee, AR. In December, an OPSEC briefing was presented to Trp
Cmd (Avn) personnel and recruit training was conducted for non-prior

service (NPS) soldiers by SGM Rogers, MSG Templin, SSG Shobert, and SSG Potemra.

An AVUM maintenance company was added to the 45th Avn Bn (SO)(A) in Sperry:

Co C (AVUM), 45th Avn Bn (SO)(A), Sperry, OK

1985

Following are some excerpts from the FY 1985 Annual Report to the Governor for the OKARNG Aviation program from pages 45-47:

Two Cessna 310 aircraft for Cmd and Staff are hangared at Norman . . . total number of aircraft is 66 with 64 authorized.

SIGNIFICANT ACTIVITIES:

- 45th Avn Bn attained 104% strength
- 45th Avn Bn became the 1st ARNG Aviation unit to be 100% NVG qualified
- During AT '85, 45th Avn Bn attained an overall rating of OUTSTANDING.
- 145th ATC Plt Enlisted man, PFC Ron Richardson[57], was Oklahoma Army National Guard Soldier of the Year.

Trp Cmd (Avn) conducted two joint training exercises with active component and reserve component aviation and pathfinder units: April 85 FTX at Camp Gruber, OK and August 85 CALFEX at Fort Chaffee, AR (8 states involved).

Co B, 149th Avn Bn conducted OUTSTANDING annual training at Fort Hood, TX in conjunction with [the] entire 49th Armored Division.

Oklahoma Distinguished Cross and Oklahoma Star of Valor presented to two aviators for heroic rescue of fellow aviators.[58]

The total number of aviators and crewmembers in the state was 134/41. The OKARNG Aviation program is in its 15th major accident-free year and has accumulated 95,000 plus accident-free flying hours.

Thus ends the reading of certain excerpts from the FY 1985 Annual Report to the Governor.

Therefore, in 1985, OKARNG Aviation was structured as shown below:

Trp Cmd (Avn), Lexington, OK

45th Avn Bn (LT HEL CBT), Sperry, OK

HQ & Svc Co, 45th Avn Bn, Sperry, OK

Co A, 45th Avn Bn, Sperry, OK

Co B, 45th Avn Bn, Sperry, OK

Co C (AVUM), 45th Avn Bn, Sperry, OK

Co B, 149th Avn Bn[59], Lexington, OK – attached to 45th Avn Bn 23 October

Det 1, HHC, 45th Inf Bde (Sep) [Avn Sec], Lexington, OK

145th ATC Platoon, Lexington, OK

OKSTARC Fixed-wing section, Norman, OK

1986

Here are some excerpts from the FY 1986 Annual Report to the Governor for the OKARNG Aviation program from pages 43 and 44:

State Safety Office consisting of State Safety Manager [(LTC James Peck[60])] and Occupational Health Nurse, has been realigned under the SAO office, located on Westheimer Field, Norman, OK.

Trp Cmd (Avn) currently leading the state in strength at 117%, has been recognized as the fourth Major Command of the OKARNG and key personnel are located at Westheimer Field, Norman, OK. Total State aircraft and full-time pers remain numerically the same.

SIGNIFICANT ACCOMPLISHMENTS:

- Scheduling of a new $6.2 million AASF and Armory on fifty acres in the vicinity of Tulsa Int'l Airport
- Construction of a new $ .5 million 2,000 foot autorotation lane at LEX
- Equipment to be received by 145th ATC Plt valued at approx. $1 million to include a portable truck-mounted aircraft flight control tower and a 'flight following' van [complete] with newest equipment.
- All UH-1 helicopters [at LEX] have been modified to NVG compatibility
- All aviators at TUL and 80% at LEX are NVG qualified
- Two UH-60s (Blackhawks) were received by the 45th Avn Bn this FY and were accepted and dedicated by the Governor of Oklahoma. Five pilots have completed [UH-60 transition tng], one currently in tng, two pilots have completed the [UH-60 MTP] maintenance course and are now qualified to test fly the Blackhawks.

(Note: CW5 Don McCarty remembered that, The first two UH-60 tail numbers (86-24501 and 86-24509) were picked up at the Sikorsky

Aircraft Corp plant in Stratford, CT. Aircraft # 501 was picked up by CWO Leonard "Dawg" Reed and a guy from AZ. Aircraft # 509 was picked up by me and TK (Klutts); WO Don Russell went with us.)

[Select] Members of the 45th Avn Bn [(SO)(A)] have attended the Airborne School and are qualified to jump from military aircraft in support of [FAARP] refueling operations.

[OKARNG] Aviation had 12 officers graduate from the Officer Candidate Class this year and eight enrolled in the new class.

Thus ends the reading of certain excerpts from the FY 1986 Annual Report to the Governor.

LTC James C. Peck was the commander of Trp Cmd (Avn) from February 1986 to 1 September 1987.

Therefore, in 1986, OKARNG Aviation was structured as shown below:

Trp Cmd (Avn), Lexington, OK was relocated to Norman (Westheimer Field) in August 1986.

45th Avn Bn[61] (Lt Hel Cbt), Sperry, OK – AAAA Outstanding Avn Unit (ARNG)

> HQ & Svc Co, 45th Avn Bn, Sperry, OK
> Co A, 45th Avn Bn, Sperry, OK
> Co B, 45th Avn Bn, Sperry, OK
> Co C (AVUM), 45th Avn Bn, Sperry, OK

Co B, 149th Avn Bn, Lexington, OK

Co B 45th Avn Bn (SO)(A) October 1986, Lexington, OK, OA 210-87(dated 15 September 1987); reorg/redesignated (formed from the former Co B 149th Avn)

Det 1, HHC, 45th Inf Bde (Sep) [Avn Sec], Lexington, OK

145th ATC Platoon, Lexington, OK

OKSTARC Fixed-wing Section, Norman, OK

1987

The most significant change in OKARNG Aviation this year was the redesignation (name change) from 45th Avn Bn (SO)(A) to 1st Bn 245th Avn (SP OP)(ABN) on 1 October 1987. This was followed by the Lexington Co B, 149th Avn becoming an integral part of 1/245th, as it was reorganized and redesignated Co B, 1st Bn 245th Avn (SP OP) (ABN) also on 1 October 1987.

Trp Cmd (Avn), Norman, OK

45th Avn Bn (LT HEL CBT), Sperry, OK

45th Avn Bn (SO) (A), Sperry, OK – redesignation/name change 1 June 1987

1st Bn 245th Avn (SP OP) (ABN) – redesignation/name change 1 October 1987 per OA 168-87

Co B, 149th Avn Bn, Lexington, OK – deactivated 30 September 1987

Co B, 1st Bn 245th Avn (SP OP) (ABN), Lex, OK – redesignated 1 October 1987

Det 1, HHC, 45th Inf Bde (Sep) [Avn Sec], Lexington, OK

145th ATC Platoon, Lexington, OK

OKSTARC Fixed-wing Section, Norman, OK

1988

Trp Cmd (Avn), Norman, OK

1st Bn 245th Avn (SP OP) (ABN), Sperry, OK

    H&S Co, 1st Bn 245th Avn (SP OP) (ABN), Sperry, OK

    Co A, 1st Bn 245th Avn (SP OP) (ABN), Sperry, OK

    Co B, 1st Bn 245th Avn (SP OP) (ABN), Lexington, OK

    Co C (AVUM), 1st Bn 245th Avn (SP OP) (ABN), Sperry, OK

Det 1, HHC, 45th Inf Bde (Sep) [Avn Sec], Lexington, OK

145th ATC Platoon, Lexington, OK

OKSTARC Fixed-wing Section, Norman, OK

1989

On 1 June 1989, Trp Cmd (Avn) was officially redesignated Det 2, HQ STARC, but remained Trp Cmd (Avn) to aviation personnel.

1/245th Avn held its official armory/facility dedication ceremonies on 26 August 1989.

Det 2, HQ STARC, Norman, OK

1st Bn 245th Avn (SP OP) (ABN), Sperry, OK

    H&S Co, 1st Bn 245th Avn (SP OP) (ABN), Sperry, OK

    Co A, 1st Bn 245th Avn (SP OP) (ABN), Sperry, OK

    Co B, 1st Bn 245th Avn (SP OP) (ABN), Lexington, OK

    Co C (AVUM), 1st Bn 245th Avn (SP OP) (ABN), Sperry, OK

Det 1, HHC, 45th Inf Bde (Sep) [Avn Sec], Lexington, OK

145th ATC Platoon, Lexington, OK
OKSTARC Fixed-wing Section, Norman, OK
There were no known or major changes in OKARNG Aviation force structure.

1990

Det 2, HQ STARC, Norman, OK
1st Bn 245th Avn (SP OP) (ABN), Sperry, OK
    H&S Co, 1st Bn 245th Avn (SP OP) (ABN), Sperry, OK
    Co A, 1st Bn 245th Avn (SP OP) (ABN), Sperry, OK
    Co B, 1st Bn 245th Avn (SP OP) (ABN), Lexington, OK
    Co C (AVUM), 1st Bn 245th Avn (SP OP) (ABN), Sperry, OK
Company A, 132d Aviation Battalion
HHC, Detachment 3, 132d Aviation Battalion
Det 1, HHC, 45th Inf Bde (Sep) [Avn Sec], Lexington, OK
145th ATC Platoon, Lexington, OK
OKSTARC Fixed-wing Section, Norman, OK

1991

MAJ Walter E. Fountain commanded Co C, 1st Bn, 245th Avn (SO) (A) from October 1991 until September 1994.

There were no known or major changes in OKARNG Aviation force structure in 1991.

1992

Det 2, HQ STARC, Norman, OK
1st Bn 245th Avn (SP OP) (ABN), Sperry, OK
    H&S Co, 1st Bn 245th Avn (SP OP) (ABN), Sperry, OK
    Co A, 1st Bn 245th Avn (SP OP) (ABN), Sperry, OK
    Co B, 1st Bn 245th Avn (SP OP) (ABN), Lexington, OK
    Co C (AVUM), 1st Bn 245th Avn (SP OP) (ABN), Sperry, OK
    Co D, 1st Bn 245th Avn (SP OP) (ABN), Sperry, OK
    Det 1, Co D, 1st Bn 245th Avn (SP OP) (ABN), Lexington, OK
Company A, 132nd Aviation Battalion
HHC, Detachment 3, 132nd Aviation Battalion
Det 1, HHC, 45th Inf Bde (Sep) [Avn Sec], Lexington, OK
145th ATC Platoon, Lexington, OK
OKSTARC Fixed-wing Section, Norman, OK

1993

NGB's Counter Drug section requested and obtained force structure for each state to stand up a RAID (Reconnaissance and Interdiction Detachment) in March 1993. The OKARNG POTO office, supported by the OKCofS, decided they would eliminate the TDA Aviation Headquarters within the state and deactivated Det 2, HQ STARC (formerly Trp Cmd (Avn) on 1 May 1993, after which all aviation assets would be under the state control of 90th Troop Command, a MACOM of non-infantry, non-artillery, combat support or service support-type units.

~~Det 2, HQ STARC (formerly Trp Cmd (Avn[62]))~~, Norman, OK – deactivated 1 May 1993

1st Bn 245th Avn (SP OP) (ABN), Tulsa, OK

H&S Co, 1st Bn 245th Avn (SP OP) (ABN), Sperry, OK

Co A, 1st Bn 245th Avn (SP OP) (ABN), Sperry, OK

Co B, 1st Bn 245th Avn (SP OP) (ABN), Lexington, OK

Co D, 1st Bn 245th Avn (SP OP) (ABN), Sperry, OK

Det 1, Co D, 1st Bn 245th Avn (SP OP) (ABN), Lexington, OK

Det 1, HHC, 45th Inf Bde (Sep) [Avn Sec], Lexington, OK???

Co A, 1st Bn 132nd Cmd Avn (CPT Bryan Palmer) Lexington, OK

Det 3, HHC, 1st Bn 132nd Cmd Avn (CW5 Jack Milavic) C-23 Sherpa element, Norman, OK

145th ATC Platoon, Lexington, OK

R.A.I.D. (Recon & Interdiction Detachment (Counter Drug), Norman, OK (CPT Roy Tackett)

OKSTARC Fixed-wing Section, Norman, OK (CW5 Tommy Klutts)

1994

The Operational Support Airlift Command (OSACOM) obtained force structure and stood up a C-12 fixed-wing detachment in each state in October 1994. The end of OKARNG Special Ops Aviation came this year with DA and NGB's orders to deactivate the 1st Bn 245th Avn (SP OP) (ABN), Tulsa, OK, in September 1994. 1/245th Avn officially deactivated, and the unit colors were cased on 28 August 1994.

~~1st Bn 245th Avn (SP OP) (ABN)~~, Tulsa, OK (LTC Terry R. Council) – deactivated[63] 1 September 1994

Co B, 1st Bn 245th Avn (SO)(A), Lexington, OK

Det 2, HHC, 45th Inf Bde (Sep) [Avn Sec], Lexington, OK???

Co A, 1st Bn 132nd Cmd Avn (CPT Bryan Palmer) Lexington, OK

Det 3, HHC, 1st Bn 132nd Cmd Avn (CW5 Jack Milavic)

145th ATC Platoon, Lexington, OK

R.A.I.D. (Recon & Interdiction Detachment (Counter Drug), Norman, OK (CPT Roy Tackett)

OSAA, Det 46 (C-12), Norman, OK

Following the U.S. Army's SOA tragedy in Somalia (Operation Restore Hope) and its short visit to Haiti (Operation Uphold Democracy) Army Aviation force structure from NGB down through the states became extraordinarily convoluted.

Immediately following the deactivation of the 1st Bn 245th Avn (SP OP) (ABN) at Tulsa, OK, on 28 August 1994, there were six OKARNG Aviation elements remaining in Oklahoma at Lexington, Tulsa, and Norman, OK. By 1997, the number of aviation units had grown in number to seven, but no growth in overall personnel strength, or in the number of aircraft. Quite the opposite – the number of authorized personnel and aircraft was dramatically reduced.

MAJ Walter E. Fountain commanded HHC, 245th AV (ATS) from September 2001 until September 2003.

By 2004, the number of OKARNG Aviation units (or elements and detachments) was at nine. But much of the OKARNG had been mobilized as individual units, elements, and/or detachments to support the wars in Afghanistan and Iraq. Not just Infantry, Artillery or Aviation, but many, many combat support-type OKARNG units were mobilized, activated, and deployed to other locations (CONUS and OCONUS) in support of Operations Enduring Freedom and Iraqi Freedom.

It is not the author's intent to try and complete the OKARNG Avn units profile after 1994, nor new units or that were organized, reorganized, redesignated and/or deactivated. However, as of December 2006, the Oklahoma State Aviation Officer, then LTC Jon Harrison, offered that the following 18 aviation units were fielded and operational within the State of Oklahoma. As of the beginning of 2007, there were approximately 430 aviation personnel authorized, of which 98 are technicians and 32 AGRs auth (only 18 on hand) and 28 aircraft in the OKARNG:

OSAA Det 46 – Norman, OK – C-12

Det 1/A/249th Theater Aviation Company (TAC) 2-C-23s

Det 1 Co A 249th Avn – Norman, OK

Det 1 Co A 1st Bn 114th Avn – Norman, OK (R.A.I.D.) 2-OH-58s

HHC 445th CS Avn Bn ASLT – Tulsa, OK

Co A 445th CS Avn Bn ASLT – Tulsa, OK

Det 1 Co A 445th CS Avn Bn ASLT – Tulsa, OK

    Det 1 HHC 2nd Bn 285th Avn – Tulsa, OK

    Co B 2nd Bn 285th Avn – Tulsa, OK 10-UH-60s

    Det 1 Co D 2nd Bn 285th Avn – Tulsa, OK

    Det 1 Co E 2nd Bn 285th Avn – Tulsa, OK

    Co B (-) 834th AVIM – Tulsa, OK

Det 2 HHC 2nd Bn 149th Avn – Lexington, OK

    Det 1 Co B 2nd Bn 149th Avn – Lex, OK 5-CH-47s

    Det 1 Co C 2nd Bn 149th Avn – Lex, OK 6-UH-60s

    Det 2 Co D 2nd Bn 149th Avn – Lex, OK

    Det 2 Co E 2nd Bn 149th Avn – Lex, OK

    Co F 211th Avn (ATS) – Lexington, OK

Along with BG Myles L. Deering's 45th Inf Bde Cbt Team, who were mobilized for Operation Iraqi Freedom on 18 October 2007, many of these OKARNG Aviation units listed above were mobilized, some for their second and third rotations! Today's ARNG isn't the same National Guard that was once and often mistakenly called weekend warriors.

Part II – Personnel

On the following pages are lists of former OKARNG Aviation units, approximate time frames and some of its members. These lists were made from OKARNG unit orders provided by numerous individuals. They are not complete unit rosters by any means. I apologize in advance if you were in one of these units and your name isn't in the list(s).

Unit	Dates Station/Duty		
45ʰ Avn Co	**May 1959**	**Apr 1963**	**Norman**
CPT Butcher[64]	1959	???	1st Cdr Off
LTC August L. Guild[65]	May 1959	Mar 1963	Div Avn Off
CPT Pete Phillips[66]	May 1959	Jan 1960	Plt Ldr
CPT Clarence L. Strance	May 1959	ca 1969	Plt Ldr
MSG L. T. Lantz	1960	???	Senior NCO
SFC C. W. Davis	1963	???	Senior NCO
MSG L. J. Bennett	1964	???	Senior NCO
1SG F. C. Shephard	1964	???	1SG
SP5 Leroy A. Wall[67]	Sep 1957	Nov 1962	Radio Mech
WO1 Leroy A. Wall	Nov 1962	Mar 1963	RW AV
CPT David L. Vaughn	ca 1960	1962	2nd Cdr Off
CPT Charles R. Jones	ca 1961		FW AV
CPT Charles R. Jones	Nov 1965	Oct 1966	Safety Off
CPT Charles R. Jones	Oct 1966	Jan 1968	Asst Div Avn Off
CPT Pete Phillips	Feb 1960	Jun 1963	S-1
CPT Coy H. McKinsey[68]	1962	1963	3rd Cdr Off
2LT Robert C. Armstrong	May 1963	Jun 1963	S-2
2LT Robert C. Armstrong	Jun 1963	Apr 1965	S-1
1LT Robert C. Armstrong	Apr 1965	Oct 1965	Safety Off
1LT Robert C. Armstrong	Oct 1965	???	S-2
CPT Pete Phillips	Jun 1963	ca 1964	Asst Div Avn Off
2LT Dana D. Batey[69]	Jun 1959	Mar 1961	Avn Maint Off
CPT Chester A. Howard[70]	May 1959	Aug 1961	Asst Div Avn Off
1LT Dana D. Batey	Apr 1963	Mar 1964	Avn Maint Off
1LT Karl M. Frank	Feb 1960	Jan 1962	Aerial Obser
2LT Jerry D. Bourassa	Jul 1959	Mar 1963	FW AV
CPT Jerry D. Bourassa	Oct 1963	Mar 1964	Cdr Hq Co
1LT Jerry D. Bourassa	Oct 1961	Oct 1962	Asst Plt Opns Off
1LT Jerry D. Bourassa	Apr 1963	Oct 1963	Avn Off
CPT Jerry D. Bourassa	Nov 1965	Jan 1968	Asst Div Avn Off
CPT Dana D. Batey	Feb 1968	Sep 1970	Aero Sct Plt Cdr

other known former unit members:

1LT B.C. Coleman*, CPT D.M. Campbell*, CPT H.B. Southern*, 1LT D.L Taylor*, 1LT J.R. Matthews*, 1LT T.E. Little*, 1LT B.E. Spagee*, SGT W.A. Hatchell*, 1LT C.H. Finch*, CPT W.F. Henry*, 1LT A. Coffin*, CPT H.H. Schaaf*, MSG D.W. Daniel*, MSG J.I. Robertson*, SFC M.W. Shears*, SP6 J.H. Coffield*, SGT M.A. Wood*, SFC R.A. Walker*, SP5 C.O. Whiting*, SFC R.A. Walker*, SFC R.I. Eades*, SP5 R. Leippe, SSG A.E. Patrick*, SSG G.W. Swanson*, PFC G.P. Lightener*, SP5 C.O. Whiting*, PFC J.L. Gregg*, SP5 H.D. Young*, PFC R.N. Bailey*, SGT T.J. Bugher*, SP4 F. Putnam*, SGT K.R. Gray*, PVT H. Fugett*, SP5 A. Tiger*, SP4 J.T. Stubbs*, PVT J.E. Cole*, PVT J. Humphries*, SP4 R.N. Wilkerson*, SFC N.W. Foster*, SP5 C.K. Stubblefield*, SP5 G.L. Sheppard*, SP5 A.W. Rames*, PFC T.A. Miller*, SP4 L.W. Bennett*, SP4 D.T. Mize*, SP5 F.G. Simpson*, PVT W.J. Mercer*, SP5 G.O. Alfred*, SP5 C.O. Vaught*, PFC D.W. Rainbow*, SP5 D.E. Simpson*, PVT O.J. Bellew*, SP5 C.P. Van Hooker*, CPT B.K. Owens, CPT R.T. Hogue, WO1 R.I. Eades, SP5 D.R. Key, SFC G. Smith, SP4 T.M. Kinslow, SP4 C.E. Sipes, SFC C.W. Davis, SP5 R.W. Rainbow, SP4 R.B. Keeling, SP4 H.A. Stokes, PFC J.M. Brown, SFC A.E. Patrick, SFC D.K. Motsenbocker, PFC M.L. Boswell, SFC L.E. Vandiver, SFC C.L. Allen, SSG C.K. Stubblefield, SSG E.D. O'Dell, SP5 J.B. Johnson, SFC D.R. Price, SP4 J.M. Hamner, SP5 J.A. Tidwell, SP4 B.C. Graham, SSG R.R. Wilkerson, SGT D.L. Kyle, E-2 T. Yarborough, PFC D.B. Hensley, SP4 D.L. Tipton, WO1 Leroy A. Wall, 2LT Dale E. Martin, 2LT Emmett D. McElwain, 1LT James L. "Bear" Smith, 1LT Charles R. Jones, MSG Ivel L. Cypert, SSG Gerald W. Swanson, SFC Floyd R. Ormiston, SP6 Lloyd R. Ormiston, SP5 Donald E. Derrick, 2LT Robert C. Armstrong, MAJ Perry H. Townsend, MAJ L. L. Glenn, SFC P. D. Farnum, CWO M. Duensing, MAJ L.L. Glenn, 1LT D.F. Ethridge, MSG, L.J. Bennett, SFC P.D. Farnum, SP5 D.L. Hellard, SGT E.R. Barnes, SGT L.D. Montague, SGT D.E. Anderson, SGT, T.K. Bray, SGT D.L. Harris, SFC J.L. La Porte, SSG E. Mabry, SSG L. Carter, SFC D. Wienoskie, SGT J. Conley, SGT I.E. Dikeman, SP4 M.F. Lloyd, SP4 W.R. Reeder, PFC J.F. DeGarimore, PFC E. Robinson, PFC R.H. Williams, PFC O.R. Mann, SP4 J.A. McElwain, PVT C.M. Crisp, PFC D.P.A. Warren, SP4 R.H. Maxwell, SP5 N.J. Phillips, SP5 K.D. Winkle

*Unit Members as of AT 1960

445th Trans Detachment	ca 1961	Norman	
2LT Dana D. Batey	Mar 1961	Sep 1961	Det Cdr

245th Trans Bn ca	1961		Norman
2LT Dana D. Batey	Sep 1961	Mar 1963	Acft Maint Off

497th Trans (Lt Hel)	ca 1962	???	Tulsa
CPT Chester A. Howard	Aug 1962	Feb 1963	XO

Co B (G/S), 45th Avn Bn	Apr 1963	ca Mar 1964	Tulsa
CPT Clarence L. Strance	Apr 1963	Feb 1964	Co Cdr
1LT Karl M. Frank	Mar 1963	Dec 1964	Aero Infrd Sec Ldr
CPT Jerry D. Bourassa	Mar 1964	Sep 1965	Co Cdr
CPT Charles R. Jones	Mar 1964	Apr 1964	Flt Opns Off
CPT Ronald L. Howland	Mar 1964	Mar 1965	S-4
CPT Ronald L. Howland	Jun 1956	Mar 1964	RW AV
CPT Charles R. Jones	Apr 1964	Aug 1965	XO
WO1 Leroy A. Wall	Apr 1963	Oct 1965	RW AV
1LT/CPT Karl M. Frank	Dec 1964	Oct 1965	Flt Opns Off
CPT Charles R. Jones	Sep 1965	Nov 1965	Co Cdr
CPT Jerry D. Bourassa	Sep 1965	Oct 1965	Aero Infrd Sec Ldr
1LT Emmett D. McElwain	Sep 1965	Oct 1965	Svc Plt Cdr

other known former unit members:

MSG Robert F. Jones Jr., WO1 Leroy A. Wall, 2LT Donald E. Derrick, 2LT Dale E. Martin, 1LT Richard E. Bailey, 1LT Marlin W. Shears, CW2 Perry H. Townsend Jr.

HHD, 45th Avn Bn	Mar 1964	ca Feb 1968	Norman/Tulsa
MAJ Chester A. Howard	May 1963	Jan 1968	Bn Cdr
MAJ Pete Phillips	Nov 1965	Feb 1970	XO
CPT Dana D. Batey	Apr 1963	Mar 1964	Acft Maint Off
CPT _____ Jackson	May 1963	???	S-4

1LT Karl M. Frank	Jan 1962	Apr 1963	FW AV
1LT Robert C. Armstrong	May 1963	Jun 1963	S-2
1LT Robert C. Armstrong	Jun 1963	Apr 1965	S-1
CPT/MAJ Clarence Strance	Mar 1964	Sep 1967	S-3
CPT Pete Phillips	ca 1964	Oct 1965	Asst Div Avn Off
1LT Robert C. Armstrong	Apr 1965	Oct 1965	Safety Off
CPT Jerry D. Bourassa	Sep 1965	Oct 1965	Aero Infrad Sec Ldr
CPT Charles R. Jones	Nov 1965	Oct 1966	Safety Off/ Tulsa
1LT Robert C. Armstrong[71]	Oct 1966	???	S-4
WO1/CW2 Leroy A. Wall	Nov 1965	Jan 1968	RW AV
CPT Charles R. Jones	Oct 1966	Jan 1968	Asst Div Avn Tul
CPT Ronald L. Howland	Feb 1968	Mar 1968	Cdr, Aero Sct Sec
1LT Jerry D. Bourassa	Oct 1963	Mar 1964	Cdr, Hq Det

other known former unit members:

SSG? Leo Keenan, SP4? Joe D'Amico, CPT Bobby D. Breedlove, CPT James L. Smith

Trp D, 1st Sqd, 145th CAV	Nov 1965	ca Feb 1968	Marlow
CPT Karl M. Frank	Oct 1966	Jan 1968	Trp Cdr
SFC Bill Ferrell[72]	Jan 1965	???	AST – Norman
1SG Lloyd Todd	Jan 1965	???	1SG – Marlow
CPT Don Harvey[73]	???	???	Last Trp Cdr
Flight Ops Sec Aero Scout Plt			
CPT Karl M. Frank	Nov 1965	Oct 1966	Plt Cdr
Service Plt			
1LT Emmett D. McElwain	Sep 1965	Oct 1965	Svc Plt Cdr

other known former unit members:

CPT Don L. Hayes, 2LT Tommie Jones, CPT Patrick M. Goerig, 1LT Gwynne L. Sheppard, CW2 John M. Johnston, CW2 Reagan E. Popplewell, CW2 Frank L. Berry, CW2 Clarence R. Clarkson Jr., CW2 Billy W. Good, CW2 Leroy A. Wall, CW2 Donald R. Key, CPT Don L. Hayes, 2LT Tommie Jones, CW2 John M. Johnston, CW2 Reagan E. Popplewell, CW2 Frank L. Berry, CW2 Donald R. Key, WO1 John R. Dollins

Co E (-) Maint 700th Spt Bn	ca1965		Ardmore/ Norman
CPT Jay T. Evans[74]	ca 1965	???	???
CPT Thomas R. Nissen[75]	ca 1965	???	???
CPT Ralph L. Mayfield	ca 1965	???	???
2LT Jimmy A. Watt	ca 1965	???	???
WO1 Don R. Heath	ca 1965	???	???
CW3 Benny E. Hurd	ca 1965	???	???
WO1 Samuel G. Yates	ca 1965	???	???

HHB, 1st ? How Bn, 30th Arty	ca 1963	Bartlesville	
MAJ Chester A. "Chet" Howard	ca 1965	???	FW AV

HHC 1st Bde 45th Inf Div (Avn Sec)	ca 1964/68		
1LT Robert C. Armstrong	Nov 1965	Oct 1966	RW AV
CPT Billy D. Imoden	ca Jan 1968	???	???
CPT Jack E. Avant		???	RW AV
WO1 Charles E. Koonce	ca Jan 1968	???	???

HHC 2nd Bde 45th Inf Div (Avn Sec)	ca 1964/68		
CPT Dana D. Batey	May 1964	Jul 1965	Plt Cdr
CPT Frank A. Cory	ca Jan 1968	???	
WO1 Frank L. Berry	ca Jan 1968	???	

HHC 2nd Bde 45th Inf Div (Avn Sec)	ca 1967/69		
1LT Robert C. Armstrong	Oct 1966	Mar 1969	Asst S-3

CPT Donald Taylor	ca Jan 1967	???	

HHB 1ˢᵗ Bn 158ᵗʰ Arty (Avn Sec)	ca 1964/68		
2LT Robert E. Bristow	ca Jan 1968	???	???
WO1 Charles E. Koonce	ca Jan 1968	???	

HHB 45ᵗʰ Inf Div Arty (Div Arty (Avn Sec))	ca 1967/68	
MAJ Donald D. Wolgamott	ca 1965/67	
CPT Bobby D. Breedlove	ca Jan 1968	???
1LT Lance Fletcher Jr.	ca Jan 1968	???
1LT Preston Perry	ca Jan 1968	???
1LT Thomas A. Naylor	ca Jan 1968	???
CWO Bill Tingler	ca Jan 1968	???
Co E, 120ᵗʰ Eng Bn (Avn Sec)	ca 1967/68	
2LT Morris W. Hale	ca Jan 1968	???
2LT David L. Russell	ca Jan 1968	???
2LT Lenton T. Stephens	ca Jan 1968	???

245ᵗʰ Med Co (Air Amb)	Feb 1968	ca May 1971	Norman
CPT Clarence L. Strance	Feb 1968	May 1968	Co Cdr
CPT Charles R. Jones[76]	May 1968	Jun 1970	Co Cdr
CPT Jerry D. Bourassa	Feb 1968	May 1970	Maint Plt Ldr
CPT Jerry D. Bourassa	May 1970	Sep 1970	Evac Pilot
MAJ Jerry D. Bourassa	Sep 1970	Jun 1973	Co Cdr
CPT Karl M. Frank	Feb 1968	May 1971	Plt Cdr
CPT Donald E. Derrick	Oct 1969	Apr 1971	3ʳᵈ/4ᵗʰ Plt – Flt Ldr
CPT Dale E. Martin	May 1970	May 1971	Maint Plt Ldr
CPT Dale E. Martin	May 1971	May 1972	Opns Off
SP6/SSG Charles H. Evans	Feb 1968	Jun 1969	Asst Opns NCO
SFC Charles H. Evans	ca 1970	Dec 1972	Opns NCO

other known former unit members:
CPT Dale E. Martin, SP4 Jack Nations

145th Avn Co	Feb 1968	ca May 1971	Norman
MAJ Pete Phillips[77]	Jan 1968	???	1st Co Cdr
1SG Ivel Cypert	Jan 1968	???	Senior NCO
CPT Ronald L. Howland	Mar 1968	May 1971	XO
CPT Frank Cory	Jan 1968	???	Flt Opns Off
CPT Jay T. Evans	Jan 1968	???	Gen Spt Plt Cdr
CPT Ralph Mayfield	Jan 1968	???	Svc Plt Cdr
CW2 Leroy A. Wall	Feb 1968	Nov 1971	RW AV
CPT Robert C. Armstrong	Mar 1969	Dec 1969	RW AV
CPT Tony E. Boyles	May 1969	Nov 1970	RW AV
CPT Tony E. Boyle	Dec 1970	Nov 1971	Cdr, Aero Sct Plt
CPT Dana D. Batey	May 1971	Nov 1971	Flt Opns Off
CPT Dana D. Batey	Sep 1970	May 1971	Tac Spt Sec
CPT Dana D. Batey	Dec 1971	Oct 1972	Aero Sct Plt Cdr
MAJ Ronald L. Howland	May 1971	Nov 1971	Cdr
CPT Emmett D. McElwain	Apr 1969	Nov 1971	Svc Plt Cdr
CPT Clarence C. Buxton III	Nov 1971	???	Svc Plt Cdr
1LT Richard W. Wilson	ca 1970/71	???	Aero Sec Tm Ldr
1LT Marvin D. Self	ca 1970/71	??? Aero Sec Tm Ldr	

other known former unit members:
CW2 Leroy A. Wall, 1LT Morris W. Hale, 1LT Tommy Klutts Jr., 1LT Richard W. Wilson, CW4 Benny E. Hurd, CW2 Warren L. Applegate, CW2 Frank L. Berry, CW4 Joe Patterson, CW2 Bobby J. Swink, WO1 Wayne R. Teague, WO1 Danny Washa, CW2 Douglas L. Gandy, CW2 William N. Jackson Jr., 1LT Morris W. Hale, 1LT Tommy Klutts Jr., CW2 Stephen R. Sneed, CW2 Bobby J. Swink, 1LT Richard W. Wilson, CW2 Douglas L. Gandy, CW2 William N. Jackson Jr.

Co D (-) Maint 700th Spt Bn	ca1969	???	Norman
CPT Robert C. Armstrong	Dec 1969	Aug 1970	Cdr, Acft Maint Plt
CPT Robert C. Armstrong[78]	Aug 1970	Nov 1971	Cdr, Co D
CW2 Clarence L. Strance	Dec 1970	Nov 1971	Acft Maint Tech
1LT Emmett D. McElwain	Feb 1968	Mar 1969	Acft Maint Plt Cdr

45th Field Artillery Gp Aviation Section[79]	ca 1971		Enid
CW2 Bobby D. Breedlove	ca 1971		???
CW2 Bill J. Hensley II	ca 1971		???
CW2 Douglas W. Jones	ca 1971		???
CW2 Stephen Sneed	ca 1971		???
WO1 Robert S. McGee	ca 1971		???

445th Avn Co (Aslt Hel)	May 1971	ca Jan 1978	Norman ('71-'75), Lexington ('75-'78)
MAJ Jerry D. Bourassa	Dec 1971	Jun 1973	Co Cdr
MAJ Karl M. Frank	May 1971	Jun 1973	XO
CPT Dale E. Martin	Jun 1972	Feb 1976	Opns Off
1LT Gary L. Elliott	Jul 1972	Feb 1976	RW pilot
CPT Tony E. Boyle	Feb 1972	Feb 1976	Avn Plt Cdr
MAJ Karl M. Frank	Jun 1973	Jul 1976	Co Cdr
1SG Kenneth Inman	ca 1973	???	Senior NCO
CW2/3 Leroy A. Wall	Dec 1971	Jul 1972	RW AV
CW3 Leroy A. Wall	Nov 1973	Jan 1978	RW Inst Exam
CW4 Leroy A. Wall	Jan 1978	Sep 1978	Flt Safety Tech
CPT Donald E. Derrick	Jun 1973	Jun 1976	XO
1SG Nate Franke	???		1SG
CPT James C. Peck	Aug 1973	Dec 1977	Sec/Plt Ldr
CPT James C. Peck	Aug 1972	Aug 1973	RW AV
CPT Tony E. Boyle	Mar 1976	Apr 1982	Opns Off
CPT Tony E. Boyles	May 1969	Nov 1970	RW AV
1LT Gary L. Elliott	Mar 1976	Oct 1976	Sec Ldr
MAJ Donald E. Derrick	Jul 1976	Oct 1978	Co Cdr

CPT Dale E. Martin	Jul 1976	Sep 1978	XO
CPT Dale E. Martin	Mar 1976	Jul 1976	Plt Ldr
CPT Emmett D. McElwain	Dec 1971	Nov 1973	Sec/Plt Cdr
CPT Gary L. Elliott	Oct 1976	Jan 1978	Flt Opns Off
CPT James C. Peck	Jan 1978	Sep 1978	Opns Off
CPT Gary L. Elliott	Jan 1978	Oct 1978	Plt Ldr
MAJ Ray Brown	1978		Last Co Cdr
CPT Donald E. Derrick	May 1971	May 1973	Plt Cdr
SFC Charles H. Evans Jan	1973 ca	Oct 1976	FT Maint NCO
WO1 Charles H. Evans	ca 1976	Oct 1978	Unit Pers WO

other known former unit members:

CW3 Leroy A. Wall, CPT Roy Brown, CW3 Clarence R. Clarkson, CW2 Alfred F. Dreves Jr., CW3 Clarence L. Strance, CPT Donald L. Nave, CWO Roy Gene Cross

Det 1, 445ᵗʰ Avn Co (Aslt Hel)	Jan 1978	Sep 1978	Tulsa
MAJ Dale E. Martin	Oct 1978	Jun 1980	Det Cdr
CPT Tony E. Boyle	Jan 1978	Sep 1978	Plt Ldr

other known former unit members:
CW3 Clarence L. Strance, CW2 Jay T. Evans, SSG Donald G. McCarty, SGT Dan Nichols, SSG Norm Crowe, SGT Donald Russell, CW2 Robert C. Lane, 1LT Garry O. Bentley

Co D (-), 149ᵗʰ Avn Bn (Attk Hel)	Oct 1978	Apr 1982	Tulsa
MAJ Dale E. Martin	Jun 1980	Apr 1982	Det/Co Cdr
CPT Gary L. Elliott	Oct 1978	Dec 1978	Flt Opns Off
CPT Vernon R. Ashbrook	Oct 1979	Mar 1980	Plt Ldr
CPT Gary L. Elliott	Feb 1979	Jan 1984	Flt Opns Off
CPT Vernon R. Ashbrook	Mar 1980	Jun 1980	XO
MAJ Vernon R. Ashbrook	Jun 1980	Jun 1982	Det/Co Cdr
CPT Garry O. Bentley	Jun 1979	Apr 1982	Svc/Plt Ldr

other known former unit members:
CW3 Clarence L. Strance, CW3 James L. Smith, WO1 Donald G. McCarty, CW2 William E. Kennedy III, CW2 Lewis W. Keller Jr., CW2 Jay T. Evans, SSG Donald Russell, 1LT Garry O. Bentley, CW2 Chance F. Whiteman III,

Det 1, Cmd & Control (HHC 145th Avn Bn)(later **PROV**)

	Oct 1978	Mar 1983	Lexington
LTC Ronald L. Howland	ca 1978	1979	Cdr
LTC Donald Derrick	ca 1979	1980	Cdr
LTC Emmett D. McElwain	ca Oct 1980	1982	Cdr
MAJ James C. Peck	Jun 1980	Feb 1983	XO
CPT Gary L. Elliott	Dec 1978	Feb 1979	Opns Off
CPT/MAJ Ronald Varner	ca 1978	1983	Admin Off/S-1
COL John Robert Dille	ca 1978	1991	Flt Surg
CW3 Bonnie Dillard	ca 1978	1982	RN
MAJ Alma Pauli	ca 1978	1982	RN
MAJ JoAnn Still	ca 1978	1982	RN
CWO Charles H. Evans	Jan 1979	1983	Unit Pers Tech

HHC (-), 45th Inf Bde (Avn Sec)			Edmond/ Norman
Det 1, HHC, 45th Inf Bde (Sep) (Avn Sec)			Edmond/Lex
Det 2, HHC, 45th Inf Bde (Sep) (Avn Sec)			Edmond/Lex
CPT Dana D. Batey	ca 1970	???	Sec/Det Cdr
LTC Pete Phillips	ca 1971		Bde Avn Off
CPT/MAJ Dana D. Batey	Nov 1972	Sep 1975	Sec/Det Cdr
PVT Walter E. Fountain	Jan 1980	Dec 1981	Hel Mech Det 1
MAJ Ronald L. Howland	Nov 1972	Jan 1976	Bde Avn Off
CPT Emmett D. McElwain	Nov 1973	Feb 1976	Sec/Det Cdr
CW3 Leroy A. Wall	Jul 1972	Nov 1973	RW AV
MAJ Emmett D. McElwain	Mar 1976	Dec 1979	Bde Avn Off
CPT Don Shroyer	ca 1978	???	Sec/Det Cdr

CW2 Paul D. 'Pete' Costilow[80]	Apr 1976	Jan 1979	OH-58 pilot
CPT Paul D. 'Pete' Costilow	Feb 1979	Jun 1982	Det 2 Cdr
MAJ Paul D. 'Pete' Costilow	Jun 1982	Sep 1986	Bde Avn Off
SGT Peggy Zumwalt	ca 1979	1981	Unit Administrator
SSG Ronald Backer	ca 1981	1989	Unit Administrator
1LT Vicki L. Glass	May 1980	ca 1981	Sec/Det Cdr
1LT/CPT Richard Sackett	Jul 1982	ca 1984	Sec/Det Cdr
CPT Roger D. Ferguson	ca 1984	Mar 1986	Sec/Det Cdr
1SG Jerry McLaughlin	ca 1984	???	Senior NCO
MAJ Jackie L. Self	Sep 1986	Oct 1987	Bde Avn Off
1LT/CPT Walter E. Fountain	Apr 1986	Aug 1987	Sec/Det Cdr
CW2 Pete Phillips	Jul 1976	Feb 1979	OH-58 pilot
1LT Walter E. Fountain	Nov 1983	Feb 1985	RW pilot Det 2
1LT Walter E. Fountain	Feb 1985	Apr 1986	RW pilot Det 1
1SG Don Morris	Apr 1986	Aug 1987	Senior NCO
CPT John M. Griffis	Sep 1987	???	Sec/Det Cdr
SGT Peggy Zumwalt	ca 1978	1983	AST

other known former unit members:

CW3 Leroy A. Wall, CW2 Wayne R. Teague, CW4 Dennis Laffick, CW3 Danny Washa, CW4 Frank L. Berry, CW4 Joe Patterson, CW3 Douglas L. Gandy, CWO Dave Huffman, CW4 Morris P. Hale, CWO Glenn Wall

45ᵗʰ Field Artillery Gp Aviation Section   Enid
other known former unit members:
(ca Aug 1971) CW2 Bobby D. Breedlove, CW2 Bill J. Hensley II, CW2 Douglas W. Jones, CW2 Stephen Sneed, WO1 Robert S. McGee

HHC, 145ᵗʰ Avn Bn (Prov)	ca 1978		Lexington
LTC Ronald L. Howland	Oct 1978	Nov 1979	Bn Cdr
CPT Roy Brown	Oct 1978	Jun 1980	S-3
CPT Roy Brown	Jul 1981	Mar 1983	S-3
MAJ Donald E. Derrick	Oct 1978	Nov 1979	XO
MAJ/LTC Donald E. Derrick	Dec 1979	Aug 1980	Bn Cdr
LTC Emmett D. McElwain	Sep 1981	Feb 1983	Bn Cdr
SSG Charles H. Evans	Jan 1979	ca 1983?	Unit Pers Tech
CPT Ron Varner	Oct 1978	???	S-1

other known former unit members:

Co B, 149ᵗʰ Avn Bn	Jan 1978	Sep 1987	Lexington
CPT/MAJ James C. Peck	Oct 1978	Jun 1980	Cdr Co B
1SG Jack Nation	Oct 1978	Feb 1986	1SG
CW4 Leroy A. Wall	Oct 1978	Feb 1981	Flt Safety Tech
CPT Alfred F. Dreves Jr.,	Nov 1979	May 1983	Flt Opns Off
CW2 Billy R. Wood	Dec 1980	Nov 1982	RW AV
CPT Alfred F. Dreves Jr.,	May 1983	Feb 1984	Cdr Co B
MAJ Roy Brown	Jun 1980	Jul 1981	Cdr Co B
MAJ Larry Graham	Jul 1981	Apr 1984	Cdr Co B
MAJ Alfred F. Dreves Jr.,	Mar 1984	Feb 1986	Cdr Co B
CPT Walter E. Fountain	Jun 1983	Nov 1983	Sec Ldr
MAJ Michael D. Whitlow	Mar 1986	Oct 1987	Cdr Co B
1SG James W. Perry	Mar 1986	Oct 1987	1SG
CPT Billy R. Wood	Nov 1982	Jul 1984	Flt Opns Off
CPT Jackie L. Self	Dec 1985	Sep 1986	Flt Opns Off
CW2 Emmett D. McElwain	Feb 1986	Mar 1989	Flt Safety Tech
SSG James Carpenter	ca 1978	1986	AST
SGT John A. Dempsey	ca 1987	???	Unit Administrator

other known former unit members:

CW2 Leroy A. Wall, CW2 Elbert R. Poole, CW2 Alfred F. Dreves Jr., 1LT Garry O. Bentley, CWO? Richard O. Murphy, CPT Henry Stone, CPT Jim Giddens, CPT Roger Gallagher, CW2 Dorothy Stenstrom, CW4 Thomas M. Clark, CW2 Mannie Beck, CW4 Samuel T. Hinch,

CW4 Clarence R. Clarkson, CW3 Don Nichols, CW2 Donald L. Taylor, CW3 Richard Slade, SFC Lee Vickery, CW2 "Sonny" Bishop, CPT Terry F. Lauderdale, CW2 Orbie J. Maddox, CW2 Thomas Heck, CW4 Robert E. Clark, CPT Mayo Elliott, CW3 Jerry King, CW3 Thomas K. McPherson

145th ATC Platoon	Apr 1979	Sep 1997	Lexington
CW2 Mike Patterson	ca 1979	???	Plt Cdr
MSG Levi Orphan	ca 1979	???	Senior NCO
CW2 William G. "Bill" Rogers	???	Dec 1982	Plt Cdr
MAJ James Crawford	Dec 1982	Aug 1984	Plt Cdr
MSG David Keating	Dec 1982	Aug 1984	Senior NCO
CPT Mayo Elliott	Aug 1984	???	Plt Cdr
SGT Wayne Campbell	ca 1985	1986	Tng NCO (AGR)
SSG Ron Richardson	ca 1986	1988	Tng NCO (AGR)
CPT Vicki L. Morgan	Jul 1987	???	Plt Cdr
SGT Douglas Riggs[81]	ca 1988	1995	Tng NCO (AGR)
CPT Ramon Claudi Rivera	ca 1988	1991	Plt Cdr
SSG Darryl Anderson	ca 1992	???	Senior NCO
SPC R. Todd Lehman	ca 1991	1995	
1LT Michael Thomason	ca 1993	???	Plt Cdr

other known former unit members:

PVT Jon Michael Harrison[82]

Trp Cmd (Avn)	1 Mar 1983	Aug 1986	Lexington, OK
	Aug 1986	Apr 1993	Norman, OK
Trp Cmd (Avn) redesignated Det 2, HQ STARC 1	Jun 1989		at Norman, OK
Det 2, HQ STARC –	1 Jun 1989	Apr 1993	(deactivated)
LTC Ronald L. Howland	ca 1983		Cdr
LTC Don Derrick	ca 1984		Cdr
LTC Emmett D. McElwain	Mar 1983	Oct 1985	Cdr
LTC/COL Dana D. Batey	various dates		Cdr
SGM William G. "Bill" Rogers	???		SGM

MAJ James C. Peck	Mar 1983	Jun 1984	XO
CPT Jackie L. Self	Mar 1983	Jun 1985	Opns Off
MSG Cleo F. Templin	ca 1978	Apr 1993	Opns & Tng NCO
CW3/MAJ Floyd Todd	ca 1980	1992	Phys Asst/Flt Surg
MAJ Roy Brown Mar	1983	1987	Afld Cdr/Opns Off
MAJ Billy R. Wood	Oct 1984	Feb 1986	S-3 (Tech/AGR)
MAJ Alfred F. Dreves	Jr., Feb 1986	Aug 1986	S-3 (M-day)
CPT Jackie L. Self	Jun 1985	Nov 1985	S-4
CPT Vicki L. Morgan	Jul 1985	Jun 1987	Flt Opns Off
MAJ/LTC James C. Peck	Feb 1986	Aug 1987	Cdr
1SG Jack Nation	Mar 1986	ca 1991	Senior NCO
CPT Walter E. Fountain	Sep 1986 –	Feb 1989	S-1 (AGR)
MAJ Billy R. Wood	Aug 1987	Dec 1990	S-3 (AGR)
CPT/MAJ Vicki Morgan/Jones	Mar 1989	Apr 1993	S-1 (AGR)
CW3/4 Barry Grove	ca 1987	Apr 1993	Admin WO
LTC Leroy A. Wall	Sep 1987	Dec 1988	Cdr (Fed Tech)
MAJ Paul D. 'Pete' Costilow	Sep 1987	Feb 1989	XO
LTC Paul D. 'Pete' Costilow	Feb 1989	Aug 1991	Cdr (M-day)
MAJ Billy R. Wood	Jan 1991	Jul 1991	XO
LTC Billy R. Wood	Aug 1991	Apr 1993	Cdr (AGR)
SGM David X. Keating	ca 1991	Apr 1993	Cmd SGM
CW4 Charlie H. Evans	ca 1983	Jul 1987	Pers/Admin WO
MAJ Jackie L. Self[83]	Sep 1991	May 1993	XO

other known former unit members:

MSG Red Rowland, SGT Mark Montgomery, SGT "Doug" Hersey, MAJ Marty Weaver, CW2 Joel K. Smith, SSG/WO1 Bozena Bo Jones, SSG Judy McBath, SSG Terry McCaleb, SGT Robert Hoover, PFC Diane Stringfellow, CPT Ramon Claudio Rivera, CW4 George Senne

other known former Aviation Medical Personnel/members:

Flt Surgeons: COL John R. Dille, LTC Mark Henderson, CPT Howard Eliason, CPT Clifton Shimmerhorn, LTC Raymond Bloomquist, LTC Charles P. Russo, CPT Joe Bob Kirk, COL Edward Y. Matheke, COL Kenneth B. Smith, MAJ Matthew Jacobson, MAJ Richard F. Chadek, COL Larry F. Wilson

Aeromedical Physicians Assistants: MAJ Floyd T. Todd, LTC Jerry E. Joern, MAJ James W. Burks, LTC Robtert L. Patrone, RN Bonnie ???

45th Avn Bn (Lt Hel Cbt)	1982		Sperry, OK
LTC Dale E. Martin[84]	May 1982	Oct 1983	Bn Cdr
CSM Charles Connell	May 1982	Sep 1994	CSM (AGR)
MAJ Vernon R. Ashbrook	May 1982	Apr 1984	Bn XO/HSC Cdr (AGR)
LTC Tony E. Boyle	Oct 1983	Oct 1985	Bn Cdr
MAJ Leroy A. Wall	Dec 1984	Dec 1985	Bn XO
LTC Leroy A. Wall	Nov 1985	Aug 1987	Bn Cdr
MAJ Gary L. Elliott	Feb 1987	Aug 1987	Bn XO

HSC/ HHC, 45th Avn Bn (SO)	1982		Sperry/Tulsa
MAJ Vernon R. Ashbrook	May 1982	Apr 1984	HSC Cdr/Bn XO (AGR)
CPT Garry O. Bentley	May 1982	Jun 1984	HSC XO/Bn S-1
MAJ Tony E. Boyle	May 1982	Sep 1983	Bn S-4
CW3 Jaime N. Smith	May 1982		Log/PBO (AGR)
CW3 Clayton Mitchell	May 1982		Tng Off/Safety (AGR)
CW4 Robert D. Graves	Jun 1982		Pers Admin Tech (AGR)
MAJ Elbert R. Poole	Mar 1983	May 1984	S-3 (AGR)
MAJ Leroy A. Wall	Dec 1983	Dec 1984	Bn S-4 (AGR)
MAJ Gary L. Elliott	Jan 1984	Jul 1984	Bn Asst Opns Off
MAJ Elbert R. Poole	Jun 1984	Jul 1987	S-2 (AGR)
MAJ Gary L. Elliott	Jul 1984	Jan 1987	Cdr, HSC
MSG Carroll McBride	???	ca 1990	Opns NCO (AGR)
MAJ Billy R. Wood	Feb 1986	Aug 1987	S-3 (AGR)
MAJ Terry R. Council[85]	Dec 1986	Sep 1987	Cdr, HSC
M AJ Terry R. Council	Oct 1987	May 1989	Cdr, HHC
MAJ Elbert R. Poole	Aug 1987	Dec 1987	S-3 (AGR)
MAJ Marvin Roberts	ca 1987	1991	S-1 (AGR)
MAJ Lewis W. Keller Jr.	ca 1986	1988	S-4 (AGR)
MAJ Arthur Kveseth	ca 1985	1987	S-1 (AGR)
CPT Joe Bob Hicks	ca 1988	1989	S-4 (AGR)

other known former unit members:

CPT Ramon Claudio Rivera, SFC Nelson Hefley, SSG Joe Bunnell, SGT "Lou" Latham, SFC Alfred Hendrix, CW4 Stephen R. Sneed, , SSG Edward Eberhardt, SSG Bryce B. Harlan, SGT Tom Wright, SSG Roger Young, MAJ Dave Walton, MAJ Phillips, CW3 Rowdy Yates, SSG Saundra Hodges, SFC Nelson F. Hefley,

Co A, 45ᵗʰ Avn Bn (SO)(A) (lift) 1982			Sperry, OK
MAJ Don G. Shroyer	1 May 1982	Jul 1984	Cdr Co A
MAJ Garry O. Bentley	Jul 1984	Sep 1987	Cdr Co A
SFC Donald Russell	May 1982	???	Senior SGT

other known former unit members:

CW4 Clarence L. Strance,

Co B, 45ᵗʰ Avn Bn (SO) (A) (atk) 1982			Sperry
MAJ Richard O. Murphy	May 1982	???	Cdr Co B

other known former unit members:

CW3 Clarence L. Strance

Co B, 45ᵗʰ Avn Bn (SO)(A)	1986		Lexington

Co C (AVUM), 45ᵗʰ Avn Bn (SO) (A)	Jul 1984	Oct 1987	Sperry
MAJ Tommy Klutts Jr.	???		Cdr Co C
MAJ Phil Johnson	???		Cdr Co C

other known former unit members:

CW3 Clarence L. Strance

1ˢᵗ Bn 245ᵗʰ Avn (SO)(A)	Oct 1987	Sep 1994	Sperry/Tulsa
LTC Gary L. Elliott	Sep 1987	Oct 1991	Bn Cdr
MAJ Garry O. Bentley	Jan 1988	Sep 1991	Bn XO
CSM Charles B. Connell	ca 1987	Sep 1994	Bn CSM (AGR)

MAJ/LTC Elbert R. Poole	Oct 1991	Nov 1992	Bn Cdr (AGR)
MAJ Terry R. Council	Oct 1991	Nov 1992	Bn XO
LTC Terry R. Council	Nov 1992	Sep 1994	Bn Cdr
MAJ Lewis W. Keller	???	Sep 1994	Bn XO

HHC, 1ˢᵗ Bn, 245ᵗʰ Avn (SO)(A)	Oct 1987	Sep 1994	Sperry/Tulsa
MAJ Marvin D. Roberts	ca 1988/89	???	S-1 (AGR)
MAJ David S. Walton	ca 1988/89	???	S-2
MAJ Elbert R. Poole Dec	1987	Oct 1991	S-3 (AGR)
MAJ Lewis W. Keller Jr.	Oct 1987	???	S-4 (AGR)
CW3 Clayton C. Mitchell	Oct 1987	???	Safety Off (AGR)
MAJ Garry O. Bentley	Oct 1991	Feb 1992	O/S Flt Opns Off
CPT Thomas D. Jesse	???	Sep 1994	S-2
MAJ Marvin D. Roberts	???	Sep 1994	S-3 (AGR)
MAJ Joe Bob Hicks	Oct 1991	Sep 1994	S-4 (AGR)
CPT Britt M. Himes	???	Sep 1994	Cdr HHC
1SG George R. Wright Sr.	???	Sep 1994	1SG HHC
MAJ Walter E. Fountain	Sep 2001	Sep 2003	Cdr HHC

Co A, 1ˢᵗ Bn, 245ᵗʰ Avn (SO)(A)	Oct 1987	Sep 1994	Sperry, OK
MAJ Garry O. Bentley	Oct 1987	Dec 1987	Cdr Co A
MAJ Arthur C. Kveseth	ca 1989	ca 1991	Cdr Co A
1SG D.R. Canole	ca 1988	ca 1993	1SG Co A
1SG Norman W. Crow	Oct 1987	???	1SG/Tng NCO
MAJ Charles E. Hammers	???	1994	Cdr Co A
1SG Joseph A. Crawford	???	1994	1SG Co A
CW3 Clayton C. Mitchell	Oct 1987	???	Tng Off
CPT David A. Vanness	ca 1987	ca 1991/92	XO
1LT Keith D. Owens	Oct 1987	???	Plt Ldr
1LT Roy K. Tackett	Oct 1987	???	Plt Ldr
MAJ David A. Vanness	ca Jun 1991	???	Cdr Co A
CPT Keith D. Owens	ca 1991	???	XO
1LT W. Briggeman	ca 1991	???	Plt Ldr
1LT R. V. Schuler	ca 1991	???	Plt Ldr

other known former unit members:

CW4 Clarence L. Strance, CW3 Phil M. Prigmore, CW4 Ron J. Ketter, SSG M.R. Delorey,

Co B, 1ˢᵗ Bn, 245ᵗʰ Avn (SO)(A)	Oct 1987		Lexington, OK
MAJ Jackie L. Self	Nov 1987	Dec 1988	Cdr Co B
CPT/MAJ Marty Weaver	Sep 1990	Sep 1994	Cdr Co B
1SG Jim W. Perry	Sep 1990	Sep 1994	1SG Co B
CPT Walter E. Fountain	Feb 1989	Oct 1991	XO
1LT Bryan Palmer	Oct 1987	???	Plt Ldr
1LT Randy W. Beene	ca 1988/89	???	Plt Ldr
SFC Thomas L. Smith	Oct 1987	Sep 1994	Plt Sgt

other known former unit members:

SGT Kevin McAnally, SSG Jerry L. Tolson, SGT Jerry D. Lea, SGT John A. Dempsey, CW2 Jerry W. Hefner, CW2 Chris A. Rau, CW4 James F. Kanzenbach, CW4 Thomas M. Clark, CW2 Kelly W. Cawood, CW2 Terry F. Lauderdale, CW2 Jerry King, SSG Gary Throckmorton, CW2 Tom Heck, CW2 Thomas K. McPherson

Co C, 1ˢᵗ Bn, 245ᵗʰ Avn (SO)(A)	Oct 1987		Lexington, OK
MAJ Phil Johnson	Oct 1987	???	Cdr Co C
MAJ Terry R. Council	Jun 1989	May 1991	Cdr Co C
1SG Joe Volpe	ca 1987	ca 1994	1SG
CW2 E. Wayne McCorkle	ca 1988/89	???	Tng Off
2LT L. M. Bradshaw	ca 1988/89	???	Plt Ldr
2LT M. Enriquez	ca 1988/89	???	Plt Ldr
MAJ Walter E. Fountain	Oct 1991	Sep 1994	Cdr Co C
1SG Ronald I. Dye	???	Sep 1994	1SG Co C

Co D (AVIM), 1ˢᵗ Bn, 245ᵗʰ Avn (SO)(A)	Sep 1991		Tulsa
MAJ Jeffery Jones	???	Sep 1994	Cdr Co D
1SG Joseph H. Volpe	???	Sep 1994	1SG Co D

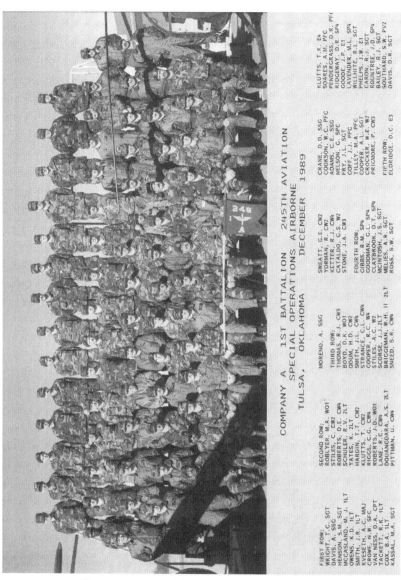

COMPANY A   1ST BATTALION   245TH AVIATION
SPECIAL OPERATIONS AIRBORNE
TULSA, OKLAHOMA   DECEMBER 1989

FIRST ROW:
WRIGHT, T.G. SGT
DAVIS, A. SSG
HENSON, S.M. SGT
MCCASLAND, M.J. 1LT
OWENS, K.D. 1LT
SMITH, J.R. 1LT
KVESETH, A.C. MAJ
CROWE, N.W. SFC
VAN NESS, D.A. CPT
TACKETT, R.K. 1LT
COX, B.A. 1LT
KASSAL, M.A. SGT

SECOND ROW:
ROBLYER, M.A. WO1
STILES, C. CW2
ROBERTS, D.E. CW4
SCHULER, R.V. 2LT
YATES, K. 2LT CW2
HARDIN, J.R. 1LT
KLUTTS, T. CW2
RIGGS, C.G. CW4
ROBERTS, J.D. WO1
LANE, R.C. CW4
DOUANGDARA, A.S. 2LT
PITTMAN, U. CW4

MORENO, A. SSG

THIRD ROW:
THOMAS, R.J. CW3
BOYD, D.K. WO1
ODUM, M.L. CW4
SMITH, J.L. CW4
STRANCE, C.L. CW4
COOPER, R.C. W4
STILES, A.C. W2
SCORSE, J.J. 2LT
BRIGGMAN, W.H. II 2LT
SNEED, S.R. CW4

SWEATT, G.E. CW2
YORMAN, R. CW2
KETTER, R.J. CW4
CATALDO, G.S. W2
STONE, J.A. CW3

FOURTH ROW:
GIBBS, R.M. SP4
GOODMAN, G.L. SP4
CLAYBROOK, D.T. SP4
MCINTOSH, J.S. SGT
MILES, A.R. SGT
ROSS, S.W. SGT

CRANE, D.D. SSG
COOKSON, W.C. PFC
ADAMS, C.E. SSG
NELSON, C. SPC
FRY, J.L. SGT
COFF, J.J. PFC
TILLEY, M.A. PFC
COOPER, A.L. SGT
CROCKER, W.E. W2
PRICMORE, P. CW3

FIFTH ROW:
ELDRIDGE, D.C. E3

KLUTTS, T.K. E4
SOARES, A.M. PFC
PENDERGRASS, D.R. PFC
RIDGEWAY, D.R. SP4
GOODE, J.P. E1
LAVENDER, M.L. SP4
WILLHITE, R.L. SGT
PHELPS, J.W. E1
CARON, R.J. SGT
ROUNTREE, J.D. SP4
BAILEY, R.J. SGT
SOUTHARD, S.W. PV2
DAVIS, D.R. SGT

Photo courtesy of BG (ret) Terry R. Council

Photo courtesy of BG (ret) Terry R. Council

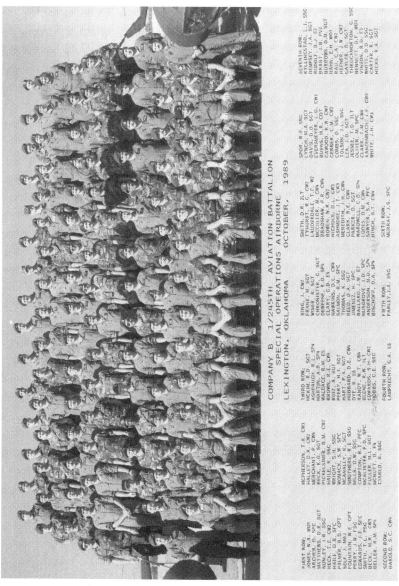

Photo courtesy of BG (ret) Terry R. Council

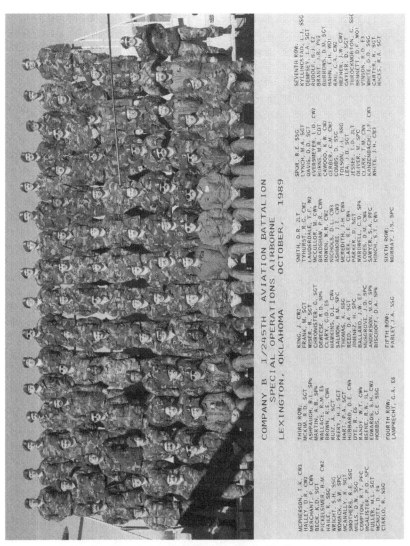

COMPANY B 1/245TH AVIATION BATTALION
SPECIAL OPERATIONS AIRBORNE
LEXINGTON, OKLAHOMA   OCTOBER, 1989

MCPHERSON, T.K. CW3
HAILEY, D.R. CW2
MERCHANT, T. CW4
BECK, K.D. SGT
PICKELSIMER, B.M. CW2
HAILE, K. SSG
WRIGHT, S.H. SSG
WOMACK, S.M. SPC
MCANALLY, K. SGT
SMOTHERS, R.E. SSG
MILLS, D.W. SSG
COMPTON, R.Y. PFC
MCALLISTER, R.D. SPC
FULLER, M.L. SGT
MCNUTT, D. E4
CIARLO, R. SSG

THIRD ROW:
MCHAM, R.D. SGT
ASHPAUGH, R.I. SP4
MARTIN, A.B. SP4
WALLACE, R.M. E5
BROWN, R.E. CW4
RUIZ, A. SGT
PEERY, H.J. SGT
HART, P.A. SGT
HUBBARD, D.E. CW4
DYE, R. E6
RANDY, W.T. CW4
BEENE, R.W. 1LT
EDWARDS, S.H. CW2
HOBBS, C.E. SSG

FOURTH ROW:
LAMPRECHT, C.A. E6

KING, J. CW2
FRANK, M. SGT
WISER, R. SGT
CHRONISTER, G. SGT
DEWEESE, R.D. SP4
CLARY, C.D. E5
HAWKINS, D.L. CW4
SALMON, R.M. SPC
THOMAS, K. SSG
REED, D.A. SGT
JIMENEZ, D.L. SGT
BALLARD, J.W. E7
MUSGROVE, J.D. SPC
ANDERSON, M.O. SP4
BISCHOFF, D.A. SP4

FIFTH ROW:
FARLEY, J.A. SSG

SMITH, D.R. 2LT
TYHURST, R.C. CW2
LAUDERDALE, T.F. W2
MCCULLOR, M. CW4
BRADSHAW, P.R. CW4
BOWEN, W.R. CW3
NICHOLS, D.J. CW3
ASHMORE, J.T. CW3
MEREDITH, J.H. CW4
CLARK, R.J. CW4
FRANCIS, D. 2LT
WARDWELL, C.D. SP4
LODES, D.M. CW4
SAWYER, S.A. PFC
HINCH, S.T. CW4

SIXTH ROW:
MURRAY, J.S. SPC

SPOR, R.E. SSG
LYNCH, M.A. SGT
DAVIS, D.D. SGT
EVERSMEYER, L.D. CW2
BURNS, M.R. CDT
CARWOOD, R.K.W. CW2
GERBER, C.M. CW2
COMBS, D. SSG
TOLSON, J.L. SSG
LEE, J.D. SGT
JRESH, D. 2LT
OLIVER, W. SPC
CLARK, T.M. CW4
KANZENBACH, J.F. CW3
WHITE, J.H. CW3

SEVENTH ROW:
KYLLINGSTAD, L.J. SSG
DEMPSEY, J.A. SGT
RUDOLF, H.J. E2
BRANT, B. PV2
BURROWS, D.M. SGT
HAHN, E.H. WO1
RAU, C.A. CW2
HEPNER, J.R. CW2
GAYER, D. SGT
THROCKMORTON, C. SSG
BENNETT, D.F. WO1
VINSON, D.D. SSG
CARTER, R. SSG
HICKS, R.A. SGT

Photo courtesy of BG (ret) Terry R. Council

COMMANDER AND STAFF
1ST BATTALION 245TH AVIATION
SPECIAL OPERATIONS AIRBORNE
TULSA, OKLAHOMA DECEMBER 1989

FIRST ROW:
BENTLEY, C.D. XO MAJ

ELLIOTT, G.L. LTC CMDR.
CONNELL, C.B. CSM
CMD SGT MAJ

SECOND ROW:
POOLE, E.R. MAJ S-3
KELLER, L.W. MAJ S-4

MITCHELL, C.C. CW3
AVN SAFETY OFF
ROBERTS, M.D. MAJ BN S-1

NOT PICTURED:
WALTON, D. MAJ S-2

Photo courtesy of BG (ret) Terry R. Council

Det 1, Co A, 114th Avn Bn ('RAID' Detachment)	1993		Norman
CPT Roy K. Tackett	ca Mar 1993	ca 2007	Cdr
CPT Clinton P. Ward*	ca 2007	ca 2009	Cdr

other known former unit members:

CW4 Thomas M. Clark, CW4 Mark Montgomery*, SFC Robert Carter*, SGT Mark Reynolds*, CW4 Dennis H. Laffick

   * current full-time RAID

Fixed Wing Sec (HQ STARC Cmd Avn)	ca 1970		Norman
OSAA, Det 46[86] (C-12)	Oct 1994		Norman
CW2 Pete Phillips	Mar 1979	Jan 1987	Cmd Pilot
CW3 Orbie J. Maddox	ca 1985	ca 1986/87	FW OIC (AGR)
CW4 George Senne	ca Aug 1987	Feb 1987	FW OIC (Tech)
CW5 Douglas L. Gandy	Feb 1991	Oct 2001	Det Cdr
CW5 Tommy Klutts	Oct 2001	Sep 2005	Det Cdr
CW5 Chris A. Rau	Nov 2005	ca 2010	Cdr (M-day)
CW4 Timothy Hardin*	Sep 2005	ca 2010	Det OIC (AGR)
CW4 Bill Stearns	fall 1987	Jun 1988	Flt Scheduler (Tech)
SGT Ralph Gibson	Jun 1988	ca 1989	Flt Scheduler (Tech)
SFC Jim Hall[87]	1979	Jun 2007	Mech/Scheduler (Tech)
SFC Jay Pierce	ca 1970	ca 1979	FW Mech (Fed Tech)
SGT Eric Wilson	ca 1990	???	FW Mech (Fed Tech)
SGT Phil Sorrom	Sep 1988	???	C-12 BASI mech
Civ Darrell Brown	Sep 1988	ca 1993	C-12 BASI mech/supr
SFC "Doug" Hersey*	Dec 1994	ca 2009	Flt Scheduler (AGR)

other known former unit members:

CW4 Orbie J. Maddox, CW3 Steve Minch, CW4 Jack Milavic, CWO Joe Tate, CW2 Joel Smith, LTC Dan Hazenfratz, CW3 John Bohan, CW4 Samuel T. Hinch, CW4 Chuck Williams*, CW4 Jeffery J. Scorse*, CW3 Todd Stark, CW4 Tom Brucker

   * current full-time OSAA Det 46

Det 3, HHC, 1ˢᵗ Bn 132ⁿᵈ Cmd Avn (C-23)	Sep 1996	Norman	
(redesignated) Det 1, Co A, 249ᵗʰ Avn Bn		Will Rogers ANG	
CW5 Jack Milavic)	1996	???	Det Cdr
CW4 Jerry King	1998	???	Det Cdr
CW4 Roy E. Brown	???	Det Cdr	
CW4 Dave Lodes	???		Det Cdr
CW4 Roy E. Brown*	???	present	Det Cdr

other known former unit members:

CW3 Dave Huffman, CW4 Don Nichols, CW4 Kelly W. Cawood* (AGR), CW4 Andy Stiles, CW4 Ken Jack, CW4 Greg Chandler, CW2 Matt McDonald, SSG Chris Self, SSG Nichols

* current full-time C-23 Det

HHC, 1ˢᵗ Bn, 245ᵗʰ Avn (ATS)	???	Lexington	
LTC Walter E. Fountain	Sep 2001	Sep 1994	Cdr
MAJ Joe Bob Hicks	Sep 1994	???	S-3/AO (AGR)

These were the aviation units in Oklahoma ARNG as of 18 Mar 2009 which were at that time under 90th Troop Command:

1/245ᵗʰ Aviation Regiment (AOB – Airfield Operating Bn), Lexington

90th Troop Command Aviation Battalion (unofficial name) Norman

    Co B 2/285th Assault (10 ea. UH-60) TUL

    Det 1 Co D 2/285th, TUL

    Det 1 Co E 2/285th, TUL

    Det1 HHC 2/285th, TUL

    Co A 777th ASB (Avn Spt Bn) (Distribution), TUL

    Co B 834th ASB (Avn Spt Bn) (AVIM), TUL

    Det 1 Co B 2/149th GSAB (Gen Spt Avn Bn) (6 ea. CH-47), LEX

    Det1 Co C 2/149th GSAB (6 ea. UH-60 Medevac), LEX

Det 2 Co D 2/149th GSAB, (Maint) LEX
Det 2 Co E 2/149th GSAB, (Airfield Services) LEX
Det2 HHC 2/149 GSAB, (Admin) LEX
Homeland Security:
Det1 Co A 1/114th S&S (4 ea. UH-72 Lakotas)
NGB:
Det 1 Co A 641th AVN (2 ea. C-23), Will Rogers
Det 46 OSA (C-12), Will Rogers

SGM Danny Matthews shared that, "Nearly all states today have small slices or detachments of a GSAB – General Support Aviation Battalion. Each GSAB is built the same, with very small detachments from the following companies:"
HHC – Personnel/Administration
Co A – Assault (UH-60)
Co B – Med Lift (CH-47)
Co C – Medevac (UH-60
Co D – Maintenance
Co E – Airfield Services

---

1. Email COL Walter E. Fountain, Dir OKPOT, 15 November 2007. The 18,695 figure is the total number of deployments of ARNG soldiers and ANG airmen from the Oklahoma National Guard as of November 2007, and it includes some soldiers/airmen who have deployed more than once.
2. Average length of rotation for an Army Guardsman is 15 months. The average length of rotation for an individual Air National Guard officer pilot/enlisted personnel is 90-120 days, although some ANG units deploy similar to an Army or ARNG unit for 12-15 months.
3. COL Fountain deployed to Operation Iraqi Freedom in November 2008 and served as the senior NGB representative at MNC-I in Baghdad.
4. National Guard "Fact Sheet"," ARNG (FY 2005) 3 May 2006.
5. While flying UH-1Ds in the 174th AHC in Vietnam(1967), the author's unit supported the 9th ROK (Republic of Korea) White Horse Division, near Ninh Hoa. Its headquarters was in Qui Nhon on the coast. They were fierce, disciplined fighting men and fearless.
6. Telephone conversation Michael E. Gonzales, Curator, 45th Inf Div Museum, Oklahoma City, OK, 8 November 2007.

7. 7 John B. Wilson, "Maneuver And Firepower (The Evolution Of Divisions And Separate Brigades)," (Washington, D. C.: Center Of Military History, U.S. Army, 1998), 266-268

8. Ibid

9. Ibid

10. A fixed-wing aircraft capable of vertical take-off and landing.

11. Telephone conversation COL Jerry D. Bourassa, 30 December 2006

12. Ibid

13. Telephone interview MAJ C.L. Strance, 30 January 2007

14. Telephone conversation COL Leroy A. Wall, December 2003

15. Telephone conversation CW4 Nate Franke, December 2006

16. OMD orders dated 16 January 1968 – provided by CPT Morris Hale, December 2006

17. Telephone conversation CW4 Lloyd Todd, 5 May 2007

18. Telephone interview CW4 Charlie H. Evans, 19 December 2006

19. Extract Spec Order No 199 dated 1 November 1965, provided by CW4 Frank Berry

20. Telephone interview CW4 Charlie H. Evans, 19 December 2006

21. 245th Med Co (Air Amb) organized under TOE 8-137E

22. Telephone conversation Ms. LaTasha Gatling, U.S. Army Center of Military History, 12 February 2007

23. Telephone interview CW4 Charlie H. Evans interview, 19 December 2006

24. Email CW4 Charlie H. Evans, 2 January 2008. Around 1977-78 Jack Nation became 1SG of Co B 149th Avn Bn at Lex and much later retired with approximately 40 years total military service. Charlie H. Evans retired on 31 March 1999 with 39 years one month, and 12 days total service; 24 years and 11 months of active duty.

25. 145th Avn Co organized under TOE 1-47E

26. 245th Med Co (Air Amb) unit history (1968 OMD)

27. Telephone conversation CW4 Morris P. Hale telephone conversation, 11 December 2006

28. State of OK Mil Dept, Special Orders # 9 dated 16 January 1965

29. State of OK Mil Dept, Special Orders # 199 dated 1 November 1965

30. This is the forerunner of commonly known [45th Inf Div] Bde Avn Sec [or Det]

31. 145th Avn Co unit history (1970 OMD)

32. Telephone conversation CW5 Donald McCarty, 20 November 2006

33. Telephone conversation CW4 Charlie H. Evans, 19 December 2006

34. State of OK Mil Dept, Special Orders Number 207 dated 26 August 1971

35. State of OK Mil Dept, Special Orders Number 285 dated 26 November 1971 provided by CW4 Frank L. Berry

36. 445th Avn Co (Assault Hel) unit history (1973 OMD)

37. AAAA awards information files, July 2007

38. State of OK Mil Dept, Permanent Orders # 84-1 dated 1 October 1978

39. Federal Recognition dated 1 January 1978. LTC Marvin Robert's *1/245th SOA History*

40. Email CW4 Charlie H. Evans, 2 January 2008

41. Telephone interview SFC Norman W. Crowe, 30 December 2007

42. Telephone interview CW4 Robert C. "Bobby" Lane, 16 November 2007

43. UH-1Ms were simply UH-1Cs with the T53-L-13B engine upgrade and had several armament systems added.

44. Personal interview MAJ Clarence L. "C.L." Strance, 31 January 2007.

45. The name "Det 2, HHC, 45th Inf Bde (Sep)" as of 1 October 1978 is from the military records of LTC Emmett D. McElwain.

46. State of OK Mil Dept, Permanent Orders # 84-1 dated 1 October 1978 – unit activated, replacing 445 Avn C0

47. 1 October 1978 Co D (-) was organized at Tulsa. LTC Marvin D. Robert's *1/245th SOA History*

48. Formerly Warrant Officer Rogers and later reverted to SGM (per LTC James F. Crawford).

49. Personal interview OKSAO LTC Jon M. Harrison, 20 December 2006

50. ASED – Aviation Service Entry Date; TFOS – Total Federal Officer Service (AR 600-105)

51. CW2 Chance F. Whiteman III, M-day aviator, was killed while flying on duty with the Tulsa Police Dept. (26 March 1982)

52. State of OK Mil Dept, Orders # 47-19 dated 11 March 1981

53. LTC Donald E. Derrick was a commercial airline pilot and Master Army Aviator from Stroud, OK.

54. State of OK Mil Dept, Permanent Orders # 88-1 dated 1 November 1981

55. Taped interview COL John J. Stanko Jr., 11 January 2007, referring to COL David Carothers, who doesn't recall making this statement.

56. State of OK Mil Dept, Permanent Orders # 7-4 dated 25 January 1982

57. SGM Ronald R. Richardson is currently the Enlisted Strength Maintenance NCOIC for OKARNG Recruiting and Retention at the JFHQ-OK.

58. 26 July 1984, CWO "Bear" Smith and CWO James Guernsey flew into Greenleaf Lake near Muskogee, OK, and were rescued by CPT Richard O. Murphy and 1LT "Randy" Smith (son of CWO "Bear" Smith). See Chapter 18 for story.

59. State of OK Mil Dept, Orders #82-1 dated 23 October 1985 – attached B/149 to 45 Avn Bn for administration and training

60. LTC James Peck was the State Safety Officer from 2 September 1987 to 31 December 1994, email from 29 December 2006

61. Cdr, LTC Leroy A. Wall; MSG Charles B. Connell, Sr. NCO

62. 605 pers auth; 517 assigned, 4 attached; 54 aircraft assigned

63. State of OK Mil Dept, Permanent Orders # 61-2 dated 24 August 1992 - effective 1 September 1994

64. Submitted by C.L. Strance 30 January 2007; also confirmed by Jerry D. Bourassa 30 December 2006

65. LTC August L. "Gus" Guild passed away 1 January 1999, OKC; he was the 1st "OIC" of OKARNG Aviation June 1965 – January 1968, before the position of State Avn Officer became official.

66. LTC/COL Pete Phillips was the 2nd OKSAO February 1972 – January 1976

67. COL Leroy A. Wall was 4th OKSAO January 1976 – October 1988

68. Telephone conversation COL Jerry D. Bourassa, 30 December 2006

69. LTC/COL Dana D. Batey was the 3rd OKSAO January 1976 – October 1988

70. LTC Chester A. Howard was the 1st OKSAO February 1968 – February 1972

71. CPT Robert C. Armstrong became the "UA" (unit administrator) at Tulsa

72. Telephone conversation CW4 Lloyd Todd, 5 May 2007

73. Ibid

74. LTC Jay Thomas "Tommy" Evans retired from OKARNG Aviation in 1990 as a full-time Fed Tech, IP/MTP, with more than 10,000 flight hours. He was an Olympic Champion wrestler from Oklahoma University, later the head OU wrestling coach and an outstanding American citizen soldier/aviator.

75. Extract Spec Order No 199 dated 1 November 1965 - provided by CW4 Frank Berry

76. Charles R. Jones was the Chief, Avn Branch NGB 3 June 1971 – 16 November 1973 and became the first Director, Army Avn Div, NGB 17 November 1973 – 1 August 1976.

77. Phillips, Cory, Evans & Mayfield are listed on OMD orders dated 16 January 1968 per CW5 Clarkson

78. CPT/MAJ Robert C. Armstrong served as S-4, HHC (-) 45th Inf Bde (Sep) from December 1971 to November 1976

79. State of OK Mil Dept, Special Orders Number 207 dated 26 August 1971 per CW4 Frank L. Berry

80. LTC Paul D. "Pete" Costilow was the M-day OKSAO June 1999 to May 2001
81. Currently MSG Doug Riggs, UA, HQs 245th ATS, Tulsa
82. 1LT Jon Harrison graduated US Army Aviation flight School in December 1989; he became the 7th OKSAO 1 July 2006 and remains as the present OKSAO.
83. LTC Jackie L. Self was the 5th OKSAO March 2000 – December 2003
84. LTC Dale E. Martin passed away 9 March 2004 Collinsville, OK
85. COL Terry R. Council was the 6th OKSAO December 2003 – June 2006; he was promoted to Brigadier General on 1 July 2006 and became the Asst Adjutant General for OKARNG, retiring in 2009.
86. Det 46 was the first ARNG officially organized by OSAA in October 1994.
87. Came to OKARNG in 1974 as RW mech; retired from FW in 2007 with 41+ years military service.

Chapter 6

Lexington Army Aviation Support Facility

(MG Hal L. Muldrow Jr. AHP—Lexington, OK)

"Behold the turtle. He makes progress only when he sticks out his neck."

James Conant

A major wild fire dances along the tops of trees, raging across yellowed pastures, and any wind becomes an enabler. It jumps roads, small and large, bodies of water and other barriers – but it began with one small, nearly invisible spark.

Every significant aviation facility, project or major unit change began with one small idea. Once conceived, these inspirations were supplemented with necessities, such as research, more planning, then sprinkled with a dash of logic and the idea or project grows and gradually becomes more conceptual. Team members and others associates are influenced by our enthusiastic desire to see it succeed and the plan grows – a little more headway is made. Eventually, with tenacity and much smart work and enthusiasm, the spark becomes a possibility; later with specifications added it becomes a plan, then along with funding and a stamp of approval it becomes a project. Incorporate the land and equipment needed, adding more funding and further man hours it becomes a dream come true. As in the entertainment field, the cliché "over-night success" is hardly the case; it often took years and years for a military project to evolve from a spark to the drawing board to open house.

A tiny spark started in the mind of visionary Major Dana D. Batey sometime between 1970 and 1972. Although Colonel Pete Phillips was SAO 1972 to 1976, the spark was Batey's. Soon the spark became a flame, then a burning desire, and a plan was born.

Batey remembered, "We had two categories of aviators in Oklahoma [in the early-mid 70s]: Vietnam returnees who were . . . already Huey qualified and the old 'Home Guard' that hadn't had the opportunity to get Huey training. I was using Tony Boyles [from Tahlequah], 'Buck' Buxton [from Ada] and [other] Vietnam returnees to go to the Bell [UH-1 Huey] plant [at Fort Worth] and pick them up. We had captains [who had just] come back from Vietnam and reverted to Chief Warrant Officer in the Oklahoma Guard [because we didn't have enough CPT slots]. Pete Costilow was one that came back and reverted to Warrant."

Our slice of the Guard pie was getting larger. Feel the synergy starting to flow with the influx of a new turbine-engine helicopter, the Huey and combat aviators, veterans just back from Vietnam. Dreams of a larger Army Guard Aviation organization in Oklahoma were now being verbalized more frequently.

"We were outgrowing [Max Westheimer Field] Norman [OK] and of course the next phase was [to establish an Army Aviation Support Facility at] Lexington," said Batey. "I asked Leroy [Wall] to put it [my plan] in writing and I said, 'There will be three locations, [which] I had already picked out in the state: Norman, Lexington and Tulsa. We'll have a command headquarters . . . I had tried to get an Attack Helicopter Battalion with command[1] structure,' but Stanko said, 'Politically, that can't happen.' I understand that, so if we just stay as we are [a couple of aviation units at Norman], as they say on the farm, 'We'll be sucking hind tit.' That's the way I briefed 'em, "We're here today [Norman] and this is where we're going to be tomorrow [AASFs at Norman, Lexington & Tulsa]."

After Korea, OKARNG aviation was located as a Flight Activity adjacent to the Air National Guard at Will Rogers Airport in southwest Oklahoma City. Beginning in the fall of 1955, OKARNG aviation assets were consolidated at Norman – all three assets. Yes, there were just three aircraft at Norman when Sergeant Dana D. Batey was hired as the fourth full-time person, in addition to LTC Gus Guild and SGTs Lloyd Ormiston and Marvin Davis. The three aviation assets were "two L-19 Bird Dogs and one OH-23B Hiller," according to Batey.

There was not an Army Aviation Support Facility or a dedicated armory there on Max Westheimer Field at Norman. LTC Guild, LTC Chester Howard and MAJ Dana D. Batey, in succession, led the OKARNG full-time aviation Flight Activities at Max Westheimer Field, Norman, OK from fall 1955 until summer of 1975. The Flight Activities at Norman were headquartered in Bldg. 7-K, a long, rectangular WWII, wooden barracks, adjacent to the State Maint Office on Westheimer Field; aircraft maintenance was in a huge, WWII, wooden Navy hangar. There was a full-time operations officer, maintenance officer, a secretary (Ms. Barbara Walker), an aviation safety officer and several mechanics and 3-4 instructor pilots.

"Leroy made this large picture board for me and I put it on an easel in flight operations [at Max Westheimer] so the pilots could see it and I called it 'Cloud Nine.' Through the breaks in the clouds you could see the [force] structure and another break you saw training at Lexington (NOE, NVG) it showed Chinooks and Hueys," said Brigadier General Batey.

"So [James] Larry Smith, [C.L.] Strance, were there one day [in the early 1970s] and I said, "Folks, the people that are going to get qualified [UH-1 Huey qualified] are the ones who [take the initiative and] get down to Rucker and get with the program. I think Buxton and Tony [Boyles], picked up two new ones at the Fort Worth Bell plant

Lexington Army Avn Support Facility

and parked them on the ramp at Norman. That new car smell [of the Huey] caused a few home-grown pilots to get off the dime and put in their requests for the UH-1 Q course."

"It took about three years to get Lexington [AASF] from the drawing board to [completion and] dedication [in 1975]. Sometime in 1972 we did a survey of the area and began working on the idea of [an Army heliport at] Lexington. We also looked at Fort Sill, the state senators loved it, but our guys didn't. I built a package on it (BOQ, ranges, ramps, etc.) and also did one on Chickasha [City Airport]. I think they [state legislators] gave us 140 acres and today the heliport [and training areas] is +/- 350 acres. So the Lexington AASF was built [completed in 1975] on the site on a World War II Naval Gunnery Range, an annex of Max Westheimer Field.

When [Major General David] Matthews came on board in 1971 [TAG October 1971 – January 1975] he put me in charge and told me to "Strike out, get with it and complete it." The survey was completed in 1972 and the [AASF] project was completed in 1975 and the [Lexington] armory a year later.

President Gerald Ford reported on 30 April 1975, that a force of 70 evacuation helicopters and 865 Marines had evacuated about 1,400 U.S. citizens and 5,500 third country nationals and South Vietnamese from landing zones near the U.S. Embassy in Saigon and the Tan Son Nhut Airfield, South Vietnam. We had withdrawn our troops and U.S. civilians from Vietnam.

"The unit I was hired into [full-time] at Norman was the 445th Avn Co and Major Jerry Bourassa was the Co Cdr. We didn't move to Lexington [AASF] until we came back from summer camp [at Fort Chaffee] in 1975. We set up a couple of tents, had a mess hall. They didn't finish the armory until 1976. [My office] was in a corner of the maintenance office downstairs in the AASF," said Charlie Evans.[2] The red clay common to south central Oklahoma was everywhere. The bottom half of local cars and pickups were covered in reddish clay and mud six months of the year; the rest of the time they were just dirty. The narrow asphalt

Muldrow AHP entrance Hwy 39

entrance road from Hwy 39E up to the new two-story hangar and later the new armory and OMS shop was permanently stained orange-red during the construction of the Muldrow Army Heliport, the new AASF and its 140 acres of training areas.

The land area at Muldrow would more than double to about 350 acres over the next ten to fifteen years. The neighbors to the east of the heliport were numerous, but by and large restricted. Most were residents of the Joseph Harp Correctional Center of Lexington, OK. Government neighbors are good ones to have. They don't complain of helicopter noise like the ostrich or emu farmers, which flourished in Oklahoma during the late 1980s and early 1990s. Even though they don't complain, we still didn't overfly the prison compound, and we avoided the known plume feather farms.

This Army Heliport, *HMY* (FAA identifier), located four miles east of Lexington, OK at Hwy 39E & 144th Ave (35-01.004417N / 097-14.018217W) was named for Major General Hal L. Muldrow Jr., a native Choctaw American, who commanded the Division Artillery, 45th Infantry Division from 10 December 1951 to 22 May 1952 in Korea and the 45th Infantry Division from 11 September 1952 to 31 August 1960. He served with the 45th Inf Div in WWII and Korea and was awarded the Silver Star for gallantry in action. He was an outstanding citizen soldier who served his state and the nation with distinction and honor.

On this 140-acre ARNG military site are included: two each (N & S) 100'x100' lighted, concrete helipads, a 2000' X 75' asphalt autorotation lane, a 75' tall man-made 30X30' pinnacle landing pad, asphalt parking areas (lanes) for 50+ helicopters, with hover-taxi lanes, numerous natural, wooded confined area training sites, multiple NOE (nap of the earth) route training areas and an external sling load practice area.

The new AASF #1 was enormous, with its combined operations and training offices and maintenance shop areas on two levels on the north side of the hangar, facing the flight line. This large, two-story, military hangar was designed to house 23 UH-1s and about 6-8 OH-58s at one time.

Then in October 1976, the brand new Armory at Muldrow AHP was completed. The 445th Avn Co (Aslt Hel) hosted the Open House and Dedication of the Armory. Approximately 1,200 people were in attendance that day.

By 1980, Cdr's/1SG's offices, training and supply rooms of Co B 149th Avn (UH-1s), 45th Inf (SIB) Avn Sec (OH-58s) and the 145th ATC Plt occupied the new armory. In addition, Trp Cmd (Avn), the Avn Medicine

Clinic, flight surgeon's office, a mess hall and large drill floor were resident in this armory.

After the Lexington Armory was completed an Organizational Maintenance Shop was added. This new OMS was located between the new armory and the AASF hangar buildings. The OMS was built for ground/wheeled maintenance.

During the spring time, when tornado warnings and sightings are a common occurrence along Tornado Alley, the AASF full-time crew could stack the hangar with all assigned aircraft +/- 29 – 31 helicopters in approximately 60 minutes. An amazing sight to behold, as all facility personnel came together and focused on one goal: bringing all our aircraft indoors safely, without damage to aircraft or injury to anyone! Several helicopters at a time were towed in from the flight line and dropped at the hangar doors, where another crew took over and manhandled the choppers into the building and with finesse, pushed carefully, then parked them nose to tail in an well-rehearsed and orchestrated effort. Damage to aircraft from a hail storm or tornado can be catastrophic and quite costly.

CW5 Clarence Clarkson

"When the new AASF at Lexington became operational, MAJ Dana D. Batey was the first facility commander [and he also became the State Aviation Officer on 13 January 1976]. Flight instructors were (I am not sure of the commissioned ranks, but I think they were) MAJ Jerry Bourassa, Major Tommy Evans, Captain Dale Martin, Captain Emmitt Doyle McElwain, Chief Warrant Officer Leroy Wall, and myself," stated Chief Warrant Officer Five Clay Clarkson.[3]

Clay had joined the OKARNG as a RW aviator in 1966, while he worked full-time as an RW IP at Southern Airways (Fort Wolters, TX). "I went to work full-time at Norman as an IP in 1972. Barbara Walker was Batey's secretary at Norman. There wasn't a full-time Operations Officer then. First Sergeant Ivel Cypert (Bde Avn Sec) was the full-time supply SGT at Norman and moved down to Lex in that position and then took over one of the lead mechanic jobs. We had three guys that worked as lead mechanics: Jim Coffield and Ivel Cypert . . . the third might have

236

been Willie Raines or one of those guys or might have been Jim Perry," said Clay.

On 19 May 1966, a group of 40 eager and daring young men enlisted in the OKARNG at the same time. They attended basic training together on the border at El Paso's Fort Bliss, TX. They were part of an Oklahoma ARNG program to increase officer strength in the Guard. They were not required to attend AIT after Basic Infantry Training, but would come back home and later begin OCS together in the future. After basic, PVT Ronald Keith Varner returned to Oklahoma and was assigned to Co C, 120th Med Bn down at Ada, OK.

The group of 40 had shrunk as some decided they didn't want to endure the trials and rigors of OCS. So in June 1967 the group of 30-35 enlisted young men began Guard OCS at the Oklahoma Military Academy (OMA) in Oklahoma City. They graduated as OCS Class #13 and Ron Varner recalled a couple of classmates – Colonel (USA ret) Leonard B. Scott[4] and Brigadier General Tom Manchino. After completing OCS, Ron attended Infantry OBC at Fort Benning in September/October 1968, then came back to Oklahoma, finished college and began teaching school.

Varner attended Officer Rotary-Wing Aviator Course (ORWAC) and graduated in April 1971. While TDY to Fort Rucker in 1974, Varner was contacted by Major Dale Martin who said, "Ron, you need to call Colonel Milligan right away at OMD, he's got a full-time job for you." He did and became the State Readiness Officer at OMD for the next five years. Milligan[5] was the DCSOPS & TNG, then moved to the DCSPER position and took Ron with him.

While working full-time at OMD, Lieutenant Ron Varner was a RW PLT LDR in the 445th Avn Co at Norman. Varner said, "[In 1972] I wrote the nomination to 5th Army recommending 445th Avn Co (Asslt Hel) at Norman, as the AAAA Avn Unit of the Year.[6] In 1976 I went to the Pentagon and did a short tour there and rewrote the Readiness Reporting Manual for ARNG units and it is still being used today."

Ron Varner became the full-time AO (Admin Off) at Lexington Armory in 1979. "That's when we formed the 145th Avn Bn (Prov). The 245th Avn Co (Air Amb) became the new Co B 149th Avn, part of the TXARNG," said Varner. 145th ATC PLT was also formed in 1979.

"They came to me and said, 'Ron, we're going to give you this ATC platoon and we want you to recruit it and fill the 50 slots. I filled that unit along with help from Charlie Evans and other aviation people."

Who else was working full-time at the Lex Armory in 1979? Well, "Charlie Evans, Jim Carpenter, plus a couple of different ASTs for Co B 149th. Monty Lamirand was the Co B AST for a while, and then worked at the Lexington prison. "He committed suicide," said Ron Varner. Sergeant John Dempsey then became the AST for Co B. Dempsey later moved to a full-time helicopter mechanic position at the Lexington AASF.

Some of you will recall that Lieutenant Colonel Ronald K. Varner retired in May 1984. "That's when my health got to where I just couldn't maintain my physical and couldn't stay in the Guard and that put me out of my work. I retired with 18 years – on physical disability. I had just gotten promoted to LTC when I had to retire, but I didn't make 180 days in grade. Had to go out as a major, replied our friend Ron Varner.[7]

Former Charlie Trp, 1/9th CAV gun driver (Vietnam 1970-71), Chief Warrant Officer Five Samuel T. Hinch related[8], "After coming home from 'Nam in May 1971 I worked at Tinker AFB and I joined the 445th Avn Co at Norman in 1973 or '74. I was hired full-time at Lex as an IP in 1978, when Richard O. Murphy left to pursue a civilian career with his daddy-in-law, doing something. I do believe at the time Dana Batey was the AASF Cdr for just a little while and then he went to SAO, then it was [Lieutenant Colonel Jerry] Bourassa. The full-time secretary Ruth Shipman followed by Mrs. Dean Raines. The other full-timers back then were Dale Martin, Tommy Evans, Clay Clarkson, Jerry Bourassa, Leroy Wall, Roger Ferguson, and John Ashmore. Then later Jack Self, Wesley Jones, Walter Fountain.

CW5 Samuel T. Hinch

Sam continued, "During those years we all were operations officers . . . we had the duty a month at a time. It was a system that worked very well until they had to manufacture a slot for a new commissioned officer that was being hired . . ."

Sam retired from the OKARNG in 2004 as a Chief Warrant Officer Five, Master Army Aviator with 11,000+ flight hours, more than 500 hrs NVG and 36 years military service.

Colonel Wall said, "I was the Flight Operations Officer at Lexington [ca 1983-84] and Colonel Jerry Bourassa the AASF Cdr. Batey was the SAAO and Dale Martin was the AAFA Cdr at Tulsa. Dale retired medically [in January 1984] and the [Tulsa AASF Cdr] job opened up. Batey had

me interview for it and they said it was mine. I turned it down because I didn't want to move at that time. Batey and Bourassa talked me into taking it. [Captain] Richard Murphy was the Tulsa Flight Operations Officer and he had also applied and thought he should have gotten the job, so there was a lot of tension [at Tulsa] for a while."

"Major Murphy was an excellent instructor pilot and operations officer. After I became the AASF Commander at Tulsa, Murphy continued serving well, but [perhaps he] never got over not being selected as the AASF Commander Technician position. About a year later Murphy got a job at the Western Army Aviation Training Site (WAATS) in Mariana, AZ," said COL Wall.

CW5 John Ashmore

"When Bourassa retired [January 1985], he wanted Batey to bring me back to Lexington, but I had been at Tulsa about six months and didn't think I had accomplished what I wanted to do. [Major] McElwain took over Lexington, and [Captain] Roger Ferguson became the Flight Operations Officer at Lex. After about a year, Lexington still had not started an NVG program. They also had failed the [5th Army] ARMS[9] (Aviation Resources Management Survey) inspection. Fifth Army said that "Lexington [AASF] had a leadership problem." Batey asked 5th Army to come back for a re-inspection in three or four months. They did and Lexington [AASF] failed again."

"[About March 1986], I moved back to Lexington and Roger Ferguson was assigned to Tulsa as the AASF Cdr. I later learned that Ferguson was a big part of Lexington's problems. The flight records all screwed up, plus he neglected [to complete] his own IP check ride and gave check rides to the other AASF IP's which led 5th Army to declare all the IP's at Lex

[AASF] invalid. I had to dive into fixing Lexington, but soon learned that Ferguson was having problems at Tulsa. This was now none of my business, except that he was a [M-day] CPT in the [45th Avn] battalion and was mysteriously absent most of the time. [I was XO of the Bn at that time] I think you know most of that story," replied COL Wall.

During the morning of 16 August 1986, we received a telephone call at the 45th Avn Bn (SO) Sperry Armory, where I was then the S-3/ Operations Officer. The call was from the Tulsa Flight Activities, Flight Operations office. The Tulsa police had found the body of Major Roger D. Ferguson in his truck. He had committed suicide the night before.

The first maintenance officer at the brand new Lexington AASF in 1975 was Chief Warrant Officer Bobby Swink. The Avionics Chief was Nate Franke. The Operations NCO was Bob Jones. [Former Sergeant Major] "Bill" Rogers was either the Shop Foreman or the Allied Shops Foreman. Rogers was both during his tenure, but I don't remember if he changed jobs at Lexington or Norman.

The maintenance side of the AASF was run by the Maintenance Officer, CWO Bobby Swink and the Maintenance Supervisor, SGM Wm. G. "Bill" Rogers. The shops at the new Lex AASF were: Engine, Prop & Rotor, Hydraulics, Avionics, Sheet Metal, Armament and Maintenance Office. The Armament Shop was deleted after the UH-1 "Charlie-Mike" guns of 445th Avn Co and Co D (-) 149th Avn Bn were gone.

COL Jerry E. Bourassa

MAJ Dana D. Batey was the first AASF #1 Cdr from 15 September 1975 to 1978, and his Operations Officer (Opns Off) was MAJ Jerry D. Bourassa. Flight Operations and Instructor Pilot offices were located on the second floor of the AASF hangar building.

The second AASF #1 Cdr was: MAJ Jerry D. Bourassa from 1978 to 1984, Opns Off – Chief Warrant Officer Four Leroy A. Wall. MAJ Bourassa was a part-time farmer from nearby Wanette, OK. "I think they had me in there as the first maintenance officer at Lexington, until CWO Bobby Swink got up to speed. Then they put me back as an IP and the Ops Officer," said Bourassa. COL Bourassa attended Wanette High School and then began his military career as an enlisted soldier in the USAF in December 1949. He served a four-year tour in the Air Force, after which he was discharged. Then in 1955 he joined the OKARNG, attending Oklahoma City University where he studied Education and graduated in 1957 from OCS at the Oklahoma Military Academy. Bourassa added, "I was commissioned in the Medical Corps and was the S-1 in a medical battalion. I transferred to the 171ˢᵗ FA Bn [because they had an aviator vacancy] so I could go to flight school. I was XO in a Firing Battery. So I went to flight school and while I was gone they had organized this Avn Co [45ᵗʰ Avn Co]. When I came back I transferred to the Avn Co. Back then [early 1960s] to transfer [or to get a slot in a unit] you had to go talk the battalion and/or regimental commanders and convince them they needed you! So I got in my car and went around to these different places that had aviation slots and found one with a slot. I told 'em 'I'll make you a good troop if you'll let me go to flight school.' And that's the way you did it back then. You had to promote yourself and go out and find those [aviation] slots and go interview for them. (laughter)

He attended the Field Artillery OBC at Fort Sill, OK, in 1958 and became an Army FW aviator in April 1959. He attended the RWQC in 1963. Later Bourassa attended the Aviation Safety Officers Course (ten weeks) at the University of Southern California in 1966 and the Avn Maint Officer's Course in 1969.

MAJ Jerry D. Bourassa commanded HQ Co, 45ᵗʰ Avn Bn at Norman in 1963, and the 245ᵗʰ Med Co (-) (Air Amb) 1970 – 1973. He went to work full-time at Norman in 1970, and recalled, "At Norman we had L-19s, L-20s, H—13s & H-23s. H-19s came in about 1970 – we didn't keep 'em long. H-34s came in 1972. Bourassa was also Cdr, 445ᵗʰ Avn Co (Aslt Hel) ca 1973.

On occasion OKARNG helicopters would be temporarily hangared at the Beechcraft FBO hangar on Tulsa Municipal Airport before any aviation units were officially stationed there. Guard aircraft were hangared overnight there on drill weekend and AFTP nights. In January 1978, Det 1, 445ᵗʰ Avn Co was formed and would be stationed at Tulsa as aircraft and full-time personnel were sorted out, hired and/or reassigned.

[In 1978/79] "Tulsa ain't fully established and they were flying Huey's from Lexington to Tulsa for drill and AFTPs," said Norman Crowe.[10]

"Who was in Det 1, 445ᵗʰ Avn Co at that time?"

"Sergeant First Class [Don] McCarty, Staff Sergeant Greg Stilwell, Staff Sergeant Wheeler Parker, Dan Crocker, MAJ Tommy Evans (State Safety Officer) senior IP. I think they were all full-timers at that time. They all transferred from Lexington [AASF] to Tulsa [Flight Activity, plus about 45 M-day personnel]. [Staff Sergeant] Gene Paine was the [Det 1, 445th Avn Co] UA (Unit Administrator). MAJ [Dale E.] Martin was the Tulsa Facility Cdr and the Det [1, 445] Cdr," added Crowe.

COL Bourassa was a temporary commander at AASF #2 at Tulsa in January 1984. He retired from Federal Civil Service and the OKARNG in January 1985 with 34 years of military service.

Lieutenant Colonel Emmett Doyle McElwain was the third AASF #1 Cdr at Lexington from 1984 to 28 February 1986, Opns Off – CPT Roger D. Ferguson.

McElwain was also a part-time farmer from nearby Byars, OK. He graduated from Stillwater High School and attended OSU where he studied history. He enlisted in the Army in 1954 as a Signal branch radio repairman and served a total of eight years as an enlisted soldier. Then in 1962 he graduated from OCS at Fort Benning and graduated from ORWAC class #63-6 in October 1963. McElwain was Aviation Maintenance Officer (AMOC) qualified in 1964. He was a civilian rotary-wing flight instructor at Fort Wolters from 1964 until 1973. He attended the fixed-wing qualification course in 1966 and he became Avn Safety Off qualified in 1973. He completed the Infantry Officer Advance course in 1976 and C&GSC in 1980.

LTC Emmitt D. McElwain

Second Lieutenant Emmett D. McElwain was a member of the original Co B 45th Avn at Norman in 1963. In 1975, CPT McElwain was the Avn Sec Cdr of HHC (-) 45th Inf Bde (Sep) 1974-75, known at Lex AASF as the Bde Avn Sec. In 1979, MAJ McElwain was Cdr of Det 2, HHC 45th Inf Bde (Sep). LTC McElwain commanded Det 1, Cmd & Control Hqs/145th Avn Bn (PROV) ca 1982-83. He then became Cdr, Trp Cmd (Avn) March 1983 – April 1985. He retired from Federal Civil Service and the OKARNG 15 March 1989 as a Master Army Aviator with a total of 9,300 flight hours and 34 years, 4 months and 17 days military service.

Lieutenant Colonel Leroy A. Wall became the fourth AASF #1 Cdr from 2 March 1986 to December 1988, Opns Off – Major Jackie L. Self.

Leroy began his military career in September 1957 as an enlisted radio mechanic. He became a WO in November 1962 and attended the WORWAC in 1965, then the FWQC in 1969. He became a RW Flight Examiner in 1973. In 1978 CW4 Wall received the 5th Army's AAAA Army Aviator of the Year Award.

Leroy applied for and received a direct commission from CW4 to MAJ/0-4 on 5 February 1981. Then in 1988 Leroy was quite busy; he attended the C-12 FWQC, the Army Air Assault Course and received a coveted Army Aviation Safety award for achieving 10,000 accident free flight hours.

COL Leroy A. Wall

CWO/COL Leroy A. Wall was a member of nearly every OKARNG Aviation unit in its history. He became a full-time IP at Norman in 1971, as well as a civilian rotary-wing flight instructor at Fort Wolters for a number of years. He attended the Army's Aviation Safety and Accident Investigation School at USC. He has served as Cdr of both AASF #1 at Lex and AASF #2 at Tulsa. He served as XO, 45th Avn Bn (Lt Hel Cbt) December 1984 to December 1985, then as the Cdr, 45th Avn Bn (Lt Hel Cbt) November 1985 to August 1987. While Cdr of the 45th Avn Bn, the Special Ops unit was honored as the Outstanding ARNG Aviation Unit of the Year 1987 by the Army Aviation Association of America (AAAA) during ceremonies held in Fort Worth. Leroy also served as Cdr, Trp Cmd (Avn) from September 1987 to December 1988, before becoming the OKARNG State Aviation Officer from December 1988 to March 2000.

COL Leroy A. Wall retired from Federal Civil Service and 43 years of military service in March 2000. Leroy is a Master Army Aviator with more than 12,000 flight hours. He continues to work and fly helicopters as an agent for the Oklahoma Bureau of Narcotics.

Lieutenant Colonel Jackie L. Self became the fifth AASF #1 Cdr from January 1989 to January 2000, Opns Off—Major Walter E. Fountain.

Colonel Jackie L. Self graduated high school at Stigler, OK and earned an Associate's Degree in Marketing from Eastern Oklahoma State College at Wilburton, OK ca 1976. He holds a Bachelor of Science Degree from the University of Central Oklahoma, Edmond, and received a master's degree from Oklahoma State University.

Jackie entered the Army as an enlisted airborne infantry soldier in May 1967 rising to the rank of SSG in Vietnam where he also earned the Combat Infantryman Badge. He was discharged from active duty in 1970. He joined the OKARNG two years after he was released from active duty and attained the rank of SFC. Self attended and graduated from Infantry OCS in 1976 at Fort Benning and then attended the Military Police Officer Basic Course in 1978.

Jackie graduated from ORWAC on 21 August 1981 and in 1985 attended the UH-1 IPC and the NVG IPC. He completed the FWMEQC in 1993 and flew the C-12 out of Norman. He was the Cdr, Co B 1/245th SOA from November 1987 to December 1988. He was the XO, Det 2, HQ STARC (Trp Cmd (Avn)) from September 1991 to May 1993.

COL Walter E. Fountain

COL Jackie L. Self became the OKARNG State Aviation Officer on 1 March 2000 and served in that capacity until December 2003. He retired from Federal Civil Service and the OKARNG as a Master Army Aviator 1 December 2003.

Lieutenant Colonel Walter E. Fountain became the sixth Lexington AASF #1 Cdr and served from February 2000 to July 2003. His Operations Officers were CW3 Wes Jones and Major Jon Harrison.

Walter E. Fountain enlisted in the OKARNG in January 1980 and became a UH-1 helicopter repairman 67N. In December 1981 he graduated from Fort Benning federal OCS. He became a RW rated aviator in 1983. He commanded Det HHC 45th SIB (Avn Sec) from August 1986 to August 1987.

In September 1986 he was hired as the full-time S-1/Admin Officer for Trp Cmd (Avn) at Norman, OK. He became the Operations Officer at AASF #1 in February 1989.

Fountain has never backed away from a challenge; he lead his class and graduated from the Air Assault School in 1988 and the following year became Airborne qualified at Fort Benning (1989). In October 1991 he became the M-day Commander for Co C 1/245th SOA and served as Cdr until September 1994. As a member of the 1/245th SOA, Emery became CH-47 qualified in 1992 and UH-60 qualified in 1998.

LTC Fountain earned a Bachelor of Science in Applied Science and Technology from Thomas Edison State University in 1996. Then he earned a Master's of Science in Natural and Applied Science from Oklahoma State University in 1998. Following his civilian post graduate work, Fountain entered and graduated from the U.S. Army War College in 2002 earning another MS in Strategic Studies.

In July 2003, LTC Fountain left AASF #1 and became the J-3 (DCSOPS), Joint Forces Headquarters of the Oklahoma National Guard.

He then became the M-day Commander of 90th Trp Cmd (MACOM) September 2003 until July 2005.

On 29 November 2008, Colonel Walter Emery Fountain deployed to Iraq as part of Operation Iraqi Freedom. Fountain is assigned to the Multi-National Corps staff working jointly for the DARNG, the Corps Commander and is the primary Guard advocate in Theater.

The seventh AASF #1 Cdr was MAJ Jon Michael Harrison, September 2003 to July 2006. His Opns Off was Second Lieutenant Michael Warren.

COL Jon M. Harrison

Jon Harrison enlisted in the OKARNG in January 1984 while in high school and was assigned to the 145th Air Traffic Control Plt at Lexington. Major Ron Varner swore him in at Lexington. After high school, Jon enrolled at Northeastern Oklahoma State College at Tahlequah, OK, where he became a member of Army ROTC and the ARNG Simultaneous Membership Program (SMP). Jon graduated from NEOS in December 1988 and went to flight school January 1989, graduating in December 1989.

After flight school, Jon remained on active duty and was assigned to Wiesbaden, Germany, H Co, 4th Bde, 8th Inf Div. "We were in Germany about a year and a half after the Berlin wall had come down," Jon said.

The Berlin Wall came down the evening of 9 November 1989, reunifying the city that had been divided for 30 bitter years of the Cold War.

"From Germany, I returned to the states and attended the Avn Off Adv course at Fort Rucker, then TDY to Jump School. From Fort Benning, I went to Fort Eustis, VA and attended the Maintenance Test Pilot and Maintenance Manager course."

Upon completion of the MTP course, "I was assigned to the 101st Airborne Div and spent about three and a half years at Fort Campbell," said Lieutenant Colonel Harrison in a December 2006 interview. After Fort Campbell, Jon's wife and kids moved back to Oklahoma and he went to Korea for a short tour. Jon was released from active duty after Korea and returned to Oklahoma, his family and rejoined the OKARNG in 1997.

Captain Cliff Pete Barger became the interim AASF #1 Cdr vice LTC Harrison, while Harrison and his unit, the 1/245th ATCS Bn, were deployed to Operation Iraqi Freedom III from August 2004 to ca September 2005.

It was Major Keith Varner[11], submitted the narrative justification for the Meritorious Unit Award 1st BN 245th AVN (ATS) covering the abundant tasks that the unit performed during period (12 December 2004 – 12 December 2005). The following is the proposed citation narrative for the MOU award:

For exceptional meritorious service to the multi-national corps-Iraq and 18th Aviation Brigade during Operation IRAQI FREEDOM 04-06. The 1st Battalion 245th Aviation Regiment (Air Traffic Services) distinguished itself through their dedication to the safety of all air operations in Iraq. Whether establishing new airfields for both Army and Air Force use, conducting space available passenger operations, or developing new flight following procedures using the airspace information center, the soldiers of this command enhanced the combat power of MNC-I, and the combat effectiveness of the 18th Aviation Brigade and in so doing brought great credit to themselves, MNC-I, their unit and the United States Army.

The Meritorious Unit Award was approved and presented to the commander, Lieutenant Colonel Bryan Palmer on behalf of the 1/245th ATCS on 4 April 2006.

At Oklahoma's Regional Training Facility, Oklahoma City, OK on 3 June 2006, LTC Harrison replaced LTC Bryan Palmer as Cdr, 1/245th Air Traffic Control Services (ATCS) Bn. The 1/245th ATCS Bn is the former the Co E 245th ATS, then another reorg as Co F 211th Avn (ATS). The

1/245th ATCS Bn originated from the 145th ATC Platoon at Lexington. The unit is today called the 1st Bn 245th Avn Regt (AOB—Airfield Operations Battalion) and has revived the former 1st Bn 245th SOA unit colors out of the museum.

From being the seventh AASF #1 Cdr, LTC Harrison, relocated his office from Lexington to the Joint Forces Headquarters at Oklahoma City and became the seventh OKARNG State Aviation Officer on 1 July 2006. LTC Jon M. Harrison was promoted to colonel 28 May 2010 and is current the OKSAO.

Captain Robert Bugner became the eighth and present AASF #1 Cdr in July 2006; his Opns Off is Chief Warrant Officer Five Wesley Jones. Both officers are presently in Iraq.

CPT Bugner, CW5 Wes Jones and all Lexington based OKARNG Aviation units were deployed in 2006 to Operation Iraqi Freedom, most for their second combat tours.

MAJ Keith Varner, a former enlisted member of the 145th ATC Plt told me, "CPT 'Bob' Bugner was an active duty ATC Co Cdr in Iraq, in LTC Harrison's 1/245th ATCS Bn. He [Bugner] liked the OKARNG units and personnel so well, that when he returned stateside he requested and received a release from active duty and joined the OKARNG and was hired full-time at Lexington."

CPT Robert Bugner

Looking back at each of the former Lexington AASF commanders there is one obvious common thread in the careers of these officers. Each AASF #1 commander from MAJ Dana D. Batey (1975 – 1978) down through the years to and including MAJ Jon Harrison (2003 – 2006) started their military careers as enlisted soldiers. It is my firm and humble opinion that each of these men having served and worked in the enlisted ranks added to their ability to provide solid leadership, beneficial guidance and achieve success in the realm of Oklahoma Guard Aviation.

Over the years, many, many men and a few women would work there at AASF #1 Lex. To name them all would be impossible. However, I'd like to mention some of Oklahoma's finest and strongest, former full-time enlisted Tech personnel[12] and I apologize if I get either the name or rank(s) incorrect:

AASF #1 Lexington Enlisted Federal Tech Personnel

SGM Wm. G. "Bill" Rogers – Maint Supvsr	SFC Jay C. Pierce
SFC Floyd Ormiston (retired ca 1981)	SFC Lloyd Ormiston (retired ca 1983)
Terry Pierce	SSG Jim Perry – Maint Office
SSG Darryl Anderson—Avionics	SFC Dave Keating—Avionics
SSG Joe D'Amico	SSG Leo Kennan
Lee Vickory	SSG Greg Stilwell—mech
SSG Wheeler W.P. Parker II Tech Insp	SSG Don McCarty—mech
SSG Don Hale – mech	SSG Ken Hale – mech
Glen Wall – Tech Insp	SFC Joe Edwards – Tech Insp
Stanley Cobb	SGT Willis Bettes
SSG Kelly (Little) Hall	SSG Jimmy Nunley – Afld Svc
SSG Don Combs – Engine Shop	SSG Danny Matthews[13]
SSG Robert Bullet Jensen—Hydraulics	SSG Rodney Green – Prop/Rotor
SSG Robert Arrington—Flight Opns	SGT Kevin Beck – ALSE

Here are the units that were there at Lexington from 1975 until about 1994:

Lexington Units from 1975 until 1994

445th Avn Co	15 September 1975 relocated to Lexington
Det 1, HHC 45th Inf Div Avn Sec	1975
Det 1, 445th Avn Co	1 January 1978 (Lex, later at Tulsa)
Co B, 149th Aviation	30 September 1978 (Co B, 45th Avn Bn (SO)
Det 1 Cmd & Control	1 October 1978–82 (145th Avn Bn (Prov)
145th ATC Platoon	1979
HHC 145th Avn Bn (PROV)	ca 1982

| Troop Cmd (AVN) | 1 March 1983–86 (moved to Norman) |
| Co B, 45th Avn Bn (SO)(A) | Oct 1986-94 (Co B 1/245th SOA) |

In addition to the full-time IPs already mentioned by Clay Clarkson and others, I also recall these Instructor Pilots: CPT Roger Ferguson, CW3 John Ashmore and CW3 Wes Jones. An M-day UH-1 IP of note was Chief Warrant Officer Four Bob Clark. He and Sam Hinch, also a 1st CAV VN veteran, would keep you in stitches with their endless jokes.

Following is a summarized list of the Lexington AASF #1 Secretaries, Facility Commanders and Operations Officers:

AASF #1 Secretaries

Barbara N. Walker	Sep 1975 – Nov 1977
Ruth Shipman	Nov 1977 – Dec 1978
Dean Raines	February 1979 – January 1986
Rhonda (McCalip) Hinch	January 1986 – October 1994
Sarah Jenkins	September 1995 – February 1998
Unknown	
Donna K. Kendall	April 2001 – January 2006
Jennifer D. Sommer	March 2006 – March 2007
Danielle L. Hamilton	November 2006 – October 2007
SGT Danielle Wells	

AASF Commanders/Operations Officers

MAJ Dana D. Batey15	September 1975 to 1978
MAJ Jerry D. Bourassa	1978 to ca September 1984
LTC Jerry D. Bourassa	
	CW4 Leroy A. Wall
LTC Emmett Doyle McElwain	1984 to 28 February 1986
	MAJ Roger Ferguson†
LTC Leroy A. Wall[2]	March 1986 to December 1988
MAJ Jackie L. Self	
LTC Jackie L. Self	January 1989 to January 2000
	MAJ Walter E. Fountain
LTC Walter E. Fountain	February 2000 to July 2003

	CW3 Wes Jones
MAJ Jon M. Harrison	September 2003 to July 2006
	2LT Michael Warren
CPT Pete Barger (interim)	August 2004 to ca September 2005
CPT/MAJ Robert Bugner	July 2006 to present
	CW5 Wes Jones

CW5 Doug Gandy

I retired in 1998, and I don't get back to Oklahoma often. Rarely do I have the opportunity to stop by the Lexington AASF. However, in March 2008, I was on my bike (Gold Wing) enroute to have dinner at the Norman country estate home of Chief Warrant Officer Five "Doug" Gandy, a VN aviation vet and long-time, dual-rated, member of the OKARNG Aviation Program. Doug had invited me and several of our mutual friends to steaks on the grill – Dana D. Batey, Leroy A. Wall, Pete Costilow, Jackie Self, John Ashmore, Gene Cross, Cleo Templin, George Droescher and several others who couldn't attend.

Having left Mena early, I decided I would stop by Muldrow AHP at Lexington and get a few photos of the armory and AASF. Much to my surprise, when I stopped at the main gate, I was greeted by a smiling security guard with whom I was already acquainted – Master Sergeant Glenn 'Red' Rowland[14], formerly of Co B 149th Avn and also of Trp Cmd (Avn). We had a great 20—30 minute visit. I'm glad I took to the time to stop and converse with 'Red.' Life is so short; don't miss an opportunity to visit an old friend. 'Red' passed away before I could stop again and visit with him.

My first visit to the Lexington Armory had been in mid-1980 at the recommendation of life-long friend and Vietnam brother, MSG Thomas L. Smith of Ada, OK. Tommy Smith[15] knew of my long-time love affair with flying. Since I had been out of the Army and military flying for ten years he could tell I missed it and thought it was time I considered getting into the Oklahoma Guard Aviation Program at Lexington. So I decided to call and talk with CW3 Charlie Evans, Unit Personnel Administrator at Lexington armory about getting into the Guard. At that time, Charlie told me, "We don't need any captains, but we *MIGHT let you* in Co B 149th as a warrant officer." I made sure he was talking about a *flying* warrant officer position and gladly accepted his offer. Having brought all my military/flight/medical records with me, Charlie did the paperwork and within about two weeks he had received my official NGB flight status orders. I began attending drill at Lex as a CW2 rotary-wing aviator in Co B 149th Avn that December 1980 (one of the best jobs I ever had).

During my March 2008 visit, I walked down the east-west halls of the old armory, where MAJs Karl Frank, Don Derrick, Jim Peck, Ray Brown, Larry Graham, CPTs Al Dreves, Michael Whitlow, Jackie Self and 1SGs Kenneth A. Inman, Nate D. Franke, Bill Rogers, Jack Nations had their Co Cdr/1SG offices at one time. I recalled numerous flight physicals and the dreaded finger wave, as I passed the old offices of Colonel John R. "Doc" Dille and physician's assistant Chief Warrant Officer Four Floyd Todd's flight surgeon clinic. At the end of the hall, I walked into the former dining hall and could almost hear the clatter of ancient, rectangular, aluminum Army food trays and visualized a few Army soldiers in cook's whites or t-shirts and BDU trousers serving chow. Several faces flashed in my mind and after too many minutes a few of their names also came to me – Sergeant James Carpenter, AST, MAJ Ronald K. Varner, the Admin Officer, Sergeant Ron Richardson, 145th ATC Tng NCO, CW3 Charlie Evans, and Staff Sergeant Bozena Bo Jones.

My visit wasn't complete until I tried to find where my old Trp Cmd (Avn) Training Office was, where Master Sergeant Cleo Templin and Captain Jackie L. Self and I used to work on a daily basis. MSG Templin formerly worked in Flight Operations at the Lex AASF.

I mustn't forget Major James Crawford. Jim had been the AGR OIC and 145th ATC Cdr at the Lex Armory ca 1983/84. Crawford left Oklahoma in the late 1980s or early 1990s and moved back to Fort Rucker, AL, where he became a contact IP for initial entry aviators. He worked as an IP for a contractor at Rucker and received his twenty-year military service letter after having joined the Alabama Army Reserve. Civilian Crawford is still instructing at Rucker as of this year (2008).

In the back of the armory, where the main drill floor is, I recalled the days of the 45th Inf Div

CSM David Keating
former OKARNG State
CSM

Bde Avn Section. With difficulty I finally remembered the names of two of the full-time AST/Unit Administrators – Sergeant Peggy Zumwalt and later followed by Staff Sergeant Ron Baker.

I also passed the offices where the 145th ATC had been and remembered a few former men of that unit: SFC Dave Keating, Staff Sergeant Darryl Anderson, Chief Warrant Officer Nate Franke, Staff Sergeant Gerald Swanson, AGR trainers, Sergeant Wayne Campbell, Sergeant Ron Richardson and Sergeant Doug Riggs. Ron Richardson is today Command Sergeant Major Richardson of the Recruiting and Retention Office at the JFHQ in Oklahoma City. Ron works as the Enlisted Strength Maintenance NCOIC. SSG Darryl Anderson, Keating, Franke and Swanson worked together in the avionics shop for 25 years or so.

Dave Keating went on to become the Oklahoma ARNG State Command Sergeant Major (October 2002 – November 2008). In 2007, Dave and his wife Sandi were visiting their son Major Ryan Keating at the U.S. Military Academy at West Point. Dave experienced a sudden heart stoppage and actually died. Ryan began CPR and called a military ambulance. Ryan's home was only seconds away from the emergency room at the USMA hospital. Miraculously, Dave was resuscitated at the hospital and has made a full recovery. He retired as the State Command Sergeant Major on 14 November 2008 with 37 years military service.

Before leaving the Lex AASF, I walked down to the facility main hangar. Since it was Monday, many of the folks I had known previously were off because they now work four tens (4 days per week, 10 hrs per day). However, I noticed the addition of a new CH-47 hangar northeast of the original operations/hangar building, a new fuel farm, new taxiways and a new autorotation lane. Things change. But the most important things in life aren't things – keep in mind, the most important things in your life are PEOPLE.

Many things have changed in the past 30 years since I joined the Oklahoma Army National Guard's Co B, 149th Avn at Lexington. Although I can no longer keep track of all of the new OKARNG

SGM Danny Matthews & SFC Houston
1/245th Aviation Regiment, Lexington
2009

aviation units, I am very thankful I can still remember many of the people and a few names.

Please accept this challenge—Make time to stop by Muldrow AHP at Lexington; visit with the security Guard; if you don't know him/her, ask if he was in the military and/or Guard. Listen to his story . . . Walk the halls of the armory and offices at the AASF. You might just recall a few of those names that you thought were forgotten. When you get home, give at least one of those persons a call and reminisce. The stories each of you may recall, might just make your day.

While you are there at Lexington, notice the unit patch on the right shoulder of those young (some not so young) aviation soldiers. You should note that nearly every one of them is wearing a combat shoulder sleeve insignia (unit patch), which they earned the right to wear while in combat in Iraq and/or Afghanistan.

Many new and significant physical changes have occurred at Lexington AASF in the past several years. A new 80,000 gallon fuel farm was added to meet the increased demand for CH-47 jet fuel. The helicopter parking ramp has more than double in surface area, with new taxi ways, new lighting and fresh stripping. It looks and is brand new.

When I joined the OKARNG, the 145th ATC Plt had a very limited amount of equipment: a portable tower mounted in the back of a 2-ton M1A1 truck trailer, a GCA radar they were attempting to get operational, and a few antique FM, VHF, and UHF radios. Men like Nate Franke, Dave Keating, Darryl Anderson and Gerald Swanson got that equipment going and eventually replaced. Today the ATC unit at Lexington is nothing less than first class, and its personnel are exceptional. At the Lexington Armory they've added an air traffic control audio/visual simulator. This device can be set up to display the visual 3-dimensional view of any Army Air Field and train ATC controllers utilizing real aircraft visuals, along with talk-back audio. Soon Lexington is to receive a new security gate house at the entrance to the Armory parking area. Change happens!

All of the Lexington units were deployed to Operation Iraqi Freedom in 2008/2009.

Not every great idea is birthed into our conscious mind through a lightning bolt experience. Not every lightning strike starts a fire in the forest. Sometimes a spark can occur during a dream; sometimes one is generated when two associates are just talking. If behind the thought or idea there is passion, a need to be met, and the effort is backed up by smart work and tenacity, you may eventually see results, unimaginable results.

Don't wait for others to bring their matches or wind-proof lighters. You bring your own flint, steel, and tender – make lots of sparks.

Look forward into the future, way out front on the horizon of OKARNG aviation. What do you see? What do you want to see . . . ?

1. Obtaining command structure for OKARNG Aviation was a large part of BG Batey's dream.
2. Interview CW4 Charles H. Evans, 19 December 2006
3. Email CW5 Clarence R. Clarkson Jr., 27 December 2007
4. Colonel Scott is the author of many acclaimed novels - *Charlie Mike, The Last Run, The Hill, The Expendables, The Iron Men,* and *Forged in Honor.* Scott, a veteran of Vietnam retired in 1994 after a 27-year career in the U.S. Army, with assignments throughout the world.
5. Colonel Curtis W. "Mike" Milligan, 45th Infantry Brigade, retired from the OKARNG as a brigadier general.
6. Awarded in 1973 to 445th Avn Co (Asslt Hel) per AAAA Awards information files July 2007
7. Telephone interview with MAJ Ronald K. Varner, 24 November 2008
8. Telephone interview with CW5 Samuel T. Hinch, on/about 29 January 2009.
9. The ARMS inspection focuses on enhancing safety, readiness, and standardization. It is a critical measurement tool for the chain of command.
10. Interview SFC Norman W. Crowe, 30 December 2007
11. MAJ Keith Varner, Army aviator, is the full-time Officer Strength Maintenance OIC for JFHQ-OK Recruiting and Retention. He is also the son of MAJ Ronald K. Varner former AO at Lex Armory.
12. SFC James A. "Jim" Hall telephone conversation 5 January 2008.
13. SGM Danny Matthew is the current SGM of the 1st Bn 245th Aviation Regiment (AOB) [airfield operating battalion] at Lexington. The 1/245th AOB is the former 145th ATC Platoon, but now holds the old 1st Bn 245th Avn (SO) (A) unit colors.
14. Retired MSG Glen "Red" Rowland passed away 8 July 2009.
15. In 1980, SFC Thomas L. Smith was a full-time AST (Admin/Supply/Tech) at C Co (-) 180th Infantry armory in Allen, OK. A few years later, the author convinced Smith to come to Lexington and get into aviation. Smith did, then attended several senior enlisted aviation maintenance courses and later retired as a MSG from OKARNG aviation.

Chapter 7

Tulsa Flight Activity 1978 - 1984 and Tulsa Army Aviation

Support Facility 1989—present

"A canyon of difference exists between doing your best and
sharing the credit, or glorify yourself."

Unknown

The state of Oklahoma encompasses 68,656 square miles of farm and ranch lands. From the eastern border with Arkansas, to the north Texas plains on the west (not counting the Oklahoma panhandle) it is 310 miles wide. From the Red River along the Texas border, north to the Kansas state line it is 220 miles. The single OKARNG Army Aviation Support Facility at Lexington would be hard pressed to handle the entire needs of the Oklahoma Guard and all state emergencies.

A short two years after the Open House and Dedication of the new Lexington Armory in 1976, a new direction and momentum came into being. Another large Oklahoma metropolitan area would be tapped for additional Army Aviation resources.

BG Dana Batey said in an interview, "Next was a satellite [facility] at Tulsa so they could support a [small aviation] unit. We went from the Beechcraft Hangar [at Tulsa International Airport] for the parking of aircraft and the 15th Street Armory at Tulsa to a brand new armory, large AASF. [Colonel Robert] 'Bob' C. Armstrong was up there [Tulsa] as a full-time trainer when we had [the first 45th Avn in 1964] Battalion. I was the Battalion Maintenance Officer."

In the late 1970s at Lexington, there were numerous members of the Guard working and drilling at Lexington, who lived in the Tulsa area. Some had even been members of the early 445ᵗʰ Avn Company while it was still at Norman.

But even before that, during the 1960s, there was a very small contingent of OKARNG Aviation personnel assigned to the Hqs Det, 45ᵗʰ Avn Bn at Tulsa. This was from 17 March 1964 to 1 November 1965. This detachment and Co B 45ᵗʰ Avn Bn were reorganized and became the new Troop D, 1ˢᵗ Squadron, 145ᵗʰ CAV at Marlow, OK in November 1965.

SFC Norm Crowe
October 2007

SFC Norman W. Crowe, the son of USMC SGT MAJ Norman W. Crowe Sr., graduated from Tulsa Central High School in May 1968. Just a few days before graduation, he enlisted in the U.S. Marine Corps. While a Marine, Norman received helicopter mechanics training and fell in love with rotary-wing aircraft and flying. Norm served in the Marine Corps until July 1978 and joined Det 1, 445ᵗʰ Avn Co, OKARNG in Tulsa on 16 July 1978.

He recalls, "In January 1978, Det 1, 445ᵗʰ Avn Co was assigned to Tulsa. They were flying [Hueys] from Lexington to Tulsa for drill and AFTPs. This included SFC Don McCarty, SSG Greg Stilwell, SSG Wheeler Parker, Dan Crocker, and Major Tommy Evans (State Safety Officer) senior IP. I think they were all full-timers at that time. They all transferred from Lexington to Tulsa. Gene Paine was the UA (Unit Administrator) for the 445ᵗʰ Avn Co. Major Dale E. Martin was the facility Cdr and the Det [1, 445ᵗʰ Avn Co] Cdr," remembered SFC Norman Crowe[1].

"That lasted until October '78 and then it became Co D (-) 149ᵗʰ Avn Bn. SGT Don Russell and me got hired [on] 26 September '78 as the first two full-time techs at Tulsa. We operated out of the north side of the main [ANG] hangar when they had A-7s. There was a break room and on the northwest side of the hangar there was an office there and that was where they operated out of and four or five desks in there."

"We didn't have a secretary [at that time]. OK, there was six of us mechanics and a shop foreman, and two full-time pilots (Tommy Evans and Dale Martin). SFC Don McCarty was the Shop Foreman.

"The other half of Co D 149th Avn was in Arizona. They had a smaller detachment in AZ, and they had the XO position, too. They may have had like one platoon there in Phoenix, AZ. Basically, we started forming up, enlisting a lot of people, getting new people in '78 and '79 we kinda built up. We started our [2.75mm] rocket program, shooting and everything. Our first AT was at Ft Rucker, AL the next year, like in July '79.

"We had a platoon of Charlie-Mike models, and we had a platoon of scouts [OH-58s Kiowa's] and . . . the facility was co-located with the ANG there at Tulsa, but the company headquarters was at the 15th Street Armory and that's where Gene [Paine] operated out of. He was the UA.

"Now then Jaime [Smith] came on . . . 'cause we took over the old range at the [15th Street, Tulsa] armory and that became our unit supply,

and Jaime and Gene had an office upstairs in the armory and we had like a training room with our training manuals. I think Jaime came on as full-time civil service Supply SGT in '79 I believe.

"I [Norm Crowe] got divorced in February 1980 and I was sorta the 'armory rat.' When I got divorced I was sleeping in the hangar. Co D (-) moved to the nose dock [at the ANG ramp] sometime in the summer of 1980. About 1979 or 1980 we added two more full-time technicians, one was Joe Volpe (retired as E-8/MSG), he was our electrician, avionics guy. And Ernest Bourget (E-7/SFC), he was our armament guy. We added a couple more mechanics, but I can't remember

CW4 Jaime N. Smith

who they were right now. We ended up with 10 or so techs by the time we became the 45th Avn Bn in 82. In June 1979 I was promoted to Sergeant First Class and I was the Aircraft Maintenance Platoon SGT [of Co D (-) 149th Avn Bn].

"Farber was the Co D (-) 1SG there for a little bit. However, something happened, he didn't do a good job and I took over in September/October of '80 as unit 1SG and I got promoted 1 October 1981.

"Dale Martin was there [in Co D (-)] until about '80, then Vern Ashbrook picked up as unit Cdr. Ashbrook picked me as his 1SG and was the one who made sure I got promoted. Then Dale went to state headquarters of course. [CW2] Chance Whiteman was our XO until he got killed.

"CW2 Chance F. Whiteman III, in civilian life was a helicopter pilot for the Tulsa Police Department when he was killed on 26 March '82 while on duty. It happened right around the [OMD] Military Ball that year," stated Crowe.

A Vietnam veteran, Norm is a soldier's soldier, an NCO who gets things done – much like Elvis - taking care of business. Norm is a true patriot. He retired from the OKARNG on 1 September 1992 as a SFC with 24 years of military service – 20 active and four ARNG.

Today you won't find Norman on his front porch in a rocking chair, or on the lake fishing. You would have to travel half way around the world to Southwest Asia, Iraq to be exact. You see, in February 2008, Norm went to work for L-3 Vertex CFT. Norm was the Maintenance Team Lead for HMLA-269, a USMC UH-1/AH-1 unit in Iraq, as a civilian contract employee. Norm just returned from working at Al Asad Marine Corps Air Station, Anbar Province, Iraq, in October 2009.

Visiting with my longtime friend CW4 Jaime Smith of Owasso, OK, he related some interesting history about the early days of OKARNG Aviation at Tulsa. "SFC Gene Payne was the AST (Admin/Supply Tech) for Det 1, 445 Avn when I first joined the guard. He stayed on as the AST for Company D (-) 149 Avn from 1978 thru 1980. I was hired on as the Supply SGT in May or June 1978. Gene Payne quit in 1980 and I became the AST at that time. "Sonny" Hendrix was then hired as the Supply SGT. At the time of the conversion to Special Ops, we were the two GS-07 and GS-05 employees for the unit (other than the AASF). The last AO I can remember was Captain Ron Varner."

Ronald K. Varner became the full-time Admin Off (AO) for the Lexington Armory in 1979. Colonel Batey, OKSAO, had Ron burning the candle at both ends. He gave Varner the additional responsibility of being the AO for the new Det 1, 445 Avn at Tulsa.

"Yes, I was AO over the detachment at Tulsa," was the response by Ron Varner. "How did I handle the duties? Some would say not very well, but that's their opinion. I made trips to Tulsa at least two times a month and many times more than that. I also sent Jack Self, Training

Officer, to Tulsa regularly. Charlie [Evans] burned up the phone lines and we had the [Tulsa] paperwork sent to us. Dale Martin would fly down to Lex often with a ton of paper work we would review and complete when necessary."

Ron added, "I recall going up and helping [the Det] get ready for their first COMET inspection. They were so far behind that a one-day trip turned into three and I scrubbed kitchen equipment for two days, as well as checking vehicles, paperwork, and such. Needless to say, after that COMET they never wanted me to come up and help them get ready for another [inspection]. I think they got the point about being ready. Oh, by the way, we failed that first one and had to have another in two weeks."

Jaime Smith continued, "I was asked by Dale Martin at the time we picked up the unit's TDA for Special Ops to decide if I wanted the Admin Warrant position or the Supply Warrant position. I was pretty tired of the admin side of the job and opted for the supply. I was still an NCO at this time."

"I was actually a Warrant Officer before. In 1979 I was an SFC and applied for Flight School. I took the FAST (Flight Aptitude Selection Test) and flight physical and was accepted. Dale Martin and Dan Batey appointed me to a W-1 in a vacant Admin Warrant positions while I awaited my school date. Saved the state a ton of money, me not going to WOC. Three of us were scheduled to go to Rucker at the same time: Don McCarty, Jackie Self from Lex, and me.

"Later, I was visiting with Dale Martin on one of our trips to Lexington and he was telling me that when I got back from flight school that he wouldn't have a [full-time] job for me; I'd be just an M-day soldier (weekend drills). At the time I was a single parent with custody of two small boys and could not afford to be unemployed—even an unemployed pilot. I later withdrew my school application and reverted back to a SFC. I still have my paperwork where I was discharged from the OKARNG as a UH-1 Pilot."

SFC Smith was hired into the 45th Avn Bn on 1 May 1982 as the full-time Supply Technician (AGR) and was appointed as a Warrant Officer W-1. Within six months or so he was advanced to CW2. Later CW2 Jaime N. Smith became the new Property Book Officer (AGR) for the unit. Jaime was a regular on most of the deployments, particularly self-deployments, as the Logistics Representative on the Advance Party.

Jaime was invaluable on our Overseas Deployments for Training (ODT) to Thailand and Honduras.

CW4 Jaime N. Smith retired from the OKARNG in September 1995. Jaime had 23½ years total military service. Jaime never went to the house after he left the military. He began working, almost immediately, for American Airlines in 1995 at Tulsa International Airport. His son, Shawn, is in the OKARNG Aviation Maint unit at Tulsa and is in Iraq. Jaime is the person I would ask to watch my six o'clock if I were to go into a dark alley, expecting danger. If Jaime said he was going to do something or was given a task – you could count on it being accomplished.

As of August 2008, both of the OKARNG fixed-wing units (C-12 and C-23) were deployed to Iraq. Also during the summer 2008, Co B, 834th ASB (AVIM) from Tulsa left Fort Sill for Iraq. Also deploying shortly thereafter was the Medevac unit from Tulsa and the Det 1, Co B, 2/149th GSAB (CH-47) unit at Lexington. Nearly 100 percent of OKARNG's aviation assets and aviation personnel have been deployed to the Gulf. I believe the U.S. Army and the Army National Guard are over-committed and under manned. Ask those OKARNG aviators, mechanics, etc. who are going back to Southwest Asia for the second or third time within the past eight years!

The units that were supported by the early Tulsa OKARNG Flight Activity/AASF were as follows:

Hqs Det, 45th Avn Bn – 17 March 1964 to 1 November 1965 Tulsa (reorg to Trp D, 1st Sqd 145th CAV)

Det 1, 445th Avn Co – 1 January 1978 – October 1978 (445th Avn Co main body at Lex AASF)

Co D (-) 149th Avn Bn – 1 October 1978 – 30 June 1982 (Gun Company)

45th Avn Bn (Lt Hel Cbt) – 1 May 1982 (later 45th Avn Bn (SO) and 1/245th Avn (SO)

On 1 May 1982, the 45th Aviation Battalion (Light Helicopter Combat) was officially organized, with its headquarters at the Sperry, OK armory. The aircraft and flight training activities were at Tulsa International Airport, Air National Guard Nose Dock ramp (initially). The Lords of Darkness, as the 45th Avn Bn (Lt Hel Cbt) was known, was a one-of-a-kind, Special Operations Aviation unit. Ninety-five percent of its mission training was at night, under NVG. This was a major change for a normal Army Aviation Flight Activity or Army Aviation Support Facility. Tulsa was not normal by any means.

Circa 1981-82, the following were the full-time personnel at the Tulsa Army National Guard Aviation Support Activity, to the best of my knowledge:

Commander MAJ/LTC Dale E. Martin (deceased) Secretary – Pauline L. Wiles

Instructor Pilots:

CW3 Robert C. "Bobby" Lane (1980)

CW2 Tommy "TK" Klutts (came to Co D (-) ca December 1981 and became Tech in April 1982)

WO Hugh D. "Hootie" Odum

Flight Operations:

CPT Richard O. Murphy – IP

CW3 Rex Bowen III—IP

SGT Sandy G. Hodges

SGT Don Keller

SGT Orville D. Cook (later WAATS CSM)

SGT Edward Eberhardt (deceased)

SGT Robert "Bob" Batson (M-day)

Aviation Life Support Equipment:

WO1/CW2 Leonard L. "Dawg" Reed – IP

SGT Eugene N. "Lou" Latham (retired as E-7/SFC)

SGT Joe R. Bunnell (retired as E-8/1SG)

Aircraft Maintenance:

CWO Jay T. "Tommy" Evans – MTP/IP

SSG Donald McCarty – helicopter mechanic (later CWO/MTP)

SFC Donald M. Russell – helicopter mechanic (later CWO)

SSG Norman Crowe – helicopter mechanic (later AGR training NCO)

SGT Daniel Crocker – helicopter mechanic

SSG Ernie Moore – helicopter mechanic (later Allied Trades Foreman)

SSG Wheeler P. Willis Parker – tech inspector

SGT Joe Volpe – aircraft electrician

SGT Ernie Bourget – aircraft armament

SGT Vick Jones – helicopter mechanic

SSG Anthony Davis – helicopter mechanic

SGT Sandra G. Hodges joined the Army Reserve in 1978 at Stillwater[2], "because that's where I lived," stated Hodges. "I met Dale [Martin] and

Captain [Richard] Murphy when they flew to Stillwater, while I was working at the college and they brought me an application (SF-171) for a technician position at Tulsa. They hired me in 1979 and I transferred over from the Reserves to the Oklahoma Army National Guard.

"CWO Rex Bowen was taking care of all the paperwork you know, the flight records and that sorta thing [in Co D (-) and the Tulsa Flight Activity]. And Rex was getting ready to retire, quit or something. Because I used to come down when they did AFTPs and fly, LTC Martin and Captain Murphy wanted me to work full-time as a Flight Ops Specialist [technician position]. After I was hired they put me in Co D (-) as an M-day soldier. Later Hodges attended the 67N helicopter repairman course.

SSG Sandra G. Hodges ca 1989

SSG Hodges' "Lunar" license plate 1995

"The ANG gave us one big hangar and it was big enough to put two of the Hueys in and one of the [OH-] 58s [Kiowas] when they were working on 'em and they gave us one office. It was real small and that's where LTC Martin did his business out of and CPT Murphy. That's where my desk was out there.

SSG Sandra G. Hodges retired from the OKARNG in 1998 while a technician at the Tulsa AASF. While in the OKARNG and a member of the 1st Bn, 245th Avn (SO), SSG Hodges had a personalized OKARNG Oklahoma license plate that read—Lunar. As you will recall, the Tulsa AASF Flight Operations call sign during the days of the Lords of Darkness was Lunar, and Sandy was the voice of Lunar.

CW5 Robert C. Lane

CW2 Robert C. Lane[3] was released from active duty at Fort Wolters, TX in 1970. He had flown OH-23Gs in Korea for a year and then was reassigned to the states. With four years active duty, he wanted to get into the OKARNG; however, they were full of aviator helicopter pilots coming back from Vietnam. Bobby finally got his name on the waiting list in 1974.

"I finally got processed in [to the OKARNG] in January of '75. April I started drilling. Then we went to AT [June 1975]. I remember my first AT was the year that the Vietnamese were at Chaffee, and we stayed in tents across the flight line. Lexington [AASF] wasn't even built yet," recalled CW4 Lane.[4]

In 1982, CW2 Lane was a member of Co D (-) (Attack Helicopter) 149th Avn Bn, a small gun company (minus) at Tulsa, with its armory collocated with the 1/279th Inf at the Tulsa 15th Street Armory.

"Before I was assigned to Co D (-), I belonged to the 445th Avn Co. Major Karl Franke was the commander. We drilled in Lexington. I drove back and forth for AFTPs and when we drilled at Lexington. In 1979 I think we moved [the 445th Avn Co] to Tulsa. We were an Army Aviation Flight Activity; we didn't have a full [AASF] facility. We used to keep one Huey up here [Tulsa] and—do Friday night AFTPs. We'd fly to Lexington, we'd pick up helicopters and bring them up here, do our drill and we'd fly 'em back down there on Sunday drill and ride back in that one Huey, cause we didn't have the facilities to prepare and do everything, we just had a Flight Activity", said Lane.

"When they finally moved them [our UH-1Ms and OH-58s] up here, they were [parked] at the Air Guard. They gave us the nose dock over there. We had that nose dock and where the security is now we had a facility over there."

"Dale Martin, Richard Murphy — they were the facility commander and ops officer. Can't remember if it was Rex Bowen, Tommy Evans was the other IP. It was when [CPT Richard] Murphy said, "You can fly this thing pretty good, why don't we send you to IP school?" So Lane went to UH-1 Instructor Pilot course in 1980 or '81.

"I think it was 1980, I went to Huey IP school. [I was] the last person to graduate the UH-1 gunnery instructor pilot school. They closed it down when all the Cobras [were fielded] . . . they phased out the Charlie-Mike models completely. The Guard was the only one that had 'em. We [Co D (-)] were in the process of getting Cobras and about to change over. When I got back, they had advertised an IP job as we started building this [new] battalion [45th Avn Bn (SO)]. I had applied for one of the Special Ops unit trainers [positions] and I got turned down; they hired [CW3] Clay Mitchell instead of me as the trainer. Then the [Tulsa Flight Activity full-time] IP job came open so I applied for that one. And I got that one," said Lane.

CW4 Leonard Reed and CW4 Jimmy Richards

"The Co D (-) armory was the old 15th Street Armory and Jamie Smith was the [Supply SGT – Tech] . . . we used to go down there quite a bit. Then as we became the 45th Aviation Special Ops, we picked up Sperry Armory and picked up a little more and started picking up the Little Birds. Then we began to shuttle back and forth to pick up all those Little Birds (OH-6s) at Gulfport, MS.

Another early member of the Flight Ops crew at Tulsa was SGT Leonard Reed. Leonard applied for and graduated from the U.S. Army Aviation Center as an Army Rotary-wing Aviator. Shortly thereafter he attended the IP course and was hired by the Tulsa folks as a Flight Operations technician and later as an Instructor Pilot at the Tulsa Flight Activity. CW5 Leonard Reed is still employed at the Tulsa AASF.

The origins of the Tulsa AASF go back a long way when OKARNG Aviation business was conducted on the tailgate of MAJ Dale E. Martin's pickup truck there at the ANG ramp. Hats Off to those guys who were treated worse than step-children for nearly ten years – before a new Tulsa AASF and Armory came into being.

Tommy Klutts Jr. was born in Okemah on 17 September 1945. As a junior in high school he joined the Oklahoma Army National Guard at the local armory in Okemah. Tommy recalled, "That was back in the old days when we drilled on every Monday night. And we did that four times a month and that's how we got our drill [four UTAs] for the month. The

old armory was actually a prisoner of war camp [for Germans] during WWII.

TK recalled, "I went to OCS, I believe it was in 1966 or actually I graduated in '66 as a second lieutenant. When I was going to OCS, Bob Morgan[5] was my company commander – Co A 2/279th."

"In about 1969, I put in an application for flight school. Of course, Chester Howard was the State Aviation Officer in Oklahoma at that time. He helped me to get in, but was honest and said 'it won't be right away!' After three years assigned to the SRF (1/279th) Infantry unit in Ponca City, I went to flight school. My first assignment as an aviator was HHC 145th

CW5 Tommy "TK" Klutts Jr.
ca 2005

Avn Bn, OKARNG, and my commander was Major Ron Howland."

TK remembered, "I really wanted to be a full-time Guard pilot, to fly and be an instructor pilot. At this time, Dana Batey was the SAO and he said 'Well, this is what you gotta do—you need to get your tickets punched first.'"

"'Number one, you need to go to IP school; number two, you need to go to safety school. You [also] need to have a maintenance background and that'll make you a real good candidate for a full-time job.' In the interim, Colonel Howard transferred to Pennsylvania ARNG. He went to Guard Bureau and was working at NGB when I was able to go to IP school first and then I went to University of Southern California – the old (accident investigation) safety course. And then I attended AMOC—all from about 1970 to about '72. Colonel Howard had become the SAO in Pennsylvania and the program was really expanding up there and they were moving fast in the direction of the turbine helicopters and at that time they were looking for other people, instructors and things like that.

"So I talked to Colonel Batey and he said, 'I don't have anything in Oklahoma right now, but Colonel Howard may have something in Pennsylvania. So go up there and get you some experience with him and then you can come back here and you can go to work for us. Five years or so after you have been up there, maybe our program will be catching up and we'll be expanding.'"

Long story short, "Colonel Howard told me to put in an application; I went up there and was selected for the job. So as soon as I finished AMOC, I gave my resignation to the Oklahoma Guard and was picked up and transferred to the Pennsylvania Guard and that's how I became a Pennsylvania Guardsman."

While at Fort Indiantown Gap, TK had become an IP, a test pilot in the OH-58, OH-6, and UH-1. He transitioned into the CH-47 and later was promoted to major and became commander of the 28th Direct Support Helicopter Co (CH-47) at the Gap.

In 1979, TK became "tired of all the cold and snow in Pennsylvania and came back to Oklahoma." For the next three years he was partners with Bobby Swink, Marcus Dunn in Consolidated Helicopters, a civilian aviation company to support the Oklahoma oil boom. They provided charter helicopter service and helicopter maintenance.

About 1982, the oil boom in Oklahoma went bust! TK sold out his portion of Consolidated Helicopters and called Batey. But there weren't any full-time flying guard positions available and to get into the guard TK would have to revert to warrant officer. He wasn't happy with that and delayed a decision to join the OKARNG for about a year.

"Tulsa was flying OH-6s and I decided that this might be my kind of deal. Dale Martin, someone I really liked, had came and talked to me. He was the Battalion Commander at that time and that's when they had started the Special Operations [45th Avn Bn (SO)(A)]. He was telling me all about it and I thought, "You know this sounds pretty interesting, I might kind of like this."

"Of course, I was an M-Day guy for a while in 1982, and then they started expanding that operation, so I took a full-time job as a CW2. I was hired as an instructor pilot in the OH-6 because I had all the experience and time in it. So I was one of the high-time OH-6 pilots at Tulsa; it was a fairly new aircraft to those guys."

Later, about 1986, TK Klutts, Bobby Lane, Don McCarty, Leonard Reed, Dave Odum, and a several other M-day Special Operations aviators, such as CW4 Ron Ketter, CW2 Andy Stiles, WO David Barr, and WO Jeff Scorse at the Tulsa AASF were known as the Road Team. Of these men, the instructor pilots were the most highly qualified, OH-6, NVG, DLQ aviators, IPs & SIPs not only in the ARNG, but in all of the Army. The M-day Guard bums who didn't have full-time jobs, made themselves available to go on any or all SOA deployments.

The standards for the 45th Avn Bn (SO) were absolutely and insanely tough. And the Lords of Darkness and the Tulsa AASF IPs and support personnel worked diligently, exceedingly long and grueling hours to meet those standards. They trained and flew at night and still had to do some daytime work. Something like burning the candle at both ends!

Although the term Road Team was in fact a group of the most highly trained SOA aviators, the use of the name was somewhat self-defeating. To some, it created much jealousy and caused many in the unit to feel like there was an us and them situation. Either you were part of the Road Team (or the in-crowd) or you weren't. If not, then you were just a flyer in the unit, perhaps not really good enough to make the team. Not everyone can fit on the high end of the spectrum. Not every aviator is blond-headed, blue-eyed and Type A, and you'd better be the best of the best to survive in the Special Ops environment.

It ain't bragging if you can do it. "Cause I'm ten feet tall and you can't touch me . . . !" There's another sage Chinese saying, "Those who have ridden the tiger can't get off."

During the period 1982 to circa 1987 it was balls to the wall, you met yourself coming and going – personalities flared, tempers exploded, but the Special Ops training continued. There were few people at OMD that we (full-time members of the 45th Avn Bn [SO]) didn't piss off in one manner or another, with the phrase, " . . . it's classified, we can't discuss that." We were special.

TK left the Tulsa AASF #2 about 1996 for the Norman fixed-wing Operational Support Airlift (OSA) Det 46 (C-12). He flew OSA missions in the C-12 out of Norman for about eight months and then was diagnosed with kidney cancer. Subsequently, the kidney was removed and he was grounded for a year. Miraculously, he and Major Floyd Todd, flight surgeons physician's assistant, were able to obtain a waiver from Mother Rucker, and he was reinstated to full flight duty status! As the Cdr, Det 46, TK took the unit and personnel to Kuwait in 2004. Klutts retired from

Federal Civil Service and the OKARNG in September 2005. He continues to fly EMS today. "Best job I ever had," TK says enthusiastically.

Late one evening during October 1986, COL Dana Batey, brought a

young Regular Army captain to the Sperry Armory. Batey wanted to introduce him to me and the other full-time staff and Headquarters 45th Avn Bn support personnel – Captain Terry R. Council. Council was still on Active Duty at that time. He was very interested in coming to the OKARNG and becoming a technician. He was born in Oakley, KS in May 1953.

CPT Council was promoted to major on 1 November 1986 while still on Active Duty. On 1 December 1986 he was released from Active Duty and came into the OKARNG on 2 December and hired as the Operations Officer of the Tulsa AASF #2. Due to the death of Major Roger D. Ferguson, Council became the acting AASF Commander and was the Operations Officer in title and pay only. He simultaneously became the M-day Commander of HSC, 45th Avn Bn (SO) at Sperry. In April 1987 he was officially hired as Cdr, AASF #2.

MAJ Terry R. Council
ca 1987

CPT Council graduated cum laude from Panhandle State University, OK in 1975 with a Bachelor of Science degree in Business Administration and was an ROTC Distinguished Mil Grad. He later obtained a Master of Arts degree in Procurement & Acquisition Management, from Webster University, St. Louis, MO.

Council held four command positions in the OKARNG Special Operations Battalion. He first commanded the HSC Co, then was the Co C (AVIM), Cdr, then became the Bn XO, and from November 1992 to September 1994 Council was the Bn Cdr, 1st Bn, 245th Avn (SOA).

Council was promoted to Colonel on 8 May 2001. He was the OKARNG State Army Aviation Officer from December 2003 to June 2006. He became the Deputy Adjutant General of the Oklahoma National Guard in June 2006 and was promoted to Brigadier General and received Federal Recognition on 1 July 2006. Brigadier General Council is a dual-rated Master Army Aviator with 4,300 + flight hours. He served as the Deputy AG, as an M-day soldier and retired 11 July 2009. BG Council devoted a total of 34 years to military service for his country.

He works full-time for the Boeing Company in Philadelphia, PA as the Senior Manager for Advanced Current Forces, Combat Systems, and Advance Networks & Net-Centric Systems. He relocated his family to Pennsylvania in May 2009.

During Council's closing remarks at his military retirement dinner in OKC, he shared with family, friends and soldiers these three things:

"If a subordinate of yours is not being successful, and is having problems, first look at what you, his/her supervisor, did or didn't do to support that person. Do this before you criticize them."

"Be an encourager, not someone who discourages (subordinates)"

"And lastly, to paraphrase someone else, if you don't care who gets the credit, you'll be amazed at what the group can get accomplished!"

Captain Barry DeFoor came to OKARNG from Active Duty and was hired as the Operations Officer for AASF #2 in early 1987. He continued in that position until approximately 1988. CPT DeFoor became disenchanted with Special Ops and the Bn, and left the OKARNG. He transferred to the Alabama ARNG as an M-day aviator and later went full-time. CW4 Tommy "TK" Klutts Jr. backfilled the Operations Officer position when DeFoor resigned; Klutts worked AASF #2 Flight Operations until ca 1996.

A former enlisted field artilleryman from Enid, OK, Lieutenant Jon R. Greenhaw graduated from flight school in 1992, came back to the 1st Bn 245th SOA and became the Asst S-2. Later, Jon was the III/V Plt Ldr and commanded HHC, 1/245th. Major Greenhaw became the Opns Off for Tulsa AASF in June 2001. Jon was also the M-Day Cdr, Co D AVIM 1/245th SOA. As the Global War on Terrorism mounted, following the tragic events of 9-11, MAJ Greenhaw and Co D AVIM deployed to Fort Campbell in Aug 2002 and supported the Night Stalkers of the 160th SOAR for a year. Upon returning from Campbell in August 2003, Greenhaw became Acting AASF Cdr at Tulsa as Colonel Council moved to OMD.

LTC Jon R. Greenhaw

Greenhaw remained Acting Tulsa AASF Cdr until he was officially hired in the AASF Cdr's position in February 2005. His first Opns Off was Captain Bill Gann. Gann resigned from the OKARNG and went to the U.S. Border Patrol. Captain Robert Walker was hired and is the current Opns Off. Both LTC Greenhaw and MAJ Walker are currently AASF Cdr and Opns Off at Tulsa AASF; CW4 Steve Phelps is the Maint. Officer.

Tulsa AASF IPs and unit IPs (including Lexington AASF), worked their butts off trying to get all of the Lords of Darkness aviators and crew chiefs MH-6/AH-6/UH-60 aircraft qualified, NVG qualified, and NVG mission qualified, in the early and mid-80s. It became an ongoing nightmare and many heated words were exchanged while attempting to get the strap-hangers like me and many M-day aviators to come to the flight line and get trained AND to maintain currency. Ninety-day currency rides rolled around quite frequently. Just ask an M-day aviator or crewmember how frequent.

There will always be the extremes at either end of the spectrum. This was true regarding aviators' training status. The Tulsa AASF had the mission of maintaining the unit's aircraft and flight training for the 45th Avn Bn and it was never easy. The Lords of Darkness mission statement was quite specific.

The mission statement read: "The 45th Avn Bn will be prepared to conduct precise, covert counter-terrorism helicopter penetration, insertions, exfils, resupply and other aviation support of CT personnel, worldwide, undetected, under low visibility, at or below 300' AGL, using the cover of darkness and NVD (night vision devices) with minimal illumination, over short to medium distances (300-600 nm), delivering CT personnel and/or cargo to their designated target within +/—50 ft and within +/—30 seconds time on target."

The aviation training of the 45th Avn Bn often required two shifts at the Tulsa AASF of maintenance, operations, ALSE and IP personnel, a day crew and a night crew to get the job done. It was almost impossible, but nobody told them that back then.

As was previously mentioned, Dale E. Martin, was said to be a great guy; everyone liked him. He retired medically from the OKARNG and his position as Cdr, Tulsa AAFA in January 1984. Sadly, Dale passed away on 9 March 2004.

CW4 Tommy J. Evans ca 1990

There was, however, another person at Tulsa who was also loved and respected by everyone – Jay Thomas Tommy Evans. Following his graduation from Oklahoma University, Tommy Evans served three years in the U.S. Air Force as a first lieutenant and later as a captain in the ANG. He then joined Port Robinson's coaching staff at OU as an assistant wrestling coach.

Evans had a legendary career with the University of Oklahoma wrestling program. As a sophomore in 1951, Evans was the NCAA runner-up. In 1952 and 1954, he won national titles and was voted the outstanding wrestler of the meet in those two national title years. He finished his collegiate career with a 42-1 record over three years and finished with 20 falls. He also won three Big Seven titles. Because of a knee injury, he didn't wrestle in 1953. He qualified for the U.S. Olympic team twice, winning the silver medal in 1952, and finishing fifth in 1956. He was a three-time National AAU title winner and was the Pan American champion in 1955.

Tommy Evans was promoted to the top spot as Robertson's hand-picked successor in 1959. As coach, his 140 career victories rank as the third most in school history. In 1968, he served as head coach of the U.S. Olympic freestyle team that finished fourth in Mexico City. He resigned as OU's wrestling coach in April of 1972, in part because of his disillusionment with the demands of recruiting. He told reporters at the time of resignation that he missed the days when athletes had to sell themselves to the school, instead of the school selling itself to the athlete.

Following his resignation from OU, Evans transferred from the ANG over to the OKARNG and later applied for a full-time job as a technician instructor pilot at the Tulsa AASF. His job duties with the military included: unit commander, IP, IFE, MTP, and maintenance officer. He flew the UH-1, OH-6 and UH-60, as well as other aircraft with the Army and Air Force. The Tommy Evans Safety Award was named after him following his military retirement.

LTC Garry O. Bentley shared a bit of humor regarding Tommy Evans, "CW3 Evans was going to give CW2 Chance Whitman his first orientation/check ride after joining the unit. They were at Lexington and CW3 Tommy Evans was the IP. After getting the helicopter started Tommy told him to hover out to the takeoff pad. Chance looked at him and said, "Are you sure?" Tommy told him to go ahead, so off they went, with Chance managing to miss all the other helicopters parked on the ramp. He got to the take-off pad and plunked it down on the Maltese cross. Tommy said something about a rough ride and Chance told him he thought it was pretty good for his first time in a helicopter. Chance was fixed-wing rated, something Tommy forgot to notice on his records before going out to fly."

Tommy Evans retired from the OKARNG in 1990 as a lieutenant colonel. He had accumulated more than 10,000+ flight hours. LTC Evans departed this life on 18 March 2008, in Norman, OK, at the age of 77.

Another great guardsman was James L. "Bear" Smith. Although Bear enlisted in the Oklahoma Guard at age 14 or 15, according to Euna Smith, his wife, he didn't serve in Korea. At the time the 45th went to Korea, Smith was attending his first semester of college at Oklahoma A&M, in Stillwater, OK. After one semester, he enlisted in the paratroopers and spent the next three years at Fort Benning, GA.

CW4 James L. "Bear" Smith ca 1990

"After being discharged [from active duty] in 1954, he returned to college and joined the Oklahoma National Guard again," said Mrs. Smith.[6]

CW4 Smith served a total of 40 years and four months military service, retiring on his 60th birthday as a major. On his last day of military service, Bear made his farewell military flight in a UH-60 Blackhawk, his co-pilot being his son Randy Smith, who served in the same unit as his father.

James L. Smith passed away on 15 June 2006. Bear's two brothers (Jerry and Mac Smith) were both colonels in the guard, and his father was Gen. J. O. Smith, also in the OKARNG.

On 22 December 2006, I asked Brigadier General Dana D. Batey at his home in Edmond, OK, "Sir, what were your three greatest accomplishments as OKARNG State Aviation Officer [1976-88]?"

BG Batey quickly replied, "Establishing aviation facilities within the state of Oklahoma at Norman, Lexington, and Tulsa. That has had a tremendous impact on our readiness, local and state emergencies, salaries (state and federal) and jobs."

"I was after a solid structure for [OKARNG] aviation. The ultimate would have been an aviation brigade with support elements. The Troop Command (Avn) [headquarters] thrilled John Stanko because we didn't have enough command structure to go all over the United States, and so even that little Troop Command [(Avn)] was kind of a 'pilot program' with a few other states. Oklahoma was the first to start that [type of TDAs Avn C&C]."

BG Batey continued, "The third thing is promotions. Look through this mass of aviation personnel, how many sergeants do we have, how many warrant officers, how many majors, lieutenant colonels and O-6s [full colonels]? How many [OKARNG aviators] made General[7]?"

Major Leroy A. Wall had been assigned as Tulsa AASF #2 Cdr in 1983 and XO, 45th Avn Bn (SO) at Tulsa in December 1984. Plans were in the works for a new facility and armory, but the OKARNG didn't own any land for these aviation projects.

Ground work began in 1985-86 to obtain the military appropriations and secure the land for these military construction projects. Wall[8] was instrumental in arranging the land deal with Tulsa for the 50 acres. In 1987 it was announced that $7 million dollars and 50 acres of land in Tulsa were available to build a new armory and new AASF at Tulsa for the 1/245th SOA[9].

BG Dana D. Batey[10] added, "We needed something in Tulsa in a good location and we need it where they [a counter-terrorism Avn Unit] can get out of there [deploy by C-5s]. The land [adjacent to HWY 169 on the NE corner of Tulsa Int'l Airport] belonged to a Tulsa lawyer. [Major General Don] Ferrell was there, I briefed the [Tulsa] Mayor, the Economic Development Director and Chamber of Commerce President. They were the three key people. The airport manager was 'Bigfoot.' I think they put him in jail later on, but he was a supporter of aviation. It was probably 6-10 people. The key play was to brief on the economic impact that this organization [would] have on Tulsa and the airport. I presented what we [the OKARNG] could place on that 50 acres, how many employees, how much fuel would be purchased, etc. When I finished that, one of the Chambers' staffers was adding that up [the figures] and what impact it would have. The mayor and [president of the] Chamber said, "Purchase the 50 acres!" The city purchased it for $1.2 million from the Tulsa lawyer and donated it to the OKARNG. The site utilities would be presented in the next briefing – getting them out to the site and "Who was going to pay for the extension of services." [The city of Tulsa bit the bullet and got the utilities to the fifty acres.]

Major C.L. Strance[11]added his point of view, "I was responsible for getting the 50 acres at Tulsa Airport for the new Armory and AASF. Bob

Moore, a friend of mine from QB (Quiet Birdmen flying organization) was on the Tulsa Airport Authority as a board member." At the meeting to present the OKARNG proposal were Wall, Batey, Strance, and Dale Martin, plus the Tulsa Airport Authority Board."

Without a doubt, it takes many people, wearing many different hats to envision and complete a project of this magnitude. This was indeed a major feat and a tremendous accomplishment.

"During this period, we (a team effort) acquired the 50 acres on HWY 169 for the new AASF [and armory] at Tulsa and completed it in 1989. We expanded the Bn from 202 personnel to 440. We began replacing MH-6s with UH-60s. The 45th Avn Bn became the 245th Avn Bn and we were the night vision and special operations force in the National Guard. [Routinely,] we deployed troops to Honduras, Thailand, Malaysia, Australia, and all over the U.S., supporting the [1st SFG,] 5th, 7th, 12th, 19th, 20th SFGs and the 75th Rangers. We had three training fatalities during this intensive and dangerous operational regime," added Wall.

On 30 June 1988, MG Donald F. Ferrell, OKTAG, announced groundbreaking ceremonies to be held for the new Tulsa Armory and AASF on Monday, 11 July 1988, at 11:30 a.m. "The AASF site is at U.S. Highway 169 and 48th Street, northeast of Tulsa International Airport."

LTC Gary Elliott

The city of Tulsa was represented by then Mayor Rodger Randle, and commissioners Gary Watts, Robert Dick, J.D. Metcalfe, and Charles King. The Tulsa Airport Trust was represented by John Bates, Chairman, and members Joseph Parker Jr., James Boese, and Brent Kitchens.

Military and other dignitaries included: MG Ferrell, OKTAG, Brigadier General Duckworth, Deputy TAG, SAAO COL Dana D. Batey, LTC Gary Elliott, Commander 1/245th Avn (SO). The governor's office was represented by State Senator Ged Wright and State Representative Calvin J. Hobson.

Just one year after ground was broken, the new facilities at Tulsa were officially dedicated on 25-26 August 1989. Tulsa's new $7 million

dollar AASF, 2,000-foot runway, fuel farm, and helicopter parking ramp/
taxiways and the new $2.2 million, two-story armory for the 1st Battalion,
245th Avn (Special Operations)(Airborne) became a reality seven years
after the original Lords of Darkness began at the old yellow sandstone
armory on Cincinnati Street in Sperry, OK.

Special guests at the AASF/Armory dedication were: LTG Herbert
Temple, CNGB; Major General Frank Kelley, USAF, Dir. of Ops for U.S.
Special Operations Command, Major General Charles Honore, Cdr, Fifth
Army, and MG Donald F. Ferrell, OKTAG.

The new AASF facility was dedicated to the memory of (and named
for) Warrant Officer David O. Barr, and the new Armory was dedicated
to the memory of (and named for) Chief Warrant Officer (CW2) Dennis
L. Barlow. "Barr and Barlow lost their lives in the line of duty on 5 March
1987 in a mid-air crash of their OH-6 aircraft while on an NVG training
mission near Wagoner, OK," said LTC Gary Elliott during an interview
with OKARNG's 145th Public Affairs Det, Captain Ron Wilkerson.

The Organizational Maintenance Shop #18 (OMS) (now called Field
Maintenance Shop #9) next to the Tulsa Armory is named in memory of
(and named) for SFC David A. Brown, who was killed on active duty 2
May 1988, during a training mission in Honduras. It was dedicated in
1990. As the communications chief for the 45th Avn Bn (SO), Dave is
remembered for his lighthearted humor, his popularity among people of
all ages, and his favorite philosophy: "Things don't matter – People do!"

Following is a summarized list of the Tulsa AAFA/AASF #2 secretaries,
facility commanders, and operations officers:

Tulsa AAF/AASF #2 Secretaries

Pauline L. Wiles	April 1982 – September 1985
Wanda J. Cleburn	August 1985 – April 1990
SP4 Susan _____	AGR (???—???)
Marilyn Reid	November 1987 – present

AASF Cdrs/Opns* Officers

LTC Dale Martin†	January 1978 – January 1984
CPT Richard O. Murphy*	January 1978 – 20 April 1986
COL Jerry D. Bourassa	20 January 1984—Tech TDY (45 dys)

	CPT Richard O. Murphy* January 1978 – 20 April 1986
CPT Richard O. Murphy	(Acting Cdr) Temporary
	CPT Richard O. Murphy* January 1978 – 20 April 1986
LTC (COL Leroy A. Wall	December 1983—2 March 1986
	(AGR December 1983—November 1985)
	MAJ Richard O. Murphy* January 1978 – 20 April 1986
MAJ Roger D. Ferguson†	2 March 1986 to 15 August 1986
	Opns Off – Vacant *20 April 1986 to December 1986*
Cdr—Vacant	16 August 1986 to April 1987
	MAJ Terry R. Council* 2 December 1986 to April 1987
LTC Terry R. Council	April 1987 to December 2003
	CPT Barry DeFoor* June 1987 to ca 1988-89
	CW4 Tommy "TK" Klutts* 1989 to ca 1999
	MAJ Jon R. Greenhaw* 2002 to December 2003
MAJ Jon R. Greenhaw	(Acting Cdr) December 2003 to 2005
LTC Jon R. Greenhaw	February 2005 to present
	CPT Bill Gann[12]*
	CPT Robert Walker* September 2007 to present

In December of 2008, the full-time picture at AASF #2, according to LTC Greenhaw, was "CW4 Steve Phelps is the Maint Off; SFC Walter Joe Rumpel is the Production Control. Let me clarify that Steve and Joe are in these positions while CW4 Don Russell, CW5 Leonard Reed and Dave Huddleston are all deployed. Supervisors have taken their places. The IPs remaining [not deployed then] were CW5 Jimmy Richards, CW4 Timmy Richards, Jimmy's brother who is coming back from Hawaii. He was a pilot here way back when. Richards is going back to Georgia in the near future. And then CW4 Jay Jones is the other IP. CW4 Dave

"Hootie" Odum retired in October 2008. CW4 Chris Kurtz, our other IP is deployed."

In an email (22 February 2009) Bobby Lane mentions, "I'm over here [Iraq] with Co B 834th ASB. Myself, CW5 Leonard Reed, CW4 Chris Kurtz, CW4 Kirk Little, CW4 Don Russell, SFC Anthony Davis, CW5 Dan Halley, SSG Brian Stillwell and SSG Shawn Smith are here [not deployed]. The 2/149th GSAB has Major Keith Owens and CW4 Richie Schuler."

Tulsa has grown into a substantial and modern AASF, armory, with its own FMS (Field Maintenance Shop). Its location is premier and highly visible to the community. Since the AASF's official opening in 1989, it has benefited not just the Special Operations client, but all units of the Oklahoma Guard, including ANG, but especially those military and state agencies in the eastern part of Oklahoma and the City of Tulsa.

Although Tulsa AASF began as a spark, that initial flame increased and was enlarged by a major lightning strike when it was announced that Special Operations Aviation would be placed at Tulsa/Sperry, OK. Without a doubt, there were several plush years at Tulsa, during the 45th Avn Bn (Sp Ops)(Abn) era. Since 1994 it's been different and challenging.

Those were exceptional days, great flying, exciting and trying times! There were days we literally felt like we were flying through hell! But that was then – this is today. The Zen Buddhists have a saying—"Now means NOW."

It's already been said that we can't live in the past, nor should we. Reminiscing is fine, remembering is good – but reality is about the NOW, knowing who we are and what we should be doing today, to achieve the goals we have set for tomorrow, next week, next year. Are we looking forward or back? We know what it was like in days gone by, but what is it supposed to be tomorrow?

Who is courageously standing up and looking out at the horizon, dreaming about what Tulsa AASF, Tulsa Guard, and OKARNG Aviation can be tomorrow, next year or five years from now?

I would proffer that what is out there, what is possible, is beyond our imagination. Don't under estimate what can be started with just a spark.

---

1. Telephone interview SFC Norman W. Crowe, 30 December 2007.

COL Billy R. Wood, U.S. Army (retired)

2. Telephone interview SSG Sandra G. Hodges, 31 December 2007

3. Robert C. "Bobby" Lane was promoted to CW5 at the mobilization station (Ft Sill, OK) prior to being deployed to Iraq in 2008. He turned 60 years of age in January 2009, obtained a waiver to stay in the Guard.

4. Personal interview CW4 Robert C. Lane, 16 November 2007; CW4 Lane deployed to Iraq November 2008 and returned the following year.

5. Robert M. Morgan later became Major General Morgan, the TAG (Adjutant General) of Oklahoma (20 November1978 – 11 January 1987)

6. Email Mrs. Euna Smith, 25 January 2007

7. As of 2008, four OKARNG aviators achieved the rank of brigadier general: Brigadier General Chester A. Howard (deceased), Brigadier General Dana D. Batey, Brigadier General Paul D. Costilow, and Brigadier General Terry R. Council.

8. Interview COL Leroy A. Wall, January 2006

9. 45th Avn Bn (Sp Ops)(Abn) was redesignated as the 1st Bn, 245th Avn (Sp Ops) in October 1987.

10. Interview Brigadier General Dana D. Batey, 22 December 2006

11. Interview MAJ C.L. Strance, 31 January 2007

12. Resigned and transferred to U.S. Border Patrol

Chapter 8

Army Aviation Advisors

"The best way to succeed in life is to act on the advice we give to others."

unknown

Life comes with many choices – until you get old. Before you get old, you can choose your own clothes, the schools you will attend, what you will or won't eat for dinner, and a career field. But you don't get to choose where you are born or who you parents will be. Similarly, in the Army National Guard, you didn't get to choose your unit advisor. You got what you were dealt. Over the past 40 years, all of OKARNG Aviation's Army Advisors were excellent!

What is an Army or military advisor? The military adviser is an expert who provides advice to a military unit or element, in a specific area, e.g. unit tactics, night flying or aviation combat assaults. This type military assignment is unique and viewed from the top down as extremely important! However, those making such assignments sometimes overlooked the expertise and importance when regarding the 45th Avn Bn (Sp Ops)(Abn).

Army Advisors came in all different shapes, sizes, ranks, branches and expertise. When in support of foreign nationals, the term advisor was quite common within the U.S. Army's Special Forces during the Vietnam War era. You may also be familiar with the term Military Advisory Group, or Joint United States Military Advisory Group such as JUSMAGTHAI – Joint U.S. Military Advisory Group Thailand, headquartered in Bangkok. Many of us have worked with, and perhaps for, an individual advisor or advisory group. However, not all who are reading this have had the experience of working with an Army Aviation Advisor for an OKARNG aviation unit.

In the past, within the ARNG, each State Area Regional Command (STARC) was authorized one COL/0-6 Senior Army Advisor and a Senior Enlisted Army Advisor. Then, at the subordinate commands within a state, the major command headquarters could request an Officer Advisor (MAJ/0-4) and/or an Enlisted Advisor (SFC/E-7). Since the total end-strength of the Army and the ARNG cannot be raised or lowered, except by Congress, the ARNG unit must 'give up' one or two full-time TOE/TDA personnel slots for the number of advisors they received. It was the exception, not the norm, for a unit to receive an active duty Army Advisor.

Major headquarters, such as the 45th Bde Cbt Team, the 45th Fires Bde and the 90th Troop Command, which oversees all aviation assets within the state, have all had Army Advisors in the past. Army Advisors for the ARNG were assigned to a battalion headquarters position, such as executive officer, operations officer or NBC NCO. They reported to the unit commander for whom they are working and to the Senior Army Advisor at the State Headquarters. Since the end of the Vietnam War in 1975, but prior to Operation Iraqi Freedom, the guidance provided by Army Aviation military advisors was very beneficial, purely from the standpoint that most ARNG units had never been activated and/or deployed. However, many officer and enlisted Guard Aviation unit members were combat veterans both prior to 1980. The Army Advisors were experienced in active duty methods, large aviation operations, coordination and activities. Normally, they had been there, done that.

The use of the term Senior Army Advisor Guard (SRAAG) began with First United States Army. Fifth United States Army used a different term, Senior Regular Army Advisor. Following the merging of all SRAAs and SRAAGs under First United States Army, the term Senior Army Advisor Guard was adopted for common use among all 50 states and the four territories with National Guard elements.

The SRAAG is a federal officer, and as such, is not subject to state authorities and has no authority to issue orders to personnel of the ARNG except when they are in a federal status (Title 10).

The goal of the SRAAG[1] is to be a productive part of the National Guard team and be a subject matter expert (SME) between the Active

Army and reserve components in order to assist in producing mission-capable Army National Guard units for mobilization and deployment to combat theaters of operation, or for Defense Support to Civil Authorities (DSCA).

The following tidbits of history are not necessarily in any order. In several cases very little information is known about former advisors, other than a last name and rank and a general idea of when they served as an Aviation Advisor to the OKARNG.

To wit: the first known active duty Army Advisor to be assigned to OKARNG aviation was Major Ned Baker. We don't know if there was

MAJ Ned Baker

an Enlisted Advisor serving at the same time with Major Baker or not. The timeframe during which he served at Norman was around 1960. How do we know the date? It was on a group aviation photograph that MAJ C.L. Strance found in an old album of his at the aviation hangar the Annex behind his house in Collinsville, OK. Some of the other more mature aviators attending the last 45th Avn Bn mini-reunion (September 2008) recalled MAJ Ned Baker serving as an advisor.

In the early days of OKARNG Aviation, at which time all aviation assets were still stationed at Norman, OK, Max Westheimer Field, we were fortunate to have had a field grade officer and former Oklahoman, as Army Aviation Advisor. His historical and elaborate story begins this chapter about Army Advisors.

Major Loren L. "Pappy" Glenn[2], and his wife Helen, came to Norman, Max Westheimer Field ca 1962. Glenn was most likely the second active duty Army Aviation Advisor for OKARNG Aviation, Ned Baker being the first. Major Glenn served in this Advisor position for three years.

His wife Helen shared, "We became great friends and travel companions with Gus and Dora Guilds." Lieutenant Colonel August Lee "Gus" Guild was the first State Avn Officer for OKARNG.

MAJ Glenn had four brothers and one sister: Lawrence was the eldest, then Loren. Another brother died at childbirth and then John, who served in the Navy. Loren's youngest brother, Fred, later served with his brother Loren in the 45th Inf Div in Korea. Lieutenant Colonel Guild finagled and got Corporal Fred Glenn assigned to the same airfield where he (Fred) became the cook for the Oklahoma Army Guard pilots!

Loren L. Glenn and his four siblings grew up just a couple of miles south of the Lake Wister Dam, in Wister, OK. They attended Glendale School. Loren's sister, Ruth (Glenn) Wilson, is still alive and resides in Poteau, Oklahoma. Lawrence, John, and Loren are now deceased.

Loren L. Glenn was born and raised in Oklahoma. He was born on 10 April 1919 in Glendale, OK, in LeFlore Co. in eastern Oklahoma. Loren was the second son of Wilbur and Ida (Balentine) Glenn. He married Helen Louise (Dobbins) in Denton, TX in February 1943.

Loren and Helen Glenn had six children; the eldest, Fred, was born in Dallas, TX, and became an Army aviator; later he retired from Northwest Airlines as a 747 captain with 30 years in the cockpit. Milton, the next to the eldest, was an air traffic controller in the U.S. Army/ARNG for several years and later became a private pilot. Milton also worked with his father's general aviation business as a general manager.

"Loren's son, Fred came into the OKARNG as an enlisted soldier in 1960. I knew him then. He and I attended Federal OCS together at Fort Benning, GA in 1964," recalled Lieutenant Colonel Donald E. Derrick.[3]

Glenn served in WWII, Korea (45th Inf Div) and in Vietnam. His initial civilian pilot training[4] took place about 1941 at Durant, OK. According to Milton Glenn[5], "Dad entered the military at Hartlee Field, Denton, TX [about 1942]. He was a civilian flight instructor one day and a second lieutenant the next. Dad was drafted into the Army at Hartlee Field, and he never went to basic training—just flew airplanes," recalled Milton.

The author was able to review the military records of Lieutenant Colonel Loren L. Glenn during a personal interview with son Milton Glenn at Bonham, TX on 6 November 2008 and found several very interesting original onion-skin copies of military orders from 1944. One of particular interest was dated 20 September 1944 and showed aviation cadet Glenn's Army Air Force service number as T-193484. The extract read "The following flight officers, AC, Class 44-ATC-6, having completed the required course of instruction at the AAFPS (Adv 2-Engine)[6] Ellington Field, Texas, are under the provisions of AR 95-60, 20 August 1942, and AAF Reg 50-7, 1 June 1944, rated Service Pilot, effective 16 Oct 44." A similar order showed that Glenn and others were TD (temporary duty) to Ellington Field, TX (Houston) from Love Field, Dallas, TX, further assigned to the 2517th AAFBU (Army Air Force Basic Unit), which was at Ellington Field.

"Dad taught me to fly in a J-5 Cub and I spent a lot of back seat hours in an L-19 [Bird Dog] and also left seat time in a [U-6] Beaver. Dad insisted that I learn in a tail dragger so that I learned to fly right."

Milton Glenn, the second son of Loren and Helen Glenn, was born in 1947 at Denton, TX. He enlisted in the Army, trained as an air traffic controller and served in the 45th Aviation at Norman (OKARNG) for several years. He works with computers as his profession and now has a satellite business in Bonham, TX. His mother Helen moved to a retirement center nearby in Denton, TX in October 2008. Milton's eldest sister, Sandra Glenn, was born in 1948 in Denton, TX.

The April 1944 U.S. Army/Navy Directory of Airfields described Hartlee Field as having a 1,500' unpaved runway, and indicated that Army flight operations were conducted from the field. The Army aviation cadet pilots in training took their ground lessons in classrooms on the North Texas campus, received their flight training at Hartlee Field and lived in Chilton Hall. Hartlee Field is about three miles west of Denton Airport, northeast of the City of Denton.

"From [training glider pilots at] Hartlee Field, Dad then went to Red Bird Field, in Dallas [ca 1942] where he was a line pilot in the Fourth Ferry Command. He ferried everything from P-38s to B-17s across the U.S."

After a period of time in the 2517th AAFBU (Army Air Force Basic Unit) at Ellington Field, TX, I suspect Glenn was assigned to the China-Burma-India theater in late 1944. Milton quite recalled that his father, Loren L. Glenn, "was assigned to India [ca November 1944 – April 1945] during WWII and flew the Hump. The best I can tell he was flying the C-109, a cargo version of the B-24 Liberator and transporting aviation fuel and supplies into China. He had at least two mishaps over there. One was running off the end of a runway in China and taking out some shacks on the end of the runway; the other was crash-landing an aircraft [a C-109] in a lake because he was loaded with aircraft fuel and the plane had caught fire."

Lieutenant Glenn would have been part of the CBI's (China-Burma-India) ATC (Air Transport Command.) His flight records indicate that he was also qualified in the C-47, which was used quite extensively in the air lift over the Hump.

While designed as a heavy bomber, the B-24 Liberator experienced many modifications and conversions for such assignments as photography, mine laying, and cargo hauling, including a C-109 fuel tanker version that flew the Hump to refuel B-29s operating out of forward bases in China. The U.S. military built more than 18,000 B-24s during WWII, more than any other American aircraft.

The Hump was the name given by Allied pilots in World War II to the eastern end of the Himalayan Mountains over which they flew from India to China to resupply the Flying Tigers and the Chinese government of Chiang Kai-shek. C-109s were dedicated fuel transport aircraft converted from existing B-24 bombers. All armament and bombardment equipment was removed, and eight fuel tanks were installed inside the fuselage so they could carry 2,900 U.S. gallons of high-octane aviation gasoline. The C-109 fuel transports were not popular with their crews, since they were very difficult to land when fully loaded at airfields above 6,000 feet elevation, and often demonstrated unstable flight characteristics with full tanks. A crash landing of a loaded C-109 inevitably resulted in a fireball and crew fatalities.

Bob Pitzer who flew the Hump stated, "Our training for hump flying was at Reno Nevada AAF Base[7]. Twelve of us flew over together after picking up our plane at Berry Field, Nashville, TN. We were issued parachutes and Colt .45 pistols. The trip over was via South America and Africa – destination Karachi, India. There, they gave us many, many shots and to our surprise, took away our parachutes! All of our trips after that were without parachutes."

At Kunming, China "there were two landing strips, both 10,000-feet long, built of crushed stone by Chinese 'Coolie' labor. The jagged gravel was very tough on our tires, often causing blowouts. On the good side, Kunming was the only place we could get fresh eggs. As soon as the engines were shut down, we headed to the line shack where the Chinese cook knew one English sentence, 'how do you want 'em Joe?' No matter what the answer, the eggs came out scrambled."

"Officers were awarded the Air Medal for participating in more than 200 hours of operational flight in transport aircraft over the dangerous and difficult India-China air routes. At that time, 500 hours qualified for the Distinguished Flying Cross.

Milton Glenn recalled that, "After WWII, Dad was discharged from the Army Air Forces and became a civilian again. He worked for a while on B-36s at Consolidated, in Fort Worth." All B-36 aircraft were manufactured in Fort Worth at Air Force Plant #4 and two B-36 wings of the United States Air Force were stationed at Carswell Air Force Base in Fort Worth.

Glenn was activated back into the Armed Forces in 1950 as an Oklahoma Army Guardsman, part of the 45th Inf Div during the Korean police action, and he flew L-19 (45th Division) spotter planes for the most part. Second Lieutenant Loren L. Glenn was reappointed as an Army aviator, through the ARNG on 15 December 1950. "It was in Korea that Dad met and worked for Lieutenant Colonel Gus Guild. Dad and Lee were the only two that flew the Navion[8]. Dad always had the 45th Thunderbird emblem on his uniform."

"Upon his return from Korea, he was a flight instructor at Fort Sill, OK [ca 1952 – 1956] until he and five other pilots went to Fort Rucker and [helped] established the [Army] flight school there. They took the Navy flight manuals and adapted them for the flight school at Rucker," stated Milton.

One of Milton's younger brothers, Dennis, was born in 1953, at Lawton, OK. Dennis is a representative for a hazardous waste company (BS in Biology). Another Glenn brother, Kenneth, was born in 1956, also at Lawton, OK. Kenneth operates a 115-foot commercial offshore [fishing] boat in the gulf.

During the Korean conflict, the Dept of Air Training at Fort Sill expanded, and in early 1953, it became the Army Aviation School[9]. As a result of the expansion of both aviation and artillery training, Fort Sill became overcrowded, and the Army decided to move the Army Aviation School to a different post. When no satisfactory permanent Army post was found, a temporary post, Camp Rucker, AL, was chosen.

The Army Aviation School began moving to Alabama in August 1954, and the first class began at Camp Rucker in September 1954. In March 1955, the Army Aviation Center was established at Rucker and in October of the same year the post was given permanent status with the name changed from Camp Rucker to Fort Rucker.

Prior to the mid-1950s, the Army Air Forces/U.S. Air Force had provided primary training for Army Aviation pilots and mechanics. In 1956, DoD gave the Army control over all of its own training. Gary AFB, San Marcos, TX and Wolters AFB, Mineral Wells, TX, where the Air Force was conducting training, were both transferred to the Army. Lacking adequate facilities at Fort Rucker, Army Aviation continued primary fixed-wing training at Camp Gary until 1959 and primary rotary-wing training at Fort Wolters until 1973.

"After a year at Rucker, Captain Glenn was transferred to Redstone Arsenal, Huntsville, AL during the summer of 1956 [and served there until ca 1959], where he flew Wernher Von Braun, General Maderis, General Barclay, and the famous Mr. Able and Mr. Baker (space chimpanzees)," added Milton. Major General John Bruce Maderis, an Army aviator, commanded the Army Ballistic Missile Agency from 1955 to 1958[10]. About mid-1958, Major General John A. Jack Barclay replaced Maderis as commander of the Army Ballistic Missile Agency at Huntsville, AL. CPT Loren L. Glenn was designated a Senior Army Aviator 4 October 1956 at Huntsville.

On 21 October 1959, the White House announced that the heart of the U.S. Army's space capability, Dr. Wernher Von Braun's Development Operations Division of the Army Ballistic Missile Agency (ABMA), would be transferred to the year-old, civilian National Aeronautics and Space Administration (NASA). With this act, President Dwight D. Eisenhower ended the first U.S. Army space program, which had begun two years before in reaction to the stunning Soviet Sputnik space launch.

Milton explained, "Dad received special orders while at Huntsville during his first tour there (1957-59) and he taught MG Jack Barclay to fly. An L-19 was transferred from Rucker for that specific task. General Barclay not only received his single engine rating, but also his multi-engine and instrument ratings at Huntsville. Later during his second tour there, Dad flew the first King Air, which the Army had, civilian tail number, N901R, leased from Beechcraft. This 1966 Model 65-A90 Beechcraft became Army (tail number) 15361, and was designated a VC-6A (VIP transport)[11].

Milton added, "My brother, Fred, who was in the ARNG at that time, requested orders to [Active Duty for Training] at no pay while we were in Huntsville, and was sometimes Dad's copilot. That's how he built his flight time that led to his working for Air America, and then Northwest Airlines."

"From Redstone, Dad [CPT Glenn] went to Fort Wolters in Mineral Wells, Texas." He attended the USAPHS (U.S. Army Primary Helicopter School) in 1959 and became a rotary-wing aviator. While there, he was awarded the Army Commendation Medal [for service at Redstone

Arsenal] by Colonel C.H. Meek on 9 June 1959. After rotary-wing school at Wolters, he went to Safety & Accident Investigation School at the University of Southern California before being transferred to Orleans, France ca 1959/60.

One of several emails received from Milton Glenn stated, "After a year in Orleans, he was transferred to Heidelberg, Germany [ca 1960]. After the Berlin Wall went up, Dad had the distinction of flying the first military aircraft up the Berlin Corridor to Berlin to determine East Germany's intentions." Milton's younger sister, Karen, was born at Heidelberg, Germany in 1961. She is a professor of Chemistry and Lab Researcher in Oklahoma (DNA specialization).

From Heidelberg, "MAJ Glenn [and his Enlisted Advisor, Master Sergeant Simpson[12],] were assigned to and worked at Westheimer in Norman as Army Aviation Advisors to OKARNG Aviation from [about] 1962 to 1965," according to Mrs. Helen Glenn.

Milton explained, "When Dad left Germany . . . the Army reassigned him to Norman, OK as the [Army Aviation] advisor to the 45th National Guard Aviation Detachment [OKARNG Aviation]. It was about this time that aviation folks started calling him Pappy."

Numerous former aviators and aviation personnel at the September 2008 OKARNG Mini-Reunion recall the name MAJ Glenn. C.L. Strance, Dana D. Batey, Charlie Evans, and Jerry Bourassa remembered MAJ Glenn flying with them and as the advisor at Norman. MAJ Loren L. Glenn received the designation of Master Army Aviator on 27 February 1963 at Norman, OK.

Another story from Milton Glenn, "After serving three years in Norman, Dad was about to be sent to Johnson County, Texas, to set up an aviation detachment for President Lyndon B. Johnson. Dad knew of LBJ's hot, volatile temper. Not wanting to place his aviation career in jeopardy, Dad looked at his options. The only assignment with a higher priority was Vietnam, so Dad requested to be sent to Vietnam."

"When Dad arrived in Vietnam in June 1966, he was sent to Vung Tau. About five months into his tour of duty, he was transferred to Saigon and became a VIP pilot. One month before his tour ended, Mom fell ill, and the Army had him return early in August 1967," said Milton Glenn. Orders indicated that Glenn was an IFE and Standardization Pilot in the UH-1 during his tour in Vietnam.

"My husband turned fifty-two years old while he was a 'Dustoff' pilot in Vietnam "He lost 42 lbs. in the severe tropical heat," said Mrs. Glenn, "but he was promoted to lieutenant colonel while serving in Vietnam."

Returning from Vietnam in 1967, LTC Loren L. "Pappy" Glenn was once again assigned to Redstone Army Arsenal. He retired from the U.S. Army at Huntsville, AL in 1969 with 30 years of military service. As an Army aviator, he had accumulated, according to his son Milton, more than 12,000 flight hours. Among the awards and decorations received during his career, LTC Glenn held the Bronze Star, Air Medal w/7th OLC, Army Commendation Medal, Korean Service Medal, Vietnam Campaign Medal, Republic of Vietnam Campaign Medal, and many other awards, including the Master Army Aviator badge.

Milton proudly remembered that, "After retiring in Huntsville, Dad started a flying service with one J-5 cub and I managed the aviation business for Dad. When he decided to move back to Texas, he sold all of the planes except his Mooney Super 21.

A few years after retiring, Loren L. Glenn and his wife Helen moved back to Denton, TX. He died there on 26 April 2006 after a long battle with Alzheimer's disease. He was 87 years old at the time of his death.

Who was the first Oklahoma Guard aviator to serve in Southwest Asia?

With the end of the ninth year of the Global War on Terror we note that Oklahoma National Guard citizen soldiers/airmen/units are still on the ground in Iraq and Afghanistan. Each of the major units of the OKARNG has served honorably overseas in Iraq and/or Afghanistan at least once since March 2003. Most OKARNG and OKANG aviators have served one or more combat tours in these locations (including Kuwait) and several Oklahoma aviation units are preparing to deploy again (as of fall 2008) overseas to provide combat aviation support to the Global War on Terror.

Today's modern Army Aviation, including the UH-60 Blackhawks, AH-64 Apaches, CH-47 Chinooks, OH-58 Kiowa, UH-1 Hueys, C-23 Sherpas, and the C-12 King Air aircraft, have been assigned to the Southwestern Asian conflict since March 2003 – with certain exceptions. Yet, we have had Army Aviation and personnel assigned to key points in this region of the world since shortly after WWII, to wit: the individual below.

Have you ever been curious who was the <u>first</u> OKARNG Aviation officer assigned to a post in Southwest Asia? Can you name him? He served as the U.S. Army Chief of Aviation for the Persian Gulf District Engineers in Tehran, Iran from January 1962 to June 1964.

(Pause . . .) Give up? Don't. Keep in mind, some individuals who later were active duty Army Aviation Advisors to the OKARNG, began as soldiers in the Oklahoma Army National Guard. Some even served in WWII, Korea, and Vietnam.

Many of you more mature aviators from the Westheimer days knew him quite well. He was assigned to the Oklahoma Military Department as the

CPT John Robert "Bob" Dome ca 1971

full-time Army Aviation Advisor to OKARNG from October 1967/68 to November 1971. He was Lieutenant Colonel John Robert Dome[13]. His unofficial duty station was Max Westheimer Field, Norman, OK. During his early 1960s tour in Iran, he flew an Army L-23 (later called the U-8) fixed-wing in Iran, Pakistan, Saudi Arabia, Iraq, Lebanon, Afghanistan – even Germany and Italy, all from Tehran, Iran.

During his 27-year military career, Bob Dome served in WWII in the U.S. Navy as an aircraft mechanic and also in Korea and Vietnam as an Army aviator. His long military career took him all over the world – to some very unique and different locales, including Nicaragua, Panama Canal Zone, Rio de Janerio, Brazil, Peru, Bolivia, Korea, Vietnam plus many stateside assignments.

Lieutenant Colonel Dome was a very "dignified and friendly officer. He was an excellent [Army Aviation] Advisor and was not pushy or condescending in any way. He was a very good aviator in both fixed and rotary-wing [aircraft]. He never seemed to put on any weight and still looked good in that white [Army Mess Dress] uniform. I last saw him when [Colonel Dana D.] Batey was promoted to Brigadier General [28 October 1988]," said Colonel Leroy A. Wall[14.]

LTC Dome considered himself a true Oklahoman, his father having made the Land Run of 1889, but he never bragged about that. As a young man, he served in the Navy as an aviation mechanic during WWII on Guam as an aviation machinist mate 2/C. He soon became an Army aviation mechanic, SGT/E-5 in the OKARNG and earned his FAA private pilot license. He attended annual training in 1950 at Camp Polk, LA with his fellow 45th Inf Div guardsmen.

"At the time the 45th Inf Div was called-up and activated, Bob was working full-time for the Oklahoma Army National Guard at Norman. He was an aviation maintenance mechanic," said Mrs. Dome.[15] The former Helen Kenley is from Skedee, OK (near Pawnee and Blackburn, OK). "I attended a boarding school and graduated from the 12th grade in 1942. "After high school, I attended college for just a little over 20 minutes and decided it was going to take way too long. I immediately got a job at Tinker AFB."

He married Miss Helen "Hedy" Kenley at the First Christian Church in Oklahoma City on 18 August 1950. Soon thereafter, Bob Dome attended Leadership School at Fort Jackson, SC in November 1950 to February 1951 and then went on to Officer Candidate School at Fort Riley, KS. After OCS he attended the Engineer Branch Officer Basic Course at Fort Belvoir, VA.

After graduating from OBC, Bob and his bride, Miss Helen "Hedy" Kenley Dome, traveled to Gary AFB, San Marcus, TX and attended Phase I of U.S. Army Flight School (fixed-wing at the time) from March 1952 to June 1952. After successful completion of Phase I, Helen and Bob moved back to Fort Sill, Lawton, OK and attended Phase II of flight school at Henry Post Army Airfield. Upon completing training at Fort Sill, Bob pinned on the silver wings of an Army aviator.

From Lawton, Bob and his new boss, Colonel Gristy Waddell, flew a U-6 Beaver from Oklahoma City to the Panama Canal Zone. Mrs. Dome drove their car to New Orleans and put it on board a ship for transport to Central America and boarded a commercial flight to Panama. Bob's first assignment as an Army aviator was to Managua, Nicaragua at Puerto Cabezas from November 1952 until August 1953 (1½ years). He was assigned to the 937th Engineer Battalion in Central America.

While a First Lieutenant, Bob was invited to the palace of Tacho Samosa, then (1953) dictator of Nicaragua. From Nicaragua, Bob and Hedy went to Rio de Janerio (Terisna) for another accompanied tour. While assigned to Puerto Cabezas, "Bob flew in every Central America country and South American country to include Peru, Bolivia, Venezuela, Columbia and also Brazil," according to Mrs. Dome.

Flying high down in Bolivia at 13,500 feet, Bob took part in Operation Bolivia and was in charge of several flight missions "to determine if it were possible to conduct a triangulation reconnaissance on the high plateau of the Andes Mountains. Successful completion of the reconnaissance [flights] required extensive contour flying and the ability to take off and land with personnel and equipment from landing strips higher than aviators have normally flown," said Mrs. Hedy Dome. The story of Bob's participation in Operation Bolivia was later published in the Army Aviation Digest, October 1957.

CPT John Robert "Bob" Dome
ca 1958

Later he flew to Toronto, Canada to train in the Army's Twin Otter. He also flew to the Sikorsky Aircraft Plant in Bridgeport, CT to pick up new Army helicopters.

In January 1957, Bob Dome was assigned to the G-4 office at the Army's Aviation center, Fort Rucker, AL. He and Hedy were assigned there until September 1958. Then Captain Bob Dome had an unaccompanied tour to Korea from October 1958 to October 1959. He was assigned to KMAG (Korea Military Advisory Group). Hedy didn't get to go, as this was an unaccompanied tour.

Syngman (Sigmund) Rhee was elected President of the Korean Provisional Government in 1919 while in exile, a post he held for 20 years[16]. In 1945 he returned to Korea, now divided into Soviet and U.S. zones of occupation. In 1948, Rhee was elected president of the new South Korean republic. He led a feeble state, beset by economic problems, Army mutiny, government infighting and, most of all, a bitter rivalry with North Korea. On 25 June 1950, North Korean troops, aided by the Soviet Union, invaded South Korea. Thanks to the assembly of a U.S.-led U.N. Army, Rhee's regime survived. Rhee strongly advocated that the U.N. forces unify his country militarily. During Bob Dome's tour in Korea, he flew Sigmund Rhee and Mrs. Dome provided the author with a photo of Rhee, his English wife, and their entourage after disembarking from the Army plane flown by Bob Dome.

Due to widespread student-led anti-government demonstrations and civil disorder in April 1960, the unrest culminated in the so-called Student Revolution, which forced Rhee's resignation. Rhee went into voluntary exile in Hawaii, where he died in Honolulu on 19 July 1965 at age 90.

In November 1959, Bob and Hedy were assigned to Fort Campbell, KY to the Airfield Operations section. There CPT Dome became a company commander. As this was prior to Aviation having become a branch, every third year a commissioned Army Aviator had to serve a ground assignment (one year), after which he would get another flying assignment.

Then in January 1962, Bob received new orders and was reassigned to Tehran, Iran. In Iran, Bob was Chief of Aviation, Engineer Gulf District. There he flew the Army's L-23. He and Hedy took an R & R (Rest and Recuperation) leave to Athens, Greece and spent a week on the Caspian Sea. He was assigned to Iran until June 1964.

"While Bob was in Tehran, he had flights to Saudi Arabia, Turkey, Afghanistan, Pakistan, Baghdad, Iraq, Beirut, Lebanon, Italy and Germany, " added Hedy Dome.

Following his tour in Iran, Bob received orders assigning him to Fort Leonardwood, MO in July 1964. At Leonardwood, Major Dome was the executive officer of the 62nd Engineer Battalion, on another ground assignment through August 1965

From Missouri, Bob and Hedy left for the Presidio at San Francisco, where Bob was the Aviation Officer for the 15th Army Corps. While in San Francisco, he attended the Aerospace college at the University of Southern California. His training included becoming an Aviation Safety Officer and Aircraft Accident Investigator. He and Hedy were at the Presidio from September 1965 to September 1966.

In September 1966, Bob got orders for Fort Benning, GA, to attend transitional training in the Army's new UH-1 Huey turbine helicopter. This training must have incorporated some preliminary air mobile operations-type training, as it lasted eight weeks, according to Hedy Dome.

In December 1966, to no one's surprise, Bob got orders and was reassigned across the pond to the Republic of South Vietnam. In country, Bob was an AMC (Air Mission Commander) in UH-1s and was also an Aircraft Accident Investigator. He was assigned to the 145th Combat Aviation Battalion – the Old Warriors. The battalion earned a Distinguished Unit Citation for its 2,700 missions flown in June 1965 during the battle of Dong Xoia. It also received the Valorous and Meritorious Unit Citations while engaging in nearly every major infantry campaign conducted in III Corps.

Dome was promoted to lieutenant colonel while stationed in Vietnam. He, like other Vietnam aviators, received a five-day R & R non-chargeable five-day leave to Hawaii to meet his wife Hedy. Later Bob met Hedy in Taiwan for another R & R, according to Hedy.

In September 1963, the 145th (Aviation) Battalion was formed from the 45th Transportation Battalion, which arrived in Vietnam July 1962, and had a HQ company, HHC, and five helicopter companies—the 8th, 33rd, 57th, 81st and 93rd Transportation Companies plus the 18th Aviation fixed-wing company. The 145th supported the ARVN 5th, 18th, and 199th Divisions plus American units in III Corps including the 173rd Airborne. In addition the 145th provided rotary-wing training for pilots of the Vietnamese Air Force. However, in 1966 the 145th Avn Bn lineup included: 68th Air Mobile Light Co, 71st Air Mobile Light Co, 118th Air Mobile Light Co, 184th Airplane Co and the 334th Air Mobile Light Co.

There are two ironies involving Bob's assignment to the 145th Avn Bn in Vietnam: First, he was assigned to the same battalion; however, at different times, as was First Lieutenant Billy E. Sprague, another Army Aviator who served as an advisor to OKARNG later in the 1970s and #2. The 118th Air Mobile Light Co was called the Thunderbirds. The 118th served in Vietnam beginning in Saigon, September 1962 as the 33rd Transportation Co. (light helicopter). It became the 118th Assault Helicopter Company June 1963 and was inactivated August 1971. Known as the "First of the Assault Helicopter Companies," the 118th actively participated in every major battle and operation in III Corps, distinguishing itself in the early years in the Battle of Dong Xoai, Operations Attleboro, Cedar Falls, and Junction City. Among the greatest claims of the Thunderbirds, and their reputation as a fighting unit, was that they were the *"first to arrive and the last to leave."* Robert Brandt wrote the book *Thunderbird Lounge* about the 33rd Trans Co days before it became the 118th. However, there is no known connection between the 118th AHC and the 45th Inf Div ARNG Thunderbirds.

Returning from Vietnam, Bob received orders assigning him to the Army's Aviation Center and School at Fort Rucker, AL. This tour was unique, in that Bob was to become the editor of the U.S. Army's Aviation Digest magazine until September 1968.

Following his short tour at Fort Rucker, Bob was reassigned to the Oklahoma Military Department in October 1968; more specifically, to the OKARNG as the Army Aviation Advisor, with duty at Norman, OK.

Bob served in this position until November 1971, at which time he retired from the Active Army.

COL Wall added, "In fact, he [Dome] was an Instrument [Flight] Examiner (IFE). He flew with Batey to pick up one of our first CH-34s. Bob lived in Norman and at one time owned a movie theater there after he retired. He and Chet Howard were great friends. Even after retirement I would see Bob at Guard [OKARNG] functions in his tropical uniform."

After the military, Bob spent some time as a business partner and pilot for Western Concrete Preservers. He was also a member of the Military Order of the World Wars (Colonel Pendleton Woods – Oklahoma City Chapter), a member of the Oklahoma Heritage Association, a member of the 1889ers Society, and a great enthusiast and member of the Ham Radio Association. LTC Robert and Hedy Dome were named Adjutants Emeritus of the Military Order of World Wars in April 2005.

Helen Kenley "Hedy" Dome has long been supportive of her husband's military service and was an active worker and leader in the Officers' Wives Club, Aviation Wives and the Society of Military Engineers Wives. Hedy served a number of years as a Girl Scout Leader and hosted for six years a daily program for the Oklahoma League for the Blind. She is a kind, compassionate, charming lady and resides today in Ardmore, OK.

LTC John R. "Bob" Dome was a dual-qualified Master Army Aviator with 8-10,000 hours and 27 years military service. He served in WWII, the Vietnam War, and many overseas assignments. He was an Army Aviation Safety Officer, Aircraft Accident Investigator, Instructor Pilot, and Instrument Flight Examiner.

Among the many certificates, awards and decorations which LTC Dome received during his distinguished military career include: the Legion of Merit, the Bronze Star, Air Medal w/Two Oak Leaf Clusters, Vietnam Service Medal, Vietnam Defense Medal, Theater Ribbon Korea, Good Conduct Medal, World War II Victory Medal, the Asian Pacific Medal, and the Master Army Aviator badge.

"At the time of his military retirement [November 1971], Bob was qualified in every airplane and helicopter in the Army inventory," said Mrs. Dome.

John R. Dome was born in Enid, OK on 18 June 1924. He graduated from Oklahoma City University and later studied Russian while assigned in Korea and business law when he was in Vietnam. He and Hedy were married 58 years. The last military award received by LTC Dome was the

Army's Legion of Merit award for his service as the Army Aviation Advisor to the OKARNG at Norman, presented at his retirement ceremony in November 1971. LTC John R. Dome died on 11 March 2008 at the age of 84 in Oklahoma City.

Lieutenant Colonel Billy Eugene Sprague followed LTC John R. Dome as Army Aviation Advisor for OKARNG Aviation. Lieutenant Colonel Sprague served in this capacity from ca January 1972 until his retirement ca 1974/75.

Billy Eugene Sprague was born 21 October 1928[17] in Chandler, OK. "My folks are country folks. There is nothin' but oil and cattle out there [Oklahoma] – and the ground won't raise nothin' anyhow[18]." His daddy was a Pontiac dealer in Chandler, Oklahoma around the mid-sixties.

LTC Billy E. Sprague
ca 1974

The ever-present red clay is seen in the many Oklahoma lakes, Eufaula, Thunderbird and Murray and most of the rivers, such as the North & South Canadian and the Red River. They are so bright red it's understandable why the native Americans called it Oklahoma—meaning red man. To get away from his red small-town world, Billy began flying at the age of 16 at the Shawnee Municipal Airport just north of town. "Flying became the love of his life," says Judith, his second wife.

Billy enlisted in the Oklahoma Guard at the Chandler, OK Armory while in high school and was a field artilleryman. He served in Korea in 1952 with the 45th Inf Div, later going on to OCS and then Army Flight School. He became dual rated in Army fixed-wing and rotary-wing aircraft. After rotary-wing flight school he volunteered to go on Active Duty and was accepted.

In December 1961, elements of the 8th and 57th Transportation Companies (Light Helicopter) arrived at the Port of Saigon, Republic of Vietnam. President Dwight Eisenhower didn't want to be involved in war, but agreed to send military advisors to the Republic of Vietnam, "but not combatants." President John F. Kennedy was also reluctant, but that too changed! Sprague volunteered in 1961 for a (combat) tour flying helicopters in Vietnam. He arrived in country during October 1962. How quickly things can change.

Towards the end of 1962, three more Transportation Companies[19]—the 33rd, the 81st and the 93rd—arrived to boost the lift support. The 93rd UTT (Helicopter Co.) flew out of Tan Son Nhut Air Base in Saigon. 1LT Billy E. Sprague was assigned to the 93rd UTT (Helicopter Co) when he arrived in country. It was quite common for the 57th, 33rd and 93rd UTT (Helicopter Cos.) to fly large missions together in the Mekong Delta.

Two significant things changed in the U.S. Army during 1962, the year 1LT Billy Sprague was in Vietnam. Neither related to him personally, but they do relate to the history of Army Aviation and our story. The first is a new tri-service (Army, Air Force & Navy) aircraft redesignation program. For example, the Army's L-19 became the O-1 Bird Dog. Secondly, the Army changed the nomenclature of its aviation transportation units to accurately reflect the true purpose of their mission.

As mentioned in the previous paragraph, in September 1962, the U.S. military went to a new tri-service aircraft designation scheme, and the HU-1A (hence the nickname Huey) became the UH-1A, while the HU-1B became the UH-1B. The UH-1B was fitted with the M-6E3 armament system, which included two M-60 machine guns mounted outboard of each door, for a total of four, and the existing eight-round rocket packs. The machine guns could be aimed by the pilot using a cockpit-mounted sight and a hydraulic actuation system.

Billy, before receiving his orders for the Republic of Vietnam was at the right place, at the right time and became a rotary-wing gunnery instructor pilot in the UH-1B. The B model Huey was a much improved aerial gunnery platform than the UH-1A could've ever been. He soon became quite proficient with the new UH-1B gunship and before he knew it, he had the orders he had volunteered for—the Republic of South Vietnam. The new UH-1B was to see tremendous usage in Vietnam.

1LT Sprague was fortunate to be flying Hueys, but the earliest Vietnam U.S. Army rotary-wing aviator weren't so lucky. The 8th and 57th flew CH-21 Shawnee helicopters to support and advise the Army of the Republic of Vietnam (ARVN) soldiers. Within days of their arrival, both units were conducting aviation support operations moving ARVN forces, along with American military advisors, into combat.

The Army's Shawnee (known as the Banana) helicopter was underpowered, limited in range, and in need of defensive armament. Its control cables, push/pull rods, fuel lines and electrical wiring were susceptible to enemy small arms fire. It also became evident that the climate and weather conditions of Vietnam had negative effects on the CH-21 with its large reciprocating engine and twin-rotor system. Even with its limitations, the helicopter did the job it was sent there to do – move +/- 20 combat-equipped ARVN troops into contact with the Viet Cong.

As U.S. presence in South Vietnam grew, so did the helicopter fleet. Utility Tactical Transport Helicopter Companies (UTTH) were issued new UH-1B Huey helicopters. The Hueys were armed with a variety of weapons systems and dedicated as fire support for the CH-21 companies.

The new Bell Huey helicopter became the aircraft of choice. While the UH-1B carried fewer troops than the Banana, the new turbine engines provided greater power and longer range than the CH-21. The Flying Bananas—CH-21B flew in VN from 1962 until the end of 1964, at which time UH-1B Hueys replaced all CH-21s in-country.

1LT Billy E. Sprague arrived at Tan Son Nhut Air Base, Saigon in October 1962, with orders assigning him to the 93rd Transportation Co., part of the 145th Avn Bn. Shortly Army (Aviation) Transportation companies were redesignated to reflect their increased role in troop movements and their secondary role in supply:

8th Transportation Co (Light Helicopter) to the 117th Aviation Co (Airmobile Light)

33rd Transportation Co (Light Helicopter) to the 118th Aviation Co (Airmobile Light)

81st Transportation Co (Light Helicopter) to the 119th Aviation Co (Airmobile Light)

57th Transportation Co (Light Helicopter) to the 120th Aviation Co (Airmobile Light)

93rd Transportation Co (Light Helicopter) to the 121st Aviation Co (Airmobile Light)

By November 1962, the 93rd, which was at Tan Son Nhut Air Base, had moved south (150 km) to Soc Trang and later became part of the Delta Battalion or 13th Aviation Battalion (Provisional) out of Can Tho. Flying gunship escort for the slow and vulnerable CH-21s, Billy's call sign was "Blue Three." His fellow pilot-in-command and Air Mission Commander (AMC) was Captain Gerry Hanson.

In the Delta, around Lai Khe, U.S. Army Advisors, later numbering 12,000 throughout VN, supported the Army of the Republic of Vietnam

(ARVN)[20]. Army Transportation Companies provided aviation support to the U.S. Advisors and the ARVN flew Boeing CH-21s [Shawnee], Cessna L-19s [Bird Dog], North American T-28 [Trojan] and the new Bell UH-1B [Iroquois]. The Air Force laughed at the Army's armed helicopters and called them pee shooters!

Billy's upbringing led to his thought, if you don't have money and can't get an education, you have to get experience – like this war. It is a practical way to look at his involvement in Vietnam. He lacked a formal education, and as a soldier in combat, a first lieutenant, his meager salary barely supported his wife Maryann and his four children[21], two girls (aged 13 and 7), and two boys (aged 9 and 5). "I had seen Billy doing his job as a gunner and pilot with endless energy and daring, I had seen his rough-cut face peering over his 7.62 gunsight in quite a few dangerous situations – and I knew that he was prepared to risk his neck for the career he had chosen. And if his personal obligations included four children, that probably was one more reason for his doing such a good job against the VCs in the hope of recognition and advancement[22]."

The author of *Vietnam Diary*, Richard Tregaskis, now deceased, was a noted and respected war correspondent and wrote throughout October, November, and December 1962 daily accounts of Eagle flights and other aviation missions by members of the 93rd UTT and other aviation companies in the delta. He mentions 1LT Billy Eugene Sprague on at least 20 occasions and with utmost praise. Tregaskis was quite impressed with Billy's gunnery skills and fearlessness.

Following Billy's combat tour in Vietnam, he returned to the states, and in 1966 Sprague attended the Accident Investigator/Aviation Safety Course at USC in southern California. While there, he met Judith. They were married in 1967 and had other children. Later he received orders to Germany for a three-year accompanied tour.

Following a tour with USAREUR in Germany, Sprague received an assignment as the Army Aviation Advisor to the OKARNG at Norman, OK in late 1971. He worked in this position until 1974/75.

Chief Warrant Officer Five Samuel T. Hinch[23], who was also a Vietnam gunship driver like Billy Sprague, remembered this Army Advisor at Norman, "Sprague was an instrument examiner. Ninety percent of us coming back from Vietnam didn't have an instrument ticket, just that Tactical Instrument Ticket. Hold the blue thing (card) up to the sky and you go fly. If it's not blue you don't fly. I think that got a lot of us killed back then. He [Billy Sprague] was an instrument examiner and I remember him giving me an instrument evaluation (check ride), when I just had gotten my standard instrument ticket. It was just almost the most horrible thing I ever endured. He made it tolerable. He'd say, 'No, this is what you gotta do . . . ' It was not just an exam; it was an instruction period for me. He was very fair, very strict, a very stern lieutenant colonel-type, [although, he was] very amiable in the cockpit."

LTC Billy Eugene Sprague retired in 1975 and returned to his hometown of Chandler, OK. He passed away on 17 October 2006 at Chandler, after a long struggle with Alzheimer's disease. Most of his family is still in the Chandler area.

Following Billy Sprague was a tall aviation soldier who loved to run, Lieutenant Colonel Leroy E. Bond. Lieutenant Colonel Bond was the first advisor to work at the new Army Aviation Support Facility at Lexington, OK. Bond came on board as the Army Aviation Advisor ca 1975/76.

LTC Bond was the only advisor to work at the Lexington AASF. "Bond was a great advisor; just a super nice guy. I flew with him quite a bit. He was a runner and bike rider," said COL Leroy A. Wall. After he retired from the Army, he worked at the Lexington Assessment and Reception Center (LARC) (formerly Lexington Correctional Facility), next door to the Lexington AASF until ca 1980/85.

LTC Leroy E. Bond
ca 1983

Lieutenant Colonel Donald E. Derrick recalls,[24] "Then came Lee Bond [at Lexington]. Good guy, very professional, pro Army Aviation, very athletic. I had a lot of respect for him. He ran all the time and was a consummate physical enthusiast. When he was on Active Duty before he became an aviator, he went through Airborne School, Ranger School; he was an infantry officer. He earned the EIB (Expert Infantry Badge). He went to flight school, then a tour in Vietnam. He came to Lexington as our Army Aviation Advisor. I think people were put off by him at first; some people were. Once they got to know him, they realized how helpful, how interested, and how he promoted the Guard and aviation. I liked him a lot. I worked with Bond quite a bit when I was commander of the 445th Avn Co."

After many attempts to find LTC Leroy E. Lee Bond, and some help from Jim Hall, I got in touch with Lee in early June 2010. Here's his story in his own words: "I was assigned as the US Army Advisor to the Oklahoma Army National Guard for all aviation matters in July 1976 upon completion of the Command and General Staff College at Fort Leavenworth. I was the successor to LTC Billy Sprague, who had already retired when I arrived. I remained in that capacity until January 1980, when I was assigned to Supreme HQ Allied Powers in Europe (Belgium)."

"When I arrived in Lexington, Master Sergeant John Kivler, the enlisted advisor, was already on station. Master Sergeant Kivler was a top notch assistant who worked well with the enlisted members of the unit. During the three and one half years I spent with the OKARNG, I witnessed a transformation from a flying club atmosphere, with very little knowledge or concern for tactical training, to a unit that ended up performing low level troop insertions at Fort Chaffee, AR during an evaluated tactical exercise. During that timeframe, the company based at Muldrow went to Fort Rucker for training one summer camp, Fort Hood for another camp, and had an aviation unit from the 101st Airborne Division come to Oklahoma for tactical training."

Bond continued, "I have to credit Major Don Derrick, the unit commander during that period, with most of that emphasis on tactical training. When I left my assignment I felt good about my small part in how far the OKARNG Aviation units had progressed. Of course, the unit was filled with Vietnam veteran pilots who had more flight hours and tactical experience than their regular Army counterparts."

"One summer camp story that comes to mind is when the Air Traffic Control Section was formed. One of the new soldiers was a very attractive young lady. The maneuvering for her affections within the unit reached a peak during an evening picnic when we were at Fort Chaffee. The result was that one of the unit members who she ignored got mad and wrapped his 240Z around a tree. I can also remember going to Army HQ in San Antonio, when Leroy Wall was recognized as the [5th Army] area Aviator of the Year. While the rest of us attended meetings, Dana Batey was out politicking. That was his forte and he was good at it. I believe that he deserves the real credit for the growth of the OKARNG aviation resources in the late 1970s and early 1980s. Of course, the talent in the units made his task of growing the resources doable."

Bond added, "When I arrived at Lexington, my office was toxic as a result of actions that occurred prior to my arrival. It took about a year before most of the unit members would talk to me beyond the rudimentary courtesies. When I left, I left many good friends, some who I still see and many for whom I have great respect.

"I first came to Oklahoma on a construction crew when I was a teenager just prior to enlisting in the Army in 1958. I spent six years in the Infantry before going to OCS at Fort Benning and later came back to Fort Sill when we staged our Birddog Company there for six months prior to my first deployment to Vietnam. During my enlisted time I went to jump school at Fort Bragg and later earned my Expert Infantryman Badge at Schofield Barracks, Hawaii. After OCS, I went to Ranger School and then Flight School within the year. I wore Infantry crossed rifles until the Aviation branch was formed. My first trip to Vietnam was in 1965, when I flew the O-1 Birddog in the area north, south and east of Saigon, including many night missions over the shipping channel. I came back to Fort Hood for 16 months, during which time I went to Fort Rucker to transition into the U-21 turboprop. Then it was back to Vietnam at Nha Trang in II Corps for a year. I flew the U-21 and Beavers that year. After that the Army was gracious enough to let me go to Bootstrap at the University of Oklahoma, which was like coming home. After college I was sent back to Fort Hood again and from there to Fort Rucker for helicopter training. Then we went to Fort Leavenworth for C&GSC, which brings us full circle to 1976 and the assignment to OKARNG. I retired in 1985 from Fort Benjamin Harrison, IN, where I was the Deputy Director of the US Amy Computer Science School, and then came back home to Oklahoma.

LTC Lee Bond's awards include Master Army Aviator, Parachutists Badge, Ranger Tab, Bronze Star w/1OLC, Defense Meritorious Service Medal, Army Meritorious Service Medal, Air Medal w/ 25 OLC, Army Commendation Medal w/V, Good Conduct Medal and various Vietnam campaign and service ribbons.

Below is an article that appeared in the *Noble News*, 3 May 1979 when MSG Kivler and Major Bond were awarded the Oklahoma Distinguished Service Medal, presented by Colonel Ron Howland.

"Two Win State's Top Military Award"

MAJ Leroy Bond, MSG John Kivler and COL Ron
Howland 1979

In what was possibly the first presentation of its kind in state history, two regular Army advisors for the 145th Aviation Battalion in Lexington, received the Oklahoma Distinguished Service Medal, the highest state military award.

MAJ Leroy E. Bond, Rt. 1 Noble and MSG John Kivler, Norman, were presented the citations and medals for dedicated service to the Oklahoma Army National Guard. The citations were signed by Gov. George Nigh and State Adjutant General Bob Morgan.

Bond has served as Army Advisor for the 145th Aviation Battalion for three years. He was instrumental in improving the operation of the battalion by developing and implementing advanced programs in the tactical use by the Oklahoma Army Guard.

Since 1976 he has assisted in the implementation of a year-long helicopter maintenance training course, was responsible for developing unit operating procedures for tactical field operations and worked closely with officers and operations personnel in training programs in command and control functions of the unit.

Bond has been in the Army since 1958 and was a staff sergeant before completing Officer Training School in 1965 at Fort Benning, GA. He is a graduate of the U.S. Army Ranger School, Fixed Wing and Rotary Wing Flight School, Infantry Officer Advanced Course, and of the Command and General Staff College. He has a degree in business management and a Masters degree in Computer Science.

He served two tours in Vietnam, during which time he earned 25 Air Medals for flying more than 1,250 hours in combat. Bond also received the Army Commendation Medal for Valor and has received two awards of the Bronze Star. During his tenure in the Army, he has served with the 82nd Airborne Division, the 2nd Armored Division, III Army Corp, the 17th Combat Aviation Group, and the 25th Infantry Division.

Kivler has been an Army Advisor for the 145th Aviation Battalion for four years. He was instrumental in improving the operation of the battalion by specializing instruction and as advisor in aircraft maintenance and accident prevention for enlisted personnel of the unit. Since 1975 he has been involved in implementing enlisted training programs in aircraft and motor maintenance, administrative and supply procedures, dining facility operations and other enlisted personnel training.

Kivler joined the U.S. Army in 1961 and is a native of New Jersey. He served three tours of duty in Europe and two tours in Vietnam, where he earned two Bronze Stars, while serving as senior aircraft maintenance sergeant.

To the best of my knowledge, LTC Lee Bond was the lone Army Advisor for OKARNG aviation units at the Lexington AASF. The next full-time, Army Advisors, dedicated to OKARNG aviation were at Sperry, OK in the 45th Aviation Battalion (Sp Ops) (Abn) Lords of Darkness.

During the 1982-94 timeframe, the main focus of our Army Aviation Advisors to OKARNG Aviation was to provide battalion staff and operations training and enlisted MOS training to our brand new Special Operations aviation unit, the Lords of Darkness. The advisors in the 45th Avn Bn (Sp Ops) worked out of the S-3 shop. They interfaced with the Bn staff, CSM, Unit 1SGs and Co Sr SGTs. They participated in aircraft qualification, NVG training, FAARP training, deployments and MOS qualification.

Major Jack "Happy Jack" Brayton was assigned as an Army Aviation Advisor to the 45th Avn Bn ca May 1982. Chief Warrant Officer Four Jaime N. Smith recalled, "I remember when he was at the Senior Army Advisor's office at State Headquarters. He went to the University of Oklahoma and completed his master's degree in psychology at the same time. I don't know why or how in hell he got the S-3 job with the 45th Avn Bn. He was a hard-headed and arrogant guy. I don't think anyone liked him. On the other hand, he did a lot of hard work for the unit, especially in the area of deployments. He was responsible for the air crewmembers getting serious about the [new Special Operations] mission and training, because some weren't.

"He especially had trouble with the pilots because they had to fly with the full-face AN/PVS 5A NVGs. The pilots didn't like them one bit, but at the time it was all we had," remembers Smith. In mid-1986/87 we were inundated with NVG goggles and at one point had close to 1,000 pair of NVG (ground and aviator goggles), from every Pentagon vendor under the sun. They gave them to us, hoping we would like them and help them sell their version to DoD.

Jaime Smith did a fantastic job of juggling the property book and excess accounts to provide us with the best available and first-class goggles! SGTs Joe Bunnell and Lou Latham, both full-time ALSE technicians, worked tirelessly testing, tweaking and maintaining NVGs, flight helmets, and survival equipment. Certain Tulsa AASF Flight Ops personnel, Staff Sergeant Sandy Hodges, Staff Sergeant Ed Eberhardt and CW3 Leonard Reed often assisted the ALSE section with maintenance tasks.

Because of the high priority of the new Special Operations Counter Terrorism aviation unit, the 45th Avn Bn at Sperry America, we didn't have just one Army Aviation advisor; we had three: two officers and an enlisted Advisor, Master Sergeant Thomas W. Rickenbach. Major Bill Barnhorst was the number two Officer Advisor; he came on board at Sperry ca 1984/86 as a liaison officer between the Lords of Darkness and Task Force 160 at Fort Campbell.

CW4 Smith remembers Barnhorst, "He was small of stature, but a Big Picture type officer. His liaison job between 45th Avn Bn and Task Force 160th might have appeared to be easy, but not exactly. He seemed competent at what he was sent to do. At first, I think there was an initial stand-off attitude with the TF 160 [the 45ᵗʰ Avn Bn?—why they're just National Guard weekend warrior aviators . . .]. Barnhorst helped bridge that problem and got us the information/coordination that we needed. (The respect we wanted came later – we earned it!) I know that he would go TF 160 and find out how they got permission to do a certain thing. He would discuss an issue with the staff at the 160ᵗʰ, find out how they resolved it and bring back that information to us. We never felt like he was sent here to keep tabs on us, or our strengths and weaknesses.

There were several interesting rumors in the late 1980s, relating that Brayton and/or Barnhorst may have been directly or indirectly involved with the CIA and the black world of Special Operations. There was one story that circulated around Sperry and the town's people, which involved Brayton and Major Vernon Asher about a brief case full of cash for a rapid deployment mission. Although all of these stories are highly titillating and interesting, none of them can be substantiated. End of message.

Major Brayton, Major Barnhorst and Master Sergeant Rickenbach had completed their tours as advisors by the time I was assigned as the S-3/Operations Officer at the 45ᵗʰ Avn Bn in February 1986. Either shortly before or after my arrival in Sperry, OK, Major Dwight Cheek was assigned as the Army Aviation Advisor to the 45ᵗʰ Avn Bn (Sp Ops).

Sergeant First Class Stan Skokowski was the Enlisted Advisor at Sperry before Major Cheek arrived. Then Sergeant First Class Todd Duncan followed as the next Enlisted Advisor; after which Sergeant First Class John Weber, a very quiet Native American, was the Enlisted Advisor. Weber left the 45ᵗʰ Avn Bn and went to the 82ⁿᵈ (Abn) Div at Fort Bragg, and was 1SG of a Chinook company, according to 45ᵗʰ Avn Bn Command Sergeant Major Charles "Corky" Connell.

"SFCs Webber and Duncan, both were professionals and heads-up guys. They helped out with training and worked with our NCOs to bring them up to speed. They were around 24/7 and didn't mind getting dirty. I have nothing but praise for these gentlemen and there are not enough superlatives to describe them," said Sergeant First Class Norman Crowe from his civilian aviation maintenance job in Iraq in 2008.

It was about mid-spring, 1986 when a lean, stern-looking, MAJ Dwight Cheek arrived in Tulsa, OK, and casually asked someone, "Excuse me . . . . do you know where the hell Sperry, OK Armory is?" Cheek was the new Army Aviation Advisor to the 45ᵗʰ Avn Bn (Lt Hel Cbt). Somehow he knew how to get some great assignment opportunities around the world, not that any of them would help his Army career, but . . . .

MAJ Cheek, an Army rotary-wing aviator, had just finished a unique assignment with the U.S. Navy. He had been assigned as the Helicopter Coordination Officer for the Navy's Tactical Air Control Squadron at Beirut, Lebanon. Dwight wasn't quite sure why, but he had been awarded the Navy's Expeditionary Medal[25] for his time in Beirut.

Prior to arriving in Sperry, MAJ Cheek stopped off (TDY enroute) at Fort Indiantown Gap, PA and somehow obtained an OH-6 transition. Then he drove his small European sports car to the old sandstone armory on Cincinnati Street in Sperry, with the same enthusiasm he enjoyed when flying the sporty OH-6 aircraft.

Prior to his Beirut Naval assignment, Dwight had been assigned to an Army Aviation (GS) Battalion at Hunter AAF, Fort Stewart, GA. There he often supported the 1st Bn 75th Rangers. Because of their special missions, their training scenarios required more than just a ride to/from the target! Ranger teams wanted to maintain a low profile, infiltrate as quietly as possible at night, and inundate the target with overwhelming force and surprise! Dwight had some experience with the dark gray side of military aviation and brought that experience, large or limited, with him to Sperry.

MAJ Cheek flew often and became NVG-qualified in the OH-6, and away from the airfield he partied just as often. When on duty, he offered a great deal of advice, much of which was right on target. He worked with CW3 TK Klutts and CW3 Leonard "Dawg" Reed on the subject of Risk Assessment. He was not one to back off his own humble position, even after it was obvious that he might be wrong.

Dwight was single, brash and had an attitude – "Do as I say, not as I do." His hubris prevented many lasting relationships. He imperiously suggested that all of the 45th Avn Bn Staff officers should complete the Command and General Staff College as soon as possible. We did, but he never followed his own advice.

Dwight was not overtly religious, except in one area – the Army's bible. His bible was FM 101-5 (Field Manual – Staff Organizations and Operations) and to his credit, he knew it inside and out. He saw our battalion staff's inexperience in preparing staff estimates and operational briefings and helped us achieve a higher level of professionalism, coordination and success than even we thought was possible. Our staff briefings became very succinct, on target, proficient presentations for our commander. Later our information or decision briefings, which we gave to the highest levels in the Special Operations community, were frequently lauded.

Lieutenant Colonel Arthur C. Kveseth, former S-1/Adjutant for the 45th Avn Bn, remembers Dwight Cheek, "He was an effective advisor for the unit. He seemed to understand Guard politics and the personalities involved. He gave some good advice on many matters, but concentrated on staff actions and planning. When he would start to talk about Field Manual (FM) this or that, I would groan inwardly because he was right, and it meant a lot of writing and research [for the S-1 office]. The man [Cheek] loved operation orders; I think he read them for entertainment. He contributed a lot and was always there to assist and some cases defend the way we did our [Special Operations] business."

MAJ Cheek was a very tall guy, and he had a nice and easy going personality. He was definitely a hands-on advisor, much more into pilot training than Barnhorst.

MAJ Dwight Cheek left the 45th Avn Bn armory at Sperry on terminal leave in October 1986. He retired officially in November 1986 from the Army at age 40. MAJ Cheek had 20 years active duty in the Army, +/- 2,800 flight hours and received his Master Army Aviator wings the day he retired. Among the several awards and decorations he received, was the Army's Meritorious Service Award, Army Commendation Medal and the Navy Amphibious Expeditionary Medal.

Dwight was an eccentric individual, somewhat arrogant and dogmatic. He unashamedly considered himself a party animal and a chick magnet. Regardless of the destination on his leave orders, permanent orders or TDY orders, Dwight always packed and carried with him his Army dress blue uniform. His philosophy was "You just never know what opportunity might present herself."

MAJ Dwight Check was a fine Army Aviation Advisor for the 45th Avn Bn. He now resides in Mt. Dora, FL. When the housing market isn't crashing, he does land surveying for spending money and because he enjoys it.

Allow me to fill in a few blanks. According to several older fellows, they seem to recall another Army Aviation Advisor, Major Fuchs (pronounced Fox) who served[26] at Norman ca 1966 following MAJ Loren L. Glenn. Nothing more was found on Major Fuchs.

Master Sergeant Simpson served as the Enlisted Advisor during the period ca 1962-65, along with MAJ Loren L. Glenn. Nothing more was found on Master Sergeant Simpson.

Master Sergeant Lee Bennett served[27] as the Enlisted Advisor during the period October 1968 to November 1971, along with LTC John R. Bob Dome. Nothing more was found on Master Sergeant Bennett.

Master Sergeant Neil Hurst served[28] as the Enlisted Advisor during the period ca 1972, along with LTC Billy E. Sprague. Nothing more was found on Master Sergeant Hurst.

SFC John H. Weber was the active duty Enlisted Advisor for the 45th Avn Bn (SO) September 1985 – July 1987. John was perhaps a Native America Indian. Although he was an aviation NCO, he was not a member of Task Force 160th, nor had he ever been. He was a very quiet individual.

SFC Todd Duncan came to Sperry/45th Avn Bn (SO) as the active duty Army Enlisted Advisor ca 1987—1990. He helped out with training and worked with the NCOs to bring them up to speed. They were always around and didn't mind getting dirty. I have nothing but praise for these gentlemen and there are not enough superlatives to describe them, said Art Kveseth."[29]

SFC Joe Stalling served as an Enlisted Advisor at 1st 245th Avn (SO) (A) ca 1988-1991at Sperry/Tulsa.

Sadly, all of the post-1980 Army Aviation Advisors to OKARNG Aviation came from Active Duty Combat Aviation Battalions and none from Task Force 160. None of the active duty Army Aviation Advisors, officer or enlisted, during the period 1982 until 1994, had any, repeat any Special Operations Aviation experience—none. Why did the Army not see fit to share its own limited, but vital experience in the 'black' world with an Army National Guard unit that was touted in the halls of the Pentagon as "a mirror image of Task Force 160?" Why?

As a result, the majority of the Special Operations concepts we learned were developed by our own 45th Avn Bn (Sp Ops) AGR Bn Staff, Company Staff and AGRs/military technicians from the Tulsa AASF. There was little that got by the 45th Avn Bn as far as Special Ops aviation techniques and/or procedures. In a word, we helped write the book, even though we've seldom been mentioned in the credits.

At the beginning of this chapter I mentioned that, "This type military assignment [Army Aviation Advisor] is unique and viewed from the top down as extremely important!" What I didn't add was that the Active Army doesn't see this job as career-enhancing at all and normally assigns an individual to this advisor position as their last military assignment. Does the later opinion give us an idea how important they, the seamless Army, view working with the ARNG or Army Reserves???

During October 2008 a military friend shared with me, " . . . . the active Army no longer supports advisors to separate reserve component units and will only resource a lieutenant colonel or a colonel [depending on the size of the State's Army Guard] for the Joint Force Headquarters Land Component[30]; many [Senior Army Advisor positions] are vacant so that many Senior Army Advisors must cover more than one state. In the office of the SRAAG, there is no [GS] secretary and no Enlisted Advisor. The active Army no longer provides advisors to individual units. The Army, being short on officers for deployments, expects NG units to go to their supporting Training Support Brigade (TSB) if they need assistance. However, the TSB seems to only be able to support units in the process of mobilizing, so if your unit is not in the process of training for a mobilization you are not likely to get support. The Army and Congress through Title 11 personnel had a great program for supporting units [in the past], but it has fallen apart . . ." Since the Army's become so over extended, and deployment cycles to Iraq and Afghanistan are so frequent, it appears that Army Advisors to Army National Guard units have become a valued resource of the past.

1. Information on the office and responsibilities of the SRAAG provided by COL Otis L. Brown II, assigned to the JFHQ-OK as the SRAAG ca 2008/09.

2. Telephone interview with the widow of LTC Glenn, Mrs. Helen Glenn, Gordonville, TX on 27 September 2008.

3. Telephone interview with LTC Donald E. Derrick, 8 December 2008.

4. Extracted from the obituary of Loren L. Glenn.

5. Emails and personal interview with Milton Glenn 27 October to 6 November 2008.

6. Army Air Forces Pilot School, advanced multi-engine bomber and navigator training at Houston, TX

7. Reprinted by permission. Charles R. "Bob" Pitzer, "Keeping China Alive" (Tales of "Flying the Hump") http://www.kilroywashere.org/003-Pages/Hump/Hump.html

8. A U.S. Army "Navion" was the last Army fixed-wing aircraft mounted on a pole at the 45th Inf Div Museum in Okla. City, OK, ca 1993.

9. Extracted from U.S. Army Aviation History at the U.S. Army Aviation Center Museum, Fort Rucker, AL

10. Heike Hasenauer, "Rocket Pioneers," U.S. Army's *Soldiers,* (October 2008)

11. Information researched by former Army Captain/VN combat aviator of the174th AHC, Steve R. Kennedy.

12. Nothing further has been determined regarding the Enlisted Advisor MSG Simpson.

13. MAJ C.L. Strance provided some 'biographical notes' on LTC John R. "Bob" Dome, as did Mrs. Helen Dome, who provided photos, articles, books, facts and memorabilia to the author.

14. Email COL Leroy A. Wall, 2 July 2008.

15. Telephone conversation with Mrs. Dome 25 October 2008.

16. Extracted from a CNN biographical article on Syngman (Sigmund) Rhee; http://www.cnn.com/fyi/school.tools/profiles/Syngman.Rhee/content.html

17. Telephone interviews with Mrs. Billy Lee Sprague o/a 11 September 2008 and Mrs. Judith Sprague o/a 20 September 2008.

18. Richard Tregaskis, "Vietnam Diary," (NYC: Henry Holt & Co, 1963), 287

19. In the earliest days of the 1960s, [Aviation] Transportation Companies were called UTTs "Utility Tactical Transport (Helicopter Companies) and then later were redesignated as Aviation companies (Airmobile Light). Information from the U.S. Army Transportation Museum website: http://www.transchool.eustis.army.mil/museum/VietnamAviation.htm

20. Interestingly, the author Richard Tregaskis, a veteran war correspondent, mistakenly called the ARVN troops "Arvin" throughout his book "Vietnam Diary."

21. Children of Lieutenant Sprague and his first wife Mary Ann.

22. Richard Tregaskis, "Vietnam Diary," (NYC: Henry Holt & Co, 1963), 287

23. Telephone interview with CW5 Samuel T. Hinch on/about 29 January 2009.

24. Telephone interview with LTC Donald E. Derrick 8 December 2008.

25. The *Navy Expeditionary Medal,* an award of the U.S. Navy, awarded to any Navy personnel who have operated in foreign territory to engage in operations, both combat and non-combat, for which no other campaign medal has been awarded.

26. The name, MAJ Fuchs, was provided by LTC Cameron Weber and verified by CW4 Charlie Evans and COL Jerry Bourassa.

27. Personal conversation with CW4 Charlie Evans on 20 September 2008, Washington, OK.

28. Ibid

29. Email LTC Arthur C. Kveseth, 16 December 2007

30. Email COL Eric C. Peck, Chief of Staff, Joint Forces Headquarters, KSARNG, a personal friend of the author. Eric Peck was the former Deputy Commander of OSACOM at Davison AAF, Fort Belvoir, VA, under Colonel Billy R. Wood, then Commander of OSACOM. Peck was promoted to brigadier general on 17 October 2010.

Chapter 9

OKARNG Aviation Medicine

*"We occasionally stumble over the truth, but most of us pick ourselves
up and hurry off as if nothing had happened."*
Winston Churchill

Aviation medicine is defined by the Department of Defense as the special
field of medicine which is related to the biological and psychological
problems of flight. It may be further defined as—the medical study and
treatment of physiological and psychological disorders associated with
atmospheric or space flight—also called *aerospace medicine.*

The necessity for aviation medicine was discovered early in our history
of aeronautics. Aviators didn't know what they didn't know, particularly
about aviation medicine. Accidents and casualties have always been and
are still costly; education and medicine would begin to reduce this deficit.
It became obvious to medical personnel that doctors, nurses and other
personnel dealing with aviators and their lofty environment, needed to
be specialized in the field which they soon called – Aviation Medicine.
However, it didn't begin in this or the last century.

Which came first – the chicken, the egg or aviation medicine? None
of the above. But if you said, the balloon, then you were correct.

Two French brothers, Joseph & Etienne Montgolfier, are credited in
the 18th century with the first unmanned hot air balloon flights. Naturally,
this soon led to manned hot air balloon flight on 21 November 1783 and
then later to medical experiments involving aerial flight.

Dr. John Jeffries, was the first American of note to conduct some
aeronautical experiments for medical scientific purposes. His book *A*

Narrative of the Two Aerial Voyages written in 1786 listed some scientific measurements such as air samples taken, pulse, breaths per minute and it was noted that one might experience a strange pressure or pain in the ears. Hypoxia was discovered during early balloon flights at higher altitudes.

It is sad, but the first century of aviation medicine was of little or no consequence. It would not be until later that the true science and new field of aviation medicine would come into being.

Aviation in the U.S. Army began in August 1907, when the Aeronautical Division of the Office of the Chief Signal Officer of the Army was established. A Captain, corporal and a private first class were first responsible for "all matters pertaining to military ballooning, air machines and all kindred subjects." In 1913, our nation's government owned but one airplane, but in 1914 it bought another. "How many airplanes does a Government need?" was the thought in Congress at the time. In our country people were convinced that we would not be drawn into the conflict, this terrible war, a World War. The dream faded and the nation which was the birthplace of the Wright Brother's airplane entered the first World War with an air service in its infancy, hardly capable of crawling and its aviation medicine in swaddling clothes.

In stark contrast, Germany began WWI in 1914 with more airplanes than France, Great Britain and the United States combined. Medical papers on aviation related subjects first appeared in 1907 and by 1910; Germany was the first country to establish minimum medical standards for military aviators.

In the darkness and emptiness of our unpreparedness, aviation medicine began in the Army's Air Service, part of the Signal Corps. For some strange reason, horsemanship was considered to be a good indication of a man's potential skill as an aviator. Soon one of the first Army aviation warnings was published – "Aviators will remove their spurs before flying."

The Germans, British and French were involved with aviation and aerial combat in the first World War, before the American's could even spell dogfight or vertigo. But soon Army Aviators and cadets were notified of physical evaluation standards for men wanting to become flyers. Although the other participants of WWI had aviation programs, the examination procedures and their importance were not standardized.

In 1908, the Wright Brothers delivered the first airplane to the U.S. Army. Our first aviators were required to meet general duty medical standards, i.e., nothing special for aviators.

Military and civilian aviation needed aviation medicine and the need grew every more intense with the increasing loss of airplanes and aviators. Two dangerous issues needed to be addressed in the military: too many pilots were being lost due to factors other than combat or equipment failure (i.e., "pilot failure") and a method of screening out physical defects in candidates without overly restricting the candidate pool. Finding this balance proved extremely difficult. Of 39,000 applicants, 11,500 were commissioned as aviators during the 21 months the United States was involved in WWI.

A few years later, 7 February 1912, the U.S. Army Surgeon General was wrestling with how to medically qualify individuals for pilot training. There were many different, quirky proposed tests for balance, vision, hearing, color blindness, etc. Eventually the Surgeon General's office determined the items which led to an Army physical exam for would-be pilots. The emphasis was on eyes, ears and heart. No one could pass the exam, therefore the Army lowered its standards (sound familiar?) and candidates began passing the entrance physical for aviation training. During the short 21 month period we were involved in WWI, less than half of the applicants for flight training passed the physical exam.

September 1917, Lieutenant Colonel Theodore Charles Lyster became the first Chief Surgeon, Aviation Section, Signal Corps. Later that month, an Air Division was approved for the Signal Corps. One the six sections of the Air Division was the new Medical Department. Lyster is later recognized as the "Father of Aviation Medicine."

During his WWI experience with aviation and medicine, he accomplished much useful research. He determined that the Army's accident rate was one crash/accident every 250 hours and one fatality every 750 hours.

A program was then soon developed for the selection and highly technical training of new medical officers and examiners at the new Air Service Medical Research Laboratory at Hazelhurst Field, on Long Island, New York. Regular participation in aerial flight by aviation medical personal was recommended. It is hard to evaluate what you are unfamiliar with or haven't experienced yourself. It was Drs. Isaac H. Jones and Eugene

R. Lewis who chose the term *Flight Surgeon* for these medical officers who were taught to counsel aviators and their commanding officers on such matters as rest, recreation, nutrition, exercise and when to temporarily refrain from flying because of medical reasons. "The Flight Surgeon has struggled from that date in the performance of his duties, because medical commanders did not see much need for a doctor, who was needed elsewhere, to spend his time flying with aviators. Aviators saw the Flight Surgeon as a danger to their career and part of the problem, but not part of the solution," said MAJ Todd.

Also at Hazelhurst Field was the new U.S. Army School of Aviation Medicine (USASAM), which opened in May 1918. By June 1918, the school was functioning and training flight surgeons. In August the first class graduated 34 officers and enlisted men, who were sent overseas to provide aviation medical support to the air squadrons of the American Expeditionary Force (AEF). Major Robert R. Hampton was appointed as the first flight surgeon in the AEF 17 September 1918. The first flight surgeon to report for active duty at a U.S. base was Captain Robert J. Hunter. He submitted a written report of his first observations of aviation cadet training at Park Field, Tennessee, which included these comments:

"Investigated the three accidents occurring since I came here. None of these were fatal. One was due to inexperience, topography of the country and mechanical difficulties. Second: uncertain cause but patient thinks he hit his head on the cowl while doing a loop. Third: machine [went] out of control while chasing a crow."

USASAM was moved in 1926 to Brooks Field, now Brooks AFB at San Antonio, TX. In 1931 it was moved across town to Randolph Army Air Field. On 25 Jun 1943, The Army Air Forces (USAAF) School of Air Evacuation was established at Bowman Field, KY. In 1944 this school was moved to San Antonio and incorporated into the USASAM. In 1947, the U.S. Air Force became a separate service and USASAM was renamed the U.S. Air force school of Aviation Medicine and moved back to Brooks AFB.

Dr. Jones was a salesman of the newly designated *flight surgeons* and traveled to tell commanders about them and how they could benefit aviation and aviators. He taught that keeping pilots mentally and physically fit to continue flying was the main purpose of flight surgeons. He was quoted, "It may take 100 years to convince pilots of this idea because pilots feel doctors are determined not to let them fly if doctors can possibly find a way to prevent their flying."

> "The first and primary duty of the flight surgeon in connection with flying personnel is the maintenance of the pilot in such a condition, that . . . the pilot is always ready for his mission . . . This is accomplished in numerous ways, such as . . . participation with them in their flying . . . The flight surgeon should know the inherent stresses and strains produced by the particular type of flying being done . . . and their effects . . . the flight surgeon should be interested in all phases of a pilot's work."
>
> Henry H. "Hap" Arnold (1886-1950)
> Five Star General of the Army Air Forces in WWII

What are the responsibilities of your *flight surgeon*? Well, more than I care to list here. Try to remember that he is your friend and does want to see you remain on flight status. Here are some of the duties of an Army Flight Surgeon:

- Maintains his own professional education through a medical continuing education program.
- Administers the primary flight physical entrance examinations and annual flight physicals for aviators and crewmembers.
- Assists in aeromedical research studies.
- Provides primary medical care for air crewmembers and their families.
- Provides consults for special treatments of air crewmembers and their families.
- Providing aeromedical support to an aviation unit during combat or peacetime deployments.
- Prevention and treatment of medical conditions and disease.
- Participates as a viable member of the unit's flight safety programs.
- Participates as a board member of the accident investigation team for aircraft mishaps.
- Evaluates air crewmembers for medical issues which may ground or disqualify them from flight status.

- Re-evaluates air crewmembers who desire to return to full flight status.
- Other duties "as assigned . . ."

After the Army Air Corps became a separate service in 1947, most of the Army Air Force Medical Officers transferred to the Air Force. The Army was left with a few officers who were qualified to carry the Army aviation medical program forward. At the Field Artillery Post called Fort Sill, the U.S. Army was left with one flight surgeon for the Army Aviation School, also located at this time (1950) at Fort Sill, OK. His name was Lieutenant Colonel Rollie M. Harrison, who was an advisor to the Director, Department of Air Training concerning matters of aviation medicine. That was until Major Spurgeon H. Neel graduated from the U.S. Air Force Flight Surgeon course in March 1951, thus doubling the Army's number of flight surgeons at Fort Sill to two. They worked out of the Aviation Clinic adjacent to Henry Post airfield, which was later named Harrison Aviation Clinic, after LTC Rollie M. Harrison. Like the old dirigible hangar there at Henry Post AAF, old Harrison Aviation Clinic is listed as a national historic landmark.

January 1943 the YR-4B helicopter was being tested for use as an air ambulance. U.S. Army helicopter procurement began in April 1944. The Sikorsky S-47 or XR-4 was delivered to the U.S. Army Air Corps in May 1942, the prototype for the first helicopter produced in quantity for the U.S. armed forces. An R-4 flew the first helicopter mercy mission through a snowstorm in January 1944, hauling blood plasma from Battery Park in Lower Manhattan to Sandy Hook New Jersey to aid victims of a steamship explosion. In November 1945, an S-51 conducted the first helicopter hoist rescue when it pulled two seamen from a sinking barge off Connecticut. In World War II, the fabric-covered helicopters flew the first combat rescue and Medevac missions. The first combat medical evacuation occurred on 23 April 1944 and the pilot was Lieutenant Carter Harmon in Burma.

The first Table of Organization and Equipment (TOE) for an aeromedical evacuation unit was published in August 1952, with 7 officers, 21 enlisted and 5 helicopters. This marked the beginning of the only dedicated aeromedical evacuation capability in any armed force in the world.

During the Korean War, MAJ Neel was instrumental in developing helicopter medical evacuation. Neel and Army Aviation Medicine take great pride in the fact that the helicopter first designated the HU-1, was developed under contract with Army Surgeon General's office as an air ambulance. The HU-1's nickname became the Huey and was later designated the UH-1. The UH-1 *Huey* was the backbone of Army air mobility and aerial medical evacuation during the Vietnam war. We in the Army are familiar with the term medical evacuation or *MEDEVAC* in lieu of aeromedical evacuation.

When the 57th Medical Detachment (Hel Amb) first arrived in Vietnam in 1962 and flew the UH-1 *Huey* in the MEDEVAC role, it was given the famous call sign DUSTOFF. The callsign epitomized the 57th's MEDEVAC missions. The Vietnam countryside was then dry and dusty and as helicopters approached and landed their rotor-wash blew dust, dirt, ponchos, tents and anything not nailed down away . . . The men on the ground had mixed emotions, disappointed with all the dirt and debris blowing, but thankful someone was there to transport the wounded to hospital. By 1966, all throughout Vietnam, all U.S. Army Medical Air Ambulance units used the callsign[1] DUSTOFF. Individual crews used DUSTOFF followed by two-numbers, e.g. DUSTOFF 34. There had to be at least one exception, the 1st Cavalry Division (Air Mobile) in Vietnam used the callsign MEDEVAC followed by two numbers.

Helicopter ambulances grew to a peak of 140 in Vietnam. From May 1962 to March 1973 900,000 patients were evacuated. By May 1966 hoists had been installed in most DUSTOFF and MEDEVAC Army aircraft. Roughly 8,000 hoist evacuations were made by the end of the Vietnam war. If you were assigned as a DUSTOFF and MEDEVAC pilot back then or today – your odds are 3.3 times greater that you will become a casualty. Hoist operations are 7 times more likely to take a hit and become a statistic.

In late October 2009, a retired Army Aviator and dear 174th Assault Helicopter Company friend of mine, Lieutenant Colonel Bernie Cobb, now deceased, formerly of Enterprise, AL, sent me an article published in the *Enterprise Ledger*, 21 October 2009, written by Michelle Mann, Ledger Staff Writer. This article was about two Army Aviation real heroes—a father/son pair of Army Dustoff Aviators, CW4 Michael J. Novosel Sr. and his son, CW4 Michael J. Novosel Jr.. Major General James O. Barclay

III unveiled a sculpted bust at a Fort Rucker ceremony of the Medal of Honor winner, Mike Novosel Sr.. CW4 Novosel, while serving in the Vietnam war air-evacuated more than 5,500 wounded soldiers during two tours in Southeast Asia, including his own son, Michael Novosel Jr. Novosel (Sr.) had accumulated 12,400 military flying hours, which included 2,038 combat hours. He served in WWII, the Korean War and the Vietnam war. Novosel (Sr.) was awarded the Medal of Honor at the age of 48 and was the Army's oldest veteran to receive the honor. He was also the last WWII military aviator in the US Army to have remained on active flying duty. After 42 years as a military aviator, Novosel retired to Enterprise in 1985 and lived there until his death from cancer on 2 April 2006. A main thoroughfare at Fort Rucker is named "Novosel Street" in his honor.

Retired CW4 Michael J. Novosel Jr., also a former UH-1 Huey pilot lost his short battle with cancer on 10 December 2009 at his Florida home[2]. He was 60 years old. The Novosel-father-son team flew Dustoff missions together while serving in the same medevac unit in Vietnam.

At the U.S. Army Aviation Center and School, which we called Mother Rucker, also had, and continues to have, its own medical evacuation aircraft and crews assigned to the school's headquarters. They are called FLATIRON and their motto is *"Always hot."* They were manned by military aviators assigned to TDA positions. Today the FLATIRON medevacs are manned by civilian aircrew members. They provided almost instantaneous aerial medical evacuation for all of Fort Rucker's numerous airfields, stage fields and landing areas. The Fort Rucker FLATIRON aircraft are also contracted to the Alabama State Department of Transportation to provide some aeromedical evacuation of seriously injured automobile accident victims in the Fort Rucker, LA (that's lower Alabama) area.

The callsign FLATIRON evolved[3] in the 1970s when Major General William "Bill" J. Maddox[4] Jr., Commandant of the US Army Aviation Center at Fort Rucker required that one rescue aircraft be in the air the entire period of time that U.S. Army Aviation Center flight students were flying and/or receiving instruction – day or night. When one FLATIRON aircraft would land to refuel or pick up an injured soldier another FLATIRON would launch immediately. The term FLATIRON refers to the flat irons our American pioneers used to iron their clothing. One flat iron would be heating on the wood stove while the other was being used.

Lieutenant Colonel Ray Collins, an Ozark, AL resident, holds the distinction of flying the very first FLATIRON MAST (Military Assistance to Safety and Traffic program) mission[5] at Fort Rucker on 18 April 1974. Collins had just returned to Rucker following a tour of duty as a Dustoff pilot with the 54th Medical Detachment in Vietnam. The MAST program was set into motion at Fort Sam Houston by General Spurgeon Neal.

On 12 November 1952, Army Regulation (AR) 40-110 established standards to be used by medical officers performing aviation physical examinations. This regulation differed slightly from the Air Force examination, but it was published on an Army-wide basis and officially designated as the bible for Army flight physicals. However, the majority of flight examinations, other than those conducted at Fort Sill, continued to be performed by Air Force Medical Officers. After the initial group, two Army medical officers were graduated from the formal Air Force course in Aviation Medicine between December 1952 and October 1954.

To offset this, the Army Medical Field Service School at Fort Sam Houston, TX added 46 hours of instruction in aviation medicine for career Army Medical Corps officers attending the primary course in military medicine.

In 1954, the first formal recognition within the Army of a separate and distinct aviation medicine military occupational specialty (MOS) was marked. The MOS 3160, Aviation Medical Officer (AMO) was established for officers who were to provide aviation and general medical service for Army aviators. The MOS did not mention flight requirements, or incentive or hazardous duty pay. This subject would be debated for a few more years to come for medical personnel.

At the end of 1955, the Army had projected a requirement of 60 to 70 AMOs. This requirement was based upon projected Army Aviation growth and a current AMO authorization policy. This policy stated that any post or installation or unit with over 30 pilots should be authorized at least one AMO. This meant that an AMO would be assigned to each Army Division, Corps, Field Army, Transportation Helicopter Battalion and major commands and schools such as the Army Aviation School.

In 1955, Colonel William H. Bryne replaced COL Harrison as the Aviation School's Medical Staff Officer before the school house left Fort Sill. At Fort Rucker he was encountering new aviation medical issues such as long hours of continuous flying, lack of adequate facilities and mental fatigue among flight instructors. Bryne was actively involved in attempting to regulate maximum individual flying hours and other recommendations for flight safety.

In September 1955, 28 Army aviation medical officers were practicing aviation medicine. This same year, a significant aviation medical document was published, TB (technical bulletin) *MED 244, Army Aviation Medicine*; it was one of the first truly Army aviation oriented medical publications. This TB MED 244 was in 1976 still in effect with minor changes. One of those changes recommended that "participation in frequent and regular aerial flights . . ." and that noncrewmember flying status be authorized for certain AMOs and that they should receive hazardous duty [flight] pay. Additionally in 1955, the Surgeon General initiated action to obtain authorization for distinctive insignia to be worn by qualified aviation medical officers. By custom, Army aviators expected their physicians to wear wings too! This authorization was secured in the summer of 1956.

By 1956, the Army's flight school had moved to Fort Rucker, AL. Most of its remaining 150 flight surgeons had been trained by the USAF, which was rapidly moving into the newly chartered field of jet aircraft and the atomic age. The Army, on the other hand, was steadily focused on front line combat and rotary-wing aviation support operations. This lead to separate research and flight surgeon training facilities which focused on Army Aviation Medicine concerns and the new U.S. Army Aeromedical Research Laboratory (USAARL) at Fort Rucker. In 1964, COL Neel established a Department of Aeromedical Education and Training or DAET to train the Army's own flight surgeons.

Colonel Spurgeon H. Neel, in 1960, completed his formal residency in aviation medicine at the U.S. Air Force School of Aerospace Medicine and was certified in aerospace medicine by the American Board of Preventive Medicine. Therefore, he became the first board-certified flight surgeon in Army history! He was assigned to Fort Rucker as Hospital Commander and continued in that position until 1964 when he was succeeded by Colonel Richard P. Austin.

In July 1962, Army AMOs were authorized crewmember flying status.

CW5 Clay Clarkson recalls, "While I was new Warrant Officer aviator in November 1961 with the Kansas ARNG, I took my flight physicals at Ft. Leavenworth, KS. This took all day. Sometimes, we had to go back on the next day to see the flight surgeon as the last part of the physical, if we didn't finish our lab work in time. When I first went to went to work for Southern Airways at Fort Wolters, TX in 1965, we were allowed to take flight physicals with civilian doctors, but since I was also in the ARNG, I was allowed to use the military facility. Sometime later all Southern Airways flight instructors were required to take physicals at the military facility at Fort Wolters. After I went to work fulltime as a RW IP for the OKARNG I took my annual flight physical at the 120th Medical Company in Midwest City, OK. Our flight surgeon was Dr. Geigerman."

Lieutenant Colonel David J. Geigerman (M.D.) was assigned to the OKARNG State Headquarters in Oklahoma City from 1965-1977. He was born in 1921 and had attended University of Oklahoma College of Medicine in 1944 and served in WWII before joining the OKARNG on 1 February 1965. Everyone that knew him consider him to be enthusiastic, very much pro-aviation. Some said, "He was an aviation buff." He was a talker, very verbose. Although he wasn't an aviator he loved to fly. During drill he would sometimes bring another doctor, a couple of nurses and medics to Norman and gave flight physicals at the flight facility at Max Westheimer.

According to CW5 Clarkson, "Dr. Geigerman was a character all right. He meant well, but had a tendency to go overboard with his preparation for flight. He used to carry what he called a first aid /survival kit. It was basically a surgeon's house call bag. He probably could have performed an appendectomy in the field."

"He talked to the point of driving everyone crazy. When he came to fly with us, we drew straws to see who had to fly with him. Sounds unkind, but you had to be there. Yes, and he was very excitable," said former State Aviation Officer, Colonel Leroy A. Wall.

LTC Geigerman, while a member of the OKARNG, was attending Annual Training the summer of 1965 at Fort Chaffee, AR when on a Sunday afternoon a motorcycle accident occurred involving an OKARNG soldier. Here's the story as told by COL Leroy A. Wall: "I was a very junior [Warrant Officer] and was the only pilot on duty that weekend. LTC Geigerman was also on duty at the medical unit. He called me and said that one of our soldiers had gone home and was on his way back to Chaffee and had been involved in a motorcycle accident near McAlester, OK. He needed me to fly him to McAlester immediately."

"Well, I called LTC Chet Howard [OKSAO] and he said to crank up an OH-23 and take Dr. Geigerman to McAlester. I flew the helicopter and he [Geigerman] did all the talking. When we arrived at McAlester he commandeered a car and we went to the local hospital. He rushed into the ER and announced that he was LTC/Dr. Geigerman of the National Guard and asked about a man who had been in a motorcycle accident. The doctors there said that there was a victim who had a severe head injury and that he needed an immediate operation but they didn't have the facilities for brain surgery."

"Geigerman made the decision to have him transported by ambulance to Veteran's Administration hospital in Muskogee, OK. At this point I was released to fly back to Chaffee. Geigerman stayed with the victim. When they arrived at the VA in Muskogee, they said that they also didn't have the facilities for that type of brain surgery and that he would have to be transported to Oklahoma City (OKC). Geigerman made the decision to have him transported to OKC."

"When they arrived [in OKC] the man was still unconscious and could not tell Geigerman who was his next of kin, so Geigerman made the decision to let them operate. They did and saved the man's life."

Shortly after these extraordinary circumstances, the actual OKARNG soldier who was first reported to have had the motorcycle accident, which began this series of events, rode into Ft. Chaffee. It seemed he wasn't seriously injured, only a little road rash. He hadn't been hospitalized; however, he apparently did make a short visit to the McAlester Hospital ER, then dusted himself off and rode the slightly bent 'bike' back to Ft Chaffee.

The question now became, "Who was the guy that Geigerman was having transported all over Oklahoma and who were the next of kin for this individual whom Geigerman had authorized brain surgery? Was the victim even an OKARNG soldier???

"As it turned out, the guy was a veteran, the operation did save his life and he didn't have any close kin. He was not a member of the OKARNG, even though he was a veteran. I don't think the Guard was very pleased about all of this. I understand that later after he went to NGB, [there might have been] some similar trouble, but I don't know the story on that one," relates COL Wall.

Geigerman was a unique individual to say the least and just like the rest of us, had a few flaws, but lack of enthusiasm wasn't one of them.

In 1971-72, he was asked to go to NGB as the first flight surgeon for the new Aviation Division of NGB at Edgewood, MD. Colonel Charlie R. Jones recalls, "When General [LaVern] Weber asked me to put together, the TDA for the first NGB Aviation Division, I included the slot for a flight surgeon. I don't remember whether David [Geigerman] contacted me or Gen Weber, but it seems to me like Gen Weber asked me, "What do think about David coming up as the flight surgeon?"" I said, "Well, that would be wonderful." David did get on orders and got a house or quarters on Edgewood Arsenal, where the NGB Avn Div was located. He and his wife moved in and he did a wonderful job. He was there while I was the Chief of Avn Div (ca 1971 – 1976)."

"Sometimes when it was impossible to get your flight physical renewed at Oklahoma City or Norman during drill weekend, Dr. Geigerman would say, "Well, just come on by my house in Nichols Hills on Monday and I'll give you your flight physical there." And we did. He was a good doctor, a patriotic soldier, a loyal supporter of the OKARNG Aviation Program and interested in getting the [flight] physicals done and approved. Any problems – he was the guy that would get them worked out. He was good friends with Chet Howard and LaVern Weber and a very likeable person. I know that LaVern liked him and that's why he brought him up to Washington," stated Brigadier General Dana D. Batey.

After Gen Weber was at the Pentagon for a while as DARNG, he had visited his ranch home in Oklahoma. While doing what he enjoyed, working at the ranch, he fell and broke his hip. According to John J. Stanko, "Dr. David Geigerman came to the NGB in some capacity, but mostly to help MG Weber. At the same time a crusty Command Sergeant Major (CSM), also from Oklahoma, came in as the NGB CSM. Weber's hip was troubling him and the old CSM had to help the General in and out of the bath tub. Walter [Reed Army Medical Center] (WRMC) had developed the procedure of hip replacement, but had yet to do the first one."

Geigerman, Weber's friend and trusted physician, held off until WRMC had performed two successful procedures and then MG Weber had the hip replacement procedure done at Walter Reed. It was a resounding success.

"It seems to me that there was a big flap [after MG Weber left and Gen Ott became the next Director of ARNG (1974-78)] Gen Ott said that Dr. Geigerman was going to have to go, that he had used up all the allocated time for this job. David went over his [Gen Ott's] head; he knew someone at [the Dept of Defense] DoD or Dept of the Army. But I don't know what happened as I left for the War College about that time," stated Charlie R. Jones.

He and his wife lived near the Chesapeake Bay in military quarters, not too far from the Operational Activity Center (OAC) at Aberdeen Proving Grounds (Edgewood, MD) until he was moved to the NGB Surgeons Office in the Pentagon. At this point, Dr. & Mrs. Geigerman moved to Mt. Vernon, VA just around the corner from COL & Mrs. Charlie R. Jones. Dr. Geigerman stayed on as Surgeon for NGB for several years until he retired from the military on 3 February 1975 and moved to Arizona. COL David J. Geigerman, formerly of Oklahoma, died on 18 September 2000 in Phoenix, AZ.

The 120th Med Co on North Air Depot Boulevard in Midwest City had doctors and technicians who gave flight physicals under the supervision of the flight surgeon prior to the Flight Surgeon Detachment being activated at Lexington in 1978. This detachment was part of the new OKARNG Det 1 Cmd & Control (145th Avn Bn (Prov)).

Back on the national scene in 1963, due to the determined efforts of COL Neel and Major James Hertzog, a new program for training Army AMOs was developed, due to the Army's rapidly expanding general aviation program, i.e., Vietnam. This training was established at the U.S. Army Aviation School as the Department of Aeromedical Education with Neel as Director and Hertzog as Deputy. They conducted the Basic Army Aviation Medical Officer's Course (BAAMOC), the Army Aviation Medical Officer's Orientation Course (AAMOCC), and several others. From 1964 until 1976 the two main courses, BAAMOC and AAMOCC graduated an average of 80 students per year, with the years 1968 through 1971 being an average of 150 students each year due to Vietnam.

In January 1970, Major William Caput completed the first Army Flight Surgeon's Manual and provided two volumes of information on both classic aeromedical subjects and Army unique aspects of flight medicine.

The flight surgeon is a military physician who has received formal training in the specialized field of aviation medicine. He is often loved and/or hated by his many clients called Army Aviators. We dreaded going to see him for fear we would be grounded because of kidney stones, bad vision or God forbid, permanently grounded for something we didn't even know we had. After we turned 40, we didn't like going for an annual flight physical/exam because of the finger wave or digital (rectal) exam. We also at times loved this medical doctor with wings on his chest. Some aviators have a flight surgeon to thank when he discovered something life threatening, such as rectal or colon cancer, high blood pressure or a bad heart.

The flight surgeon's mission includes the prevention and treatment of disease, injury, and mental or emotional deterioration among aviation flight, ground crew, and maintenance personnel. He monitors the programs of flyers and is expected to participate in frequent flights. He is confronted by the problems of traumatic injury; of acute and chronic disease, ranging from the common upper respiratory infections to the most uncommon of tropical diseases; of psychiatric disorders, which run the gamut from occupational fatigue through the minor disorders of personality to overt psychoses; and of personal hygiene and environmental sanitation, including dietetics, venereal disease, insect control, and a multitude of bizarre and worrisome matters.

The flight surgeon treats physical and mental conditions that might endanger pilots or passengers. Whether in the examination room or out on the flight line, he must be able to readily detect major and minor disorders of personality in men/women who, in their zeal to fly, frequently try to conceal the disorders.

He administers and prescribes medications and treatment, and he reviews and studies the case history and the progress of the patient. He also acts as consultant in his specialty to other medical services and provides aeromedical staff advice. In addition, the flight surgeon serves as medical member of aircraft crash investigation teams and, when possible, contributes to aeromedical research and development.

Traditional aeromedical philosophy on the use of drugs by flying personnel is conservative. AR 40-501 and AR 40-8 specifically limit their use. The flight surgeon's duty was to promote a state of individual fitness that allowed the flyer to meet the myriad stresses of combat flying. Ideally, the use of systemic therapeutic agents should have been prohibited in Vietnam, as they are elsewhere, but realistically, the unit commander needed the maximum number of personnel to carry out his mission. It was the duty of the flight surgeons to evaluate the risk of using therapeutic and prophylactic agents against the impact of losing personnel to flying duties while undergoing treatment. On this basis, the flight surgeon frequently administered certain drugs without restricting the aviator from flying, and other drugs after careful evaluation of the pilot's condition and his particular response to the drug. When the acute medical condition of an aircrewman did not prohibit flying status, he was often allowed to fly after a period of drug use to determine his susceptibility to side effects. Antibiotics and decongestants were used but antihistamines, sedatives, and tranquilizers were prohibited.

Accidental injury was a source of significant personnel loss during Vietnam. Aircraft accidents, until the spring of 1968, caused more aircrew injury and death than did enemy action. Less spectacular but also significant were those casualties caused by weapons accidents, vehicle mishaps, and sports. Simple injuries removed the patients from flying duties for the duration of treatment.

Prior to the OKARNG Aviation program having its own flight surgeon and medical clinic, all military medical services were provided by the 120th Medical Battalion in Oklahoma City. Dr. (Lieutenant Colonel) Rodney Dwight Steward was Commanding Officer of the 120th Med Bn and was also a flight surgeon. Born 6 February 1932, Steward's first love was always flying, and he always looked for an excuse to go out to Wiley Post Airport and fire up his plane. He continued to actively practice medicine as a Senior Aviation Medical Examiner until his death. He belonged to multiple flying organizations – to include serving on the Board of Directors for the International Civil Aviation Medical Association. Dr. Steward passed away on 25 March 2009 at the age of 77.

The first OKARNG Aviation Flight Surgeon Detachment was authorized in 1978. This TDA detachment was located at the Lexington, OK Armory and heliport. Lieutenant Colonel J. Robert Dille was the first official flight surgeon.

John Robert Dille was born in 1932 in Pennsylvania. From 1949 to 1956 he received a deferment from the military, until he completed Medical School at the University of Pittsburgh. Concerning the military, "The Army wasn't my first choice – it was my third choice." He had heard about a commissioning program at Fort Detrick, MD and in 1955 he became an Air Force second lieutenant while in his senior year of medical school.

Dille served two years active duty in the Air Force from 1957 to 1959. Then the FAA offered him a Guggenheim Foundation Fellowship to attend the Harvard School of Public Health in Boston (1959-60). He accepted and earned a Masters of Industrial Health at Harvard which is the first year of residency in Aerospace Medicine. However, at the time of the FAA fellowship offer he almost declined because all of his contemporaries were being told they could go to T-33 (Tweety Bird) training. The FAA wasn't about to let him get away and said, "OK, no problem you can do both, go to Harvard and to T-33 training."

After his Air Force service, Doc Dille was offered a position with the FAA's Aeromedical Institute in Oklahoma City. He accepted and came to Oklahoma, becoming a GS-17 as the Director of the Federal Aviation Administration's Civil Aeromedical Institute for twenty-two years. By the way, GS-17 is the military equivalent of a Lieutenant General and yes, Doc Dille shared with me, "There are perks which go along with the rank."

Colonel J. Robert Dille told me[6], "It was Batey, McElwain and Tommy Evans who sweet talked me into joining the OKARNG. I spent the last 14 years of my military career in the Oklahoma Army National Guard. I have fond memories of that time and the individuals."

Although Dr. Dille says he is retired, he is serving as the Flight Surgeon for the Oklahoma Reserve Officer's Association and attends meetings at Tinker AFB, OK. It would be a mistake for me to attempt to list all of the awards and accolades given to COL Dille, perhaps an embarrassment to him and I'd surely leave one or more out. Suffice it to say, he is a patriot extraordinaire, a wonderful individual and the most knowledgeable medical officer we have known in the OKARNG. He lives in Norman and continues to write about aviation medicine as we speak. He is the author of many books and articles regarding aviation medicine.

The Purcell Register newspaper, 27 July issue 1978 carried an article with the headline "Flight Surgeon Moves Unit to Lexington." The article addressed the fact that OKARNG aviation unit personnel would now be able to receive flight physicals and other medical services at Hal Muldrow heliport.

"A flight surgeon's detachment, formerly stationed on North Air Depot Road in Midwest City, has relocated at this Army National Guard Aviation Center six miles east of Lexington, OK.

"The unit is commanded by Lt. Col. J. Robert Dille, the flight surgeon for the Oklahoma Army National Guard and director of the Civil Aeronautical Institute at the Federal Aviation Administration in Oklahoma City. He has four (and is seeking more) medical professionals to assist him in providing medical examinations and some consultation services on a weekend per month basis," said the article.

"The detachment temporarily has the services of two active Army servicemen from Fort Sill, OK to assist on drill weekends . . . . Dille expects the unit to perform an average of 16 flight physicals per month.

"Lt. Col. Dana Batey, State Aviation Officer, sees the flight surgeon's relocation as a plus for the pilots and other Guard members stationed at Hal Muldrow. He believes, "It is another advancement toward making the heliport the complete aviation center for the Guard's flying units."

The aviation medical detachment

OKARNG Aviation Flight Surgeon Section—Annual Tng 1980 L-R: SSG Jesse Ahdunko, CW2 Bonnie Dillard, COL J. Robt. Dille, MAJ Joann Stil & MAJ Alma Pauli

at Lexington Armory had at one time three additional flight surgeons: Captain Clifton Shimmerhorn, Lieutenant Colonel Raymond Bloomquist, and Lieutenant Colonel Charles P. Russo. Lieutenant Colonel Shimmerhorn, a psychiatrist and flight surgeon is renowned for having the largest (circumference) index finger of any Army Flight Surgeon in modern history! In the late 1970's and early 1980s, the OKARNG Flight Surgeons detachment included one female PA, CW2 Bonnie Dillard and two (former OKANG) Registered Nurses assigned to the Aviation Medicine Clinic: Major Alma Pauli and Major Joann Still. Also

Staff Sergeant Jesse Ahdunko worked as a medical specialist in the clinic during this early beginning of the aviation flight medical clinic era. They were transferred to a new nursing platoon ca 1981/82 which had been assigned to the Oklahoma Military Department. Later there were several Aeromedical Physician Assistants within this detachment: Major Floyd Todd, Lieutenant Colonel Jerry E. Joern and Major James W. Burks. MAJ Todd remained at Lexington the longest of any medical personnel.

[Sometime in 1977/78] "I flew Doc Dille down to Ft Rucker and we went into Clothing Sales to get him an Army Officer's [dress green] uniform. We purchased his Class "A" uniform and his brass, because the next day he's going before the Army Aviation Medicine Board to be certified and sanctioned as an Army Flight Surgeon. So the next day the board is about to convene and the President of the Board [an Army Colonel] came up to me and said, "Do you know who you have here?" And I (COL Batey) said, "I beg your pardon." He said, "Dr. Dille is a renowned surgeon, and prominent physician in aerospace medicine, he's the head of aviation medicine in the FAA!?!?!?" And I said, "Yes, and now he's an Army Officer in the OKARNG and I want him approved by this board as our Flight Surgeon!" He signed the paperwork right then and there. Dr. Dille didn't have to go before the board at all!"

CW4 Floyd T. Todd—
PA—1988

The 1980s brought true advances for the Army Flight Surgeon with the addition of flight training in the TH-55 training helicopter. The new doctors were given flight training up to and including solo proficiency as part of the Basic Army Flight Surgeon's Course.

MAJ Floyd Todd, former fulltime Flight Surgeon Physician's Assistant with the OKARNG at Lexington, OK recalls, "The Aviation Clinic [at Lexington Armory] was augmented in 1982 with an AGR (Active Guard and Reserve) Aeromedical Physician Assistant [MTOE position] to help in the support of a Special Operations Aviation Battalion, following the failure and events that came out of the desert in Operation Eagle Claw in 1980. I went to work full-time at Lex around 1982. The military lacked aircraft and crews that were trained and prepared to perform Special Operations missions. The organization established to perform this mission encompassed the greatest number and variety of helicopters of any unit in the Army and the Oklahoma Army National Guard became a part of this rotary wing Special Operations capability and aviation medicine was part of this process."

In the late 1980s, a civilian secretary, Mrs. Jeannie Salmon, was hired for the medical clinic at the Lex Armory. The clinic operated by MAJ Todd and Mrs. Salmon existed until around 2000 when Todd retired. It had become a split operation, half their time was spent at OMD and the other at Lexington.

The initial aeromedical phase of this process was preparing crews for deployment with immunizations and medications, which included deployments of the 45th Avn Bn (Lt Hel Cbt) and later 1st Bn 245th Avn (SOA) to a variety of locations in Central America, Puerto Rico, Southeast Asia, Central Asia and other points of interest. This process required the Aviation Medicine Clinic at Lexington to give large numbers of vaccinations, sometimes with vaccines that had not been approved for use in the United States, which required our aeromedical activity to become a part of the study program at Walter Reed Military Hospital. One such study was an anti-rabies vaccination and required multiple inoculations prior to deployment. These new special operational aviation demands had aviators stressed to extreme limits and we in aviation medicine struggled to keep up.

Aeromedical concerns include both fixed-wing and rotary-wing flight parameters. With the advent of the automatic pilot and today's flight directors, some of the aviator's work load is definitely reduced. However, Army helicopter pilots often fly extended hours during nap-of-the-earth (NOE) flight profiles, using night-vision goggles, enduring climatic temperature extremes, and carrying out difficult and sensitive tactical missions. These areas create stress and add to the flight surgeon's concern and need to be abreast of what his aviators are doing – not only in the cockpit, but the time spent planning, limited time for recreation and/or rest. Although, reasonable rest before flight was always considered wise, it had not previously been regulated, e.g. the Vietnam era. From this point forward, the term *crew rest* becomes paramount in the life of an Army aviator.

Each and every Army Aviator must be medically qualified and certified to be placed on flight status. In the past this process of getting the flight physical completed was the initial step before getting in the cockpit. Long ago when Army National Guard Aviation began in 1948 Army Aviators had to take the dreaded flight physical. Why was it dreaded? Well, if you were perfectly healthy, could see and hear normally, it still took a full two days to complete the flight physical ordeal and then you still had to wait!

Colonel John J. Stanko recalls the unbelievable amount of time involved, "About 1952, I was an M-day aviator in the Pennsylvania ARNG after transferring in from the Air Force Reserves. Mr. Pennypacker was the IP that checked me out in the L-19 Birddog; it took nine months to get my flight status back from the National Guard Bureau. There were 32 endorsements back and forth, back and forth. In those days it took two full days just to take a flight physical. I took two days off work, then went to Olmenstead AFB for the flight physical and 6 months later had to do it again. The Class I flight physicals were only good for six months! Nine months later I get my silver wings in the mail and shouted, "Now I'm an Army aviator.""

Thanks to a great Army National Guard aviator, COL John J. Stanko Jr., who fought through the red tape (read – bull hockey or Pentagon bureaucracy, your choice) to get a flight physical approved and certified which they were able to eventually reduce to just a few hours. This was one of the greatest achievements that the Aviation Division of NGB ever accomplished for the 54 states and U.S. territories. What a service was done by COL Stanko for all ARNG aviators today!

Our greatest surge in U.S. Army aviation was during the Vietnam war. The aeromedical problems that faced Army aviation units in Vietnam provided a challenge to their supporting flight surgeons. No problem, however, was more common yet more elusive than that of flyer fatigue. It became more pronounced after 1965 when the buildup of U.S. forces gained momentum and remained a significant limiting factor in the conduct of airmobile operations. By the end of 1966, aviators were flying 100 to 150 hours or more per month, and the need to know how much an aviator could fly before he was so fatigued that he was no longer effective or safe was evident.

Army aviators were assailed by a multitude of stresses, each to some extent capable of endangering their missions. The stress from hostile fire was aggravated by such factors as heat, dehydration, noise, vibration, blowing dust, hazardous weather, exhaust from engines and weapons, and labyrinthine stimulation. Additional stress was caused by psychic elements, such as fear, insufficient sleep, family separation, and frustration. These stresses, acting on the aviator day after day, combined with the physical exertion of long hours of piloting an aircraft, caused fatigue.

The ever-increasing requirements during the years 1967-68 for aviation support caused the accrual of extremely high aviator flying times in all units. Night operations, with their extra demand upon the critical judgment of the aviator, increased. The shortage of crews often forced an individual to undertake both day and night missions without adequate rest.

In response to expressed concern of the unit commanders and of aviation safety officers, flight surgeons at all levels of aeromedical support studied every aspect of the fatigue problem. Because fatigue was the result of many variables, it defied easy definition and precise measurement.

Major General Spurgeon Neel[7], when assigned as Chief Surgeon US Army Vietnam (USARV), noted in the Command Health Report for August 1968 that about 70 percent of aircraft accidents were found to be the result of pilot error and that pilot fatigue had been implicated as a contributing factor in a large proportion of accidents. He indicated that the only way to cope with pilot fatigue was prevention by reducing the aviator's flying hours. His recommendation was "that immediate action be taken to provide additional aviators to USARV insuring at least 100 percent authorized aviator strength to reduce the degree to which pilot fatigue is contributing to the loss of lives and expensive aircraft." This was never done.

Some flight surgeons, notably Captain Philip Snodgrass, MC, of the 269th Aviation Battalion at Cu Chi, believed that the relationship of days flown to days off and, particularly, the provision of a scheduled on-off work cycle were more important than the total number of hours flown. Captain Snodgrass's staff study of a goal-directed flying-hour schedule indicated that a series of five or six days flown, followed by a scheduled day free from flying and from other duties, resulted in a unit that evidenced less fatigue and could fly even greater numbers of hours. This idea was adopted by many units and proved workable and effective.

Fatigue in the enlisted crew members was said to be a less obvious, though very real, threat. These individuals, who accompanied the aircraft on all its missions, returned to their base camps and worked many additional hours in providing required maintenance and preparing for the following day's missions. With the added requirement of aiding in perimeter defense and in the multitudinous other details of combat aviation, they performed under great stress. Efforts by the unit flight surgeons in their behalf centered upon improving their living conditions, eliminating some extra duties, and increasing their numbers.

The problem of performing periodic physical examinations on flying personnel began with the first Army aviation unit in Vietnam. Equipment and facilities were not available for an adequate examination. This handicap was partially overcome by Department of the Army waiver of the requirement for routine periodic examinations for rated aviators in Vietnam; however, despite the waiver, many still requested them. Periodic examinations for crew chiefs, flight surgeons, and aerial observers were also waived; required initial examinations were performed as well as available equipment allowed. Modifications of organization and the addition of equipment helped eliminate these difficulties. Aerial door gunners were not given a complete examination. After reviewing their medical records, the flight surgeon gave them a general examination which included visual tests and their "Adaptability Rating for Military Aeronautics." A statement of medical qualification was then issued by the flight surgeon.

By 1970, fatigue as an entity was still no better defined nor more capable of measurement than before. Moreover, the attempt at limiting aviator flying hours by regulation had been proved ineffective in the combat environment, and the requirement for continued study of the problem was needed.

In 1974 the Department of Aeromedical Education and Training (DAET) mission was transferred from the Aviation Center to Health Services Command under the (Theodore C.) Lyster Hospital Commander at Rucker. It is ironic that almost 60 years after the father of U.S. Army Aviation Medicine (Lyster) fought to stay organizationally close to the aviation community, this function was now placed back under medical jurisdiction at a hospital named after him. In 1984 DAET was again transferred and the resultant was renamed the "U.S. Army School of Aviation Medicine (USASAM).

In the 1970s, women were accepted into pilot training, which caused the beginning of new research into issues related to accommodating women, who are on average smaller, have less upper body strength, and into military aircraft and escape systems.

Following Vietnam, in 1976, the title *AMO* (Aviation Medical Officer) was deleted and replaced with the title *Flight Surgeon* and the MOS was changed from D3160 to 61N9D.

The Oklahoma Army National Guard, like other states, has had a traditional part-time aviation medicine program manned by medical officers, and at times we have had medical officers trained specifically as Army Flight Surgeons. One of the very first was Dr. David J. Geigerman, a Flight Surgeon in the OKARNG. Many excellent Flight Surgeons followed Geigerman and later staffed the OKARNG Aviation Medicine Clinic at Lexington, OK.

The Oklahoma Aviation Medicine Clinic has over its history, received some notoriety in that Dr. J. Robert Dille (retired Colonel) received the prestigious "Society of U.S. Army Flight Surgeons" Flight Surgeon of the Year Award for 1986-1987. Dr. Dille later went on to be President of the Aerospace Medical Association. MAJ Floyd T. Todd received the "Society of U.S. Army Flight Surgeons" Aeromedical Physician Assistant of the Year Award for 1987-1988. "However, the greatest reward that a Flight Surgeon can receive is to keep his aviators flying with an accident free record," said MAJ Todd.

Here are just a few, quite significant medical success stories of OKARNG aviators who encountered medical circumstances which were not only grounding conditions, but in a few instances, were life threatening also.

Colonel Ronald L. Howland remembers, "I flew Chief Warrant Officer Frank L. Berry in a Bde Avn Sec OH-58, during AT, from Ft

CW2 Frank Lillard Berry 45th Inf Bde Avn Sec

Chaffee, AR to Ft Rucker, AL in 1975. The purpose of this flight was so Frank could take a check ride with the Aeromedical Services Flight Surgeon at Rucker, hoping that he might get back on flight status. Frank had lost 3 fingers on his right hand in an oil field V-belt accident in Oklahoma. I went up in the tower at Rucker so I could watch. It was a three hour check ride. Frank was such a good guy, I was a Sec Cdr of the Bde Avn Sec at the time. The Flight Surgeon from Rucker that flew with Frank and the DES

(Department of Evaluation and Standardization) IP was the reason for a three hour check ride – he needed his flight time for the month!"

"The ole Flight Surgeon at Rucker was a Major. I had been grounded for about six months when I went to his office for the evaluation on my waiver request to get back on flight status. He looked at my X-rays and then at my hand and then said, "The surgeon that took care of it did an excellent job." Then he handed me a five pound fire extinguisher and said, "Pull the pin and use it." So I took it with my right hand, pulled the pin and fired the white powder into a trash can. Next he handed me a .38 caliber pistol and said, "Fire it." I took it with my left hand and he said, "No shoot it with your right hand." I told him I shot left handed. But he wanted me to use my right, so I first opened the cylinder and checked to make sure no cartridges were in the chambers. This made me extra points with him, he liked that a lot! Then he said, "Let's meet at the flight line, it's going to be a three hour check ride because that's how much time I need for flight pay this month!" recalls CW4 (ret) Frank Lillard Berry from Konawa, OK.

Frank passed the UH-1 with auxiliary tank check ride with flying colors. His waiver was approved and he was put back on flight status.

"Later I recall Frank Berry and the problem he had with his heart. He developed a positional heart murmur, which is very unusual. Frank had noticed a shortness of breath while TDY in Germany. Fortunately he had a doctor who pursued it and diagnosed a myxoma, which is a growth inside his heart. These are usually found on autopsy after sudden death," said MAJ Floyd Todd.

In 1988 Frank L. Berry was told he needed to have surgery to remove his myxoma tumor inside his heart and that in four or five years he would probably have to have a bypass. "So I told them "No, go ahead and let's do it at the same time." Two weeks after surgery I was at Lexington laying out a compass course for drill weekend. They (Aeromedical Services, Ft Rucker) sent me a letter saying they were going to medically retire me, after 39 yrs military service. If it hadn't been a bypass I could have stayed until age 60. They retired me 9 months after the heart surgery," said CW4 (ret) Berry.

Our Lexington, OK Flight Surgeon's clinic was the first Aviation Medicine Clinic in the Army to return an aviator to flight status that had been disqualified for coronary artery disease.

Chief Warrant Officer Five (CW5) Paul Merchant received an aeromedical waiver for cardiovascular disease. Paul was a real aviation medicine miracle I believe. As for as I know, he was the only aviator to receive a waiver after disqualification for what the aeromedical activity at Fort Rucker considered significant coronary artery disease. Paul, as many aviators do, felt that the flight surgeon's office was not on his side and wanted to see him off flight status. "CW5 Merchant, with his desire to prove us wrong and get back on flight status, started a very rigorous physical development program as well as a severely strict diet. That caused him to lose a significant amount of body fat. I could see significant changes in his body fat composition over time. He started climbing mountains and joined the 14-Peak Club, I believe. When he came back later he asked to be re-evaluated for flight status. Although he didn't feel we wanted too, I had to give him the opportunity. After all that he had done, I wanted to know if the plaque in his coronary arteries had changed. We pursued his desire to be re-evaluated at Brooks AFB in San Antonio, Texas. I didn't believe at first we would be successful. We had a cool reception to our request at first. Mother Rucker was very serious about aeromedical safety but agreed and Paul went back to Brooks AFB for his re-evaluation and went through a complete evaluation from head to toe. This included a complete examination from all the specialists at Brooks. His heart evaluation included a cardiac catherization. This, as I was told, was given to different physicians for evaluation and measurement and all agreed he had plaque regression and did in fact meet standards for flight status. Brooks AFB made the recommendation to the Army that CW5 Paul Merchant be returned to flight status and a waiver was granted by NGB," recalled MAJ Floyd Todd.

Todd continued about OKARNG flight status waivers, "CW4 Tommy Klutts Jr. was another miracle. I don't think TK quite knew what to make of me at first. His kidney cancer in 1997 was a surprise to all of us in aviation medicine. We knew we were going to have a significant problem going through the waiver process with him because it would be complex medically and lengthy. I was afraid he might not survive his cancer and he had lost one kidney to the cancer. Fortunately TK listened and was able to understand the aeromedical process. He was able to communicate to his attending physician the need to provide those necessary documents and tests needed to document his medical progress with his cancer. This would later prove he would not likely be a cause of concern or problem to aviation safety. This is always the bottom line in requesting a waiver for any disqualifying medical condition. Dr. Urbauer, a Urologist and Flight Surgeon from Nebraska, was able to advise us and guide us through the process for TK's waiver.

When TK and I were discussing his kidney cancer he said, "Doc Todd . . . God bless his heart. I almost drove him nuts. The army said, "OK, you're grounded for a year." So at about the nine month mark I started beating on Todd's door, saying, "Hey look – there's nothing wrong with me. Let's get me back on flight status." But he did everything in his power and he got it done. I don't know how he did it, but I got back on flight status after a year. Boy, I owe it all to him."

CW4 Tommy Klutts Jr., OKARNG aviator, was only the eighth U.S. Army aviator returned to flight status with a single kidney.

Some aviators from other states had aviation medicine support that was less able go the extra mile to push issues. Many aviators have lost flight status, or the process took an extraordinarily long period of time, which meant a prolonged period of grounding. This was not because the flight surgeon didn't care, but because most flight surgeons in the Army National Guard are traditional guardsman and are therefore part-time soldiers.

We were instrumental in Oklahoma in changing some to the policies and returning to flight status aviators and flight crew that probably would not have returned to flight duties without our efforts. The following are some of these occasions of which we are very proud.

On one occasion, we in aviation medicine were successful in expressing our concerns with individuals resulting eventually in having the aeromedical policy dealing with renal stones changed and updated. The old policy required some prolonged periods of grounding and extensive unneeded evaluations. This change greatly benefited aviators with these aeromedical problems.

Todd recalled a conversation he had with a Flight Surgeon from Nebraska who was then the NGB Surgeon. The problem was that Army National Guard personnel returning to flight status, requiring an aeromedical waiver, that had been waivered in the past, had to remain grounded until a new waiver was granted. This process could take a year while the aviator remained grounded and unproductive. "I was lectured on how difficult it was to change policy at NGB. A few months later, the NGB Surgeon changed the policy which allowed personnel to return to flight status, under some conditions, pending the waiver process. This benefited many aviators in the Army National Guard."

Numerous aviators disqualified for complicated aeromedical problems were guided through the waiver process by the Aviation Medicine Clinic and in some cases, their attending physicians were educated about the aeromedical requirements that would allow these aviators to return to flight status, thus allowing aviation medicine to meet the requirement of a waiver process from the Aeromedical Activity at Fort Rucker and National Guard Bureau.

All Army Flight Surgeons participated in the Flight Safety Program at all levels of command. In addition to their constant fatigue monitoring and their vigilant protection of the mental, emotional, and physical health of all aircrews, they served as advisers in evaluating and proposing protective armor for both aircraft and aircrew. The OKARNG began its safety program long ago in the early days of Westheimer Field at Norman, OK. OKARNG began conducting an annual Aviation Safety Standdown, at which all aviation personnel, the TAG, SAO, the OKARNG state level Safety Office, aviation medical and all unit aviation personnel attended. The first was held at Fountain Head State Lodge, Eufaula, OK about September 1987. Special guest speakers were invited to speak and present aviation topics of importance.

There could not, and there cannot be a viable Aviation Program without the dedicated professionals of Aviation Medicine . . .

1. Information on DUSTOFF callsign provided by Michael W. Basler, former SP5 U.S. Army Medic on Dustoff aircraft in Vietnam. Airline Capt. Mike Basler flies today for United Parcel Service.

2. Excerpt from a short article in Army Aviation magazine, January 2010, ref death of Retired CW4 Michael J. Novosel Jr.

3. Information on FLATIRON callsign provided by USAR COL John R. Dabrowski PhD., U.S. Army Historian, USAACS, Ft Rucker, AL

4. MG Wm. J. Maddox Jr. was Commandant at Ft Rucker from 22 September 1973 to 30 June 1976. A veteran of Korea and Vietnam, Maddox was affectionately known as the "Grey Ghost." Maddox was awarded eight Distinguished Flying Cross awards and accumulated over 10,000 flight hours of which 4,000 were combat hours flown in Korea, Vietnam and Cambodia. He was inducted into the Army Aviation Hall of Fame in 1976 to represent the period 1960 to 1969.

5.   Excerpt from a news article in the *Enterprise Ledger* and the *Dothan Eagle,* AL, October 2007, provided to the author by LTC Bernie Cobb, a noted Vietnam veteran, former aviator member of the 174th AHC "Sharks" and personal friend. Bernie passed away on 24 February 2010.

6.   Telephone interview COL John Robert Dille, 23 March 2009

7.   Major General Spurgeon Neel, "Medical Support Of The U.S. Army In Vietnam 1965-1970," (Washington, D.C.: Department of the Army, 1991). Much of the material from this chapter is credited to MG Neel.

Chapter 10

"No, We Are Not Invincible"

"Victory is reserved for those who are willing to pay its price"
Sun Tzu

Part One

In 1978, Co D (-) 149th Avn Bn, OKARNG, became one-half of an Attack Helicopter Battalion whose headquarters was in the Arizona Army National Guard. Throughout 1979 it continued its recruiting effort and a training program to bring the new recruits and appointees up to speed. Co D (-) 149th Avn Bn trained for its Assault Helicopter anti-armor mission, based on the 1950s doctrine from the Cold War and war against the Soviets in the European Theater.

This attack company (-) minus, equipped with antiquated UH-1M aircraft and armament, and quite a few Vietnam era vets, tried to maintain a traditional gun company attitude – We're ten feet tall and you can't touch me!

June 1979, Co D (-) went over the 100% authorized strength mark for the first time since it had been reorganized as a company. In July the company conducted Annual Training (AT) at Fort Rucker AL; each non-MOS qualified member of the unit attended a formal Military Occupational Specialty (MOS) producing school or received Operational Job Training (OJT) alongside an active duty soldier of the same MOS.

The following year, July 1980, Co D (-) 149th self-deployed to Ft. Chaffee, AR for Annual Training. Training at annual training 1980 was on ARTEP tasks and unit readiness. There at Fort Chaffee, AR, the gun company soldiers curiously observed a large group of Cuban exiles, criminals, drug addicts, homosexuals and thugs, being held behind barbed wire on Main Post, awaiting further disposition instructions from the Carter administration.

Little did the older vets, gun bunnies and armament personnel in that small gun company at Chaffee know—how significant the influence of future world events would be. Some of these events had already taken place and would initiate dramatic force structure changes and bring in totally new mission statements for Army units and especially OKARNG Aviation. A few broad shouldered, no-nonsense, out of the box type thinkers would lead Army aviation to the beginning of an innovative era—Special Operations Aviation.

Who would have ever imagined it was going to be right in your backyard, in Oklahoma Army National Guard Aviation?

Can today's military achieve even higher standards of combat readiness and still meet our nation's deployment and show of force requirements for all possible threats to America and its allies? Can we continue to send both active duty and reserve component forces back into today's combat zones with little or no re-equipping and retraining time in between rotations? Can today's military achieve the unrealistic recruiting goals, two wars and deployment objectives of each service? Or will they continue to dumb down, lowering their enlistment standards to meet an annual recruitment goal.

They (our senators and representatives) say that we don't need a military draft. They say that our 'all volunteer military' is meeting today's demands. That is pure hog wash in my opinion. It appears to me, the Army is about ready to recruit convicted felons and enlist them into today's modern Army as volunteers!

I served in the U.S. Army with bonafide draftees in the early 1960s and they were some of the best soldiers I've ever seen and/or served with in uniform. I am definitely for reinstating a national draft in the U.S.A. Yet again, that subject is for another book, another day; but don't hesitate to ask me about it next time we meet.

How long can Reserve Component soldiers maintain their civilian jobs, careers and families when they are called back to serve two and three combat tours within five to seven years? How can the military increase the length of normal combat deployments from 12 months, already difficult to deal with for most citizen soldiers, to longer terms of 15-18 months (depending on the service)? Why can't they tell Congress that the Army is broken and must raise dramatically its own endstrength. Your response(s) may awaken old memories of a tragic event that came to symbolize our nation's depressed military of the post-Vietnam era. It was caused by the administration's edict to have a reduction in force (RIF).

How did our nation's military deal with new and unforeseen difficulties in the 1970s and early 1980s? How did the Pentagon recognize some dramatic new requirements for highly specialized capabilities, new skills, new means of doing old tasks (intelligence), creating new agencies – but in particular, create new aviation capabilities in a new scenario? Some of the lessons learned from a politically driven reduction in force were learned the hard way . . .

In 1975, the voters of our nation elected Jimmy Carter as the 39th President of the United States. He won election by 297 electoral votes to 241 for Gerald Ford. Soon our military forces' endstrength were dramatically reduced by the Democratic Carter administration, along with a reduction in the Central Intelligence Agency's (CIA) ability to conduct covert operations overseas, particularly in the intelligence gathering arena. Carter served one term as President (1976-1980).

In the late 1970s, one of the U.S.'s mid-east allies, Shah Mohammed Reza Pahlavi of Iran, was diagnosed with cancer, later forced to abdicate and flee into exile. On 4 November 1979, two weeks after President Carter had allowed the Shah to enter the U.S. for cancer treatment; some 200-300 radical, Iranian, Islamic students invaded the U.S. Embassy in Tehran. They took 66 Americans and Iranian employees hostage. Chief of the U.S. Mission in Tehran, L. Bruce Laingen, and two aides were also captured and held separately at the Iranian Foreign Ministry. The students demanded that the Shah be returned to Tehran for trial. Ayatollah Khomeini's supporters blocked all efforts to free the hostages.

We, the U.S. military and America, anticipated that President Carter, a graduate of the U.S. Naval Academy at Annapolis, would secure the safe release our American hostages in the matter of just a few days or weeks at most.

Although the United States had provided billions of dollars in foreign aid to the Southwest Asia region, not a single country offered any assistance or military help to the U.S. Anwar Sadat of Egypt offered words of support, but no action! To my knowledge, this became the first incident in which the U.S. was confronted by the new hostile force of radical Islamic fundamentalism. Sadly it may not be the last.

Thirteen black and female hostages were later released as a gesture of humanitarian goodwill by the Ayatollah Khomeini. The humiliating captivity for the other 53 American hostages would drag on for 14 months.

President Carter, facing a re-election battle in 1980, favored a diplomatic solution, but his national security advisor, Zbigniew Brzezinski, directed the Pentagon to begin planning for a rescue mission or retaliatory strikes in case the hostages were harmed. In response, the Chairman of the Joint Chiefs of Staff, Air Force General David C. Jones, established a small, secretive planning group, dubbed 'Rice Bowl,' to study American options for a rescue effort.

It quickly became crystal clear how difficult a hostage rescue would be, if not improbable. Inside the Pentagon such a task was super classified and on the main floor it was Top Secret.

A major consideration at this juncture, was the condition of the U.S. military, which had plummeted in size and quality in the seven years since it had staged a near-total withdrawal from Vietnam. Among the casualties of the post-Vietnam cutbacks was the once-powerful array of Army and Air Force Special Operations Forces that had performed feats of great bravery and military skill in Southeast Asia. This included the once elite Special Forces which had been formed in 1952, and later brought to the nation's attention by President John F. Kennedy, when he approved and authorized the wearing of the Green Beret; they too had suffered major cutbacks in manpower and funding.

One exception was a little known group of Army Warriors organized specifically for counter-terrorism. General Edward C. "Shy" Meyer, Army Chief of Staff, had pushed for a new Army counter-terrorist commando organization under the command of Colonel Charles Beckwith, a combat-tested Special Forces Officer. President Carter authorized the initial formation of Delta in 1977 to combat terrorism worldwide.

On occasion the military performs for dignitaries, foreign government officials and/or the White House administrators. On 3 November 1979, the day before the Iranian students invaded the U.S. Embassy in Tehran, Delta Force was performing for senior White House/CIA officials and European/Mid-east special commandos. The next day Delta was put into the initial planning for a hostage extraction from the U.S. Embassy headquarters in Tehran.

One immediate question seemed to be paramount – "How do we get Delta close enough to the U.S. Embassy in Tehran to do its job?" Obviously, it would have to be by air, but . . . how?

The joint task force hostage rescue mission is given the code name Operation Eagle Claw. Red tape, bureaucracy and too much compartmentalization clogged the pipes of effective planning and progress. Neither logic nor common sense seemed to be included in the plan. This was to be a 'joint mission,' meaning four different military services trying to coordinate and work together. These were guys who had never before worked together and later didn't even rehearse together—pilots of one service, flying aircraft of another service . . .

The Joint Task Force (JTF) Rice Bowl key players were Secretary of Defense–Harold Brown, National Security Advisor—Zbigniew Brzezinski, Secretary of the Army – Clifford L. Alexander Jr., USAF Chairman, Joint Chiefs of Staff—General David C. Jones, JTF CDR—Major General James Vaught, USAF Air Planner—USAF Colonel James Kyle, 'Delta Force' Commander—COL Charles Beckwith, H-53 Bluebird Flight Commander – USMC Lt. Col. Edward Seiffert, Chief of Staff Army (CSA)—GEN Edward C. Meyer, Army Deputy Chief of Staff Operations (DCSOPS) – Lieutenant General Glenn Otis. Lieutenant General LaVern E. Weber, from Oklahoma, was Chief National Guard Bureau (Chief NGB), Major General Emmett H. "Mickey" Walker was Director Army National Guard (DARNG), Major General Robert M. Morgan was the Oklahoma Adjutant General (OKTAG) and Colonel John J. Stanko Jr. was Director of NGB Aviation and Safety at this time.

To the dismay of COL Beckwith and MG Vaught, there was no viable intelligence coming out of Iran, "Zip, nada, null, zed, none." Carter had dismantled the CIA's network of spies due to the agency's former involvement in overthrowing governments in Vietnam and Latin America. It would be months before agents could be inserted into Iran to supply the detailed intelligence Beckwith said was, " . . . the difference between failure and success, between humiliation and pride, between losing lives and saving them."

When Beckwith ruled out a parachute drop, helicopters were chosen as the best option for reaching Tehran, despite the doubts Beckwith and other Vietnam veterans had about their reliability. The Navy's RH-53D

Sea Stallions were chosen because of their superior range and load-carrying capability and their ability to operate from an aircraft carrier. However, not even the Navy Sea Stallions could fly from the USS Nimitz carrier deck in the Indian Ocean to Tehran, about 1,000 SM, without refueling. After cussing, discussing, testing and rejecting many other alternatives, the JTF planners opted to use Air Force EC-130 Hercules transports rigged with internal 18,000-gallon fuel bladders to perform on the ground as a Forward Refueling and Rearming Point (FAARP) for the RH-53D helicopters enroute to Tehran. The site selected was a dirt landing area suitable for C-130s and would be given the code name Desert One. What we failed to consider was that the desert environment could change in a few hours and cover the landing zone with fresh new sand and completely change the characteristics of the landing zone! This happened, but was not a mission stopper however.

Operation Eagle Claw was to have been a surgical extraction mission, to bring our hostages home alive from Tehran. To meet Air Force and Navy objectives of total surprise, the rescue force would train to operate at night without lights – totally blacked out, as stated by JTF CDR MG Vaught. This was a new idea for C-130 aircrews, heretofore not having been accomplished by the Air Force. At the outset, none of the C-130 units had any night vision goggles; nor were there procedures/SOPs (Standard Operating Procedures) for their use. Some of the Air Force crews had seen these awkward devices and were not excited about using them[1]. The same was true for the Navy RH-53 units, pilots and all but a few USMC pilots.

Secrecy during the planning of EAGLE CLAW was ridiculously tight and created a snot storm. One section was precluded from knowing what was being planned or considered in another. Joint planning and full-blown joint rehearsals did not happen. The Pentagon can at times be brilliant; at other times it can be a cauldron of gross stupidity!

By mid-March 1980 the JTF Rice Bowl had developed what they considered a workable plan and that plan looked like this:

On the first night, six USAF C-130s carrying 132 Delta commandos, Army Rangers, and support personnel and helicopter fuel for the H-53s, would fly from the island of Masirah, off the coast of Oman, more than 1,000 miles to the FAARP at Desert One. The C-130s would be refueled in-flight from Air Force KC-135 tankers. Eight Navy RH-53Ds would lift off the aircraft carrier deck of the USS Nimitz, about 50 miles south of the Iranian coast, and fly more than 600 miles to Desert One.

After refueling at Desert One's FAARP, the mission 'minimum of six' (6) RH-53Ds would carry the rescue force to a hideout in hills about 50 miles southeast of Tehran, then fly to a separate hiding spot nearby. The C-130s would return to island of Masirah, once again to be refueled in-flight again.

The next night, Delta Forces' commandos would be driven to the embassy in vehicles obtained by the agents. A team of Army Rangers would go to rescue the three Americans held in the foreign ministry. As the ground units were freeing the hostages, the helicopters would fly from their hiding spot to the U.S. Embassy and the Foreign Ministry. Three USAF AC-130 gunships would arrive overhead to protect the rescue force from any Iranian counter-attack and to destroy Iranian jet fighters at the Tehran airport. The RH-53Ds would fly the rescue force and the freed hostages to an abandoned air base at Manzariyeh, about 50 miles southwest of Tehran, which was to be seized and protected by a Ranger company flown in on C-130s.

At Manzariyeh the U.S. Navy RH-53D helicopters would be destroyed and USAF C-141s, flown in from Saudi Arabia, would then fly the entire Operation Eagle Claw group to a base in Egypt.

In the Joint Operations Division at the Pentagon, there was a Counter-Terrorism Branch, which was in the Current Operations Division. Tragically, this group of specialists was never asked to be involved in any of the planning for the rescue mission.

Shame on the Pentagon hierarchy that allowed a plan to be approved that was so complicated, convoluted, unrehearsed and had holes in it large enough to fly a C-130 with the gear down through it! Shame on me for restating the obvious.

Push Fast Forward . . . .

Mid-late April 1980, President Jimmy Carter and his administration had a lot more concerns than just Fidel Castro's insult to U.S. immigration. On 24 April, Carter had given the OK to execute Operation Eagle Claw. The waiting at the White House and Pentagon must have been almost unbearable. The desire for success was exceedingly high! Everyone with knowledge of Eagle Claw waited anxiously to hear the words, "Mission complete Sir. All hostages and mission personnel are coming home!" Those words were never spoken . . .

At 7:00 a.m. 25 April 1980, Carter announced to the American public that Operation Eagle Claw had failed. Eight U.S. service men were killed in a fiery inferno at Desert One and four survivors severely burned, none of which were due to enemy action or fire. The elaborately complex, super Top Secret mission had not gotten beyond the FAARP at Desert One, still 200 miles southeast of Tehran. Two aircraft (one C-130 and one RH-53) had been totally destroyed, and another five (5) RH-53Ds left on the ground.

Once the order to 'abort mission' had been given through a complicated chain of command, another order to 'destroy the remaining Navy choppers' was given, but in their haste to leave, the order was never carried out. As a result, our rescue team abandoned and left behind five (5) RH-53D Navy helicopters intact. The very next day the Iranians discovered Top Secret plans left in the RH-53 choppers. Our American agents (operatives) recently placed in Iran to help the Delta Commandos were compromised and nearly captured as a result.

Should we criticize the brave men who participated in Operation Eagle Claw? Air Force COL John Kyle didn't pull any punches when he said, "All that was lacking was the guts to try . . ."

After the president was notified that Eagle Claw had been aborted one can only imagine Carter's chagrin, as he demanded of Pentagon officials that a new plan be immediately pursued.

> "We are ten feet tall and you can't touch me!"
> The days of the "Ugly American" haven't ended, have they?
> Wait a minute, are we really as naïve as a typical 16 year old teenager?
> Do we really think we are invincible?

Sure we do, just like the 16 year old kid down the block from your house, the one who just got his driver's license and feels that it is his right to drive a car at 100 mph on a back road, believing he is invincible!

Just because we may be the world's greatest power, (so we think) are we immune to terrorism? Is it impossible for us to fail???

We are indeed unprepared for the unexpected—EMP; total loss of electric power (lights, household appliance, cars—anything with electronics); destruction of our financial and economical wireless networks and your ability to have access to them; total loss of nation communications. All of these items and more, which can be accomplished by domestic and/or external foreign terrorism. This nation is in the dark and without knowledge how to survive independent of electricity and the indefensible national grid which provides this quiet energy to your house and mine. We don't realize we are on the brink of a major catastrophe should a rogue nation detonate an EMP (electronic-magnetic pulse) nuclear device over the heart of this country, which would push us back into the dark ages . . .

Richard M. Nixon's greatest fear as he took office as the President in 1968 from LBJ was – becoming the first President of the U.S.A. to have lost a war! Although he didn't start the war in Vietnam, he is often credited with losing it. We may think we're ten feet tall, but we are not invincible!

We are not as invincible as we tend to think.

The Monday Morning Quarterbacks at the Pentagon couldn't wait to 'suit up,' they each had at least two, perhaps three or more ideas which, "If only they had been included in the OPPLAN for Operation Eagle Claw it *would have been successful,*" or so it goes. If there had been a suggestion box in the Pentagon it would have needed to be as large as the Lincoln Monument to hold all of the new ideas people had and wanted to offer.

Within forty-eight hours of the disaster, a new effort was already under way; President Carter authorized the Joint Chiefs of Staff to begin planning another rescue operation. This time the Pentagon was determined not to make the same mistakes. The most salient flaw of the first mission—as pointed out by an investigative commission led by Admiral James Holloway—was that the entire operation had been mostly improvised. Disparate units and forces had been quickly assembled and forcibly integrated, never achieving mission capability. In other words, they had not been ready.

Indeed, the units had not even exercised together in a full-dress rehearsal of the mission. Other problems included the absence in the military inventory of both long-range and quick-insertion helicopters, the unwillingness or inability of the CIA to provide tactical intelligence to the Army, the absence of long-range covert transport to carry American forces secretly from one country to another, the inadequacy of the training and selection program for the helicopter pilots and bitter competition among the different military branches which had each demanded a piece of the action.

During the planning of Operation Eagle Claw, the Defense Department was quite pleased with itself, having given each of the services part of the mission. In the end this was the most horrendous of errors. Having worked with more than one service at a time on different missions while on active duty, I can assure you, joint service operations are never easy. Radio communications are hardly ever compatible. Jargon and acronyms are confusing and misused. Additionally, I never saw an occasion where one service's aviators were told to fly another service's aircraft during a combat mission.

Operation Eagle Claw was reviewed later by the Holloway Commission. Major General Vaught, who as the commander of Task Force 179, in retrospect, saw the use of Navy helicopters as a big problem. He felt that the Navy viewed helicopters as an annoyance, which had to tolerated, but to which they attached little importance.

Vaught was not without fault regarding the helicopter issue. He had on two occasions, prior to the mission's execution, dispatched a captain from the Army to visit the Navy carrier to which the MH-53s were assigned. The captain returned with limited information regarding maintenance and upkeep on the aircraft, all of which was negative. Inspections were not being conducting in accordance with written Navy technical manuals; nor had the aircraft been flown regularly. As you will recall this was a major reason the mission failed—poorly maintained equipment—helicopters. The Navy did not appreciate the Army captain's visit and implied they didn't need the Army to tell them how to maintain their equipment. Apparently, they did. Why didn't Vaught make changes when he could have prior to the mission's launch?

One common theme, a major issue concerning this hostage rescue attempt had bothered the military planners from the get-go. There was no dedicated counter-terrorism aviation element or unit(s) to transport our counter-terrorist Delta Force Commandos to their objectives and to provide close fire support during the extraction.

President Carter later appointed Admiral James L. Holloway III, the former Chief of Naval Operations, to head a commission to study the sad and costly deficiencies in the failure of Operation Eagle Claw. Among the findings was the simple, but obvious fact that the military lacked aircraft and crews who were dedicated and specifically trained and prepared to perform this complicated type of mission. The services would formally address the findings of the commission, but in the short term, the focus remained on recovering the hostages.

In the days that followed in and around northern Virginia and the District of Columbia, several significant events are taking place simultaneously, at the Pentagon, within the Army and at the CIA's Langley headquarters. These events involve the planning of a second rescue attempt to free the American hostages in Iran.

The second rescue attempt was called Operation Snow Bird. Army General James Vaught remained commander of the joint task force, and he appointed Air Force Major General Richard Secord, a veteran of many classified special operations, as his principal deputy. Secord was a combat pilot with experience in Vietnam. He had worked closely with the CIA on many sensitive projects, including secret air missions over Laos and Zaire during the early 1960s. He also commanded several units in Air Force Special Operations. In 1975 Secord became the chief American adviser to the Iranian Air Force and managed much of the U.S. military assistance to that country. His work in the Middle East, said one associate, led Secord to "develop closer connections in Iran and Saudi Arabia than anyone else in the services." In two decades of black operations, Secord gained a reputation for cutting bureaucratic red tape, getting things done . . .

Albert Einstein stated that the definition of insanity is, "doing the same thing over and over again and expecting different results." There were lessons learned from the failed hostage rescue attempt. The follow-on operation, Snow Bird, began its planning with a new thought process—innovation, not re-creation. Different, new units were visualized in the fields of aviation (helicopters and transport), counter-terrorism and intelligence. It takes years to design, appropriate funds and build new helicopters, but mods and upgrades can take place much more quickly. As the planning proceeded, the Army initiated Operation Honey Badger as part of Operation Snow Bird. Counter-terrorism and special operations tactics, including new aircraft and flight techniques were developed.

It was recognized by aviation staff planners that supporting the customer's needs such as accurate delivery to the target location and at a precise time, these requirements were paramount. This led to the mission parameters for the about to be formed Task Force 160 and the 45th Avn Bn (Lt Hel Cbt)—" . . . delivering CT personnel and/or cargo to their designated target within +/- 50 ft and within +/- 30 seconds time on target." As in the Army's Field Artillery—"accuracy first, speed second."

The Army's unique, counter-terrorism unit, Delta Force, was formed post Operation Eagle Claw. These one hundred or so commandos and another one hundred support personnel, selected from Army Rangers and Special Forces, included sharp-shooters and other experts in combat-skills, prepared to perform surgical strike missions and hostage rescues silently and under adverse conditions. Their motto remains, "Surprise, Speed, Success."

Army Lieutenant Colonel James E. Longhofer was selected to be in charge of training the new helicopter pilots in Honey Badger. Longhofer had served under Vaught in the 24th Infantry Battalion at Fort Stewart, Georgia. A brilliant aviator, instructor and take-charge leader, Longhofer helped structure and coordinate an intense pilot training and selection program.

Change is not readily accepted in most services, especially in the regular Army. And flying was seen as an old and traditional type skill. Don't try to teach me new ways to fly, I like doing it the old way; the way we've always done it.

Immediately upon coming into the joint task force, the short, energetic Longhofer saw firsthand the problems that existed with current helicopter pilot training. Many paradigms had to be broken. Putting an inexperienced, but new aviation Captain in charge of leading a large, highly complex, multi-ship, night aviation mission, instead of placing an older, more qualified Chief Warrant Officer aviator in charge of the flight is just the first bad example! Some Army policies and methods change extremely slowly.

It is dramatically slow to get a new aircraft from the drawing board to units in the field. Seven years is a long, long time to fulfill a military requirement for new equipment/aircraft and or a new unit. So it's not often and certainly not in a crisis situation that you would chose to start from scratch and to design, or build a new stealth helicopter. That wasn't the idea during Honey Badger either. Stealth and helicopter are not usually used in the same sentence anyway!

"In the last dark nights of the Vietnam War, however, a secret government organization did develop and use a modified, secret helicopter for a single, covert, stealth-type mission. But it was no ordinary aircraft. The helicopter, a limited-edition model from the Aircraft Division of Hughes Tool Company, was adapted to be stealthy. It was called 'Air America's black helicopter' or the Quiet One— also known as the Hughes 500P, the "P" standing for Penetrator."[2]

"The Quiet One grew out of the Hughes 500 helicopter, known to aviators in Vietnam as the OH-6A Loach, after LOH, an abbreviation for light observation helicopter in 1968. The idea of using hushed helicopters in Southeast Asia came from the CIA's Special Operations Division Air Branch, which wanted them to quietly drop off and pick up agents in enemy territory. The CIA bought and then handed over two of the top-secret helicopters to a firm—by all appearances, civilian—called Air America. Formed in 1959 from assets of previous front companies, Air America was throughout its life beholden to the CIA, the Department of State, and the Pentagon."

CPT Joe Bob Hicks—Lop Buri, Thailand
1987

The classified mission on which the CIA would use the black helicopter known as the Quiet One/OH-6 was a one-time wire tape mission and installation of a 'spider relay' with solar panels. The wire tap was of NVA communications on the North Vietnam/Laotian border. The tactics of surprise, stealth and speed were all necessary to insure complete success.

"The slapping noise that some helicopters produce, which can be heard two miles away or more, is caused by blade vortex interaction, in which the tip of each whirling rotor blade makes tiny tornadoes that are then struck by oncoming blades. The Quiet One's modifications included an extra main rotor blade, changes to the tips on the main blades, and engine adjustments that allowed the pilot to slow the main rotor speed, making the blades quieter. The helicopter also had extra fuel tanks in the rear passenger compartment, an alcohol-water injection system to boost the Allison engine's power output for short periods, an engine exhaust muffler, lead-vinyl pads to deaden skin noise, and even a baffle to block noise slipping out the air intake.

The extensive alterations did not blank out all noise. Rather, they dampen the kinds of noise that people associate with a helicopter. Noise is very subjective. You can reduce the overall noise signature, but not eliminate it altogether. You don't hear the lawnmower next door, but a model airplane is easily heard. It has a higher frequency and seems irritating.

This early 1972 CIA stealth mission was carried out following long delays caused by heavy monsoon rains, lack of training and poor lunar illumination. This was also one of the first missions to be flown using NVG and FLIR. In the end it was a success, no loss of life, or equipment. It was the predecessor for Special Operation Aviation mission training and equipment development for Operation Honey Badger.

"I was assigned to Alpha Co, 229th Attack Helicopter Bn at Ft Campbell at the time, and some strange things were starting to happen," stated Brigadier General Lester D. Eisner. BG Eisner became the Deputy Joint Force Land Component

Commander (Army) South Carolina ARNG in February 2006, a 'post Vietnam' Army aviator and friend of the author.

Eisner graduated from Mercer University as a distinguished military graduate in 1976 with a regular Army commission in Infantry. In February 1979, he graduated from the Initial Entry Rotary Wing Course at Fort Rucker, AL, as the honor Aeroscout graduate and was then assigned to

BG Lester D. Eisner

the 229th Attack Helicopter Battalion, 101st Airborne Division serving as a Scout Section Leader, Platoon Leader, and Staff Officer. He also served with the original Task Force 158 from late 1979 until 1981. Eisner resigned from the Active Army in September 1985 to join the South Carolina Army National Guard. September 1995 and then became the Deputy Director, Aviation and Safety, Headquarters (-) State Area Command, Columbia, South Carolina. In Sep1999, he became the Commander, 51st Aviation Group. He relinquished command in March 2004 and became the South Carolina Army National Guard Director of Aviation and Safety. BG Eisner continues to serve as of August 2010.

"We aviators were hearing these strange statements/questions from some of the senior chain of command about . . ."Tracking the guys who had flown Little Birds during VN; they began accessing some of the junior company grade officers." I was a first lieutenant [active duty aviator] at the time."[3]

"We were involved in a 101st Airborne Div FTX and this is how it started. I had flown an aircraft in from the field to put it into Phase [Maint] and getting ready to go back to the field during this FTX. I was one of the few first lieutenant aviators during 1979. I had served two years as an Infantry Officer then went straight to Flight School graduating in December 1978. As I was getting ready to go back to the field another officer said, "No, the Bn Cdr wants to talk with you," and about that time a bunch of aviators were dragging their duffle bags along the tarmac coming back in from the field. "What's going on? Why does the Bn Cdr wants to talk to us?"

"The [229th] Bn Cdr was at the time a guy named Lieutenant Colonel Drew. LTC Drew became the leader of the Little Bird portion of Operation Honey Badger. And I can't remember Drew's first name. So Drew takes us all down to the conference room at hangar # 11 at Campbell Army Airfield and says, "I don't know what you guys are doing, I don't know how long you are going to be gone. I just know that some of you are leaving tomorrow, some of you are leaving two or three days from now."

"Part of the guys that had already been identified as Little Bird qualified had already been told they were going to be Little Bird pilots. The remaining guys that had not been qualified in Little Birds – to the best of my memory were told, "Alright you guys over here go with this group, you guys over here are going with that group."

"I was assigned to the UH-60 group, Charlie Company of Task Force 158. Doug Brown[4] was my company commander.

Brown enlisted in the U.S. Army in 1966. He served on an A-team and in 1970 he attended Officer Candidate School and then went to flight school at Fort Rucker, Ala. It was also the year he married his wife, Penny. He commanded a battalion of the 160th Special Operations Aviation Regiment during Operation Desert

LTG Bryan D. "Doug" Brown ca 2000

355

Storm in the 1991 Persian Gulf War. He later commanded the 160th Special Operations Aviation Regiment. In the course of his career, Brown rose from private to general – the first Army aviation officer to wear four stars. Among his several military qualifications, GEN Brown is a Master Army Aviator. GEN Brown retired on 9 July 2007 from USSOCOM, where he had served as Commander since September 2003. He retired with 40 years service to this nation.

Eisner continued, "My first mission [during Honey Badger], my first training task, I was assigned to be a UH-60 navigator. You know, we were deployed to Norton AFB, but we didn't know where we were going. They put us on a C-5 at Campbell and told us "You're going to a classified location and will be told where you are when you get there." We landed and as we taxied in we could see automobiles with tags on them, so we figured you were in California. [They] kinda briefed us on what was going on and the next couple of days we were told to go buy a CONEX full of NVGs (full-face goggles). They issued us our NVGs and in the next few days we started doing NVG qualification training, crew training and then soon started doing navigation training. Pretty long legs, 800 – 1,000 mile legs . . . eventually. There were some 12 hour training missions."

"That's where we started, the aircraft were modified and [we] put [additional] fuel in the back, and had satellite communications (SATCOM) gear onboard. They were modified . . . the navigator's station [jump seat with table] was modified to allow the navigator to do fuel management and navigation. And some of them that had satellite communication onboard you could also be a communications guy!"

Over the next few months, Longhofer endured until he had restructured the entire pilot training program. Together with Bruce Mauldin, an irrepressible Army major with endless energy and no respect for regulations, he also helped develop this new unit of helicopters capable of conducting clandestine insertions as required by Operation Honey Badger. Most of the helicopters of Task Force 158, which included OH-6 Little Birds, UH-60 Black Hawks, and cargo-carrying Chinooks, were taken from the 101st Airborne Division at Fort Campbell, Kentucky, and from Army National Guard units.

The 101st Airborne Division possessed the greatest number and variety of helicopters of any unit within the Army, and thus had the greatest potential for the rapid development of a rotary-wing special counter-terrorism aviation capability.

Some say, size matters. And I would agree when it comes to quietly infiltrating a rescue force without being discovered—the smaller the better! The Army decided that smaller and quieter were greatly desired characteristics in respect to getting our Delta Force in and out of Tehran. As previous demonstrated by Air America's black helicopter, the OH-6 Little Bird was about to be reborn!

Just down the outer hallway called the "E ring" in the Pentagon, the Army National Guard just happened to have a small, but operable fleet of OH-6 aircraft on its books. Aviation Staff members of DCSOPS (Dept of the Army, Deputy Chief of Staff Operations and Plans) asked the NGB to loan twenty (20) OH-6s to the 101st for a special test program.

The NGB OH-6s were Vietnam era, low-skid, 1st CAV scout type helicopters. Right now the Army wanted to put a few modifications on these Little Birds. Soon the ARNG's Gulf Port, Mississippi AVCRAD (Aviation Classification Repair Activity Depot) was directed to initiate a classified program called "Nine-Whiskey-Whiskey" to modify the +/—20 ARNG OH-6s. "The person running Nine-Whiskey-Whiskey inside the Pentagon, the holder of the Army's SOA check book, was Lieutenant Colonel Harvey Browne, today a GS-13 branch chief in NGB-AVS at Arlington Hall. Only 18 OH-6s were ever modified and loaned to the 101st Abn Div's 158th Avn Bn that became Task Force 158, then Task Force 160," stated Brigadier General Alberto J. Jimenez.[5] Jimenez was the NBG-AVN project manager of Nine-Whiskey-Whiskey. BG Jimenez served as Director of NGB-AVN from June 1999 to July 2001 in Federal Civil Service status. He later served from July 2005 to June 2008 as a Special Assistant to the Director, Army National Guard at Arlington Hall and also served as the Assistant Adjutant General of Maryland from June 2008 until his retirement in June 2010. BG Jimenez served aviation and the nation for 41 years.

BG Alberto J. Jimenez

Colonel Robert Toobie Johnson at the Mississippi TARS was at point for Nine-Whiskey-Whiskey at Gulf Port. Toobie also personally delivered these modified Little Birds to the 158th Avn Bn.

COL John J. Stanko Jr. remembers that, "An Army officer, Major Jacobs, walked into my office [at Edgewood] one day. He said, "Do you [NGB Aviation] have a facility where a C-5 could land and not draw a lot of attention?"

And I said, "Sure, for openers, Buckley Air Force Base out in Colorado."

Jacobs then said, "Yeah, that's great. You, being the Guard, have all of the OH-6's don't you?"

Stanko replied, "Yeah, 400 of them. All of the OH-6's in the Army – we had 400 of them in the Guard at this time. The only mistake I've ever made in my life—Colonel Dave Carothers [at this time Chief, DAMO-FDV in the Pentagon] talked me out of keeping the OH-6's [instead we later gave 'em up] for the OH-58's. [We should've kept the OH-6s] because we could rebuild those things . . . We had all of the jigs and airframe alignments and fixtures, etc."

So MAJ Jacobs says, "How long would it take to offload an OH-6 off of a C-5 and take off and fly it away? From the time the C-5 lands until the OH-6s depart, how long would it take?"

"Well, I have no idea. I guess we could find out."

MAJ Jacobs responded, "Okay, let's do that."

"So we went out to Buckley, we got some OH-6's, got a C-5, put them on board—put the OH-6's on board the C-5; took off, went around the pattern. The C-5 landed, moved off the runway, and punched the stopwatch. It was just amazing how fast the guys could do that [approx. 20 minutes]. And they eventually got it down to even faster times."

He, MAJ Jacobs, then asked a bunch more questions and says, "You know I have a *Special White House clearance . . .*" in essence meaning, if I say, 'Do this,' you know that it means the President is saying, "Do this!"

"Okay MAJ Jacobs," COL Stanko replies, "Well, I've been through that before with the White House. So naturally I understood that he has some kind of a blessing from the White House and a *Special Clearance* to do this and ask these questions. So at this point I said, "You know something Major, I've gone just about as far as I can go with you. Even farther than most people would do. I just can't go any farther with you until you accompany me down the hall and explain to General Walker what this is all about and tell him what's going on."

"I'm sorry, I can't do that," blurted Jacobs.

Stanko countered and said, "I'm sorry too. You and I are finished talking."

He looked at me and said, "Did you not understand that I have *Special White House Clearance*? Didn't you understand what I'm telling you?"

A few minutes later they got General Walker and took him downstairs to the special 'Tank' at DCSOPS, [a secure, guarded briefing room with bells and whistles]. Walker was down there for a couple of hours.

"So Gen Walker comes walking up to my office and sticks his head and says, "Hey Bub!" That's what he called me (Stanko). So General Walker said to me, "Hey Bub, I can't tell you everything that's going on, but whatever these guys ask you to do, you do it. Whatever it is, don't question it.""

So I said, "Well then Sir, you have to do one thing for me."

Walker said, "What's that?"

"Sir, I need you to call the Adjutant General of Mississippi and have him tell Jim Burns, Director of the MS AVCRAD, that he (Jim Burns) is to do anything that I tell him to do down there. No ifs, ands or buts."

"Jim Burns is the type of guy that dots every "I," crosses every "T" and doesn't do anything unless it's authorized," recalled Stanko.

"So a couple of hours later I get a call from Jim Burns. And he says, "Okay boss, what's first?"

"Okay Jim, the first thing we have to do is, you have to seal off part of the hangar down there at Gulfport. Make it secure. Nobody can go in that secure area unless they have *Special Clearance*, a pass and permission. Your enlisted people are going to be working on OH-6's on a classified Special Operations project. It's authorized by a high, high power. I need you to get me a list of names of those who will be working on this, send it to me because I've got to get them cleared by the FBI. We're going to have to get their security clearance elevated."

He said, "How long's that going to take?"

"Hell, I'll get 'em a security clearance in 48 hours. Hell, when the President says, "Jump," damn it we jump!" "I was just amazed," said Stanko, "I was amazed at what was happening."

"So about two days into this [special project] Jim Burns calls and says, "Hey Colonel, there's this guy down here—Charlie Smith (or something) from such and such a newspaper . . . He's a newspaper reporter and he's out in the parking lot and he's checking every car, every car tag, looking over the fence, trying to see what's going on. And he's gotten word from somebody in Washington, DC that something's going on down here at the Mississippi AVCRAD. He wants to take a look at it.'"

"How the hell that got out so quick, I don't know."

"So Jim Burns tells me—he walks out to the parking lot and says, "Hey, 'Charlie Reporter,' how ya doing? Come on in here. Let me tell you what's going on here.'"

And so Jim Burns takes him by the arm and walks him waaaay up the parking ramp there to an OV-1 Mohawk airplane. Jim says to the reporter, "See that? That's a Mohawk." And he starts describing the Mohawk to him and says, "See this is a rare airplane and it does intelligence and surveillance. That airplane is from the Georgia Army National Guard and when they can't fix that airplane, they send it down here to Mississippi and we fix it and we do the maintenance and we test fly it. And then he walks him waaaay down to the other end of the ramp, parking ramp, and said, "Charlie Report, you see that helicopter? That's a Huey and that belongs to the Florida Army National Guard. And when they can't fix it, they send it here to Mississippi." Jim talks real, real slow and goes into a lot of detail regarding the nomenclature, horsepower, radios, blade lengths, etc about each of the aircraft he had shown the reporter.

Later that afternoon, the reporter goes back and writes up his story, convinced that maintenance is the real story and sends it in.

The Army's special project known as Operation Honey Badger would center on the Army's 158th Aviation Battalion. Companies "C" and "D" of the battalion had acquired the Army's new UH-60 Blackhawk assault helicopter which would serve as the primary lift/assault force for the project. The Blackhawk was an easily deployable and highly capable assault helicopter with its superior power and ability to carry large payloads at high speeds.

The 229th Attack Helicopter Battalion would provide Army aviators for the light assault and attack OH-6A scout helicopters. These highly maneuverable and quiet Little Birds were chosen for the light assault role because of their small size and ease of transport. At this time the OH-6 Little Birds could carry only three soldiers and a single aviator. However, they could land in the bed of a Chevy pickup, on a moving barge, train or on top of your hometown's water tower!

Personnel at Fort Rucker, AL developed, tested and created armed AH-6 Little Bird gunships as a separate part of the project. Selected 229th personnel would team with the Fort Rucker element toward the end of the initial project as Company B, 229th Attack Helicopter Battalion became the Little Bird organization of the Task Force.

Company A, 159th Assault Support Helicopter Battalion would provide the heavy lift element of the new organization. CH-47C Chinooks, although not as deployable as the other aircraft, were capable of moving large numbers of personnel and much heavier payloads. The Chinooks would prove most effective in the project by establishing forward area refuel/rearm points (FAARPs) for long-range operations.[6] Together, these men and aircraft formed Task Force 158.

Operation Honey Badger began with separate training deployments. The Blackhawks were moved to Norton Air Force Base (AFB) in San Bernardino, California, on Air Force C-5 transport aircraft. At Norton AFB, the Blackhawk aircraft were modified to increase their range and improve long-range navigation capabilities. Meanwhile, the crews were given intensive training over the California desert.

Few of the 101st aviators were qualified to fly with night vision goggles (NVG), and no one was qualified for NVG flight in the UH-60. In fact, the aircraft instruments and cockpit lighting were not NVG compatible, and modifications would have to be made before training could begin. Once the aviators completed a 10-hour NVG syllabus, they progressed to long-range navigation training. Training flights consisted of up to seven and one-half hours of night flying with AN/PVS-5 night vision goggles (NVG). Pilots who completed the designated route, known as Black Route, three times with the NVGs were considered qualified.

The Chinooks self-deployed and stopped at Reese AFB in Lubbock, Texas, and Luke AFB in Phoenix, AZ, for refueling and crew rest, and then joined the Blackhawks at Norton AFB.

BG Eisner added, "When we went to Norton AFB, it was just the UH-60 guys and the Little Birds were off training at their location. If my memory serves me right, they were training at Yuma [UT], although I didn't know that at the time. It wasn't until the Black Hawk guys left Norton AFB and went to Dugway, UT. Once we got to Dugway, UT, we were joined by the Air Force Special Operations Pave Lows[7] and started doing some multi-ship operations with the [AF] Special Operations guys out of Hurlburt AFB."

Aviators selected for the Little Bird helicopters were sent to the Army National Guard Aviation Support Facility (AASF) at Gulfport, MS for

COL Billy R. Wood, U.S. Army (retired)

two weeks of training on the OH-6A helicopters. Following aircraft qualification, the Little Bird aircraft and crews were loaded on Air Force C-141 aircraft and moved to Fort Huachuca, AZ, for two weeks of mission training.[8] Armed OH-6 aircraft would join the training program at Dugway, UT later in the fall of 1980. Ultimately, aircrews would perform missions over routes as long as 1,000 nautical miles. Little Birds would load on C-130 transports and move to appropriately located forward staging areas to train for their role in the mission.

"I remember during those long training periods, much of which was just trial and error, wearing full-face goggles. We would take off as the sun was going down and land when the sun was coming up. Severe headaches, neck strains and all that other stuff . . . they had everything jury rigged from curtain rods running across the Black Hawk cockpit to . . . finally a bunch of inventive Army Aviators said, "Hey, let me cut these sons of bitches in half!"

Eisner remembers, "And that was what it was—trial and error back then. What we have now—goggles built for aviation purposes [not ground/Infantry type goggles] and cut-aways. There were the navigation techniques; SOP's to be rewritten, night operations that were totally new, NVG FAARP operations, and planning. Some of our over water flights – you couldn't drive a pin up our rear ends with a sledge hammer . . . We were developing new techniques for overwater flights when we were training out of Hurlburt and flying off the coast of the Gulf of Mexico, some of that was pretty tense. All of the detailed planning we did didn't exist in an organized fashion within Army Aviation prior to then."

"Although the UH-60 was new, big, fast and interesting, after Honey Badger was rolling, all I wanted to be was a Little Bird guy flying around with my hair on fire!

All of the units continued extensive training throughout the summer and fall of 1980 in desert environmental skills and long-range, close-formation, precision navigation with NVGs in preparation for the unspecified mission.

Nine months later we still didn't know the where the American hostages were, except that they had been moved to several locations. Operation Snow Bird had gained the confidence of Pentagon leadership. At this time, aviators and crewmembers from the 101st volunteered to stay with Task Force 158.

Then came a break in October 1980. General Secord was advised that the CIA said in knew the location of the American hostages. They were now, supposedly, back at the U.S. Embassy in Tehran. Secord wanted to validate the CIA information. He fought the issue all the way to the White House, without identifying the source. Now President Carter was becoming concerned that another failed attempt would be catastrophic. He had received an operational briefing that a sizeable number of hostages and commandos might be killed in the rescue effort. This late in the game Carter called off the Tehran rescue operation.

Regan's GOP comrades were pleased and felt this would insure a win in the November election. Although the operation was put on shelf, the special operations agents, Delta Force, Navy Seals and Task Force 158 were kept on standby.

The year 1980 ended with Ronald Reagan being elected as our 40th President. During December 1980, the Joint Special Operations Command (JSOC) was organized and stood up (at the recommendation of Army COL Charles Beckwith). Delta Force and Navy Seals were placed under JSOC at this time.

On a crisp Tuesday, 20 January 1981, on the steps of the U.S. Capitol building, President Jimmy Carter shook hands with the newly sworn in President Ronald Reagan. Just minutes after President Ronald Reagan received the oath of office on the steps of the U.S. Capitol building, and after last-minute delays over U.S. release of Iranian banking assets and fund transfers, the American hostages are released and leave Tehran on the 444th day of their captivity. By holding out until Reagan is sworn in, the radical Islamic Iranians had succeeded in giving Carter one last slap in the face.

Once the hostages were released and flown to Germany, Operation Snow Bird/Honey Badger was cancelled. The test program was ended at 1400 hrs. EST, 20 January 1981.

Naturally, the men of Task Force 158 expected to disband and return to their former units and homes at Fort Campbell. However, Army leadership determined that this new Army Special Operations Aviation unit was needed to meet future counter-terrorist contingencies. It now consisted of a Headquarters and Service Company (HSC), a Light Assault Company (MH-6s), and a Light Attack Company (AH-6s) and with the addition of two Blackhawk companies and a company of Chinooks, Task Force

160 was formed. Soon Task Force 160 would be redesignated the 160th Special Operations Aviation Battalion. Sometime later, a maintenance company was developed from the maintenance platoon of HSC and added. The Task Force continued to train and develop specialized skills while operating from diverse locations on Fort Campbell to minimize the appearance of a non-standard unit.

The 160th Aviation Battalion was activated at an open ceremony on the Fort Campbell Division Parade Field on 16 October 1981 following the change of command ceremony for the 158th Aviation Battalion. Lieutenant Colonel Jacob B. Couch, outgoing commander of the 158th, became the first commander of Task Force 160. Six months later, on 1 April 1982, the 160th Aviation Battalion was officially added to the Army's rolls. The new battalion's stated mission would be to provide additional flexibility to the commander of the 101st Airborne Division (Air Assault) while experimenting with new and improved air assault tactics, techniques and procedures.

In reality, the Army's first Special Operations Aviation unit had been quietly but openly activated. The reason was quite deceptive, as we will see later. While the 160th has grown and evolved over the past 20 years, many still refer to today's 160th SOAR (Special Operations Aviation Regiment) as Task Force 160.[9]

160th SOAR unit crest

The seeds had been planted for the development of Army Aviation in support of counter-terrorism or what would be called Special Operations Aviation (SOA). What those men back at Co D (-) 149th Avn Bn, Tulsa, OK, didn't realize was – their Vietnam style gun company was about to undergo such dramatic change that it would no longer be recognizable. At the Tulsa Air National Guard hangar on the northeast side of Tulsa International, the question of the day was, AH-1 Cobras or OH/AH-6 Little Birds? Did they even have a choice?

The aforementioned events and the failed hostage rescue mission, Operation Eagle Claw, were in fact the catalysts which led to the organization and Federal recognition of the OKARNG aviation unit called Lord of Darkness – the 45th Aviation Battalion (Light Helicopter Combat), at Sperry, OK on 1 May 1982. This occurred one month after the 160th Avn Bn was officially added to the Army's list of new units.

"We are ten feet tall and you can't touch us – we will own the night!"

Part Two

Following Operation Eagle Claw and the Department of Defense's recognition of the need for dedicated Special Operations Aviation, DoD also made another dramatic realization: It must have dependable, timely and credible intelligence. That almost sounds too simple.

Ask COL Charlie Beckwith and he would have reminded you of one problem that plagued the first rescue attempt Eagle Claw. It was the lack of reliable updated intelligence from inside Tehran. In 1980, the CIA proved unable to provide the critical intelligence Delta Force needed, such as: are all hostages in one location, the number of guards, the type of weapons they were using and what kinds of locks were on the doors.

The other most obvious shortcoming of Eagle Claw was the lack of a uniquely trained aviation organization, skilled in all aspects of counter-terrorism, to insert and exfil our Delta Force anywhere in the world on short notice.

These two items caused the most dramatic changes in the Army in the last 20 years, since the airmobile concept was created prior to Vietnam.

There was such a climate of change, one didn't know if what appeared to be white or overt really was, or was it actually black or covert and all was just a mirage. In some cases that was exactly the case. What once was the only means of gathering covertly human intelligence, the CIA, became non-effective, untrustworthy and not seen as capable of doing the job in the time allotted and manner desired. Today the same non-effective, non-productive view of the CIA is causing the executive and legislative branch leaders to discuss the disbanding of the CIA and the reinstitution of an OSS-like, post WWII, organization.

Special Operations was hailed by the majority as the means to originate and implement those changes necessary to bring about success in the future environment of counter-terrorism. Can you guarantee success? No, but you can stack the deck in your favor. Waiting and/or betting on the luck of the draw is for kids. The Army would not accept another failure and it was going to make sure it could deliver, on target, on time whatever it took to rescue any future American hostages and bring everyone safely home!

The process begun to implement new change was indeed for the better, but anything taken to the excess can become as malignant and deadly for individuals and/or careers. When staying too long in one place . . . you may become the target! I believe Will Rogers said it differently, "You may be on the right track, but if you stand there too long, you'll get hit by the darn train!"

The second rescue force's Operation Snow Bird and its Army Aviation slice called Operation Honey Badger was not going to be affected by the same problems. Senior leadership in the Pentagon tasked the Army to build the aviation capability to conduct counter-terrorism operations in a foreign country and gave them the blue chips necessary to play the game, minus 99.9% of the military red tape, briefings, required signatures and bureaucracies. A number of black organizations were established which were seen as necessary to gather and disseminate intelligence, others to build and support clandestine aviation units. Several were known only by Top Secret code words, some of which still exist today.

On 17 December 1981, Army Brigadier General James Dozier, the highest ranking American Army officer in the NATO southern European Command was kidnapped from his home in Verona, Italy, by members of the Red Brigade terrorist faction. Under the code-name Operation Winter Harvest, a small team of Delta Force operatives were dispatched to Italy to provide assistance with the search for Dozier. After a massive effort, including remote viewers from the United States, turned up nothing, a team of ISA signals intelligence specialists was sent to Italy to provide assistance, along with sophisticated equipment and specially outfitted helicopters. The ISA technicians were instrumental in the tracking and capture of a number of Red Brigades terrorists, and the location of Dozier himself. BG Dozier was rescued by Italian Special Forces after 42 days in captivity. He is later promoted to Major General and became the Deputy Cdr of III Corps and Fort Hood, TX.

Plan as a team, rehearse as a team and execute as a team. Some NCOs I looked up to in 1963 at Basic Infantry Training, Fort Polk, LA, told my basic training platoon – "Plan your work, then work you plan!" Very basic, very simple, yet sometimes we have forgotten and overlooked that sage advice. Still today, this tidbit remains critical to every military operation, not just in the Army, but in the other services and in life as well!

Military intelligence will remain one of the most critical elements to the success of any covert mission or defensive plan and certainly an offensive attack. Doesn't that include almost everything? Luck has very little to do with success. The more completely and imaginatively we plan, the more we rehearse, including all elements involved, especially military-intel, the more positive, effective and successful our execution will be.

Regarding intel-security, an old Army cliché is recalled, "If you don't have a need to know then I can't tell you." Later it became, "If I tell you, I'm going to have to kill you – How bad do you want to know?" Funny – Yes! Serious – Absolutely!!!

The need for and importance of current, viable and reliable intelligence will never cease. It is essential to most everything to be accomplished in our Special Operations Aviation and SOF communities. Plan your work, and then work your plan! You cannot possibly be successful without intelligence, even though,

"You may be ten feet tall and nobody can touch you . . . ."

1. Reprinted by permission. Colonel James H. Kyle, USAF, with John Robert Eidson, "The Guts to Try," (Phoenix, AZ: Renaissance House Publishing, 1995). This is a most excellent book about the planning and execution of Operation Eagle Claw and the commission which reviewed the failed mission.

2. James R. Chiles, "America's Black Helicopter," *Air & Space* (March 2008). http://www.airspacemag.com/

3. Telephone interview Brigadier General Lester D. Eisner, 29 January 2008

4. General Bryan Douglas Brown, former U.S. Army Commander, USSOCOM September 2003 - July 2007

5. Personal interview Brigadier General Alberto J. Jimenez, Arlington Hall, VA, 10 January 2007

6. http://www.nightstalkers.com/history/origin.html

7. MH-53J/M "Pave Low" – the Air Forces 20th Special Ops Wing's twin-engine, medium lift, all-weather, armed helicopter, used to covertly infil/exfil its pax/resupply into enemy territory, low-level, day or night, with a 486 nm range. Sikorsky MH-53s have operated since Vietnam (Son Tay Raid) and were to be retired in September 2008 and replaced by the Osprey tilt-rotor aircraft

8. Interviews conducted for 160th SOAR by Dr. Ronald E. Dolan with CW4 "Frenchy" LeFavor, CW4 Steve Koester, CW5 Charlie Weigandt, and CW5 Bob Fladry, 16 July 2001. http://helpingsoar.com/history160.htm

9. Ibid

Chapter 11

Jackpot at Caesar's Palace

"The soldiers fight, and the kings are heroes."
Yiddish proverb

In January 1978, Det 1, 445 Avn Co[1] received Federal Recognition. This detachment was located at the 15th Street armory in Tulsa, OK with the parent 445th Aviation Company headquarters located in Lexington, OK. Det 1 was a small gun element with 50 personnel, 3 UH-1M gunships and 2 OH-58 aircraft. Sergeant First Class Gene Payne was the AST (Admin/Supply Tech) for Det 1, 445 Avn when Sergeant Jaime Smith first joined the guard. "Payne stayed on as the AST for Company D (-) 149 Avn from 1978 thru 1980. I was hired on as the Supply SGT in May or June 1978. Gene Payne moved out in 1980 and I became the AST at that time. Sonny Hendrix was then hired as the Supply SGT," remembered CW4 Jaime N. Smith.

Army Guard aircraft at Tulsa were at the ANG ramp of Tulsa International Airport. Tulsa did not have an Army Aviation Support Facility at this time; however, there was a Flight Activity. The OIC or Commander was Major Dale E. Martin who was an IP. Two other IP Technicians worked at Tulsa then – Chief Warrant Officer Jay T. Tommy Evans and Captain Richard O. Murphy. The other known full-time Techs there at this time are: Norm Crowe – Helicopter Mechanic, Don Russell – Helicopter Mechanic, Don McCarty – Helicopter Mechanic, Greg Stilwell – Helicopter Mechanic, Daniel Crocker – Helicopter Mechanic, Wheeler Parker – Tech Inspector, Joe Volpe – Electrician and Ernie Bourget – Armament Tech.[2]

"Joe Volpe was from New Jersey and we called him "Jersey Joe." Ernie's last name was Bourget. He was a Frenchman from Massachusetts and he was short. He was later on the AGR First Sergeant of HHC. We called him "Frenchy," recalled Chief Warrant Officer Robert D. Graves.[3]

Det 1, 445th Avn Co was deactivated on 1 October 1978 and a new unit, Company D (-) 149th Aviation Battalion was formed and redesignated from the former Det 1, 445 Avn Co. The new unit had an authorized strength of 127 personnel and remained located in Tulsa. Its attack battalion headquarters and parent unit were in the Arizona Army National Guard (AZARNG). Major Dale E. Martin was the unit commander. Captain Vern R. Ashbrook was a Plt Ldr until March 80 when he became the XO. He also owned a chicken farm in Stillwell, OK and often brought fresh eggs[4] to drill and gave them to his soldiers. SFC Gene Paine was the AST (Admin/Supply Tech) with Det 1, 445 and stayed on in Co D (-) as AST from 1978 until he temporarily quit in 1980. At that time SFC Jaime Smith was hired as the new AST.[5] About the same time Staff Sergeant Alfred "Sonny" Hendrix became the Supply SGT Tech. "The last admin officer (AO) I can remember was Captain Ron Varner,"[6] stated Chief Warrant Officer Smith. Varner's duty station was at Lexington, OK, but he was the AO Technician for Co B 149th Avn Bn at Lex and Co D (-) at Tulsa.

Co D (-) 149th OKARNG Instructor Pilots (IPs) and aviators became qualified on the weapons systems mounted on the OKARNG UH-1M aircraft[7]. These armament subsystems included the M158 – 7 tube 2.75 in. rocket launcher, the M5 – 40mm grenade launcher and the M21 – 7.62mm mini-gun. Co D (-) 149th Avn had 7 or 8 UH-1Ms and 6 OH-58s[8].

"There was a rumor of us getting AH-1s Cobras. As a matter of fact, I believe we went down to Fort Hood, [TX] and spent some time flying the AH-1 Cobras at one summer camp," stated Chief Warrant Officer Four Uriah W. Roy Pittman.[9]

MAJ Martin was replaced as Cdr of Co D (-) 149th Avn Bn on 16 June 1980 by Major Vern R. Ashbrook.

At the end of 1979 and beginning of 1980, OKARNG Aviation was now in three distinct and different Oklahoma locations: Norman, OK (KOUN) – Max Westheimer Field, Lexington, OK (KHMY) – Major General Hal Muldrow Army Heliport (AHP) AASF #1 (Army Aviation Support Facility) and the Tulsa Flight Activity at Tulsa International

Airport (KTUL) – co-located with the Air National Guard. Co D (-) 149th Avn Bn (gun company) was at Tulsa, OK. The Tulsa AASF had not yet been built, nor even envisioned at this time.

"In about 1980, Lieutenant Colonel Dana D. Batey, OKSAO, convinced Major General Bob Morgan, OKTAG, to take aviation units out from under the command and control of OKARNG ground unit Hqs (Inf Bde, FA Bde and Eng Bde) and put them under an OKARNG TDA (Table of Distribution and Allowances) Aviation Headquarters where they could train as an aviation entity, and have their own aviation safety program," related[10] Colonel Leroy A. Wall, former State Aviation Officer (1988-2000).

MG Robert M. Morgan
OKTAG 1978-1987

"MG Bob Morgan throughout his tenure as the Adjutant General of Oklahoma National Guard (20 November 1978 – 11 January 1987) resisted attempts by his staffers and NGB staffers to put OKARNG aviation back under a ground command. Other States followed Batey's lead and soon Oklahoma Aviation was the model for progressive aviation force structure in the Guard during the 1980s. I believe this is one of the reasons that the OKARNG was given the Special Operations Aviation Battalion. It is also one of the reasons that it was lost later on," added[11] COL Wall.

Following the failed Operation Eagle Claw on 24 April 1980, two individuals in the Carter administration, Secretary of Defense Harold Brown[12] and Secretary of the Army Clifford L. Alexander Jr., were under extreme pressure to pull the military from the ashes of Desert One. On the morning of 25 April they were tasked with creating not only a new concept, but to physically establish an original special aviation unit. This type unit was designed to perform complicated, undetected infiltrations, exfiltrations and armed helicopter support of Delta Force and other U.S. military SOF operatives world-wide!

As discussed in the previous chapter, a classified test program conducted in the autumn of 1980 within the Army's 101st Airborne Division proved to be very successful. National Guard OH-6As were intensely modified, then loaned to and utilized by the Army in this test.

In September 1980, Guardsmen from all 50 states and U.S. Territories gathered on the edge of the desert at the dazzling oasis known as Las Vegas, NV. At this time Sin City or Las Vegas was a mere 164,674 population; today it borders on 560,000 souls. These military men and women were there to attend the Annual Convention of the National Guard Association of the United States (NGAUS). The brilliant white, five-star hotel, known as Caesar's Palace, a Roman-style city within a city, with its enormous casino, multiple restaurants, shops and ballrooms, hosted NGAUS' members and their guests on the glittery, neon strip. The highlighted guest speaker for the main banquet during the NGAUS convention was the second ranking member of the Senate Armed Services Committee and a staunch supporter of military aviation, senior Sen. (D-NV) Howard W. Cannon.

Sen. Howard W. Cannon

Senator Cannon was a USAF Reserve Major General, and a highly decorated pilot from World War II, Korea and Vietnam and a good, good, friend of many aviation defense contractors. Cannon received the French Legion of Honor for his heroism after being shot down over Holland during the Allied invasion of Europe in 1944. During WWII Cannon spent twenty months overseas and evaded capture for 42 days before reaching Allied lines, after being shot down. He served in the Combat Engineers – Army Air Corps 1941-46. His awards included Legion of Merit, Distinguished Flying Cross, Air Medal with Two Oak Leaf Clusters, Purple Heart, European Theater Ribbon with Eight Battle Stars, French Croix de Guerre with Silver Star and Presidential Citation. The Howard W. Cannon Aviation Museum at Las Vegas attests to his legacy and is located inside the McCarran International Airport.

His bio stated that Sen. Cannon was " . . . so committed to maintaining American military superiority that he managed to test fly nearly all new aircraft before voting for money to develop them."

Unnoticed by several thousand guests, an important conversation was taking place to one side of the ballroom at Caesar's Palace, between Lieutenant General LaVern E. Weber, CNGB, Major General Emmett H. Walker, DARNG, Major General Robert M. Morgan, OKTAG, Lieutenant Colonel Dana D. Batey, OKSAO and Colonel John J. Stanko Jr., Director of NGB Aviation and Safety.

"In a quiet corner of the Caesar's Palace in Las Vegas during the NGAUS Annual Convention 22-24 September 1980, we, the men you have mentioned[13], created the 45th Special Ops Bn[14]," according to COL John J. Stanko Jr.

It was perhaps in mid-June or July, that Dana D. Batey and John J. Stanko Jr. had an informal conversation via telephone. Neither Batey, nor Stanko can recall the exact date. The Director of Aviation at NGB, John J. Stanko[15] called LTC Dana Batey[16], Oklahoma State Aviation Officer in the months before the NGAUS convention and told his protégé that he needed to discuss a classified force structure subject right away and they did[17]. This dialogue was the first time that anyone in the OKARNG was to hear of the possibility that NGB might ask Oklahoma to accept a new, classified counter-terrorism aviation battalion.

It may have been suggested by Stanko, Chief of NGB Avn & Safety, in the confidence of their private telephone calls, "Dana, this conversation never took place and if you later say it did, I'll deny it. I'm going to tell you that Oklahoma might have the opportunity to enlarge that little attack helicopter element at Tulsa, Co D (-) 149th Avn to a full company MTOE, and replace your UH-1M gunships with AH-1 Cobras. This alone would have caused most State Aviation Officers to jump at the opportunity and say, "Yes, Sir, I'll take it, yes Sir!"

But Stanko wasn't finished talking . . ."Or you have the chance to replace Co D (-) with a much larger, new, classified aviation battalion and be on the cutting edge of something they are calling counter-terrorism." Then John J. Stanko Jr. would have spent at least another hour describing to Batey the complexity of standing up a new "CT" (counter-terrorism) aviation battalion, training 60 aviators in new aircraft to fly under Night Vision Goggles, and the multitude of other problems which were going to occur. What Stanko didn't tell Batey during this conversation would have shocked the Pope, and wasn't spoken of until only recently.

The friend and mentor of Dana D. Batey, John J. Stanko Jr. had to walk the tight rope of friendship and OPSEC; at the same time not divulging classified material. There was little doubt that this new aviation unit would be a clandestine operation, along the same order as the rotor-wing resources used during Operation Eagle Claw. For certain the hint had informally been dropped by Stanko to Batey. More subtly though, the hint formed several rhetorical questions which Stanko passed to Batey, "Dana, can you guys do this? It's not going to be easy. Most of the training and flight time will be at night. Do you want to do this?"

It is regretful that we don't know what exact words were spoken, as neither man can now recall precisely what was said or in what time frame. I'm speculating as to what LTC Batey did next. Based on my working relationship with him (BG Batey), I would not have been surprised if he had told me, "I was on the next plane to BWI (Baltimore International Airport, MD) . . ." before the ink was dry on his DD 1610 [travel orders].

See in your mind's eye, this 49 year old Oklahoma State Aviation Officer, listening to his mentor tell him he is being offered larger force structure, more manpower, new, modern airframes. Then there was that very special force structure word 'battalion' that Dana Batey loved to hear. The variety, intrigue and potential of each option – Cobras or counter-terror aviation was beyond good fortune and was hard to fathom.

Stanko, in his wisdom, knew this was not a question which should be answered quickly or without serious thought. He also felt his younger protégé should digest and study the impact on Oklahoma Aviation and discuss the possibilities with the OKTAG and OMD staff. I believe Stanko knew Batey well enough that he already knew which option Batey would chose, but both would have to wait for the time being. I also believe that John J. Stanko Jr. knew Batey, his talents, leadership abilities and the tenacity to get things done, well enough to have great confidence that if Oklahoma said "Yes" to the counter-terrorism mission, they would in fact get it done!

Very candidly, Stanko was hoping that his dear friend, Batey, would simplify and make it easy for NGB to centralize the new, proposed attack helicopter battalion force structure in Arizona's ARNG Aviation program. Remember, in the big ball game you never get something for nothing—there is no free lunch. To get something new, bigger and better, you must be willing to give up something.

COL Stanko would not have lied to his friend, nor would he have told him "This is going to be a bird's nest on the ground!" He would have been honest with Batey and told him how, "This might be the most interesting, challenging and at the same time difficult thing with which you are every involved. Young men, your fine Oklahoma aviators and soldiers might die just training to achieve the high standards. This unit could be called up to active duty for another hostage rescue in the future. It isn't going to be easy Dana. Think long and hard before you tell General Morgan [OKTAG] that this will be good for Oklahoma."

Sometime during the wee hours during which this conversation took place, John Stanko would have mentioned two other significant factors: first, "There'll be a golden spigot from which money will flow from the black world [Special Operations] to Oklahoma" and secondly, "If Oklahoma decides it does not want to do this counter-terrorism aviation battalion, your Co D (-) 149th Avn will probably be in line to receive AH-1 Cobras to replace the UH-1Ms you now have in Tulsa."

And before Batey could open his mouth, Stanko replied, "No, Dana, you can't do both!"

Is it possible that I might be overlooking the bright side of these two points? Doesn't this scenario (Cobras or Little Birds) appear to be a win-win situation for Oklahoma?

Back in Oklahoma City, LTC Batey had a plan, but first he wanted some more information and he wanted a second opinion. I think Batey already had made up his mind; he knew what he wanted – bigger and better, traditional MTOE force structure. How could he ignore the 200+ personnel and 25-30 new aircraft with the CT mission, a battalion size aviation unit?

He also needed to know how the gun company boys in Tulsa would respond to this Little Bird idea, before he presents a decision briefing for the TAG, MG Bob Morgan. From his home in Purcell, Batey called MAJ Dale Martin, the Tulsa Flight Activity Commander and MAJ Vern Ashbrook, Commander of Co D (-) 149th Avn. Batey did his best to maintain OPSEC (Operational Security) and walked the proverbial tight rope attempting to tell Martin and Ashbrook what might be coming down the pike, without breaching the classified aspects of the CT mission and possible new unit at Tulsa. But he communicated a heads up to them regarding making a choice between Cobras or Counter-Terrorism (Little Birds). He asked Dale to discuss the options with the Co D (-) guys and " . . . get back to me as soon as possible."

In 1980-81, a lot of full-time aviation personnel, with very good intentions, would often go over their boss's head and would call National Guard Bureau aviation directly and talk straight to the well-informed action officers at Edgewood, MD. Let us speculate that's probably what Martin, Ashbrook and Murphy did as soon as Batey had told them what he knew. Each of these key Tulsa players probably pumped everyone at NGB-AVN and friends at the Pentagon they could get to answer the phone about this possible new counter-terrorism mission and unit being offered to OKARNG. Can you blame them?

Throughout 1981 soldiers of Company D (-) 149th Aviation continued to train with the expectation of the formation of an attack helicopter battalion and the receipt of AH1 Cobras. Some pilots of the unit had completed AH1 transitions at Ft. Hood during the summer of 1981.

CW4 Robert C. "Bobby" Lane was a former active duty rotary-wing aviator, having served overseas in Korea in 1968-69 and a member of the OKARNG since 1975. He had placed his name on a waiting list in 1974 to get into an OKARNG aviation unit. When he joined the Guard in April 1975 he was assigned to the 445th Avn Co at Norman. Now in 1980 he was a gun driver with Co D (-) 149th Avn Bn at Tulsa, flying UH-1Ms. Lane remembers[18], "We'd just gotten back from annual training at Ft. Hood flying Cobras, shooting stuff, learning about the Cobras. When we got back from AT, I guess there was this offering to pick up this Little Bird Special Ops mission, in lieu of the Cobras. It was the first time I ever saw the democratic process work in the Guard. Dale Martin, our Flight Activity Commander and CPT Richard Murphy our Operations Officer (both full-timers at Tulsa), got us all together there at the ANG hangar. At this briefing there was myself, Tommy Evans, C.L. Strance, David Kerbow, Wes Foutch, Rick Yorman, Roy Pittman, Bear Smith, Dave Walton and some others I can't remember. Dale Martin and Richard Murphy, both Technicians, presented us with two options regarding us and our gun detachment at Tulsa. The first option was for us to remain as a gun company (-) minus and the possibility we'd be getting AH-1 Cobras. The second option was and they said, "We've been offered this other mission should we choose to accept!" It was this new, classified, counter-terrorism mission. The new secret aviation battalion would have about 25 OH-6 Little Birds, 17 MH-6 lift birds and 8 AH-6 armed attack birds. They told us how hard it was going to be, who our customers would be and about flying with Night Vision Goggles. We took a vote and opted for the Little Birds."

There are always a few folks you and I didn't get to meet. I don't recall having met Wes Foutch, but later I learned he was co-pilot with Ron Ketter the day they lost a tail rotor and gearbox on a UH-1 over Coffeyville, KS. C.L. Strance recalled that "Wes Foutch was a former Naval Officer that was working for Getty Oil in Tulsa. I flew quite a bit with Wes. Out of the blue several days ago [in 2008], I got an e mail from him. When Getty Oil moved to Houston, he chose not to move there and so he moved to Rhode Island where his wife's folks lived. He says he has a sister that lives in Sand Springs so he get back to the Tulsa area every once in a while."[19]

Although Bobby didn't recall, MAJ Vern Ashbrook, Cdr Co D (-) 149th Avn Bn was most likely there at this meeting also. Ashbrook was still an M-day soldier at this time. Former Marine SGT, Norman Crowe, was the 1SG of Co D (-) and also a full-time Tech at Tulsa. Twenty-four year old Bryon L. Barnhart enlisted in the Army, attended basic training and then was reassigned to Mother Rucker where he became 67N (helicopter repairman) qualified. He returned to Tulsa as a UH-1 Huey crewchief in Co D (-) 149th Avn Bn. Later in 1984 he attended rotary-wing flight school and becomes an aviator in Co A 45th Avn Bn at Sperry.

MAJ Martin called Batey and told him of the men's decision – Little Birds!

Just a few weeks before the NGAUS Convention (1980) at Las Vegas, Batey prepared what he calls an "Arm Chair Briefing" for the TAG, MG Morgan. He assures Morgan that he has verified with the Tulsa boys their desire to do the Little Bird covert mission and more. He had managed to get some demographics from Tulsa County on aviation personnel within a 100 mile radius of Tulsa International Airport. The OKARNG Recruiters in Tulsa provided info which fortified Batey's desired outcome. "Morgan was very excited and saw the tremendous opportunities for Oklahoma. MG Morgan knew he was going to be asked 'Yea' or 'Nay' at Las Vegas," said[20] Batey. And very likely, just before LTC Batey made his recommendation to the TAG, he told him about the golden spigot[21]" and how the governor might like to hear this good news personally from MG Morgan.

LTC Dana D. Batey then recommended to MG Morgan that Oklahoma should enthusiastically take this counter-terrorism Little Bird mission and fly with it!

The marble floored ballroom of the NGAUS banquet sparkled and the speaker's voice resonated, as did the loud, protracted applause. The guest of honor, Sen. Cannon was given a long, sincere, standing ovation, following his patriotic speech. After the ovation died down and the crowd began to rise from their white linen covered tables, Cannon lingered in the ballroom, moving away from the head table area to chat with his close Guard friends.

At the Oklahoma table in the ballroom, John J. Stanko Jr. suggests to his dear friend, LTC Dana D. Batey that they go and get a Coke from the bar. Three men remaining at the table are conversing quietly, but seriously: LTG Weber, MG Walker and MG Morgan. Before COL Stanko and LTC Batey left the table, the discussion was about what happened during Operation Eagle Claw and since then. As the two left, perhaps Gen Walker also mentioned the upcoming international summer Olympic Games to be held in Los Angeles in 1984 and the real threat of terrorism in a large metroplex. The subject of counter-terrorism couldn't be mentioned without remembering the Israeli hostages taken and killed by Arab terrorists at the Munich Olympics in 1972. Ten to fifteen minutes of polite conversation occur and then MG Mickey Walker asks the Adjutant General of Oklahoma, "Bob, I know that Oklahoma can do this counter-terrorism aviation thing, but do you realize the magnitude of this mission – the significance of this type unit? Are you confident you can recruit the right kind of aviators and train them for a bona fide counter-terrorism mission? I'd like to see you guys succeed!"

LTG LaVern E. Weber—
CNGB 1974-1982

Imagine the electricity and opportunity in those words, not to mention the many millions of dollars which would flow through Oklahoma within the years to come. And as municipal pundits remind us, a dollar spent in your local community will turn-over in the same community seven times!

With LTG LaVern Weber, MG Mickey Walker at the table, MG Bob Morgan gave Walker his answer—a resounding "YES Sir! We can do this mission." Being the southern gentleman he is, MG Walker rose to shake the extended hand of MG Morgan and likewise Weber rose and congratulated both men.

About the same time, Batey returns to the table, "Gen Weber was just smiling and Morgan says to me, "Well, Batey, looks like you're gonna get your chance!" remembered BG Batey[22].

"I remember the Caesar Palace meeting and Stanko told me about how they did a handshake deal at Caesar's; that's the way Stanko did

MG Emmett H. Walker—
DARNG 1978-1982

business," stated Brigadier General Alberto J. Jimenez in his office when interviewed on 10 January 2007. Stanko and Batey knew the outcome before the question was asked.

Thus a behind the scene deal was sealed with a handshake and instead of a pair of dice rolling at the Caesar Palace Casino, it was Special Operations Aviation that began to roll in northeastern Oklahoma. The decision formally created a new Special Operations Aviation unit in Tulsa, OK with a specific mission of providing clandestine aviation support to counter-terrorism. This unit was first constituted and designated the 45th Avn Bn (Light Helicopter Combat), federally recognized on 1 May 1982 at Sperry, OK per OA 81-82 dated 2 September 1982. They would be known as the Lords of Darkness.

Co D (-) 149th Avn Bn was the nucleus from which this new black, counter-terrorism aviation organization arose.

"This new ARNG counter-terrorism aviation unit was specifically requested by the Chief of Staff of the Army and the DCSOPS." COL John J. Stanko Jr. recalls emphatically that the statement "It [45th Avn Bn] will be a mirror image of Task Force 160" was stated to him in the hallway of the DCSOPS at the Pentagon.[23]

"Yes, we heard that everywhere we went, from everyone, "The 45th Avn Bn (SO)(A) will be a 'mirror image of TF 160," said COL Leroy A. Wall.[24] In the community of Special Ops it was a given that the 45th Avn Bn (Sp Ops)(Abn) was to be a "mirror image" of Task Force 160.

Task Force 160 was officially recognized on 16 October 1981 when it was designated as the 160th Aviation Battalion. The 160th became known as the Night Stalkers because of their capability to strike undetected during darkness and their distinguished performance in missions throughout the world[25].

One evening in September 1980, a small, influential group of high-ranking officers stood face-to-face, in a Caesar Palace ballroom, and with a 'hand shake' formed a one-of-a-kind, Counter-Terrorism aviation unit in the Army National Guard.

For a moment, just image the excitement, the ideas, thoughts and thousands of valid questions that the Tulsa OKARNG aviators would have when they received the news – the U.S. Army, National Guard Bureau and the Oklahoma Army National Guard were going to stand up a new, Special Operations Aviation Battalion, with a real-world mission of counter-terrorism at Tulsa International Airport.

The news sped from the towering white, stone-tiled walls of Caesar's Palace, to a small, innocuous, pastel sandy-yellow, 1937 WPA Armory.[26] The town of Sperry, OK, which had a farming population of 900 was alive with speculation in May 1982. So was the Oklahoma Military Department's headquarters.

Hardly eighteen months had passed from semi-formal discussion to orders of Federal Recognition. Thus the agreement which confirmed that Oklahoma had accepted the challenge of organizing, equipping and training a new Aviation Battalion for a classified counter-terrorism aviation mission came to fruition. Official State of Oklahoma Military Department, Permanent Orders 24-2, dated 27 April 1982, partially read, "Files, records and orders for Co D (-) 149th Avn Bn will be closed out as of 30 April 1982 and forwarded to HQ OMD, ATTN: OKPA-A, NLT 1 June 1982." Co D (-) 149th Avn Bn became the new 45th Avn Bn (Lt Hel Cbt) 1 May 1982 having 3 companies initially. Permanent Order 24-2 was signed by Colonel Robert E. Clark, ACofS Personnel at the OMD Headquarters.

Winner, winner – chicken dinner! OKARNG Aviation is a winner!

1. Federal Recognition 1 January 1978. LTC Marvin D. Robert's '1/245th SOA History'

2. Telephone conversation SFC Norm Crowe, 10 December 2007

3. Email CW5 Robert D. Graves, 11 December 2007

4. Email MAJ Ramon Claudio Rivera, 28 November 2007

5. Email CW4 Jaime Smith, 30 November 2007

6. Ibid

7. UH-1Ms were UH-1Cs with T53-L-13B engine upgrade and one or more armament systems.

8. Personal interview CW4 Robert C. "Bobby" Lane, 16 November 2007

9. Telephone conversation CW4 Roy Pittman, 28 November 2007

10. Email L Leroy A. Wall, 30 January 2006

11. Ibid

12. Sec Def Brown and Sec Army Alexander served 1977-1981

13. CNGB Weber, DARNG Walker, OKTAG Morgan, OKSAO Batey and NGB-AVN Stanko

14. Telephone conversation COL Stanko, 2 December 2006

15. COL John Stanko was NGB, Director of Aviation from 1 July 1976 to 3 August 1993

16. COL Batey was OKARNG State Aviation Officer from 1976 to 1988

17. Telephone conversation Brigadier General Dana D. Batey, 26 November 2007

18. Personal interview CW4 Robert C. "Bobby" Lane, 16 November 2007

19. Email MAJ Clarence "C.L." Strance, 14 January 2008

20. Telephone conversation Brigadier General Dana D. Batey, 26 November 2007

21. This "unlimited" money/ mandays may have been "a major factor" which ultimately caused such a tremendous chasm/conflict between OKARNG aviation and OKPOT in the late 1980s.

22. Telephone conversation Brigadier General Dana D. Batey, 26 November 2007

23. Telephone conversation COL John J. Stanko Jr., 2 December 2006, 12 January 2007

24. Telephone conversation COL Leroy A. Wall, 2 December 2007

25. Extracted 160th SOAR unit history, http://www.specialoperations.com/Army/160th_SOAR/default2.html

26. Telephone conversation Larry Briggs, historian, city of Sperry, OK, 4 December 2007

Chapter 12

Golden Palace on Cincinnati

"Always do right. This will gratify some people and astonish the rest."

Mark Twain

The spring in Oklahoma usually is quite mild, but brings a hint of things to come in the months ahead, like blistering heat. On this day there were daffodils and jonquils reappearing throughout the rusty town with plush, green leaves and blossoms of white and golden-yellow. The Sperry, OK *Pirates* boys and girls basketball had finished another ordinary season and now the track teams concentrated on District meets with high hopes. The high school is located on N. 4th Street. The *Pirates* were a Class 2A school and had competitive wrestling and baseball teams.

On the sidewalk in front of the Post Office, a yellow, metal newspaper stand held about 20 copies of the *Tulsa World* newspaper for 1 May 1982. Hidden several pages deep was a story about British planes carried out raids on two airstrips near Port Stanley, the capital of the Falkland Islands which were then occupied by Argentinean forces. The article also mentioned that a British submarine sank an Argentinean naval cruiser. Neither item would affect events in Sperry this day.

Each morning down at the Kountry Kitchen Café on East Main Street there was a constant buzz in the early months of 1982. The old geezers' club arrived habitually each morning at the café on East Main and considered their normal seats as reserved for them and them alone. The geezers were early risers, first light regulars addicted to strong cups of scalding Folgers coffee; they sipped from heavy mugs and gossiped about

" . . . this here new Army unit coming to Sperry" and boasted that it was "gonna have helicopters all painted black so you couldn't see them at all!" During lunch at the small hamburger bar and grill behind the armory on Hwy 11, the conversations over a greasy cheeseburger basket were much the same.

Bow-legged men with sun-burnt faces, bent at the waist, wearing John Deere green ball caps lingered at the one-man, one-window Post Office just next door and north of the Sperry Armory on Cincinnati Avenue. They checked their post office mail boxes every morning, as regular as a railroad engineer's pocket watch, then stayed to gab and speculate with other old men. They parked their ancient pickups, faded sky-blue Chevys or washed-out black Fords, in front of the blue mail drop boxes – one labeled "Local" the other "Out of Town." It was almost difficult to ignore the words rolling from their tobacco stained lips, "I hear that half of this here helicopter unit is gonna be CIA and the other half regular army, disguised as Guard soldiers. Them pilots are supposed to wear black all the time they fly 'em there black choppers. And I suspect they got something to do with 'em UN folks back east somewhere, don't you?" Some of the old farmers could recall days when they themselves drilled at the old WPA armory as members of the National Guard; some were former artillerymen.

Imagine all of the rumors and gossip floating around. Too bad someone didn't write them down and save them. One of the occasional subjects heard around town had to do with the 45th Avn Bn's new counter-terrorism role and the upcoming 1984 City of Los Angeles summer Olympics. Although we don't have any documentation, the timelines fit that the 45th Avn Bn may have been designed and developed with support of that event in mind. "Our [initial] training progress did not allow us to make that goal."[1]

Sperry's Sunday morning religious choices were similar to Baskin-Robbins – they got one of each flavor! There was the First Baptist Church, the Christian Church, Assembly of God, Church of Christ and a few others. There was an automobile repair shop in town and several auto salvages along North Cincinnati Avenue. The general dry goods store was on West Main and there was a pizza parlor, a small drug store, gas station, a convenience store and a funeral parlor.

Major Phil Johnson, an Oklahoma Army National Guard aviator and former Charlie Company Cdr, was the local funeral home director of Johnson Funeral Home. In his words, "He would be the last guy in Sperry to let you down." And when I recently called and asked how business was doing? He replied, "Dead."

MAJ Phillip Johnson

Sperry America—an ideal town for a unique military unit headquarters – out of sight, out of mind. Not quite literally, but almost.

Not much was happening at the small, but ultra-quiet city library, just a few doors west of the Tag Agency on West Main Street. However, the City Fathers of Sperry were counting on the financial boom that the reopening of this old, golden-yellow, WPA armory would bring. Who could blame them? For certain, just think of the size of the payroll for the full-timers that would work every day at

45th Avn Bn (SO)(A) Armory, Sperry, OK

the armory. This was going to be a God send to the local businesses. Drill weekend would be like manna from heaven. Since a government mess hall was not available, there would soon be a contract with the local café for soldier's drill weekend meals. The owner of the local gas station was also seeing dollar signs in his sleep each night. Even the town librarian, Miss Mary Ann, was anxious to see a little action!

This potential economic boom for Sperry America—the reopening of the old golden WPA armory was what State officials had told them they could expect. The armory had been built in the late 1930s, officially dedicated in 1940, and had no central refrigerated air and little if any heat, but sufficient space inside and out including a large drill floor. It also had good, fenced parking for the unit's wheeled vehicles and two parking lots for drilling soldiers. The offices and work areas were Spartan with concrete floors and steel framed windows, many of which would later be painted black. After many telephone calls and visits to OMD (Oklahoma Military Department) Maintenance we obtained window air conditioning units. If your desk happened to be right in front of the window you stayed cool. If not it was your own fault.

The metal front doors of the Sperry Armory were ancient, dented and covered with untold layers of oil based enamel, now chipped, faded and cracked. The newly cut master key was hard to turn, but it finally opened the industrial grade dead bolt lock. At long last, the doors swung open for military business once again. Stepping indoors from the sunny western foyer, you were greeted by a cool and somewhat familiar musty odor in the air, like granddad's damp old cellar. There we were in Sperry America and the old armory didn't even have an Arms Room to secure our individual weapons, ammunition, NBC equipment, field gear (gas masks, test equipment), etc. The previous military occupants had been a Medical unit which has no weapons authorized; therefore the lack of an Arms Room was of no consequence to them.

The 120th Medical Company was the former unit at the old Sperry Armory. The unit had been transferred to Broken Arrow, probably having something to do with a better recruiting base on the south side of Tulsa. The armory sat waiting upon the Lords of Darkness.

One of the first things you noticed once inside was that none of the desks matched each other or anything else in the room. The military furnishings throughout the building appeared to have been donated from the last big yard sale at the high school several blocks to the west. There were a few new Remington electric typewriters which had been recently dropped off by OMD USPF&O (United States Property and Fiscal Office) courier, stacked side-by-side on one desk. There was little else in the offices, except a few OD (olive drab) folding metal chairs and a couple of three and four drawer metal filing cabinets and layer upon layer of dust. Notice what was missing? There were no government computers. The Army hadn't begun to contract for or purchase and distribute PCs to units in the field just yet. This next generation of modern technology was perhaps a half dozen years down the road.

The very first Friday evening before drill, was a large celebratory party, or what we used to call a G.I. party! A G.I. party was a sarcastic term or name for a major clean up of the barracks and/or office area on a military installation. The Sperry armory was long overdue being given a top to bottom cleansing! It would take Friday afternoon and all night to get rid of the dust, rust, mold, corrosion, rat's nests and junk which had accumulated over the years. It was going to take another day just to clean the white porcelain bathroom lavatories, commodes and their standard black split seats. Someone was overheard saying, "I'm damn glad this old armory doesn't have a kitchen, or they have us pulling KP for the next month solid. Out in the drill floor area, there were a half dozen old Pabst Blue Ribbon beer cans lying on and around a dirty military bunk mattress that some enterprising teenagers must have trashed there from a Friday night's big adventure.

On 1 May 1982, 45th Aviation Battalion (LT HEL CBT) was officially constituted using the unit spaces from Co D (-) (Attack Helicopter) 149th Avn Bn as the nucleus for this new black, counter-terrorism aviation organization. The 45th Avn Bn was federally recognized at Sperry, OK with 203 personnel authorized per OA 81-82 dated 2 September 1982. The battalion headquarters armory was open, clean, but just not quite ready for inspection.

The National Guard Bureau federal recognition order is signed (1 May 1982) by Lieutenant General Emmett H. "Mickey" Walker, CNGB.[2] The old Co D (-) 149th Avn Bn unit headquarters was moved from the 15th Street armory in Tulsa to the larger WPA stone armory located in downtown Sperry, OK, about 12 miles NNW of the Tulsa International ANG ramp. The basic structure of the battalion consisted of a Headquarters and Service Company and two line companies, "A" Lift and "B" Attack. The Bn Cdr, CSM, Bn Staff, staff sections and each company had offices within the Sperry armory.

Equipment authorized for the old D (-) 149th Aviation was transferred by its Commander, Major Vern R. Ashbrook, to the parent unit headquarters in Phoenix, AZ. Drill periods and AFTPs for the remainder of 1982 were utilized for night vision goggle qualification training in the new OH-6s and the development of night low level navigation training in the local flying area. Throughout this year, motivation and morale were exceptionally high within the unit and all personnel felt a common urgency to achieve tactical proficiency in the shortest time possible.[3]

OH-6 Little Bird

The remainder of 1982 did indeed bring about drastic and dramatic change for Tulsa OKARNG aviation personnel and the entire Oklahoma Army Guard Aviation Program. OH6 aircraft were picked up and ferried back to Oklahoma. Large quantities of new military equipment began to arrive: FAARP (Forward Arming and Refueling Platoon) pumps, hoses, nozzles, parachutes, trucks, tankers, trailers, NVG and ALSE. The Property Book Officer (PBO)[4] was busier than the proverbial _____ (you fill in the blank).

Recruiting began with an unusual twist for an ARNG unit.

"We took what we had originally in the unit [Co D (-)] and put those people we thought were good into the key positions. We made Don Russell the "A" Co Senior SGT. Ron Freeman was running the guns at this time and took over "B" Co, which was the gun company. We brought the new guys into the office, [and told them] this is what we're gonna do. We're no longer a traditional Guard unit, you're gonna do this, you're gonna do that. We're gonna require a little bit of extra time from you, this and that," stated SFC Norm W. Crowe Jr.[5]

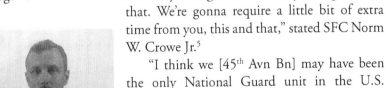

LTC Arthur C. Kveseth

"I think we [45th Avn Bn] may have been the only National Guard unit in the U.S. that reserved the right to interview and reject personnel brought to us by our recruiters. We got some top quality people that way. All incoming enlisted [soldiers] and WOC [Warrant Officer Candidates] candidates [had to meet our] standards [which] were Honor Graduate or Distinguished Honor Graduate from MOS producing schools," added Lieutenant Colonel Art C. Kveseth, former Adjutant.[6]

All of the 45th Avn Bn's aircraft were first based at the Tulsa Flight Activity, ANG base, Tulsa, OK. Initially the new unit had a handful of full-time Techs at the Tulsa Flight Activity, 12 full-time (AGR) personnel at the armory, and a few M-day soldiers assigned to the new Battalion Headquarters at the Sperry Armory.

The first 45th Avn Bn (LT HEL CBT)[7] full-time Command & Staff personnel list (shown below) is based on the terrific memory of Bob Graves and some amazing recollections from 25 years ago of a few good men.[8] "At the start we were authorized 12 [full-time] AGR positions, plus a full-time RA (regular Army) [active duty advisor] S-3 Officer. The Bn Cdr, Major Dale E. Martin, Bn XO, MAJ Vern R. Ashbrook and new active duty advisor, Major Jack "Happy Jack" Brayton, did the interviewing for the AGR Military Personnel Technician position and hired me on the spot, but my battalion (1/179th Inf) made me go to summer camp with them [due to the short notice]. They [DA/NGB] later

CW5 Robert D. Graves

added many more AGR positions [within the Bn] . . . ," stated Chief Warrant Officer Five Robert D. "Bob" Graves, former Mil Pers Tech (MPT).[9] CW4 Bob Graves was hired as the AGR Personnel Warrant on 1 June 1982. The new 45th Aviation Battalion (LT HEL CBT) had an authorized strength of: (OFF/WO/EM) Hqs & Svc Co 14/8/114(136); Co A (MH-6s) 4/18/19(41); Co B (AH-6s) 3/14/9(26); totals 21/40/142 = 203.

First Cmd & Staff Members of 45th Avn Bn (Lt Hel Cbt):

Cdr – Major/Lieutenant Colonel Dale E. Martin[10] (Tech at Tulsa Flt Activity)

AO/Bn XO/HSC Cdr – Major Vern R. Ashbrook (AGR)

Sup Tech – Sergeant First Class Jaime Smith (AGR)

Sup SGT – Staff Sergeant Alfred "Sonny" Hendrix (AGR)

MPT – Chief Warrant Officer Four Robert D. Graves (AGR)

PSNCO – Sergeant First Class Gene Paine (AGR)

Commo NCO – Specialist Four David A. Brown (AGR)

Motor NCO – Sergeant Melvin Merley (AGR, later Tech when OMS was authorized)

Ops NCO – Sergeant First Class Charles "Corky" Connell (AGR) (later became CSM)

Co A Tng Officer – Chief Warrant Officer Four Rex Bowen III (AGR)

Co A Tng NCO—Sergeant First Class Norman Crowe (AGR)[11]

Co B Tng Officer – Chief Warrant Officer Four Dennis L. Stedman (AGR)

Co B Tng NCO – Sergeant First Class Ron Freeman (AGR)

S-1 – (initially Captain Garry O. Bentley[12] (M-day); not an authorized AGR position.) Later auth/filled as AGR by Major Arthur Kveseth (October/November 1983). Major Marvin D. Roberts later replaces Kveseth as S-1 AGR ca 1987/88 and remained as the S-1 in the 1/245th.

S-2 – (initially Captain Dave Walton[13] (M-day); not an authorized AGR position.) First AGR S-2 was Major Elbert R. "Ray" Poole.

S-3 – Major Jack L. Brayton (AD Army Advisor – May 1982 to ca January 1985; later filled as AGR by Major Larry Graham from Cache, OK. Graham was the S-3 for approx. one year. Major Billy R. Wood was the AGR S-3 from January 1986 to August 1987. Captain Bryon L. Barnhart was hired AGR as the Plans Officer ca May/June 1986.

S-4 – (initially not an authorized AGR position[14]) Major Tony E. Boyle[15] (M-day) 1 May 1982 – 21 September 1983,

MAJ Lewis Keller

then Major Leroy A. Wall (M-day effective 11 December 1983) (FT – Tech Cdr at TUL AASF; later Major Lewis "Lew" Keller (AGR ca 1986)

Safety – (FT AGR position not authorized until 1/245th) CW3 Clay Mitchell (AGR)

Auto Maint Tech – CW3 Donald Roush (M-day) (Oklahoma Highway Patrolman)

CW3 Jaime N. Smith

Co A (MH-6 Lift) Cdr – Major Don Shroyer (M-day)
Co B (AH-6 Attack) Cdr – Major Richard Murphy (M-day/Tech AASF #2)

The Bn Cdr's, CSM's, Army Advisor's office and recruiter's cubby hole was on the immediate left as you entered the main, west entrance of the armory and the latrine was opposite on the right. Next on the left or north side of the hall was the S-1/Admin shop. On the right hand or south side of the hall was the larger S-3/Operations shop. "The S-4/Logistics office was adjacent to the S-3 complete with a walk though door which we blocked with a desk and dead bolts. Our Supply room took up two bays of the motor pool [We built the new] Arms Room in the S-4 office made from 8"X8"X16" cinder block filled with reinforced concrete and topped with a solid concrete cap or top with we sometimes used for storage," stated former supply SSG Alfred L. "Sonny" Hendrix.[16] The Commo area was near the Supply storage area.

"The last offices on the north side were used by the Unit Trainers (CWO Bowen, SSG Crowe, CWO Stedman, SFC Freeman; later Mitchell & Arnold). The drill floor was chipped and broken and had basketball goals/nets at each end. Next to the S-4 office was the S-2 Intel Office. To the south of the drill floor was the [enclosed] motor pool area. It had an office and [make shift] living quarters where CW4 Bob Graves stayed [during the week]," remembered CW4 Jaime N. Smith.[17]

LTC Garry O. Bentley

"We froze in the winter (I had to brush snow off my desk some mornings) and baked in the summer. In between, we rescued locals from the flooding caused by Sperry Creek. The [armory] facility was inadequate in every way the OKARNG could make it. Didn't impress too many visitors even if we tried to clean it well, the sandstone just flaked off the walls and dusted down everything. It was a busy time though; we were building and training the unit. We were always busy trying to make the next training operation [or deployment] go or running unit schools. The staff meetings were always bloodshed, commanders blaming the staff for problems and proposing solutions in their favor. The early years were highly emotional and charged with politics and empire building . . . Coordination was difficult at Sperry; we had limited telephone and AUTOVON lines. Seems the S-3 was always on the AUTOVON or wanted us to get off so he could make a call. Even the distance between the [Tulsa] AASF [#2] and Sperry caused miscommunication problems. Not being face to face made things more difficult by an order of magnitude," said LTC Kveseth.[18]

SFC Norman Crowe

Many 45th Avn Bn soldiers either came from career military families and/or were career military themselves. One such soldier's soldier was Norman Wayne Crowe Jr. Norm's father (NWC Sr.) was a retired USMC SgtMaj. Norm was born at Camp Pendleton, CA, but graduated from Tulsa Central High School in May 1968 and joined the Marine Corps as he left high school. After 10 years active duty (USMC) including one tour in Vietnam, he got out of the USMC on 12 July 1978. Norm returned to Oklahoma and joined the OKARNG on 16 July 1978 as a member of Tulsa's Det 1, 445th Avn Co.

Norm recalled, "We replaced the 120th Med Bn in Sperry and they moved to Broken Arrow. We moved from the 15th Street armory and the flight facility [Tulsa Flight Activity] was still located at the nose dock [at the Tulsa ANG]."

"I was the Cmd SGM at the time for Dale Martin. Vern [Ashbrook] went from being the unit Cdr of Co D (-) [149th Avn Bn] to the Bn XO. I think he was the Bn XO/HSC Cdr. Also at the same time he was the OIC of the armory," Norm continued.

At this time Corky Connell was the Operations NCO and later he and Crowe swapped positions.

"Jack Brayton, who was our Army Advisor for the State of Oklahoma, he moved in to be the Operations Officer. A lot of people didn't like Jack. I had my run-ins with him and we kinda had a mutual respect of each other. Basically, we were on the same sheet of music. We were moving from the traditional Guard concept to a new Special Operations concept. We had a little bit of feed [back or help] from Task Force 160th back then . . . they weren't a [SOA] regiment [yet]."

"We were trying to build this unit and get it together. So Jack stepped on a lot of toes, but at the same time he held their feet to the fire. Trying to get these guys away from what I called a Flying Club. It definitely was that, they flew to White Horn Cove [on Fort Gibson Lake] to get dinner, flew up to other places, like the Red Barn I forget where that is . . ."

" . . . Vern had a lot of [prior] active duty, I think he had about ten years of active duty before he got out and came to the Guard. Jack Brayton of course was a Major and had about 10-12 yrs in . . . he knew what was going on. I myself was full-time – I had 10 yrs active duty—of course I had the Marine Corps concept, "Kill 'em first and let God sort 'em out," in my mind."

"MAJ Martin was a good commander, but he was your traditional guard guy, but also he kinda understood the concept of where we needed to go to . . . OK. But also I think he was a good politician too. For the first year we were trying to develop concepts. Build a training program that was operable, because when we started out as counter-terrorist force, working towards having a mission during the 1984 Olympics in LA."

"The first year was doing all the exceptional planning and how we were going to do the mission. Because we didn't have an ARTEP (Army Readiness Test and Evaluation Program) [for a Special Operations or counter-terrorism aviation battalion]. We had no MOS producing school for the OH-6. In May [1982] we only had two or three vanilla birds.[19] They weren't special mission operating birds. They started the flight training [OH-6 qualification for pilots] with those birds getting people up to speed."

How did the unit qualify and train the enlisted mechanics to become 67Vs?

Norm recalled, "OK, the first AT we went to Gulf Port, MS. All those 67N [UH-1 repairman from Co D (-)] and 67Vs which was also the MOS for OH-6, but they were all OH-58 guys [from Co D (-)]. All the mechanics went through a Familiarization School there on the OH-6 for 2 weeks. The pilots at the same time started their flight training there. At Gulf Port what happened [was], the Task Force 160th sent down their old birds, we picked those birds up at Gulf Port and flew 'em to Tulsa. There was like 18 birds we flew back to Tulsa. I might be wrong but that's what I remember."

"Of course, [SSG Don] Russell was already MOS qualified [as a 67V] on the OH-6 because that was what he did in Vietnam. He got a Bronze Star with a combat "V." After that [Gulf Port] what we did was OJT training [home station] and it was kinda hap-hazard the first couple of years. The full-time guys picked it up a lot faster because they were doing the maintenance all the time."

"In September of 1982, I went AGR and I became the Plans & Tng NCO for the battalion. I dropped a rank from 1SG to SFC. I was in charge of all the training for all the MOSs. What we tried to do was send those who could go – send 'em to a full-time [residence] MOS producing school to get trained."

"Our second AT was Yuma, AZ and we started doing our mission planning. I started working on the mission cells; I made the routes, time, distance and heading type of deal, navigation. We still didn't have GPS back then. Everything was done by dead reckoning, using major points on a map. What Jack did – he held them to task and what we'd do is draw up these missions. I'd be in a jeep with a radio. At each check point they (aircraft) were supposed to call in "Lunar One-One" at ACP (aerial check point) One or Aerial Checkpoint Two," whatever the point was along the route. I would stand there with a [stop] watch and a clipboard and see 'em fly over and as they reported in I'd write it down."

The original names on the roster were from varied places, backgrounds and of course had mixed skills and abilities. Most of them are no longer living or working in Oklahoma and several are deceased. I thought you might be interested in some of the comments about them, from those who knew them.

First Bn Cdr – MAJ/LTC Dale E. Martin (1 May 1982 to 2 October 1983) Dale was a full-time ARNG Technician (Tulsa Flight Activity Cdr) and had been in Tulsa for several years. Previously, he had commanded Det 1, 445th Avn Co (guns) and Co D (-) (Attack Hel) 149th Avn Bn at Tulsa. He was promoted to Lieutenant Colonel on 27 September 1982. Many consider Dale Martin "one of the nicest guys I ever met." However, he had a problem which, " . . . had a negative effect on his ability to function as an officer." Dale had a brother, Doyle, who was also an Army aviator in the OKARNG. Dale later retired to Shawnee, OK and died on 9 March 2004.

Bn XO/HSC Cdr – MAJ Vern R. Ashbrook (May 1982 to 7 April 1984) He graduated Army flight school in Warrant Officer Class # 69-5 and served in Vietnam with Trp A, 228th CAV, during 1969-70. He came to the OKARNG at Okmulgee, as a Sec Ldr in HHC (-) 120th Eng in February 1978. He became a Plt Ldr in Co D (-) in October 1979. He followed MAJ Dale Martin as the next and last commander of Co D (-) 149th Avn (16 June 1980—31 June 1982). As an M-day soldier Ashbrook lived in Stillwell, OK and farmed there; he became AGR in May 1982 and relocated to Claremore, OK. He was married and had two sons in high school during the days at Sperry. "Yes, he was a chicken farmer who wore his coveralls to drill and changed [into his uniform] there. "He'd bring farm fresh eggs and give them to soldiers at drill." He was tall 6" 2", weighed about 212 lbs and shaved his head. Those are the unbiased comments. Other comments were all quite biased, but still quite interesting. At least half of those asked liked Ashbrook. "He was pretty much liked and respected." Some even said, "Ashbrook was a GREAT leader, supervisor and ass kicker and was well liked by all of the AGR personnel at Sperry." Others commented about Ashbrook, "He could be abrasive, was bullheaded and locked horns with his superiors a couple of times. He was fair and I think everyone who knew Vern knew exactly where you stood with him, especially the people at OMD headquarters." One individual recalled, "You have to remember, back in the early 1980s, the people who ran the Operation (OKPOT I think) were [M-day personnel] from the 45th (SEP) Infantry Brigade and the [OK] USP&FO [branch] was ran by [M-day soldiers from] the 45th Field Artillery Brigade. The implication was that OMD, the 45th Inf Bde and some in the 45th FA Bde were not in favor of OKAVN being in charge of or in control of anything, certainly not their own destiny. Vern always had trouble with the politics of the State Headquarters. I think that was his demise." He had quickly adapted to the 45th Avn Bn's classified mission and supported it possibly with too much enthusiasm.

This was the beginning of the ongoing conflict with OKPOT which we in OKARNG aviation created unwittingly. When a higher headquarters staff officer asks a question about your unit's mission, its night training, its next deployment and night vision goggle training, even though your mission is classified SECRET, you don't have to respond with a cute or sarcastic reply, like "It's classified, if you don't have a need to know, I can't tell you!" Thus began what we'll later refer to as the 45th Avn Bn's Turnpike War with OMD. Tulsa to OKC via the Turner Turnpike was about 120 miles and you logged two hours windshield time enroute. However, it was like visiting behind the Iron Curtin during the Cold War.

Additionally, it's not nice to fool Mother Nature! And it's also not nice to go over the heads at OKPOT. The Deputy Chief of Staff for Plans and Operations, or any higher headquarters, active or ARNG for that matter doesn't like it when one of their subordinate units communicates directly with National Guard Bureau Headquarters and especially directly with Department of the Army. To make the situation worse, the golden spigot (black Special Ops money, officially called P-11 funds[20]) direct to the 45th Avn Bn only exacerbated the problem between OMD and the Little Bird unit at Sperry-America.

"... There was a lot of direct communications between our unit, namely Martin, Ashbrook, Brayton, Barnhorst and Batey [directly with NGB] and DA. And OMD did not like it one little bit. There was some talk about OMD ciphering off some of the funds [P-11] that were authorized specifically for the [45th Avn Bn] unit and using it for other Oklahoma assets. I know that OMD was going bananas because for a period of time DA was talking directly to the Big Four[21] in Sperry and OMD was being left out of the picture. I think it was eventually resolved, but for quite a time there was quite a bit of animosity between OMD and the SOB (Special Operations [Avn] Battalion)," said CW5 Robert D. Graves.[22]

For reasons some deemed correct and others did not—it was suggested to MAJ Vern R. Ashbrook that he resign from the OKARNG. He did and left the 45th Avn Bn officially on 7 April 1984.[23]

Active Duty Army Advisor – MAJ Jack L. Brayton (November 1982 to June 1984)—was a tall, white headed and an serious officer. He had previously been assigned in the Senior Army Advisor's office at OMD. Brayton was said to have been a great organizer. While at Sperry, he completed a master's degree in psychology at Oklahoma University. Some said that he was a hard headed and arrogant guy and I don't think anyone liked him. On the other hand he did a lot of hard work for the unit. He is credited with having lots of enthusiasm for the new mission and was quite serious about the training necessary to meet the standards. Initially, as the S-3 he had major trouble with the OH-6 pilots, due to the fact they had to learn NVG flying with the incredibly unsafe and uncomfortable, full face, AN/PVS-5A NVGs. The pilots didn't like it one bit, but at that time the 5s (NVGs) were all the Army had—period.

Active Duty Army Liaison/Advisor – Major Bill Barnhorst (May 1982 – ca May 1983) – was assigned to Sperry simultaneously with Brayton and Weber. "He was a small guy. Here we are again seeing human nature at work – some see the glass half empty, some see it as half full. Some members of the Bn seemed to think, he was pretty competent at what he was sent here to do. His liaison job was pretty easy and I think there was an initial stand-off attitude from the 160th towards the 45th Avn Bn. You know – active duty guys (TF 160) working with those weekend warriors! Barnhorst helped bridge that problem and got us the information we needed. He would go to TF 160th and [find out] how they got permission [or a waiver] to do something . . . [then] he would let us know. We never felt like he was sent here to keep tabs on us and our abilities or to do anything but help," said LTC Kveseth.

And then there were these comments from the other side of the room and I paraphrase: He was supposedly an Army major assigned to Task Force 160th; however, no one ever saw him in an Army uniform. His principal job was to be our aviation liaison with TF 160. He was purported to be an OH-6 and logistics SME (subject matter expert). He spent very little time working at Sperry or at the Tulsa Flight Activity. He was gone more than was normal and never where he said he'd be. Most former Lords of Darkness say that Barnhorst was not OH-6 qualified, nor was he NVG qualified.

One of his several nicknames was the "Ghost." More than a few former early unit members were convinced that "MAJ" Barnhorst was at least involved with, if not an agent of the CIA. Certain sources alluded to a bank account or safety deposit box having in it the sum of $100,000, designated for use by MAJ Ashbrook and the 45th Avn Bn in the event the 45th was called up on short notice to be deployed for a major event (mission) overseas. One source recalls that "He often picked up two men in civilian clothes at the Tulsa airport and would meet with them behind locked doors at the armory. He also rode a motorcycle to work, although to my knowledge that is not a prerequisite for being a CIA agent.

I asked one senior individual if he had heard this rumor and if he thought Barnhorst might have been a CIA agent? And his reply was, "I seriously doubt it. I don't think he was smart enough to be CIA."

He went on to add, (paraphrased) ' . . . he [Barnhorst], Ashbrook and Brayton seemed convinced that in the near future the Army would control the 45th Avn Bn and that NGB and OKARNG would not have any say about it. The new chain of command would be direct to Task Force 160th and DA. They [same three guys] had been pretty much undercutting Dale Martin.'

"Barnhorst and Brayton? You bet I remember them, from day one! Brayton was a military smartass; I offered to whip Brayton's ass more than once when I was S-4 in the BN," stated Colonel Tony E. Boyle[24] the second commander of the 45th Avn Bn, Tahlequah, OK.

[MAJ Bill] "Barnhorst, Advisor and LNO to TF 160th had tried [unsuccessfully] to get OH-6 NVG qualified on four or five previous occasions. He'd hit the 90 day wall and come back to fly again on day 95. The IPs would tell him, "Nope, you gotta start all over." So one night I flew with him all night and signed him off as "NVG qual." The guys were asking me, "Why did you sign him off?" I signed him off, because we'll never see him again! He won't come back and fly NVG, I know what I'm doing," CW5 Tommy Klutts.[25]

CW5 Tommy Klutts Jr.

The following quote points out the intensity, immediacy, high priority and deep, deep pockets of this little black aviation unit located in Sperry in 1982: "I can tell you that Ashbrook, Brayton, Barnhorst and myself were at one time on worldwide, open, travel orders. We were issued DD Form 1610s that allowed us to travel anytime, anywhere in the world, by any means of transportation, up to and including chartering aircraft," statement by CW4 Jaime Smith.[26]

Active Duty Army Advisor – Major Dwight C. Cheek (spring 1984 – November 1986) – MAJ Cheek, before coming to the 45th Avn Bn and the Sperry Armory, attended OH-6 transition at Fort Indiantown Gap, PA. In my opinion he was smart, but also very egotistical. He was easy going and primarily beneficial to our battalion headquarters' staff. One of the staff officer subjects on which MAJ Cheek felt he was highly qualified to teach was the Army's *FM 101-5 Field Manual – Staff Organizations and Operations*. He was able to get through our thick heads the benefit of preparing a proper staff estimate, a logistics estimate, a full blown staff briefing, etc. To his credit, our battalion staff studied, learned and became very adept at researching, preparing and presenting an outstanding military staff briefing for upcoming 45th Avn Bn events, operations and large scale missions to our battalion and company commander(s). His love for FM 101-5 amazed me because he himself, even as a bachelor, never found the time to complete the Army's CGSC (Command and General Staff College) mandatory course (mandatory only if you wanted to be considered for promotion to LTC/0-5).

"[MAJ Dwight Cheek] . . . was an effective advisor for the unit. He understood NG politics and the personalities involved. He gave some good advice on many matters, but concentrated mainly on staff actions and planning. When he started talking about FM this and that, I would inwardly groan because he was right and it meant a lot of writing and research. The man loved Operation Orders; I think he read them for entertainment on the 'Crapper'. He contributed a lot and was always there to assist, and in some cases defended the way we did our business," said LTC Art C. Kveseth.[27]

MAJ Cheek retired from the Army to Florida and does survey work for large housing developments.

Throughout the first 60-90 days the battalion concentrated on hiring a skeletal full-time staff, recruiting unit aviation personnel, making the restationing move and moving OH-6A aircraft from various points all across the United States to Tulsa, OK. Enlisted personnel attended AT

CW5 Donald McCarty

in Gulfport, Mississippi in order to learn maintenance procedures on the OH6 aircraft. Pilots performed their 15 days of AT by transitioning to the OH6 at numerous different locations such as Fort Indiantown Gap, PA, Long Island, NY, Tupelo, MS, and Denver, CO.

"Yes, it was Islip [Long Island MacArthur Airport], NY and there were three[28] of us who went to pick up the OH-6s . . . The [OH-6] aircraft [tail numbers] were 140 and 249; the Task Force [TF 160] still has 249, and 140 was crashed while at Tulsa," recalls CW5 Don McCarty.[29]

Don asked me this bit of trivia: "Did you know that all U.S. Department of Defense aircraft, receive their tail number assignments from the U.S. Air Force?" No and I was surprised.

Morale was extremely high and the intensity of standing up this one of a kind aviation organization was unbelievable. Yet there were some fun times during those days. Ms. Jeanne Ulrich, former secretary and Action Officer for John J. Stanko Jr. at Edgewood, MD recalls, "Oklahoma's Special Op unit was working so hard and diligently, picking up OH-6 aircraft from many different locations to fill their new unit. They came to Maryland to pick up another OH-6 Little Bird and were shocked to later find out that this particular aircraft had been scheduled to become a permanent static display aircraft on a pole in Maryland!"

"Well, we were . . . out of the way. No one just happened to stop by; you have to make it a point to go to Sperry. The town's people liked us being there from the start. We were certainly a boost to the local economy and we were by far the largest employer," stated Don McCarty.[30]

The first and initial 45th Avn Bn (Lt Hel Cbt) Table of Distribution and Allowances (TDA) was NGW7QQAA issued with an effective date (EDATE) of 1 May 1982. This TDA showed the battalion having an H&S Co (136 pers), Co A (41 pers) and Co B (26 pers) for a total of 203 officers/warrant officers/enlisted required and authorized. The Avn Unit Maint (AVUM) Co was added in July 1984 as Co "C" (AVUM), 45th Avn Bn (Lt Hel Cbt). Within the next three—four years the total strength of the 45th Avn Bn would exceed 440 personnel and additional AGR positions were added each year until ca 1987/88.

An advanced copy of a new TDA NGW7QQAA with the CCNUM NG0284 was issued with an EDATE of 1 April 1982. This new organization had a Headquarters and Service (H&S) Co, Co "A" (lift) w/15 ea. OH-6, Co "B" (attack) w/8 ea. OH-6, and Trans Acft Maint Co. This advanced copy (printed on 840404 2047 hrs, showed 23 officers, 45 warrant officers and 162 enlisted personnel required/authorized for a total of 230. This document was exciting and decidedly inaccurate. It contained numerous errors: mathematical totals, was lacking things needed and included many things not needed.

Over the years untold changes were forthcoming from NGB and the Pentagon. Requests for changes to existing and/or future TDA/MTOEs came from the battalion on a regular basis. Like the old saying, change doesn't necessarily mean progress, but progress necessitates change! CWO Jaime Smith became the unit SME (subject matter expert) on formulating changes to the TDA or MTOE documents. He was often assisted by MSG Carroll B. McBride and/or the author.

In 1983 someone, perhaps at NGB or OMD decided it was un-American for a unit, especially a battalion not to have a Mess Section (cooks, pots and pans)! On 14 April 1983, LTC Dale E. Martin, Cdr 45th Avn Bn sent a letter to the Oklahoma Military Department, Attn: ACofS Aviation, Subject: Elimination of Mess Section from Proposed TO&E (table of organization and equipment), with the following justifications:

2. b. "Present and future training for IDT[31] will continue to require elements of the 45th Avn Bn to perform IDT on at least two separate weekends per month."

3. "The duration of drills are from 1800 hrs, Friday, through 2000 hrs, Sunday and require personnel to report at various locations and times, i.e. the armory at Sperry, the AASF, which is 15 miles away and then proceed to various field locations."

4. b. "One flying company reports at 1500 hrs, Saturday and are released on completion of mission, Sunday evening, with the other flying company personnel supporting the following weekend."

Naturally the OKARNG ACofS Avn (State Avn Officer, Colonel Batey) recommended approval and forwarded the request up to NGB. It was approved. The 45th Avn Bn never had a TDA Mess Section and was either provided support by the customer or by contract meals.

Other items of note/dates of interest:

1 November 1983 – 45th Avn Bn (LHC) was officially attached to Trp Cmd (Avn) (OMD orders 90-11)

February 1985 – counter-terrorism mission changed to support of SOF

1985 – 45th Avn Bn was CAPSTONE aligned to 1st SOCOM, Ft Bragg

16 January 1985—TF 160 transferred from 101st Airborne Division to 1st SOCOM.

16 October 1986—Task Force 160 was redesignated 160th Special Operations Aviation Group.

1 November 1985 – Co B 149th Avn is attached to 45th Avn Bn (LHC)

1 October 1986—Co B 149th Avn is reorganized into 45th Avn Bn (LHC)

1 June 1987—45th Aviation Battalion (LT HEL CBT) was redesignated 45th Aviation Battalion (SP OP) (ABN).

1 October 1987—45th Aviation Battalion (SP OP)(ABN) was re-designated 1st Battalion 245th Aviation (SP OP)(ABN).

Why Tulsa? Did Tulsa, Oklahoma, its location and many fine qualities have anything to do with NGB selecting Oklahoma to be home for the counter-terrorism aviation unit which became the 45th Avn Bn (LT HEL CBT)? I would be hard pressed to prove it one way or the other, but I do believe that John Stanko was aware of the potential that Tulsa had with its existing commercial aviation resources in the area. He knew from Batey's many conversations that recruiting would not be a problem and that many advantages existed.

Stanko, Weber and Walker knew Oklahoma and they knew of Batey's enthusiasm and ability to get things accomplished.

MG Mickey Walker, DARNG at this time and from Mississippi, had first hand military experience in Oklahoma just prior to WWII. He had been sent to Camp Gruber (just east of Muskogee, OK) to train up before he was shipped overseas as a Combat Infantry Officer in WWII. In the mid-1980s, the author personally flew him from Tulsa International Airport down to Camp Gruber, OK, on the east side of the Arkansas River. His eyes glistened with tears, as foregone memories of early days in the military reappeared in his mind; he pointed as he looked down out of the UH-1 at what had been the original streets of the Army training camp long ago of Camp Gruber in the early 1940s.

First, the decision to give OKARNG the new counter-terrorism aviation unit and mission had already been made. Perhaps Tulsa was a factor in that determination, or not. Tulsa was and still is the second largest city in Oklahoma, and by far the most progressive. For certain there was an excellent Recruiting base there and in the surrounding areas. And military facilities were available and already existing – Tulsa ANG ramp, hangar and limited office space. The old WPA Sperry armory was also vacant and available.

The Oklahoma Air National Guard (OKANG) already existed on the north end of the Tulsa International Airport. Their military ramp could handle C-130s, C-141s and also C-5As. They also had ANG Military

COL Billy R. Wood, U.S. Army (retired)

Security there and additional USAF Military Police from Tinker AFB were available if and when needed. Therefore, future 45th Avn Bn deployments of Little Birds and personnel on USAF C-130s or 141s would draw little additional or unusual attention. Since there was an ANG base and certain Air Force facilities, Air Force aircrews would find Tulsa a convenient place to stop in on deployments – it was already user friendly to the boys in blue.

Tulsa International was (and still is) an American Airlines hub and within a 30 mile radius, there are many varied aviation businesses and support facilities in existence. Thus there was already a sizeable pool of possible aviators, mechanics, avionics personnel and other skills available on the spot. Some of these people were prior military service individuals who wanted to complete their military time in the Guard so that could retire after 20 years of service. Maintaining unit strength for the 45th Avn Bn over the next 12 years wasn't going to be a problem and most often we were authorized to be over strength and usually were.

As those of you familiar with the 45th Avn Bn know, it was a covert unit, we weren't looking for publicity, we didn't advertise our existence and we tried not to draw unnecessary attention. Therefore, the WPA Armory in Sperry America was ideal. Sperry was small, secluded, and was 12 miles from our front door to the ANG ramp at Tulsa International Airport, a 20 minute drive.

It was so quiet at Sperry and those 20 inch thick stone walls were so sound deadening that we hardly drew any attention from the local police and passersby when we would occasional shoot a new, young soldier who was reported as AWOL (absent without leave) for missing a drill weekend. We didn't have to shoot too many,[32] then word got around quickly and attendance at drill became every soldier's priority!

Another major advantage of our physical location was the relative short distance from Tulsa to military/civilian training sites nearby:

a. Camp Gruber, OK—approx. 60 miles

b. Davis Airfield, Muskogee, OK – approx. 60 miles

c. Fort Chaffee, AR – approx. 140 miles

d. John Zink Ranch, 10-15 miles SW of Sperry

e. LZ Disney, near Disney, OK and Lake of the Cherokees – 65 – 70 miles NW

If any discussion occurred at Department of the Army or at National Guard Bureau about where to locate this new unit, it might have been in regards to quick response time and time to reach a target located within the contiguous 48 states or anywhere US personnel and assets were located and/or deployed. Assuming this discussion involving times and distances might have taken place, here are some interesting stats:

a. Approximate air miles from Tulsa to San Francisco, CA – 1,470 sm

- +/- 3.9 hrs via C-130H
- +/- 2.6 hrs via C-141B

b. Approximate air miles from Tulsa to Boston, MA – 1,390 sm

- +/- 3.7 hrs via C-130H
- +/- 2.5 hrs via C-141B

c. Approximate air miles from Tulsa to Houston, TX – 435 sm

- +/- 1.2 hrs via C-130H
- +/- 0.8 hrs via C-141B

d. Approximate air miles from Tulsa to Minot, ND – 865 sm

- +/- 2.3 hrs via C-130H
- +/- 1.6 hrs via C-141B

e. Approximate air miles from Tulsa to Miami, FL – 1,170 sm

- +/- 3.1 hrs via C-130H
- +/- 2.1 hrs via C-141B

It seems possible, if not probable, that a military planner or strategist might look at a map of the United States and notice that Oklahoma is almost dead center of the lower 48 states. Tulsa, for all of the other reasons stated above, is also equal distance from the left and right coasts. OK, it isn't exactly half way north and south, but name one large city of strategic importance in North or South Dakota, Minot AFB is admittedly of strategic importance, but the population there is almost nil.

Whether there was any discussion about Tulsa before Oklahoma found the jackpot at Caesar's Palace in 1980 we will never know. Yet as a former planner and operator, the question will remain one of interest to me, an old military retiree with a growing interest in history.

Just like Adjutant Generals, armories come and go; sometimes they might be resurrected. As of December 2006, there were 130 different OKARNG Army organizations from the JFHQ (Joint Forces Headquarters—OKC) down thru the detachment level in the state of

Oklahoma, located in sixty-three different locations (armories, aviation and maintenance facilities) and/or cities. Tulsa has eleven and Lexington has eight of those 130 entities, however, those numbers are fluid and change frequently.[33]

Today the old 1937, WPA Sperry Armory is in use as a Community Center for the residents of Sperry America. It is located on the east side of N. Cincinnati Ave, a half block north of East Main Street.

45th Avn Bn (SO)(A) Armory (May 1982—August 1989), N. Cincinnati St, Sperry, OK

Take time some weekend and drive over to Sperry. Walk through the old WPA armory; get a burger at the café. It's an interesting little place.

Although the old armory has changed very, very little since 1940, many other things changed dramatically. This extremely small, complicated, covert aviation battalion grew and matured over the first few years. Army Advisor, MAJ Dwight C. Cheek made the comment to COL Dana D. Batey, OKARNG SAO, in late 1986, "Sir, you don't need an Active Duty Advisor anymore! This unit can do the job!"

---

1. LTC Arthur C. Kveseth

2. Original Federal Recognition certificate Perm Order 24-2 dated 27 April 1982

3. From 1/245th Avn (SO)(A) unit history by LTC Marvin D. Roberts

4. CW4 Jaime N. Smith became the first and only PBO for the 45th Avn Bn and 1/245th SOA.

5. Telephone conversation SFC Norman W. Crowe Jr., 30 December 2007

6. Email LTC Arthur C. Kveseth, 16 December 2007

7. Not until April 1987 was (Lt Hel Cbt) dropped and (SO)(A) added.

8. CW4 Jaime N. Smith, CW5 Robt. D. Graves, SFC Norm Crowe, SFC "Sonny" Hendrix, CW4 Bobby Lane, CW5 Tommy Klutts, BG Terry Council, CSM Charles Connell, MAJ Ramon Claudio Rivera, COL Gary Elliott, LTC Arthur Kveseth and LTC Mike Bedwell.

9. Email CW5 Robert D. "Bob" Graves, 1 December 2007

10. MAJ Dale E. Martin was promoted to LTC effective 27 September 1982, data provided by email COL David W. Brown, 27 November 2007

11. Full-time Tech at Tulsa Flt Activity, then AGR Plans NCO at Sperry in September 1982 per email Norm Crowe 27 November 2007; Crowe and Connell 'flip' positions, Connell became CSM and Crowe became Ops NCO

12. Email CW5 Robert D. "Bob" Graves, 27 November 2007

13. Ibid

14. Email CW4 Jaime N. Smith, 28 November 2007

15. Email CW5 Robert D. "Bob" Graves, 27 November 2007

16. Email SFC Alfred L. "Sonny" Hendrix, 12 December 2007

17. Email CW4 Jaime N. Smith, 16 December 2007

18. Email LTC Arthur C. Kveseth, 16 December 2007

19. OH-6A aircraft that was not a 'mission' bird configuration, just plain 'vanilla'

20. Department of the Army funds specifically designated for Special Operations Forces equipment, training, etc.

21. LTC Martin, MAJs Ashbrook, Brayton and Barnhorst

22. Email CW5 Robert D. Graves, 11 December 2007

23. Orders 61-3 OMD 840323 amended by orders 72-10 OMD 840401

24. Telephone conversation COL Tony E. Boyle, 20 November 2006

25. Telephone conversation CW5 Tommy Klutts telephone, 18 December 2007

26. Email CW4 Jaime N. Smith, 9 December 2007

27. Email LTC Arthur C. Kveseth, 16 December 2007

28. LTC Michael Bedwell, CW5 Don McCarty and LTC Garry O. Bentley

29. Email CW5 Don McCarty, 20 November 2006. CW5 McCarty retired as a Tech from the Tulsa AASF #2 in 2001; remained in OKARNG. Called back to activate duty in 2002; assigned as an MTP - Task Force 160th at Fort Campbell, KY for 14 months. Don retired again December 2003.

30. Email CW4 Jaime N. Smith, 9 December 2007

31. Inactive Duty Training (normally drill weekends)

32. Just kidding!

33. Email MAJ Hiram Tabler, Force Integration Readiness Officer, JFHQ-J3-MR, 2 December 2006

Chapter 13

Counter-Terrorism or Special Operations?

"What gets us into trouble is not what we don't know, it's what we know for sure that just ain't so."

Mark Twain

The new aviation battalion stationed at Sperry, OK on 1 May 1982, with its *Little Birds* hangared at Tulsa International Airport was to have a unique name, yet definitely one that was richly and deeply associated with the 45th Infantry Division of WWII and Korean fame.

The 45th Avn Bn (LT HEL CBT) was the official, first, unit name given. This was the first military unit with a sub-name Light Helicopter Combat. This covert or black specialized helicopter unit had something else quite unique. It was specifically designated as a counter-terrorism aviation organization. This was right before the term *Special Operations* came into popular use. The phrase " . . . it will be a mirror image [of the Army's Task Force 160]" was heard often in the halls near the offices of Deputy Chief of Staff for Operations (DCSOPS) in the Pentagon in 1981/82.

Nearly thirty years after the unit was 'Federally Recognized' at Sperry, we Americans are all too familiar with the word/term terrorism. In the early 1980s, as a result of terrorism against Americans, this small aviation battalion was baptized not by 'fire,' but 'desire' – the 'desire to serve.' We made the team, but didn't get to play in the finals.

We watched on television the events of 5 September 1972 in the Munich Olympic Village after five Palestinian Arab terrorists wearing track suits climbed a tall fence and in the early morning hours and were met inside the fenced area by three others who used fake credentials to gain entrance. During the next 24 hours, 11 Israeli athletes/staff, five terrorists and a German policeman were dead.

The Islamic terrorists made demands for the release of 200+ Palestinian prisoners held in Israel and for safe passage out of Germany. A hostage rescue plan was formulated as negotiations proceeded, which included moving the hostages and terrorists by helicopter to a nearby air base to board an airliner.

Around 3:00 a.m. 6 September, the rescue plan failed miserably at the NATO air base, as a bloody firefight ensued between the Palestinian terrorists and the Germans. During the rapid exchange of bullets, the Palestinians exploded a grenade in one helicopter, killing all aboard. Terrorists onboard the second helicopter executed the remaining, blindfolded Israeli hostages. Three of the Palestinian Arab terrorists were captured alive and held in Germany.

On 29 October 1972, a Lufthansa jet was hijacked by Palestinian terrorists who demanded that the Munich Muslim terrorist killers be released. The Germans capitulated and the imprisoned terrorists were freed.

Seven years later in November 1979, hundreds of angry, militant Iranian students in Tehran enveloped the American Embassy and took 66 hostages. Six months later on 24 August 1980, a U.S. Joint Military Force implemented a hostage rescue mission known as Operation Eagle Claw. It ended in disaster at the FAARP called Desert One, 300 miles south of Tehran. The failed rescue attempt was very costly – " . . . in the flaming funeral pyre of Eagle Claw's shattered hopes, they left the bodies of eight brave men."[1]

Fifty-three[2] of the original 66 American hostages in Tehran would languish in isolation and imprisonment until 20 January 1981 when they were released after 444 days in captivity.

""The nation was embarrassed, the Army was embarrassed, special ops was embarrassed," a retired Special Forces colonel said. Desert One was a disaster. For 25 years, the message that has been given to the senior leadership of the special operations community has been: No matter what else you do, no matter how much it costs, we will never have another Desert One. . . . It is not surprising that for 25 years . . . that has been the priority."[3]

Desert One wasn't the first use of special commandos or special operators. It all began many generations, many ages ago, but not long after the first battle between early warriors.

"During the 15th century B.C. on an unnamed day between the years 1475 and 1449, the Egyptian King Thutmosis III decided to attack the port of Jaffa. He entrusted the operation to a Captain Thute . . . Thute had a fine sense of the economics of warfare. The perfect operation . . . was one in which the gains were out of all proportion to the numbers of men and material used . . . Instead of pitting his men against the port's substantial defenses, he decided to take it from within . . . He selected 200 crack troops . . . baled [them] in flour sack[s] [while] others disguised as laborers, carried them from the docks to a point well within the walls. The parceled warriors . . . cut themselves loose and took the garrison by surprise. Jaffa fell at a moderate cost. Captain Thute can be fairly described as the world's first commando leader."

The utility and benefit of hand selected, skillfully and specially trained, highly motivated and organized *Special Operations Forces* to achieve tactical advantage has been recognized since even before the time of Thutmosis. When properly employed they are combat multipliers by achieving surprise, exercising economy of force, outmaneuvering the enemy, attacking his most vital facilities, and destroying or capturing areas critical to his operations.

Place yourself in Sperry Oklahoma, fifteen months following the release of the American hostages from Tehran, May 1982. It is not hard to imagine that soldiers and town's people are speculating as to what connection may exist between this new 45th Avn Bn with its classified counter-terrorism mission and the upcoming 1984 summer Olympics to be held in Los Angeles, CA.

The major west coast newspapers of Simi Valley headlined stories about what might happen at the Olympics. City fathers of the Los Angeles metroplex, the governor and state legislators of California, heads of the Los Angeles Olympic Planning Committee, conducted hundreds of hours of closed door meetings in Sacramento and other key locations, with the International Olympic Committee officials, Interpol, FBI, CIA, ISA and Pentagon officials. The subject of those meetings was one in the same as concerned private citizens of LA, local government officials and the

International Olympic Committee – possible terrorist attacks at the Los Angeles Summer Games of 1984.

Does the term counter-terrorism or anti-terrorism come to mind?

Was there any connection between the fielding of the 45th Avn Bn (LT HEL CBT) in 1982 and the known possibility of terrorist attacks at the LA Games in 1984? Perhaps? It seems feasible, doesn't it? Can I prove? No.

The military defines *terrorism* as "the unlawful use or threatened use of force or violence against people or property to coerce or intimidate governments or societies, often to achieve political, religious, or ideological objectives." (*JCS Pub 1-02*)

Then how do they define *counter terrorism (CT)*? "Offensive measures taken to prevent, deter, and respond to terrorism; taken to oppose terrorism throughout the entire threat spectrum." Let's also include a short definition of *anti-terrorism* – "the defensive measures taken to reduce the vulnerability to terrorist acts."

Is there a major, significant difference between counter-terrorism and special operations? Not anymore. What began as the highly specialized, resource-intensive mission of counter-terrorism some thirty years ago is the essence of the Global War on Terrorism (GWT) performed by SOF. Although the Joint Pubs still list a definition of *CT*, it isn't often verbalized. More prevalent is the use of the generic special operations.

The term *special operations* or *Special Operations Forces* sound relatively new, yet strangely familiar when you watch the evening network news. The term isn't really new at all. We are not the only nation whose military uses these terms. The meaning, however, is less specific and many older soldiers might have to tap dance a little if asked to define *special operations*.

Department of Defense (DOD) defines *Special Operations* as operations conducted in hostile, denied, or politically sensitive environments to achieve military, diplomatic, informational, and/or economic objectives employing military capabilities for which there is no broad conventional force requirement. These operations often require covert, clandestine, or low visibility capabilities. Special operations are applicable across the range of military operations. They can be conducted independently or in conjunction with operations of conventional forces (Afghanistan and Iraq) or other government agencies and may include operations through, with, or by indigenous or surrogate forces. Special operations differ from conventional operations in the degree of physical and political risk, operational techniques, mode of employment, independence from friendly support, and dependence on detailed operational intelligence and indigenous assets. The term is also abbreviated SO, e.g. 45th Avn Bn (SO) (A) and the (A) is of course for Airborne.

Army Special Operations Forces — those Active and Reserve Component Army forces designated by the Secretary of Defense that are specifically organized, trained, and equipped to conduct and support special operations. Army SOF is also called ARSOF (JP 3-05).

Covert Operation — An operation that is so planned and executed as to conceal the identity of or permit plausible denial by the sponsor. A covert operation differs from a clandestine operation in that emphasis is placed on concealment of the identity of the sponsor rather than on concealment of the operation. (JP 3-05)

The term *Counter-Terrorism* might be easier to define and perhaps require less tap dancing. DOD defines *counter-terrorism* as operations that include the offensive measures taken to prevent, deter, preempt, and respond to terrorism. It also is the defensive measures used to reduce the vulnerability of individuals and property to terrorist acts, to include limited response and containment by local military and civilian forces.

1st Special Forces Operational Detachment – Delta (SFOD-D) is one of two of the U.S. government's principle units tasked with counter-terrorist operations outside the United States (the other being Naval Special Warfare Development Group – formerly SEAL Team 6). *Delta Force* or just Delta, was secretly organized in October 1977 and continues today as a counter-terrorism element, capable of performing surgical actions around the globe, to include aggressive hostage rescues or other scenarios. They are also utilized as special operators/agents on the ground in unconventional warfare such as Afghanistan, Iraq, Kuwait and other lesser known trouble spots on the globe.

They, Delta, are not the only agents or special operators in this field of U.S. military players. More often the 45th Avn Bn (LT HEL CBT) and later the 1st Bn 245th Avn (SO) (A) supported various special operators/agents such as Special Forces Groups (SFG) (Green Berets) and Navy *Seals* (SEAL Team 6 at Coronado, CA) over the 12 year period 1982 to 1994. The Special Forces customers we supported included: 1st SFG, 5th SFG, 7th SFG, 12th SFG (USAR), 19th SFG (ARNG) and 20th SFG (USAR). Any of these above mentioned operatives, can perform counter-terrorism missions today and at the same time are always considered *Special Operations Forces* or SOF.

A unit's mission statement, sometimes its unit designation or how a unit is employed or utilized today determines if it is specifically counter-terrorism or other. Case in point, the original Department of the Army directives or mission statement for the 45th Avn Bn (LT HEL CBT) at its inception in 1982 was counter-terrorism and was classified SECRET. Note—I have paraphrased the original mission statement; it is not intended to be word for word as issued in 1982. The 45th Avn Bn's official mission statement was changed in 1987 from *CT counter-terrorism* to the broader role of *Special Operations*, yet the words of the mission statement hardly changed.

(former classification)
SECRET
"COUNTER-TERRORISM" MISSION STATEMENT
45th Avn Bn (LT HEL CBT)
1 May 1982

The 45th Avn Bn will be prepared to conduct precise, covert counter-terrorism helicopter penetration, insertions, exfils, resupply and other aviation support of CT personnel, worldwide, undetected, under low visibility, at or below 300' AGL, using the cover of darkness and NVD (night vision devices) with minimal illumination, over short to medium distances (300-600 nm), delivering CT personnel and/or cargo to their designated target within +/- 50 ft and within +/- 30 seconds time on target.

(former classification)
SECRET

The definition of *unconventional warfare* is "a broad spectrum of military and paramilitary operations conducted in enemy-held, enemy-controlled or politically sensitive territory. Unconventional warfare includes, but is not limited to, the interrelated fields of guerrilla warfare, evasion and escape, subversion, sabotage, and other operations of a low visibility, covert, or clandestine nature. These interrelated aspects of unconventional warfare may be prosecuted singly or collectively by predominantly indigenous personnel, usually supported and directed in

412

varying degrees by an external source or sources during all conditions of war or peace. (JCS Pub 1-02) Also called UW.

From the beginning of warfare, clandestine or covert military operations have been incorporated into the preparation for and conduct of war—before, during and even after battle. What has changed? Well, for certain today's military special operations forces are trained in very unique, very specific military skills and trades, such as aviation, armament, parachuting skills, medical, communications, shooters, swimmers, demolition, language and another list of additional skill identifiers, ad infinitum.

Under the umbrella of counter-terrorism today there are different branches of the services which have a few different specializations, e.g., the Army has Delta Force, officially known as the '1ˢᵗ Special Forces Operational Detachment – Delta (SFOD-D). The Navy has the *Seals* and the Air Force has the 1ˢᵗ Special Operations Wing and 27ᵗʰ Special Operations Wing including MC-130s, AC-130 Gunships, MH-53Js[4] and CV/MH-22s—assigned primarily to Hurlburt Field, Eglin AFB, FL and as of August 2007 to Cannon AFB, NM.

I admit it, I'm very biased, but, "Why does the USAF have a 6ᵗʰ Special Operations Squadron – the US Air Force's (own) equivalent of the Army's Green Berets." They have never wanted us (the Army) to have fixed-wing aircraft and I'm against them owning helicopters. However, don't let me hear you call them wasteful spenders of taxpayer's money. There must be a damn good USAF-reason that we have a duplication of effort betwixt and between the services.

U.S. Special Operations Force is the official category under which the U.S. DoD lists the U.S. military units that have a training specialization either in unconventional warfare and/or special operations. There are some 50,000 soldiers, airman and Naval special operations personnel resident in the Army, Navy and Air Force branches of service.

"U.S. Army General Bryan "Doug" Brown, as USSOCOM Commander, . . . worked to transform special operations, which included a 20 percent increase in the size of the force and a 50 percent increase in the budget. It also includes a mindset that brings with it a tenacity that says, "I have a job to get done. How can I best get it done?"" said USMC GEN Peter Pace, Chairman of the Joint Chiefs of Staff (September 2007 to September 2009) at Brown's retirement.[5]

United States Special Operations Command (USSOCOM) MacDill AFB, FL

Army:
- US Army Special Operations Command (USASOC) Ft Bragg, NC
  - U.S. Army Special Forces Command (USASFC—Green Berets)
    - 1ˢᵗ Special Forces Group – Ft Lewis, WA (PACOM)
    - 3ʳᵈ Special Forces Group – Ft Bragg, NC (EUCOM)
    - 5ᵗʰ Special Forces Group – Ft Campbell, NC (CENTCOM)
    - 7ᵗʰ Special Forces Group – Eglin AFB, FL (SOUTHCOM)
    - 10ᵗʰ Special Forces Group – Ft Carson, CO (EUCOM)
    - 19ᵗʰ Special Forces Group – ARNG – UT & WV (PACOM)
    - 20ᵗʰ Special Forces Group – USAR – AL (SOUTHCOM)
  (12ᵗʰ Special Forces Group (USAR) was deactivated 1995)
  - 75ᵗʰ Ranger Regiment (Rangers)
  - 160ᵗʰ Special Operations Aviation Regmt (Abn) (Night Stalkers)
  - US Army John F. Kennedy Spec Warfare Center (USAJFKSWCS)
  - 95ᵗʰ Civil Affairs Brigade (Airborne)
  - 4ᵗʰ Psychological Operations Group (Airborne)
  - 528th Sustainment Bde
  - Spec Ops Support Command (SOSCOM)

Navy:
- US Navy Special Warfare Command (USNSWC) Coronado, San Diego, CA
  - Naval Special Warfare Group 1, Coronado, CA (Seal Teams 1/3/5/7)
  - Naval Special Warfare Group 2, Little Creek, VA (Seal Teams 2/4/8/10)
  - Naval Special Warfare Group 3, Coronado, CA (SDV Team 1)
  - Naval Special Warfare Group 4, Little Creek, VA (Special Boat Teams 12/20/22)

- Naval Special Warfare Group 11, Coronado, CA (Seal Team 17/18)
- Naval Special Warfare Center, Coronado, CA
- SEALs (Sea, Air, Land)
- Naval Special Warfare Development Group (formerly SEAL Team 6 – CT unit)
- SEAL Delivery Vehicle (SDV) Teams
- Special Warfare Combatant – craft crewman (SWCC boat teams)

Air Force:
- Air Force Special Operations Command (AFSOC) Hurlburt Field, FL
- 23rd Air Force, Hurlburt Field, FL
- 27th Special Operations Wing (27th SOW) Cannon AFB, NM
    - 3rd Special Operations Squadron (MQ-1 Predator UAV) Cannon AFB, NM
    - 73rd Special Operations Squadron (MC-130W) Cannon AFB, NM
    - Air Force Special Operations Command (AFSOC) spokeswoman 1st Lt. Amy Cooper said "CV-22s and Hurlburt-based AC-130s also would move [from Hurlburt to Cannon]."
- 919th Special Operations Wing (AFRES) (919th SOW) Duke Field, FL
- 193rd Special Operations Wing (ANG) (193rd SOW) Harrisburg, PA
- Air Force Special Operations Training Center, Hurlburt Field, FL
- 720th Special Tactics Group, Hurlburt Field, FL
- 352nd Special Operations Group, RAF Mildenhall, U.K.
- 353rd Special Operations Group, Kadena AB, Japan

Marine Corp:
- Marine Forces Special Operations Command
- Marine Special Operations Regiment
    - 1st Marine Special Operations Battalion
    - 2nd Marine Special Operations Battalion

415

- • 3rd Marine Special Operations Battalion
- • Marine Special Operations Support Group
- • Marine Special Operations School

In reference to the catastrophic events at Desert One and the failed rescue attempt, "Now all of that changed on Sept 11, [2001]," a retired SF colonel said. "The number one priority of the nation for special operations was no longer episodic direct action (DA) to surgical standards. . . . Everybody recognized we had to be able to do unconventional warfare like we did in Afghanistan, but many places at the same time. And everybody understood that it was no longer about airplane takedowns and ship recoveries and these episodic events, it was about a sustained presence in a country to destroy an infrastructure."[6]

It would be very naive to not expect any changes to have occurred in Special Operations Aviation (SOA) during the past 25 years. I don't claim to know of all the changes made and won't attempt to list them. There have been more than we can discuss at this time. However, the golden spigot, that unending flow of U.S. Congressional dollars into the black world for new equipment, more training and more troops, has not even slightly been reduced. However, one has reason to believe with the 2009 economic downturn it is possible the flow may be slowed. Yet with the GWOT (now called *Overseas Contingency Operations* by the new Obama administration) still going on, who's to say that it might even be increased?

One can read various newspapers, magazine articles and Congressional Reports on what the Senate Armed Services Committee plans for FY 2010 and you'll be hoping your 'one-aspirin-a-day' regiment will indeed prevent a heart attack.

It all started with the Little Birds (AH/MH-6s) in TF 160 and 45th Avn Bn ca 1980. The Boeing (McDonald-Douglas) (former Hughes model 369) OH-6 Cayuse was first test flown in 1963 and fielded in Vietnam in 1968. It was resurrected for Special Ops in 1979, refurbished, and modified repeatedly. The versions used today are based on the civilian MD500/530MG series of helicopter built by Hughes and then McDonnell Douglas. The 500/530 (AH/MH-6J) can be distinguished by its five bladed main rotor and "T" shaped tail and are used today by the 160th SOAR.

The Sikorsky UH-60 Black Hawk was first flown in 1974 and later UH-60s reached operational status in 1978 and were fielded to priority Army units soon after. In the 1980s the MH-60s became the prime movers for Army SOF.

The Army triad of SOA helicopters was completed with the addition of a tried and true heavy lift workhorse, the Boeing MH-47D Chinook and later with the fielding of the MH-47E with its long range/aerial refueling capability and some with the new All Weather Capability (AWC). The CH-47 was delivered to U.S. Army units in Vietnam during 1962. There were 12 MH-47D produced, eleven of which are still in service. Boeing produced 23 MH-47E (aerial refueling probes) and delivered the upgraded MH-47G in 2008. Many MH-47s are forwarded deployed.

During the aforementioned timeframes the USAF has depended on two stalwart, aircraft – the C-130 Hercules and the MH-53J Pave Low helicopter. Both have continued in service for the Air Force SOA until recently. The MH-53J was also refuelable in flight, but it is an ancient airframe and destined for retirement soon, after 25+ years of service to SOA. The MH-53s were scheduled to be replaced in September 2008 by the new CV-22 V/STOL tilt-rotor aircraft. The same is basically true of the C-130 but its latest upgrade the "J model" continues to be procured by USAF and DoD into FY 2008. As of 2010, you'll still see MH-53s flying for the Air Force.

What will be the predominant new SOF airframe/capability for the 21st century? DoD authorized R&D for a new conceptual vertical take-off and landing (VTOL) aircraft in the 1990s – a combination of rotary-wing versatility, vertical lift/flight, with the speed and long range of fixed-wing aircraft. It was developed as the CV/MV-22 Osprey and built by Boeing.

About 1992, Lieutenant Colonel Billy R. Wood, Major Terry R. Council and Major Jackie L. Self, all members of the OKARNG (Self and Council both Oklahoma AASF Commanders at that time, were also members of the 1st Bn, 245th Avn (SO) (A)), flew to Pennsylvania at the invitation of Mr. Harry Frazier, Boeing Military Sales Representative. The purpose of the visit was to tour the Boeing CH-47D production line at the Ridley Park, PA plant on the Delaware River near Philadelphia. OKSOA was anticipating receiving CH-47Ds for the 1/245 SOA and we all were interested in learning about future enhancements from the factory.

While there, Harry arranged for our group to tour a V-22 Osprey prototype. The Osprey had first been flown in 1989. At that time six prototypes had been built by Boeing, but aircraft #5 was the subject of a fatal crash which killed one of the Boeing test pilots. All V-22s were grounded and the future of the program was in doubt. We visited the somber test flight section area and walked through a V-22 prototype. The size of the engines/rotors compared to the fuselage was so out of proportion; it is a very unusual airframe.

While attending a 174th AHC Association Vietnam annual reunion in Fort Walton Beach, FL years later in May 2006, Carolyn and I were riding our 'bike' west on US Hwy 98 towards Hurlburt Field at Eglin AFB. The former 20th Special Operations Squadron (USAF) is located near the approach end of runway 36 at Hurlburt. Over the field about 1,000 ft AGL and flying northward were several CV-22 Osprey tilt-rotor aircraft. In September 2006, my wife and I were on another one of our motorcycle adventures, this one to the Grand Canyon. As we approached the east side of Amarillo, TX on I-40, I noticed two aircraft about 2000 ft AGL and making about 150 kts toward the Amarillo International Airport and pointed them out to Carolyn. The aircraft turned out to be Ospreys from the Bell manufacturing plant at Amarillo.

It was some 16 years ago, ca 1991/92 that I saw firsthand the new tilt-rotor V-22 aircraft during early prototype testing. And how long have we seen the UH-1 Huey or the C-130 Hercules in service? Well over 40 years each! It takes lots of time and fists full of dollars to field a new airframe. Sometime up to 10 years for development. Once an airframe is fielded you can anticipate a 25 year useful life program. Then the SLEP (Service Life Extension Program) kicks in to give you another 10—15 years of additional use. Yes, the pendulum swings, but it does so very, very, very slowly.

The CV-22Bs have been fielded to the USAF train the trainers facilities at 58th SOW, Kirtland AFB, NM and to the Air Forces first CV-22 combat squadron, the 8th Special Operations Squadron at Hurlburt Field, Eglin AFB, FL. Their SOA primary mission is "to insert, extract and resupply unconventional warfare forces inside hostile territory. The Air Force plans to have 50 CV-22 by FY 2017.

However, the biggest "Hoorah" comes from the USMC guys, the primary customer for the CV-22. In September 2007, the first combat squadron, USMC VMM-263 Squadron (the Thunder Chickens) deployed to Iraq with 10 operational CV-22Bs at Al-Asad Airfield, +/- 100 miles west of Baghdad. VMM-263 Squadron is U.S. based at New River Air Station,

Camp Lejeune, NC, where the USMC has about 40+ CV-22s. To date the USMC has received more than 52 Ospreys from Boeing.

The military originally planned to operate 458 Ospreys, with 360 in the Marines and the others between the Navy and Air Force. The Osprey costs taxpayers roughly $89—100 million each, including R&D. The CV/MV-22 has a cruise speed of 230/240 kts, a range of more than 2,500 miles and can carry up to 24 combat equipped troops or 20K lbs of cargo.

"The current SOF aircraft inventory consists of modified C-130s and a variety of Army and Air Force helicopters which provide tremendous combat capability to the warfighting CINCs. However, none of these combine the speed, range, survivability, and vertical lift capabilities required to conduct SOF missions. The current C-130 fleet has the required speed and range, but lacks the ability to land on unprepared airfields and landing zones used routinely by helicopters. SOF's existing helicopter fleet is among the most technologically advanced in the world, but lacks the speed and unrefueled range necessary to conduct sensitive missions deep in enemy territory within one period of darkness, or without the requirement of refueling in hostile or denied areas."[7]

"The CV-22 alone combines combat capabilities needed on the modern battlefield with speed and range of fixed-wing aircraft and vertical performance of a helicopter. This combination will enable it to fill a niche no other aircraft can approach. Increased SOF mobility in terms of range, speed, survivability, and rapid responsiveness is more critical than ever for meeting difficult operational environments, both current and projected."[7]

"USSOCOM has now been resourced across the FYDP (future years defense program) with a plus-up of more than $7 billion and 4,000 additional personnel to develop the additional capability required to build a robust capability aimed at fighting a global war on terrorism over a sustained period of time."[7]

"Our Air Force Special Operations rotary-wing capabilities must remain safe, sustainable and relevant. We are working to ensure the airworthiness and defensive system capabilities of our MH-53 helicopters to allow them to fly in the threat environments they face on the battlefield."

"The heart of our future rotary wing capability as we transform Air Force special operations to the CV-22 is the rotary-wing upgrades and sustainment funding provided for critical improvements to our Army special operations aircraft. These aircraft must be capable of operating at extended ranges under adverse weather conditions to infiltrate, reinforce, and extract SOF. The FY04 budget provides ongoing survivability, reliability, maintainability, and operational upgrades as well as procurement and sustainment costs for fielded rotary-wing aircraft and subsystems to include forward-basing of MH-47 helicopters. In FY04, the Department made a concerted effort to mitigate our most pressing problems associated with SOF low density/high demand rotary-wing assets. In particular, the MH-47 inventory was increased by 16 aircraft in FY04 by diverting CH-47D aircraft from the Army's service life extension program (SLEP) production line to the SOF MH-47G production line to help alleviate USSOCOM's critical vertical lift shortfall due to battle damages. We are grateful to the Army for their support. The MH-60 fleet begins a major program in FY04 to extend its useful life, which will upgrade our MH-60 fleet. Improvements to both fleets will enhance SOF's ability to conduct both medium and long range penetration into denied or sensitive areas. These programs will keep our Army rotary-wing relevant well past 2020."

Special Operations and Special Operations Forces are indeed a costly segment of our U.S. military. Yet they have been and will continue to be a specific priority. The average civilian has no earthly idea of the billions of dollars involved with the recruiting program, training, maintenance of specialized skills and unique equipment, aircraft, boats, overseas training deployments, R & D and payroll of SOF annually. The cost is not just measured in dollars, but also in the sacrifices of the men and women who have chosen this profession. They did so not because of pay or for glory, but because of their love of American freedom. Some have sacrificed a little, some gave it all . . .

Desert One was, in my memory, a long time ago. In reality, it has been 30 years since we heard Carter announce news of the failed rescue attempt and since we saw the horrifying photos of the burned out EC-130 Cow (18,000 gal JP-5 fuel bladder inside) and those six RH-53D Bluebirds left behind at the FAARP near Yazd, Iran.

"No matter what else you do, no matter how much it costs, we will never have another Desert One . . ."

1. Otto Kreisher, "Desert One," *Air Force Journal* (January 1999, Vol. 82, No. 1).

2. Thirteen of the original hostages (mostly blacks, a few women, and several with medical conditions) had been released early on as a sign of good will by the student terrorists.

3. Sean D. Naylor, "Support Grows for Standing Up An Unconventional Warfare Command," *Armed Forces Journal*, (2 November 2007).

4. USAF planned to retire the MH-53J in 2008, (1st Special Operations Wing).

5. Retirement of U.S. Army Gen Bryan "Doug" Brown, Cdr USSOCOM in July 2007.

6. Sean D. Naylor, "Support Grows for Standing Up An Unconventional Warfare Command," *Armed Forces Journal*,(2 November 2007).

7. Statement by GEN Charles R. Holland, USAF, CINC, USSOSOM, Before the House Armed Services Committee, U.S. House of Representatives on the State of Special Operations Forces 12 March 2003.

Chapter 14

Troop Command (Aviation)

"Success is not final, failure is not fatal: it is the courage to continue that counts."

Sir Winston Churchill

From the beginning of OKARNG aviation history, each successive State Army Aviation Officer wanted a legitimate MTOE battalion, regimental, brigade or group aviation headquarters under which all other ARNG state aviation assets could be placed – for command and control. It never quite happened as desired. However, what was achieved, a TDA called Troop Command (Avn), was none-the-less a stroke of genius, applauded by NGB-AVN Director John J. Stanko Jr., and emulated by other ARNG states' SAOs.

The first attempt at an OKARNG aviation headquarters was a TDA organization, formed on 1 October 1978, known as Det 1, Command and Control (CAC) Headquarters, OKARNG. Permanent Order[1] 84-1 formed UIC W7SUA1 as a detachment of W7SUAA, CAC, with 21 personnel plus attachment of 14 more from the CAC. Det 1, Cmd & Control, located at Lexington, OK AASF #1. The first Det 1, Cmd and Control commander was Lieutenant Colonel Ronald L. Howland of OKC ca 1978-1979, followed by Lieutenant Colonel Donald Derrick ca 1979–1981.

Also on 1 October 1978, Major Donald E. Derrick became the Executive Officer (XO) of Det 1 Command and Control and served as XO until 30 November 1979. On 1 December 1979, MAJ Donald E. Derrick who had been the XO, was reassigned to the Bn Cdr position. He was promoted to lieutenant colonel in September 1980 and stayed as Bn Cdr until 31 August 1981.

The 14 attached personnel to Det 1, Cmd & Control (1978) were the Flight Surgeon's Detachment, Aviation Fire/crash rescue, and avionics Direct Support Maintenance Team. On 1 November 1981, Permanent Order 88-1 increased the total to 35 personnel with no attachments. It also included a name change to HHC 145th Avn Bn (Provisional). Lieutenant Colonel Emmett D. McElwain, from Byars, OK was commander ca October 1981–1982.

On 1 March 1983, Permanent Order 21-6 a reorganization which changed the name to Troop Command (Aviation). All detachments of the CAC came under one TDA NGW8A8AA. Troop Command (MACOM Headquarters at 23rd Street Armory, OKC, supported miscellaneous combat support elements, the band, PAD and PAO of OKARNG) became Detachment 1, HQ STARC and Troop Command (Aviation) became Detachment 2, HQ STARC. Strength of Troop Command (Aviation) was now 19 personnel, plus attachment of 20 personnel from HQ STARC, the Flight Surgeons section, Fire/Crash rescue, and Avionics Maintenance.

The mission of Troop Command (Aviation) was to provide command and control, administrative and logistical support, training guidance, training assistance, and day to day supervision for all ARNG aviation assets within the state of Oklahoma. The overall objective for Oklahoma Army National Guard Aviation has been to develop, train, qualify, and sustain aviation personnel at the highest levels of combat readiness.

On 1 August 1984, OMD Permanent Order 60-2 kept the 19 personnel, but changed the accounting by dropping the attachments.

1 October 1985, Permanent Order 74-6 shows Troop Command (Aviation) growth from 19 personnel to 38. On the same order HQ STARC dropped from 312 to 291. OKARNG SAO, Colonel Dana D. Batey had somehow talked the OKTAG (Major General Robert Morgan) out of 21 spaces, which came out of HQ STARC. Troop Command (Aviation) moved in 1985 from the Lexington armory to a wooden, WWII, two story, airplane hangar at Max Westheimer Airfield, Norman, OK.

On 1 March 1988, Permanent Order 20-3 reduced the strength of Troop Command (Aviation) from 38 to 34 due to the move of two flight safety technicians to HQ STARC into the State Safety Office, one warrant officer slot to HQ STARC supply section and one NCO slot to the State Aviation Office. In November 1988, Permanent Order 111-1 shows the strength of Troop Command (Aviation) to be 33 personnel total, located in Norman, OK.

The Troop Command (Aviation) Commanders were: Lieutenant Colonel Ronald L. Howland ca 1983, Lieutenant Colonel Don Derrick ca 1984, Lieutenant Colonel Emmett D. McElwain ca 1984, COL Dana D. Batey (all actual dates of Batey's command are unknown), Lieutenant Colonel James C. Peck 28 February 1986 to 1 September 1987, followed again by COL Dana D. Batey, then Lieutenant Colonel Paul D. Costilow February 1989 to August 1991, then

Troop Command (Aviation) Deactivation—25 April 1993, Norman, OK

Lieutenant Colonel Leroy A. Wall 1 September 1987 to 30 September 1991 and Lieutenant Colonel Billy R. Wood 1 August 1991 to 25 April 1993.

Oklahoma Army National Guard Aviation began an extraordinary era in its history on 1 May 1982, when the 45th Avn Bn (Lt Hel Cbt) was activated. The next eleven years were the most exciting, challenging, unbelievable, exasperating and trying years to be remembered. They were fantastic experience building and developmental years. Everyone involved in Oklahoma Guard aviation at the unit level gained at least the equivalent of a bachelor's degree in aviation force structure and management. Each staff member at the State Aviation Office, Troop Command (Aviation) headquarters and aviation battalion headquarters during these times gained the equivalent of a master's degree in special operations aviation evolution and concept plans.

On 12 July 1989, the Oklahoma National Guard forwarded the initial version of its visionary Special Operations Aviation (SOA) Group Concept Plan through 1st Special Operations Command (Abn) (Brigadier General James A. Guest), Special Operations Command Pacific (Brigadier General Barry J. Sottak), to NGB/DA (Major General Donald Burdick) for staffing, consideration and approval. A refined version was submitted on 14 October 1990 which updated the original SOA GP concept, over the signature of then Adjutant General, Major General Donald Ferrell. It received tremendous support from the special operations community, not including the 160th.

The purpose of the Oklahoma *Special Operations Aviation [Group] Concept Plan* was to show a way to field a critically needed special operations aviation group headquarters AND a second special operations aviation battalion within the Army National Guard. "Additionally, the purpose is to show feasibility and the economics of fielding such units in the Oklahoma Army National Guard," stated the memorandum to the Chief, National Guard Bureau, date 11 July 1989.

A summary of the proposal included the assumption that wartime mission requirements existed for:

- 245th Avn Gp Hqs (SOA) (new – replacing Trp Cmd (Avn))
- 1st Bn 245th Avn (SOA) (existing at Tulsa/Lex)
- 2nd Bn 245th Avn (SOA) (new BN which would include:)
- HHC 2/245th – 2 MH-6B
- Co A 2/245th – 10 C-23B fixed-wing (dedicated procurement)
- Co B 2/245th – 8 MH-6 (existing assets)
- 4 MH-1 (existing assets)
- Co C 2/245th – 1 UH-1 (existing asset) Maint. Co.

The 145th Air Traffic Control Platoon at Lexington would be organic to the 245th Avn Gp Hqs. Facilities for the new units and headquarters were available at Muskogee Davis Field, Muskogee, OK (across the Arkansas River west of Camp Gruber) and Fort Sill, OK in southwestern Oklahoma, as well as Norman, OK.

The most logical idea of this concept plan, in the view of its originators, was its economy of force. The majority of assets already were on-hand in

Oklahoma. The experience of growing the first and only SOA battalion, the 1/245th Avn, had been accomplished and those personnel with the SOA experience remained in the OKARNG. The cost savings to the Army by placing not only a second SOA battalion in the reserve component, but also placing an SOA, functional headquarters in the RC would have been astronomical, in our most humble opinion.

Of course there were negatives or disadvantages inherent to approving the concept plan. First and foremost, the Army would have had to allocate to the ARNG additional manpower slots/spaces, thus increasing endstrength of the Guard, which they are always reluctant to do. Secondly, this was prior to the code being broken on how to get the Army to request that the NGB mobilize/activate a portion of or an entire ARNG aviation unit, i.e., 1st Bn 245th Avn (Sp Ops)(A) to be utilized in a LIC (low intensity conflict) or less than an all out declared by Congress war. This would be seen as saying, "We (the Army) can't do our job without help from little brother." Today activating a National Guard Army or Air Guard unit isn't a problem. It seems now to be done quite often!

BG Barry J. Sottak made the following endorsement in 1989 of the OKARNG SOA Group Concept Plan, "As Commander, Special Operations Command, Pacific (COMSOCPAC) and former commander of Task Force-160, I am well acquainted with special operations forces (SOF) aviation matters—requirements, capabilities and issues. In my view, the single greatest deficiency in the SOF arena today is the shortfall in suitable airlift platforms and trained crews with which to infiltrate, resupply and exfiltrate our forces. The [OKARNG SOA GP] plan, featuring both fixed and rotary wing assets blended into a single SOF organization, offers a cost-effective, near-term capability that will benefit our nation, USPACOM (U.S. Army Pacific Command) and the Army tremendously. Some of the principal advantages that I see follow (edited for brevity by author):

"The Group headquarters could better manage and support training requirements for all SFGs, with primary emphasis[2] on the 1st, 12th and 19th SFG — resulting in improved training readiness and wartime preparedness.

"The proposed fixed wing company adds a totally new and sorely needed dimension to support LIC requirements in Southeast Asia and elsewhere.

426

"In closing, I firmly support and applaud the OKARNG SOF aviation initiative. On behalf of USCINCPAC and CDRWESTCOM, we in USPACOM would like to see such a concept plan proceed without delay," signed Barry J. Sottak, Brigadier General, USA, Commanding.

MG Donald Burdick, Director, Army National Guard at the time, made the following (edited) comments in his response to OKTAG regarding the OKARNG SOA GP Concept Plan submission – " . . . this process will require lengthy coordination . . . We recognize the excellent work Oklahoma is doing in the Special Operations community. Every effort will be made to accommodate your plan in the overall program," signed Donald Burdick, Major General, GS, Director, Army National Guard.

As of 1990, Troop Command (Aviation) had nine officers, five warrant officers, one each E-9, three each E-8s, four each E-7s, three each E-6s, six each E-5s, and two each E-4 positions. These positions were utilized as follows: four in the Command Section, six in Admin/Personnel, six in Operations and Training, ten in Logistics and seven in Airfield Operations. The State Aviation Office had grown from four in 1987 to ten as of April 1990. This was due in part to the addition of three C-12 pilots.

As of the same timeframe, NGR 10-2 provided three possible locations within a HQ STARC for aviation personnel: para. 003G, Staff Aviation Section (SAOs office); para. 003H, Army Aviation Operations Facility (AASFs); and an Aviation Division (position) in para. 006H, Operations and Training (OKPOT). Apparently, OKPOT felt there was a probability that OKARNG was going to receive an SOA Group Headquarters or a Combat Aviation Group Headquarters in the near term. This was also an assumption of OKPOT-MR as of April 1990.

"With the conversion (1987) of the 45th Avn Bn (Sp Ops)(Abn) from TDA NGW7QQAA to the 1st Bn 245th Avn (Sp Ops)(Abn) MTOE 17085HNG30, the staff assets exist to operate effectively without Troop Command (Aviation)," stated the memorandum (for record) to Oklahoma Military Department's Deputy Chief of Staff for Operations and Training from the office of OKPOT-MR (mobilization and readiness office). Albeit technically accurate, thus began the demise of Troop Command (Aviation) – for better or worse.

Regressing several years, I very much want to discuss the subject of the C-23 Sherpa fixed-wing aircraft and how they came to be in the ARNG.

In 2007, the author requested and received from the office of Senator Robert C. Byrd (D-WV) information on the late 1980s procurement of C-23 Sherpas for the ARNG. Information received included excerpts from a 1988 article from *Aviation Week & Space Technology*, "U.S. Army has ordered 10 Short Brothers C-23 Sherpa turboprop transport aircraft to equip units of the Army National Guard. Value of the order is $60 million (plus) and first deliveries are scheduled for early 1990. The C-23 aircraft will replace DeHaviland Canada C-7 Caribou transports." The order was bumped to 30 aircraft with an initial price tag of $144 million." This price didn't include logistical maintenance costs for multiple sites, nor for a C-23 simulator and transitional training for ARNG aviators. Sen. Byrd went on to build a plant in Clarksburg, West Virginia to convert the Shorts SD-360 commuter/transport aircraft into C-23B+ Sherpas. The ARNG also built the FWATS (Fixed Wing Training Site) at Clarksburg, WV and it was manned and operated under the command and control of OSACOM (Operational Support Airlift Command).

It was reported that the mission of the original 16 Sherpa aircraft supplied to the ARNG during 1990-1992 would be "transporting Army Aviation spare parts between NG bases and repair facilities." The author recalls being given the opportunity by NGB-AVN to submit any ideas we (OKARNG) might have regarding use and missioning for the C-23s before they arrived in the Guard. What a wonderful opportunity for Special Ops Aviation.

You see, between 1986—1988, each of the active and reserve component Special Forces Groups lost their internal UH-1/UH-60s (four/SFG) and their fixed-wing (two/SFG) U-6 Beavers, C-7 Caribous or UV-18 DeHaviland Twin Otters. These aircraft not only had provided resupply & log support, but were used for infil/exfil of ODA teams and jump platforms for training and proficiency. Where would the SFGs get their aviation support now? The 1/245th Avn (SOA) provided endless SOA support to the SFGs all across the nation from Fort Richardson, AK to Fort Lewis, WA to Camp Williams, UT to Camp Blanding, FL to Fort Bragg, NC and including Panama, Honduras, Thailand, Australia and other locations. Several of these SFG UH-60s came to 1/245th Avn at Tulsa.

Troop Command (Aviation) saw an opening to demonstrate how we could assist in meeting the Special Forces mission requirements, but also to support National Guard Bureau in finding a legitimate way to utilize the unrequested C-23 Sherpas. These aircraft did not have a statement of need, nor did the Guard or the Army request these aircraft from Congress. They would not have been selected specifically to fill an Army fixed-wing role. We worked nights and weekends, developing, formulating new concept plans which incorporated the C-23s into the special operations arena. Although none of them were approved, all of them got a lot of attention. Yes, I understand that "close doesn't count . . ."

> A "Congressional action in FY 88 and FY 90 directed procurement of 16 C-23 Sherpa aircraft to replace the aging C-7 Caribou fleet at the ARNG Aviation Classification and Repair Activities/Depots (AVCRADs)," stated Major General Raymond F. Rees, DARNG, in a memorandum, dated 6 July 1992, Subject: ARNG Theater Airplane Companies. Included in the memorandum and also in an NGB-AVN Information paper, dated 7 August 1992, by Major Dray, NGB had determined that OKARNG would be the Headquarters for the new first of two C-23 Theater Aviation Company and get two detachments, a total of five aircraft. Operation Support Airlift Command (now OSAA[3]) eventually was responsible for the stationing and issuing of the Theater Avn Co C-23s based on their use and scheduling for OSA missions on a daily basis, through centralized scheduling.

From the beginning of Oklahoma's Special Operations Aviation program in 1982, the GAO reported that the Army Class "A" Flight Mishap Rate was 3.0 mishaps per 100,000 flying hours. This figure dropped to about 1.6 in 1994. These figures are nearly the same as the DoD rate for the same period. The number of Army Class "A" Flight Mishaps in FY 82 was 52 and 20 in FY 94. This was a dramatic improvement and it is also stated that increased Optempo does not necessarily relate to an increase in the rate of Class "A" incidents. However, in 1994/95 it was noted that 73% of the Army's Class "A" Flight Mishaps were attributed to human error.

In July 1991, Oklahoma Army Guard Aviation had a tremendous Flying Hour Program and it was 100% funded by NGB. The Fixed-wing Flying Hour Program projected for FY 92 was 1,600 hours (C-310 750hrs,

U-8F 250hrs and C-12 600hrs). The Rotary Wing Program was 11,657 hours (UH-1 5,089hrs, OH-6 2,968hrs and UH-60 3,600hrs). Support of Special Operations Forces received the majority of the Rotary Wing flight hours: UH-1 75%, OH-6 75%+ and UH-60s 97%+.

We basically got what we asked for in flying hours, fuel and maintenance. And we flew what was received. In my opinion, our higher headquarters considered Oklahoma a viable, reliable and honest broker. We valued our customers and gained their respect.

During the mid-late 1980s and early 90s, OKARNG aviation experienced major shortages of UH-60 and CH-47 AQC quotas, shortages of SOF communications equipment, lacked sufficient Air Force airlift for 1/245th Avn (SOA) for Pacific Theater exercises and a lack of official CAPSTONE affiliation. July 1991, Troop Command (Aviation) briefed expected developments which included:

- CH-47 loaners from 160th (2 A/C)
- MH-47E distribution (16 A/C)
- MH-60K distribution
- C-23 B/C Cmd Avn Co F/W (5 A/C)*
- Delivery of 2 ea U-8F F/W from 1/132nd
- LTOE delay
- Redesignation of 1/245th Avn to become 4th Bn 160th SOAR

As the cliché goes, "Nothing is certain, but death and taxes." It was not certain that Oklahoma would get a Special Operations Aviation Group Headquarters. In the end we didn't. You are told, "Don't take it personal, it's just business, the military way . . ." The 160th became a Special Operations Aviation Regiment (160th SOAR) and they eventually added the 3rd and 4th Battalions of the 160th SOAR. The only way they could afford to add the 3rd and 4th Battalions was to deactivate the 1st Bn 245th Avn (Sp Ops)(Abn).

"Casing the colors"—L-R: SGM David Keating, Cdr LTC Billy R. Wood, SAO COL Leroy A. Wall, Dep TAG BG Donnie Smith

He who has the most marbles gets to make the rules. The 1/245th Avn (SOA) cased its colors in August 1994.

"By direction of the Adjutant General, State of Oklahoma," Oklahoma Military Department, DET 2, HQ STARC, Troop Command (Aviation) was officially deactivated 1 May 1993. All former units of Troop Command (Aviation) were reassigned under the command and control of DET 1, HQ STARC, Troop Command, commanded by Colonel Jerry Grizzle.

The last formation of DET 2, HQ STARC, Troop Command (Aviation) was held at its headquarters/hangar, located at 1625 Westheimer Drive, Norman, OK 73069 at 1500 hrs. 25 April 1993. In attendance was a good friend of ours, Brigadier General Donnie Smith, Assistant Adjutant General and Commanding General 45th Separate Infantry Division.

The Troop Command (Aviation) units at the time of its deactivation were: 1st Battalion, 245th Aviation (Special Operations) (Airborne), commanded by Major (P) Terry Council; Company A, 1st Battalion, 132nd Command Aviation, commanded by Captain Bryan Palmer; 145th Air Traffic Control Platoon, commanded by Lieutenant Michael Thomason; and DET 3, HHC, 1st Battalion, 132nd Command Aviation, commanded by Chief Warrant Officer Jack Milivic. Troop Command (Aviation) was commanded by Lieutenant Colonel Billy R. Wood of Ada, Oklahoma. Sergeant Major David L. Keating of Noble, Oklahoma, was the senior noncommissioned officer. Troop Command (Aviation) had thirty-three personnel. As a MACOM (Major Command) of the Oklahoma Army National Guard, Troop Command (Aviation) was authorized a total of 605 personnel, with 517 assigned and four attached. Fifty-four (54) aircraft were assigned to the various aviation units.

At approximately the same time period, ca 1993/94, Det 1, 45th Sep Inf Bde Avn Section is disbanded.

It has been nearly twenty years since Trp Cmd (Avn) at Norman was deactivated. In the spring of 2009, I asked the Deputy TAG of Oklahoma, Brigadier General Terry R. Council for a list of OKARNG Aviation units. He provided the list and a few days later I was visiting with Sergeant Major Danny Matthews who was at an Aviation Leadership Conference in Fort Rucker, AL. SGM Matthews, formerly a member of the 145th ATC Platoon at Lexington, was explaining the new OKARNG Aviation units, their size, aircraft (or not) and mission. And he began to describe a new aviation battalion-like TDA headquarters. This new unit is called the 90th Troop Command Aviation Battalion, an unofficial name. SGM Matthews said, "Sir, it's like the old Trp Cmd (Avn) headquarters down at Norman."

It is amazing, everything changes, but in the end, it all comes round – full circle. Seems like the truth never changes, " . . . there is a time and a season for all things."

---

1. All Permanent Orders referenced here regarding Trp Cmd (Avn) are Oklahoma Military Department permanent orders.

2. Brigadier General Sottak, Commanding General U.S. PACOM, was of course primarily interested in 1st SFG, 12th SFG and 19th SFGs because they were all apportioned to the Pacific Theater in the wartime OpPlan, as was the 1/245th Avn (Sp Ops)(A).

3. Operational Support Airlift Agency (OSAA) fixed-wing assets as of March 2007 included: 57 C-12s, 41 C-23s, 11 C-26s and 4 UC-35s. Thirteen of those aircraft were deployed to Iraq and Kuwait at the time.

Chapter 15

The Stories You May Not Have Heard . . .

"No storyteller has ever been able to dream up anything as fantastically unlikely as what really does happen in this mad Universe."

Robert A. Heinlein

Sometimes the best things come in very small packages and some of the best aviation stories I've ever heard were quite short. In this chapter I have the opportunity to share with you some of our Oklahoma aviation history in short story form. Most of these OKARNG aviation tidbits didn't exactly fit into another chapter, but were too good to omit. Here's an example . . .

Seven Foot Tall Yucca Plants
LTC Mike D. Bedwell

"Our first Little Bird deployment to Yuma, AZ—damn that was scary," said Mike Bedwell in a long email back in 2003. "We were taking SF guys to a simulated target in the mountains, which they were to blow. The first flight out that night went to the AO, but returned after they couldn't see the mountain pass they were to fly through. I led the flight on the second try and you could not see those mountains at all. I remember seeing a lighted tower on the top of one of the mountains and kept it close off my right for bearing and made it through this time."

"The SF guys blew hell out of the building; you could see it burning for miles. But what I remember most about that mission was the Yucca plants. Once arriving at the AO, our 3 ship MH-6 formation approached and landed in the LZ and off loaded the pax without incident. When I looked out my door I couldn't believe my eyes! Just a couple of yards away were seven foot tall Yuccas—all around us. To this day, I don't know how we landed three aircraft amidst those tall Yuccas and didn't damage a single rotor blade!

"After returning to base, we celebrated at the Marine Corps Officer Club pool that night for lots of reasons! I don't remember who did it, perhaps Bobby Lane, but he rubbed 'chem light' juice all over himself and swam in the pool—funniest thing I've ever seen. I don't know how we managed not getting kicked off the base!

Difference Between a Captain and a CW2
CW5 Tommy "TK" Klutts

Tommy Klutts and I were visiting one day on the telephone and TK was telling me how he got hired as a full-time IP at Fort Indiantown Gap, by Colonel Chet Howard, the Pennsylvania SAO. Howard had been the OKSAO and helped TK get into flight school. During the conversation Howard said to TK, "Hey, I want to you to think about becoming a Warrant Officer." Of course, you know I was a young Captain at this time (1972) and I didn't want to step down to become a Warrant Officer; I wanted to stay a Captain. I was a Captain and a fairly good Captain. Soon I was hired, went to Pennsylvania and went to work at Capital City Airport (New Cumberland AASF)."

Then "TK" said to me, "Billy, do you know the difference between a Captain and a CW2? The only difference between a Captain and CW2 – the CW2 is going to beat that Captain to CW4."

An Orange Inferno Rising from the Brazos River

During the early years of the war in Vietnam, nearly every flight school class of Primary Rotary-Wing Students included several Vietnamese Army or Air Force Flight Cadets. In my ORWAC Class # 66-8 we had five Vietnamese students along with fifty-seven American U.S. Army Officers. In 2004, I was able to contact four of the five Vietnamese classmates; all living now in the U.S.A. except one who now lives in Sydney, Australia.

After some dual instruction out in the confined area and pinnacle areas west of the main helipad at Fort Wolters, TX, the flight instructors would require their students to do some solo work in the confined areas.

After giving his Vietnamese *Flight Cadet* several hours of dual confined area instruction in the OH-23C/D model, the IP would have the student land at the stage field. The IP would get out and off the student would go, heading back to the confined areas.

This one student, whom we'll call Nguyen, was a pretty proficient aviation student. He made a perfect steep approach into confined area. His touch down point was also right on the edge of a high cliff above the Brazos River. Nguyen was in a bit of a hurry to catch the bus that morning at the BOQ and was not able to take his normal morning constitutional . . .

He rolled the throttle to flight idle, tightened the friction on the throttle, centered the anti-torque pedals and cyclic and again tightened the cyclic and collective friction. Although the collective was nearly all the way down, he gave the friction sleeve just one more slight twist and bailed out of the aircraft, with a few paper towels which he carried for checking the engine oil during pre-flight.

Nguyen ran away from the idling helicopter into the tree line along the south edge of the landing zone. He quickly unzipped and lowered his flight suit, leaning his back against a small Mesquite tree about as tall as he was. The wind was to Nguyen's back, blowing toward the helicopter. He couldn't see the aircraft, but could just hear it between gusts of the Texas wind – he left his flight helmet on to save time.

The surface of the LZ is white, chalky, sandstone rocks, a little dirt and even less grass, surrounded by scrub oaks, small, twisting Mesquite trees and some cactus of several varieties. The soft rocks beneath the skids of the OH-23 crunched and the chopper moved left about two inches, which caused the friction on the throttle and collective to loosen. The engine RPM increased a couple of hundred RPM and a gust of wind increased the lift of the rotor disk – just enough.

What had began as a practical exercise in confined area operations – had suddenly deteriorated. However, Nguyen was doing quite well and oblivious to what was happening nearby.

The tail boom and rear of the rotor disk lifted, the skids slid forward as the nose was now dipping towards the river below. Another hot gust was all it took. Imagine the chopper as it tittered briefly and then in slow motion

435

slid over the edge, trimming scrub brush and rocks all down the face of the cliff. As the OH-23 slammed into the reddish brown Brazos River, the cockpit canopy exploded, as the main rotor blades were disintegrating into small slivers of aluminum and honeycomb.

The instruments and radio console flashed yellow sparks, with small clouds of white smoke and disappeared beneath the shallow water. The super hot piston engine ignited the one-third full tank of AVGAS as the tail boom folded and became unrecognizable. The flames immediately formed a brilliant orange-white ghostly ball with lashing wisps of black smoke rising over the river, up the side of the cliff.

Don't worry – no one was onboard! The IP was safely back at the stage field with another student, and Nguyen, well he's OK, but wasn't yet finished with his paperwork in the woods.

Within 30 seconds, another aircraft, this one having two souls on board – another IP and his student flew into the same training area. They saw the smoke, which was now becoming less and less visible, due to the fuel tank being under water. They expected the worst—a deadly crash. It was obvious to the IP, as he lowered the nose of his aircraft; they were going to need help. He expedited getting to the scene of the crash, as he radioed the main helipad and requested "Flat Iron" (Medevac) out to the confined area, "Get them out here immediately, we have an OH-23 that's crashed into the Brazos River."

There wasn't a suitable landing site near the crashed OH-23 in the river. So, the civilian IP elected to land in the same confined area nearest the crash site where he and his student would climb down to the injured men and give first aid. He put the aircraft right in the skid marks of where Nguyen's OH-23 had been, right on the edge of the cliff in the confined area.

Quickly, the Southern Airways IP locked down all the controls and frictions, as he and his student bolted from the cockpit. They didn't remove their helmets, nor their gloves; but heroically begin their dissent down the cliff to the now smoldering aircraft.

As soon as these two began climbing down toward the river Nguyen finished his business in the woods. He zipped up his flight suit and began walking back to his aircraft. "Sure nuff it's still there . . ." He was relieved to see that he did a good job and his "heli-chopper" is sitting right where he left it.

He climbed in, buckled up, released all the frictions on the controls and brought the throttle up to 2300 RPM, completed his before take-off checklist. "Clear left, right, overhead . . ." staring straight ahead at the north Texas horizon, he made a picture perfect pinnacle take-off, oblivious to what was occurring 100 feet beneath the nose of his aircraft.

He waved at the UH-1 Huey "Flat Iron" Medevac aircraft racing past him in the opposite direction, as he nonchalantly flew back towards the main Fort Wolters heliport. What a feeling of satisfaction and confidence Nguyen must have had at this moment. "Isn't this a great country?"

I wonder if Nguyen made it through the war in Vietnam and where he is today.

Somebody Should've Told Me the Gov. Doesn't Like to Fly!
CW5 (ret) Samuel T. Hinch

"Our M-Day gunnery Instructor Pilot, Chief Warrant Officer H.D. Buster Bass, was leaving the 445th Avn Co; Buster was going to college at the time. He recommended to Captain Jim Peck that I go to IP School. Buster was a great guy," said Chief Warrant Officer Samuel T. Hinch.

In June 1976, after returning from UH-1 IP/Gunnery IP training at Fort Rucker, Hinch and his Lexington unit, 445th Avn Co, attended annual training at Fort Chaffee, AR. Former OKARNG Captain David L. Boren, had been sworn in as the new Oklahoma Governor in January 1975. He was visiting the Oklahoma Guard troops at Chaffee and was visiting the aerial gunnery range on this particular morning.

Commander, CPT Jim Peck had assigned the newest gunnery IP, CW2 Hinch to take Gov. Boren out for a gunnery demonstration. Captain Richard O. Murphy was the full-time gunnery IP at the time and Sam was giving Murphy instruction on the new low-level running fire gunnery techniques and procedures he had learned at 'Mother Rucker.' Young Sam Hinch was a Vietnam veteran, who had served with Charlie Troop, 1st Sqd, 9th CAV, 1st CAV Div during 1970-71. He wanted to impress Gov. David Boren, knowing that he had been in the Oklahoma Guard before running for governor. This was a great photo op for Boren and the Lexington gun drivers!

Sam did what every young Army helicopter pilot would have done with the new governor onboard. On take-off he pulled the collective pitch up under his left arm pit, leaned the Huey's nose over and hauled ass. Taking off from the gunnery rearming pad Sam said, "I did a sixty-degree pedal turn as I buried his butt in the observer's seat with collective. Finishing the last low level gun run, I hadn't noticed Boren's white knuckles and that he was leaving finger prints in the armrests where he was seated. After landing, Boren didn't make small talk and left rather quickly. "Somebody should've told me that the Gov. didn't like to fly . . ."

"CPT Jim Peck was watching from the staging area during Gov. Boren's ride along and as we came roaring over the area around 25 feet and 100 kts he was heard to say, "Well, there goes the Governor and my IP . . . It's sorta sad to say, but it'd be easier to replace the Governor that would be to replace my IP.""

Sam wrapped up the story, "This statement was a testimony of the difficulty he [CPT James C. Peck] had getting me funded to attend the IP course at Ft. Rucker. Jim had actually offered to pay my travel expenses since the [Oklahoma] Military Department couldn't come up with the funds until the very last minute . . . But they did come up with the funds and history was made . . ."

The Dirt Drug Strip in Florida
SFC (ret) Melvin Merley

This FAARP story was told to me by Sergeant First Class Melvin Merley, former OMS #18 Shop Chief, Tulsa, OK. Melvin was one of the original members of the 45th Avn Bn (Lt Hel Cbt) and a charter member of the S-4/Logistics Section. He always accomplished whatever mission he was given.

During the days of the *Lords of Darkness*, say around 1984, maybe 1985, Major Jack Brayton was one of the Active Duty aviation advisors for the 45th Avn Bn at Sperry, OK. Jack was also the S-3/Operations Officer for a while and everyone learned to hate him equally well.

The battalion was conducting at least one deployment for training each month, sometimes two. Brayton had scheduled two this particular month. Three C-130s had landed at the Tulsa ANG ramp and the on-loading had begun. Jack Brayton was out to impress everyone.

He had invited COL Batey, the OKARNG SAO, to go along. It was as if, "everyone should enjoy a 4 hour, low-level, flight in a packed C-130. In the cramped, red-lit cargo bay, were two *Little Birds*, their five thin blades neatly folded back, some 15 or so empty five gal jerry cans and a few odd crew members. Their faces were smeared with camouflage paint. There were two other C-130s in this formation, each with two more OH-6s, enroute to Camp Blanding, Florida. Blanding is a Special Forces training camp, airborne drop-zone, and a neat little third world-like runway.

There was the usual Special Ops advance party along with this deployment: an Operations person, several Logistics personnel and sometimes an Admin guy. SSG Melvin Merley and CW3 Jaime Smith, from the S-4/logistics section being two of the key personnel. MAJ Brayton had secretly given SSG Merley his instructions for a special NVG flight by the six *Little Birds* and to set-up an enroute *gas can FAARP* at a little known airport (or runway) he had spotted on a map. Jaime may have been the ranking individual on the advance party and was taking care of business when Melvin left Blanding.

Melvin was to take the rental car van, the fifteen or so five gal cans, fill them with JP-4 and then make haste to the designated remote landing sight Brayton had designated for the FAARP. Once there he was to spread out the cache of gas cans into six locations, one for each OH-6 and place a chem light on each of the six locations. Flight lead, Captain Mike Bedwell, would bring the NVG formation into the landing zone and all six *Little Birds* would land at the same time. The passenger would assist the co-pilot in the refueling their aircraft. Once the entire formation was refueled, Bedwell would give a light signal and the flight would simultaneously take-off for the final target and then back to Camp Blanding. There they would do an engine-running (C-130) on-load and then the USAF air mission commander would tell his three crews to "shut it down for the night. We are now in crew rest!"

Well, that's the way Brayton had hoped it would go. It turned out almost deadly, and lives could have been lost!!!

Melvin got the rental van, filled the cans with JP-4 and left for the landing site where he would set-up the *gas cans FAARP*. He got a little bit disoriented and stopped in a nearby town. When he saw a local constable, he figured he'd just ask for directions. As Melvin asked for directions, the constable slowly moved his right hand over the holster of his 9mm Glock and unsnapped the hold-down strap and gripped the pistol – if Melvin made another move he was dead!

SSG Merley, being from Collinsville, OK and claimed to be a lover—not a fighter! He began explaining why he was wearing camouflage fatigues and had 15 jerry cans with aviation fuel in a rental van – enough to blow up a small five story building. His green military identification card and his TDY orders may have kept him from being shot and bleeding all over the street.

The constable finally laughed and said to Melvin quite seriously, "You know that's a drug landing strip and if you go in there, especially at night, someone's going to get killed! You just need to call your helicopters and tell them to turn around.

Well, Melvin knew the *Little Birds* were already in the air, he didn't know what frequency they were on and he didn't have a radio. Up the ole creek, huh? "Too late to turn back now." (Somebody ought to write a country western song about that.)

He thanked the constable and got back into the van and headed for the landing strip anyway. "How could it be a drug dealer's airport – it's marked on the map?"

Thirty minutes later, he turned the van south, off the main highway onto a soft, sandy dirt road. The palmettos became thicker the farther south he drove, lining both sides of the old road. He drove and drove and finally saw a pale-blue house about where he should make the next turn. As he pulled into the yard, a large, well-dressed, Cajun-looking man with a Panama hat stepped out onto the long front porch. A rifle was cradled in his right arm and it had a nice looking dark leather sling. But what impressed Melvin most was the scope. It was probably a 150X power scope, but it had 'night vision' on it also! Melvin thought to himself, "I'll bet he doesn't hunt crows with that!"

"Who are you? What the hell brings you down my road my man?" Mr. Panama spoke slowly.

"Well sir," Melvin started to say, "I'm with the military . . ." But then he thought maybe he better not. He decided to take the good ole boy approach.

"Sir, I'm here doing some navigational training with . . . ah, for the National Guard. We're not with the Army Sir, I'm from Oklahoma and I live on a farm. I do lots and lots of farming and just a little bit of this Guard stuff, you know?!?!?"

Melvin must have talked so long and slow that Mr. Panama just gave up and interrupted him, rather abruptly.

"Look here young man, I don't know who the hell you are, but I'll tell you this . . . you're standing on Holy Ground! If you go on out to my dirt strip and your fancy little whopper choppers come cruising in here tonight – you all – every one of you'll be plum full of Holy holes! And I don't even plan to follow your dumb ass down there."

Long story short – Melvin is between a Cajun and a tight spot. The *Little Birds* will be on their *low fuel* warning lights when they get here. They have to have fuel. They won't make it back to Blanding without these cans of JP-4. He got in the van and headed through the tall cane toward to Cajun's private landing strip, drug drop-off point and frequently used entry point for illegal immigrants. He saw 'Mr. Panama' shaking his head in the rear view mirror of the van.

It was still just nautical twilight (just before dark), so Melvin drove out onto the dirt strip and set-up his *gas can FAARP*. He decided he wasn't going to wait in the van. He'd just hide in the tall cane until the Lords of Darkness flight arrived.

The next two and a half hours took three days to pass. About 2 minutes before the target time when they should arrive – Melvin heard the sounds of . . . ."That isn't an OH-6 chopper, that's a big mudder. That's a pickup with tires five foot tall and two foot wide. They make a loud, helicopter-like noise when they cruise down the road." Company's coming to visit . . .

One minute before target time he heard the familiar sound of advancing rotor blades slapping against the air. It was the six *Little Birds* no doubt about it! Then a few breathes later, he saw the rotating beacon on the trail aircraft . . .

Mike Bedwell brought the flight perfectly down the west edge of 'Mr. Panama's' dirt strip and was turning onto final . . .

A vehicle's horn beeped, two or three more times. Someone turned on the headlights of a pickup truck. Melvin knew the headlights on the flight would cause the PVS-5 NVGs to shut down, but Bedwell only hesitated a moment, then accelerated to the chem lights by the gas cans and slammed his bird on the ground. Each of the remaining OH-6s did a similar landing.

Melvin thought he heard several shots fired as he ran out to Bedwell's lead aircraft. Once there he gave a brief account of what had taken place. Bedwell broke radio silence and told the flight to load up the gas cans. They would fly away and land five miles down the route and continue refueling.

As the *Little Birds* lifted off and headed east toward Camp Blanding, Melvin did what any TDY Army soldier would do in his rental vehicle

– he gave it the Lords of Darkness rental car test. He revved the engine to about 5,000 RPM, crammed it into reverse, made a new road through the tall cane, turned the wheel 420 degrees left, slammed the transmission back into *Drive* and floored the gas pedal.

Melvin was going about 120 miles per hour when the constable's red lights got his attention.

The constable asked Melvin, "License and registration . . . and do you know you were doing 118 miles per hour when my radar went off???"

"No sir, but . . . ," said SSG Merley.

"No buts young man! This ain't Interstate 10 or any other highway. This is a city street. You must be from Oklahoma!"

Melvin made it back to Camp Blanding after some time and several cups of coffee with the Constable of Stark, FL. He had some new words and a few new names for MAJ Jack Leonard Brayton. COL Dana Batey and MAJ Vern Ashbrook were bent double with laughter and couldn't sleep before the C-130s headed back to the Tulsa ANG ramp next morning.

It was terribly hard for Melvin to trust anyone above the rank of CW4 for a long, long time. He was still a little bit leery of commissioned officers for several years!

I Hear You Sir!
as related by BG (ret) Paul D. Pete Costilow

The Air Commerce Act of 1926 ushered in airline regulation. In 1929 the city of St. Louis hired Archie League, the country's first air traffic controller. The second person hired was Pete Costilow. He used two signal flags to direct airplanes. A red one meant to hold and a black-and-white meant go! In the '30s radios are installed in airplanes and airports. World War II brought radar and the first women to air traffic control. Pete discovered color radar on a slow afternoon at work at Will Rogers.

On more than one occasion Pete and I flew together. One of these flights was in the C-12, I was co-pilot flying right seat and Pete was the PIC in the left. Leaving Oklahoma City airspace, Pete contacted Fort Worth Center, who responded, "Army Guard 24149, you have traffic at 10 o'clock and six miles.

In his normally slow, low voice, Pete replied, "Fort Worth, could you give us another hint, we both have digital watches!"

When interviewing retired BG Paul D. Costilow, I asked him to name one of his most memorable fellow aviators he had served with in the

OKARNG. Pete has one of the keenest minds and most marvelous sense of humor of anyone I've had the pleasure to know. In civilian life Pete was an FAA radar control supervisor for the Will Rogers International Oklahoma City Approach Control segment of responsibility for many years. Pete replied to my question and named Chief Warrant Officer Four Joe Patterson, WWII pilot and former member of the 45th Inf Bde Avn Sec. "Joe was kinda my hero ya know. He was always in a good mood. Always willing to fly, he'd come in on Saturday morning at drill and we were assigning missions. We might have one with a 5:30 take-off in the morning and we were trying to get somebody to volunteer to fly the early take-off mission . . . all the young guys would kinda look at their feet. Joe would say, "Yeah, I'll go." Always had a good sense of humor, kept everybody kinda loose. I heard he had like 30,000 flight hours when he retired."

Pete then told this story about Joe – "I was working one day on the approach control radar board. Joe wasn't even on the picture (radar screen). He wasn't talking to us [OKC Approach Control] or anything. I got a little busy and nobody was answering me – I needed some people [aircraft] to do what I'd told 'em to do. Even the air carriers weren't answering ya know. And I'm thinking, "What the hell is going on . . . ?" And finally I just got frustrated and I said [over the approach control frequency] "Does anybody out there hear me?" And just out of the blue came Joe Patterson's voice, "I hear you Sir!"

Before I could stop laughing, Pete said, "Wait a minute I gotta tell you about this ole guy who flew a red and white Cessna 320 out of Oklahoma City, and I'd seen the airplane down there ya know and the tail number stuck with me. And he'd call OKC approach control all the time. I'd say to him, " . . . this is OKC approach control . . . is that airplane red and white? He comes back saying, "How'd ya know that? And my reply was always, "Well, we do have color radar ya know."

The Honduran Deployments
MAJ (ret) Ramon Claudio Rivera

The Lords of Darkness were making many deployments to Central America beginning in about 1986. At that time, Captain Ramon Claudio Rivera was our Communications Officer for the battalion. Ramon was an M-day aviator who as a civilian worked at Tulsa International Airport approach control for the FAA and later at Will Rogers International in Oklahoma City. In Dec 2007 he shared the following story.

"Recall that on the first deployment we stayed in the city of La Ceiba in the Honduran Army 4th INF Bn compound. Then all other subsequent deployments [to Honduras] we were at Palmerola Air Base, near Tegucigalpa," related Claudio.

"Enroute to La Ceiba joint-use airport, we were in a C-141 and I was in the cockpit talking with the pilots, we were at FL 220 about 100 miles from La Ceiba. The pilots asked the Center controller if they should be talking to the tower by now. The [Honduran] controller came back and asked the pilots to see if they had communications with the tower. They checked the frequency and reported back that they had contact with the tower.

"At FL 220 they switched us to the tower and at 100 miles away the tower cleared us to land. What a country!

"The next day I was asked to go to the airfield and speak with the Honduran Air Force Base Commandant to see if I could solve a problem for them. It turns out that a small detachment of an active duty Army Aviation Unit was operating out of La Ceiba airport and every night they would crank up and go flying NVG.

"The problem with that was in Honduras anything flying between 6 p.m. and 6 a.m. is considered hostile unless you have special authorization. Well, it took some negotiating, but I was able to get the Army guys to come up with a schedule, which the Hondurans approved and they agreed on some special [transponder] beacon codes to use during their night flights. They were one day from getting shot down by the *Super Mistres* that were based at La Ceiba.

"It turns out that one of these [Night Stalkers] Blackhawks went down to the beach one day and decided to play close to the water and their rear wheel hit the water and they almost lost the aircraft. The pilot was the Unit Commander and the Co-Pilot was the Unit Safety Officer. They were both sent home.

"On our second deployment we were at Palmerola AFB. One day Captain Byron Barnhart and I took two *Little Birds* down to La Ceiba to support the 4th INF Bn again. On the way to La Ceiba we stopped at San Pedro Sula Airport to refuel. The gas truck guy didn't want to fuel us because it wasn't worth it for him to drive his truck for a few gallons of gas.

It took a lot of talking and promising him that more *Little Birds* would be showing up in the near future.

"All the Honduran Battalion Cdrs had a big meeting with the head of the Honduran Army at Tela, a place about 50 miles west of La Ceiba. The 4th INF Bn Cdr asked me if I could fly him down to the meeting place. I jumped at the opportunity to give back a little for their hospitality.

"All other commanders arrived in jeeps, pick-up trucks and buses, then all of a sudden here comes this chopper and lands and off came the 4th Inf Bn commander. He had the biggest smile I've ever seen on anybody. Needless to say, he was the envy of all his colleagues.

"A few days later, Lieutenant Colonel Gary Elliott and Colonel Leroy A. Wall show up and visit with us and wanted to fly back with us in the *Little Birds*. We had the *Little Birds* inside the 4th Bn compound and so we had to make a quick flight to La Ceiba to top off.

"Gary jumped in and asked me if he could fly and so I gave him the controls. I was in the right seat and after he took off, he asked which way to turn. Since we had to go in the opposite direction of our current heading, I told him he needed to turn 180 degrees—so it didn't matter. He decided to make a right turn and so we fly to the airport and after landing, I start unbuckling my seatbelt only to find out I never had it on. Had Gary made a left turn, I probably could have gone out the door; because we always flew those *Little Birds* like jet fighters making tight turns.

"After we fueled up and I changed my shorts, we headed out towards Palmerola. Remember the '6 p.m. rule'? Well, we were delayed and 6 p.m. came upon us so we had to think fast. It turns out that we had special permission to fly a bird every night for perimeter security. Since it was somewhat dark when we arrived in the area, we contacted the guys flying perimeter and they flew to where we were and one by one we followed them in and the Hondurans never even knew that there were actually three aircraft flying. All the time they thought that they were seeing the same bird.

"The tower at Palmerola was divided into two sections. On one side there was a Honduran AF controller and on the other there was a USAF controller. If you called the tower and spoke English, then the USAF controller would answer and if you spoke Spanish then the Honduran would answer. The problem was that the Hondurans would forget to tell the American they had just cleared someone for takeoff or to land; consequently, there were many 'go-arounds' at that airport.

Stormy Night at Camp Gruber

"Masterful Sergeant" (MSG) Cleo Franklin Templin's face was nearly always the home of a wide, honest smile. He always had a good word to say and would try to be helpful, especially with new soldiers. He was a great NCO; tell him what you wanted and then get the hell outta the way!

He was a good mentor for the younger soldiers in Troop Command (Aviation's) flight operations section at the Lexington Armory. In the spring of about 1984/85, recruiting was going well and we enlisted a new soldier, a female, Private First Class Diane Stringfellow. She had already attended Basic Infantry Training and was assigned to Trp Cmd (Avn) at Lexington, OK. She was soon going to attend MOSQ and become a flight operations specialist. PFC Stringfellow was very attractive and quite tall, about 6' 2".

Trp Cmd (Avn) had scheduled a Multiple Unit Training Assembly (MUTA) – four UTAs, for later in the spring at Camp Gruber, in the eastern part of Oklahoma. Other units included Co B 149th Avn, commanded by Captain Alfred Dreves and Det 1, HHC, 45th Inf Bde, which was familiarly called the Bde Avn Sec, commanded by Captain Roger F. Ferguson. We had built a training scenario around several 279th Inf units from Tulsa and were planning to do Air Assault troop movements, C & C and some sling-loads for the Infantry with UH-1Ds and OH-58s. The 145th ATC Platoon, commanded by Captain Mayo Elliot, was also incorporated into the training and provided some excellent night air space control and approaches. Everyone involved was looking forward to this exercise.

MSG Templin would occasionally become so focused on his project that everything else sat idle, unless someone else noticed and picked up the slack. That was the case j. MSG Templin had adopted this new soldier and she was to be part of Cleo's Flight Ops Section. He had been a flight operations NCO in the 1st Cavalry Division in Vietnam, around 1965/67. He wore the 1st CAV patch proudly on the right sleeve of his fatigues. Cleo became very concerned about PFC Stringfellow's going to the field (Camp Gruber) with us.

As a mother hen does with her chicks, Cleo watched over the fledgling flight ops specialist. He began planning how he could provide a clean, dry, private sleeping area for Ms. Stringfellow at Gruber and still have everyone in the field. To his credit, he determined that he could convert the flight ops section's M-35A3 2½ ton truck's single axle trailer, after it had been unloaded, into a miniature, olive drab (OD) Holiday Inn Express. He assured her a standard Army issue cot would fit the bed of the trailer, the canvass would provide privacy and that he would string a light bulb to the trailer from the section's 5KW generator.

The week of our MUTA-4 arrived, road convoy clearances had been obtained a week before, ground vehicles and aircraft were loaded, JP-4 fuel tanker filled and checked out, flight plans filed – a small string of olive drab vehicles departed the gate at Muldrow AHP, Lexington onto Hwy # 39 East and the operation began. Aircraft would infiltrate the perimeter of Camp Gruber later in the day, in small groups to avoid detection by the rebels at Bragg, OK. The heart of Bragg, a convenience store which sold beer, was marked on the area of operations map in red grease pencil, and its coordinates briefed to the flight crews as a small, armed, enemy outpost. It was not to be fired upon, nor was it to be captured!

The Trp Cmd (Avn) Cdr and S-3, after having arrived at the AO on Camp Gruber, had obtained an up to date FAA weather briefing for that first evening. The various aviation sections began securing the immediate area, putting out a perimeter of defense, camouflaging tents, vehicles, as ATC began to erect antennae and get their radios up on the net as quickly as possible. The Cdr wanted to get a message out to all of the aircrews that a storm front would be passing through our area later that evening. A tentative aircraft and vehicle evacuation plan was passed on to all of the units/sections commanders.

MSG Templin and crew unloaded the truck and trailer. He gave orders for the location and erection of the GP medium in which most of Trp Cmd (Avn) would sleep. As that was being accomplished, he went to work on the Holiday Inn Express deuce and a half trailer.

Tents, rotor blades and antennae must be nailed down for the possible storm. The sky was black, with the exceptional blinding flash of hot light. The S-3 checked with range control every 5-10 minutes at the Gruber block house on the status of the storm. It was evening and a few soldiers were heating water for their MREs (Meals Ready to Eat), while the old timers used P-38s to open a can of Vienna sausage or Spaghetti-Os and shared crackers from a red and white cardboard container.

The two 100 watt light bulbs hanging from the horizontal ridge pole of the GP medium tent flickered, as the 5KW generator roared to life. Cleo, flash light in hand, ran into the tent to see if he had connected the wiring correctly. The wind outside had become much stronger and howled. The S-3 issued a stand-down order for the evening; further training was cancelled for the night due to weather. The threat of strong winds and storms still lingered.

Lieutenant Colonel Jim Humphrey, the full-time OIC at Camp Gruber, was a good friend of aviation and he too was keeping a watchful eye on the weather. He drove out to our training sight to visit. As he pulled up to our Trp Cmd (Avn) flight operations tent, Cleo was frantically stringing that single light out to the Holiday Inn Express trailer for PFC Stringfellow.

The winds had become stronger and the rain was almost horizontal. Jim Humphrey called back to the block house at Camp Gruber's range control to check on the latest tornado warning. All flights and training had already been cancelled, but crews were on standby just in case we needed to evacuate the aircraft. Everyone else was about to settle in for the night, spreading OD fart sacks on their aluminum cots.

Cleo finished the Holiday Inn Express trailer and had told PFC Stringfellow she could retire to her private sleeping quarters for the evening. She gathered her personal gear and headed out to the trailer.

LTC Humphrey advised us the tornado warnings for our area had been cancelled, even though we were still experiencing some strong wind gusts and lots of rain. Before he could head back out to his pickup, the sky became as bright as daytime. And three seconds later was followed by a rolling, thunderous explosion equal to a case of dynamite. Two more tremendous flashes of hot, white light and ear shattering claps of thunder followed in short order.

Before the echo of the storm's rumbling had subsided, through the door of the tent exploded PFC Stringfellow wrapped in her OD Army blanket. Drenched by the blowing gale and with eyes full of fright, she looked like a lost puppy. She walked hesitantly a few steps further inside our tent, very much embarrassed and pleaded, "MSG Templin, I'm afraid of the storm. Do you think it would be OK if I stayed here—in this tent—with you guys tonight?"

How I Got to Flight School
CW4 Frank L. Berry

Frank Lillard Berry talks kinda slow, but he's smart as a whip. He tells it this way, "I transferred from Co B 180th Inf to 45th Bde Hqs in Ada,

OK and Colonel Barnes was the commander. As a Post Office employee, I would have to take vacation time off to attend some military schools. I still had a couple of weeks vacation time left and I was looking at the military schools catalog and saw Aviation listed in the book. Sergeant Josh Nunley was the AST (full-time Administrative-Supply Technician) there at the Ada armory. I told him I wanted to go to flight school. He said, "You do? Well, let me talk to COL Barnes." He did and pretty soon COL Barnes wanted to talk with me."

"I went in and he asked would if I wanted to go and I told him "Yes, I'd really like to go!" "Well, you've got more than enough points to qualify as a Warrant. If you'll go, I'll get you a Warrant commission!"

So in 1963 the guys at Bde Hqs, they helped me put in my paperwork. I still had to wait on my Warrant Officer commission before I could go. In the mean time the Army's flight school was closed down to National Guard personnel [due to Vietnam]. I loaded up my family and went to Washington, D.C. I marched straight into the Pentagon and found a COL Johnson who was responsible for Army Flight School applications.

Johnson told me how sorry he was and that, " . . . One day Army Flight School will again be available for National Guardsmen." He told me, "Keep your application on file and you will eventually get in."

The problem I faced was that I was 28 years old. In the meantime, Lieutenant Colonel Chet Howard was the OKSAO up at Norman and he said I couldn't go to flight school because it was Oklahoma's policy that our guys had to go through the WOC (Warrant Officer Candidate) program.

COL Barnes and I went before Major General Dougherty who had been my company commander at one time. The decision was made to let me go through flight school as a Warrant, but after that everyone had to go through WOC program.

Soon I got my Warrant (WO1), was still waiting to go to flight school. I served four years as a WO1. We were attached to this unit at Marlow and I asked when I'd ever get promoted to CW2. This guy there at Marlow said, "We can't promote you because you're not MOS qualified. I kept after him and we called NGB and they said, "Yes, you will promote him, because it's not his fault that he can't get into flight school.

I was promoted to CW2 and in 1969 the Army re-opened flight school to the Guard. I went to flight school in Sep 1969 as a CW2 and graduated May 1970.

Abandoned FAARP at Fort Bliss
CW4 Jaime Smith

Jaime Smith gets a bit upset when he recalls this story, but that just shows his loyalty to his men and comrades. Here's the way he remembers the events, "Our new Operations Officer came to the 45th [Avn Bn (Lt Hel Cbt)] right after Jack Brayton left. The new guy was working [full-time as a Federal Civil Service tech] at Fort ___ when he took the job with us. After Brayton, what an enormous let down. We went from the ultimate, confident, hard pressure guy to a . . ."

Have you ever been left behind? Truly left behind – in the desert, with cactus providing what little shade you have and you don't even know if anyone is aware of your dilemma. It can drop to freezing at night in the desert.

This story occurred in June 1985, when the 45th Avn Bn (SO)(A) went to Fort Bliss, TX for annual training. Jaime is still angry as he related this story and it's been abridged quite a bit . . ."From home station [at Tulsa] we deployed our MH/AH-6 aircraft in C-141s to a desert stage field near El Paso. We had the III/V FAARP Platoon make a night [airborne] drop to set up a rearming site. The logistical guys on the advance party (me, Sonny, Merley and others) were picking up the ammunition for a *Little Bird* AH-6 live fire exercise during the first night's mission. The new guy was on the Ops roster for the advance party.

"The deployment started. We had buried a cache of five gallon fuel cans of JP-4 at designated sites. The mission was to land [the C-141s, off-load], fly a selected route, refuel enroute at the five gal can cache, go to the FAARP, arm and then conduct a live fire [exercise] on the firing range. Great idea! The fuel was there; the aircraft flew their route and then rearmed, and then the problems started. The new Ops guy hadn't gotten the [firing] range cleared as planned [and required]. The AH-6 *Little Bird* gunships got to fire a couple of hours late; but not before they got some other unit off the range. It was raining like hell that night. We were all pissed because we had already put in about 14 hours at that point.

[After the AH-6 'live fire' and] "We all got back to garrison, I told Sonny Hendricks to give me a weapons count. We still had 14 weapons not checked in. I had Jim Gaston (my armorer) and Sonny give me the names of the people who had weapons out. It was my FAARP guys. Captain Lew Keller was then the III/V (FAARP) Platoon Leader; I could not find him or anyone else from the FAARP Platoon. I called over to the

S-3 Operations office and got Gary Elliott, the Bn XO. Gary was pulling duty as the SDO (Staff Duty Officer) that evening. EVERYONE in the Ops section had gone to the barracks and called it a night.

"I knew that with the down-pour of rain the desert could be very dangerous. I sent Staff Sergeant Melvin Merley and Sergeant David Brown out in a military pickup to look for the guys. When they didn't find them, I got Sonny and we took the unit's 44 passenger bus out on the range road close to where the FAARP was to be set up. We couldn't find Lew or the platoon either. Now I was really scared for them. We had no radio contact with Lunar Flight Ops, so after about an hour and a half we headed back to the post Ops to see if they had any new information. Still, Gary Elliott was the only person there.

Within the hour we found out that Lew and the platoon had hitch-hiked back to Fort Bliss in the back of some guy's pick-up and was safe. While at Lunar Ops, I asked Gary where the new Ops guy was? He told me that he was in bed, because he had to leave in the morning to go to a JA/ATT (Joint Airborne/ Air Transportability Training) Conference. I told Gary I was going to his BOQ room and . . . I went to the barracks looking up and down the hall with Gary yelling at me, "Come on Jaime—settle down—don't hurt him."

"Then I found out he had already left the building to go to the airport. Closing down Lunar Ops before everyone was accounted for and back to post safely was not acceptable to me," said Smith.

He was later terminated from his AGR job. End of story.

Humor – By the Slice
related by COL (ret) Charles R. Jones

Retired Colonel Charles R. Jones, former OKARNG aviator, first Director of NGB Aviation and Washington D.C. Aviation Officer (SAO), shared some humorous tidbits when we were doing several long taped interviews in February 2007.

Jones told this one about his mentor, Major General LaVern Weber – "When I flew Weber he was always asking questions: "What about this? Charlie, what about that?" We were flying a helicopter out to a Boy Scout Camp and we landed. He said, "Come on and go up here with me." There were these wild flowers growing everywhere and he said, "Charlie, what kind of flowers are these?" There was only one that I knew, and I said, "Sir, I think these are "Indian Paint Brush." He gave me that look that he had,

"Sounds like B.S. to me!" We got up to the Boy Scout Camp and after a while he said rather loudly to the Scout Executive, "By the way, I see a lot of these wild flowers around here. What are they called?" The Scout Executive says, "General, those are Indian Paint Brush.""

Then this one about aerodynamics – "This ARNG aviator fellow down in the south somewhere, was flying an OH-13 and he had both medevac liters attached with the hood up front over the liters on each side. He's at summer camp and he sees several large fields of watermelons. He said, "I thought my buddies back at summer camp would just love some watermelon; nobody could see me, not a house, not a person within miles. So I landed and loaded those melons into the liters. I picked it up to a hover to see if I could still hover. "All's well." I moved the cyclic forward to start my takeoff and those melons rolled forward. I yanked back on the cyclic and they rolled aft! Before I could level my skids and land again, the main rotor blades are beating me and this damn helicopter to smithereens!"

Well, We Cheated Death Again!
related by CW5 (ret) Samuel T. Hinch

Sam began this story trying to recall the timeframe it had occurred, "Captain Jim Peck hadn't yet become the commander of 445th Avn, so this may have been about 1975. Our unit was ferrying UH-1 aircraft over to Fort Chaffee, AR for annual training, like we always did. That evening they called me about 6 o'clock and said, "We have a problem – we have an engine chip detector light [illuminating].

"Of course there's no one still at the Lexington facility and I'm already at home. So I dutifully put my flight suit on and go down to flight ops at the hangar. The only maintenance person that I could get hold of who was Sergeant First Class Floyd Ormiston. He meets me at the hangar and we fly east to where they are – they had landed in a field near Arrowhead State Park, east of Hwy 69 on Lake Eufaula, OK.

"We landed and Floyd did all his magic stuff. We looked at the oil contents. He cleaned the chips from the chip detector plug and reinstalled it. We check the engine oil and if I ever see it again, I'll know – that engine oil was a brass/copper color.

"After inspection, we buttoned up the engine cowling and I put everybody in the other aircraft, to include Floyd. Jim Peck and I got in the aircraft, cranked it up, preparing to come home. It was dark. Our thinking was everybody has to get home and be back at 5:30 or 6 o'clock in the morning. Considering that it is summer, it's already 8:30 or 9 o'clock in the evening.

"As I'm climbing out on take-off from the field site, the engine chip detector light flickers and comes back on *JUST AS BRIGHT* as could be. The light almost hurting your eyes it was so bright. Jim Peck reset the chip light on the dash and I called the other aircraft. Engine failures in an aircraft most often occur when you make a power change—either increasing or decreasing power. If I had known what I know now, that Huey would have stayed right there.

"No longer are we headed for Lexington, but now we're following the prescribed "emergency procedure" for an *Engine Chip Light*, we are looking to land immediately. I had just pushed the collective down to begin my landing and we both saw the lights of Arrowhead Lodge landing strip which was lit up like Christmas.

"I told everybody, "This engine chip light is back, just turn around and follow us back in. But give us some room." So we're making a good, rather quick approach down to Arrowhead, and it's pitch dark. We've got the landing lights on, we see that we've got it made with the glide ratio, we're not going to drop off into the trees anywhere. As I get down close to the runway, I pull in just a little bit of power to help slow down as I'm starting to decelerate – at which point the engine blew up! You could see the flash in your peripheral vision on the trees on each side. It went KA BLAM and of course the nose yawed, every light on the caution panel came on. At least it looked like they did.

"Of course, I had planned ahead, I was over the runway. I was about 50 or 60 knots at about 40 or 50 feet. I just said, "Jim, the f___ing thing has quit!" As I completed the autorotation, we landed on the center line and slowly slid to a stop. There were sparks everywhere – it was so dark. You could see all the sparks coming off the aircraft and our lights were all on. Screw everything else, until we get fully stopped. As the old flying adage says, "Keep flying the aircraft until everything has come to a complete stop."

"I put the pitch entirely down, looked at the dash and of course there was nothing on the engine tach and RPM gauges and the blades were swinging to a halt. I said, "Well, you know what? We cheated death again!"

"Jim Peck and I unbuckled and got out, the others landed behind us. Of course we can't move the aircraft and we can't leave it here 'cause if someone comes in to land, they can't see this dark OD Huey in the middle of the runway. We sent a crew back to Lex in the other aircraft to get the ground handling wheels. I think we got home about two o'clock in the morning and I had to turn around and be back there at 6 a.m.

"I used to say all the time, after every flight, "Well, we cheated death again." After that engine failure I decided, "I'm not going to say that anymore. I will no longer use that expression.

"Flying is so many parts skill, so many parts planning, so many parts maintenance, and so many parts luck. The trick is to reduce the luck by increasing the others."

David L. Baker

Mexican Border Violation – 1986

While conducting a split-annual training period at Ft. Huachuca, AZ, members of the 45th Avn Bn (Lt Hel Cbt) participated in a hostage 'Snatch' exercise during LABEL VISTA II with 3rd Bn, 7th SFG. The 160th SOAR had several MH-60s in the exercise playing as aggressors.

During the final extraction by our MH-6 *Little Birds,* the 160th's MH-60s attacked the hostage area where the extraction was taking place and our AH-6s began to pursue them. I think Chief Warrant Officer Bear Smith was one of the AH-6 gun drivers and TK Klutts another. The MH-60s tried to out run our *Little Birds* and headed south beyond Miller Peak, down towards San Pedro – Mexico.

Yes, there still exists a political border between the U.S. and Mexico just south of Fort Huachuca. Most U.S. Army aviators see it on their maps, but not everyone!

Later that night, the author received a phone call at our BOQ at Huachuca from the Post Commander. As I recall he was an Army two-star, Major General.

"Wood, what the G__ damn hell were your helicopter flyboys thinking when they flew across the Mexican border tonight? Do you have any idea how serious an illegal border penetration like this is?"

"Sir, do you have the time of this incident and precise number of aircraft involved? You did say helicopters, correct, Sir???"

"Wood, you'd better not get smart with me. You know damn well it was two of your [Oklahoma] Guard helicopters that crossed the border tonight. You've created an international incident and it's my name that's currently on the line. Yours will be there before morning!"

"Excuse me Sir, do you happen to have the tail numbers from those careless helicopters that committed this crime tonight?" It was difficult to sit on the edge of my bunk. I'm sure the General wanted me standing at attention!

"Hell no, I don't have the tail numbers . . ." at which point I interrupted him . . .

"Sir, would you like to have the tail numbers of the two MH-60 aircraft, belonging to the 160th SOAR which crossed the border tonight?" My sarcastic smile must have shown through the phone that night.

"What do you mean Wood? My staff said, "It was . . . it must've been your Guard choppers!"" The word "Guard" was stressed strongly.

"Sir, our AH-6 and MH-6 aviators have the military tail numbers of the two 160th aggressor aircraft and I believe if Nogales ATC were to run their radar tape back a couple of hours, it would show that our *Little Birds* did in fact chase a couple of Blackhawks, more precisely MH-60s, south to the border near San Pedro at which point our helicopters did 180 degree turns returning to home base at Fort Huachuca. As witnessed by our aircraft commanders, the 160th Blackhawks proceeded straight south into Mexico. Sir, in their defense, it is awful hard for NVG'd Blackhawk drivers to see that dotted red line (border) on the ground."

The general slammed the phone down, causing my left ear to ring for about two minutes. I hardly noticed though, as I was laughing so hard I got cramps in my abdomen! We didn't hear any more about the border incident. Earlier, during our internal After Action Review in the twilight hours of morning, our AH-6 and MH-6 drivers had given me precise details, times and the tail numbers for the Blackhawks and our *Little Bird* guys knew exactly where the border was!

This wasn't the Lords of Darkness first rodeo, nor would it be our last!

I've Got the Controls . . .
LTC Mike Bedwell

"We're all are getting older and remembering dates is just too damn hard. This particular deployment/mission (ca 1984/85) was one of our biggest deployments because it involved the full logistics train, staff estimates and processes. The mission was to on-load two *Little Birds*, plus 45th Avn Bn personnel, onto each of three C-130s at Tulsa International ANG ramp, fly to a staging base in remote Florida, off load and prepare for flight under goggles, and then proceed on a long NVG route, with FAARP operations enroute, to a pick-up point. We'd load up the Special Forces A-Team in the swamps and transport them to Camp Blanding, FL.

"When we arrived at the staging area and pulled the MH-6's out of the back of the C-130s under goggles with about 30% illumination, we were in the middle of a three-ring circus, surrounded by C-130s and groups of VIP observers, none of whom could see us! At one point I watched a taxing C-130's wing go right OVER the top of a *Little Bird*! I almost s___ my pants!

"Once at operating RPM, I instructed the flight to lift-off, over fly the C-130s and VIPs in order to get us to the route's take-off point. I'll never forget looking down under goggles and seeing the C-130s and confused people who could hear us, but couldn't see us. It must have really impressed them hearing, but not seeing those six MH-6s hovering over them in pitch black darkness! By some miracle, we managed to get to the take-off point at the exact start time required and proceed on the route.

"The route that night included a 55 gal drum hot refueling stop at a theoretically abandon airfield. That's where we learned a little about Florida and the drug trade. When we arrived at the FAARP check point, even though this place was WAY out in the boonies, swamps, etc., it was obvious that we were not alone on that grass strip! We could see flashlights and I'm sure we were on some drug runner's turf because I know they were not ours!

"We hand pumped the fuel and readied for departure. I picked the aircraft up to a hover and turned 90 degrees to the flight to alert them to prepare for take-off. I wish I could remember the name of my co-pilot on that night and the others who witnessed what came next. I'm sure they would remember.

"I was studying my knee board route card and preparing for the next leg. I instructed my partner to pick up the aircraft and position for takeoff, pause 10 seconds, then go. With my head buried in the map I noticed and felt the aircraft slipping sideways. All of a sudden I hear from my co-pilot, "You've got the aircraft." To my dismay, he was experiencing spatial disorientation (vertigo). I desperately grabbed the cyclic and collective, and shouted, "I've got the controls," but forgot to place my feet on the pedals! We must have spun 6 or 7 times to the left towards a line of trees. Then suddenly I remembered how to fly a helicopter and got my damn feet on the pedals! I'll bet the other crews got a real kick out of that one. During the ride my co-pilot said he had the aircraft again and I said to the asshole, "You have to be kidding!"

"At any rate, we survived the FAARP and continued on the route to the pick-up point. When arriving at our LZ we were shocked on final approach to see what appeared to be a lake! We knew we were at the right coordinates, but there was nothing down there, but water. We found out later that it had rained hard and our LZ was flooded. The SF Team had sent new coordinates, but they never got to us. While on the missed approach from the original LZ, I caught a glimpse of the dim glow of a chem light off my right and adjusted the flight to the right and there in front of us were our SF guys in an alternate LZ. Unfortunately it was RIGHT THERE and caused us to make a very nervous six ship steep approach.

We landed and were feeling pretty good about finding these guys when all of a sudden these idiots started throwing simulators everywhere! Scared the crap out of all of us! To make matters worse, all the flying around to an alternate LZ taxed our fuel loads and Chalk Four called fuel critical and decided he couldn't make it to Blanding. We left him and his pax in the LZ and flew on to Camp Blanding. Another OH-6 flight brought him fuel later and he got home. He was right to make that decision. We had nothing left when we landed!

We loaded back onto the C-130s and flew back to Tulsa early after a couple hours of sleep, with a lot of pride and the respect of the 12th Special Forces, but that was one hell of a long night!! It remains one of my favorite missions because lots of things went wrong, but we managed to get it done right and on time in spite of ourselves.

TULSA BOAT SHOW
related by COL (ret) Leroy A. Wall

"Back during the early helicopter days at Max Westheimer Field, the city fathers of Tulsa were hosting a large Boat Show. They had contacted one of the OKARNG Aviation patriarchs and requested that they bring an

Oklahoma Army Guard H-19 helicopter up to Tulsa for the Boat Show. Somehow, Major Charlie R. Jones, a real Felix Unger type guy collected the mission request and headed for Tulsa.

"Although MAJ Charlie R. Jones was at this time the full-time instructor pilot at Norman, and a school teacher by trade from Enid, OK, he didn't have much rotary-wing experience besides the OH-23 Raven. But he got Chief Warrant Officer Four Gerald Pappy Devine to accompany him as co-pilot in the H-19 Chickasaw. Just so you'll not have any preconceptions about Jones leadership, Pappy was not a rotary-wing kinda guy either. He had flown P-47's in the European Theater of Operations during WWII; he was later recalled and flew F-86's in Korea. He also served three (3) tours in Vietnam. He was a terrific O-1A Bird Dog pilot and lived in Cleveland, OK.

Jones, Pappy and their enlisted crewchief (full-timer Sergeant Lloyd Ormiston) flew their H-19 to downtown Tulsa and made a routine safe landing in a large parking lot. This landing area didn't seem all that big to either Jones, or Pappy. The two aviators stepped down to the ground and watched as the crewchief had to climb over a somewhat large amount of sisal rope, which he had brought along. Waiting nearby, was the Boat Show point of contact. He began to discuss what he wanted the helicopter and crew to do during the show.

"As the story goes, the ring-leader of the Boat Show wanted these guard guys to suspend one of his 14' aluminum, V-bottomed boats, with a 15 horse-power outboard motor and a male mannequin dressed in fishing attire and driving the boat, beneath their helicopter and fly low and slow over the city of Tulsa. Yes, of course, he had a sign duct-taped to the side of the dinghy which read "TULSA BOAT SHOW." Beads of sweat had already begun to form beneath the toupee of MAJ Jones and Pappy was just getting real excited . . . . !

"The four men unload the rope and begin to rig the aluminum boat sling-load. On an H-19, a bridal sling is used; they carefully situated the rear of the boat/motor, under and to the cargo hook on the belly of the aircraft. The front of the load was then tied by the crewchief to the bridal (with a "Y" in front) and subsequently tied over the main landing gear. The crewchief would hold the end of this bridal and be prepared to pull and untie it in the event of an emergency and the pilot would press the cargo hook release button to jettison the entire load. Good plan.

"The guard guys secured the load and told the Boat Show coordinator how to help them get this load into the air. They will take it up for a short spin and see how it hangs, etc. There is already a crowd of people gathering, lining the edges of the streets, some on the sidewalks watching all this business with the chopper and the boat.

All aboard, "Rotor clear?" Jones held down the start button and the loud, reciprocating, radial engine of the H-19 backfired, coughed and roared to life, soon the rotor blades to spin faster with each revolution. The wide, red tie worn by the man holding the ropes tied to the boat was waving wildly, being blown away from his neck by the rotor blast.

Jones brought the H-19 engine and rotor RPM up to the green arc and each crew member is queried over the intercom, " . . . We all set back there?" Jones applied more power, increased collective pitch and they rose to a low hover. He slowly lifts the boat off the ground, it wanted to spin, but the ground guy is holding it by the outboard motor. He gave them a hardy thumbs up and they took off . . .

They had barely cleared the light poles on the perimeter of the parking lot, when Ormiston, the crewchief, starts yelling at Jones, "The boat is swinging wildly! It's going to hit the blades." Jones turns hard right, back over the parking lot as the crewchief let's go of his rope. The mannequin fisherman in his plaid shirt, falls suddenly from the boat, arms flailing, helplessly to the asphalt parking lot below. The crowd gasps loudly and many turned away as the mannequin crumpled on impact! Now the boat is suspended only by rope to the main cargo hook. Jones heroically manages a hover near the point of origin, but the boat is vacillating and banging the bottom of the helicopter. Jones wants to land immediately, and tries to jettison the boat from the cargo hook. It fails to release and again fails on the second and third try also.

Ormiston shouts over the intercom to Jones, "Stop, don't go any lower, the boat is hanging vertically and is preventing you from landing."

Pappy who was used to life-threatening emergency situations in military aircraft, can almost imagine red tracers zinging past the helicopter. He takes charge of the situation and heroically climbs out onto the right main landing gear wheel, with a three foot machete in his hand. If his arms were only four foot longer, he'd somehow reach out and cut the rope . . .

"About this time, Jones remembers you aren't supposed to land an H-19 or CH-34 with the main gear (wheel) brakes in the locked position.

So he wisely releases the parking brakes, the wheels are now free to turn and Pappy takes a 15-20 foot nose dive. He defied death only by hitting the suspended boat first, then tumbling on down to the pavement below! The crowd gasps loudly as they are drawn closer to the drama . . .

Ormiston shout again to Jones, "He isn't dead, but he's bleeding like a stuck pig!"

Pappy gets to his feet and with some assistance from a now leery Tulsa Boat Show guy; they climb up the boat and cut the rope.

"Jones slides the H-19 to the left and safely lands. Everyone is thankful to be back on terra firma!

This should be the end of the story . . . . but it wasn't.

About three weeks later, a very interesting and official looking envelope arrived at the office of MAJ Charlie Jones at Norman. It had a return address from the Tulsa Boat Show and along with a letter; it had a photograph of a mannequin's arm protruding from a sandbox! The letter invited the Oklahoma Army Guard to please come back to Tulsa real soon and bring your H-19 Clown Show for one and all to enjoy!!!

Supposedly the letter was signed (or forged) by Captain C.L. Strance, an Oklahoma Guard Aviator from Tulsa. However, C.L. continues to deny that he sent the letter.

"Some persons are likeable in spite of their unswerving integrity."
Don Marquis

Chapter 16

1st Battalion, 245th Aviation (Special Operations)(Airborne)

"Life is what happens while you are busy making other plans."
John Lennon

1/245th Avn (SOA) Lineage

It is so important to know and understand where a unit came from, where it began, how it got its designation, which operations, conflicts and wars it has participated in, what battle streamers it has received. These items are part of what is called the 'historical lineage.'

Oklahoma's original Special Operations aviation unit was indeed the 45th Avn Bn (Lt Hel Cbt) which became the 45th Avn Bn (Sp Ops)(Abn) and was in 1982 equipped with MH and AH-6 helicopters. On 1 October 1987, the unit was redesignated the 1st Bn 245th Avn (SO)(A) and was eventually equipped with MH-60s at Tulsa and destined to additionally receive MH-47s at Lexington.

Wouldn't it be great to be able to see a distinct and formal lineage of the 1st Bn 245th Avn (SO)(A) back to a specific early OKARNG aviation unit, yet that isn't possible. Regular Army and Army Reserve units follow the general military custom in recognizing that a unit has a corporate identity that transcends the individuals assigned or attached to it. The military organization's history is traced through the intangible spirit of the unit itself, regardless of changes in the personnel that comprise it. Through this process, a unit retains an existence even during periods of inactivation.

461

Army National Guard units, however, use local identity as the basis of organization. All legislation since the colonial period has based units in specific geographic areas, because armories and companies normally didn't move. Therefore, Guard lineages are based on the stability of "personnel from a specific location," regardless of changes in the unit's branch or designation. Deviations from these principles are rare. The lineage of an Army National Guard unit is unlike the other components of the Army. They are based on an individual organization in a specific community or geographical area of a state. Regardless of redesignation, the lineage of an ARNG unit is the history of that unit and its personnel in a specific geographical location.

During my research on OKARNG aviation unit histories and their organizational dates I worked closely with two individuals at the U.S. Army Center of Military History (CMH) at Fort Lesley J. McNair, Washington, D.C.: Mr. Joseph Seymour, Army National Guard Historian and Ms. LaTasha Gatling[1], a former contract employee of IIF Data Solutions. Mr. Seymour is a gregarious, enthusiastic ARNG historian. The following is his January 2009 explanation of how the lineage issue works for Guard units:

"Your question regarding Company B, 45th Aviation Battalion is one of the reasons why I find ARNG organizational history so fascinating, and that's no joke. The answer to your question is a question: which Company B are you talking about? The current Detachment 1, Company G, 149th Aviation and Company D, 1st Battalion, 279th Infantry Regiment were both once designated as Company B at one time. When the current Company D reorganized as Headquarters Detachment, 45th Aviation Battalion, the current Det 1 Company G reorganized as Company B. That is because in the Guard, designations come and go, but the personnel remain the same, and it is through personnel and localities that we trace the history, not the designations."

Mr. Seymour continued, "The 245th Medical Company would be the 245th Air Ambulance (Clearing Company). Army units are usually better known by their parenthetical designations or mission, CMH (US Army Center for Military History) uses the formal long name designation."

"The 445th Aviation Company was located at Oklahoma City in 1971 [later Norman] and at Lexington in 1975-78, but was eventually redesignated as different units in the Oklahoma Army National Guard. Again, an ARNG unit's 'historical lineage' is traced by personnel and to a lesser extent, geography. Organizational Authority (OA) 98-71, 14 May 1971 reorganized the 245th Medical Company as the 445th Aviation Company in 1971 in Oklahoma City."

Therefore, the true and traditional historical lineage is the Army National Guard's method of tracing its history by personnel. The Regular Army and the Reserves were the ones who deviated. It's very awkward to trace and a bit confusing too. However, it did begin over 230 years ago and "because the Guard has maintained permanent stations in a way that the Regular Army and Reserves have not."

Even though we can't begin with an early OKARNG aviation unit and follow it logically forward to our 1st Bn 245th Avn (SO)(A), there is something I can share with you, which Joseph Seymour[2] and I were able to put down on paper. OA #48-59, dated 21 April 1959 reorganized and redesignated Co A 179th Infantry into the HHC 120th Engineers. OA #88-67, dated 1 February 1968 reorganized the HHC 120th Engineer Battalion into the 245th Air Ambulance (Clearing Company). Later, elements of another Oklahoma aviation element, Trp D, 1st Sqd, 145th CAV, forms the 145th Avn Co (OA #88-67); then the 145th Avn Co is reorganized into the 445th Avn Co (OA #98-71) 14 May 1971 and the 245th Air Ambulance Co is also reorganized into the 445th. In September 1978, OA #234-78 effects the change of 445th Avn Co into Co B, 149th Avn. In May 1982, OA #56-82 established the 45th Avn Bn (Lt Hel Cbt); then in September 1987, OA #210-87 redesignates/reorganizes Co B 149th Avn into Co B 45th Avn Bn.

Mr. Seymour added, "Organizational Authority OA #56-82 and 81-82, 3 September 1982 organized and federally recognized the 45th Aviation Battalion (Lt Hel Cbt). OA #168-87, 5 August 1987 reorganized the 45th Aviation Battalion as the 1st Bn 245th Aviation, effective 1 October 1987."

Regarding the numeric designation of the 45th Avn Bn (SO)(A) and the 1st Bn 245th Avn (SO)(A) – it was derived from the original 45th Infantry Division, Army National Guard.

How so? Well, the following is a bit long, but I find it interesting.

"The United States Army first implemented the current system[3] of numbering blocks for its units at the start of U.S. involvement in World War I. In 1917 Army National Guard units were still identified by state designations, such as the 1st Pennsylvania Infantry, and the 2nd Texas Infantry. With the mobilization of the National Guard for World War I, having so many like-named units was not feasible. At the same time, 500,000 men filled the Army's ranks through a selective service system."

"These soldiers eventually formed organizations that collectively became known as the National Army. All of these units needed to be numbered in a way that made sense. To this end, the War College Division of the Army General Staff devised a numbering scheme for divisions, brigades, and regiments that would indicate the component to which the unit belonged (Regular Army, National Guard, or National Army [called USAR today]) just by its number.

"With War Department General Order (WD GO) #88, dated 11 July 1917, Secretary of War Major General Tasker H. Bliss ordered the implementation of the unit numbering system developed by the War College Division in 1917.

"In this system, _Regular Army divisions_ were to be numbered from one to twenty-five. _National Guard division_ numbers started at twenty-six and _National Army division_ numbers began at seventy-six.

"For _brigades_ the Regular Army was allotted the numbers from one to fifty; National Guard brigades started at fifty-one; and National Army (USAR) brigades began at 151.

"The system also allotted _regimental numbers_ as follows: the Regular Army started numbering at one; the National Guard at 101; and the National Army at 301. The initial GO was rescinded and replaced by WD GO #115, dated 29 August 1917, which kept the same numbering scheme, but provided more detailed information. This order addressed a variety of units such as Engineer trains (1st Engineer Train), Balloon squadrons (1st Balloon Squadron), and Bakery companies (Bakery Company No. 301).

"The experience of mobilizing for World War I showed that having one numbering system across all components of the Army was necessary. Keeping this numbering system allowed the Army to devise detailed mobilization plans by keeping units on inactive lists, instead of disbanding them as was the practice at the end of earlier wars. This retained a structure in place for the next major mobilization.

"The numbers allotted to the National Army were reallotted to the Organized Reserves (the predecessor to the Army Reserve) in WD GO #5, dated 22 January 1921. The National Defense Act of 1920 also impacted unit designations. The act stated that "the names, numbers, and other designations, flags, and records of the divisions and subordinate units thereof that served in the World War between 6 April 1917, and 11 November 1918, shall be preserved as such as far as practicable." With this directive the numbering system kept in place and it helped advance the idea that units maintained the lineage and honors of past units.

The World War I-era numbering system continues to be used as a starting point when considering new unit designations, and is applied as new branches and new types of units are added to the Army. After ninety-two years, the unit numbering scheme first developed in 1917 is still in place. There have been many exceptions to the system over the intervening years, but the system is still visible.

So for the historically inclined reader, you can say the 1st Bn 245th Avn (SO)(A) links back by lineage to Co A 179th Infantry and its numeric designation from the 45th Inf Div, ARNG. For the rest of you, just go back and re-read Chapter 5 "Name That Unit . . . ," Part I – "Chronology." It will not convince you about the Guard way regarding lineage, but it should help you with unit names and dates.

1/245th Avn (SOA) Table of Distribution and Allowances (TDA)

From its humble beginning, the 45th Avn Bn (Lt Hel Cbt) was originally authorized 203 spaces, which came from the old Co D (-) 149th Avn Bn, plus another small source. The new TDA NGW7QQAA was supposedly designed by NGB, specifically for Special Operations (45th Avn Bn), yet every single line item and paragraph of the new TDA needed a tremendous amount of attention. Specific line items on the TDA, MOS identification, special equipment, NVGs, aircraft – everything needed to be air-deployable and self-deployable. The new 45th Avn Bn didn't exactly hit the ground running. The TDA was continually worked on, changed and improved, up through 1987.

Following the 14 November 1986 enactment by Congress of Public Law 99-661 section 1311, to revitalize special operations and correct deficiencies identified in the nation's ability to conduct special operations. This law was to ensure that special operations were adequately funded and Congress later directed the Department of Defense to include a new special operations budget category, major force program-11 (MFP-11), in its future year's defense plan. MFP-11 provides the Special Operations Command with funding authority for the development and acquisition of equipment, materials, supplies, and services peculiar to special operations.

Effective 1 October 1987, the 45th Avn Bn (Sp Op)(Abn) is reorganized (MTOE 17085HNG30 1 November 1986) and becomes 1st Bn 245th Avn (Sp Op)(Abn). The authorized battalion strength is 372, spread between four companies: HHC, Co A, Co B, and Co C, all at Tulsa.

Manpower, equipment and aircraft are major areas which required much attention. On numerous occasions, members of each primary Bn Hqs staff sections worked hours, upon hours, utilizing their active duty experiences, combat aviation and infantry talents, personal ingenuity and backgrounds, sprinkled liberally with large quantities of tenacity and determination to keep working, "until we get it right!" Then these recommended line item changes to the TDA would be put into proper Army TDA change format and hand carried to the staffs at NGB and the Pentagon. We spent days buried in the basement bowels of the Pentagon, where DAMO-ODF (Pentagon office symbol—Army Operational Force Structure—Special Operations Aviation), Room BF722, working TDA personnel and equipment issues. Room BF722 was home of the Army's Special Operations Aviation section. Lieutenant Colonel Johnny Shepherd was the first active duty HQ DAMO-ODF Special Ops Avn staff member we worked with in the dungeon at the Pentagon from 1986 until he rotated in March 1987. Later, from March 1987 until spring 1992, we spent weeks working with Lieutenant Colonel Harvey Brown at DAMO-ODF. Following Harvey was Lieutenant Colonel Ken Hemilrick toward the final days of 1/245th.

"To understand the story of the 45th Avn Bn (Lt Hel Cbt) you must take a look at the total Army picture and what was going on at the time across the board," said Colonel Johnnie Shepherd in his January 2003 email.

Shepherd went on, "It [45th Avn Bn development ca 1986/87] was a real struggle most of the time for the Pentagon staff. One of our best friends, Colonel Rich Kiper [DA Staff], wasn't even an aviator, but was absolutely essential in helping us hand jam the force structure and force requirements into the Army's program."

"As you will recall, the Army was in a period of change regarding SOF aviation. Some of the drivers were:

- Removal of aviation elements from SF Groups [UH-1s, UH-60+'s & UV-18As]. Some SFG UH-60+'s were transferred to 1/245th Avn. The "plus" suffix on the SF Groups UH-60s "was an unofficial designation of these aircraft that were in nonstandard configurations," said Brigadier General Terry R. Council.
- Consolidation of SOF aviation assets into units subsequently affiliated with 160th SOA Gp [45th Avn Bn; 129th Avn [Hunter AAF] And 617th SOAD [Panama]
- Alignment of SF aviation units to JSCP (Joint Strategic Capabilities Plan) requirements
- Competition with the USAF staff when they covertly attempted to disrupt Initiative 17 by quietly changing the designation of their SAR units to Special Operations
- Evolution of the MH-47E and MH-60K [into the SOF communities]
- Struggles to find CH-47 airframes to feed into the CH-47D modification line to release D's for [SOF] "E" modification
- Creation of Special Operations Command
- Struggle undertaken by the fine leaders of the OKARNG to be accepted as an SOA team member by Army SOCOM at Ft Bragg and by 160th at Ft Campbell
- Obtaining resources to upgrade the airfields in Oklahoma and to modernize the 45th Avn Bn companies to MH-60 and MH-47 aircraft

To realize the complexity of developing Special Operations Aviation in Oklahoma you must remove all blinders and get rid of all personal bias. You had to be objective on the critical issues and not let your own pride be your down fall. It was difficult for me to do, as I took such satisfaction in working toward our major goals – the objective design and the SOA Group Concept Plan.

Here are a couple of very important points (ca 1987) which played into "Why we weren't more successful getting newer and modernized equipment more quickly and higher priorities for MTOEs, ODTs, etc":

1. 1/245th – our <u>Force Activity Designator</u> (FAD) was a FAD 2, much higher than an average ARNG unit. We would like to have been a FAD 1 which would have increased our priority used for supply requisitions. FAD defines the relative importance of the unit to accomplish the objectives of the Department of Defense.
2. 1/245th – our <u>Dept of Army Master Priority List</u> (DAMPL) was a DAMPL 23102. The DAMPL is the standing order of precedence list approved by the senior Army leadership to guide the distribution of personnel and equipment resources used or controlled by Department of the Army (DA).
3. 1/245 Avn was <u>Capstone</u> aligned through 1st SOCOM to WESTCOM. This was good. We were considered a valued asset by WESTCOM.
4. 1/245 Avn was apportioned to USPACOM (Headquarters Camp Smith, HI) in FY 87-88 JSCP, Annex E, 16 January 1987 and inserted in TPFDD 5000-88 (Time Phased Force Development Data) to support PACOM's (United States Pacific Command) OPLAN (Operational Plan) 5000 with priority of deployment to OPLAN 5000-88 (SE Asia) and 5027 (Korea). The assigned geographical area of responsibility was Southeast Asia.

This is a complicated and convoluted subject, except for those who worked in MOBPLANs (mobilization planning). At the Oklahoma Military Department the subject matter experts were MAJ Mike Miller and LTC Paul Jones, down in the basement at OKPOT.

Here's my understanding of how this all worked: United States Transportation Command (USTRANSCOM) was responsible for generating and maintaining the plans which determined how U.S. military forces were deployed (who goes first, second, etc and with how much equipment). TRANSCOM had to determine the transportation needs for each military scenario on the shelf. This was an enormous effort. Then representatives from the various services and commands involved in a plan had to agree how to allocate the limited transportation resources (aircraft, ships, trucks and trains) to achieve the goals of the mission. The end of this process results in an Operational Plan (OPLAN) which specifies how, when and where the forces involved in a mission are to be moved. Add another piece to the puzzle—associated with an OPLAN is the Time Phased Force Deployment Data (TPFDD's) for each specific unit. This priority number described what, when, and how the forces for a mission would be moved and deployed. The OPLANs and TPFDDs are stored and maintained until they are needed. OPLANs, DAMPLs, and TPFDDs change and are modified to fit the current situation.

The bottom line—the 1st Bn 245th Avn (SO)(A) numbers (DAMPL & TPFDD) were not high enough. The Lords of Darkness were destined to continue to be a step child or a little brother to the active Special Ops Aviation units. Although our CAPSTONE headquarters, USPACOM, wanted us badly and even some parties in the Pentagon wanted us for Operation Prime Chance, Army/TRANSCOM planners didn't place our priority at the top.

What was Initiative 17 which LTC Shepherd mentioned at the Pentagon? Joint Army and Air Force Initiative 17, dated 22 May 1984, was a convoluted Memorandum of Agreement supposedly to transfer responsibility for Special Operations Forces (SOF) rotary-wing airlift mission support from the Air Force to the Army and to get the Army to agree to stay out of fixed-wing SOF mission support. Negotiations drug on for years, and Initiative 17 was seen for what it was – in my opinion, an interminable, disguised attempt by the Air Force to get the Army out of the Special Operations Aviation support business for SOF—period. In the end, hardly anything changed – the Army still has its rotary-wing SOA regiment (160th SOAR) at Fort Campbell, KY, with its old MH-60s and MH-47s, and the Air Force currently has the new tilt-rotor CV-22 V/STOL transport Special Operations Wing at Hurlburt Field, FL and those new MH-130 E/H Combat Talons.

At times it seem like we battled over nickels and dimes. At other times, we couldn't use all the money, contracts, etc. they gave us. One of this country's prolific special operations adventure authors was quoted on a subject near and dear to each of us; I've taken liberty to change just one word, without, in my humble opinion, changing the meaning—"I believe that *Special Operations* is one of the most beautiful, natural, wholesome things that money can buy," said Tom Clancy.

Regarding the TDA, working on modifications, corrections and changes—this area required much time and a strong desire to become fluent in and knowledgeable with the intricacies, terms and procedures by which the Army functioned. It is a military truism that, "Just about the time you think you've discovered the answer, they change the questions."

With our TDA it was often two steps forward, one back. As Winston Churchill once said, "Success is going from failure to failure, without loss of enthusiasm."

1/245th Avn (SOA) Unique Identity

Perhaps less important, but having a great deal of importance in the area of tradition were a 'name,' a 'mascot,' patches, unit crests, coat of arms and unit colors for this unique Counter Terrorism aviation battalion which later became a unique Special Operations Aviation unit.

When treading water in a sea of sharks, these items of 'traditional value don't carry a high priority. However, as a motivator and morale builder, these things find their way onto the Commander's, CSM's or the Staff's "To Do List."

Oklahoma' 45th Inf Div shoulder sleeve insignia

From the very beginning, May 1982, the Army's plan was to CAPSTONE align the 45th Avn Bn to the 160th Special Operations Aviation Regiment (SOAR). However, since the 45th Avn Bn was an ARNG unit, specially the OKARNG, it was to wear the should sleeve insignia (SSI) of its parent organization. Although there was no parent aviation organization in the OKARNG, it was determined that the 45th Avn Bn would wear the 45th Inf Div Thunderbird patch or SSI on the left sleeve.

In 1982, a new headquarters was formed at Fort Bragg, one which was to be the Special Operations Command headquarters for all active component Army Special Operations units, ground and aviation – 1st

Special Operations Command or 1st SOCOM. The first commander was Brigadier General Joseph Lutz, followed by Brigadier General James Guest. First SOCOM also had the responsibility for preparing all reserve component SO units to meet their wartime missions. It was in February 1985 when the CAPSTONE alignment of the 45th Avn Bn to 1st SOCOM occurred. These responsibilities later transferred to a new headquarters in 1987, U.S. Special Operations Command (USSOCOM). The 1st SOCOM Headquarters was deactivated and replaced by a new Army headquarters, U.S. Army Special Operations Command (USASOC) in November 1990. Lieutenant General Gary E. Luck was appointed as USASOC's first commander.

In 1985/86 45th Avn Bn staff began to discuss the idea of creating a new, distinctive, motto, mascot or logo for the new unit in Sperry. Several ring leaders in this discussion were MSG Carroll McBride, S-3/Ops NCO, Command Sergeant Major Charles Connell, Major Art Kveseth, Adjutant, Sergeant First Class Norman Crowe, Co A, Training NCO and Major Dwight Cheek, Army Advisor. Others joined in as interest grew.

Dwight worked with some of the folks at the Tulsa Flight Activity (Bobby Lane, TK Klutts and Leonard Reed) and some those at the armory.

Dwight said, "One night in my apartment, I was watching public television and they were presenting a documentary on the owl as a predator—a nocturnal, quick and silent killer. Then it hit me – *Lords of Darkness*. That was the name they needed and the logo would be an owl in flight!" MAJ Cheek can be credited with proposing the name Lords of Darkness and coming up with the idea of the owl as the mascot. Rebecca

Original artwork by Rebecca Bond

Bond, daughter of Staff Sergeant Gregg[4] and Bunny Bond, drew the original artwork for the 45th Avn Bn's owl with the Oklahoma Native American shield.

SFC Norm Crowe and Major Carroll McBride also remembered the PBS television program by Marty Stouffer called "Wild America." There was a special episode by Stouffer called "North American Predators" in which Stouffer presented the great horned owl and called them, as did the Native Americans, *The Lords of Darkness*. Cheek brought the suggestion to work the next day at Sperry and as they say, "The rest is history!"

Several full-timers at the Sperry armory got interested in designing a special patch for flight suits and/or helmet bags. There was a local, informal contest, within the battalion, to come up with a unit patch for the *Lords of Darkness* which could be worn on flight suits, sewn on helmet bags and also used as a logo. Norm Crowe did a lot of drawings and eventually a friend of Dwight's helped with a professional circular drawing of two owls, with a setting lunar body in the background. This circular patch drawing incorporated a nocturnal scene with the text *Lords of Darkness* on the

45th Avn Bn (SO)(A) pocket patch

bottom arc, then two owls in flight in front of a rugged horizon. The lunar moon sets before a dark field behind the owls. The birds of prey holding their talons opened, ready to kill. The Tulsa AAFA's full-time Flight Operations section used the radio callsign Lunar Flight Ops, as did 45th Avn Bn aircraft during training. It was decided to go with the corporate design to the left.

In January 2003 Carroll McBride recalled, "The great horned owl . . . The best I remember, the owl mascot was born at the Sperry armory. The owl, a known predator, was an excellent night flyer and deadly hunter. At a shop in Welch, OK, I found a ceramic owl, bought it and took it home. Pat, my wife, painted it and it became a hit. We purchased the mold in Kansas City and fired many of them in our kiln and gave one to almost everyone in the Special Forces." Carroll and

"Hootie" stencil

his wife Pat operated a ceramics shop from their home in Claremore, OK.

The theme of the owl as a mascot for the 45ᵗʰ Avn Bn (SO)(A) grew and was carried into many parts of the world by certain special operators. The credit for coming up with the (non-official) "Hootie" stencil goes to Master Sergeant Carroll McBride. Carroll was the best Operations and Training NCO I've ever had the pleasure to work with. Besides his skill and dedication to his military job, he was very artistic. When internal deployments were the norm, Carroll came up with Hootie, which was a creatively designed stencil of an owl's determined eyes, eyebrows and beak.

The Hootie eyes were soon being stenciled on footlockers, olive drab T-shirts, sea containers, footlockers and other things everywhere we went. While in Central America on an ODT exercise called Cabanas '86, two unidentified men were photographed allegedly in the act of painting the Hootie eyes on a local Honduran farmer's pig at Palmerola, Honduras. As the story is told, it took about two hours to catch the pig and

"Hootie" stencil in use—LaCeiba, Honduras

only two minutes to do the painting. That night the pig found its way home outside the wire at Palmerola AFB. The local farmer complained to the local airbase commander, who in turn wanted an explanation from our commander.

With the official name change in April 1987, from 45ᵗʰ Avn Bn (Lt Hel Cbt) to 45ᵗʰ Avn Bn (SO)(Abn) and recognition of the "P" MOS qualifier on the TDA for the III/V Forward Arming And Refueling Point (FAARP) Platoon as airborne, parachute qualified soldiers, the unit was also authorized to wear the maroon beret headgear. This was a tremendous morale booster for the ARNG Special Ops aviation unit in Sperry, OK. It was also a very beneficial recruiting tool and

1st SOCOM patch

important to the enlisted soldiers, Warrant Officers and Commissioned Officers. The Special in Special Operations was showing, not only in our skill, our pride, but through our uniforms. In October 1987, another name change occurs. The 45th Avn BN (SO)(A) officially became the 1st Bn 245th Avn (SO)(A).

After a great deal of gnashing of teeth, much discussion and several high level decisions, the CAPSTONE alignment of the 45th Avn Bn to 1st SOCOM leads to the authorization for unit members to wear the 1st SOCOM SSI on their left breast pocket. This 'patch' was the dark green shield with a black horse's head silhouette centered and a diagonal lightning bolt behind it.

Also occurring in 1987 was the unit's request for and authorization of a "distinctive unit insignia" (DUI) and a "coat of arms" for the 245th Aviation. The Department of the Army's Institute of Heraldry, at that time located at Cameron Station, Alexandria, VA, describes the symbolism of the new 245th Aviation Regiment DUI: "Ultramarine blue and golden orange are colors traditionally associated with U.S. Army Aviation. The chevron signifies strength and support; with an invected edge it simulates a cloud structure and denotes the unit's theater of operations. The bow and drawn arrow, pointing down, imply aerial strike capabilities and defense preparedness. The arrow emphasizes swift, silent and deadly attack as well as highlighting the unit's heritage and location, and its mission and role as a

1st Bn 245th Avn (SO)(A) distinctive unit insignia

National Guard unit in the defense of home and country. Black recalls solidity, cohesion and strength. The black and blue together suggest the capability of both night and day operations. The distinctive unit insignia was authorized effective 1 October 1987.

1st Bn 245th Avn (SO)(A) Coat of Arms

The Coat of Arms is described by the Institute of Heraldry below.

474

Blazon:

Shield: Azure, a chevron enhanced invected Argent above a bow and arrow in full draught, point to base of the like barbed, flighted and detailed Tenné. Crest: That for the regiments and separate battalions of the Oklahoma Army National Guard: On a wreath of the colors (Argent and Azure) an Indian's head with war bonnet all Proper.

Motto: ***NOT FOR OURSELVES ALONE.***

Symbolism:

Shield: Ultramarine blue and golden orange are colors associated with U.S Army Aviation. The chevron signifies strength and support; with an invected edge it simulates a cloud structure and denotes the unit's theater of operations. The bow and drawn arrow, pointing down, imply aerial strike capabilities and defense preparedness. The arrow emphasizes swift, silent and deadly attack as well as highlighting the unit's heritage and location, and its mission and role as a National Guard unit in the defense of home and country.

Crest: The crest is that of the Oklahoma Army National Guard.

The coat of arms was authorized effective 1 October 1987.

With the authorization to wear the maroon beret, the OKARNG Special Ops unit began wearing the 1ˢᵗ SOCOM Airborne Flash on the front of the berets. The issue of obtaining our own 1/245ᵗʰ distinct Airborne Flash for the maroon berets and Airborne Oval to be worn behind a paratrooper's airborne wings on his dress green (Class A) or dress blue uniforms was soon

1ˢᵗ Bn 245ᵗʰ Avn (SO)(A) "Oval"

addressed. The U.S. Army Department of Heraldry issued approval on 30 August 1990 for the distinctive beret Flash and for the Airborne Oval. The flash and oval have a dark blue field with orange borders. "Two

1ˢᵗ Bn 245ᵗʰ Avn (SO)(A) "Flash"

475

bends sinister, yellow above red representing the colors of the 45th Infantry Division's Thunderbird SSI," once again tying the 1st Bn 245th Avn (SO) (A) back to the 45th Inf Div.

1/245th Avn (SOA) CSM Charles B. Connell submitted the unit's request for organization colors on 6 October 1987. The actual date that the official 1/245th Avn (SOA) organization colors were received by the unit is not known.

Military *challenge coins* are seen by commanders and leaders to be morale builders, to create esprit de corps and are used to honor service performed. Said to have begun during World War I in the flying squadrons, the tradition of carrying a military unit coin saved the life of a downed aviator. Shot down behind enemy lines and captured, the Germans stripped him of all his belongings except the small leather pouch around his neck with his bronze unit coin in it. Later he escaped and found his way to a French unit. The French didn't recognize his American accent and thought he was a saboteur and were about to execute him. One of the French soldiers noticed the leather pouch and opened it. He recognized the aerial squadron's insignia on the coin, giving the American time enough to explain who he was and how he got there. His life was spared.

Today, throughout the military, not just the Army, the traditional of the unit *challenge coin* continues. The rules of challenging apply to individuals from the same or a sister unit, who are also authorized to carry the same *challenge coin*. A coin holder may challenge any individual who is known to have a coin. The challenge is begun by withdrawing a coin and raising it in the air or by tapping it

Front—1st Bn 245th Avn (SO)(A) unit coin 1987—Back

476

on a bar or table. The individual being challenged is required to produce their coin within 60 seconds. If he produces the coin, the challenger is obligated to buy the person he challenged a drink. If the challenged individual fails to produce the coin, they are obligated to buy. Coin challengers may be sneaky and are known to strike anywhere at any time.

Shown above is the original 1/245th Avn Bn (SO)(A) coin from 1987. It is also customary today to have new coins made for very special exercises or Operations. Shown below is a special 1/245th Avn (SOA) coin minted during an ODT period ca 1991 with the Royal Thai Army.

Front—1st Bn 245th Avn (SO)(A) Thailand unit coin—Back

45th Avn Bn (Lt Hel Cbt) Concept Plan

On 20 December 1985, the first Concept Plan to reorganize the 45th Avn Bn (LHC) was drafted by the author, over the signature of then Battalion Commander, Lieutenant Colonel Leroy A. Wall. Although 95% complete at the time, the author and Chief Warrant Officer Three Charles H. Evans of Trp Cmd (Avn) hand carried the second generation of proposed reorganization MTOE documents to the Pentagon's DAMO-ODSO, LTC Johnnie L. Shepherd, 5-7 November 1985.

> "The purpose of this concept plan is to provide a means for the 45th Aviation Battalion to transition from current TDA organization to an MTOE organization which would be capable of performing as a special operations aviation battalion. The unit is not capable of performing the assigned mission under current structure due . . . to the

lack of company level force structure and utility helicopters. This plan presents a concept for the evolution of the cited unit to a TRADOC (Training and Doctrine Command, Fort Monroe, VA) produced, HQDA (Headquarters Dept. of the Army) approved objective design for a special combat aviation battalion as the long-term goal. The near-term interim design is necessary to allow for the orderly progression of unit structure, in accordance with TAA 92 (Total Army Analysis FY 92) decisions, while simultaneously contributing to enhanced combat capability and readiness."

The original TDA was quite limited, but it was a place from which to start. We had to identify its shortcomings and fill in the blanks. The original TDA was 25% self-deployable by wheel-vehicles; it was not capable of self-sustainment, we were dependent upon an SFG's FOB (Forward Operating Base) for mid to long term support. Additionally, the OH-6s with C-20 engines in a high-hot area of operations were only single soldier transporters (but what fun to fly).

This interim design within the Concept Plan was necessitated by the then existing lack of a TRADOC approved SOA Brigade or Regimental TOE. We thought we were thinking out of the box, perhaps a couple of light years ahead of the 160th SOAR in the mid-late 1980s. However, the score was advantage 160th. This particular plan requested quick staffing and concurrence due to the HQDA Management of Changes (MOC) window for FY 87 actions which would close on 31 March 1986.

It also requested that assets of Co B 149th Avn be incorporated into the TDA/MTOE of the 45th Avn Bn (LHC) to achieve stabilization in ARNG aviation stationing by accelerating the activation of a UH-1 helicopter company in the 45th Avn Bn using an existing company, manpower and aircraft currently in the Oklahoma ARNG. Co B 149th Avn was programmed to convert to a combat support aviation company (CSAC) in a Louisiana ARNG aviation battalion which was to be activated in FY87. By the authority of the Adjutant General of Oklahoma, Co B 149th Avn was then attached for training to the 45th Avn Bn (Sp Ops)(A) in October 1985.

Year-Round Training (Y-R-T) for the 45th Avn Bn was requested by Trp Cmd (Avn) in February 1986 and was approved by OKPOT. This enhanced our capability to train with the SOF community and provide real time support and pertinent ODTs (overseas deployments for training) to coincide with theater specific exercises such as PACOM's Cobra Gold, or Erawan '87 and SOUTHCOM's Cabanas series. Then in October 1986, approval was granted by NGB-AVN to incorporate the Lexington UH-1 unit, known as Co B 149th, as an official, integral part of the *Lords of Darkness* SOA Bn.

The interim design in the 45th Avn Bn Concept Plan was to have been structured with an H&S, two utility helicopter companies, one medium lift helicopter company, and an aviation maintenance company. Total aircraft were to have numbered 50.

Shown below is the Interim Design (FY 87-88) from the Concept Plan:

INTERIM DESIGN
FY 87-88

	Pers	Aircraft
H&S, 45th Avn Bn	210	
Co A, 45th Avn Bn	92	25 MH-6
Co D, 45th Avn Bn	182	2 UH-60
Co B, 45th Avn Bn	92	23 UH-1
	576	50 A/C

Then the Object Design based on 1st generation TRADOC TO&E (strengths were expected to change)

OBJECTIVE DESIGN
FY 89

	Pers	Aircraft
H&S, 45th Avn Bn	94	

Co A, 45th Avn Bn	114	15 MH-60
Co B, 45th Avn Bn	114	15 MH-60
Co C, 45th Avn Bn	126	17 MH-47
Co D, 45th Avn Bn	223	2 UH-60
	681	49 A/C

There were portions of the concept plan approved right away. This plan to include incorporating CH-47s and C-23s into SOA MTOEs, other major additions, and was briefed to all major Special Ops headquarters. On 5 December 1989, the OKARNG SOA Concept Plan was briefed to USSOCOM at Tampa, FL. Attendees included: Major General Lutz (USA) USSOCOM CofS; CAPT West (USN) SOJ8; CAPT Bailey (USN) SOJ3; Lieutenant Colonel Leiberschaf (USA) J4/8; Colonel Bortner (USAF) J3 Rqmts/Tng Div; Colonel Niddiffer (USAF) former Tulsa ANG; Colonel Bob Dolan (USA) RC Advisor).

At one point OKARNG Aviation proposed and the Army was considering adding a Special Ops company of C-23 Sherpas to the 1st Bn 245th Avn (SOA). Even though OKARNG submitted several major, visionary proposals, only a portion of several were approved or implemented for Oklahoma. However, the 160th SOAR became what it is today as a result of the a few proposals and suggestions made by the *Lords of Darkness* and OKARNG aviation staff.

We were ready, willing . . . but not called

"When are they going to call us up? Are we going? Will they call up the whole unit or just a few of us?" These questions were as common in the summer of 1987 as bacon, eggs and toast are for breakfast.

It was during the Iraq-Iran War, Iran's attacks on oil tankers prompted Kuwait to ask the United States in December 1986 to register 11 Kuwaiti tankers as American ships, so that they could be escorted by the U.S. Navy. The United States has had for a long time a written National Security Policy which states that we would go to war to protect the energy reserves in the Persian Gulf, if necessary and would protect access to these same reserves for the west – meaning the U.S. and its allies.

President Reagan agreed to the Kuwaiti request on 10 March 1987, hoping it would deter Iranian attacks. Operation Earnest Will was initiated by the United States Navy to ensure that neutral oil tankers and other merchant ships could safely transit the Persian Gulf during the Iran-Iraq War.

The protection offered by U.S. naval vessels, however, didn't stop Iran, which continued to lay mines and use small boats to harass these tanker convoys steaming to and from Kuwait. Army Special Ops helicopters, Navy SEALs and Special Boat Units, had the best trained personnel and most suitable equipment for monitoring hostile activity, particularly at night when the Iranians were conducting their missions. The 160th SOAG's helicopter crews were suited to the task. MH and AH-6 helicopters are difficult to spot on radar and relatively quiet, allowing them to get in close to a target.

In late July 1987, six Mark III Patrol Boats, other *Special Boat* assets, and two SEAL platoons deployed to the Persian Gulf. At the same time, two MH-6 and four AH-6 aircraft and 39 men from the 160th SOAG received orders to the Persian Gulf in a deployment called Operation Prime Chance.

At this point, I feel we there are two similar terms which need to be defined—activation and mobilization. As we read, we see that individuals and/or units are mobilized first, then activated (placed on active duty). They are often used almost interchangeably. According to (Joint Publication) JP 1-02, DOD Dictionary of Military and Associated Terms:

Activation—Order to active duty (other than for training) in Federal service.

Mobilization

1. The act of assembling and organizing national resources to support national objectives in time of war or other emergencies.

2. The process by which the Armed Forces or part of them are brought to a state of readiness for war or other national emergency. This includes activating all or part of the Reserve Components as well as assembling and organizing personnel, supplies, and materiel. Mobilization of the Armed Forces includes but is not limited to the following categories:

a. *Selective mobilization*—Expansion of the active Armed Forces resulting from action by Congress and/or the President to mobilize Reserve Component units, Individual Ready Reservists, and the resources needed for their support to meet the requirements of a domestic emergency that is not the result of an enemy attack.

b. *Partial mobilization*—Expansion of the active Armed Forces resulting from action by Congress (up to full mobilization) or by the President (not more than 1,000,000 for not more than 24 consecutive months) to mobilize Ready Reserve Component units, individual reservists, and the resources needed for their support to meet the requirements of a war or other national emergency involving an external threat to the national security.

c. *Full mobilization*—Expansion of the active Armed Forces resulting from action by Congress and the President to mobilize all Reserve Component units and individuals in the existing approved force structure, as well as all retired military personnel, and the resources needed for their support to meet the requirements of a war or other national emergency involving an external threat to the national security. Reserve personnel can be placed on active duty for the duration of the emergency plus six months.

d. *Total Mobilization*—Expansion of the active Armed Forces resulting from action by Congress and the President to organize and/or generate additional units or personnel beyond the existing force structure, and the resources needed for their support, to meet the total requirements of a war or other national emergency involving an external threat to the national security. Also called MOB.

There in the sweltering Oklahoma summer heat at the Sperry Armory, the 45th Avn Bn Operations office telephone started to ring. LTC Harvey Brown "needed to speak with us over a secure line." The author called him back on the STU-II secure telephone.

"We may need you guys to help out. Do you think the Adjutant General would allow you to be called up," asked Harvey, not officially, but more as a feeler. He also asked if they only requested some helicopter crews, would our guys be willing to volunteer individually?

Operation Prime Chance[5] (August 1987—June 1989) was a U.S. Special Operations Command operation intended to protect U.S.—flagged oil tankers from Iranian attack during the Iran-Iraq War. Prime Chance took place roughly at the same time as Operation Earnest Will (July 1987—December 1988), which was a Navy effort to escort the tankers through the Persian Gulf.

The two operations were intertwined – 160th helicopters flew nighttime search-and-destroy missions from Navy frigates, destroyers and from two leased barges in the northern Gulf. Navy SEALs operated from the barges as well. Operation Earnest Will was publicized in reaction to Kuwaiti pleas for help, however, Operation Prime Chance was classified SECRET.

The full-time battalion staff at Sperry went to work in four different directions and a classified staff briefing was prepared for then 45th Avn Bn (Sp Ops) Commander, LTC Leroy A. Wall and his Executive Officer, Major Gary L. Elliott. Elliott became the Bn Cdr on 1 September 1987. Both men were in 100% agreement that the 45th Avn Bn should work with LTC Harvey Brown, DAMO-ODF and Major Ron Johnson, NGB-ARO-Y, Special Operations Forces Staff Officer, regarding a call up of the unit to deploy and participate fully, if requested, in Operation Prime Chance.

Over the next several days, the staff began intensively looking at maps, mobilization packets, mob requirements and anticipated that we might be called up. Harvey called numerous times over the next 10 or 12 days. We called in our most qualified and high time NVG and NVG gunnery aviators, who signed Standard Form 189—Classified Information Nondisclosure Agreements. Then they were briefed and interviewed regarding the possible call up of selected individuals, which might become replacements for 160th SOAG MH and/or AH-6 aviators in the Persian Gulf.

Simultaneously, a classified briefing regarding a unit call up was prepared for the OKTAG and Dir, OKPOT to be given by LTC Wall at the Oklahoma Military Department. Major General Donald F. Ferrell was reserved but supported aviation in most cases. However, Ferrell didn't like the idea of individual fillers. The USAR does individual mobilizations, but not the Guard. The Director of Oklahoma ARNG Plans, Operations and Training at the time was Colonel Charles D. Houston, who was somewhat neutral as I recall. However, Houston's staff was less quick to offer support, which was appropriate at that time.

NGB was slightly willing to send the entire unit, but only if DA formally requested the 1/245th. They would not volunteer the unit. OKPOT communicated with NGB, who would later state, "DA will have to make a formal request, requesting the 1/245th be activated." NBG couldn't initiate an action to volunteer a unit. This would have to come from the top down. The problem – Department of the Army wanted 1/245th Avn SOA mission qualified individual fillers for the 160th. To DA, they didn't see why NGB couldn't accommodate their desire, but which had yet to be formally requested of NGB.

They, DA, were accustomed to calling up individuals with a particular MOS, qualification or special training. The USAR utilizes Individual Ready Reserves (IRR) and Individual Mobilization Augmentees (IMA). An IMA is an individual reservist who is preassigned to an active duty organization and trains/serves with it periodically. An IRR can be called up to fill any position need necessary by DA. There are many Special Forces officers in the IRR and/or serving on active duty with Special Ops as IMAs. This remains one of the major differences between ARNG and USAR.

Operation Prime Chance was supported by the 160th SOAG. In the end, DA didn't ask NGB to mobilize 1/245th. We were trained, fully capable, ready and willing. We just weren't asked. This was a real disappointment, especially for those who were fully trained, fully qualified and willing to volunteer.

Just a few years later, the situation in the Gulf had only continued to turn sour. The stench carried far and wide, even worse than before. Saddam Hussein had occupied Kuwait and said he didn't intend to leave. President Bush ordered Operation Desert Storm to begin. Now, unlike Operation Prime Chance, the OKARNG was actually mobilizing many guard units.

BG Terry R. Council, former Cdr, 1/245th remembered, "On at least two separate occasions I was told that the AVIM [Co C 1/245th] of which I was commander at the time, was going to be activated—in the August timeframe of 1990 for Desert Shield. Then in January 1991 while on our AT in support of the 25th [Inf Div (light) Tropic Lightning Division at Schofield Barracks, HI], Lieutenant Colonel Elliott and Major General Joseph C. Boyersmith, Deputy Commander (ARNG Affairs) from USASOC (Army Special Ops Command, Ft Bragg) came to Hawaii to personally tell me that my unit was going to be mobilized to support the 160th in [the Pacific] theater, as soon as we returned to the U.S. from our annual training [in Hawaii]. Also, we were going to be co-located with the 3rd Bn/160th in Iraq. They even told us that they had allocated space for us in their maintenance hangar."

Oklahoma provided units which served in Desert Storm in 1991. These units were: 1st Bn 158th (MLRS), 120th Med Bn, 1120th Maint Co (NTC), 2120th Supply and Service Co, 1245th Trans Co, 1345th Trans Co, 745th MP Co and 445th MP Co. A few of our Oklahoma units gained high praise for their unit capabilities, tenacity and the ingenuity of the certain commanders, such as Lieutenant Colonel Gary D. Haub of the 1/158th (MLRS). Haub, of Hydro, OK, later retired from the OKARNG as a brigadier general.

As of January 2009, there isn't a single Oklahoma Army National Guard Aviation unit which has not served in either Operation Iraqi Freedom (Iraq) or Operation Enduring Freedom (Afghanistan). Most OKARNG aviation units have been deployed on two or three rotations. Some things never change; some things never stay the same.

How would you (1/245th) like to become the 4th Bn 160th SOAR?

The 1/245th was not your traditional weekend warrior type guard unit, far, far from it. What a negative connotation that phrase had back in the '60s and '70s, when college age boys and a few men sought to avoid going to war in Vietnam. It is wrong to generalize and imply that everyone in the National Guard or Reserves during that timeframe was unpatriotic, disloyal or cowardly – they weren't. But the average American used the term weekend warrior disrespectfully to label someone as belonging to the guard or reserves so they could play war on weekends – or to circumvent going to combat.

As you are already aware, the average 1/245th aviator was not a pup, nor was he an old man. Our SOA guys averaged 39 years of age. Crew chiefs/engineers were slightly younger. The average aviator had about 4,700 total flight time, of which +/—350 hours were NVG. This Army National Guardsman had on average 14 years of military service.

Whereas your normal Reservist or non-SOA Guardsman would drill one weekend per month and attend two weeks summer camp, not so for our Guardsman. He too performed weekend drills, but in conjunction with other types of mandays, such as dditional Duty for Special Work (ADSW), Active Duty for Training (ADT), Deployment for Training (DFT), Overseas Deployment for Training (ODT) and/or Additional Flight Training Periods (AFTPs). In an average year, your Special Operations aviator, crew chief/flight engineer, or soldier performed <u>100 to 120 days active duty for pay</u>. Weekend warrior? – I don't think so.

Special Operations Aviation trained extremely hard. In the early days, March to October 1983, Task Force 160th suffered the loss of four aircraft and sixteen personnel while training. Because of these accidents, the Army convened a blue ribbon panel at Fort Campbell, Kentucky in

October 1983. The accidents were catastrophic. We too suffered fatalities and can empathize with the Night Stalkers. The panel recommended the creation of a dedicated training program, which became known as the Green Platoon. The program would later evolve into the dedicated Special Operations Aviation Training Company.

The SOA standards, " . . . on target plus or minus ten meters and on time plus or minus thirty seconds," were exacting. NVG formation flying is demanding, exhilarating, dangerous and stressful. In the beginning, flying with full face PVS-5 NVGs was utterly consuming, almost crazy. But train they did.

The 1st Bn 245th Avn (Sp Ops) (Abn) met the demanding standards. We were accepted in spirit as the 4th SOA battalion when the 160th was a Special Operations Aviation Group (160th SOAG), commanded by John N. "Coach" Dailey. We were shown on organizational charts (September 1990) and diagrams as the 4th battalion (NG) of the 160th (yet listed as 1/245th) when the Special Operations Aviation Regiment (160th SOAR) was commanded by Colonel Billy Miller and Zeandrew Farrow was Command Sergeant Major at Fort Campbell. LTC Gary L. Elliott was commander of 1/245th at that time. Lieutenant Colonel Bryan D. "Doug" Brown was commander of 1st Bn 160th, Lieutenant Colonel Gordy Hearnsberger commanded 2nd Bn 160th, and Lieutenant Colonel Dell L. Dailey was commander of 3rd Bn 160th.

Because of the respect the 1/245th had earned from the SOF community and because we were touted to be a mirror image of Task Force 160th (except in the area of equipment), DAMO-ODF put out informal feelers in 1989 asking if the TAG-OK would support a request for the 1/245th to become one of four battalions of the 160th SOAR. This was a request that the 1/245th change its name to 4/160th. Can you imagine the enthusiasm and arguments this question created in Tulsa, Lexington, Troop Command (Aviation), OKSAO and OKPOT? However, in our naivety "we couldn't see the forest for the trees."

Besides the initial reactions, the opinion of the SAO's office was to non-concur. Why? Because Oklahoma was working to obtain approval on its own Special Operations Aviation Group (concept plan). Oklahoma's plan was to have its own Special Operations Aviation Group Hqs and a second SOA Bn in the OKARNG.

However, it was no surprise when the commander, 1/245th Avn received a memorandum from 1st SOCOM (Abn) dated 5 January 1989, subject: Integration of 1/245th into the SOF Aviation Regiment.

The 1st SOCOM memorandum stated, "1st SOCOM has initiated a proposal to reorganize available aviation assets to form an SOF Aviation Regiment. The [new] Regiment will consist of three active component [aviation] battalions and, of course your unit [1/245th Avn]. An important concern of 1st SOCOM is the full integration of the National Guard into the training, standardization and readiness of worldwide Special Operations Forces." The new proposed aviation regimental commander would be Colonel John N. Dailey, then current commander of the 160th Special Operations Aviation Group (Abn), Fort Campbell, KY. This memorandum was signed by Colonel Mercer M. Dorsey Jr. Dep Chief of Staff, Operations, 1st SOCOM, with copies furnished to TAG Oklahoma, NGB and Cdr 160th Avn Gp.

By mid-year 1991, Oklahoma had received word that the SOA Group Concept Plan was disapproved. The Army had already reorganized the 160th SOAG (group) into the new 160th SOAR (regiment) in June 1990. When the 160th became a regiment John Dailey was promoted to brigadier general.

Then in June 1991, Cdr, USASOC, Fort Bragg, sent an unclassified message to TAG OK, Subject: Redesignation of 1/245th SOA to 4/160th SOAB (A). The message was concise. "This action, when approved, will contribute immeasurably towards developing total unit cohesion, establish one unit support for all special operations ground forces and better facilitate training and support between regimental organizations. The esprit de corps and cohesion that will develop based on this redesignation certainly will be advantageous to all," stated Lieutenant Colonel Ryan, USASOC POC for this message.

In retrospect, I see that none of OKARNG Aviation fully understood or foresaw, at the time, the complications and traditions which would preclude renaming a National Guard unit as part of an active duty regiment. Yes, we have regimental affiliations today and can even wear the *Night Stalkers* unit crest. In 1990/91 however, renaming of the 1/245th to 4th Bn 160th SOAR (Abn) was not going to happen.

Because of the Army's unit numbering system developed by the War College Division in 1917 (discussed earlier), National Guard's traditions of numerical designations would not allow the 1/245th to become 4/160th

SOAR. Perhaps this was seen by some in Special Operations as "Oklahoma not wanting to play ball." This was not the case at all. However, this may have driven another nail in our coffin, leading to the demise of the 1/245th SOA.

1/245th Avn (SOA) Airborne and FAARP Operations
"If everything seems under control, you're just not going fast enough."
Mario Andretti

When the unit was formed in May 1982, out 200 soldiers and aviators assigned, only a very small handful of them were already airborne qualified. In fact, at that time, there was no one in the Oklahoma Army National Guard on active jump status. That was about to change and change it did! During the period 1982 until 1994, the 45th Avn Bn (SO)(A) was the only unit in the OKARNG that had active parachute qualified slots authorized and assigned.

SGM Mike Kittrell

Sergeant First Class Mike Kittrell, born in Chelsea, OK in 1958, was the nucleus for the 45th Avn Bn's III/V (FAARP) airborne operations. Mike joined the National Guard on 8 November 1975 while still a senior in high school. His first unit was the Scout Platoon, 1st Bn 279th Inf in Tulsa at the old 15th Street Armory. SFC Kittrell joined the 45th (Light Helicopter Combat) in January 1986 as the AGR Mobilization and Training NCO and remained with the unit August 1994 when it was deactivated. He had made his first parachute jump as a member of the 45th Avn Bn (LHC) on 29 April 1986 at Arrowhead DZ, Fort Chaffee, AR. By summer 1986 Kittrell was Service Platoon Sergeant.

SFC Kittrell completed jump school at Fort Benning, GA in January 1985 and attended Pathfinder School in April 1985. The 45th Avn Bn's TDA changed and the HQ & Svc Co's Airfield Service Platoon, which were refueling specialists, were required to be jump qualified. "I took a correspondence course and became 76 Whiskey (76W) MOS qualified, then later the MOS became 77 Foxtrot (77F). The full MOS would be 76

Whiskey 4P (76W4P); 4 for E-7 and P for parachute qualified," related Kittrell.

"When the job in the Avn Bn came open, they wanted two things: #1—I was replacing a guy that they didn't want and #2—they wanted a guy who was a strong Readiness NCO because the unit had never passed a 5th IG Inspection. So me being one of the very first [Mob & Tng NCOs] in the Oklahoma Guard, I was the most experienced. And then it just so happened that I had the MOS's to get the job. So I was brought in to do that. Two months after I got there we had a 5th Army IG Inspection and we passed that inspection," stated Sergeant Major Mike Kittrell in a 17 November 2007 interview.

MAJ Carroll D. McBride, 279th Inf Bn Operations Officer had told Kittrell that he ought to get qualified in that MOS because they were going to have a job sooner or later. "Carroll was a strong mentor for me," stated Kittrell. McBride soon reverted from Major to MSG and was hired by the 45th Avn Bn as the S-3/Operations and Training NCO.

Mike talked about the original staff at the old armory in Sperry, "I shared an office. We were all AGR full-timers — two full-timers in each company. There was an AGR Training NCO and an AGR Training Officer. The Training Officer was a rated warrant officer aviator. We had four companies in Tulsa then, with one company at Lexington. There was SFC Norman Crow and Chief Warrant Officer Three Clay Mitchell in Alpha Company. Sergeant First Class Ron Freeman and Chief Warrant Officer Two Ralph "Hap" Arnold were in Bravo Company. Charlie Company [Maintenance] was Chief Warrant Officer Four Dave Young and Sergeant First Class Jerry Kibby. Then me and Chief Warrant Officer Three Mark Yates were at Headquarters Company."

"Over at the S-1 Admin shop there was MAJ Art Kveseth, the Adjutant, and Chief Warrant Officer Four Bob Graves was the personnel tech. Sergeant First Class Roger Young was the top personnel NCO. Sergeant Brett Hodges, Sergeant Clyde Blue, Sergeant Randy Glenn all worked in the 'Admin office.'

"In the S-3/Operations shop, was Major Billy Wood, as S-3, Captain Byron Barnhart, Asst S-3, MSG Carroll McBride, Operations SGT, and Sergeant First Class Nelson Hefley. On the S-4/Logistics side it was just Chief Warrant Officer Three Jamie Smith. Clyde Blue was working for Roger Young at the time when I first came over. Major Lew Keller came on board about six months later. Jamie, Sergeant First Class Sonny

Hendricks and Sergeant Tom Wright – made up the S-4 shop. Major Ray Pool was the S-2/Intel Officer. Sergeant Dennis Barnes came to work for him around 1987, then later SSG Gregg S. Bond. That pretty much was it until we moved to the new armory at Tulsa in 1989. In 1989 I think Clyde Blue ended up going to work over in the S-4 shop. Roger Duncan came on board. Sergeant Joe Bunnell, who had been working ALSE at the facility, came to the HHC at Sperry. Sergeant Lou Latham, ALSE came on board—I guess Lou was working at ALSE at the facility. But then he came over to the battalion side as a Supply SGT," recalled Kittrell.

"When we first started out I was the only 45th Avn Bn FAARP guy jump qualified, so my first mission was to get guys in jump school and get them qualified. It took us about a year before we had four of us on jump status. The original four was me, Sergeant Dave Looper, a young man named Tim Biles, he was one of our originals and then another guy, Chuck Lacrone. Those were the original four—on jump status with the battalion by the end of the first year. So we began jumping with 2nd BN 12th SFG, Army Reserves out of Tulsa. The first multi-personnel jump of

Thai jumpers—Lacrone, Biles, Looper and SFC Kittrell

the 45th Avn Bn was 13 December 1986 at Spike DZ, Lexington, OK, by Kittrell, SPC Chuck Lacrone and PFC Tim Biles. We formed a reciprocal airborne relationship with those guys. They helped us by providing Jump Masters and we provided jump platforms.

"Around mid-1987 myself and Lew Keller went TDY to Fort Campbell and spent three days hanging out with 1st Bn or 2nd Bn 160th's Airfield Service Platoon sergeants. While at Campbell they gave us the 160ths SOPs and manuals – *How to Rig Loads*; we got to see new equipment that they were using—off the shelf equipment. So, throughout that whole period we were doing refueling missions and I had suddenly become an expert.

"It was around 1990 or 1991, when the 3rd BN 160th came to Camp Gruber, OK. We (1/245th and 3/160th FAARP guys) were going to jump into Camp Gruber. Sergeant Mike Stewart and I, we were at the time the only two jump masters in the 1/245th Avn Bn. Mike and I were the drop zone (DZ) safety officers. I attended Jump Master School in August 1987 at the 12th Special Forces Group school at Fort McCoy, Wisconsin and a year later Mike Stewart went.

RTA Master Parachutist wings   RTA Master Aviator wings

In May 1987, we worked and jumped with 2nd Bn 19th SFG in Thailand during a Joint Exercise called Erawan 1987. Those who jumped at Erawan were awarded the Royal Thai Army parachutist badge. Aviators from Bn Hqs, Co A (Tul) and Co B (Lex) which flew while in Thailand were awarded the Royal Thai Army Aviator wings.

In October 1987, we supported an exercise called Label Vista at Fort Huachuca, AZ. May of 1988 we went to Honduras; then in October (1988) we did a month long Label Vista exercise again with the 7th SF Group. In July 1989 we worked with 2nd Bn 19th SF Group from Utah, right after we moved into the new Tulsa armory & AASF facility. There were a lot of little missions we did in the late 1980's and 1990's when we were supporting SF groups going into Fort Chaffee at JRTC—JRTC was tough.

FAARP at LZ Disney

"During a typical JRTC rotation our guys and the SF guys deployed and flew out of Fort Sill, OK. We sat up FAARPS enroute. Since we were using modified UH-1 Huey's, they had no way to get gas between Sill and Chaffee, unless it was bought at FBO [fixed base operator]. So we'd put a 1/245th Avn Bn FAARP down around Stigler in a farmer's pasture.

491

We did this off and on for two or three years, which became our standard for a JRTC mission. In fact, the old man that owned the Stigler property was Lieutenant Colonel Jackie Self's uncle.

When we finished the move to the new armory (1989), we turned around and began our internal deployment to Utah to support the 19th SFG out at Camp Williams. The challenge was to move everything I needed to run a FAARP by ground in one big truck and everything else in about eight or nine trucks. We convoyed the advance party to Camp Williams and set up an FOB at Camp Williams. When the rest of FAARP my guys showed up, we built some small loads for airdrops, which we would jump out of MC-130's owned by the 20th Special Operation Wing (20th SOW), Hurlburt Field [Eglin AFB, FL]. I was 30 or 31 years old when we jumped into the DZ in Utah and I felt like an old timer. My platoon leader was First Lieutenat Jay Jones. The subsequent FAARP operations were going to take place about 50 miles west of Milford, Utah. Our location was in the southwest corner of Utah, down in an area that's called the "Wah Wah Valley," which is listed on the maps that way.

The plan was for us, the FAARP platoon, 1LT Jones and me, to jump in doing a Mass Tactical jump, including a bundle with some FAARP equipment. Our unit was flying the 19th SF guys, and would fly into our FAARP, get fuel and then insert the Special Forces 60 or 70 miles away. What made this one a key deal, if they didn't get fuel with us, those helicopters weren't going to go anywhere else—they were too far away. That made the FAARP an absolute must on this mission. We couldn't air drop the total amount of fuel required for this AT mission due to real world environmental restrictions. So what we had to do was borrow 5,000 gallon tankers out of the Utah [Army Nat'l] Guard POL unit. We orchestrated getting fuel and managed our own diesel fuel along with the missions. We jumped in with everything for our eight soldiers; our food and equipment went in with us for an eight day mission. They were a good bunch of guys.

The valley elevation was 6,000 feet. On the first jump, we jumped Special Forces parachutes that had been designed for higher altitudes. But what they didn't tell us, was that these with chutes—there were no delays in opening. When they opened, they opened fast and hard. On this particular jump in I got airsick inside the airplane; it was dark around 11 o'clock at night. I didn't adjust my harness correctly and when I jumped out of the airplane, the opening was so hard that my reserve parachute flew up in my face and broke my nose. Due to the darkness, we didn't know when we'd hit the ground because of the overcast that night. The 20th SOW MC-130 aircrew just forgot to tell us this part. We jumped through the clouds. Our DZ party was waiting on us and never saw us come out of the airplane; they never saw us hit the ground because we were in the clouds. I think there's a name for that, it's called AWADS (All Weather Air Delivery System). Special Ops aircraft can do that. The only issue we had with it was the fact if you're doing an AWADS drop, there's a few more things you got to do in your pre-jump planning/training. We were totally unprepared.

We lost a couple of rucksacks on opening. One of the jumpers inadvertently cut lose his rucksack, when the lowering lines had come unconnected from their harness. When he went to lower their rucksack, it just kept right on going and impacted the ground from about 800 foot which destroyed the rucksack and the contents. The Air Force—I'll never forget that first drop because when I talked to the navigator before we took off, he told me he was going to put me 21 yards from the fence. You see there was a fence running perpendicular to our flight path in the DZ. I was the first man out of the aircraft and when I hit the ground I turned around and walked in the direction of the fence. Twenty-three steps and I walked into the fence. I didn't see it on the way down, but I was thinking about it on the descent to the ground. Those Air Force Special Ops guys were damn sure accurate that night.

The first members of the unit to receive the Master Parachutist Badge were SFC Mike Kittrell and SGT Mike Stewart. These awards were presented on 7 November 1993, during drill at Tulsa. The second and last awards of Master Parachutist Badges were presented to SGTs Bryon Fry and Greg Long.

"Before our last Avn Bn Annual Training in 1994, we knew the 1st Bn 245th Avn (SOA) was going away. I asked for Fort Hood Aerial Delivery Equipment Repair Section parachute riggers and they helped us rig parachutes for AT. We jumped about 15 per day at Annual Training. We ran seven or eight airborne operations in that final week and at the same time cleared our property book accounts. So the last day of AT I was no longer the hand receipt holder of any government property. At the headquarters company, I had more stuff than anybody—about 15 trucks. I had two pickups, four each five ton trucks with ton and a half trailers, eight 5,000 gal. tankers, and one HEMMET (Heavy Expanded

Mobility Tactical Truck) cargo, a 6,000 pound forklift and a 4,000 pound forklift. I probably had 10 different kinds of refueling systems with all the hoses, fittings, tools, and parachutes. I had 60 personnel parachutes and umpteen cargo parachutes—I had beau coup equipment.

On our very first air drop, a heavy drop of FAARP equipment, we used our parachutes that were packed by Air Force Aerial Port personnel from 137th ANG at Tulsa International. They assisted us in building a bundle.

We just called it an Air Force drop. Later a couple of our guys qualified as parachute riggers. Our first rigger was Sergeant First Class Ken Simpson, an experienced civilian skydiver and master rigger. Another who got qualified as a rigger was Brian Fry. I was to Brian what Carroll McBride was to me—a mentor. Brian Fry was promoted to Sergeant Major on/about 7 November 2007.

We also used the Aerial Delivery Equipment Repair Section out of Fort Hood, Texas. By army regulation, they were to support us with direct support, packing and also maintenance on our parachutes. The parachutes above anything else had to be maintained. When we got ready to do a drop, the week before the drop we would start building the load. The aerial delivery people out of Fort Hood would come up to Tulsa with parachutes and then they would bring an E-7 or a Warrant Officer to supervise and we would build the load through the week. Then on Friday night an airplane would come in and we'd put the load on board the aircraft, either jump on Friday night or early on Saturday morning.

I asked Mike Kittrell, what impressed him most about the 45th Avn Bn (SO)(A) or its personnel?

"Most outsiders always complain about the Army aviators. I know that for a fact, as an Infantry soldier before and after my years in the Avn Bn, but from the inside, it was totally different. Those guys were willing to do anything, anytime, anywhere. With the right planning and coordination, Special Ops aviators always put us on target, exactly where they said they were going to or where we wanted to be. It was also the customer's (SF, Seals, CIA or whoever) ability to coordinate with our flight crews and get the job accomplished – on target, on time! The crews would fly anytime, anywhere and it was just a 100% Can Do, Will Do Attitude. From 1986, all the way up to about 1990 or 1991, we had become world travelers, TDY a lot. We were out there supporting all of the Special Ops community. We had some salesmen on our staff that were real good about selling us and getting us out there and working.

"We were all on the same team"—whether it was doing PT at Sperry, whether we were out there sweeping the drill floor, or on a deployment—it was a team effort. It wasn't us and them. You had your part and we had our part. Then occasionally our parts all intermingled and we worked together as a one team and one big family. I think that carried on because of the selling you were doing. It was in that period that we were world travelers. We were a new ARNG Special Ops unit; you got us out there with our customers and in view of the public. That's when we were doing the big stuff.

During the period May 1982 until August 1994, 38 Airborne qualified members of the *Lords of Darkness* made over 678 military parachute jumps in the United States, Thailand and Honduras. SFC Mike Kittrell led the way with 108 total jumps; he also made the battalion's first and last jumps. These soldiers were (listed by date of airborne qualification; * indicates individual was present at the deactivation of the 1/245th Avn (SOA)): SGM Mike Kittrell*, Thailand, Honduras; Sergeant Chuck Lacrone*, Thailand; SPC Tim Biles, Thailand; Sergeant David Looper*, Thailand, Honduras; 1LT Jay Jones, Honduras; Staff Sergeant Mike Stewart* Canada; SPC Paul Wallace (broke his back at Par DZ, Camp Gruber, OK September 1989, medically retired), Honduras; Sergeant Terry Harper; SPC Steve Schiemlpfenig; Sergeant Greg Long*; Sergeant First Class Ken Simpson, parachute rigger; Sergeant Stanley Mason; First Lieutenant Craig Mullen; SPC Matt Hoover (later CW2, CH-47 pilot); SPC Tom Schulze (injured in tanker wreck, June 1990, medically retired); Sergeant Richard McCorkle, parachute rigger; SPC Ed Jost (later SSG w/20th SFG); Staff Sergeant Chuck Hannah*; Sergeant Robert Caron; SPC John Rountree; SPC Damon Eyerly; Sergeant John Price; Sergeant Jeff Smith; First Lieutenant Lance Bradshaw; Sergeant Alan Martel; SPC John Tunnell; Sergeant Bryon Fry (later SFC); Captain Joe Bob Hicks; Captain Glen Phillips; Sergeant First Class Joe Crawford* (later CSM); SPC Tim Farlow*; SPC Frankie Howe; PFC Tom Gilliland*; Sergeant Bill Scavezze* (later SSG) parachute rigger; SPC Eric Schlemme*; PFC Chris Moore (later SSG) parachute rigger; PV2 Leo Sawyer*; SPC Sergio DeLeone*.

Last official parachute jump by a member of the *Lords of Darkness* – 19 August 1994, Holiday DZ, Camp Gruber, OK, by SFC Mike Kittrell.

Among many other military awards, ribbons and honors, SGM Kittrell also was awarded the Pathfinder Badge in April 1985.

"Airborne, All the Way, Sir!"

Deck Landing Qualification (DLQ) and Dunker Training –
"A good time to keep your mouth shut is when you're in deep water."

Unknown

Due to the 1/245ᵗʰ SOA Bn's mission parameters, the unit was required to be prepared to conduct Special Ops missions to and from the decks of U.S. Navy vessels. The requisite training was called *deck landing qualification* or DLQ and was conducted by the Navy in deck certified aircraft. Before DLQ training could be conducted by a member of the 1/245ᵗʰ Avn, you must complete the academic training and pass the Navy's dunker training. This involved a helicopter shaped fuselage which was submersed in an indoor pool. You were strapped into the seat of the training device (helicopter) about 25 feet above the water's surface, wearing your flight suit and flight helmet, and then the fun begins. The helicopter-device is released and slams into the water with terrific force and sinks rapidly. Only after the instructor in scuba gear gives you a signal can you begin to make an egress from the submerged aero machine.

Once you have successfully passed the sunken helicopter hurdle you learned about HEEDs (Helicopter Emergency Egress Device system) – a compact lightweight breathing apparatus, which provides for up to two minutes of emergency air. It can be carried either in the pocket of the pilot survival vest or in a holster container worn on the side of the leg like a sidearm holster. It requires a cool, calm personal that can avoid panic and has received proper training in its use. Passing the HEEDs exercise you could begin the next step for DLQ.

Dunker Training and DLQ were just two more items for which a Special Ops aviator would receive additional training in and have his ticket punched. My first landing on a U.S. Navy vessel occurred in the South China Sea in April 1967. As a UH-1D Aircraft Commander in Vietnam I received a mission to fly

CW3 Jimmy Richards & CPT Glenn Phillips—Dunker Training

some Army Artillery officers five miles offshore from Duc Pho to a U.S. destroyer. At the time DLQ hadn't been thought of; since then it is used to prevent good intentioned guys like me from landing on Navy ships.

U.S. Navy requirements for Shipboard Operations (landings/take-offs) by Army aircraft, especially Army rotorcraft, require a waiver from God, which the Navy was quite reluctant to approve; otherwise you had to attend Deck Landing Qualification. It was their boat and they got to make the rules. In our case the training was conducted at NAS Jacksonville and/or NAS Pensacola, FL.

Here's an excerpt from a U.S. Navy aviation manual (AV1525) on DLQ for Army helicopter aviators: b. Deck-Landing Qualification Training

(1) Before conducting deck-landing qualification training, pilots of self-deploying helicopters must meet the following prerequisites:
(a) Be a designated PC with 50 PC hours.
(b) Have 500 total helicopter hours.
(c) Have 50 night and 50 instrument hours (actual or simulated).
Five night and five instrument hours must have been within the last 60 days (for night deck-landing qualification only).
(2) In addition to those prerequisites listed in (1) above, Army deck-landing qualification instructors will meet the following prerequisites:
(a) Be qualified as an instructor pilot.
(b) Have 500 pilot hours in the type of helicopter in which qualified.
(c) Be instrument qualified and current. c. Initial Qualification, Requalification, and Currency Requirements
(1) Multi-spot, Air-Capable Ships
Qualification requirements for operations from multi-spot, air-capable ships are —
(a) For initial and requalification requirements, five day and five night shipboard landings will be made per year. This training will be under the direction of a deck-landing qualification instructor.
(b) For currency requirements, two day and three night shipboard landings will be made per year. One day landing will be made within 24 hours before conducting a night landing.
(2) Single—and Dual-Spot, Air-Capable Ships
Qualification requirements for operations from single—and dual-spot, air-capable ships are —

(a) For initial qualification, 10 day-field landings and 6 day-shipboard landings will be made within a 2-day period. This training will be under the direction of a deck-landing qualification instructor.
(b) For requalification, pilots whose currency has lapsed within the last six months will be trained by a deck-qualified mission commander. Pilots also will make 10 day-field landings and 6 day-shipboard landings within a 2-day period. For those pilots whose currency has lapsed six months or more, currency requirements are the same as those for initial qualification.
(c) For currency requirements, four day-shipboard landings will be conducted within 90 days.

Without reproducing the entire, lengthy document, let me suffice by saying it would cause you more pain if I listed the night requirements. If we listed NVG Shipboard Ops it would cause you to go blind and you wouldn't believe another word I wrote.

Lieutenant Colonel Art Kveseth, a former USMC helo pilot, said in his email from December 2006, "Our first dunker training was at NAS Pensacola. This was during an Annual Training period [ca 1986] that was to end up being in support of an SF training operation out of Ft. Bragg. The SF mission fell through, but we got [dunker] training just the same. I went through initial qualification at Pensacola and I think we qualified 12—14 pilots. I also went through requalification at NAS Jacksonville, FL a year later. The normal group was 10-12 crewmembers at a time."

MAJ Joe Bob Hicks recalled that a number of personnel from Lexington's Co B 1st Bn 245th Avn (SOA) attended DLQ at NAS Jacksonville. Some he remembered were: himself, Chief Warrant Officer Three Jerry Hefner and Chief Warrant Officer Four Don "Dirt Doctor" Hubbard.

"The initial DLQ for the Bn was also done at NAS Pensacola during the same AT. We were not allowed to use our MH-6's we had along as they were not deck certified on the HLT (Helicopter Landing Trainer). The 10 or so pilots that did get qualified flew U.S. Navy UH-1N's that were provided by HC-6 [Sqd] based at Pensacola. The instructor pilots from the HC-6 Squadron flew left seat. LCDR Zen Hac, a flight school buddy of mine played a major role in getting the training coordinated and completed for us," added Kveseth.

Maintaining DLQ currency was next to impossible, unless you lived in the panhandle of Florida or passed through weekly, at night. A few of the 1/245th Avn instructor pilots received DLQ recurrency on the East coast later, and perhaps a few others during mission support for Seal Team 6 at Naval Base Coronado and/or NAS Whidbey Island, CA.

Art reminds me, "Remember our DLQ percentage was higher than it looked. We had a number of qualified, but not current aviators from the Marines in the unit." As the sounds of the U.S. Marine Corps hymn begin to fade away, it's time to get the SERE portion of your ticket punched . . .

SERE – Survival, Escape, Resistance and Evasion

"Do something every day that you don't want to do; this is the golden rule for acquiring the habit of doing your duty without pain."

Mark Twain

In July 1963, the author attended Basic Infantry Training for eight, humbling weeks at Fort Polk, LA. The heat and humidity of Louisiana were more irritable and severe than the hot and dry periods between monsoons later in Vietnam. It was a requirement which I recall, that we recruits learn by memory the six articles of the Military Code of Conduct. In addition to those periods of instruction given during Basic Training, there were more classes in AIT (Advanced Individual Training) and OCS (Officer Candidate School) on the Code of Conduct. You were taught to have pride, dedication and loyalty in the Army, your country and in yourself.

"I am an American, fighting in the forces which guard my country and our way of life. I am prepared to give my life in their defense."

"I will never surrender of my own free will. If in command, I will never surrender the members of my command while they still have the means to resist."

"If I am captured, I will continue to resist by all means available. I will make every effort to escape and aid others to escape. I will accept neither parole nor special favors from the enemy."

"If I become a prisoner of war, I will keep faith with my fellow prisoners. I will give no information or take part in any action which might be harmful to my comrades. If I am senior, I will take command. If not, I will obey the lawful orders of those appointed over me, and will back them up in every way."

"When questioned, should I become a prisoner of war, I am required to give only name, rank, service number, and date of birth. I will evade answering further questions to the utmost of my ability. I will make no oral or written statements disloyal to my country and its allies or harmful to their cause."

"I will never forget that I am an American, fighting for freedom, responsible for my actions, and dedicated to the principles which made my country free. I will trust in my God and in the United States of America.

In accordance with the Geneva Convention, we were told that (Article 5) if we were captured and interrogated that, "we only had to give name, rank, service number and date of birth." During OCS and in flight school we were given the opportunity to put our training and our ability to resist to the test in dramatically real escape and evasion field training exercises.

Since WWII we have learned in Korea, China, Vietnam, Somalia, the Gulf, Iraq, Afghanistan and elsewhere that the reality of being starved, beaten, tortured and often executed as a POW, can be expected. Today's guerilla, Jihadist, Taliban, Al Qaida war fighter doesn't give a damn about the Geneva Convention – you are nothing—an infidel. What must we know to remain alive, protect our fellow POWs and at the same time keep from divulging classified information to the enemy?

Colonel James N. "Nick" Rowe[6], a Special Forces Officer was captured early in the Vietnam War and held for five years as a POW. Rowe was brutally tortured by the Viet Cong and finally escaped. Later he introduced SERE and RTL (resistance training lab) training based on his own experiences from Vietnam to Army Special Operations Forces. His lessons learned are the core of the SERE training provided to all branches of the military and especially Special Operations operators.

In accordance with Army Regulation 350–30 Training Code of Conduct, Survival, Evasion, Resistance, and Escape (SERE)[7] there are three levels of intensity of SERE training which are based on risk and perceived threat of capture:

Level A training is initial entry level training included in the program of instruction at basic enlisted training and at all courses of instruction designed for officers [ROTC, Officer Candidate School and Officer Basic Courses]. It gives the new soldier/officer the basics of how he/she should act in the event he/she is captured. Level A training includes: developing a knowledge and appreciation of national, Army, and unit history and traditions; the strengths and advantages of the Nation's democratic institutions so as to develop resistance to enemy political and economic indoctrination; understanding the mutually supporting relationship between the Code and the UCMJ; peacetime conduct of U.S. military personnel in detention, captive, or hostage situations, and the goal of achieving a full understanding of the Code, its purpose, and its meaning.

Level B training is for officer and enlisted personnel or any military occupational specialty (MOS) operating (or anticipated to operate) forward of the division rear boundary and up to the forward line of own troops (FLOT). DoD 1300.21 lists these examples, "members of ground combat units, security forces for high threat targets and anyone in the immediate vicinity of the forward edge of the battle area or the forward line of troops." Service members deploying to Iraq and/or Afghanistan is in this category. Level B training can be completed by correspondence course, video courses and is done at the home station unit level.

Level C training is for soldiers whose wartime position, MOS, or assignment has a high risk of capture and whose position, rank, or seniority make them vulnerable to greater than average exploitation efforts by a captor. Examples include personnel who operate forward of the FLOT such as special forces, pathfinders, select aviators, flying crew members, and members of ranger battalions. Peacetime level C personnel are those who, due to assignment or mission, have a high risk of being taken hostage by terrorists or being detained by a hostile government in a peace time environment. Examples include special forces, selected military attaches and members of ranger battalions, and anyone in special support missions near conflict areas.

DoD Instruction 1300.21 [Guidance For Instruction In Support Of The Code Of Conduct] requires: "As a minimum, the following categories of personnel shall receive formal Level-C training at least once in their careers: combat aircrews, special operations forces (e.g., Navy special warfare combat swimmers and special boat units, Army Special Forces [Special Ops Aviation] and Rangers, Marine Corps force reconnaissance units, Air Force special tactics teams, and psychological operations units) and military attaché."

There are four SERE Level-C training facilities: Air Force conducts training at Fairchild AFB, WA, Navy locations are in Brunswick, ME, and at North Island, CA; U.S. Army at Camp Mackall, NC; and at the Army Aviation Center, Fort Rucker, AL. All IERW (initial entry rotary-wing) students must successfully complete the course before beginning flight training.

With the exception of minor periodic adjustments in content and length, SERE instruction at Camp Mackall has changed little since Lieutenant Colonel Nick Rowe conducted the first Level-C course in 1986. The course spans three weeks with three phases of instruction, with the first phase consisting of 10 days of academic instruction on the Code of Conduct and in SERE techniques that incorporate both classroom learning and hands-on field craft.

The second phase is a five-day field training exercise in which the students practice their survival and evasion skills by procuring food and water, constructing evasion fires and shelters and evading tracker dogs and aggressor forces for long distances.

The final phase takes place in the RTL (resistance training laboratory), a simulated prisoner-of-war camp, where students are tested on their individual and collective abilities to resist interrogation and exploitation and to apply the six articles of the Code of Conduct in a realistic captivity scenario. The course culminates with a day of debriefings in which the students receive individual and group feedback from the instructors. These constructive critiques help students process everything they have been through to solidify the skills they applied and to correct areas that need adjustment.

"SERE—Level "C" is specifically required of Special Operations aircrews, Special Forces, Army Rangers, Pathfinders, Delta Force, Seals and those of a high risk of capture and exploitation. Due to the nature of our mission, the airfield service guys were also required to attend. I went to lead the way," said SGM Mike Kittrell, January 2003.

Active duty Army soldiers attend resident courses as the rule. National Guard and Reserve soldiers normally can't attend the longer resident courses provided by Army schools, due to their civilian jobs and limited time off. Correspondences courses developed over the years, but are focused on academics or class room instruction and can't replace an exercise in the field. Therefore the ARNG and USAR came up with innovative ways to put together field training in digestible packages, such as MTT (Mobile Training Teams). The active duty trainers come to us. This isn't possible for all courses, but for some it is and saves training and travel funds. MTT was one alternative for the 1/245th Avn to get SERE training, without sending everyone to Fort Bragg for the resident course. However, some did go to Fort Bragg initially.

"We had two IDT sessions at Tulsa/Camp Gruber conducted by an MTT from FT Bragg. The course culminated in an eight or nine day session at Camp Mackall, NC.

"The first IDT session was three or four days long and consisted of classroom and practical exercises. The classroom material included Code of Conduct Training, survival, evasion, resistance (classified), and escape (classified). The practical exercise portion included knot tying and combatives (we beat the s___ out of each other for fun).

1/245th air crewmembers in SERE Training at Camp Gruber, OK

"The second IDT session was four or five days long and focused on survival techniques, large and small game and fowl preparation, traps and snares, individual and team movement techniques, and horizontal obstacles both above and below the ground.

"The ADT (active duty for training) portion at Camp Mackall, NC consisted of vertical obstacles, evasion planning and preparation, the evasion FTX (field training exercise) and clandestine linkup, and finally, the Resistance Training Laboratory. The evasion FTX and the RTL were the tough parts. During evasion, we moved at night (10-15 km), had to scrounge food and water, and avoid enemy contact. It was hot and dry, and then it rained in biblical proportions. Once captured, there was the RTL. We started tired, hungry, sore, and with various injuries and it only got worse!!!!

Many aviators and crewmembers from Co B 1/245th at Lexington attended SERE and RTL. "It was tough. I can remember, besides me, there was Chief Warrant Officer Five Paul Merchant, Chief Warrant Officer Four Chris Rau, Sergeant Kevin Beck, Chief Warrant Officer Three Don Hubbard, Sergeant Robert Hicks and others from Lex and Chief Warrant Officer Four Mark "Rowdy" Yates from Sperry, recalled Joe Bob Hicks, 6 February 2009.

In January 2003, LTC Art Kveseth recalled, "Strangely enough, there was an in-depth report on Army SERE training on NBC a couple of weeks ago. I was in the first group [from 45th Avn Bn] to attend. I also had the honor of being the SRO (senior ranking officer). Since we could not break people free for the full (as I recall) six weeks of training in residence [at Camp Mackall], we had MTTs (Mobile Training Teams) came to Tulsa and taught the classroom work for us in MUTA 6 status. The classes were combined from Co A (Tulsa) and Co B (Lex) units. We spent three days at Camp Gruber in February (1986 or 1987) for static survival training before going to the RTL (Resistance Training Lab) at Fort Bragg, NC. The thing I remember most about Static Survival was the seeming endless ice fog and ice storm we had for those three days.

"MAJ Lew Keller (S-4) provided rabbits, chickens and a goat for the kill class. We were all to have the opportunity to kill an animal and prepare it for food. Since we were mostly country boys, we had been eating a lot of roasted Armadillo for the previous days. We weren't hungry in the least! Besides, the chickens and goat Keller bought were in the neighborhood of 12,000 years old and tough as shoe leather. We ate the rabbit and buried the chickens and goat when the SF (Special Forces) instructors were not looking. (Back to BBQ'd Armadillo.)

"I can remember a few of those who went to the first class. Among the ones I do remember are: Bobby Lane, Joe Bob Hicks, David Barr, Mark Yates and Andy Stiles. Yes. It is worth it. I believed that as a Company Commander, and still believe it today. You should not be able to be SOA qualified without attending SERE and RTL.

Some other recollections from Kveseth regarding the MTTs at Camp Gruber and Greenleaf Lake, "One of the events we had to pass was the wire obstacle course. It was built by our AGR personnel and some M-Day folks. It was a series of barbed wire obstacles you had to work your way through. I remember a grid of wire about 12 inches off the ground. The object was to make a set of forked sticks to prop the wire with so you could negotiate passage under. Needless to say, it was tough passage for the larger members of the unit.

"Bobby Lane was a member of my team. We were cold, tired and didn't feel like crawling around in the freezing mud to play under barbed wire. Bobby got hung up and wanted to go back to the start and give up. I got back under the wire and between the two of us got him through to the finish. Not everyone who started SERE finished . . .

"One of the biggest problems during one of the weekends was the placement of the hidden fishing lines in Greenleaf Lake. We made the set lines with sticks and some cord provided. The problem was to plant them under water to avoid detection. I waded hip deep into the freezing water in February and placed the sticks. Picture this scene, you can see the fog in the background. It was so hopeless, there wasn't a fish in the lake gonna bite on that line unless they had a fur coat!

"I think it was about a month after the static survival that we traveled to Camp Mackall at Fort Bragg to do the remainder of the SERE training that could not be accomplished at Tulsa. Camp Mackall conducted the attack dog training and high obstacle training followed by the evasion practical exercise and the RTL (Resistance Training Lab). We flew to Bragg by commercial air and were bussed to Mackall. The next morning we went to the high obstacle training area and commenced class work and rappelling exercises/various methods of climbing vertical walls.

"While this was all well and fine, our age [older than your average recruit] and lack of proper [physical] conditioning became a small problem. We were aviators, not 18 year old SF candidates. The last event was a walk around the top of a couple of abandoned concrete water storage tanks. The edges were about a foot wide, rough and uneven. I followed directly behind the instructor. I was determined that he would not show us National Guardsmen up since he had only one functional eye and no depth perception to speak of. I stayed right on his heels, so close I even stepped on them a couple of times. That didn't even unnerve him one little bit. The rest of the group followed at their own pace. Finishing that, we went back to Mackall and had lunch followed by attack dog training that evening.

"The attack dogs [practical exercise] were unbelievable. The handler had a German Shepherd that we all took turns with. We got dressed up in the padded suit and had armor for our forearms. He would command the dog to attack, we would offer our protected forearm and she would gnaw on it while we practiced slitting the dog's throat with an imaginary knife. I remember looking down at her eyes while she had my forearm. Her look was one of "just business, nothing personal," while she held me. I never believed a dog could run up a seven foot wall, but this one could.

Kveseth continued his recollections of SERE training, "The night before the evasion phase we finished our movement plan and were broken down into four or five man teams, with enlisted, warrant officers and commissioned officers on each team. The next morning we got up and packed. We had no breakfast and were expected to live off the land for the next three days.

"It was February or March, damp and cold; we had to find food along the way, but all that was available seemed to be wild onions. I ate a lot of them. Each team had a minimal amount of personal gear: our BDU's, a rain suit, a web belt and canteens. We could also carry one knife, most of us had the traditional Swiss Army knife with its many blades. Each team was also required to carry a military radio in case of a serious incident.

Each of the teams were dropped at separated points along the sandy, orange, foreign roads outside of Fort Bragg. Team tactics were to wait until nightfall and then move during the night to the next designated rendezvous point. There was one map and one compass per team.

"The thing I remember most," said Kveseth, " . . . was all the water obstacles that we had to cross. At 0100 hrs we encountered a creek; I remember crawling across a deadfall, [log] the tree trunk was so big we could walk most of the way across and then straddle it to slide the rest of the way. Even with our rain suits on, we were freezing. Bobby Lane was crossing a deep ravine on a deadfall log; it broke and he fell into waist deep muddy, cold water. When we pulled him out he was shaking from the icy water. He was not in the best of spirits, nor frame of mind. To hell with the aggressors they had looking for us. We built a fire and dried him out. Of course we were so far out in the bush no aggressor would be stupid enough to come searching for us – we hoped.

It is amazing what you can do and what you can find when you want and if you are hungry enough. Your mind is much weaker than your muscle and bone. Mentally, your head says, "I can't go any further . . ." but your physical body will keep going long before total exhaustion.

Kveseth and his team said, "We found a hide site so good that even the Special Forces instructor was impressed. Our team burrowed into the brush deeper than a deer would go, it was a bramble with a couple of bedding areas where local wildlife had slept. We heard aggressors all around, but they never found us.

"The second night was more of the same. By this time we were out of fresh water and drank water from the local stream, which we made potable using water purification tablets. The water and partially dissolved tablets tasted terrible. We were cold, tired and extraordinarily hungry. The team crossed an area where loggers had cut timber. It was filled with wait-a-minute vines and deadfalls. Oh, did I mention it was still raining? We stopped deep in the forest that night and built another fire just to dry out.

"We arrived at our designated hide site area in the dark and drizzle. No moon or stars – only darkness. We arrived early, sacked out. The next thing I remember is being awakened by an alarm clock! It was Saturday morning and we were sleeping in the front yard of a farmhouse! We had no idea a few hours before that the structure was even there!

"That afternoon, we had a DOR (drop on request), an OKARNG sergeant from my team. He also quit the 1/245th Avn shortly after we got back to Tulsa.

Losing a team member is emotional, but Kveseth continued, "We moved out the third night pretty tired and looking forward to the end of the movement. The next day was Easter Sunday. I noticed on the map that our next hide site would be across a river from a State Park. I remember thinking – "we could cross over and steal some Easter Baskets!" Yes, we were getting hungry! By doing a map recon we also found some chicken farms along our route of movement. We decided to detour and see if we could pick up a couple free chickens. No such luck, all the chicken houses were empty.

"However, there were some fresh water taps in the barns, and we got clean water! The down side? It continued to rain all day long. We arrived at our hide site and found a collapsed chicken coop to provide shelter from the driving rain in the dark. We woke up Easter Sunday with cold, muddy water running down our necks.

"Early in the day we were visited by the SF instructors, who reminded us to prepare our link-up plans with the local partisans. That event was to take place that afternoon. Well, we reviewed the link-up procedures. Andy Stiles was the designated contact. As dusk fell, we moved into position and waited for the friendlies to arrive. As luck would have it, the first person they walked up to was me. Fortunately, we all had the passwords and information and I was able to complete the verification. They placed hoods over our heads and loaded us into a van. For the first time in 3 days we were warm and didn't shiver.

"After being transported to an unknown site we were allowed to sleep. The partisans directed each team to keep a [guard] watch all night long. My team made a big pile of leaves and snuggled up to each other. We took turns of one hour watches during the night. We were checked frequently. The next morning we were again placed in the back of a van and moved. Along the way, the van was ambushed. The bad guys captured us and the RTL phase (simulated POW Camp) was about to begin.

The RTL phase is a ball-buster, the training methods and course cannot be discussed. I remain proud of Art Kveseth, Mike Kittrell, Joe Bob Hicks and each member of the 1st Bn 245th Avn (SOA) who attended and completed SERE Level – C and the RTL. You are indeed Special.

NVG, Mission Qualification & Training and Risk Assessment

From the days of full-face night vision goggles (1978—1983), involving endless hours of night flying; yet living in a day light operations world. The job of aircrew members of the 1/245th included multitudes of various task, such as maintaining aircraft currency, night currency, NVG, DLQ, basic and final mission qualification, instrument qualification, maintaining a marriage, supporting a family and a civilian job – it all adds up. It's called STRESS.

In addition to the requirements for mission qualification mentioned above, all of which are stressful, imagine sitting in a Commander's Call with key members of the 45th Avn Bn (SO)(A) listening to their new Bn Cdr, MAJ Leroy A. Wall. The following are my notes from an After Action Report of the meeting, which was held on 17 November 1985 at the Quality Inn, near Tulsa International Airport:

"The new 45th Avn Bn Commander, Major Leroy Wall opened the Cdr's Call at 1235 hrs. He first stated his overall goals for the entire battalion:

1. [We have] a mission to support the Special Forces, continue to train at night, increase our capability to plan, execute and develop concepts to support Special Operations.
2. Staff will continue development of tactical and administrative SOPs, to be in hard copy NLT 1 February 1986.

3. S-3 will prepare a plan to have 12 personnel in the FAARPs section airborne qualified NLT FY 87.
4. NBC training will begin battalion wide . . . I want each Cdr to take a personal look and interest in NBC . . . I'll look for it (NBC) on your training schedules, NBC testing and weapons qualification in MOPP4 gear. Use your imagination. NBC training will become commonplace in this battalion.
8. I want a long range deployment every other month.
9. Last, but certainly not the least, . . . I want all of this done as SAFELY as possible.

Then MAJ Wall gave specific guidance to each of the battalion's company commanders as follows:

HSC – "Work on training the many low density MOS personnel, explore ways such as unit schools, EAATS, to bring up MOS qual; devise ways to work with Co B 149th Avn on movement of your FAARP.

Co A [MH-6 lift] – "Continue your low-level, night [NVG] operations and deployments; stress Omega training and longer range missions.

Co B [AH-6 guns] – "100% gunnery qualification . . . lead the way in concept development of Special Operations Aviation [doctrine]."

Co C [Maint] – "You are getting two new aircraft [UH-60] in April, train for these aircraft and the aircraft we have [today], emphasis on common soldier skills and NBC."

Co B 149th – " . . . you've already started NVG training, by the end of May 1986 I want one airlift platoon NVG Mission Qualified. My staff and I will assist you in overcoming the problems in the area of Mission Training vs Mission Support (IDT/AT). The S-3 will involve you in air-loading training of your UH-1s in the next year and hazardous cargo training . . . I would expect you, NLT AT 1986 to be able to provide a limited one ship NVG mission capability.

Everyone in that conference room could feel the tension and stress level rising. This unit wasn't going to be a place for good ole boys or free loaders. If you were going to play in the game, and not sit on the bench, then you were going to have to work your ass off and do one helluva lotta training! Yes, you were going to get stressed – not a just a little, but to the max.

Stress is cumulative, meaning if not addressed, or released, it continues to worsen with time and continued stress. It can lead to inaccuracies during planning, disorientation, bad judgments, accidents or fatalities – those things, contributors or causes we often see labeled as human error.

During this same Commander's Call, CW2 Tommy Klutts Jr. presented a very informative and well organized *Night Vision Goggle Risk Assessment* management program briefing. This program has been presented to 5th Army and NGB. MAJ Wood asked that this presentation be included in the *Ground Commander's Course for Army Aviation* being conducted by Trp Cmd (Avn) in Stillwater on 25 January 1986 to the 1st Bn 179th Infantry," as stated in the After Action Report. It's a new game and we've noticed that we don't have all the necessary equipment or experience – and nobody was going to just give it to us.

Most flight instruments used on early helicopters were designed for fixed-wing aircraft and respond quite poorly to helicopter maneuvering at slow speeds, or at a hover. Disorientation can occur when helicopters are hovered over snow, sand or loose dirt that may be picked up by the rotor wash, leading to loss of visual reference—referred to as a white-out or brown-out. Automatic hover mode on newer generation helicopters greatly reduces disorientation and accidents. However, situational awareness is essential in all times, along with specific aircrew coordination training.

The requirement for all-weather day and night operational capability has provided the impetus for major advancements in light amplification systems. In the 1970s, Army aviation adopted second-generation AN/PVS-5 night-vision goggles which were first developed for the infantry. These were mounted to the flight helmet and used as the primary means to acquire visual information so that flights could be conducted during darkness down to quarter moon levels.

With the help of some of our 45th Avn Bn instructor pilots, and at their suggestion, most specifically Chief Warrant Officer Leonard Reed, the U.S. Army Aeromedical Research laboratory (USAARL) designed a modification to the full face goggle to allow much of it to be removed and provide a look under capability for peripheral target detection and the reading of aircraft instruments.

More recently, the aviation night-vision imaging system (ANVIS) was developed specifically for aviation. The principle improvement in these new systems is the third generation light amplification tube with enhanced sensitivity and extended range to the near infrared region. The ANVIS allows operations down to starlight levels. Night-vision devices do not turn night into day. Visual acuity with high-contrast targets varies from 20/40 to 20/60 depending on ambient illumination. Field-of-view is restricted to 40 degrees and both stereopsis and color vision are essentially eliminated.

Thus, aviators using night-vision devices must operate with visual information quite different from the normal daytime unaided input. Operations involving night vision devices require different flight rules. Preflight planning and coordination become vital for mission safety and success. Aviators must be trained to know the capabilities and limitations of these devices. Most importantly they must be taught that constant scanning using head movements to clear airspace is absolutely essential to compensate for the reduced field of vision.

Helicopter operations in and out of unimproved landing sites, with or without sophisticated electronic aids can be highly stressful and demanding. Thus increasing the burden of decision making on the pilot. The threat of unintentional ground or surface contact is much higher during confined area, pinnacle operations, slope landings and over-water operations.

Risk Assessment/Management

"Flying is inherently dangerous. We like to gloss that over with clever rhetoric and comforting statistics, but these facts remain: gravity is constant and powerful, and speed kills. In combination, they are particularly destructive."

Dan Manningham

For the new aviator or air crewmember, it is most difficult to imagine the lumps, bumps, cuts and scrapes that have been endured by your predecessors. From those bad experiences (training mishaps, errors and accidents in TF 160 and the 45th Avn Bn) came good judgment. We learned from most of our mistakes. What we learned came to be called "lessons learned." Were they all original ideas? Can't say for sure, but I believe that a few actually were . . .

The Army's Aviation Risk Assessment Program – well, perhaps it began in Oklahoma, maybe Tulsa. We know it had already been briefed to the 45th Avn Bn (SO)(A), 5th Army and NGB by November 1985.

Here's what Chief Warrant Officer Five Tommy Klutts told me, "The original idea came to me from the days I flew helicopters in the oil field. The company I worked for gave each employee a little portion [percentage] of each [oil] well they successfully produced. One day I asked one of the owners how he knew the probability of any given new well producing?

He said, "We do an assessment of all the factors and make a highly educated guess as to the probability of it coming in!" That started the idea for aviation risk assessment.

"One day at the facility, late summer 1984, there were four of us sitting around talking: Richard Murphy, Leonard Reed, Dwight Cheek and myself. We were discussing the 26 July 1984 incident at Greenleaf Lake, where Bear Smith and that guy from Arkansas [Chief Warrant Officer James Guernsey of Fayetteville, AR], flew an OH-6 [during NVG training] into the lake. We talked about what could have be done that might have prevented that incident."

"We started listing the factors which might have contributed:
- reduced illumination
- divided attention
- formation
- crew rest
- other, etc.

"I came up with idea that we should list these factors, add more, such as temperature, pucker factor and give each one value on a scale. The idea being if the illumination decreases, then the risk factor [number] increases and vice versa."

"Together we designed a Risk Assessment matrix. The AMC or Flight Lead would arrive at a final risk assessment of Low, Medium or High Risk and brief this to the commander. Then commander then was to decide whether to allow this mission to be flown or not."

"Later, Lieutenant Colonel Barefoot, 5th Army Aviation Officer came to Tulsa and did an ARMS (Avn Readiness Maintenance Survey) inspection. I briefed the new Risk Assessment matrix and program. He liked it and invited me to come to 5th Army and brief it. I briefed it to 5th Army and also to the NGB Avn & Safety Conference at NG PEC (National Guard Professional Education Center) at Camp Robinson, AR. They liked it and the NGB Safety guy, Major Kenneth Boley, wanted to take it and the credit [for developing it]."

"NGB and Dept of the Army adopted my Risk Assessment program and it is still in use by military and civilian aviation worldwide. Mr. NGB Aviation Safety, Al Carrigan, always gave credit to me and the *National Guard for the Risk Assessment Program*," stated CW5 Klutts.

"Tough, realistic training conducted to standard is the cornerstone of Army warfighting skills. An intense training environment stresses both soldiers and equipment, creating a high potential for accidents. The potential for an accident increases as training realism increases, just as it does in combat. The end result is the same; the soldier or asset is lost. Commanders must find ways to protect individuals, crews, teams, and equipment from accidents during training and combat. How well they do this could be the decisive factor in winning or losing. Risk [assessment/] management is a commonsense tool that leaders can use to make smart risk decisions in tactical and everyday operations. It is a method of getting the job done by identifying the areas that present the highest risk and taking action to eliminate, reduce, or control the risk. It is not complex, technical, or difficult. It is a comparatively simple decision making process, a way of thinking through a mission to balance mission demands against risks[8].

Deactivation – August 1994
"The difference between fiction and reality? Fiction has to make sense."
Tom Clancy

Soldiers in the unit began to hear the rumors which had started around late 1990 or 1991. Some said they got mixed messages. Perhaps the aviation leadership in Oklahoma was too optimistic. The action officers at Dept of the Army in the Pentagon were quite the opposite. Yet, we leaders had been trained that confidence was 90% of the battle. If you talked to some of the more cynical, realistic guys—they were saying, the deactivation of 1/245th, was going to happen.

There were optimists and there were pessimists everywhere you looked. It was impossible to get a clear reading at any level. Some in Oklahoma were ready for Special Operations Aviation to end. It was seen as a jaded idea, too expensive, too compartmentalized and too classified.

In 1987, we never got an official invitation to participate in Operation Prime Chance in the Persian Gulf. They wanted us, but getting us called up was a nut that was too tough to crack. We can't assume that was the case during Operation Desert Storm, yet we weren't called upon to participate in that fight either.

At times it seemed as if Oklahoma Special Operations Aviation had been blessed with almost an endless source of funding for the SOA mission. At a point in time, circa 1990, the scales became unbalanced. Someone many pay grades above us made the decision that 1st Bn 245th Avn (SO) (A) had become too costly and/or too distracting. We were to become a bill payer for other options out on the table.

If you are interested in military history you perhaps have heard General Westmoreland, former military commander of U.S. troops in Vietnam, who said, "We never lost a military battle in Vietnam."

You may also have heard of former infantry commander, historian and instructor at the U.S. Army War College, Colonel Harry G. Summers Jr., who was discussing the Vietnam war with a North Vietnamese Army counterpart. Summers made the following comment to the Vietnamese officer, "You never defeated us in the field."

To which the NVA officer replied: "That may be true. It is also irrelevant."

At 1400 hrs. on 28 August 1994, the 1st Bn 245th Avn (Special Operations) (Abn) formed one last time on the concrete ramp of the Tulsa Army Aviation Support Facility and the deactivation/casing of the colors ceremony of the *Lords of Darkness* took place.

At the time of the deactivation the Bn Cdr was Lieutenant Colonel Terry R. Council and the Bn CSM was CSM Charles B. Connell. The Bn Executive Officer was MAJ Lewis W. Keller. The following names and unit positions are taken from the 1st Bn 245th Avn (SO)(A) deactivation program handout dated 28 August 1994.

Members of the Bn Staff were:

S-1 – vacant
S-2 – Captain Thomas D. Jesse
S-3 – Major Marvin D. Roberts
S-4 – Captain Joe B. Hicks

Headquarters and Headquarters, 1/245th Co Cdr was Captain Britt M. Himes. The First Sergeant was First Sergeant George R. Wright Sr.

Company A, 1/245th Co Cdr was Major Charles E. Hammers. The First Sergeant was First Sergeant Joseph A. Crawford.

Company B, 1/245th Co Cdr was Major Martin E. Weaver. The First
Sergeant was First Sergeant James W. Perry II.

Company C, 1/245th Co Cdr was Major Walter E. Fountain. The
First Sergeant was First Sergeant Ronald I. Dye.

Company D, 1/245th Co Cdr was Major Jeffery Jones. The First
Sergeant was First Sergeant Joseph H. Volpe.

---

1. Ms. LaTasha Gatling provided numerous emails regarding OKARNG aviation history, which included great detail such as OA #s, dates, unit designations, reorganizations, locations, etc.

2. Joseph Seymour, a native of Philadelphia, PA and a former PA Army National Guardsman, holds a Bachelors degree from Penn State in International Politics and a Masters in History from Temple University

3. Information on the history of the Army's method of numeric designations for new units was provided by Mr. Joseph Seymour, 30 January 2009, with a reference from Jennifer Nichols, AAMH-FPO, 26 January 2009, Subj: Numbering Blocks for Army Units, Center for Military History.

4. SSG Gregg S. Bond, former major and Army Aviator, was a valued member of the 45th Avn Bn's S-2/Intelligence staff section.

5. Some info on Operations Earnest Will and Prime Chance are excerpts from the website http://www.specialoperations.com/

6. Nick Rowe had become a Viet Cong POW in 1963 and was held for 5 years, but he never gave up and finally escaped. He was later killed by terrorists in Manila, Philippines on 21 Apr 1989.

7. Excerpts from Army Regulation 350–30 Training Code of Conduct, Survival, Evasion, Resistance, and Escape (SERE) - Training Headquarters, Department of the Army, Washington, DC, 10 December 1985

8. Excerpt from Army FM 3-04.513, Appendix D, Battlefield Recovery and Evacuation of Aircraft, Department of the Army, Washington D.C., 27 September 2000

Chapter 17

Lest We Forget . . .

(Heroes, Memories and Memorials)

*"The world is divided into people who do things and people
who get the credit. Try, if you can, to belong to the first class.
There's far less competition . . ."*

Dwight Marrow

Did we recognize every significant event or heroic action that occurred
during our watch? Probably not. And perhaps that was the norm, rather
than the exception. Could it be apathy that causes us to ignore unselfish
acts of courage or other heroic events, thinking, " . . . someone else will
recognize them; or sadly, it wasn't that big of a deal."

It should always be our desire to give credit where such is due and
recognition for service above oneself. Yet, I know that sometimes I've
overlooked the efforts of others. Although it may not have been intentional,
it still was a lack of recognition. While serving in the military we often
have seen those who have sacrificed a little, some who sacrificed a lot. Let
us not forget those comrades who have sacrificed it all. Let us not forget
the men at the bottom of the totem pole who were seldom recognized,
but were always there giving 110% effort, even when we didn't notice.
Without him completing his job, we couldn't have done ours.

Many aviation soldiers should be recognized for the sacrifices they
have made and continue to make. I will make no claim that I have

516

included in this chapter ever note worthy act of valor, heroism or unselfish courage by an OKARNG aviation soldier, but I pray that these heroes and memories will not slip by unnoticed, and importantly, that their memory and accomplishments will not be forgotten.

It is also a pleasure to include several interesting news articles from the years past which pertain to OKARNG Aviation and the 1st Bn 245th Avn (SOA). Also included in this chapter are some short memories which are appropriate for inclusion.

Not everyone in this chapter necessarily received great honors or awards. Some of the real aviation heroes in our OKARNG history are those who were here at the beginning . . . Most of their high flying tales and real war stories are lost in time.

During a visit at the home of Brigadier General Dana D. Batey in Edmond, OK several years ago, I had asked him to recall some of the names of our Oklahoma Guard aviation pioneers. Since then, I dug a little deeper, and consider the following aviators as heroes of our past . . .

- Chief Warrant Officer Two Perry H. Townsend Jr. – Aviator in OKARNG Avn before Korea. Went with 45th INF DIV to Korea, returned to OK w/Div and remained in OKAVN (OKARNG "Long Service Medal[1], Armed Forces Reserve Medal and 15 yr LS Ribbon" 2 November 1942 – 24 December 1961) [Co B 45th Avn Bn] died ca 2003.
- Captain Jack Ray – Aviator in OKARNG Avn before Korea. Went with 45th INF DIV to Korea, stayed on active duty and retired; died ca 1996.
- Lieutenant Colonel Gus Guild—w/45th Inf Div in Korea, later in Div Arty Avn Sec, then 45th Inf Div Hqs; died 1 January 1999.
- Colonel Karl M. Frank – post-Korea, went through Guard aviation program, was in 45th Avn, his wife was a CWO admin type; she passed ca 1996. He passed 4 April 2009 in Norman (Parkinson's).
- Colonel Ron Howland – Korea before OKARNG; MG (Judge) Dougherty was a federal judge who helped Ron. First an admin law clerk, then he became a judge. Ron retired as a Colonel from OKARNG; still a runner/jogging, marathoner, big OU basketball fan. Stepped down from the bench (ca 2008) . . .

- Chief Warrant Officer Four Gerald "Pappy" Devine—flew P-47s in the ETO in WWII, later called back and flew F-86s in Korea and then did three tours in Vietnam flying O-1As. Ended his aviation career at Tulsa; now deceased.
- CWO John Mitch Johnston – Navy Ace during WWII, he came from Navy Reserves into OKARNG, was an civilian Instructor Pilot at Mineral Wells, later retired from OKARNG and went to work at LEX as a security guard. Passed away ca 1987.
- Captain Jack Avant – came into OKARNG as an aviator, he spent time at Norman, he was from Tulsa, (OKARNG "Long Service Medal[1] and Armed Forces Reserve Medal" – 2 February 1947 – 30 January 1958) [Avn Sec 1, Bde 45 Inf Div] got his 20 yrs in, makes C.L. Strance's reunion, still in Tulsa area.
- Major Donald D. Wolgamott—was an Instructor Pilot at Mineral Wells, retired as a MAJ/LTC. (OKARNG "Hourglass Device[2] to Armed Forces Reserve Medal" – 30 November 1942 – 29 November 1962) [HHB 45 Inf Div Arty (Avn Sec)] Passed away ca 1997.
- Warrant Officer Chas. E. Koonce – was in 45th Bde/Div Avn Sec, post-Korea, went to regular Army. Whereabouts unknown.
- Billy M. Bodem – was in OKARNG Div Arty Avn Sec after Korea, retired from OKARNG.
- Richard E. Bailey – post-Korea, didn't stay very long, 2 or 3 yrs.
- Robert Bristow – came out of the FA and was in Div Arty Avn Sec, post-Korea; retired.
- Marvin Shears – Co B, post-Korea, he stayed around for 5 or 6 yrs and went to Alaska, Batey said, "Don't think he got his 20 yrs in, may have been enlisted, then got his commission."
- Thomas Naylor – came out of Div Arty Avn Sec, post-Korea, went regular Army and retired.
- Frank L. Berry – a dedicated guardsman; worked for the postal service. Lives near Konawa; retired.
- C.L. Strance – a 1950s active Army aviator, joined the guard and made Major, then reverted to Chief Warrant Officer, retired as MAJ/CW4.

- Frank Cory – was in the 445th Avn Co and 45th Inf Bde Avn Sec, post-Korea, made lieutenant colonel, then USAR and retired as colonel.
- Lieutenant Colonel Jay Tommy Evans – "one hell of a man," died 18 March 2008.
- Captain Ralph Mayfield – was USAR aviator came into OKARNG became Cdr, Co E 700th Maint Bn as a captain, went to work at Mineral Wells as IP, then committed suicide. Worked out of Norman in Avn business.
- Chief Warrant Officer Four Joe Patterson—flew B-24s in WWII, joined the OKARNG in 1964. Quit logging flight time after he had accumulated 25,000 plus hours while a member of Det 1, HHC, 45th Sep Inf Bde Avn Section at Lexington.

In an email from Colonel Leroy A. Wall, he remembers that, "John Mitchell Johnston was a Naval Aviator in WWII and a double ace, having shot down 11 Japanese aircraft, two in one day. I know he flew Hellcats, from the USS Bon Homme Richard (CVA31), an Essex class attack carrier, which I'm sure you know is the name of John Paul Jones' old ship. After WWII Mitch lived in Boise, Idaho and was a home builder. He told me that one day in the 1960's he was working on the roof of a house and a National Guard recruiter, who somehow found out about his prior service climbed the ladder and talked to him about joining the Idaho Army National Guard. Mitch joined up and went to the Army Rotary Wing Course."

"In about 1967 Southern Airways at Ft. Wolters TX was looking everywhere for helicopter pilots and Mitch moved to Mineral Wells and transferred to the Oklahoma National Guard. Mitch didn't like instructing and became a maintenance pilot for Southern. After a couple of years his wife decided to go back to Boise and they divorced. In 1972 Mitch moved to Oklahoma to be closer to the Guard and built a big mobile home park in Nicoma Park, OK. Another divorce later, Mitch became the head grounds keeper at the heliport at Lexington. Later he became a security guard. Mitch lived a few miles east of the heliport on acreage on the North side of State highway 39. After he retired from the Guard, he hurt his back lifting a bale of hay into his pickup. He spent the last years of his life in a wheel chair."

In 1973, under the command of Major Karl M. Frank, with First Sergeant Kenneth Inman as the Senior NCO, the **445ᵗʰ Aviation Company (Assault Helicopter)** won the national, prestigious and coveted AAAA Outstanding Aviation Unit (RC) of the year award. MAJ Karl Marx Frank, commander of the 445ᵗʰ attended the AAAA Award Banquet in San Antonio, TX, and accepted the award presented by the 5ᵗʰ Army CG, Lieutenant General Seneff.' Some have stated that it was your typical rubber chicken banquet and Karl fretted all day about what remarks he would give at the banquet. He wound up thanking everyone, one-at-a-time. Then he would pause, waiting for the audience' applause to die down and he'd begin once more. However, as humorous as that may sound, he did share the credit.

Karl M. Frank was born 19 July 1930 at Duncan, OK and graduated from Bethany High School in 1948. Karl's military career covered all the bases—he enlisted in the Air National Guard 9 November 1948 and stayed until 21 March 1949, and then he joined the Navy March 1949 for a two year hitch. Following active Navy duty he entered the Naval Reserves from March 1950 to 1954. In March 1954 he joined the OKARNG and attended Infantry OCS in 1957/58. As an officer Karl attended FW and RW flight school in 1962-64. He also worked for the U.S. Postal Service, retiring after 37 years. Karl earned a bachelor's degree from Southeastern State University in May 1981 and retired from the military as COL/0-6 on 28 March 1983.

Below are a few highlights from 1973:

It was a very busy year for the 445ᵗʰ. Instrument Flight Training Classes would be conducted at the Army Aviation Support Facility Norman, OK; six separate classes of thirty days duration were scheduled to qualify all assigned aviators on instruments by December 1973.

"Reactions were quick on the afternoon of 27 July 1973 when the call for assistance came. A full blown riot was underway at the Oklahoma State Penitentiary at McAlester, OK. Selected individuals with Riot Control equipment were in the air and the way within minutes." The 445ᵗʰ Avn Co furnished support and assistance from 27 July through 3 August. The unit left Oklahoma on 4 August for annual training at Fort Carson, CO.

Mountain Flight Training was the major area of concentration at Summer Camp 1973 for the 445ᵗʰ. The unit successfully completed all training requirements and was cited by the Fort Carson Aviation Safety Officer as follows:

"The score of "Satisfactory" does not do justice to the 445th Avn Co (Aslt Hel) as this unit, with the exceptions as noted, is the most outstanding unit I have ever inspected."

A Crew Chief Standardization (67N) program, designed by the 445th, was adopted by OKARNG as the State Standardization program for training and qualification of Crew Chiefs.

At 2330 hrs, 28 September 1973, another call came. This time for a search and rescue mission. A Texas International Airlines, Convair CV-600 (N94230) passenger plane, Flight # 655, with eight or nine Army Officials from the Red River Arsenal aboard was missing. The Arkansas National Guard responded first to the call with two of their aircraft. during dense fog and rain, one of the Arkansas ARNG aircraft crashed. Three Arkansas Guard air crewmembers answered the call for help and made the supreme sacrifice that day while conducting the search for the missing airliner.

Lieutenant Colonel Emmitt Doyle McElwain[3] recalled this unfortunate accident, "Those Texas International guys got into a thunder storm coming out of Magnolia, AR or somewhere around there. You know the [black box] tape was just horrible. One minute they are smoking and joking around; they should've never taken off. Finally one of them says, "Hey you know the ground is 2,700 feet here . . ." and about that time they impacted. And they had [tuned in on] the Rich Mountain VOR at the time of the accident. I think I had just gone to work for the Guard [aviation]."

Here's the tragic part of it – they knew these [Texas International Airlines] guys had crashed and they sent the Arkansas [ARNG AASF] facility commander, who was also the State Avn Officer, a full colonel, in the front aircraft [UH-1] and the maintenance officer in the back aircraft. They were dispatched down there early in the morning in the fog. They were following the road . . .

McElwain sadly continued, "I think his name, the maintenance officer, was John Grisham. I had just gone to Aviation Safety School [at USC] with him. I knew him. He didn't like to fly instruments. It was like he was scared to death . . . we talked about that in Safety school. Well, what happened was they kept digging in deeper and deeper [into this bad weather]. The last thing that he said is, he called the colonel by name and said, " . . . I'm in trouble." They crashed [that UH-1] into the ground, a lieutenant over there in the left seat, my friend CWO Grisham in the right . . . at about 110 knots."

"And then they called us [OKARNG aviation from Lex] down there. We had to take care of all that mess. To include all those people on that airplane. It was bad! I didn't get in on that at all. I think I had just gone to work [full-time with aviation].

Members of the 445th Avn Co (Aslt Hel) continued the search for the airplane and its eleven passengers. On 1 October, a civilian pilot on a routine flight reported sighting what he believed to be the wreckage of the airliner. Our 445th Avn Co. helicopters went to the reported site, found the wreckage, but there were no survivors. All eleven were later found and had died in the crash near Rich Mountain at Mena, AR on 27 September 1973. Three Arkansas ARNG aviation personnel died in their UH-1 while in search of Texas International Airlines Flight # 655.

The OKARNG crews helped with the evacuation of the bodies, later flying in some of the Texas International Airline personnel to the crash site. Tired and weary, the 445th's "Can Do" crews from Oklahoma came home to Norman to rest.

October 1973 was cold, wet and miserable in Oklahoma. During the heavy fall rains another disaster occurred. The Oklahoma Military Department activated selected individuals from the 445th Avn Co on the morning of 11 October flood waters were raging in Alfalfa, Kay, Grant, Noble, Major, Garfield, Kingfisher and Logan counties in North-central Oklahoma. For the next seven days, helicopters of the 445th Avn Co churned the air, while muddy flood waters raged below. The activated aviation personnel assisted with aerial searches, evacuations, ferried supplies, equipment and personnel in various parts of the affected area.

The year 1973 was nearly over and things looked like they would settle down, but on the 19th of November another catastrophe occurred. Mother Nature blew a tornado into the Blanchard and Moore areas. Once again the 445th Avn Co. (Aslt Hel) was called upon to assist. At 2300 hrs on 19 November the unit was on the move, sealing off the area, setting up check points and assisting local authorities in the search for missing persons following this tornado. OKARNG aircraft and personnel responded and were on station until released on the morning of 21 November. Once again the 445th's "Can Do" attitude stood tall as did its members.

December 1973 brought another AGI (Annual General Inspection) and a sigh of relief as the year came to an end. But what a year!

Looking back, the year 1973 began with Major Jerry D. Bourassa as commander, and Captain Karl M. Frank as Executive Officer. The Operations Platoon was headed up by Captain Frank A. Cory and Captain James C. Peck was the Asst Ops Officer.

Captain Nathaniel Ray Brown was the PLT CDR of the First Airlift PLT. Chief Warrant Officer Three Clarence R. Clarkson Jr. was the Flight Safety Tech. Sergeant First Class Charlie H. Evans was a UH-1 crewchief; Chief Warrant Officer Two Robert E. Clark and Chief Warrant Officer Two Roy G. Cross were RW pilots.

Second Airlift PLT was commanded by Captain Donald E. Derrick. Specialist Five Donald G. McCarty, Captain Tony E. Boyle, Specialist Five Jack Nation, Chief Warrant Officer Two Gary L. Elliot, First Lieutenant Dan E. Hasenfratz, Chief Warrant Officer Two Delbert E. Meier, Specialist Five Wheeler Parker II, and First Lieutenant James L. Giddens were a few others in Second Flt PLT.

Armed Helicopter PLT was commanded by Captain James L. Smith. Specialist Five John T. Ashmore, Chief Warrant Officer Three Donald L. Day, Chief Warrant Officer Two Richard O. Murphy, Captain Dale E. Martin, Chief Warrant Officer Two C.L. Strance, Chief Warrant Officer Two Jack E. Avant and Warrant Officer One Donald L. Nave were some of the crew in the Armed Helicopter PLT.

Service PLT was commanded by Captain Emmett D. McElwain. Sergeant First Class William G. "Bill" Rogers and Specialist Six Leo Keenan were part of the Service PLT Hqs.

Aircraft Maint Section was commanded by Chief Warrant Officer Two Bobby J. Swink. Staff Sergeant Rudie Leippe was the Maint Supervisor. Staff Sergeant Willis G. Bettes was the Aircraft Armament SGT. In charge of the Avionics Repair Section was Chief Warrant Officer Two Oren L. Peters. Sergeant First Class Nathan D. Franke and Specialist Six Gerald W. Swanson were part of the crew in avionics.

In the Flight Surgeon Detachment (Augmented) were the Avn Med Off Lieutenant Colonel David J. Geigerman, Specialist Five Robert D. Hudgins, Specialist Five Jackie L. Pinion, Specialist Four Michael L. Williams and PFC Jon T. Ledlie.

On 11 June, Captain Karl M. Frank replaced MAJ Jerry D. Bourassa as Commanding Officer and CPT Donald E. Derrick became the Executive Officer. Many other platoon and section officer changes occurred during the summer and early fall.

"Boy, that was a lot of work; [CWO] Bobby Swink and [CPT] Dale Martin did 80% on that AAAA [award] they worked with the Senior Army advisor [Lieutenant Colonel Billy Lee Sprague]. Bobby worked full-time [in Maint at Norman] and left the guard about the time we went down to Lexington (1975)," recalls Charlie H. Evans[4].

"Congratulations to each member of the 445th Aviation Company (Assault Helicopter), you are a definite asset to our Nations' Defense and a great credit to the Oklahoma Army National Guard." Those were the words of Colonel Curtis W. Milligan, Assistant Chief of Staff-Operations for Oklahoma as the unit [445th Avn Co] was presented with the National Guard Bureau's Superior Unit Award for 1974 during the March 1975 drill assembly.

With the awards over, successful completion of the COMET Inspection, and range firing near completion, the unit went back to the classroom for instruction and MOS-OJT training. Armed UH-1s fired rockets and mini-guns at Fort Chaffee during March while conducting Aerial Gunnery Qualification.

The 445th Avn Co (Aslt Hel) was the premier aviation unit in OKARNG for its time – 1971 until 1978. It is a rich history with many, many accomplishments.

COL Leroy A. Wall

Chief Warrant Officer Four Leroy A. Wall was honored in **1978** by AAAA and received the 5th Army Area Reserve Component Aviator of the Year Award. He applied for a direct commission and was promoted from Chief Warrant Officer Four to Major. As a lieutenant colonel, he commanded the 45th Avn Bn (Sp Ops)(Abn) the year it was awarded the AAAA Aviation Unit of the Year award 1986. COL Wall and his wife, Tommy, reside in Norman, OK. He continues to fly rotary-wing and fixed-wing in his civilian job today.

Colonel John J. Stanko Jr. received many accolades during his years of military/civilian service to aviation. In **1980** COL Stanko received the AAAA Joseph P. Cribbins DAC of the Year Award. COL Stanko and his wife, Pinky, resided in the beautiful town he settled in after WWII, Danville, PA. He was promoted to the rank of Brigadier General in the state of Pennsylvania.

COL John J. Stanko Jr.

17 February 1980 Broken Wing Award[5] – excerpts from a National Guard Bureau article and *Tulsa World* articles. Note: The requirements for this award, as stated in Army Regulation 672-74, specify that, "An aircrew member must, through outstanding airmanship, minimize or prevent aircraft damage or injury to personnel during an emergency situation. The aircrew member must have shown extraordinary skill while recovering an aircraft from an in-flight emergency situation."

Three Oklahoma Army National Guardsmen escaped injury Sunday, (17 February 1980) when they made an emergency landing on a street in Coffeyville, KS. Oklahoma Guardsman Chief Warrant Officer Three Ronald J. Ketter, 32, of Owasso, was awarded the Army's prestigious Broken Wing Award for saving three lives by piloting a severely damaged and disabled UH-1M (gunship) helicopter to safe landing at Coffeyville, KS while on a training flight out of Tulsa. The award was presented by Major General Robert Morgan, the Adjutant General of Oklahoma in September 1980.

Ketter was flying a UH-1M at 2,000' when a tail rotor blade disintegrated, causing the 90° gearbox to separate and then it hit the horizontal stabilizer before failing further. The gearbox fell through the roof of an abandon house, where children had been playing moments earlier. They heard the helicopter and came outside to watch, before the incident. Ketter said he heard what " . . . sounded like an explosion" at about 11:40 a.m. and he immediately began emergency-landing procedures. Ron Ketter managed to land his aircraft on an 80-foot wide Coffeyville, KS city street, avoiding power lines, tree limbs and cars.

"The Broken Wing Award is given by the regular Army to 12 to 15 aviators annually worldwide. CW3 Ketter is the first to receive this award in OKARNG aviation," according to Lieutenant Colonel Dana Batey, OKSAO. Ketter, a Vietnam veteran worked for Cities Service Oil Co, Tulsa and was a member of Co D 149th Avn at the time of this incident.

Others on board were Chief Warrant Officer Wes Foutch, 37, copilot from Wagner and Sergeant Lee Taylor, 26, crewchief of Tulsa."

15 May 1982 Army Commendation Medal[6] – excerpt from award certificate and *Tulsa World* – On 15 May 1982 a flight of two UH-1H Aircraft enroute from Tulsa to Ft Sill observed an explosion and fire at a gas oil rig in the distance, near Rush Springs. A bulldozer had hit a gas line, setting off the explosion which injured eight men. As the aircraft

Tulsa World photo—L-R: CW2 Arnold, CW2 Booher, CW2 Baines, CW2 Barlow, CPT Murphy, CPT Bentley, CW2 McCarty & CPT Sleeper

neared the burning gas line several injured men signaled the aircraft for assistance. They landed and gave assistance to burn victims and transported injured to Reynolds Community Hospital at Ft Sill, resulting in the saving of lives. Medals were awarded to eight aviators (CPT Richard O. Murphy OIC, Captain Garry O. Bentley, Captain Earl Sleeper, Chief Warrant Officer Two Ralph Arnold, Chief Warrant Officer Two Tom Baines, Chief Warrant Officer Two Dennis Barlow, Chief Warrant Officer Two Timothy Booher. Chief Warrant Officer Two Don McCarty and CPT Richard O. Murphy, the OIC, was given an Army Commendation Medal, the others Army Achievement Medal.

CPT Richard "Rick" Read

3 October 1982 – Broken Wing Award – Captain Richard A. Read, pilot-in-command and Chief Warrant Officer Three Donald E. "Dirt Doctor" Hubbard, co-pilot, both of Co B, 149th Avn, while supporting the 45th Inf Bde (Sep) on a drill weekend near Fort Chaffee, AR, were the lead aircraft in a formation flight of five UH-1 Hueys. During the routine troop movement/combat assault training mission, the audio warning signal beeped and the RPM warning light momentarily blinked, then came on steadily and interrupted what thus far been a routine mission. CPT Read increased collective pitch to reduce the rotor RPM which was sky-rocketing and simultaneously stated to his co-pilot, "I think we've got a problem." Then he transmitted to the flight, "Engine Overspeed." Read made the decision to autorotate and successfully landed in a very small landing area. The Broken Wing award was presented to CPT Read by MG Robert M. Morgan, Oklahoma Adjutant General at the Skirvin Plaza Hotel, OKC, during the annual military ball on Saturday, 26 March 1983.

Rick wrote in a recent email, "After being on stage, I'll never forget the walk back to our table and the standing ovation. It was one of my proudest moments."

During primary rotor-wing flight training at Fort Wolters, TX, I recall someone defining helicopter flight as, "Hour upon hour of shear boredom, marked by moments of stark terror." Having been there I have to agree and I'm sure Rick and "Dirt Doctor" will also. Today, however, is a new day and there is another thought which comes to mind – "Life isn't measured by the breaths we take, but by the moments that take our breath away."

26 July 1984 Oklahoma Distinguished Cross Medal – excerpt from award certificate—CPT Richard O. Murphy and First Lieutenant James Randy Smith were awarded the Oklahoma Distinguished Cross and Oklahoma Star of Valor for the heroic rescue of fellow aviators. CWO Larry "Bear" Smith of Tulsa and CWO James Guernsey of Fayetteville, AR, escaped serious injury in a nighttime OH-6 crash at Greenleaf Lake. The OH-6 was on a classified mission for the 45th Avn Bn flying under NVGs along a low-level NVG route, when the pilots lost reference to the terrain and could not detect their altitude above the ground. Luckily for them, they were over water, Greenleaf Lake, and crashed into the water at 100 Knots. CPT Murphy and 1LT Smith rescued the two men from about six foot of water as they held onto the skids of his OH-6 until they reached shallow water. A Poteau fisherman, Monroe Henson, took the men to shore in his private boat. Another aircraft had called a Tulsa Life Flight helicopter for medical evacuation of the injured pilots. They were treated and released from a Tulsa hospital.

1985-1986 – Outstanding Contributions—Colonel Robert J. Dille, Senior Army Flight Surgeon for the OKARNG, and Director of the Federal Aviation Administration's Civil Aeromedical Institute in Oklahoma City for twenty-two years was recognized for outstanding contributions to Army Aviation Medicine for 1985-1986. The following year Doc Dille received the Society of U.S. Army Flight Surgeons U.S. Army National Guard Flight Surgeon of the Year Award for **1986-87**.

COL J. Robert Dille

19 October 1986 – Army Commendation Medal – excerpt from award certificate—Captain David G. Orr, Co A, 1ˢᵗ Bn 245ᵗʰ Avn (SO)(A), while supporting the 7ᵗʰ Special Forces Group (Abn) during exercise Label Vista II, conducted a night Search and Rescue mission [in an OH-6] into hazardous terrain of the Huachuca Mountains in an effort to locate members of the 7ᵗʰ SFG who were lost and feared to be injured or possibly in other danger. Putting himself at great personal risk, CPT Orr was successful in locating the missing soldiers and ensuring their safety.

5 March 1987—MH-6 NVG Midair Kills Two Guardsmen[7]—excerpts from the *Tulsa World.* WAGONER [OK] During a multi-ship, NVG, training mission, two Oklahoma Guardsmen were killed in a mid-air collision on 5 March 1987. " . . . the deaths are the first in the 30 years [since] helicopters have been used by the Oklahoma National Guard," said Guard spokesman Colonel Gary Jackson. Killed in the crash were Chief Warrant Officers David O. Barr, 24, and Dennis L. Barlow, 43, both of Tulsa.

Two other Tulsa fliers in the other helicopter – Warrant Officers Mark R. Desjardins, 25, and Hugh D. Odum, 27 – were treated and released at St. Francis Hospital.

Gov. Henry Bellmon ordered flags flown at half staff in honor of the guardsmen.

The crash of the two OH-6 helicopters of the 45ᵗʰ Avn Bn based at Tulsa International Airport occurred about 9:20 p.m. Thursday, about four miles south of Wagoner along U.S. Hwy 69.

Chief Warrant Officer Three Dennis L. Barlow, married and father of three children, taught seventh grade science at Nimitz Middle School for 12 years.

Warrant Officer One David O. Barr was working full-time at the Tulsa unit's flight facility at the time of the accident. Barr was the honor graduate of his 1984 WORWAC flight school class. A military selection board had just promoted Barr to Chief Warrant Officer Two, but he had not yet been informed of the promotion.

Services for CWO David O. Barr were held at First United Methodist Church. Services for CWO Dennis L. Barlow were conducted at Central Church of the Nazarene. Burials included full military honors and a military missing man formation flyby salute.

1987 – Broken Wing Award The United States Army's Broken Wing Award recognizes an individual who demonstrated a high degree of professional skill while recovering from an in-flight failure or malfunction requiring an emergency landing. Warrant Officer Hugh D. Odum, pilot-in-command of the lead aircraft, one of the two OH-6 aircraft involved in a mid-air collision, 5 March 1987, was awarded the Army's Broken Wing Award as he and his co-pilot, Warrant Officer Mark Desjardins successfully autorotated their OH-6 following total engine failure.

45th Avn Bn (SO)(A) MH-6

Spring 1987 Aviation Unit Honored—"The 45th Avn Bn Special Ops unit was honored as the AAAA Outstanding ARNG Aviation Unit of the Year by the Army Aviation Association of America during ceremonies held in Ft. Worth in the spring of 1987. The award is . . . given to outstanding aviation units . . . that have demonstrated the highest degree of professionalism and accomplishment."

""The 45th Aviation Battalion, headquartered in Sperry, was given the award for their performance of mission citing the unique organization of the unit. The 45th Aviation Battalion is one of the most innovative aviation units in the Army National Guard," said Lieutenant General Charles D. Franklin, commander of the First U.S. Army and presenter of the prestigious [AAAA] award."

"Accepting the award was Battalion Commander Lieutenant Colonel Leroy Wall and Sergeant Major Charles B. Connell. "We are proud to accept this honor on the behalf of the men of the 45th Aviation Battalion," Wall said. "The men have worked long, hard hours enduring many hardships and I'm proud they are being recognized for their efforts.""" (Extracted from the OKARNG *On Guard* publication, Spring issue, 1987, by Captain Pat Scully, Asst PAO, 145th PAD).

2 May 1988 Guardsman Killed in Electrical Accident[8]—excerpt from article in *Tulsa World*—Palmerola Air Base, Honduras – An Oklahoma Army National Guard sergeant from Claremore died Monday in an electrical accident while on a training mission in Honduras, Guard personnel said Tuesday. Sgt. 1st Class David Alvin Brown, 31, was electrocuted about 2 p.m. while putting up a radio antenna. The antenna may have struck a high voltage line during the procedure, said Chief Warrant Officer Robert Graves, a communications officer in the Guard office in Sperry.

Brown was a radio communications chief on a routine training mission in Honduras with the Headquarters Company 1st Battalion 245th Aviation Special Operations Airborne Unit.

The Sperrybased unit is an airborne unit equipped with helicopters, Graves said. The training mission is an annual exercise for the unit in Central America.

Brown is survived by his parents, Oliver and Jennifer Brown of Claremore; three brothers, Ted Brown and Jim Brown, of Claremore, and Ben Brown, of California; and a daughter, Carrie Lynn Brown of Barnsdall.

8 May 1988 – Todd Named PA of Year – article in the Oklahoma National Guard *On Guard* magazine. "Chief Warrant Officer Three Floyd T. Todd, a Physician's Assistant [Flight Surgeon] in the Oklahoma Army National Guard, has been named the 1988 Aeromedical Physician Assistant of the Year for the ARNG by the Society of U.S. Army Flight

Surgeons. The award was presented at a special awards luncheon 8 May, during the organization's annual meeting in New Orleans, LA.

Todd is a Physician Assistant with Troop Command Aviation, Lexington. He joined the Oklahoma Guard in 1964 and later attended the Air Force Physician Assistant School at the University of Oklahoma. He received his PA certificate in 1979 and has been the full-time Physician

MG Don Ferrell, Sandy Todd & CW3 Floyd Todd

Assistant at Troop Command Aviation since 1984.

He was selected for the honor because the Society felt he was the Physician Assistant "who best represents the high ideals and standards set forth in Army Aviation Medicine," according to Major John V. Barson, secretary of the Society [of U.S. Army Flight Surgeons,] based at Fort Rucker, Alabama.

12 September 1988 Memorandum of Commendation – Departments of the Army and the Air Force, National Guard Bureau – "The assistance your State rendered during a recent classified operation involving the 160th Aviation Group (Airborne) has been recognized by Major General James D. Smith, Director of Operations, Readiness and Mobilization . . . the high state of readiness and the integrity and security of the operation were maintained by the personnel and professional vigilance of the following members of the OKARNG:

Major Billy R. Wood, Operations Officer

Chief Warrant Officer Four Robert Lane, ARNG Aviation Support Facility

Chief Warrant Officer Two Hugh Odum, Oklahoma Military Department

Signed, Donald Burdick, Major General, GS, Director, Army National Guard

27 August 1989 National Guard Complex Dedicated[9]—excerpt from *Tulsa World* article—The Oklahoma National Guard on Saturday dedicated a new $6.5 million complex that which will house a special battalion, a support center and a vehicle maintenance shop. The new Tulsa Army National Guard Aviation Complex is located at 4220 N. Mingo Valley Expressway. It will serve as the headquarters for the helicopter support center and 1st Battalion, 245th Aviation.

"We work under special operations throughout the United States and we support airbornetype units," said Sergeant Gregg Bond of the armory aviation support center. "We react to threats against the defense of the United States and the state of Oklahoma."

The three buildings were dedicated in honor of guardsmen killed while on duty. Guardsmen Dennis Barlow and David Barr were killed in a March 1986 helicopter crash in Wagoner, OK. Barlow was a seventh grade science teacher at Nimitz Middle School. Barr was a fulltime guard technician. The National Guard Armory was dedicated in honor of Barlow and the Army Aviation Helicopter Support Center in honor of Barr. The headquarters and armory was formerly at Sperry, OK.

The Army National Guard Battalion supported by this new facility includes a group of 30 helicopters that work with the Rangers, Green Berets and other special operations teams. The facility was relocated because the unit needed more space, said Captain H.R. Holman [OKARNG PAO]

Plans are under way for a new Organizational Maintenance Shop to be constructed in the next year. It will be dedicated in honor of Sergeant David A. Brown of Barnsdall [OK], who was killed in 1988 while on duty in Honduras.

14 October 1989—Rappelling Accident[10]—Specialist Fourth Class Ross Duncan, an OKARNG soldier, was killed during a military rappel demonstration at an air show in Topeka, KS. SP4 Duncan was the brother of State Rep. (OK) Rex Duncan. The accident occurred on 14 October 1989. In accordance with the Oklahoma Air Assault School SOP, a rehearsal had been conducted prior to the actual mission and went off without a hitch. The Senior AAS Instructor for this demonstration told all members involved that the Rappel Master would "cut ropes" as part of the demo. A crew chief change was conducted prior to the actual mission and the new crew chief was not properly briefed on his responsibility concerning the team members. The Rappel Master was doing a rope cut on one side of the aircraft after he had cleared the rappellers as being on the ground. It appeared that the crew chief decided to help the Rappel Master and cut the ropes without looking below the aircraft to make sure the men were safely on the ground. SP4 Duncan had a rope entanglement at a height of 65-70 feet and while he was attempting to free the entanglement he was tragically cut loose from the aircraft . . .

16 January 1990 News from the Oklahoma Army National Guard by Colonel Bill Francis and Major Pat Scully, OKPAO—An Oklahoma Army National Guard Aviation Battalion from Tulsa will get more than an even break by the time it completes swapping its Blackhawk helicopter for newer models.

The unit, 1st Battalion, 245th Aviation (Special Operations Airborne) of the Oklahoma Army National Guard, began trading in its Blackhawks this month, said Lieutenant Colonel Gary L. Elliott, Battalion Commander. Currently, the unit has 10 Blackhawks.

By October 1990, the unit will have traded all of its current Blackhawks for newer ones, he said. But instead of having only 10, the unit will have 16 of the newer MH-60 Blackhawks, Elliott, a Mustang resident, said. Other helicopter changes will come later, he said.

In 1992, 19 UH-1 Hueys at the Battalion's unit at Lexington, will be replaced by the MH-47 Chinook helicopter, he said. Besides Blackhawks and Hueys, the unit has 13 MH6 aircraft.

The Battalion has more than 400 people, is in excess of 100 percent strength, and probably could recruit up to 150 percent strength if it were allowed to do that, Elliott said.

"The success in keeping this unit at full strength is to keep personnel busy and involved. The lowest grade kid is involved because if his job isn't completed, the missions don't go," Elliott said.

For example, he said, the unit has a Forward Area Refueling Point (FAARP) unit. The personnel are airborne qualified. They jump out of a C130 with 500 gallon fuel bladders to provide refueling in the forward area, he said. The aviation unit also supports various Oklahoma Guard missions including the Air Assault School at Camp Gruber, he said.

"The average pilot puts in about 110 days a year, is 28 to 32 years old and has flown between 1,100 and 1,500 hours," he said. Elliott, who was a helicopter pilot in Vietnam, joined the Oklahoma Guard in 1972.

2 June 1990 Fuel Truck Crash[11]—From an article reported in the *Tulsa World*: On 2 June 1990, an Oklahoma National Guard fuel truck crashed on Oklahoma Highway 59 in the vicinity of Grove, OK in Delaware County, during a refueling exercise by the Tulsa-based 245th Aviation Battalion. Fuel truck passenger Thomas Shulze of Chelsea was reported in fair condition today at St. Francis Hospital in Tulsa, a hospital spokesman said. Driver Gregory Long of Tulsa was reported in good condition at the hospital. A second truck passenger, Alan Martel of Tulsa, was treated at an Arkansas hospital and released a few hours after the accident Saturday afternoon, said Guard spokesman Colonel William Francis in Oklahoma City.

COL Francis said an obstacle created by a highway construction project sent the 5,000-gallon tanker off Oklahoma 59 in Delaware County. "I don't know if it got in a rut or what, but they tried to correct it and the truck flipped," Francis said. The truck rolled three times, the Oklahoma Highway Patrol said. One of the compartments carrying some of the tanker's 3,500 gallons of JP-4 jet fuel ruptured, forcing the patrol to close the highway for more than two hours. About 1,500 gallons of fuel spilled, said Jack Shields of Tulsa-based Sooner Emergency. The private company had heavy equipment at the site Sunday, scraping up dirt contaminated by the fuel.

2 June 1990 MH-6 Crash[12]—Also reported on 2 June 1990 by the *Tulsa World*: MH-6 Crash south of Claremore (engine failure) – COL Francis said, "Hours after the truck crashed, a Guard observation helicopter crashed in a field south of Claremore in the same refueling exercise. Pilots Roy Tackett of Bixby and Keith Owens of Wagoner were not injured. They were the only ones aboard the OH-6 helicopter when the craft lost power in an engine at about 8 p.m.," he said.

The two kept the helicopter from spinning out of control, but the hard landing damaged the helicopter's tail rotor blades, Francis said.

The accidents occurred as the Guard trained in Oklahoma and Missouri in exercises meant to hone its forward refueling abilities, Francis said.

4 May 1990 – Guardsman Receives MacArthur Award[13]—excerpt from a *Tulsa World* article. WASHINGTON—A member of an Oklahoma National Guard unit based in Lexington has received a MacArthur

Leadership award from Gen. Carl E. Vuono, Chief of Staff of the U.S. Army. Captain Walter E. Fountain, a member of Co B, 245th Aviation (SO)(A) unit, was one of 28 junior officers given the award, named for the late Gen. Douglas MacArthur. The officers represented both active and reserve units as well as each of the Army's major commands and staff agencies.

27 July 1991 – Heroism excerpt from Recommendation for Award On 27 July 1991, at Fort Bragg, NC, at approximately 0300 hrs SERE Team #5 was negotiating a rain swollen creek. While acting as a point man, Staff Sergeant Robert E. Jensen, was swept 25 meters downstream by the swift moving current. First Lieutenant Randal W. Beene, Co B, 1st Bn 245th Avn (SO)(A), without hesitation or reservation, with great risk to his own safety, dove into the water and rescued Staff Sergeant Jensen. The rescue and assistance rendered by 1LT Beene to SSG Jensen without any doubt prevented injury and saved SSG Jensen's life.

17 August 1991 – Guardsmen Mistaken for Drug Runners[14]—excerpt from a *Tulsa World* article. EDNA, KS—Two Tulsa-based Oklahoma National Guard helicopter crews practicing nighttime combat maneuvers were mistaken for drug traffickers and briefly captured by Labette County, Kan., law officers. Numerous sheriffs' officers and a Kansas Highway Patrol trooper, suspecting they might be interrupting a drug drop, arrested the crews of two Blackhawk helicopters at gunpoint Thursday at the former Edna airport.

"We thought we had a booger," Sheriff Tom Bringle said Friday. "We didn't know if we had good guys or bad guys." Bringle said citizens had reported hearing or seeing helicopters taking off and hovering in southern Labette County. "There's reason to cause suspicion. It has the makings of a good drug drop site," Bringle said. Officers tried to intercept the helicopters Wednesday and on other occasions, but they had disappeared.

MAJ Pat Scully [Public Affairs Office] of the Oklahoma National

Tulsa World photo—CW4 Jerry Farlin

535

Guard said the 245th Aviation Special Operations unit based in Tulsa had permission from the Kansas property owners to land at the abandoned airstrip. Guardsmen had been landing there all week and were using night vision equipment Thursday when the local officers converged on them, guns drawn. "It got pretty tense," Scully said. "It could have developed into something pretty serious."

26 August 1991 – Flying Leap[15]—excerpt from a *Tulsa World* article. BRAGGS, OK—Two Special Operation units from the Army Reserve and Army National Guard joined forces recently to get up in the air above Camp Gruber—only to jump back to earth.

The airborne operation was conducted by the Army Reserve's 2nd Battalion, 12th Special Forces Group (Airborne) and the Army Guard's 1st Battalion, 245th Aviation (Special Operations). Both units are headquartered in Tulsa.

The airborne parachute jump for about 200 members of the Special Forces was just one day of a two-week annual training exercise at Camp Gruber, according to Major Steve Ecker. The aviation battalion provided the air support and more than 20 members of the unit's refueling section participated in the jump.

The 1/245th is the only National Guard aviation battalion in Special Operations. The 2/12th is in one of two Special Forces groups in the Army Reserve.

The Army Reserve group is a unit of the 86th Army Reserve Command headquartered in Forest Park, IL. The 86th Infantry, the forerunner of the 86th Army Reserve, trained for World War II at Camp Gruber. They were known as the Black Hawk Division.

26 June 1992 Oklahoma City Pilot Killed in Crash[16] – excerpt from article in the *Tulsa World*—KONAWA—An Oklahoma City man died Thursday when a twin-engine airplane he was flying from Oklahoma to Florida crashed in a field south of Konawa.

Oklahoma Highway Patrol spokesman Chris West identified the victim as Pete Phillips, 65. Phillips was an experienced pilot and a retired Colonel with the Oklahoma National Guard. He

COL Pete Phillips

also was a part-time helicopter pilot for Oklahoma City television station KWTV.

A Seminole police officer spotted the crashed plane and directed ground searchers to the site. They found the plane resting with a portion of the tail section in a tree and the nose of the plane on the ground. Parts of the tail of the plane were found more than a mile away. Dispatcher Mike Weeks at the patrol's office in McAlester said the cause of the crash isn't known, but weather may have been a factor. Thunderstorms were reported in the area of the crash in south central Oklahoma.

Weeks said the Aero Commander was registered to a Springfield, Mo., company. The plane was sold Wednesday to Aircraft Services Inc. of Fort Lauderdale, Fla., and the pilot was flying the plane to Florida when it crashed.

Phillips, who was the only one on board, had stopped in Norman a short time before the crash, apparently to check the weather conditions.

22 August 1993 SPECIAL GUARD UNIT STAYS ON THE MOVE[17] – excerpt from an article in the *Tulsa World* by John Klein—The UH-60 Blackhawk helicopter skims just above the surface of the Kerr-McClellan Navigation channel at 150 mph in total darkness. Chief Warrant Officer 4 Jerry Farlin and Warrant Officer 3 Tommy Klutts Jr. are piloting the helicopter, one of the most advanced and sophisticated in the U.S. arsenal. A tiny infrared pen flashlight has been left behind at a landing site in grass that is nearly 4-feet tall. "No problem," said Farlin. "We'll just head back down the river and find it."

When the helicopter approaches the landing zone, they pilot the craft up out of the channel and just over the top of trees on the bank. It comes to a quick stop and hovers over the landing zone.

In less than a minute, the flashlight has been located, retrieved and the three crew members and three passengers are on their way back to Tulsa.

Another mission accomplished for Tulsa's Army National Guard aviation unit, the only special operations aviation unit in the nation among Guard or reserve components. The unit, 1st Battalion of the 245th Aviation Regiment, operates some of the military's most advanced technology. All of the unit's flight crews are trained with specially designed aviator's night vision goggles, ANVIS-6. ANVIS stands for Aviator's Night Vision Imaging System.

The goggles, which cost $15,000 each, illuminate the landscape, allowing pilots and crew members to fly in total darkness. The goggles, which cost $15,000 each, illuminate the landscape. "It is a lot like watching a black and white television except that everything is in green tones," said Warrant Officer 3 Dave Odum. "You are actually looking at an image, but it is not a true image. Everything is in shades, shapes and contrasts of green.

All of the helicopters are equipped with special infrared spotlights, which help crew members with night goggles search the landscape. To those without goggles, there's nothing but darkness.

The unit operates from its headquarters on the east side of Tulsa International Airport. It has 15 Blackhawk helicopters, all are designed for the unit's mission, which includes support of special operations, conventional missions and counter-narcotics programs.

Special operations units are trained to fly hundreds of miles at night at tree-top level and land Special Forces within a few feet of the objective and within a few seconds of the scheduled time.

"I'm sure people think of us as part-time soldiers because this is a Guard unit," said Klutts. "In this case, it isn't true. We have to meet the same standards as pilots on active duty in Special Ops units. "It is definitely not part time. When you climb into this helicopter, it is a profession. This helicopter doesn't care if you are a full or part-time pilot. It only knows me as a pilot." Members of the unit are among the busiest guardsmen in the nation. The air crews of the Tulsa battalion averaged more than 122 paid days last year.

"This is very technical aircraft and we're performing technical missions," said Farlin. "So, we are required to undertake the same training as the pilots on active duty. "We have to perform the same tasks at the same skill levels as those on active duty. You have to be pretty motivated [to remain] in this unit."

Farlin, who flies helicopters for Air-Evac in Tulsa, is typical of many members of the unit. Some members fly for American Airlines, Tulsa Police and oil companies. "The biggest misconception about the National Guard is everyone looks at us as part-time," said battalion commander Lieutenant Colonel Terry Council of Broken Arrow. "I am often asked, "how do these guys stay proficient by attending training one weekend per month and one annual training period (15 days)?'

"Our pilots are flying on the average of once a week, which is probably as much as a lot of active-duty people. We do 15 exercises a year, for an average of two exercises per air crewman, and conduct 12 drill weekends per year. So tell me, is that really a part-time force?" But no one is complaining.

"We have a reputation to maintain," said Council. "We believe our working relationship with the 160th Special Operations Aviation Regiment at Fort Campbell, KY, is a good one that we must work hard to uphold." Members of the unit stay on the move, too.

The unit has already trained this year in Indonesia and Bangladesh. Several members returned from training Thailand helicopter pilots in Special Operations techniques. Some members of the unit are in Australia this month for a major exercise with the Australian Special Forces Group. That mission includes training with the Navy Seals, Army Special Forces and Air Force Special Operations units. Annual training this summer was conducted at Fort Campbell, KY, and Camp Gruber near Muskogee. A 50-person contingent from the unit will participate in a Joint Readiness Training Center mission this fall at Fort Polk, LA.

"We do stay pretty busy," said Sergeant Steve Decoster, a mechanic and crew chief for the unit. "But you get into this unit because you are motivated. I still get a rush when we're doing a mission. These helicopters can do some amazing things. It is even more of a thrill because you are doing it in total darkness."

Klutts added, "With the night vision goggles, you can use the terrain to your advantage. You can use the trees to mask yourself. You get down in those river beds, between those trees, and you can literally sneak right up on them." Special Operations Aviation units have four primary uses. They are used for internal defense and supporting local forces. The units also provide training for local forces. The air crews are used for special reconnaissance to gather intelligence and provide the information to headquarters. Sometimes the units are used for direct action. On those missions, the crews are instructed to destroy a target. The fourth type of operation is counter-terrorist. Little wonder members of the unit are required to do so much training. Last year, the unit recorded 6,298 hours in actual missions and support of Special Ops.

"Our pilots have more night vision goggles experience than any unit in the reserve component, and more than any conventional aviation unit in the active Army," said COL Leroy Wall, Oklahoma National Guard State Aviation Officer.

"When we do our job right, no one knows where we came from or where we're going," said Decoster. "We're in and we're out. It's a real experience. You have to do it. This isn't something you can really describe."

1993 Order of Aeromedical Merit COL John Robert Dille was honored and presented the prestigious Order of Aeromedical Merit by the U.S. Army's Society of Flight Surgeons. The Aeromedical Order of Merit "recognizes individuals who have selflessly contributed to the advancement, growth, or maintenance of US Army Aviation Medicine."

15 June 1994 Thai Soldiers Take Part In Camp Gruber Exercises[18]—excerpt from an article in the *Tulsa World*—CAMP GRUBER—Training exercises at Camp Gruber have taken on an international flavor during the past several days.

Elements of the Royal Thai Army are conducting exercises with the National Guard's 1st Battalion, 245th Aviation crews as part of the Joint Combined Exchange Training program. CPT H.R. Holman [OKPAO] said the Thai soldiers arrived in Oklahoma on June 4 and, after spending some time in the classroom, began working on maneuvers in the middle of last week.

Elements of the 245th have trained in Thailand with the Royal Thai Army for the past seven years. This year's exercise is designed to train U.S. Special Operation Forces. During the exercise, the Thai Army and the National Guard crews work on

COL "Roger" Palad Puknoi

perfecting various tasks involved in Special Operations missions. Those include low-level navigation, formation flight and rappelling.

28 August 1995 – Crash[19] –excerpts from the Tulsa World—Chief Warrant Officer Four Dennis H. Laffick, 49, an AGR member of the OKARNG RAID team and Mike G. Miller, 33, OK BIA Drug Enforcement, were killed in an OH-58 crash during Operation Deep Thrust in Tulsa County on 28 August 1995. While conducting anti-drug operations in the vicinity of a marijuana 'farm' near Tulsa, the OH-58 piloted by Laffick struck a power line and crashed. CW4 Laffick, was a decorated, long time Army helicopter pilot and former member of the 45th Inf Bde Avn Section. At the time of the crash he was on active duty as an AGR member of the OKARNG's Reconnaissance and Interdiction Detachment (RAID) Team. Dennis Laffick was born on 3 September 1946. A memorial service was held on 1 September 1995 for Dennis at the First Baptist Church, Norman, OK. He was laid to rest a few days later at Arlington National Cemetery, Washington D.C. with full military honors. At the time, the author was stationed at Fort Belvoir's Davison AAF. Me, Jackie Self, other Oklahoma friends and family walked behind the U.S. Army's Old Guard caisson which carried Dennis' remains to the site where he was laid to rest. An Old Guard soldier, walking on foot, held the bridle of a black, rider-less horse and led the procession. An empty pair of highly polished black cavalry boots rode backwards in the stirrups – in honor of this fallen soldier.

May 1996 – Captain Keith D. Owens[20] was one of twenty-eight Army Officers to receive the MacArthur Leadership Award at Ground Zero (courtyard) of the Pentagon from GEN Dennis J. Reimer, Army Chief of Staff (from Medford, OK). The General Douglas MacArthur Leadership Award for exceptional leadership skills is awarded each year since 1987 to twenty-eight Army officers were presented by Army Chief of Staff. The competition is open to Active and Reserve Component company grade officers serving in the Army, ARNG, and USAR. A total of 28 awards are distributed as follows: (1) Active Army: 14 awards (13 officers and one warrant officer). (2) ARNG: seven awards (six officers and one warrant officer). (3) USAR: seven awards (six officers and one warrant officer). The selection is based on overall leadership performance that exemplifies the ideals of Duty, Honor, and Country.

Duty, Honor, Country—those three hallowed words reverently dictate what you want to be, what you can be, what you will be. They are your rallying point to build courage when courage seems to fail, to regain faith when there seems to be little cause for faith, to create hope when hope becomes forlorn.

Gen Douglas MacArthur

July 1996 – An Old Dog Learns – and Can Teach – a Lot of New

Tricks from an article in OKARNG's *On Guard* by Major Ron Wilkerson. "CWO Robert Duane Graves was recently promoted to Chief Warrant Officer Five in the Oklahoma Army National Guard. The Perry, OK resident went to the school [Ft Rucker Senior Warrant Officer Staff Course] with 38 years of military experience under his belt, but you're never too old to learn, he discovered." At the time of his promotion Graves was the OKARNG's manager of officer personnel and drove (61 miles each way) five days a week from Perry to the Oklahoma Military Department complex in NE Oklahoma City. The first Chief Warrant Officer Five in Oklahoma was Chief Warrant Officer Five Richard Wrede, actually pinned the new CW5 on the shoulders of Graves. "Only 3.4% of the Army's warrant officers will ever achieve that rank. Graves' military career began in 1958 and included service with the 45th Avn Bn (Sp Ops)/1st Bn 245th Avn (SOA) from 1982 until 1991, when he transferred to OMD. Bob Graves is a great man, a tremendous soldier and was always willing to help other soldiers.

CW5 Robert D. Graves

22 January 2002 – Death of Casey C. Stiles—Casey Stiles, 41, Harrodsburg, KY, husband of Luanne Gibson Stiles, died Tuesday, 22 January 2002. Casey was born 18 April 1960 in Tulsa and raised in Broken Arrow, OK. He was the son of Sue White Stiles and the late William Henry Stiles. He was a 1979 graduate of Broken Arrow High School. Casey enlisted in the Army National Guard in 1981 and received his Rotor-wing Pilot Wings after completing U.S. Army helicopter flight training at Fort Rucker, Alabama in 1985. He continued service to his country as a Warrant Officer in the Army National Guard until 1993 when he was honorably discharged. In 1991 he moved to Harrodsburg, KY to begin a commercial helicopter pilot career flying for Kentucky

CW2 Casey C. Stiles

Utilities. His hobbies included his love for flying helicopters and his personal gyrocopters, which he used for training many sport aviation enthusiasts. Casey's hobbies also included playing the bagpipes and his art. He was President and founding member of the Brotherhood of Ultra-light and Rotary Wing Pilots Association. In addition to his wife and mother, survivors include a daughter, Corey Nicholle Stiles, Harrodsburg; and three brothers, Andrew, his twin brother of Broken Arrow, James of Coweta, and Scott, also of Broken Arrow. Memorial service will be held at 3 p.m., Wednesday, January 30 at Rose Hill Funeral Home Chapel.

18 September 2008—Mechanical Failure Eyed In Iraq Helicopter Crash That Killed Three Oklahoma Soldiers[21] excerpts from the *Tulsa World* news article by Manny Gamallo – Three Oklahoma Army National Guard soldiers attached to a Lexington battalion, along with four soldiers with the Texas Guard, were killed Thursday morning when their helicopter crashed in southeastern Iraq, according to the military.

The accident occurred as the Chinook, part of a four-helicopter convoy, was traveling from Kuwait to the Balad Air Base, located around 40 miles north of Baghdad. The seven who died were based at Balad and . . . were the only ones aboard the downed helicopter.

The Oklahoma National Guard said the soldiers killed were: CPL Michael Thompson – Kingston, OK , CWO Brady Rudolf – Moore, OK and Sergeant Dan Eshbaugh – Norman, OK. These troops were all attached to Detachment 1, Company B, 2nd Battalion of the 149th Aviation at Lexington.

Colonel Scully [OKPAO] said the Texas Guard troops were also part of Company B, 2nd Battalion of the 149th Aviation unit. The unit, made up of about 200 Texas and Oklahoma Guard members, were mobilized in June and left for duty in Iraq in late August [2008].

MG Harry M. Wyatt III, adjutant general of Oklahoma shared, "Our hearts, thoughts, prayers and support go out to their families, friends and fellow soldiers during this difficult time."

Gov. Brad Henry also was quick to react to news of the deaths. "Today we mourn the loss of three Oklahomans who made the ultimate sacrifice," the governor said. "They were courageous men of duty and honor, and our thoughts and prayers are with their families and loved ones during this challenging time." Henry said the "brave men and women of the Oklahoma Army and Air National Guard have an awesome responsibility.

They place themselves in harm's way for the sake of the country they love. The tragic deaths of three Oklahoma Guardsmen remind us of the dangers they routinely face so that Americans can enjoy the freedoms upon which this nation was founded."

Along with the Lexington battalion, the Oklahoma National Guard currently has around 3,000 of its troops in Iraq. The bulk of them, around 2,600 Oklahoma Army National Guard soldiers, have been in Iraq, mostly around Baghdad, since January [2008] and are due to start returning home in two weeks.

Just a week ago, on Sept. 11, around 225 Air Guard troops with the Tulsa-based 138th Fighter Wing left for Iraq. Those troops were headed to Balad Air Base, 40 miles north of Baghdad. Another three-dozen Air Guard troops were due to join them in the ensuing days, bringing the total contingent of Oklahoma Air Guard troops at Balad to around 300.

In July [2008], 90 troops with the Tulsa-based 834th Aviation Support Battalion of the Oklahoma Army National Guard also left for Iraq. The battalion is a helicopter maintenance unit.

The Chinook crash was the worst helicopter accident for U.S. troops since August. 22, 2007, when a UH-60 Black Hawk helicopter crashed in northern Iraq, killing all 14 U.S. soldiers aboard.

[COL Patrick] Scully [OKPAO] said the latest three deaths bring to five the number of Oklahoma Guard soldiers who have died since the war in Iraq began five years ago.

Among the thousands of individual pages from which these chapters are derived, one faded and nearly obscure Disposition Form (DF 2496) cannot be overlooked. The unselfish act in writing this DF is as important as the intended outcome. This DF dated 5 June 1985, was addressed to the Cdr, XO, AO, S1 and CSM, 45th Avn Bn and the subject was Super Troopers.

"While screening and reviewing records, I couldn't help but notice that we have an extra ordinary number of personnel that are returning from training who have been designated as Outstanding soldiers. I recommend . . . an Honor Roll . . . for all to see what the Aviation Personnel in Oklahoma are achieving," signed Robert D. Graves, Chief Warrant Officer Three, OKARNG, Military Personnel Technician [45th Avn Bn (SO)(A)].

The attachment to the DF was a list of 21 aviation soldiers, crew chiefs, and aviators who during recent MOSQ or other required military training had been designated as Distinguished Graduate, or Honor Graduate of their respective military class. The list dated back to 1979 when Sergeant Randy S. Glenn graduated 35K – Avionics Mechanic Course as Distinguished Graduate and came forward to 1985 when Sergeant Sandra Hodges graduated OMA, BNOCC as Honor Graduate and Staff Sergeant David A. Brown was Honor Graduate of his COMSEC Custodian Course at NGPEC.

Keep in mind, Grave's list of Super Troopers was a mere snapshot in time and only included the 45th Avn Bn (SO)(A) at Sperry. Just imagine the total number of Super Troopers if we add the distinguished young aviation lads from Lexington and updated the list through 1994.

Not only did Chief Warrant Officer Bob (Duane) Graves recognize the many, many soldiers and aviators who were at the top of their class, his largesse gives us cause to reflect on his unselfish character. Besides being a long-time soldier, Bob is also a golfer and a sports writer in his hometown of Perry, OK. He is at the top of his game when he is helping or giving accolades to other soldiers and their accomplishments.

On the walls of the Tulsa AASF, down towards Flight Operations, hangs several wooden plaques with the inscribed names of heroes who flew hundreds, even 1,000 plus flight hours under Night Vision Goggles. When you see these men, don't miss an opportunity to thank them for their dedicated service to Oklahoma, the Army and to Special Operations. They deserve much more than just our thanks!

500 hour NVG Club Tulsa AASF

CW4 Robert C. Lane – Nov 1985	CW2 Jimmy Richards – Oct 1990
CW2 Tommy Klutts – Jun 1988	CW4 Lowell Kennedy – Nov 1991
CW2 Leonard Reed – Jan 1989	CW3 Andrew Stiles – Feb 1992
CW4 Larry Smith – Jan 1989	CW3 Chris Kurtz – Feb 1992
CW2 Dave Odum – May 1990	CW3 Clayton Mitchell – Aug 1993
CW4 Ron Ketter – Oct 1990	CW2 Tim Hardin – Dec 1993

500 hour NVG Club Tulsa AASF

"In recognition of having flown 500 hours of Night Vision Goggle flight. This is an outstanding achievement that is an example to all those who would strive for excellence in Army aviation."

CW2 Leonard Reed	CW3 Rick Yorman	CW2 Tim Hardin
CW3 Andrew Stiles	CW4 Ronald J. Ketter	SSG R.E. Dennis
CW2 Jeff Scorse	CW3 Clayton Mitchell	
CW4 James L. Smith	CW2 Randy Teague	
CW3 Chris Kurtz	CW4 Lowell Kennedy	

250 hour NVG Club—Army Aviation Support Facility (Tulsa) Non-rated Crewmember

SPC Donald C. Eldridge – Oct 1992	SSG Danny R. Davis – Feb 1999
SPC Mark E. Loud – Dec 1993	Kyle J. Worden – Apr 1999
SSG Stephen B. Decoster – Sep 1994	SGT Walter J. Rumple – Apr 02
SSG Richard E. Dennis – Nov 1994	SGT Bruce N. Korn – Oct 2002
SGT Frank J. Montgomery – Nov 1996	SSG David R. McNair – Sep 04
SGT Jon J. Goff – Dec 1996	

Millie Hora Club Tulsa AASF

"In recognition of having flown 1,000 hours Night Vision Goggle flight. This is an outstanding achievement that is an example to all those who would strive for excellence in Army aviation."

CW4 Robert C. Lane	CW4 Randall R. Teague
CW4 Kris E. Kurtz	CW4 Jimmy H. Richards
CW4 Tommy Klutts Jr.	CW3 Hugh D. Odum

1,500 hour NVG Club Tulsa AASF
(currently not on a plaque in the AASF)
CW5 Robert C. Lane

At an OKARNG Aviation Safety Standdown, Brigadier General Terry R. Council awarded several plaques: One to Sergeant First Class Richard E. Dennis, CE, 1,000 hour NVG Club and one to CW4 Randy Teague, 1,000 hour NVG Club.

1,000 hour NVG Award Lexington AASF

CW4 John Ashmore	CW5 Samuel T. Hinch

500 hour NVG Club Lexington AASF

Lords of Darkness

"500 hours Night Vision Goggle Flight. This is an outstanding achievement that is an example to all those who would strive for excellence in Army aviation."

CW4 Thomas M. Clark	CW4 Henry G. Bryant
SSG Martin R. Frank	CW5 Dan R. Halley
SSG Kevin R. McAnally	SGT David L. Tillman
CW3 John T. Ashmore	CW4 Richard C. Cooper
SSG Robert E. Jansen	CW4 James F. Kanzenbach
SSG Jerry D. Lea	CPT Jonathan L Lund
CW3 Wesley A. Jones	CW4 Samuel T. Hinch
CW3 Jerry F. King	CW4 David M. Lodes
CW3 Larry D. Eversmeyer	CW3 J. Mike Griffis

Oklahoma Army National Guard Armory
Tulsa, Oklahoma

In Memory Of

Chief Warrant Officer (CW2) Dennis Lee Barlow
Senior Army Aviator

CHIEF WARRANT OFFICER DENNIS LEE BARLOW, a former United States Army Reserve Captain and veteran combat helicopter pilot, enjoyed a most distinguished military and civilian career.

His active military service began as an enlisted man in October 1968. From 1969 to 1972 he served his country as an Infantry Officer and as an Army helicopter pilot, receiving his wings on November 3, 1970. From 1970 to late 1971 Chief Warrant Officer Dennis L. Barlow flew as an aircraft commander and flight leader on numerous combat support, medical evacuation, and resupply missions in the Republic of Vietnam, returning to Tulsa, Oklahoma where he later served as Civil Affairs Economics Officer with the 486th Civil Affairs Company from 1975 to 1981. He joined the Oklahoma Army National Guard and this Battalion as a UH-1 helicopter pilot at the rank of Chief Warrant Officer CW2 on December 17, 1981. He performed his flight duties with honor and distinction, serving first as a member of Company B in Lexington, Oklahoma until April 1982 and then with Company A, previously headquartered in Sperry, Oklahoma. On February 1, 1986 he was awarded his Senior Army Aviator Wings.

On March 5, 1987, Chief Warrant Officer Barlow was tragically killed while in the performance of his duties on a specialized training mission for this Battalion. He was one of the most proficient, experienced, and respected pilots and officers ever to serve in the Oklahoma Army National Guard.

Born on July 11, 1944 in Stigler, Oklahoma, DENNIS LEE BARLOW was the son of Chester Barlow, now of Indianola, Oklahoma, and Gladys Rowena (Spence) Barlow of Tulsa. He was married on May 27, 1979 to Debra Jean (Satterfield) Barlow. A devoted and loving father, he cherished his family. Their three children include their boys Lance L. Barlow, age 17; Erin A. Barlow, age 8, and Blake L. Barlow, age 6. His three sisters include: Barbara Spencer, Judy Bond, and Diana Holcomb, each of Tulsa. He was equally proud of his several nieces and nephews, as well as his many friends and fellow Guardsmen, and their families. He was a member of the Tulsa Central Church of the Nazarene.

A graduate of Northeastern State University with a Bachelor of Arts degree in 1967 and the University of Tulsa in 1968, where he received his Master of Arts degree in History, CW2 Dennis L. Barlow was a dedicated and highly loved junior high school teacher. In 1972 he started his illustrious teaching career at Nimitz Middle School in Tulsa. Then, in 1973 he taught Science subjects at Foster Junior High, until, in 1975, he was able to return to Nimitz (his pride and joy), where he proudly taught Geography. Barlow was a self-appointed counselor and friend to all of his students. As a special memorial to their beloved teacher, his junior high students released 12 balloons in his honor: one for every year of his service at Tulsa's Nimitz Middle School. He was particularly fond of and dedicated to helping seventh graders grasp his enthusiasm, love, and hunger for learning.

A skilled amateur photographer CW2 Barlow applied his photographic talents to his love for flying, contributing immeasurably to the still and aerial combat photography capabilities of this Battalion. His attention to detail and profound dedication to duty are reflected in his many awards and decorations. They include: the Bronze Star for distinguished service; the Air Medal; the Army Commendation Medal; the Army Achievement Medal, and the Army Reserve Components Achievement Medal. Additionally, he was awarded the National Defense Service Medal, Vietnam Service and Campaign Medals, Armed Forces Expeditionary and Reserve Medals, the Human Services Medal, the Army Services Ribbon, and the Oklahoma National Guard Long Service Medal.

Army Aviation Support Facility
Tulsa, Oklahoma

In Memory Of

Warrant Officer (WO1) David Owen Barr
Flight Instructor and Technician

WARRANT OFFICER DAVID OWEN BARR received his appointment as an Army Reserve National Guard Warrant Officer and was awarded his Army Aviator Wings on the same day: March 29, 1984. He was permanently assigned to Company A, First Battalion, 245th Aviation (Special Operations)(Airborne), which was then headquartered in Sperry, Oklahoma. Throughout his military and civil service careers he served with distinction and honor.

A dedicated and enthusiastic helicopter pilot, his highest goal as an Army Aviator was finally attained when, on February 1, 1987, he was promoted to and appointed as a certified instructor pilot for this Battalion. Warrant Officer David O. Barr was serving as a full-time National Guard Technician and as a flight instructor engaged in a specialized training mission when, on March 5, 1987, he was tragically killed while in the performance of his duties. His enthusiasm for his job, his attention to detail, and his dedication both as a National Guard Army Aviator and as a Civil Service Technician served as an inspiration for all who knew him, worked with him, and flew with him.

Born on May 10, 1963 in Muncie, Indiana, DAVID OWEN BARR graduated in 1981 from Central High School in Tulsa, Oklahoma. For the next five years his education and primary interests centered around his military flying duties and the technical aspects of Army Aviation. In 1986 he attended Tulsa Junior College, where he began his formal studies in computer programming, hoping to enhance his future military and civil service careers.

The oldest of three sons, Warrant Officer Barr is survived by his father, David K. Barr of Tulsa, Oklahoma, and his mother, Diane (Owen) Barr, an educational prescriptionist (DODDS) now stationed in Bitburg, Germany. His brothers include Bruce Alan Barr, age 23, and Christian Alexander Barr, age 21, both of Phoenix, Arizona.

Warrant Officer David O. Barr's recognition as an outstanding soldier and individual began early in his career. At basic training he was singled out and awarded the Soldier Stakes Award for exemplary skills and competency. In addition to his Army Aviator Wings, Warrant Officer Barr also qualified for and was awarded the Aircraft Crewman Badge.

Among his many awards and decorations for distinguished service and dedication to duty are the Army Achievement Medal, the Army Reserve Components Achievement Medal, and the Army Reserve Components Overseas Training Ribbon. His Oklahoma decorations include the Oklahoma Long Service Medal, the Good Conduct Ribbon, and the 100 Percent Drill Attendance Badge, earned as a conscientious and dedicated member of the Oklahoma Army National Guard.

A young, energetic officer and a talented, hard working helicopter pilot, Warrant Officer David O. Barr contributed immeasurably to the success of his Battalion and his Army Aviation Support Facility, for which he was extremely proud to be a part of.

Organizational Maintenance Shop 18
Tulsa, Oklahoma

In Memory Of

Sergeant First Class David Alvin Brown
Communications Chief

SERGEANT FIRST CLASS DAVID ALVIN BROWN, an Active Guard Reservist (AGR) and full-time electronics technician with the First Battalion, 245th Aviation (Special Operations) (Airborne), previously headquartered in Sperry, Oklahoma, was born on August 24, 1956, at Ft. Leavenworth, Kansas, the son of Sergeant Major Oliver D. Brown (U.S. Army - Retired) and Mrs. Jennie L. (Lingenfelter) Brown, now of Claremore, Oklahoma. Raised in El Paso, Texas, he graduated from Orange High School in southern California. Later, he attended the Tri County Vo Tech Center in Tulsa, Oklahoma, where he began his formal studies in electronics.

DAVID ALVIN BROWN was married on January 16, 1976 to Paulette Elaine (Garrett) Brown of Barnsdall, Oklahoma, now a Licensed Practical Nurse in Barnsdall. Their daughter, Carrie Lynn, age 12, lives with her mother and attends the 6th grade at Barnsdall Grade School, where she enjoys studying history, riding horses, and a wide variety of outdoor sports and activities, like her father. Carrie's lifelong goal is to be a qualified pediatrician.

His three brothers include Sergeant Ted Brown of Claremore, Oklahoma, who continues to serve full-time as an Oklahoma Army National Guardsman and a maintenance technician with this Battalion; Ben Brown of Sacramento, California, and Jim Brown, also of Claremore. Other close relatives by marriage include Virgil and Hazel Garrett of Barnsdall, and his brother-in-law David McMullen of Olive, Oklahoma.

With this unit, Sergeant First Class David A. Brown deployed to Honduras where he served with honor and enthusiasm until his tragic death on May 2, 1988 while in the performance of his duties. He was a dedicated and devoted Guardsman and a skilled Communications Chief who contributed immeasurably to the success of his unit's mission.

Sergeant First Class Brown began his Army National Guard service in Oklahoma on July 7, 1979. He served for more than eight years with distinction, excelling in electronics and avionics maintenance and repair and in establishing ground and air Communications Security for this Battalion. He performed his many and varied duties in such remote assignments as Lop Buri, Thailand, as well as in various outposts and locations across the United States.

Known and respected as an individual who never met a stranger and one who went out of his way to help others and to offer special attention to those in need, particularly the elderly, Sergeant First Class Brown will be revered for his lighthearted humor, his popularity among all ages of people, and his favorite philosophy: "Things Don't Matter -- People Do!"

Sergeant Brown prided himself in his personal appearance, his military bearing, top physical conditioning, and in his ability to accomplish his job under all conditions. He was especially keen in upgrading and maintaining his communications and electronics equipment, and he took special pride in keeping his work areas, whether in the field or in garrison, always organized and ready for on-the-spot inspections or for emergency 24-hour operations, if needed. His many commendations reflect such attention to detail.

Among his awards and decorations are the Army Commendation Medal, the Army Achievement Medal, Army Reserve Components Achievement Medal, Armed Forces Overseas and Reserve Medals, the Army Good Conduct Medal, Oklahoma Commendation Medal, Non-Commissioned Officer Professional Development Ribbon with Numeral 3, and the Oklahoma Long Service Medal and 100 Percent Drill Attendance Badge, earned as a conscientious and dedicated member of the Oklahoma Army National Guard.

IN
MEMORY

Dennis H. Laffick
03 September 1946
to
28 August 1995

Chief Warrant Officer Four Dennis H. Laffick

1. St of OK General Orders No. 19, dated 18 February 1965 provided by CW4 Frank Berry
2. Ibid
3. Telephone interview LTC Emmitt D. McElwain, 24 February 2009
4. Telephone interview CW4 Charlie H. Evans, 19 December 2006
5. Reprinted by permission, Tulsa World article, Tulsa, OK, Joe Worley - Executive Editor, 17 February 1980
6. Reprinted by permission, Tulsa World article & photo, Tulsa, OK, Joe Worley - Executive Editor, 15 May 1982
7. Reprinted by permission, Tulsa World article, Tulsa, OK, Joe Worley - Executive Editor, 5 March 1987
8. Reprinted by permission, Tulsa World article, Tulsa, OK, Joe Worley - Executive Editor, 2 May 1988
9. Reprinted by permission, Tulsa World article, Tulsa, OK, Joe Worley - Executive Editor, 27 August 1989
10. As related by former Sergeant Jack Duncan, OKAAS Rappel Master (no relation to Specialist Duncan)
11. Tulsa World article, Tulsa, OK, Joe Worley - Executive Editor, 2 June 1990
12. Ibid
13. Reprinted by permission, Tulsa World article, Tulsa, OK, Joe Worley - Executive Editor, 4 May 1990
14. Reprinted by permission, Tulsa World article, Tulsa, OK, Joe Worley - Executive Editor, 17 August 1991
15. Reprinted by permission, Tulsa World article, Tulsa, OK, Joe Worley - Executive Editor, 26 August 1991
16. Reprinted by permission, Tulsa World article, Tulsa, OK, Joe Worley - Executive Editor, 26 June 1992
17. Reprinted by permission, Tulsa World article, Tulsa, OK, Joe Worley - Executive Editor, 22 August 1993
18. Reprinted by permission, Tulsa World article, Tulsa, OK, Joe Worley - Executive Editor, 15 June 1994
19. Reprinted by permission, Tulsa World article, Tulsa, OK, Joe Worley - Executive Editor, 28 August 1995
20. MAJ Keith D. Owens served two tours in Iraq as a Medevac pilot and member of Co C, 2nd Bn 149th Avn (GSAB) as of February 2009.
21. Reprinted by permission, Tulsa World article, Tulsa, OK, Joe Worley - Executive Editor, 18 September 2008

Chapter 18

Don't Forget to Turn Out the Lights

"It was the best of times, it was the worst of times, it was the
age of wisdom, it was the age of foolishness, it was the epoch of
belief, it was the epoch of incredulity, it was the season of Light,
it was the season of Darkness, it was the spring of Hope, it was
the winter of Despair, we had everything before us, we had
nothing before us, we were all going direct to heaven, we were
all going direct the other way . . . (from "A Tale of Two Cities")
Charles Dickens (1812-1870)

Everything depends on leadership. Without leadership, determination and drive, we would never have had all of the astonishing aviation units, tremendous tactical training and sensational Special Operations Aviation in Oklahoma.

We must never forget how far we've come and from what points it all started. The success you've seen glowing in the eyes of our soldiers, in the accolades expressed about our units and in the accomplishments achieved as part of OKARNG aviation came from lonely, fiery and nearly forgotten beginnings – far distant from Lexington and Tulsa, Oklahoma.

Sixty years ago, a time when communists north of the DMZ were indoctrinated by their Soviet occupiers, invaded Southern Korea. It was 1950, before Army aviation companies, troops, battalions, and aviation regiments existed. The naked mountains were then covered in crusted snow, the rivers frozen, as were the feet of our soldiers. It was bitter cold and terrifying beyond imagination at the same time. A few of our OKARNG aviation patriarchs experienced firsthand the civil war battlefield adage,

" . . . I've seen the elephant," meaning he had been in and was a veteran of combat. This was one beginning . . .

Thirty years after Korea, in the dark, bleak, blindness of blowing, abrasive sand, far from civilization and six hundred miles inside the border of an enemy, Islamic governed country, eight U.S. soldiers/ aircrew were killed and five were nearly burned alive, in an unsuccessful joint U.S. military attempt to rescue American hostages. This was another beginning . . .

[Operation] "Eagle Claw was a successful failure," said retired Lieutenant General Jim Vaught, overall commander of the super secretive, joint rescue mission. "We wanted with all our being to rescue the Americans [in Tehran].

Out of the unabashed, self-inflicted flames of failure, our military organized, trained and equipped the appropriate Special Operators and Aviators to be successful in this type mission in the future, and to do it well and with extreme prejudice. It isn't often we hear of their silent, surgical successes, but the media will inundate you repeatedly with their few, but well documented failures.

In retrospect, some of those responsible for the planning of Eagle Claw have since admitted it was too complicated, immersed in too much secrecy and overly compartmentalized. We attempted to do a Joint mission without training jointly and without compatible equipment or communications.

Almost within hours of loading all of our servicemen involved in Operation Eagle Claw onto another C-130 and abandoning the RH-53 helicopters at the isolated location called Desert One, a new concept was sought, which would lead to a new type unit called Special Operations Aviation.

"No matter what else you do, no matter how much it costs, we will never have another Desert One . . ."

Task Force 160 began the summer of 1980 and evolved from Task Force 158, formerly elements of the 101st Airborne Division. These SOA units were training in anticipation of a second rescue attempt up and until the Iranians released the hostages within hours of President Reagan's inauguration.

In 1981 the Department of Defense in conjunction with the National Guard Bureau, saw the logic of placing a very unique aviation unit in the ARNG. In my opinion, DA and NGB had already determined that placing a counter-terrorism aviation organization in the reserve component, particularly the Oklahoma ARNG, a leader in its own right, would save money—lots of money. Being centrally located didn't hurt anything either.

Creating a mirror image of its own 160th Aviation Battalion in the reserve component was a stroke of pure genius on behalf of the Army. You gained a second, highly skilled, specially trained SOA unit, but it doesn't count against active Army endstrength – it comes straight out of ARNG total endstrength. Yet they still had, what was perceived to be ready access to this new mirror image capability in the event of war or if the TF 160 was spread too thin.

You've heard the buzz words/slogans, "One Seamless Army (Active, Guard & Reserves)" and the Total Army. I'm convinced that it never was seamless. If it had been seamless, each component would have the interest of the whole at heart – "one for all and all for one." The Guard and Reserves were always considered as step-children – we got seconds, ninety percent of the time.

If the Army tried to enlarge its own active duty SOA force structure too fast this would have been seen by politicos as being too greedy. They couldn't increase their own endstrength to build a new SOA unit, without Congressional approval. That wasn't going to happen. Or they could eliminate some other unit(s) with a total endstrength equating to a battalion level strength – that wasn't likely to happen either. Placing this new SOA unit in the ARNG was a good example of a win-win situation. Oklahoma felt like it had won the lottery. At first I assume the Army did also.

Therefore, brought forth by a gentleman's agreement, sealed with a handshake and backed by millions of dollars of forthcoming funds – the 45th Aviation Battalion (Light Helicopter Combat) counter-terrorism unit was formed at Sperry, OK – May 1982.

The cost savings were subtle at the beginning, but real. You achieved the capability of a Special Operations Aviation Battalion with part-time pay and allowances vice active duty full-time funding. In the ARNG you don't have soldiers rotating to another duty station ever 24 to 36 months – saving moving costs. Other cost savings? – flight pay, quarters allowance (housing), aircraft and avionics maintenance costs. In the ARNG, your aviation maintenance cost per flight hour is much less. National Guard technicians and mechanics are basically stationary; they rarely move, nor change jobs. They will work in the same job three to four times as long as or longer than active duty maintenance soldiers. They become expert at what they do. In the end, our ARNG aircraft maintenance was at the exceptionally high end of the spectrum. Net result – reduced maintenance, training and flying hour program costs.

In the ARNG your personnel base of aviators, crew chiefs, mechanics, flight engineers, etc. are often prior service, and frequently combat experienced soldiers. Flight experience was much higher both in the enlisted and officer ranks in the ARNG. Net result – reduced maintenance, training and flying hour program costs.

Flight facilities were a mixed-bag when talking cost savings. On one hand, many hangar facilities already existed at Norman and Lexington. Many more were within close range, such as Henry Post Field, Fort Sill, OK and Muskogee Davis Field, Muskogee, OK, just to name a few. These were available to the OKARNG aviation program for a nominal annual lease. And just east across the Arkansas River from Muskogee Davis was the mid-sized training area known as Camp Gruber, which was a former WWII Infantry mob-site, and training area. Therefore, cost savings were indeed available when addressing aviation facilities for SOA. On the other hand new construction would typically require a minimum of three years planning, budgeting, land acquisition, architectural planning and finally – contracting and construction. And that occurred – the new armory, Army aviation support facility and Organization Maintenance Shop, all at Tulsa. Later there would be a new CH-47 maintenance hangar built at Lexington. Each of these projects was for the 1st Bn 245th Avn (SO) (A), although the completion of the CH-47 occurred after the unforeseen deactivation of the 1/245th.

Today there has been much additional new construction completed at Lexington.

Constant change was the norm in the Special Operations Forces arena from 1985 to 1990. To wit: 14 November 1986, Congress enacted Public Law 99-661, section 1311, to revitalize special operations and correct deficiencies identified in the nation's ability to conduct special operations. The law directed the President to establish a unified combatant command for special operations[1] to ensure that special operations forces were combat ready and prepared to conduct specified missions. The law required the

Secretary of Defense to assign all U.S.-based active and reserve special operations forces to the Special Operations Command and special operations forces stationed overseas to the Atlantic, Pacific, Southern, Central, and European combatant commands, PACOM, in the case of the 1/245th Avn (SOA).

Were there obstacles to our development, equipping and permanence? You better believe that there were. Issues such as Initiative 17 were monumental, nocuous obstacles which we alone could have never overcome. This issue called Initiative 17 was a beautiful example of how one military service can engage another, present a dazzling, but false argument to occupy the opposing service, while they go behind the scenes to accomplish their own self-serving objectives.

Ever since the 1980 failure of Operation Rice Bowl/Eagle Claw at Desert One, too much jointness was considered a primary contributing factor. The jointness with the Air Force, Army, Navy and Marines, caused competition; each branch clawing to get a bigger piece of the pie! It was not the norm.

During 1983, Congress made statements that they wanted the SOF aviation issue resolved and recommended that the Air Force purchase additional PAVE LOW and Combat Talon aircraft. This was soon to be in total contradiction to the Army-Air Force Initiative 17. The conflict about who was responsible for rotary-wing SOF missions and fixed-wing SOF missions caused the pot to boil, and the two arch rivals (Army and Air Force) squared off for another round. The initial ball buster as seen by the Army was the Air Forces intention to procure an additional nine Pave Low (MH-53) helicopters.

At the outset of addressing corrections, changes and additions to the initial TDA for the 45th Avn Bn (Sp Ops) (A), Initiative 17 was a part of nearly every discussion with Dept of the Army Special Operations Aviation personnel in the Pentagon. When a request was made by Oklahoma for modernized aircraft in 45th Avn Bn, the answer included a response such as, " . . . at this time we cannot approve any additional SOF aircraft enhancements due to Initiative 17.

In May 1984 the Army Chief of Staff and Air Force Chief of Staff announced an agreement which was designed to advance cooperation between the services. The intra-service agreement contained 31 initiatives to reduce waste and provide better joint operations. Initiative 17 addressed the decision to transfer sole responsibility for rotary-wing support of SOF to the Army and was briefed to the Secretary of Defense in 1984.

As any high school student of Government should have been able to see, duplication of effort existed between the four major military services in various areas. SOF airlift was (and remains) a major area of duplication between the armed forces. Initiative 17 may have been intended to reduce the duplicity of SOF airlift support between the Army and the Air Force, but it didn't happen. The supposed intent of this initiative or agreement was for the Army to assume responsibility for helicopter lift support to SOF. However, the Air Force was not willing to give up the fixed wing support for SOF forces. Initiative 17 meant that the Army would have to develop its own methods and provide aircraft for long range SOF mission support vs the Air Force's MH-53Js (range 900 km/486 nm). Its largest helicopter, the CH-47 was considered to be medium range. This led to the development of the air-refuelable MH-47D and the MH-47E with a new range of 555 km/300 nm. Behind closed doors the Air Force continued to lobby for their wish list and additional MH-53 PAVE LOWs.

At the Pentagon, Noel C. Koch was Deputy Assistant Secretary of Defense for International Security Affairs until March 1981, when he took charge of the Office of Special Plans at the Department of Defense. Koch was opposed to Initiative 17, although he was a devout supporter of SOF and a tireless fighter. Koch often criticized the Air Force and its regular failure to support SOF airlift requirements. As a strong proponent of SOF rebuilding in the 1980s, Koch said, " . . . on the subject of special operations force revitalization, . . . when they [DoD officials] say "no," they mean no; when they say "maybe," they mean no; and when they say "yes," they mean no, and if they meant anything but no, they wouldn't be there." This well describes the level of absurdity we faced while trying to promote and advance Army Special Operations Aviation from Sperry to the Pentagon.

"Sensing that the largest obstacle to the agreement was to be U.S. Army aviation objections, representatives from AFSOC[2] (Air Force Special Operations Command) and USSOCOM met with representatives of the US Army Aviation Center (USAAVNC) regarding the aviation—FID (Foreign Internal Defense) initiative. The meeting concluded with mixed results; USAAVNC and TRADOC supported the fixed-wing portion of the concept (AF would continue to provide SOF fixed-wing support), but expressed reservations about any Air Force special operations rotary-wing

FID efforts; especially given the perceived prospects of overlap between USAAVNC and AFSOC missions."

Much of the reluctance had its roots in Army and Air Force squabbles regarding helicopters in general. The Air Force decision, however, had been made without AFSOF input. In 1986, after two years of heated debate, the House Appropriations Committee decided the expense of transfer outweighed any advantages and directed that Initiative 17 not be implemented. With the stand—up of USSOCOM in 1987, all SOF aviation assets fell within its purview and for all intents and purposes under a single joint commander. Consequently, in 1991 the CINCSOC Joint Special Operations Aviation Board Report averred that "Initiative 17 is no longer an issue.[3]"

Initiative 17 proved to be a most expensive and troublesome hindrance to progress in the Special Operations Aviation environment. It was extremely detrimental to Army SOA procurement programs; yet, it resulted in just another go-round with the guys in blue.

In the end, we had the Air Force telling the Army they wanted to give us their rotary-wing SOF mission, while their senior level managers were lobbying for more newer C-130s and additional MH-53s. They did just that, plus they got the bonus of 50 CV-22 V/STOL tilt-rotor transports, which they now have at the 8th Special Operations Squadron (SOS), 1st Special Operations Wing (SOW) at Hurlburt Field, FL. It appears to me, that the Air Force's lobbying to get more aircraft seems to always work. Take this as it is offered – my personal, but strong opinion.

Initiative 17 was one of many examples of the ludicrous battles between the services. As a lieutenant colonel and later a colonel, stationed at Fort Belvoir, VA, between 1993 and 1998, I had the distinct pleasure of helping to build, organize, and activate the Army's (Active, Guard & Reserve) Operational Support Airlift Command. I later served as the second commander of this organization. In 1995, the Chief of Staff of the Army, placed all 107 of the Army's fixed-wing passenger aircraft into one organization and used the Army's own Centralized Aircraft Scheduling System (CASS) to mission each aircraft on a daily basis. The aircraft were stationed across the nation from Hawaii to Alaska, the lower 48 states, Puerto Rico and Panama, with Army jets (Learjets and Gulfstreams) stationed in Hawaii and at Andrews AFB, MD.

At the time the Army consolidated all of its fixed-wing aircraft, DOD directed that the four services, Army, Air Force, Navy and Marines, including Guard and Reserves, place all service OSA fixed-wing into one resource pool and jointly centralize the scheduling of all of these DOD aircraft. Which services scheduling system would be utilized and who would make the final, hard scheduling decisions on a day to day basis? These were paramount issues.

What ensued for nearly three years was one giant pissing contest. Each service wanted to do its own thing, even though the Secretary of Defense's office gave us a charge to accomplish this efficiently, smoothly and transparently. I'm quite biased and prejudiced against the Air Force, and to a lesser degree the Navy and Marines. We fought almost real battles between the Army and Air Force and the outcome was not pretty, nor cost effective. The Navy lied and said their JALIS scheduling software (Joint Air Logistics Information System) could be modified for less than one million dollars and up and running within one year. DOD believed them and later we were all sorry. The Air Force won too. The new JALIS software and joint personnel to run, operate and maintain it, were later stationed at Scott AFB, IL. Sometime I'll have to tell you that whole story. This is just another example of the turf wars between the services, which most soldiers never see or even hear about.

Were there obstacles to our (1st Bn 245th Avn (SO) (A)) progress during the years? Yes, many obstacles were faced. Some included insufficient school quotas and modernized equipment issues. Others were doctrine and procedural issues. In Oklahoma we were doing full touch-down autorotations with older, full-face NVG, waiting on newer, more effective goggles. Much of our progress and evolution was self-taught, self-learned. It was like your daddy's money – we earned it the hard way!

In my estimation the summer of 1987 was the beginning of the 1/245th's downfall. It was not because of what we had done or not done. It was because neither the Department of the Army, nor OKARNG aviation had foreseen any problem should the new reserve component SOA unit, 1/245th Avn (SO)(A), be called up in a low intensity conflict (LIC) such as the Persian Gulf (Operation Prime Chance). It appeared early on that everyone assumed we could and would be called-up. No one at DA would admit that then, however.

Were we, inclusively, DA, NGB and Oklahoma, too naive to think we could secretly mobilize a specialized SOA unit, 45th Avn Bn (SO) (A)? The 45th was specifically trained and nearly equipped as a mirror image of the 160th SOA. Our sister unit, the 160th, was already engaged in actual combat in the

Persian Gulf to protect our nation's foreign energy resources when DA began to ask – could you . . . ? Yes, each level of authority overlooked the one hard to do question—how do we covertly mobilize and send a single Army National Guard unit into combat, during a LIC, without a full mobilization?

Once again, it is my humble estimation that the 1/245th Avn (SO) (A), wanted to be called up and utilized. When you put so much of yourself, blood, sweat and tears, into something as demanding as this training and mission qualification, it is normal to want to test yourself against the challenge and the enemy. I would say, almost to a man, everyone was hoping we would be activated that summer of 1987. We wanted to prove that the Army was correct in building this reserve component mirror image of the 160th in the Oklahoma Army National Guard.

Was it in the too hard to do box, to get the 45th Avn Bn and later the 1/245th SOA, mobilized for deployment? Or was it that the Department of the Army felt like it might appear as if they needed help from their little brother to get the job done? *Pride,* one of the seven deadly sins, may have contributed to our not getting called-up, and it may have also led to the deactivation of the 1/245th Avn.

Or was it *Greed,* another one of the seven deadly sins? I know for sure that it wasn't because the 45th Avn Bn wasn't ready, willing or able—they were. They had met all of the standards required of them. Yet time seems to change everything; change was the name of the game.

Soon after, in 1991, during the mobilization for Operation Desert Storm and then again beginning on or about 20 March 2003, all ARNG units, plus USAR units suddenly became available and many reserve component units were mobilized and activated for combat in Kuwait, Iraq and Afghanistan. The pendulum swung to the other extreme.

Had the 1/245th Avn become too expensive? Perhaps, but why would you suppose that? The 1/245th Avn was doing what it was programmed to do and what was requested to do by USASOC and USSOCOM. We were in support all of the RC SOF units, a majority of JRTC iterations and some AC SOF units. Albeit there was a perpetual problem for us (1/245th) to get sufficient or often any USAF airlift to support Army SOF in overseas JSCP areas of responsibility.

The following is another major obstacle, but takes on a different color – green. Not as you might guess – Army green, but the color of money. Was it too expensive for the Army to keep us warming the bench, especially after

Operation Prime Chance (LIC)? They couldn't admit publicly that they were wrong to stand us up back in 1982. But was that the opinion now. How could they gracefully close the books on the 1/245th Avn?

A February 1990 Government Accounting Office (GAO) report to the Honorable William V. Roth, U.S. Senate, entitled "SOF – Army Plans to Buy More MH-47Es Than Needed:" "The Army's plan to buy 34 additional MH-47E SOF helicopters in fiscal years 1990 to 1994, at an estimated cost of $532 million for procurement and support costs, is without a sound mission-based justification," stated the GAO report.

The report continued, "In 1987, the Office of the Secretary of Defense determined that medium-range SOF missions would be met with 17 MH-47E helicopters procured by the Army and 41 MH-53J helicopters procured by the Air Force. The Army, however, now plans to buy a total of 51 MH-47E helicopters because it inappropriately believes that this number is still needed to implement a 1984 Memorandum of Agreement between the Army and the Air Force Chiefs of Staff, even though it was determined that only 17 MH-47E helicopters were needed. Because both the Army and the Air Force have already contracted for the needed quantities of helicopters, there is no basis for procuring an additional 34 MH-47E helicopters."

Did you happen to see who or what the bill payer for that $532 million would be? The report didn't say did it? Do you suppose the Army had already decided in 1990, that the 1st Bn 245th Avn (Special Operations) (Airborne) would become the bill payer for its additional MH-47s? No, we didn't have any CH-47s in Oklahoma in 1990.

In addition, we need to look at this March 1994 GAO report to the Chairman, Committee on Armed Services, House of Representatives—*Special Operations Forces – Force Structure and Readiness Issues*: "Excess Reserve Forces could cost millions to maintain." Although the GAO report was prepared in 1994, it references budget guidance from 1990 . . .

"In November 1990 the Department of Defense developed budget guidance that directed the deactivation of three Army National Guard and three Army Reserve Special Forces battalions. The Department rescinded the deactivation plans for the three Army Reserve battalions pending the results of the Command's joint mission analysis. Conferees for the 1993 Department of Defense Appropriations Act included in their report the expectation that the Army Special Operations Command would maintain existing Army National Guard Special Operations units through fiscal year 1993 and reject any plan or initiative to expand the active component special operations forces to replace these National Guard units. The conferees further noted that in the fiscal year 1992 Defense Appropriations Act, Congress had limited any conversion of National Guard missions to the active components."

"The Command's analysis validated the need to deactivate the six battalions and identified further reductions of reserve units. Table 3.1 lists the reserve forces that the Command identified for deactivation. The six battalions [in addition to the 1/245th Avn] are in the 11th and 19th Special Forces Groups."

Table 3.1 Reserve Forces the Command (Sp Ops Cmd) Identified for Deactivation

Unit Reserve spaces

Unit	Reserve spaces
1-245th Special Operations Aviation Battalion	463
19th Special Forces Group	1,040
5th Psychological Operations Group	495
11th Special Forces Group	1,266
Total	**3,264**

Source: Special Operations Command

The GAO reports continued, "According to the Command, the forces listed in table 3.1 are linked to the drawdown of conventional forces in Europe and the Soviet threat and are not needed to meet contingency mission requirements. Moreover, according to the Command, maintaining the excess reserve structure will cost about $355 million through fiscal year 1999. The Command stated that using funds to maintain excess force structure is adversely affecting the operating tempo of special operations forces."

According to the Department of Defense, " . . . it has a plan to inactivate the excess units by the end of fiscal year 1994. The specific units will be announced by the Department in the second quarter of fiscal year 1994."

"*FINDING H: Excess Reserve Forces Could Cost Millions to Maintain.* The GAO reported that in November 1990 the DOD developed budget guidance that directed that three Army National Guard and three Army Reserve Special Forces battalions be deactivated. The GAO noted that the DOD rescinded the deactivation plans for the three Army Reserve battalions pending the results of the Command's joint mission analysis. The GAO pointed out that the DOD request for authorization to deactivate the three National Guard battalions was denied by the National Defense Authorization Act of Fiscal Year 1992. The GAO reported that subsequently the Command's analysis validated the need to deactivate the six battalions and identified further reductions of reserve units. The GAO noted that the six battalions are in the 11th and 19th Special Forces Groups. The GAO indicated that the Command identified the following reserve forces for deactivation:

- 1-245 Special Operations Aviation Battalion – 463 reserve spaces
- 19th Special Forces Group—1,042 reserve spaces
- 5th Psychological Operations Group – 560 spaces
- 11th Special Forces Group – 1,279 spaces.

The question remains, "Was the 1/245th Avn (SOA) too expensive? We requested modernized equipment, but only that which was already authorized on our MTOE, we never asked for more dollars, other than training quotas, those authorized by new aircraft on the MTOE, such as CH-47 AQC (aviation qualification courses) and CH-47 flight engineer quotas, tech inspectors and Maintenance Test Pilot quotas. All of which were authorized to meet readiness requirements.

It appeared in 1993 that the 1/245th would not be receiving its authorized CH-47Ds for a long, long time. The conversion of CH-47D aircraft to MH-47Es for the 160th SOAR was done at the Boeing factory outside of Philadelphia at Ridley, PA, along the Delaware River. Naturally the 160th had the priority and was to receive the newer, modified 47E's, before we began receiving any of the older CH-47Ds.

It felt like we were always swimming upstream, especially when it came to new major end items such as aircraft and/or JAAT airlift support. Therefore, we had begun to plan ahead and negotiate. As of July 1992, the 1/245 had swapped, traded, and connived to get 22 aviators, 10 CE/FE, 3 IPs and 1 MTP CH-47 AQC'd (aircraft qualified). We had already obtained concurrence from NGB-AVS Director, John J. Stanko, USASOIC, and Director, ARNG, Major General Rees to work with the 160th on this CH-47 issue. A Memorandum of Agreement (MOA) was signed and sent overnight express to Ft Bragg. Lieutenant Colonel Gary Elliott, commander of the 1/245th at this time, was at Bragg and picked up the document, briefed and obtained Major General Downing's signature.

MG Downing briefed Lieutenant General Steiner at USSOCOM on 24 August 1992. We were gaining some momentum.

On 29 July 1992 we offered the 160th SOAR commander, Colonel Joe Fucci, a deal he could hardly turn down. We offered to perform at the Lexington, OK AASF phase maintenance on his 160th CH-47 aircraft (two at a time) and in return he would allow us to fly-off 20-30 hours flight time, per aircraft, to maintain flight currency for our 1/245th Avn CH-47 personnel. Can you say, "Win-win?"

Through ongoing enthusiasm and ingenuity, Lexington CH-47 personnel, such as Maintenance Officer, Chief Warrant Officer Three Rick Coburn, contacted nearby CH-47 units at Fort Sill, Olathe, KS, and Grand Prairie, TX. Other MOAs and gentlemen's agreements were worked out and ongoing CH-47 training and currency for the 1/245th took place. All of this in anticipation of the 1/245th receiving its authorized MTOE issue of CH-47s.

This continued until circa spring of 1994. In the meantime, a new CH-47 maintenance hangar was built at Lexington AASF, which was programmed, designed and approved based on the 1/245th Special Operations MTOE. The 1/245th never received any Special Operations CH-47 aircraft. It was after the deactivation of the 1/245th Avn in August 1994, that NGB gave OKARNG one-half of a CH-47 aviation company's aircraft. Lexington received eight CH-47D aircraft.

In 2004, the Army decided to end the RAH-66 Comanche Reconnaissance/Attack Helicopter procurement program, after having spent $7 billion on R&D and two prototypes by a joint venture with Boeing/Sikorsky Helicopters. The Army considered it now had $14 billion dollars it could spend elsewhere. Was the 1/245th Avn (SO) (A) still not affordable?

In 1981, under U.S. Army leadership, the Department of Defense began the "Joint-service Vertical take-off/landing Experimental (JVX)" aircraft program. The Army later dropped its role and request for such an aircraft, while the U.S. Navy/Marine Corps later took the lead.

The U.S. Air Force was scheduled to acquire the new CV-22 Ospreys and then begin replacing its aging fleet of MH-53J Pave Low helicopters used to insert and extract special operations forces covertly from hostile areas in September 2008. The CV-22 Osprey V/STOL transport aircraft is manufactured by Bell and Boeing Helicopters.

Planned production quantities initially totaled 458 V-22s, including 360 for the Marine Corps, 48 for the Navy, and 50 for the Air Force at an average cost of $110 million per aircraft, including development costs. CV-22 training was/is being conducted at 58th SOW at Kirtland AFB, NM. The 8th SOS (Special Operations Squadron) at Hurlburt Field, Eglin AFB, FL equipped with the new CV-22s replaces the MH-53 SOW which was there.

Many words and many issues have been mentioned to say this—the Air Force is expert at lobbying for and getting what they want. When I was stationed in Vietnam in 1966/67 we made jokes that " . . . when the Air Force builds a new base, they start by building the Officer's Club first, the base swimming pool, then the NCO Club, then the Base Exchange and Commissary and lastly the runway. Of course they run out of funds before completing the runway. They go back to Congress, request additional funding to complete this new Air Force Base and they get it! I shouldn't gripe, I never complained when I was sent TDY to an Air Force base.

We, the Army, send our soldiers to the U.S. Army's War College at Carlisle Barracks, PA, and learn war fighting skills for senior soldiers and leaders. At the Army's War College senior officers learn about logistical supply trains, battle field intelligence, maneuver units, warfighting skills, politics and diplomacy as relates to the military and more. They learn about leadership through the examples of Bradley, Eisenhower, Schwarzkopf, MacArthur, Patton and Petraeus.

When they, the Air Force's field grade officers, reach top management levels, it appears to me they go to business school/colleges and earn degrees in business management and salesmanship. They learn to lobby and let someone else do the dirty work of combat.

It isn't difficult to notice, there seems to be a lot more time spent between wars than conducting wars. Therefore, are they (blue-suits) educating their leaders more appropriately? Or is the ancient art of warfare an outdated philosophy. Can the next conflict or war be won by air power?

As I'm thinking back to the invasion of Baghdad, I recall that the Air Force leadership told President George W. Bush that, "We can win this and get Saddam with air power; you won't even have to send in the Army!"

We've got some awesome UAV's now (unmanned aerial vehicles) that can do many different and exciting things. They can gather Intel, real time and certain ones can deliver some heavy and hot steel on target. But I've yet to see or hear of one that can plant the American flag in the ground or question a captured enemy soldier, or pick up and comfort a crying child of war. It still takes boots in the dirt. You won't see anything in their arsenal which can replace the Army fighting man – NOTHING!

When nearly three-quarters of all guardsmen and reservists have been 'called-up' at least once in the past ten years, you'd think the nation's employers would support our military. These employers should not only support our service members while they are serving overseas, often being in combat, but especially when they return home.

Today the active Army is broken and won't admit it. They can't meet all of the real world threats and requirements for American military presence with existing manpower levels. I'm sure you've heard of several Army programs such as Stop Loss and extended tours? What was once a 12 month tour in Iraq or Afghanistan became a 15-18 months tour, not only for active soldiers, but for their National Guard brothers as well, during stop loss in 2006-2008.

There are several other ways to reduce the frequency of active and reserve component rotations. Encourage Congress to approve a total Army endstrength increase in manpower. When the Army has met the military and strategic political goals in Iraq and Afghanistan, then implement a reduction in force. It's not a new idea; it was done in WWII, Korea and Vietnam. Why can't it be done again?

While we're on the subject of force structure, I want to take this one last opportunity to express my personal opinion. Yes, I know everyone's got one, but here's the idea. My charming and beautiful sweetheart is also a tremendous cook. Her culinary talents in the kitchen are known far and near. She even has a sign on the wall near our dinner table which reads, "Many have eaten here – Few have died." My very favorite desert is her mouth-watering, low-fat, low-sugar, cherry pie. This relates to the National Guard Bureau and my perception of how they distribute aviation force structure today.

Here's the problem—there isn't enough pie to go around. We don't have enough to share with neighbors down the road, with folks at church; there's just not enough to give everyone a large slice they can enjoy and fully taste such a treat!

Today's Army National Guard Aviation force structure is reminiscent of an old and antiquated organizational adage, supposedly stated by the aviation hierarchy for wholesale success, which says, "Give everybody a piece of the pie!" Well, when you give everybody a piece of the pie—you need 54 pieces (50 states, the District of Columbia and the territories of Guam, Puerto Rico, Virgin Islands). Once the pie is cut and divided up, you then have bits, pieces and crumbs that aren't remotely recognizable as pie, cake or cookies.

To say these pieces of pie are lacking sufficient command and control, administration, service and maintenance support elements does not fall on deaf ears. Each state would like to have either a battalion, regiment, group or brigade aviation headquarters and the senior grades (personnel positions) that come with that organizational MTOE.

A very common problem of Army aviation within each state, is that if you only have detachments, platoons or companies you will not have any authorized positions for officers above first lieutenant or captain (if you are lucky). Whereas the older H-series MTOE for aviation units had major slots for company commanders and captain slots for platoon leaders. A young guardsman/woman that gets to go to Army Aviation Flight School will likely be either a first lieutenant or a captain by the time he/she nears graduation and receives the silver wings of an Army Aviator! Today the average is 17 months to complete rotary-wing flight school with the additional courses now associated with pilot training. This includes time spent completing the SERE Level "C" and RTL course, Dunker or Overwater Training and advanced aircraft qualification. What are State Aviation Officers to do when a promising young aviator wants to stay in Army National Guard Aviation and eventually get promoted above the rank of captain and major without having to move up and out? Thus another reason many commissioned officer aviators decide to become warrant officers – they can't move on up the ladder of commissioned rank because of a lack of TOE positions in higher grades. It becomes up and out or request permission of the WOPA (Warrant Officer Protection Association) and see if you might become a Warrant Officer (just kidding).

It would be criminal of me not to recognize that NGB can't be totally blamed for this situation. They receive authorization to field (man and equip) only a certain limited number of new units periodically. And thus far they have never been authorized to field 54 aviation companies and/or battalions at one time. Nor do they get to pick and choose what type units to field, as if they were in a candy store. This is regretful, but true.

Whereas in the late 1970s, through the early 1990s, very few states with ARNG Aviation had complete TOE units, and what they did receive did not come necessarily with a great deal of senior grade positions. To wit: in 1980, the OKARNG had an Avn Command & Control Hqs (TDA), Co B 149th Avn (TOE w/23 UH-1s), Det 1, HHC, 45th Inf Bde Avn Sec (TDA w/1 UH-1 and 6 OH-58s), and the 145th ATC Platoon (no aircraft). Each of these units was almost autonomous. Most states back then didn't have the clutter and confusion of a Det 1, Det 2 or Det 3 of Company A, B or Z this or that and such 'n' such Co. (-). I must admit that looking at OKARNG aviation's piece of the pie back in December 2006, which included no less than seventeen (17) detachments, a company, and a company (minus), I am truly confused and incapable of comprehending any continuity whatsoever!

Today it is slightly less confusing, but not better. As of March 2009, there are 16 separate aviation units in the OKARNG. Two are fixed-wing units (C-12 and C-23) and the others are a mix of rotary-wing units (CH-47, UH-60, and OH-58s – eventually to be replaced with the new UH-72 Lakota by Eurocopter). Most of those (11) are small detachments. However, the size doesn't prevent them from being deployed.

The old joke regarding 54 pieces, is sad, but true. The Army National Guard, our constitutional militia, is quite political. However, don't take it personal, it's just business.

Therein lies part of the problem – for way too long our NGB forefathers have attempted to appease everyone and fought the good political fight. I do not envy NGB-AVN, now NGB-AVS, nor do I know the answer or best way to divide this big pizza and give everyone what they want. Hell, I'm not sure we can even give a portion of the states exactly what they want. OK, let's admit that first, and then take the second step.

What is available to be shared, divided or given separately? Does NGB necessarily have to divide and split up every aviation organization before it is fielded in several diverse states? Det 1 this and Det 2 that – let's put politics aside and make some hard decisions. What is best for the military? Could it be – solidarity and consistency of training and equipment?

For the good of the whole (is this idea unique or what?), what if Battalion Headquarters and above, plus aviation companies, were left intact and would be issued to the most deserving states ONLY? What if an

Aviation Battalion with three helicopter companies were assigned to three adjacent states: the Bn Hqs plus one flying company to one state and the other two flying companies to the other two states? This may sound like a political stink bomb to most, but humor me a little longer.

What if we based the distribution of new aviation units to states on the merit system? Those states who have shown they can recruit and maintain aviation force structure at or above 100% strength and at or near 100% MOSQ, who utilize their FHP most efficiently, who utilize AFTPs and Annual Training to the mutual benefit of their states major commands and the aviation unit's own combat mission training and who have the best aviation safety record – these states would be placed at the top of the NGB Aviation Force Structure Distribution Merit List.

Yes, this new way of doing business would mean there would be certain states that would not have any aviation force structure. You may read the word any to mean zip, ned, null, nadda, zero—no combat aviation units. *C'est la vie!*

Forget politics and the good ole boy system. Give the best states some credit for excellent work and reward them with some force structure that is relevant and has continuity and upward mobility within that states area(s) of excellence and experience.

Oklahoma doesn't have any experience with the old CH-54 flying crane, like Kansas and Pennsylvania do, so don't offer them a piece of that pie. However, they do have much knowledge and understanding of fixed-wing aircraft and years of expertise with Special Operations in *Little Birds*, both guns and lift. Plus they have years of experience with medium lift in UH-60s and CH-47s. Oklahoma deserves an aviation Group Headquarters, at least an aviation Battalion Headquarters and full companies. Not crumbs left on the plate as those 54 slices were politically and routinely divided.

The fact that the nation's Federal Aviation Administration's headquarters and its Mike Monroney Aeronautical Academy are located at Will Rogers International Airport ought to be recognized. Then there is the fact that American Airlines hub is located at the second international airport in Oklahoma, that being Tulsa International Airport. There are also no less than five active duty military bases in Oklahoma – Fort Sill Field Artillery Center and School at Lawton, OK; McAlester Army Ammunition Depot, McAlester, OK; Tinker AFB, Midwest City, OK – headquarters for the Air Force's Material Command; Altus AFB, Altus, OK – the 97th Air Mobility

Wing, C-17 training and Vance AFB – 71ˢᵗ Flying Training Wing, Enid, OK. This is an excellent base of personnel, former military and civilians with military aviation skills and background. This Sooner State has a great potential for future growth in aviation in the Army National Guard.

Oklahoma State Aviation Officer, Colonel Jon Harrison[4] said, "I'd like to see us pick up a flying battalion headquarters, because we currently don't have a lot of field grade positions. With the units that we got sitting here today, I've got one lieutenant colonel slot and two major slots [TOE]. In September 2007 there'll be a major aviator slot in the Inf Bde and one in the FA. Since the H-series MTOE where we had majors as company commanders, captain platoon leaders . . . The Chinook unit that we have here, the Det . . . the highest [officer] grade is first lieutenant. Which will be very hard to deal with . . . getting a guy into the National Guard through flight school, he's about ready to make captain and we'll have to keep him over-grade in a lieutenant slot."

In life we are faced with many challenges, some mental, some physical, some emotional or a combination of these. Some come with real barriers or obstacles. Some have artificial barriers. In aviation we are taught to maintain our focus and to be situationally aware of our aircraft, its instrumentation, attitude, altitude, airspeed, RPM, communications, etc, things surrounding or near us and the big picture out there. There are situations in which we can input change, accept change and/or alter our course. In the arena of ARNG aviation force structure we are faced with monumental challenges. How do you deal with that?

If you personally cannot make the decision which will affect the results you desire – seek a situation which will make change possible. Or at least seek the solution that will give you (your unit, your state) the best advantage. It never hurts to get one of your pawns to the other side of the board, so one can become a king and continue to fight for your side. Well, it doesn't hurt to get one of your aviation players pushed up to the top, where you can then have more influence on the desired outcome.

Surely you've dealt with *political* situations and I for one dislike having to do so. Or you've heard, "Don't take it personal, it's just politics." I believe in opportunity and achieving results based on credibility and your own track record. Well, you can play the hand you were dealt and hope for luck. Or you can fight smartly and influence the outcome rather than waiting on chance. Having a positive attitude is a wonderful way of doing business, especially if you are selling cosmetics for Mary Kay. Yet it takes *positive action* to achieve positive results! I'm not suggesting a move motivated by or for power. I'm suggesting that you strive for excellence in all that you do and all that you can influence!

Ask Brigadier General Dana D. Batey, Colonel Leroy A. Wall, Brigadier General Paul D. Costilow or Brigadier General Terry R. Council, how they were able to influence and achieve positive results. They didn't do it sitting on the bench.

Become imaginative – what do you see out there, who do see in charge next year and the year after. How can you make a difference? Do not be willing to accept mediocrity. Challenge your people, your staff, yourself. People don't do what you expect; they will do what you *inspect*. Raise the bar, tell them what their job is and when you expect it to be completed. Then remind them again and then again. Show them you're interested in their success. If you help them succeed, you'll be amazed at what happens to your own career.

I'm sure you know your job. But do you know what your boss's job is, its complete description, how it must be accomplished and the smartest way to do it? Do you know the job of your boss's superior? How can you help your own boss become more successful? Plan ahead. Midnight oil is cheaper by the barrel – burn some, do your homework.

Always aim for the stars! If you fall a little short of that goal, you'll still be in the heavens. Aim at what you intend to shoot. If you must attack, then do so with severe prejudice. If you're having trouble with your aim or in selecting the correct target, perhaps you need a strong mentor.

Prayer is simply communication with God. There are many parts of communication, but the main two are sending (talking) and receiving (listening). The hardest part isn't talking with God – it's listening to/for Him. With mentorship, whether you are being a mentor or a superior is mentoring you – the hardest part is listening. Practice listening, often and teach others the lesson. Understanding doesn't come from hearing yourself talk; it comes from listening to others. Listen with an open mind and seek to understand. It's OK to ask questions, even of God. But listen very, very carefully to the answers. Then heed the advice offered.

Please make a note—... heed the advice offered! One more time—heed the advice offered.

When you are the mentor and offering a suggestion, such as " . . . perhaps you would benefit from taking this military education course by correspondence." Then ask the individual if they are interested, if they would commit to taking the time and effort to complete the course. If they do, then ask them to set a date that they will be able to complete the course or goal.

Display confidence in your work, your actions, in your teammates and your dreams. Share your wildest dreams not only with your spouse, but with your teammates, your boss and your mentor. You'll get lots of feedback, some of which you might be able to use to improve your idea or dream.

Be bold, take the lead, and don't wait on others. Remember it's easier to pull a rope up a hill than push it. Work smartly and wisely. Be special – look for special things in others. Don't worry about who gets the credit as long as the team does!

And in every single thing you do, at home, at work and on the job – show others that safety is the only way business gets done in your company. Similar to gravity, safety isn't just a good idea; it's a way of living and working. When others see you reading aviation safety literature they will do the same. When they see you cleaning up a wet spot or spill in the hall way, they do the same next time. When they see how much time you spend planning your flight mission, digesting the current and forecast weather, doing a brand new weight and balance, they will emulate you.

Be the best example of a Leader in Safety as you can be. When you least expect it, someone, somewhere is watching to see if you do as you say or not. And when you see a good example of someone else doing their job safely, praise them publicly. If you see a bad example, stop it right then, but correct them in private if at all possible.

From the earliest days of my military career and training, leadership has been a recurring, necessary, hard-to-define and challenging subject. It is one thing, military or otherwise, which continues to interest me in life; a subject about which I love to learn more each day.

In Basic Infantry Training we were taught to follow our leaders and obey their orders. In Officer Candidate School we were taught that as leaders, we were to be honorable, courageous, never to ask others to do what we weren't willing to do ourselves; lead from the front, and maintain integrity; adhere to moral and ethical principles, soundness of moral character and honesty. Leadership is difficult, if not hard to define.

During an interview about the book *Undaunted Courage* (Lewis & Clark Opening of the West), on March 1996 on PBS, Charlie Rose asked the author, Stephen Ambrose, what was the single common characteristic of the many leaders he had written about over the years, Ambrose stated, "There isn't any [common characteristic]. They are all different!"

Rose: "If I look at all those books [you've written] is there a theme there, is there something in all of those stories, which brings historian Stephen Ambrose to the pen?"

Ambrose: "LEADERSHIP! I am fascinated by leadership. It is something I don't do. I'm a college teacher and a writer. But I am fascinated by leaders. How do they do it? Their techniques vary enormously. Eisenhower and Nixon couldn't have been more different for example. . . . . With regard to Meriwether Lewis, he was in my mind . . . , I've been studying [the] United States Army all my career; [he was] as a good a company commander as the U.S. Army ever produced!"

Rose: " . . . looking at leadership – what defines leadership? What do all these different people have, at least in one common denominator of their capacity to lead?"

Ambrose: "That's what's fascinating. There isn't one!"

Rose: "None!?!"

Ambrose: "None! MacArthur and Nixon, both of them lied all the time [yet were still great leaders]. Eisenhower hardly every lied, except to Nikita Khrushchev."

Albert Switzer one stated, "Example is not the main thing in influencing others . . . it is the only thing." Part of creating an appealing climate is modeling leadership. People emulate what they see modeled; positive model—positive response, negative model—negative response. What leaders do, the potential leaders around them do. What they value, their people value. Leaders set the tone. Leaders cannot demand of others what they do not demand of themselves. Begin learning today and watch others around you begin to grow.

Who will be our leaders tomorrow, in aviation, in Oklahoma? Surely they are already here, on station, being groomed for the job. Here is my challenge to you – "Mentor your soldiers, they are your future leaders."

1. Do your soldiers truly know what their job is . . . have they heard their job description from your lips?
2. Have you personally told them? If not, do so.
3. Do they know what your expectations of them are (from your lips)?
4. Have you personally told them?
5. What is the education level, militarily and civilian, of the soldier(s) you are mentoring?
6. What do you expect from him/her and when? Give him/her something quantifiable and within reasonable, but challenging time limits . . .
7. Raise the bar; they will rise to your expectations and make you proud!
8. Do they know how much you care for them individually and as an organization? Your actions will speak louder than words in this respect . . .
9. Did you know, "People do what you inspect, not what you expect."
10. Ask for a commitment – "Will you do your best, all the time?" "Can you complete your degree by _____ (a specific date)?"

In his book *The One Minute Manager,* Ken Blanchard says, "There's a difference between interest and commitment. When you are interested in doing something, you do it only when it is convenient. When you are committed to something, you accept no excuses." Don't equip people who are merely interested, equip those who are committed."

Commitment is the one quality above all others that enables a potential leader to become a successful leader. Without commitment, there can be no success. Football coach Lou Holtz pointed out, "The Kamikaze pilot who was able to fly fifty missions was involved—but never committed." To determine whether your people are committed, first you must make sure they know what it will cost them to become a leader. That means that you must be sure not to undersell the job. Let them know what it's going to take to do it. Tell them if it's going to be dangerous or long hours, or demanding. Only then will they know what they are committing to. If they won't commit, don't go any further in the equipping process. Don't waste your time.

While discussing excellence, I would also like to address power. Do you have a passion for excellence or a passion for power? What is the difference? The desire for excellence is a gift from God. It is much needed by society, our military establishment and our national leaders. It is characterized by a great respect for quality. It is also characterized by the acceptance of responsibility for one's own mistakes and generously sharing the credit for success.

Excellence doesn't occur by accident, it happens as a result of liberal amounts of oversight, not micro-management, but strong, responsible management at all levels and inspired workmanship at the lowest levels, up through the organization.

My favorite Christian author, Max Lucado, says, "There is a canyon of difference between doing your best and sharing the credit (doing something and not caring who gets the credit) or simply glorifying yourself."

The quest for power, rank, command and/or responsibility are not necessarily in the same category regarding excellence. A passion for power, though, is childish, if it is for self-glorification alone. Eisenhower did not seek power, nor did he seek the position of Supreme Allied Commander during WWII. It sought him.

The quest for excellence is a mark of maturity, while the seeking of power is a sign of immaturity.

General Dwight D. Eisenhower was a true leader and demonstrated his unique leadership ability in the monumental decisions he made. Extreme care went into making those decisions because they were going to affect the lives of thousands of soldiers, civilians and the future of many generations. He collected as much factual information and intelligence as was available, then thought through the possible scenarios and outcomes. Only then did he make his decision(s). We should choose to emulate his example of decision making and leadership.

A friend of mine from OMD, Colonel Gary W. Jackson was an extraordinary individual and officer. He was multi-talented and worked in the Oklahoma Military Department's POTO (Plans, Operations and Training Office) shop for years in the 1980s and 1990s. He was a valued friend of OKARNG aviation. When I first met him in the mid-late 1980s he was the Training Administrator of OKPOT. Gary was later the Director, OKPOT, from 10 July 1994 to 28 February 1996 and then served as the OKARNG Chief of Staff for several years. As the Director of Personnel, COL Jackson conducted many leadership seminars at OMD for mid and senior level officers and NCOs. Leadership must be seen as an on-going process, always being further developed. Don't quit learning. Encourage learning in your subordinates as you do in your family.

COL Gary W. Jackson was a respected military and civilian leader from Purcell, OK. During his 36 years in the National Guard, Jackson earned numerous awards and citations. Having retired from the military in 1996, he worked as an executive assistant to the Oklahoma Adjutant General from 1997 to 2007. He passed away at age 66, unexpectedly on 13 May 2008. Those who knew him will not forget his example of positive leadership.

Ever been in a position of leadership? Were you successful? Will you for the first time or once again be in a position of leadership? If you are in the military, most likely you will have the opportunity to lead.

What is the key to successful leadership? For a team, a squad, a platoon, a company, a battalion or larger – they must have cutting edge leadership! Your organization cannot be successful by accident. Each element or unit must have a leader and he/she must exemplify LEADERSHIP!

I believe that leadership encompasses many things and brings out the best in people. I believe that . . . .

- Personnel determine the potential of the organization.
- Vision determines the direction of the organization.
- Work ethic determines the preparation of the whole.
- Leadership determines the success of the organization.
- "Everything rises and falls on leadership.5"

Our Secretary of Defense Robert M. Gates, stated at a 27 January 2009, Senate Armed services Committee hearing, "The spigot of defense spending that opened [up] on September 11 is closing." Everything changes. The Oklahoma Guard in 2009 totaled 10,358 personnel – 7,953 Army Guard and 2,405 Air Guard. Due to strength reductions the 2010 end-strength is now 7,601 Army Guard and 2,342 Air Guard—9,943. Since the GWOT began Oklahoma has mobilized more than 7,147 soldiers and airmen. During this time, almost 300,000 Army Guard soldiers have deployed overseas, out of 366,000 total. Another change is that we, the National Guard, now have a four star general as the Chief, Gen Craig R. McKinley – a decision maker and a leader.

People follow leaders and not by chance, but purposefully. A very dear friend of mine, Lieutenant Colonel Mike Bedwell is a leader and was somewhat typical of a Citizen Soldier Special Ops Aviator. He led when given the responsibility and followed when that was his job. We shared many experiences and worked for years together in the field of Special Operations Aviation. Mike shared with me his fears, his hopes and his pride of the days we spent in the *Lords of Darkness* as we worked together toward a higher plain.

Mike's last tour in Vietnam was as a CH-47 pilot 1968-69 (TET) in the Delta. He had previous tours in 1963 as a signalman and 1965 with Special Forces (communications specialist) in the Central Highlands. Mike joined the OKARNG at Tulsa when they still had UH-1 Mike-models. This was right after he returned from working as a contract instructor pilot in Libya flying for Ed Wilson, the "Ice Man," a real bad character Mike later learned. He reverted to Warrant Officer to get a slot in the unit then later was given his commission back as a Captain. He became the 45th Avn Bn (SO) (A) Signal Officer.

Mike related, "When I first joined the Guard at Tulsa, I was flying as a civilian pilot off-shore, working/supplying oil platforms in the Gulf, out of Paterson, LA. I would work for two weeks flying off-shore, and then have two weeks off. I'd come north to Oklahoma and fly AFTPs with the 45th Avn Bn back when we had lots of them," said Mike. About 1982, Mike became the General Manager of Perma Jack Foundation Company in Tulsa and settled down for a couple of years and continued to fly M-Day with the unit. "I was with the unit when we fielded the OH-6's, the deployment missions to Fort Bliss, Yuma, Camp Blanding, etc. Those were the days when were cutting up the PVS-5's so we could see. We were still doing NVG full touch-down autorotations, which the Army had ceased doing. We thought that the Litton 909s [NVGs] were the best things in the world."

"In 1985 I choose to go into the Inactive Guard and shipped out for Saudi Arabia for a two year civilian Instructor Pilot job in CH-46s (Boeing KV107s). In 1986 I returned home from Saudi to attend the funerals of our 45th Avn Bn boys, Barr and Barlow . . . . that broke my heart. I married Sandi in 1987 during my last year in Saudi. We came home with bundles of money, started a business and went broke in a year. Then in 1988 I got a job as a truck driver; then you called, God bless you, offering me the Special Operations Aviation Liaison job at Fort Bragg as a Major.

"You know the history from there . . . . I served as OKARNG's Special Operations Aviation LNO at Fort Bragg until about 1990, then worked with you for a short time at Troop Cmd (Avn) at Norman. When we lost the Special Operations mission [1994], I'm afraid I lost interest. I can't tell you how disgusted I was with those politics—I blame the Guard!

"Soon I accepted a full-time Federal Civil Service job with HQ OKSTARC as Communication and Automation Manager and then in 1993 made what many at STARC said was a stupid decision, I accepted the challenge to become the Director" of the new [NGB] Youth Challenge Program at Pryor, OK.

"As it turned out, it was the best decision of my life. As Director of the OKNG Youth Programs Division, I had the pleasure of working with about 300 dedicated people in five major statewide youth programs (two residential, three reintegration/non-residential). Our STARS (State Transition and Reintegration System) was considered the most innovative and successful in the nation.

"So that brings me to now, January 2003. I intend on retiring next year (2004) from the Guard with 36 years in the military and maybe from the State with 16 years (counting Vietnam credit). I have a custom framing and awards/engraving shop in Pryor, OK.

"What are my feelings about the 45th Avn Bn? Why yes, I miss the hell out of it! Like you, I've got many war stories from Nam, many near misses, a lot of soul searching and a lot of friends made, but somehow, despite my pride at being a Vietnam veteran, I didn't have the same feeling of excellence and accomplishment about Vietnam, as I felt working for and flying with the 1st Bn 245th Avn (SO)(A).

"The reason for this may have had something to do with our country's embarrassment after Iran and the desperate need for Special Ops Aviation expertise and our realization that, as a Guard unit, we could play an important role in that solution. My view was a little different than that of many. I often spoke with Brigadier General Garrett, a cigar hanging out of his mouth always, in staff meetings at 1st SOCOM. He and Lieutenant General Gary E. Luck respected our unit as did most active duty aviators. They wanted to do business with us . . . I just don't think the Guard (NGB) as an organization was up to it.

How many Guard units ever had the intensity of training we did? How many ever pushed the edge of the envelope as many times as we did? How many ever got as good as we were? You may remember Chief Warrant Officer Three Robert C. "Bobby" Lane at one time was the entire military's high time goggle pilot! The 160th SOA learned a lot from us. I had that validated on my recent trip to the 160th SOAR, regimental headquarters at Fort Campbell to see my son, Sergeant First Class Mark A. Bedwell. Our guys are still there and many of the names from the past are on their walls.

I think those days (before Thailand, etc.) were so special because our specific [CAPSTONE] mission hadn't been defined yet. We all had visions of being used in real world conflicts or at least doing real world support missions around the world. It was special and we were special. People in the Army Guard knew who we were no matter where you went. We were beginning to gain respect like the ANG Solant Volo people on the east coast. Most importantly, we were doing it with hand-me-downs (old OH-6s, PVS-5s, etc.) and still making mission standards and parameters!

MSG Mark A. Bedwell

Like many older OKARNG soldiers, Mike has a son, who is also a soldier. Mike's son, Mark Andrew Bedwell, was handpicked in 1994 for the 160th SOAR while serving as an airframe repairman with Co B 3rd Bn 501st Avn, Camp Eagle, Korea. He was selected because he had [previously] served with the 1/245th at Tulsa and he has now been there for over eight years and will be there for at least another four; they created a slot for him to get him promoted to E-7. His Commander told me they are still benefiting from the relationship with that unit (1/245th SOA).

Author's note: MSG Mark A. Bedwell was promoted to E-8 and is still a Night Stalker with the 4th Bn 160th SOAR at Fort Lewis, WA. He will soon be taking charge as First Sergeant of one of the 4th Battalion's companies. Mark has deployed three times to Afghanistan in 2001, 2007 and 2009. He also has deployed to Iraq twice in 2003 and also in 2008.

"My time during the 1960s in Special Forces was something I was very proud of. The 1/245th SOA brought it back. When I wore my green beret at Fort Bragg the ACofS OKPOT hated me for that, but I was authorized and it was right! The feeling of being special was not that common in the military during that period. We, the 1st Bn 245th SOA, not only had the title (Special Ops Avn) . . . *we were Special.*"

Mike Bedwell ended his comments by adding, "I drive a Corvette. Now don't laugh. I have the 160th SOA plate on the front of it. I'm getting old . . . but *I don't think those 'Special' memories will ever go away.*

Why are they special? Whether you are talking about the special aircraft, the aviation crew members or the special operators who eventually put their boots in the dirt—they are indeed all quite extraordinary. These exceptional humans are a cut-above your average career soldier. They didn't achieve their wings via correspondence courses or at a community college.

Theirs is a road less traveled for certain. They didn't learn their skills at summer school, but during long, intensive, academic, physical and hands on, challenging training. We are talking about extraordinary individuals who have displayed and been evaluated to have an unusual ability to deal with high levels of stress and an inbreed quality and desire to get the mission accomplished.

Earlier I talked about the Survival, Evasion and Resistance and Escape, Level "C" course required of all Army Special Operations Forces. In a study by Dr. Andy Morgan[6] of Yale Medical School conducted in a real-world laboratory (Camp Mackall, Fort Bragg, NC) he looked at something now called, "stress inoculation."

Dr. Morgan explains, " . . . they expose you to pressure and suffering in training so you'll build up your immunity. It's a kind of classic psychological conditioning: the more shocks to your system, the more you're able to withstand." This is why you don't graduate from flight school the day after you solo. There are more experiences and lessons to be learned.

These special operators have heart and determination. Dr. Morgan says that students during mock interrogations at the RTL (resistance training laboratory) phase of SERE " . . . their bodies pump more stress hormones than the amounts actually measured in aviators landing on aircraft carriers . . . The levels of stress hormones are sufficient to turn off the immune system and to produce a catabolic state, in which the body begins to break down and feed on itself. [In cases of extreme stress] the average weight loss in three days is 22 pounds."

Dr. Morgan found, "One very specific reason that Special Forces are superior survivors: they produce significantly greater levels of NPY [a chemical in the brain called neuropeptide Y] compared with regular troops. Special Forces soldiers really are special and different from the rest of the Army."

As we were taught in flight training – should you experience an emergency during actual flight YOU MUST KEEP FLYING THE AIRCRAFT UNTIL EVERY THING STOPS. Why? Maintaining your focus in an emergency and control of the situation will greatly increase your chances of living one more day.

During combat, should you be captured, you've been trained to survive and escape. In the soldier's Military Code of Conduct we were taught, "If I am captured, I will continue to resist by all means available. I will make every effort to escape and aid others to escape. I will accept neither parole nor special favors from the enemy." You must continue the fight until there's no breath remaining.

Our fellow Special Operations Aviation brothers and sisters, members of the elite 160th Special Operations Aviation Regiment are called the Night Stalkers. They have a motto, one which they live by – "Night Stalkers Don't Quit!"

Having had the absolute pleasure of serving in the United States Army for nearly 30 years (enlisted, warrant officer and commissioned) and the privilege of being a very small part of one special organization called the 45th Aviation Battalion (Special Operations) (Airborne) which existed for twelve years (1982 to 1994), I salute the soldiers and airman who called themselves the *Lords of Darkness*. It is my desire that you will remember them, their history and their motto: "Not For Ourselves Alone."

Please, don't forget to turn out the lights . . . .

1. USSOCOM 1987
2. Lt Col Wray R. Johnson, USAF, "Whither Aviation Foreign Internal Defense," *Airspace Journal* (Spring 1997)
3. HQ AFSOC/XPF background paper, subject: Initiative 17 (I--17) and SOF Aviation Command and Control, 25 August 1992.
4. Interview with OKSAO, Lieutenant Colonel Jon Harrison, 20 December 2006
5. Reprinted by permission. John C. Maxwell, "Leadership Promises For Everyday (A Daily Devotional)," (Nashville, TN: Thomas Nelson Inc.), 15. All rights reserved.
6. Dr. Andy Morgan, "Lessons in Survival," *Newsweek*, (23 February 2009): 56-57

Appendix A

Military Abbreviations and Acronyms

(A) or (Abn)	Airborne
(SO)	Special Operations
1LT	First Lieutenant (pay grade O-2)
1SG	First Sergeant (pay grade E-8/E-9)
2LT	Second Lieutenant (pay grade O-1)
67N	Military Occupational Specialty for UH-1 Huey helicopter repairman
67V	Military Occupational Specialty for OH-6 Cayuse and OH-58 Kiowa helicopter repairman
A/C	Aircraft
AAA	Anti-Aircraft Artillery
AAAA	Army Aviation Association of America
AAF	Army Airfield
AAFA	Army Aviation Flight Activity
AASF	Army Aviation Support Facility – e.g. NG helipad at Lexington or Tulsa
AC	Active Component
AC	Aircraft commander
AC-130	US Air Force Armed C-130 Hercules (20mm, 40mm & 105mm)
ACU	Army Combat Uniform—the current desert camouflage uniform
ADF	Automatic Direction Finder (basic radio 'homing')

ADSW	Active Duty for Special Work—a type of manday
ADT	Active Duty for Training – a type of manday and term for budget personnel
AFB	Air Force Base
AFN	Armed Forces (Radio) Network
AFSOC	Air Force Special Operations Command
AFTP	Additional Flight Training Period
AG	[the] Adjutant General
AGR	Active, Guard & Reserve, full-time active duty guardsman, Title 32 & Title 10
AH – 6	Attack Helicopter (U.S. Army prefix of designation) Cayuse
AHP	Army Helicopter (Aero) Port
AIT	Advanced Individual Training (normally 8 weeks of specialized training immediately after Basic Infantry Training (BIT)
ALCE	Airlift Control Element (Air Force) 12 man teams
ALSE	Aviation Life Support Equipment, e.g. survival vest, mustang suits, chem. lts
AMC	Air Mission Commander
AMOC	Aviation Maintenance Officer Course
ANVIS—6	Aviator Night Vision Imaging System, 6th generation
AO	Area of operation; also Action Officer; also Admin Officer
APART	Annual Proficiency and Readiness Test
AQC	Aviation Qualification Course (aviator/CE/FE/IP or MTP)
ARI	Aviation Restructuring Initiative[1]
ARMS	Aviation Resource Management Survey[2]
ARNG	Army National Guard
ARTEP	Army Readiness Training and Evaluation Program
ARTY/Arty	[Field] Artillery
ASA	Army Security Agency
ASED	Aviation Service Entry Date
ASOG	Army Special Operations Group

AST	Administration and Supply Technician – worked as unit full-timer
AT	Annual Training
ATC	Air Traffic Control (normally a platoon or company)
ATS	Air Traffic Service
AUSA	Association of the United States Army
AVCRAD	Aviation Classification and Repair Activities/Depot
AVN/ Avn	Aviation
AWADS	All Weather Aerial Delivery System
BDE/ Bde	Brigade
BDU	[Army] Battle Dress Uniform—green camouflage; ACU (Army Combat Uniform) is the current desert camouflage uniform
BG	Brigadier General (1 star); paygrade O-10
BIT	Basic Infantry Training (8 weeks of fundamental, initial military indoctrination and Army combat infantry training)
Bluebirds	RH-53D flight callsign during EAGLE CLAW
BN Bn	Battalion
C-130	US Air Force Hercules cargo & passenger transport (carried 2 MH-6s +)
C-141	US Air Force Star Lifter cargo & passenger transport (carried 3 MH-6s +)
C-5A	US Air Force Galaxy heavy cargo & pax transport (carried 2 UH-1s +)
CAA	Civil Aeronautics Administration (ca 1926 to 1985)
CAB	Civil Aeronautics Board
CAS	Combined Arms and Services Staff School (at Fort Leavenworth)
CCT	Combat Control Team (Air Force) 6 man team
Cdr	Commander
CE	Crew chief—abbreviation & symbol used by Army in logging flight time
CENTCOM	United States Central Command—responsible for the Middle East, Egypt and Central Asia

CGSC	Command and General Staff College (correspondence or Ft Leavenworth)
CH-47	Cargo Helicopter (U.S. Army prefix of designation) Chinook
CH-34	Cargo Helicopter – Sikorsky Choctaw ca 1955-72 Curtis-Wright R-1820-84C radial engine, 1425 hp, cruise 98 kts
CIA	Central Intelligence Agency
CINC	Commander in Chief
CINCPAC	Commander in Chief, Pacific
CLRT	Combined Logistics Review Team
CNGB	Chief, Army National Guard (Gen position)
CO	Commanding Officer
CO/Co.	Company
COL	Colonel 0-6
COM/ COMMO	Communications
Combat Talon	MC-130 Hercules specially equipped for SOF missions
COMJTF	Commander Joint Task Force
COMSEC	communications security
CONUS	Continental United States
CP	Co-pilot—abbreviation & symbol used by Army in logging flight time
CPL	Corporal E-4; replaced by the rank of Specialist E-4 (paygrade E-4)
CPT	Captain O-3
CSA	Chief of Staff, Army (Gen position)
CSM	Command Sergeant Major E-9
CV/MH-22	Boeing's Tilt-rotor Osprey 230/240 kts, 2,500+ nm range, up to 24 troops or 20K lbs of cargo
CV-22	Boeing's Tilt-rotor Osprey 230 kts, 2,500+ nm range, up to 24 troops or 20K lbs of cargo
DA	Department of the Army
DAET	Department of Aeromedical Education and Training
DAMO	Department of the Army Management Office

DAMO-FDF	Dept of the Army Mgmt Office, Force Development, Force Structure
DAMO-FDV	Dept of the Army Mgmt Office, Force Development, Aviation
DAMO-ODF	Dept of the Army Mgmt Office, Force Development, Operational Development Force Structure
DAMPL	Dept of the Army Master Priority List
DARNG	Director, Army National Guard (LTG position now; former MG)
DAS	Director of the Army Staff (LTG position at DA level)
DCSOPS	Deputy Chief of Staff, Operations and Plans (LTG position at DA level)
DCSPER	Deputy Chief of Staff, Personnel
DEA	Drug Enforcement Agency
DES	Department of Evaluation and Standardization—located at USAACS, Ft Rucker
DFT	Deployment for training (orders)—a type of manday
DIA	Defense Intelligence Agency
DIV	Division
DOD/DoD	Department of Defense
DOR	Drop on request. To quit a course, either due to injury or lack of motivation.
EC-130	USAF C-130 Hercules with internal 18,000 gal fuel bladder – EAGLE CLAW
EDATE	Effective date
EDRE	Emergency Deployment Readiness Exercise
ENG/Eng	Engineer
EUCOM	United States European Command—area of responsibility: Europe, Russia, Iceland, Greenland and Israel
FAA	Federal Aviation Administration (enacted 1958)
FAARP	Forward Arming And Refueling Point (for aircraft)
FAD	Force Activity Designator
FAST	Flight Aptitude Selection Test
FBO	Fixed base operator – civilian avgas/jetfuel provider at a civilian airport

FE	Flight engineer—abbreviation & symbol used by Army in logging flight time
FHP	Flying Hour Program
FM 101-5	Field Manual—Staff Organizations and Operations
FOB	Forward Operating Base – used by Special Forces Groups
FORSCOM	Forces Command, Hqs at Ft McPherson, GA
FRIES	Fast rope insertion/extraction system
FT	Full-time [employee or position]; abbreviation for Fort
FTX	Field Training Exercise
FW	Fixed-wing, as in airplane
GAO	Government Accounting Office
GCA	Ground Controlled Approach (azimuth, glide path and distance monitored)
GEN	General (4 star) O-13
GO	General Order (sometimes used to refer to general officer)
GPS	Global Positioning System mounted in aircraft
GSG-9	Border Guard (German counterterrorist) equivalent to US Army Delta
GWOT	Global War on Terrorism
H-19	Utility/Cargo Helicopter – Sikorsky Chickasaw ca 1951-68 Pratt & Whitney R-1340-57 radial engine, 600 hp, cruise 98 kts
HEED	Helicopter Emergency Egress Device
HEMMET	M977, 8WD, Heavy Expanded Mobility Tactical Truck
HHC	Headquarters and Headquarters Company
HQDA	Headquarters, Department of the Army
HSC	Headquarters and Service Company
HUMVEE	HMMWV, High Mobility Multipurpose Wheeled Vehicle
ICAO	International Civil Aviation Organization 4-letter airport identifier codes uniquely identify individual airports worldwide. Used in flight plans to indicate departure, destination and alternate airfields: KOUN = Norman, KHMY = Muldrow AHP, KTUL = Tulsa
IDT	Inactive Duty Training (normally drill weekends)

IFE/IE	Instrument Flight Examiner—abbreviation & symbol used by Army in logging flight time
IMA	Individual Mobilization Augmentee (USAR) preassigned to an active org
INF/Inf	Infantry
IP	Instructor pilot—abbreviation & symbol used by Army in logging flight time
IRR	Individual Ready Reservist (USAR) can fill any position desired by DA
JA/ATT	Joint Airborne/ Air Transportability Training
JALIS	Joint Air Logistics Information System – DOD OSA aircraft scheduling software, one system for all services' VIP passenger fixed-wing
JCS	Joint Chiefs of Staff
JCS/SOD	Joint Chiefs of Staff – Special Operations Division
JFHQ	Joint Force Headquarters, e.g. JFH-OK
JRTC	Joint Readiness Training Center located at Ft Polk, an MRE (Mission Rehearsal Exercise) normally lasts 12 days
JSCP	Joint Strategic Capabilities Plan
JSOC	Joint Special Operations Command
JTF	Joint Task Force
KIA	Killed in action
KTS/Kts	Originally a Naval term; 1 Knot = 1 Nautical mile per hour – measurement of Airspeed (multiply knots by 1.15 to get MPH)
L-15	Liaison (Observation Airplane) Boeing Scout, single engine
L-19	Liaison (Observation Airplane), single engine later O-1, Cessna Bird Dog; DoD ordered 3,200 L-19s between 1950—1959
L-20	Later U-6, DeHaviland Beaver, single engine, 4 passenger
L-23	Later U-8, Beechcraft Queen Air, twin engine
L-5	Liaison (Observation Airplane) Stinson Flying Jeep, single engine
LA	Lower Alabama, more particularly Ft Rucker, sometimes Los Angeles
LIC	Low Intensity Conflict, such as Grenada, Haiti or Somalia

Litton 909s	Night vision goggles produced by Litton Corp., early generation
LNO	Liaison Officer
LTC	Lieutenant Colonel O-5
LTG	Lieutenant General (3 star) O-12
MAJ	Major O-4
MARS	Military Affiliate Radio Systems (used in VN to talk via Ham Radio to wives at home and/or parents.
M-A-S-H	Mobile Army Surgical Hospital
MC-130	US Air Force 'Modified' C-130 Hercules
MD-500/530	McDonnell-Douglas 1984 production version of the old Hughes OH-6; this and later versions, used by TF 160 , could carry 7 combat troops.
M-day	Man-day soldier, traditional member of guard, not fulltime, Title 32
Med	Medical
MG	Major General (2 star) O-11
MH-47E	Modified Helicopter (U.S. Army prefix of designation) Chinook
MH-6	Modified Helicopter (U.S. Army prefix of designation) Cayuse
MH-60	Modified Helicopter (U.S. Army prefix of designation) Blackhawk
MOA	Memorandum of Agreement
MOI	Method of Instruction – military course for instructors (instructor pilots – IPs)
MOS	Military Occupational Specialty; numeric job descriptor
MPT	Military Personnel Technician – Warrant Officer/Admin
MSG	Master Sergeant E-8
MTOE	Modified Table of Organization and Equipment—A Modification table of organization and equipment (MTOE) is an authorization document that prescribes the modification of a basic TOE necessary to adapt it to the needs of a specific unit or type of unit.
MTP	Maintenance Test Pilot
MV-22B	Modified Tilt-Rotor (DoD designation) Osprey

NAS	Naval Air Station
NCO	Non Commissioned Officer, i.e. a sergeant
NG	National Guard
NGAUS	National Guard Association of the United States
NGB	National Guard Bureau
NGB-AVN	National Guard Bureau Aviation Office
NGB-AVS	National Guard Bureau Aviation & Safety Division
NOE	Nap of the earth – flying 50' above the terrain, water or tree tops
NVG/NVD	Night vision goggle or night vision device
O-1	Observation Airplane Cessna Bird Dog, Continental O-470, 213 hp, cruise +/—110 kts
OA	Organizational Authority
OAC	Operating Activity Center (primarily the Edgewood, MD NGB-AVN location)
OBN	Oklahoma Bureau of Narcotics
ODT	Overseas Deployment for Training
OH–13	Observation Helicopter (U.S. Army prefix of designation) Sioux production 1946 to 1976 Franklin 157hp cruise 70 knots
OH–23	Observation Helicopter (U.S. Army prefix of designation) two & three seat configuration Raven Continental O-335-5D engine, cruise 80 kts, production ca 1949 to 1965; primary R/W Army trainer until 1965.
OH-6	Observation Helicopter (U.S. Army prefix of designation) Cayuse, later nicknamed Loach in VN; Allison T63-A-5A 252 shp; cruise 120 kts, max 147 mph, production 1963 to ca 1970.[3] Also see MD-500/530.
OJT	On the Job Training – sometimes in lieu of MOS producing school when such is not available, i.e., OH-6 67V school didn't exist in 1982 or after.
OKARNG	Oklahoma Army National Guard
OKPOT	Oklahoma Plans, Operations and Training; Office of G-3, J-3
OKTAG	The Adjutant General of Oklahoma

OMS	Organizational Maintenance Shop (ground/wheeled vehicle maintenance)
OPLAN	Operational Plan
OPSEC	Operational Security – preventing the unintended release of classified mat'l
OSAA	Operational Support Airlift Agency, Hqs Ft. Belvoir – Army's VIP/Pax FW unit
P	Pilot symbol used by Army in logging flight time
P5	Special funding from DOD for use only by Special Operations units
P A C C O M / PACOM	United States Pacific Command—area of responsibility: People's Republic of China, Mongolia, N & S Korea, Southeast Asia, India/Pakistan coastal border, Antarctica; Madagascar, Australia, New Zealand, and Hawaii. Sixty percent of the earth's population.
PAX	Passenger(s)
PBO	Property Book Officer – maintains lists of units equipment, a/c and property
PCs	Personal computers
PFC	Private First Class E-3
PIC	Pilot-in-command
Plt/Platoon	smaller military segment of a company; normally about 16-44 men. They are three squads in an infantry platoon. Normally 3 plts of +/- 30 men in a company.
POTO	Plans, Operation & Training Office (normally the G-3 section)
PVS – 5	Pilot Visioning System, 5th generation
PVT	Private E-1/E-2
RAID	Reconnaissance Air Interdiction Detachment
RC	Reserve Component
Regmt	Regiment
RH-53D	USN heavy lift helicopter, General Electric T64-GE-416/416A turboshaft engines, 4,380 shp; used in Operation EAGLE CLAW, cruise 140 kts
RIF	reduction in force; reducing the size of a military without asking if soldiers want to stay in or not.

RON	Remain over night
RPG	Rocket Propelled Grenade
RTA	Royal Thai Army
RTL	Resistance Training Lab, a portion of SERE training
SAO	State Aviation Officer
SAS	Special Air Services (British counterterrorist) equivalent to Delta
SATCOM	Satellite communication/radios used by Special Operations Forces
SEAL	US Navy—Sea, Air, Land (Seal Team VI – counterterrorism unit)
Sec/Section	A small military unit, similar to a platoon; an Aviation Section; +/- 12 persons
SECDEF	Secretary of Defense
SF	Special Forces
SFC	Sergeant First Class E-7
SFFOB	Special Forces Forward Operating Base
SFOB	Special Forces Operations Base
SFTS	Synthetic Flight Training System (UH-1 simulator – 2B24; US Army also has CH/MH-47 and UH/MH-60 simulators. C-12 simulators are civilian contracted w/Flight Safety.)
SGT	Sergeant E-5
SME	Subject Matter Expert
SMO	State Maintenance Office or State Maintenance Officer
SPT	Support
SOA	Special Operations Aviation
SOAR	Special Operations Aviation Regiment
SOCOM	Special Operations Command – Army (formed 1 Oct 1982)
SOCPAC	Special Operations Command Pacific
SOF	Special Operations Forces
SOSCOM	Special Operations Support Command, Fort Bragg, NC
SOUTHCOM	United States Southern Command—area of responsibility: all of Central and South America
SOW	Special Operations Wing (Air Force, e.g. 1 SOW at Hurlburt Field, FL)

SP4/SP5	Special 4 class E-4 or Specialist 5 class E-5 differs from CPL or SGT as a technical skill, opposed to a squad leadership position.
SPC	Specialist, normal indicates SP4 E-4
SPIES	Special Patrol Insertion/Extraction System—a method of insertion and extraction of small teams. The descendant of STABO operations, SPIES is safer and more effective allowing an entire team to be extracted on the same rope.
Sqd	Squadron
SRAA	Senior Regular Army Advisor – term used by 5 USA, which later became SRAAG
SRAAG	Senior Army Advisor Guard – term first used by 1 USA; now used by all USA & NG
SRO	Senior Ranking Officer
SSG	Staff Sergeant E-6
SSI	Shoulder Sleeve Insignia
STABO	Personnel extraction system via helicopter (derived from the first letter of the surnames of the five individuals who invented the helicopter extraction system) An old system of extracting one to four soldiers by 150 foot ropes dangling from a helicopter. Primarily used for jungle extractions over short distances. It has been replaced by the SPIES system now.
STARC	State Area Regional Command; formerly ARNG term for State Hqs; today the State Hqs is normally referred to Joint Forces Headquarters (JFH-OK)
TAA	Total Army Analysis
TAC	Theater Aviation Company
TAG	The Adjutant General, a National Guard general officer in charge of the State's Army & Air National Guard units; normally a Major General (2 star)
TARS	Tactical Aircraft Repair Shops
TC(A)	Troop Command (Aviation) – TDA Avn Hqs in OKARNG
TDA	Table of Distribution and Allowances
Tech	Federal 'Technician' employee, Gov. Service , e.g. GS-11 fulltime Tech
TFOS	Total Federal Officer Service

TOE	Table of Organization and Equipment—The Table of Organization and Equipment (TOE) is a document that prescribes the wartime mission, capabilities, organizational structure, and mission essential personnel and equipment requirements for military units. Also see MTOE.
TPFDD	Time Phased Force Development Data
TRADOC	Training and Doctrine Command – Fort Monroe, VA
Trp	Troop
Trp Cmd (Avn)	Troop Command (Aviation) – TDA Avn Hqs in OKARNG 1984—1993
U-3	Utility Airplane – Cessna 310 twin engine, 4 passenger, produced 1953 to mid-1960s, Continental O-470-Ms of 240 hp, cruise 156 kts
U-6	Utility Airplane – DeHaviland, Beaver, Pratt & Whitney 450 hp R985 Wasp Junior SB-3 reciprocating radial engine4 passenger; production 1948 to 1968; cruise 110 kts
U-8	Utility Airplane – Beechcraft Queen Air, Seminole twin engine, Lycoming IGSO480 A1E6 flat-6, 340 hp, cruise 144 kts
UA	Unit Administrator – full-time Federal Technician or AGR person in charge of Armory and day to day business for a specific unit.
UAV	Unmanned aerial vehicle
UCMJ	Uniform Code of Military Justice—a federal law, enacted by Congress. Its provisions are contained in United States Code, Title 10, Chapter 47
UH-1	Utility Helicopter (U.S. Army prefix of designation) Huey produced by Bell 1959 to 1976; Lycoming T53-L-13B, 1,400 shp; cruise 100 kts.[4]
UH-72	Light Utility Helicopter – EADS North American/Eurocopter Lakota 2007 2 each Turbomeca ARRIEL 1E2, 738 shp, cruise +/- 125 kts
USAABAR	United States Army Aviation Board of Accident Review
USACRC	United States Army Combat Readiness/Safety Center (formerly USAASC US Army Avn Safety Center, redesignated USACRC 31 Jan 2005)
USAJFKSWCS	U.S. Army John F. Kennedy Special Warfare School, Fort Bragg,NC

USARV	United States Army Vietnam
USASOC	United States Army Special Operations Command (reorganized from 1st SOCOM and formed 1 Dec 1989)
USNSWC	U.S. Navy Special Warfare Center
USSOCOM	United States Special Operations Command – formed Apr 1987
USMC	United States Marine Corps
USP&FO	United States Property and Fiscal Officer
UTA	Unit Training Assembly (4 hrs period of unit training. 1 drill wknd = 4 UTAs)
VCSA	Vice Chief of Staff, Army
VTOL	Vertical Take-off and Landing
WD GO	War Department General Order
WESTCOM	Western (Pacific) command before redesignation as PACOM
WPA	Works Projects Administration – set up to provide jobs by FDR
XO	Executive Officer or Exec
Y-R-T	Year Round Training (as opposed to regular 15 consecutive days of Annual Training)

---

1. ARI improves on the Army of Excellence (AOE) structure, reduces logistics, lowers costs, and retires old aircraft within available resources. It also corrects the AOE organizational deficiencies for maint. and hqs personnel. This concept moves the majority of USAR units to the ARNG. Additionally, a large portion of the cargo helicopter and fixed wing fleet moved from the Army's Active Component to the ARNG..

2. Commanders receive assistance from the FORSCOM ARMS Team to make assessments of their management programs and capability to conduct their wartime mission. The ARMS inspection focuses on enhancing safety, readiness, and standardization. It is a critical measurement tool for the chain-of-command.

3. The Army initially ordered 1,438 OH-6As for use during the Vietnam conflict. First flown in February 1963, the OH-6A Cayuse entered service in September 1966, establishing 23 world records for speed, distance and altitude. The Cayuse was Hughes' longest-running helicopter program and, during the Vietnam conflict, as many as 100 OH-6As were built a month. The OH-6D was an improved version with more advanced electronics and heavier armament. The OH-6 also was exported as the Model 500 Defender (MD-500). It served in Granada and Panama during the 1980s, as well as in the Gulf wars, Somalia and the Balkans.

4. The last "Hueys" were produced in 1976 with more than 16,000 made in total, of which about 7,000 were deployed in Vietnam. In Vietnam, 2,202 Huey pilots were killed and approximately 2,500 aircraft were lost, roughly half to combat and the rest to operational accidents. The last UH-1s in the ARNG were finally retired in 2009.

Appendix B

OKARNG State Aviation Officers

Name	Remark	From	To
LTC August L. "Gus" Guild[1]	1st Facility Supervisor, Max Westheimer Field, Norman	10 Jun 1965	16 Jan 1968
LTC Chester A. "Chet" Howard[2]	1st SAO	1 Feb 1968	11 Feb 1972
LTC/COL Pete Phillips[3]	2nd SAO	12 Feb 1972	12 Jan 1976
MAJ/COL Dana D. Batey[4]	3rd SAO	13 Jan 1976	27 Oct 1988
LTC/COL Leroy A. Wall[5]	4th SAO	1 Dec 1988	1 Mar 2000
COL Paul D. "Pete" Costilow[6]	M-day SAO	22 Jun 1999	May 2001
LTC/COL Jackie L Self[7]	5th SAO	1 Mar 2000	1 Dec 2003
LTC/COL Terry R. Council[8]	6th SAO	2 Dec 2003	30 Jun 2006
MAJ/COL Jon Michael Harrison[9]	7th SAO	1 Jul 2006	present

Executive Secretaries to the OKSAO

Jody (McClain)	Roberts Sep 1986 – Sep 1989
Sondra R. Doucet	Jul 1989 – Oct 1994
Rhonda (McCalip)	Hinch Nov 1994 – Dec 1996
Portia R. Yongbanthom	Sep 2000 – Nov 2001
Gaylene T. Hernandez	Feb 2002 – Dec 2005
Shameka L. King	May 2007—present

1. LTC Guild was defacto "SAO" before the ARNG position "State Aviation Officer" came into being.
2. LTC Howard departed Oklahoma as a colonel; he was promoted to BG in the PAARNG.
3. COL Phillips was killed in a civil aviation accident 25 Jun '92 near Konawa; promoted to COL before he retired from the OKARNG.
4. Dana Batey was appointed and promoted to BG as Asst OKTAG on 28 Oct 1988, he retired as BG with full federal recognition.
5. Leroy Wall was promoted to COL on 15 Dec 1988; he retired Mar 2000.
6. Pete Costilow was promoted to COL on 2 Mar 1998 and to BG on 12 May 2001, he retired as BG.
7. Jackie Self retired as COL.
8. Terry Council was appointed and promoted to BG as Asst OKTAG in Aug 2006, he retired as BG.
9. Jon Harrison was promoted to LTC 27 Aug 2006. Promoted to COL ca 2009.

Appendix C

The Adjutants General of the Oklahoma National Guard

Territorial Period

Adjutant General	From	To
Harry Clark[1]	1889	
BG James Carson Jamison	23 Dec 1894	10 Jul 1897
BG Phil C. Rosenbaum	10 Jul 1897	26 Mar 1899
BG Bert C. Orner (Acting)	26 Mar 1898	11 Mar 1899
BG Harry C. Barnes	11 Mar 1899	1 Aug 1899
BG Bert C. Orner	1 Aug 1899	4 Sep 1901
BG E.P. Burlingame	4 Sep 1901	28 Feb 1906
BG Alva J. Niles	1 Mar 1906	16 Nov 1907

Since Statehood

Adjutant General	From	To
BG Frank M. Canton	17 Nov 1907	30 Jun 1916
BG Ancil Earp	1 Jul 1916	30 Jan 1918
BG E.P. Gipson	1 Feb 1918	30 Jan 1919
MG Charles F. Barrett	1 Feb 1919	28 Jan 1923
MG Baird H. Markham	28 Jan 1923	30 Jun 1925
MG Charles F. Barrett	1 Jul 1925	19 Sep 1939
BG Louis A. Ledbetter	20 Sep 1939	13 Sep 1940

MG George A. Davis	14 Sep 1940	6 May 1947
MG Roy W. Kenny	7 May 1947	7 Mar 1965
MG LaVern E. Weber	8 Mar 1965	30 Sep 1971
MG David C. Matthews	2 Oct 1971	12 Jan 1975
MG John Coffey, Jr.	13 Jan 1975	19 Nov 1978
MG Robert M. Morgan	20 Nov 1978	11 Jan 1987
MG Donald F. Ferrell (ANG)	12 Jan 1987	13 Jan 1991
MG Tommy G. Alsip	14 Jan 1991	19 Jun 1992
MG Gary D. Maynard	20 Jun 1992	31 Mar 1995
MG Stephen P. Cortright (ANG)	1 Apr 1995	21 Oct 2002
MG Harry M. Wyatt III[2] (Acting) (ANG)	22 Oct 2002	12 Jan 2003
MG Harry M. Wyatt III 313 (ANG)	13 Jan 2003	3 Feb 2009
MG Myles L. Deering	3 Feb 2009	present

The Assistant Adjutant Generals of Oklahoma National Guard[3]

Assistant Adjutant General	From	To
BG Charles V. Wheeler	1 Feb 1968	30 Apr 1968
BG Harry W. Barnes	1 May 1968	30 Jun 1970
BG Edward Moses Frye	1 Jul 1970	15 Oct 1971
BG William L. Youell	16 Oct 1971	Jan 1976
BG Paul W. Reed	Jan 1976	Mar 1976
BG James M. Bullock	Mar 1976	Jan 1978
BG William Rex Wilson	Jan 1978	Oct 1978
BG William H. Henderson	Nov 1978	30 Jun 1983
BG Norman E. Duckworth	1 Jul 1983	27 Oct 1988
BG Dana D. Batey	28 Oct 1988	30 May 1991
BG Donnie Smith	1 Jun 1991	7 Jun 1993
BG John Hubbard	8 Jun 1993	20 Jun 1997
BG Jim Morford	21 Jun 1997	9 Jul 2000
BG Thomas Mancino	10 Jul 2000	11 May 2001
BG Paul D. "Pete" Costilow	May 2001	Jul 2006
BG Terry R. Council	Aug 2006	Jun 2009
vacant	Jul 2009	Nov 2009
BG Ricky Adams	Dec 2009	Present

Command Sergeant Majors of the Oklahoma National Guard

Command Sergeant Major	From	To
1st – Billy J. Ferguson	1 Aug 1969	30 Nov 1971
2nd – John C. Marcy	1 Dec 1971	30 Jun 1972
3rd – William E. Nichols	31 Jul 1972	11 Jun 1976
4th – Edgar A. Siewert	1 Aug 1976	30 Oct 1977
5th – Sam Cluck	1 Nov 1977	30 Jun 1980
6th – William G. "Bill" Evans	1 Jul 1980	20 Aug 1988
7th – Carmon L. Allen	21 Aug 1988	9 Nov 1992
8th – David J. Willingham	10 Nov 1992	30 Nov 1993
9th – Gerald S. Plaster	1 Dec 1993	31 Jan 1995
10th – Marvin L. Barbee	1 Apr 1995	30 Sep 2002
11th – CSM David Keating	1 Oct 2002	14 Nov 2008
12th – CSM Steve Jensen	14 Nov 2008	present

---

1. Harry Clark is listed as the "Adjutant General" for the "1889 Land Run," however he was a federal agent and no Oklahoma Territorial government was yet established. Congress passed the "Enabling Act of 1890" on 2 May 1890, creating the Territorial Government of Oklahoma. BG James Carson Jamison, formerly the Adjutant General for Missouri from 1885 to 1889, was named the first Adjutant General for the Oklahoma Territorial Government by the first Territorial Governor, W.C. Renfrow, on 23 December 1894. Jamison left Missouri to take part in the 1889 land run and then campaigned to be appointed as the first territorial governor by President Grover Cleveland. When he lost this endeavor, the winner, W.C. Renfrow, appointed him Adjutant General and he organized Oklahoma's first regiment of Militia. (Information provided by Mr. Allen M. Beckett, Historian, 45th Infantry Division Museum).

2. Promoted to Lieutenant General and reassigned to NGB, Washington D.C. as the Director of the Air National Guard 3 Feb 2009.

3. The known OKARNG records listing former Assistant Adjutants General only go back to 1968 when the 45th Infantry Division was retired. "…the [Oklahoma] State Statute mentions the [position of] Assistant Adjutant General goes back to 1951," stated Mr. Allen M. Beckett, Historian, 45th Infantry Division Museum. However, a listing before 1968 appears not to exist.

About the Author

Colonel (ret) Billy R. Wood retired from the U.S. Army in 1998, with 28 ½ years total military service, 22 years active duty and 6 ½ years Army National Guard. He is a former member of the 45th Avn Bn, the Lords of Darkness.

Colonel Wood enlisted in the Regular Army in July 1963 at Ada, Oklahoma. He attended basic infantry training at Fort Polk, LA and advanced individual training as a field artilleryman at Fort Sill, OK. He attended and graduated the U.S. Army's Field Artillery Officer Candidate School in 1964/65. Later he attended U.S. Army Officer Rotary Wing Aviator Course at Fort Wolters, TX and Fort Rucker, AL, graduating in June 1966.

In July 1966, 1LT Wood was assigned to the 1st Air CAV's A Battery 2/20th Aerial Rocket Artillery unit at An Khe, Viet Nam, flying UH-1C Hogs (gunships) with ARA. In early 1967, he flew UH-1D slicks with the 174th Assault Helicopter Company at Qui Nhon and Duc Pho. Wood was reassigned from Viet Nam to the 35th Field Artillery Group Headquarters, Bamberg, West Germany. He served three years in Germany as the 35th FA GP Aviation Officer and the Bamberg Army Airfield Commander.

Colonel Wood was stationed at Davison Army Airfield, Fort Belvoir, VA from 1993 to 1998. He served as the first Deputy Commander and 2nd Commander of the Operational Support Airlift Agency. OSAA was the Army's 100 plus fixed-wing airplane organization encompassing twelve Regional Flight Centers in the contiguous U.S. plus Hawaii, Alaska, Panama and later Puerto Rico.

The author received his Bachelors of Science degree in Aviation from Southeastern Oklahoma State University and a Masters of Science degree in Natural and Applied Science from Oklahoma State University. In May 1998 he was inducted into the U.S. Army's Field Artillery Officer Candidate School Hall of Fame at Fort Sill, OK.

DECORATIONS AND AWARDS: Legion of Merit; Distinguished Flying Cross; Soldiers Medal; Bronze Star Medal; Meritorious Service Medal w/1 Oak Leaf Cluster; Air Medal w/22 Oak Leaf Clusters; Good Conduct Medal; Army Commendation Medal w/2 Oak Leaf Clusters; Army Service Ribbon; National Defense Service Medal; Republic of Viet Nam Campaign Medal; Viet Nam Service Medal; Overseas Ribbon; Viet Nam Unit Award; Viet Nam Cross of Gallantry w/Palm (2nd award); Presidential Unit Citation; Army Reserve Component Achievement Medal; Army Reserve Component Overseas Ribbon (2nd award); Army Overseas Bars (2); Armed Forces Reserve Medal; Army Achievement Medal; Master Army Aviator Badge; Aircraft Crewmember Badge; Air Assault Badge; Royal Thai Army Master Aviator Badge; M16/.45 cal Expert Badge, Rev .38 Cal Expert Badge; Viet Nam Counter Offensive II & III; Oklahoma Long Service Medal (10 yrs).

Colonel Wood and his wife, Carolyn, are both originally from Ada, OK, where they were high school classmates. They taught an adult Sunday School class, sing in their church choir and do local volunteer work. They each have two grown children and a total of four wonderful grandchildren. Billy and Carolyn are often at home in the beautiful Ouachita Mountains near Mena, Arkansas, except when they are touring the United States and Canada on their Honda Gold Wing motorcycle.

Made in the USA
Lexington, KY
28 April 2012